P9-CRN-440

Photoshop® CS2
ALL-IN-ONE DESK REFERENCE
FOR
DUMMIES®

Barbara Obermeier

Wiley Publishing, Inc.

Photoshop® CS2 All-in-One Desk Reference For Dummies®

Published by
Wiley Publishing, Inc.
111 River Street
Hoboken, NJ 07030-5774
www.wiley.com

Copyright © 2005 by Wiley Publishing, Inc., Indianapolis, Indiana

Published by Wiley Publishing, Inc., Indianapolis, Indiana

Published simultaneously in Canada

No part of this publication may be reproduced, stored in a retrieval system or transmitted in any form or by any means, electronic, mechanical, photocopying, recording, scanning or otherwise, except as permitted under Sections 107 or 108 of the 1976 United States Copyright Act, without either the prior written permission of the Publisher, or authorization through payment of the appropriate per-copy fee to the Copyright Clearance Center, 222 Rosewood Drive, Danvers, MA 01923, (978) 750-8400, fax (978) 646-8600. Requests to the Publisher for permission should be addressed to the Legal Department, Wiley Publishing, Inc., 10475 Crosspoint Blvd., Indianapolis, IN 46256, (317) 572-3447, fax (317) 572-4355, or online at http://www.wiley.com/go/permissions.

Trademarks: Wiley, the Wiley Publishing logo, For Dummies, the Dummies Man logo, A Reference for the Rest of Us!, The Dummies Way, Dummies Daily, The Fun and Easy Way, Dummies.com, and related trade dress are trademarks or registered trademarks of John Wiley & Sons, Inc. and/or its affiliates in the United States and other countries, and may not be used without written permission. Photoshop is a registered trademark of Adobe Systems Incorporated in the United States and/or other countries. All other trademarks are the property of their respective owners. Wiley Publishing, Inc., is not associated with any product or vendor mentioned in this book.

LIMIT OF LIABILITY/DISCLAIMER OF WARRANTY: THE PUBLISHER AND THE AUTHOR MAKE NO REPRESENTATIONS OR WARRANTIES WITH RESPECT TO THE ACCURACY OR COMPLETENESS OF THE CONTENTS OF THIS WORK AND SPECIFICALLY DISCLAIM ALL WARRANTIES, INCLUDING WITHOUT LIMITATION WARRANTIES OF FITNESS FOR A PARTICULAR PURPOSE. NO WARRANTY MAY BE CREATED OR EXTENDED BY SALES OR PROMOTIONAL MATERIALS. THE ADVICE AND STRATEGIES CONTAINED HEREIN MAY NOT BE SUITABLE FOR EVERY SITUATION. THIS WORK IS SOLD WITH THE UNDERSTANDING THAT THE PUBLISHER IS NOT ENGAGED IN RENDERING LEGAL, ACCOUNTING, OR OTHER PROFESSIONAL SERVICES. IF PROFESSIONAL ASSISTANCE IS REQUIRED, THE SERVICES OF A COMPETENT PROFESSIONAL PERSON SHOULD BE SOUGHT. NEITHER THE PUBLISHER NOR THE AUTHOR SHALL BE LIABLE FOR DAMAGES ARISING HEREFROM. THE FACT THAT AN ORGANIZATION OR WEBSITE IS REFERRED TO IN THIS WORK AS A CITATION AND/OR A POTENTIAL SOURCE OF FURTHER INFORMATION DOES NOT MEAN THAT THE AUTHOR OR THE PUBLISHER ENDORSES THE INFORMATION THE ORGANIZATION OR WEBSITE MAY PROVIDE OR RECOMMENDATIONS IT MAY MAKE. FURTHER, READERS SHOULD BE AWARE THAT INTERNET WEBSITES LISTED IN THIS WORK MAY HAVE CHANGED OR DISAPPEARED BETWEEN WHEN THIS WORK WAS WRITTEN AND WHEN IT IS READ.

For general information on our other products and services, please contact our Customer Care Department within the U.S. at 800-762-2974, outside the U.S. at 317-572-3993, or fax 317-572-4002.

For technical support, please visit www.wiley.com/techsupport.

Wiley also publishes its books in a variety of electronic formats. Some content that appears in print may not be available in electronic books.

Library of Congress Control Number: 2005923071

ISBN-13: 978-0-7645-8916-4

ISBN-10: 0-7645-8916-4

Manufactured in the United States of America

10 9 8 7 6 5 4 3 2 1

1K/SZ/QW/QV/IN

WILEY

Photoshop® CS2
ALL-IN-ONE DESK REFERENCE
FOR DUMMIES

Cheat Sheet

Finding Your Way Around Photoshop

Options bar   Tools palette   Image Document window   Palettes   Palette well

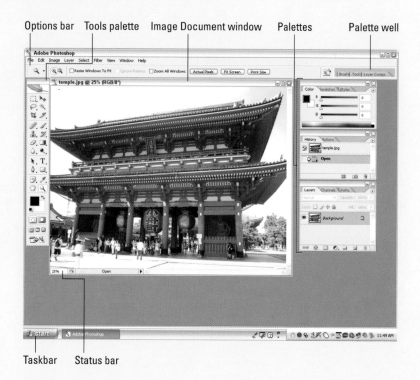

Taskbar   Status bar

- Launch Photoshop by clicking the Start menu or an icon on the taskbar (Windows) or clicking the Photoshop icon on the Dock (Mac).

  TIP You can also double-click a Photoshop shortcut or alias on your desktop.

- Open an image by choosing File⇨Open. If you have several images open at a time, cycle through them by pressing Ctrl+Tab (Windows) or Control+Tab (Mac).

- Sometimes you need to see more detail in a photo. Zoom in by pressing Ctrl (⌘ on the Mac)+spacebar+

click and when you're done editing, zoom out by pressing Alt (Option on the Mac)+spacebar+click.

- Scroll an image by pressing the spacebar and then dragging.

- Set your preferences by choosing Edit⇨Preferences (Windows) or Photoshop⇨Preferences (Mac).

- Combine palettes, position dialog boxes, customize the Options bar, and set font sizes to how you work best. Then save your workspace to use again by choosing Window⇨Workspace⇨Save Workspace. (See Book I, Chapter 5 for more info.)

For Dummies: Bestselling Book Series for Beginners

Photoshop® CS2
ALL-IN-ONE DESK REFERENCE
FOR DUMMIES

Cheat Sheet

Accessing the Tools Palette through Shortcuts

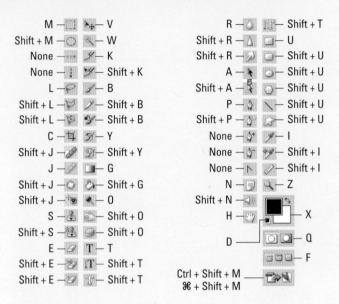

M — | +— V
Shift + M — | — W
None — | — K
None — | — Shift + K
L — | — B
Shift + L — | — Shift + B
Shift + L — | — Shift + B
C — | — Y
Shift + J — | — Shift + Y
J — | — G
Shift + J — | — Shift + G
Shift + J — | — O
S — | — Shift + O
Shift + S — | — Shift + O
E — | T — T
Shift + E — | T — Shift + T
Shift + E — | T — Shift + T

R — | T — Shift + T
Shift + R — | — U
Shift + R — | — Shift + U
A — | — Shift + U
Shift + A — | — Shift + U
P — | — Shift + U
Shift + P — | — Shift + U
None — | — I
None — | — Shift + I
None — | — Shift + I
N — | — Z
Shift + N — |
H — | — X
D — |
| — Q
| — F

Ctrl + Shift + M
⌘ + Shift + M

Making Selections

	PC	Mac
Draw straight lines	Alt+click with Lasso tool	Option+click with Lasso tool
Add to selection outline	Shift+drag	Shift+drag
Deselect specific area	Alt+drag	Option+drag
Deselect all but intersected area	Shift+Alt+drag	Shift+Option+drag
Deselect entire image	Ctrl+D	⌘+D
Reselect last selection	Ctrl+Shift+D	⌘+Shift+D
Hide extras	Ctrl+H	⌘+H
Fill selection with foreground color	Alt+Backspace	Option+Delete
Fill selection with background color	Ctrl+Backspace	⌘+Delete
Reapply last filter	Ctrl+F	⌘+F
Adjust levels	Ctrl+L	⌘+L
Free Transform	Ctrl+T	⌘+T

Copyright © 2005 Wiley Publishing, Inc. All rights reserved. Item 8916-4.
For more information about Wiley Publishing, call 1-800-762-2974.

For Dummies: Bestselling Book Series for Beginners

Wiley, the Wiley Publishing logo, For Dummies, the Dummies Man logo, the Dummies Man logo and all related trade dress are trademarks or registered trademarks of John Wiley & Sons, Inc. and/or its affiliates. All other trademarks are property of their respective owners.

About the Author

Barbara Obermeier is principal of Obermeier Design, a graphic design studio in Ventura, California. She's the author of *Photoshop Album For Dummies*, coauthor of *Adobe Master Class: Illustrator Illuminated*, *Photoshop 7 For Dummies*, and *Illustrator 10 For Dummies*. She has contributed as coauthor, technical editor, or layout designer for numerous books. Barb also teaches computer graphics at Brooks Institute; the University of California, Santa Barbara; and Ventura College.

Dedication

I would like to dedicate this book to Gary, Kylie, and Lucky, who constantly remind me of what's really important in life.

Author's Acknowledgments

I would like to thank my excellent project editor, Becky Huehls, who kept me and this book on track; Bob Woerner, the world's best Acquisitions Editor; Andy Cummings, who gives Dummies a good name; David Busch, for his great contribution to the first edition; David Herman, Technical Editor Extraordinaire; and all the hard-working, dedicated production folks at Wiley. A special thanks to Ted Padova, colleague, fellow author, and friend, who always reminds me there is eventually an end to all those chapters.

Publisher's Acknowledgments

We're proud of this book; please send us your comments through our online registration form located at www.dummies.com/register/.

Some of the people who helped bring this book to market include the following:

Acquisitions, Editorial, and Media Development

Project Editor: Rebecca Huehls

Senior Acquisitions Editor: Bob Woerner

Copy Editor: Rebecca Senninger

Technical Editor: David Herman

Editorial Manager: Leah Cameron

Editorial Assistant: Amanda Foxworth

Cartoons: Rich Tennant (www.the5thwave.com)

Composition Services

Project Coordinator: Maridee Ennis

Layout and Graphics: Lauren Goddard, Denny Hager, Lynsey Osborn, Melanee Prendergast, Heather Ryan

Proofreaders: Laura Albert, Melissa Buddendeck, Leeann Harney, Betty Kish, Jessica Kramer, Carl William Pierce, Sossity Smith

Indexer: Richard T. Evans

Publishing and Editorial for Technology Dummies

    Richard Swadley, Vice President and Executive Group Publisher

    Andy Cummings, Vice President and Publisher

    Mary Bednarek, Executive Acquisitions Director

    Mary C. Corder, Editorial Director

Publishing for Consumer Dummies

    Diane Graves Steele, Vice President and Publisher

    Joyce Pepple, Acquisitions Director

Composition Services

    Gerry Fahey, Vice President of Production Services

    Debbie Stailey, Director of Composition Services

Contents at a Glance

Table of Contents

Introduction

There's a reason why Photoshop is the world's industry standard in image-editing software. The depth and breadth of the program is unheralded. Photoshop immediately sucks you in with its easy-to-use interface and powerful tools and commands. It is so feature rich that you soon begin to lose track of time and start blowing off your commitments just to try one more thing. And just when you think you've finally explored every nook and cranny and mastered the program, you suddenly read a tip in a book or magazine that enlightens you about something you didn't know. Or even more likely, you stumble upon some great effect while working on a late-night project. That's the beauty of Photoshop. It's the program that just keeps giving.

The depth and breadth of Photoshop has downsides, too, of course. You must make a major time commitment and invest much effort to master it — hence the large number of books written on the program. Walk into your neighborhood bookstore or type `Photoshop` in the Search field at any online bookseller's site, and you see a barrage of choices. Some books are general reference books, some are targeted toward the novice user, and others focus on a specific mission, such as color management or restoration and retouching.

About This Book

This book is written for the person who has a good grasp of using a computer and navigating the operating system and at least a cursory knowledge of Photoshop. It is intended to be a comprehensive reference book that you can read cover to cover or reach for when you're looking for specific information about a particular task.

Wherever I can, I sneak in a useful tip or an interesting technique to help you put Photoshop to work for your project needs.

Sometimes, knowing *how* to use a tool doesn't necessarily mean that you know *what* to do with it. That's why this book contains several Putting It Together exercises that help you make a connection between the multiple Photoshop tools at your disposal and the very specific task you need to accomplish. Want to get the red out of a subject's eyes or create a collage? Just check out the Putting-It-Together sections in Books III through IX. These sections present info in easy-to-follow numbered steps, in a hands-on style, building on what's presented in the chapter so that you can go to the next level, put concepts to work, and move on to the next task.

You can find images that appear within the Putting It Together sections on this book's companion Web site (`www.dummies.com/go/photoshopcs2`), so you can follow along precisely with the steps.

What's in This Book

This book is broken into minibooks, each covering a general topic. Each minibook contains several chapters, each covering a more specific topic under the general one. Each chapter is then divided into sections, and some of those sections have subsections. I'm sure you get the picture.

You can read the book from front to back, or you can dive right into the minibook or chapter of your choice. Either way works just fine. Anytime a concept is mentioned that isn't covered in depth in that chapter, you find a cross-reference to another book and chapter where you find all the details. If you're looking for something specific, check out either the Table of Contents or the Index.

The Cheat Sheet at the beginning of the book helps you remember all the shortcuts you'll use most often. Tear it out, tape it to your monitor, and glance over it when you need to.

And finally, I have pictures. Lots of them. And this time they're in full, living color. Many of these pictures have callouts that point to specific steps or identify important concepts, buttons, tools, or options. With a program like Photoshop, an image often speaks louder than words.

This book contains nine minibooks. The following sections offer a quick synopsis of what each book contains.

Book 1: Photoshop Fundamentals

Ready to get your feet wet with the basics of Photoshop? Head to Book I. Here's where you get familiar with the Photoshop environment — the desktop, menus, and palettes. I also briefly introduce the key tools and explain what each one does.

Photoshop has such an abundance of tools — and so many ways to use those tools — I can't possibly cover them all in this book. But if you're looking for details on the less commonly used features or perhaps more information about using tools you're already familiar with, you'll find them on this book's companion Web site (`www.dummies.com/go/photoshopcs2`).

In this book, I cover how to get started on Photoshop and how to view and navigate your image window. Here's also where I give you all the important details about the o'mighty Adobe Bridge and how to customize your workspace and preference settings.

Finally, I go into the bare basics of printing, and then how to save files and close Photoshop.

Book II: Image Essentials

This book covers all those nitpicky — but critical — details about images, such as size, resolution, pixel dimension, image mode, and file format. Turn to this book to find out how to safely resize your image without causing undue damage.

You can also find out how to crop images and increase their canvas size. In addition, I breeze through basic color theory and get you started using and managing color.

But wait, there's more. I give you the lowdown on the History palette and brushing and erasing to history. And, if that's not enough, I throw in a chapter on using and creating actions for enhanced productivity.

Book III: Selections

This important book gives you all the juicy details and techniques on creating and modifying selections and paths. You find out about each of the selection tools and also the powerful — albeit sometimes unruly — Pen tool and its accompanying Paths palette.

Book IV: Painting, Drawing, and Typing

If you want to know about the drawing and painting tools, this book is for you. Here I cover the Brush and Pencil tools, along with the once again improved Brushes palette. I also show you how to create vector shapes by using the shape tools, and how to fill and stroke selections.

Head to this book to find out how to create both gradients and patterns and, last but not least, become familiar with the type tools and how to use them to create and edit standard type, type on and in a path, and type with special effects.

Book V: Working with Layers

Layers are an integral component in a Photoshop image, and Book V is where I explain them. In this book, you discover how to create and edit layers and how to use multiple images to create a multilayered composite image. You find out various ways to manage layers for maximum efficiency, including using the Layer Comps palette. I also show you how to enhance layers by applying different blend modes, opacity settings, layer styles, and styles. Finally, I introduce you to working with the new Smart Objects feature.

Book VI: Channels and Masks

This book gives you all the how-tos you need to work with channels and masks. I show you how to save and edit selections as alpha channels so that you can reload them later. And I show you how to work with the various kinds of masks — quick masks, layer masks, and channel masks — and how you can use each to select difficult elements. I also cover other masking techniques, such as erasing and using the Color Range command.

Book VII: Filters and Distortions

I filled this book with tons of handy tips and techniques on using filters to correct your images to make them sharper, blurrier, cleaner, and smoother — whatever fits your fancy. You also find out how to use filters to give your image a certain special effect, such as a deckled edge or water droplets. Next I introduce the Liquify command so that you can see the wonder of its distortion tools — and how they can turn your image into digital taffy. Finally, you get some tidbits on how to work with the new and fascinating Vanishing Point feature, which can make editing and compositing images a whole lot easier.

Book VIII: Retouching and Restoration

You find everything you need to know about color correction or color enhancement in Book VIII — getting rid of colorcasts, improving contrast and saturation, remapping, and replacing colors.

In addition, I include a chapter on using the focus and toning tools to manually lighten, darken, smooth, soften, and sharpen areas of your image. You get to see how you can use the Clone Stamp tool, and the two Healing Brushes and Patch tool to fix flaws and imperfections in your images, making them good as new. I also show you the Color Replacement tool and how to replace your image's original color with the foreground color. And finally, I introduce you to the new and long-awaited Red Eye tool.

Book IX: Photoshop and Print

This book gives you the lowdown on preparing your images for print. You find details on how to get the right resolution, image mode, and file format. You also discover how to set up both process and sport color separations for those offset print jobs. For good measure, I also throw in a chapter on creating contact sheets and picture packages from your digital masterpieces.

About the Web Site

For those Web graphics, you find lots of great material on this book's companion Web site (`www.dummies.com/go/photoshopcs2`). Find out how to optimize your images for maximum quality and quick download times. You also find information on slicing and animating your images and creating a photo gallery that you can easily post on the Web.

Conventions Used in This Book

You'll find that this book is cross-platform. Windows commands are given first, followed by Mac commands in parentheses, like this:

Press Enter (or Return on the Mac) to begin a new line.

And occasionally, text is specific to one platform or another. You'll find that figures are divided into both platforms as well.

Often the commands given involve using the keyboard along with the mouse. For example, "Press Shift while dragging with the Rectangular Marquee tool to create a square," or "Alt+click (Option+click) on the eyeball to redisplay all layers."

When you see a command arrow (➪) in the text, it indicates to select a command from the menu bar. For example, "choose Edit➪Define Custom Shape" means to click the Edit menu and then choose the Define Custom Shape command.

While this book has been written using Photoshop CS2, you can still glean valuable info if you're using Version CS or 7. It may take a little more time to understand how a palette or options have changed, and of course, the topics covering new features won't be applicable. But hey, when you see the cool Version CS2 features, you may get the impetus you need to go out and upgrade!

Icons Used in This Book

While perusing this book, you'll notice some icons beckoning you for your attention. Don't ignore them; embrace them! These icons point out fun, useful, and memorable tidbits about Photoshop, plus facts you'd be unwise to ignore.

Seasoned users will appreciate this icon, which kindly points out new features introduced in Photoshop CS2.

This icon is a reminder of things that I already mentioned and want to gently re-emphasize. Or I might be pointing out things that I want you to take note of in your future Photoshop excursions.

This icon marks eggheady graphics or Photoshop info that goes beyond the basics.

This icon indicates information that makes your Photoshop experience easier. It also gives you an icebreaker at your next cocktail party. Whipping out, "Did you know that pressing the bracket keys enlarges or shrinks your brush tip?" is bound to make you the center of conversation.

The little bomb icon is a red flag. Heed these warnings, or else Photoshop may show its ugly side.

This icon points to related content you'll find on this book's companion Web site, which you can find at `www.dummies.com/go/photoshopcs2`.

Book I
Photoshop Fundamentals

The 5th Wave   By Rich Tennant

SINCE INSTALLING PHOTOSHOP, THE 4th PRECINCT BECAME NOTED FOR ITS CREATIVE WANTED POSTERS

"Ooo – look! Sgt. Rodriguez has the felon's head floating in a teacup!"

Don't know where to start? Well, unless you have a burning question on something very specific, this is a great place to dive in. And I promise you won't flounder. There's nothing like a general overview to get you feeling confident enough to tackle more sophisticated features.

In this book, I introduce you to the Photoshop environment with all its components, from the desktop to the many palettes. I show you each of the 58 tools and briefly explain what each tool does. From there, I show you how to open existing files or create new ones and then how to save and print those files, as well as how to view and navigate around your image window. In that same chapter, I give you details on using the new Adobe Bridge, a powerful browser and file management tool. Finally, I explain how to customize your workspace and preferences so you can tailor Photoshop to better suit your personal image-editing needs and interests. I guarantee you won't find a more accommodating image editor around.

Wright Beach, Ca

Chapter 1: Examining the Photoshop Environment

In This Chapter

✔ Starting Photoshop

✔ Working with palettes

✔ Examining the Photoshop desktop

✔ Investigating the menu bar

✔ Discovering the Options bar

As environments go, the Photoshop working environment is pretty cool: as inviting as a landscaped backyard and not nearly as likely to work you into a sweat. Each of the many tools in Photoshop is custom-designed for a specific chore and chock-full of more options than a Swiss Army knife. When you're familiar with your surroundings, you'll be eager to make like Monet in his garden, surrounded by palettes, brushes, buckets of paint, and swatches of color, ready to tackle the canvas in front of you.

Getting a Warm Welcome

When you launch Photoshop CS2 for the first time, you're greeted by Photoshop's rendition of the friendly neighborhood welcome wagon. The handy Welcome Screen, shown in Figure 1-1, provides a virtual plethora of goodies for everyone from the beginner to the advanced user. New feature descriptions, tutorials, tips, and tricks are all at your fingertips. Don't worry about exploring every item when you first launch Photoshop. You can call up the Welcome Screen anytime by choosing Help⇨Welcome Screen. Some information is available via the Help Center while other information is available through links to the Adobe Web site. Video clips allow you to see features in action. So grab some popcorn and enjoy.

If you prefer to access the Welcome Screen at your own leisure and don't want it to appear every time you launch Photoshop, deselect the Show This Dialog at Startup option in the bottom-left corner of the Welcome Screen window.

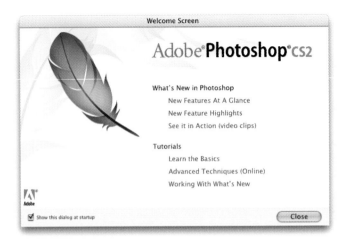

Figure 1-1: Photoshop's Welcome Screen goes beyond a friendly greeting and offers lots of tips, techniques, and tutorials.

Launching Photoshop and Customizing the Desktop

You start Photoshop just as you launch any other program with Windows or the Mac OS. As with other programs, you can choose the method you find the easiest and most convenient. In Windows, you can launch programs from the Start menu or an icon on the taskbar. In Mac OS X, you may have a Photoshop icon on the Dock. In either Windows or Mac OS X, you can double-click a Photoshop shortcut or alias icon if you have one on your desktop. Finally, you can double-click an image associated with Photoshop, which then launches Photoshop along with the file.

When you launch Photoshop, the desktop workspace, shown in Figure 1-2, appears. Like the real-world desktop where your keyboard and monitor reside, the Photoshop desktop is a place for you to put all the images you're working with.

Within the main Photoshop window, you see a variety of other windows and boxes, such as the *image document window* that enables you to view and edit images. The main window contains the stuff you're probably used to seeing in other programs — a title bar at the top of the window, a status bar at the bottom (unless you have it turned off) if you're a Windows user, and menus to help you execute commands and get important information about your image files. But the arrangement of controls may be a little unfamiliar to you. Photoshop arranges controls into groups called *palettes*.

Tools palette
Options bar   Document window

Palettes
Palette Well

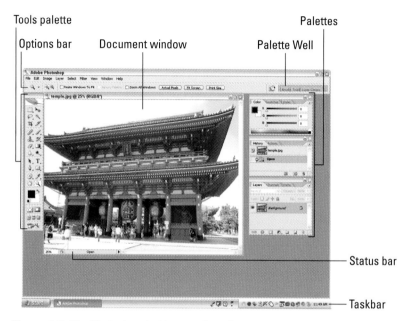

Status bar

Taskbar

Figure 1-2: The Photoshop desktop consists of many components, including an image document window, palettes, and bars.

Your virtual desktop can become as cluttered as the real thing, but Adobe has built in some special features (located on the Options bar, which I discuss later in this chapter) that let you keep stuff close at hand but tuck things away so they're not constantly underfoot (or undermouse, so to speak). After you arrange your Photoshop desktop just as you like it for a specific project, you can even save the desktop and reuse it whenever you work on that project. See Book I, Chapter 5.

Every document you ever work on appears within the confines of the image document window and can't leave its borders. You can move around some other components, such as the various palettes and the Options bar, both inside and outside the Photoshop application window.

 Windows users can close, minimize, and restore the main Photoshop window, just as you can with most windows in other programs. Mac users can choose Photoshop➪Hide Photoshop. To display Photoshop again, simply click the icon on the Dock.

 The Photoshop window hides one cool secret for Windows users: If you double-click anywhere in the gray empty area, the Open dialog box pops up, so you can navigate to a file you want to work on without wandering up to the File menu, using the Ctrl+O keyboard shortcut, or using Adobe Bridge.

The following sections show you how to customize the main working area so that you can get to work.

Setting display settings with the Window menu

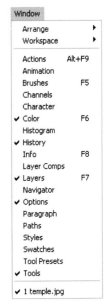

The Window menu, shown in Figure 1-3, controls the display of palettes and some other elements of the Photoshop working area. (Find out more about maneuvering palettes later in this chapter.)

The top two entries on the Window menu enable you to control the display arrangement of your open documents and manage your workspaces. On the Window➪Arrange submenu, you can tell Photoshop to cascade (stack) or tile (butt them edge to edge) all open documents. Table 1-1 gives you the lowdown about the other options on the Window➪Arrange submenu.

On the Window➪Workspace submenu, you can save your current desktop arrangement, load or delete a stored arrangement, or reset your palette locations.

And now in Photoshop CS2 you can load preset workspace setups designed for specific workflows. For step-by-step instructions, see Book I, Chapter 5.

Figure 1-3: Access all palettes via the Window menu.

The remaining bulk of the Window menu contains a list of palettes in alphabetical order.

Table 1-1	The Window➪Arrange Submenu
Menu Command	*What It Does*
Match Zoom	Takes all your open documents and matches the magnification percentage of your currently active document.
Match Location	Takes all your open documents and matches the location of your currently active document. In other words, if you are viewing the lower-left corner of your active document and choose Match Location, all your open documents are also displayed from the lower-left corner.
Match Zoom and Location	Employs both commands simultaneously.

Menu Command	What It Does
New Window	Opens another view of the same image, allowing you to work on a close-up of part of the image while viewing results on the entire image.
Arrange Icons (Windows only)	Takes minimized files and arranges the title bar icons in a neat row directly above the status bar.
Minimize (Mac only)	Hides the image while placing the image's thumbnail on the Dock. Click the thumbnail to restore the image in Photoshop.
Bring All to Front (Mac only)	If you have multiple applications launched and document windows open, this command brings all Photoshop documents to the front, ahead of any open document windows from other applications.

Setting up the status bar

Adobe has eliminated the Windows application status bar in favor of individual status bars for each document window. If you're a Mac OS user, of course, this is the way it has always been.

Many people tend to associate status with wealth, so I think there's a good reason to accept the free wealth of information that the status bar offers:

✓ At the far left is a box that displays an active image's current zoom level (such as 33.33%). Incidentally, the title bar of the document itself also shows the zoom level.

If you installed Photoshop to a networked computer and you activate the workgroup features, which enable file sharing and other perks, you see the icon for the Workgroup Services pop-up menu just to the right of the zoom info box.

✓ Next is the file and image information display area, which, by default, shows the document size information. You can customize this area to display other information. Click the size value to display a preview of how your image fits on your selected paper size.

Because Photoshop files can get pretty hefty in size, your status bar shows the file size of the active image by default. To display other types of information, click the right-pointing arrow in the status bar, slide down to Show and select one of the following options from the menu that pops up, shown in Figure 1-4:

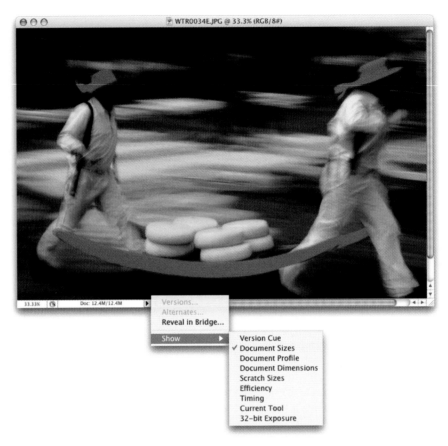

Corbis Digital Stock

Figure 1-4: The status bar provides a wealth of vital information about your image.

~ **Version Cue:** If you have Version Cue enabled, Photoshop displays Version Cue information, such as if another user is using the file. What's Version Cue? It is a program (which works across all CS2 applications) designed to increase productivity in a collaborative environment. Version Cue identifies and organizes files into projects. You can have various versions and alternates of the same project file. It also provides file security, file status, and allows for commenting by multiple users.

~ **Document Sizes:** When you select this option, Photoshop displays two numbers to approximate the size of the image. The first number shows you the size of the file if you were to flatten (combine) all the layers into one and save it to your hard drive. The number on the right shows the size of the file, including layers, channels, and other components, and how much data Photoshop has to juggle while you're working on the file. You want this option active when you need to keep track of how large your image is.

✓ **Document Profile:** When you select this option, the status bar displays the name of the color profile that the image uses. You probably won't use this option unless you need to know the profiles of all the open documents while making complex color corrections. You can find more information about profiles in Book II, Chapter 3.

✓ **Document Dimensions:** When you select this option, the status bar shows you the size of the image by using the default measurement increment you've set in Photoshop's Preferences (pixels, inches, picas, and so on). You might need this for instant reference to the physical dimensions of your open files. For information on setting preferences in Photoshop, see Book I, Chapter 5.

✓ **Scratch Sizes:** *Scratch space* is the virtual memory set aside on your hard drive to simulate RAM and make editing large files easier. Enabling this option shows two measurements for an active image. On the left, you see the amount of real memory and virtual memory that all open images are using. On the right, you see the total amount of RAM available for working with images. Photoshop needs a lot more memory and disk space to work on an image while it's open, and that's what's shown by the Scratch Sizes display, as opposed to the Document Size display that shows only the file size of the document itself.

✓ **Efficiency:** This indicator helps you gauge whether you really have enough RAM to perform a task. It shows the percentage of time Photoshop spends actually working on an operation, compared to the time it must spend reading or writing image information to or from your hard disk. If the value dips below 100 percent most of the time, you need to allocate more memory to Photoshop (if you're using a PC). For more information on parceling out RAM, see Book I, Chapter 5.

✓ **Timing:** This number shows you how long it took you to complete your last incredible feat.

These four features on the menu are new in Photoshop CS2:

✓ **Current Tool:** This option shows you the name of the tool currently in use.

✓ **32-bit Exposure:** This option is for adjusting the preview image for viewing 32-bit High Dynamic Range (HDR) images. The slider control is only available if you have an HDR image open.

✓ **Versions:** If you are a Version Cue user, you can select this option, which allows you to select other versions of your file. For example, you may want to select a version with comments or one with a specific version date. Versions provide a good way of storing work that was executed in different stages. At each progress point, you can save a version of that file, thereby creating a snapshot of the file at that point in time.

✓ **Alternates:** Again, if you are a Version Cue user, you can select this option, which allows you to select alternates of your file. For example, you may

have variations of a design for a project. By using alternates, your original
file is untouched.

✔ **Reveal in Bridge:** This command transports you to the Adobe Bridge,
where it then physically locates your active image wherever it resides on
your system.

Playing with Palettes

Many image-oriented programs use palettes of a sort, and Photoshop itself has
had palettes since version 1.0, released in January 1990. However, since
Photoshop 3.0, the program has used a novel way of working with palettes.
Instead of stand-alone windows, Photoshop uses grouped, tabbed palettes,
which overlap each other in groups of two or three (or more, if you rearrange
them yourself). To access a palette that falls behind the one displayed on
top, click the palette's tab. By default, some palettes, such as Brushes, Info,
Layer Comps, and Tool Presets, appear alone.

Palettes may contain sliders, buttons, drop-down lists, pop-up menus (as
shown in Figure 1-5), and other controls. You also find icons at the bottom
of many palettes. For example, at the base of the Layers palette are icons
that let you create a new layer, add a layer style, or trash a layer that you no
longer want.

Many palettes, such as the Brushes, Styles, Actions, and Colors palettes,
include options for defining sets of parameters (called *presets*) that you can
store for reuse at any time.

Here's how to open, close, and otherwise manipulate a palette group from
the Window menu:

✔ **To bring a palette to the front of its group:** When the palette group is
open, the palette that's visible is the palette that has a check mark next
to it on the Window menu. In this mode, you can select only one palette
in any group because only one tab in a group can be on top at one time.
When you select a palette from the Window menu, you have no way of
knowing which palettes are grouped together because Adobe lists palettes
alphabetically instead of by groups.

✔ **To move a palette out of its group:** Grab the palette's tab and drag to its
new location, such as another group, the Palette Well, or the Photoshop
desktop. If you move the palettes out of their groups or drag them onto
the desktop so that they stand alone, any of them can be check marked.

✔ **To hide a palette:** Select a check-marked palette on the Window menu or
click the Close button at the top of the palette. Note that the whole palette
group closes.

✔ **To access a palette from the desktop:** Find its group and click the
palette's tab to bring it to the front.

Playing with Palettes **17**

Book I
Chapter 1

Examining the
Photoshop
Environment

Figure 1-5: Palettes contain various types of icons and controls for editing and managing your image.

Here are some palette-manipulation tips:

- **Save space by keeping palettes in groups.** You can drag all the palettes in a group by dragging the group's title bar. Access an individual palette by clicking its tab to bring it to the front. As a result, several palettes occupy only the screen space required by one.

- **Use the Window menu if you can't find a palette.** On the Window menu, select the palette's name to make it visible or to bring it to the top of its group.

- **Rearrange groups by dragging.** If you'd like to move a palette to another group or to display it as a stand-alone palette, drag and drop its tab.

- **Customize, customize, customize.** After you use Photoshop for a while, creating your own custom palette groups based on the palettes you most often use can be a real timesaver. For example, if you don't use the Paths palette very often but can't live without the Actions palette, you can drag the Paths palette to another group or the Palette Well and put the Actions palette in the same group as the mission-critical Layers and Channels palettes.

✓ **Minimize palettes to save even more space.** You can double-click a palette's title bar (or tab if you're using the Mac OS) to shrink the palette or palette group down to its title bar and tabs alone. You can also click the Minimize button at the top of palette.

✓ **Restore default palette locations whenever you need a change.** If you decide you don't like the way you've arranged your palettes, you can choose Window➪Workspace➪Reset Palette Locations to return them to the default configuration (the way they were when Photoshop was installed).

Many palettes, such as the Swatches and Character palettes, allow you to reset the settings back to their defaults. Select Reset from the palette's pop-up menu located in the top-right corner.

Working with Your First Photoshop File

So many menus, so little time! The second you begin working with Photoshop, you may be convinced that Adobe's flagship image editor has somewhere on the order of 8,192 different menu selections for you to choose from. In truth, Photoshop has only about 500-plus separate menu items, including some that are duplicated. That figure doesn't count the 100 or so entries for filter plug-ins (which can expand alarmingly as you add third-party goodies). However, even 500-plus menu items are considerably more than you find in the most ambitious restaurants. Basically, if you want to do something in Photoshop, you need to use the menu bar (or its equivalent command snuggled within a palette menu). If you're using the Mac OS, the Photoshop menu bar may share space with Finder components, such as the Apple menu.

The following sections offer a summary of what you can find and where you can find it.

Photoshop also helps you by providing efficient context menus, which change their listings depending on what you're doing. You don't see options you don't need and do see options appropriate to what you're working on. Right-click (Ctrl+click on the Mac) to bring up the menu.

Opening, printing, and saving files

The File menu offers a cornucopia of file options, from opening new images and opening saved files to browsing existing files, closing files, and saving files. You find the page setup, preview, and printing commands, too. To open a file, choose File⇨Open and navigate to the folder containing the file you want to open. Select the file and click Open. For detailed instructions on all the many different ways you can open files, see Book I, Chapter 3.

Making selections

Selections let you work with only part of an image. You can choose an entire layer or only portions of a layer that you select with one of the selection tools, such as the Marquee or Magic Wand tools. The Select menu offers several commands to modify your selection from capturing more pixels to softening the edges of the selection. The Select menu (shown in Figure 1-6) is short and sweet, but the capability and control that the menu unleashes is nothing short of an image-editing miracle.

Understanding selections is such an important cornerstone to your Photoshop knowledge that I devote an entire book (Book III) to showing you how to use them.

Figure 1-6: The Select menu offers commands for making, modifying, saving, and loading your selections.

Making simple image edits

The Edit menu contains tools that enable you to cut, copy, or paste image selections in several different ways. You can fill selections or *stroke* their outlines (create a line along their edges), which I explain in more detail in Book IV, Chapter 2. And you can use this menu to rotate, resize, distort, or perform other *transformations* (changes in size or shape) on your selections (see Book III, Chapter 3). You can undo the change you made in Photoshop, fade a filter, check your spelling, or find and replace text.

Adjusting size, color, and contrast

You'd think the Image menu (shown in Figure 1-7) might have something to do with making changes to an image document as a whole, wouldn't you? In practice, some of the entries you find here do apply to the whole document, but others apply only to particular layers or selections.

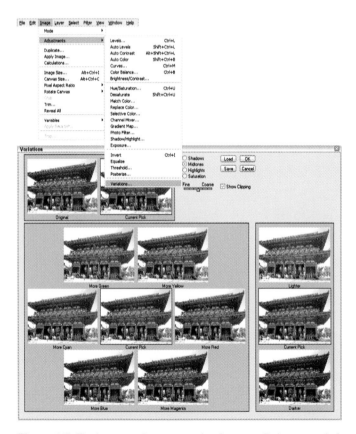

Figure 1-7: The important Image menu is where you find commands for adjusting the size, color, and contrast of your image.

For example, the Mode menu item allows you to change an entire image from color to grayscale. The Image Size, Canvas Size, Rotate Canvas, Crop, and Trim selections all change the whole document in some way. On the other hand, you can only apply the changes wrought from the Adjustments sub-menu to an entire image if the document consists of only a background and has no layers. If the document has more than one layer, adjustments such as Color Balance, Hue/Saturation, or Levels work only with a single layer or a selection on that layer.

The new Variables and Apply Data Set commands are reserved for working with data-driven graphics. Briefly, data-driven graphics make it possible to quickly produce multiple versions of an image for print and Web projects. Multiple versions allow for target audience customization for projects such as direct mail pieces. For example, you can prepare hundreds of versions of a brochure or Web banner based on a single template. The Variables define which elements in a template change. A Data Set is a collection of variables and associated data.

You'll find yourself turning to the Image menu more often than many of the other menus, partially because it's so useful, and partially because, for some reason, many of the options don't have keyboard shortcuts that let you bypass the menu.

Creating layers

Layers give you a way of stacking portions of an image — like sheets of acetate — on top of one another so that you can work on individual pieces separately. Then, when you're satisfied with your changes, you can either combine the changes into a final image or leave them in layers for maximum editing flexibility.

The Photoshop Layers feature, which gets an entire book of its own (Book V), lets you create new and duplicate layers, delete one or several layers, change layer properties (such as a layer's name), or add special features, such as drop shadows or beveled edges, to objects in a layer. You can also create special kinds of layers to make adjustments or mask out portions of an image. The menu has selections for changing the order of the layers (moving a specific layer to the front or top of the stack, and so on) and grouping layers. Figure 1-8 shows an image that has three layers: The first layer is the symphony image, the second layer is the instrument, and the third layer contains the type.

You also can merge layers down, combine them with all other visible layers, or flatten them into one single-layer image (or background). Although con-solidating your layers makes the file smaller, flattening is irreversible after you close the file. Storing an unflattened version of a file is always a good idea in case you want to make more changes later on.

PhotoSpin

Figure 1-8: Layers enable you to easily edit elements individually in your document.

Applying filters

A *filter* is an effect that changes an entire layer, channel, or selection. Some common filters include the Blur and Sharpen filters as well as the Distort filters, such as Spherize. The Filter menu, shown in Figure 1-9, consists almost entirely of cascading categories of image-transmogrifying plug-ins. You can wade through this menu to find the perfect effect to apply to an image or selection. Book VII has everything you need to know about filters.

After you apply a filter, Photoshop copies the filter command to the top of the Filter menu for easy accessibility in case you want to reapply the filter with the exact same settings.

The Filter Gallery command allows you to apply several filters simultaneously in one neat editing window.

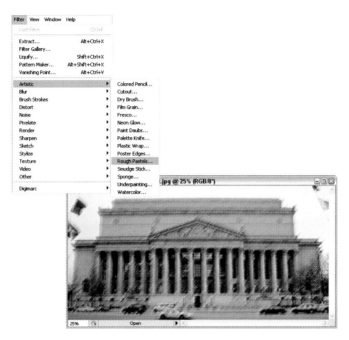

Figure 1-9: The Filter menu is bursting at the seams with plug-ins to improve, enhance, or completely transform your image.

Extract, Liquify, Pattern Maker, and Vanishing Point are more like mini-programs than filters. The rest of the Filter menu consists of 14 different filter categories, each containing from two to a dozen or more options:

- Single-step filters are pretty basic to use but can make a huge impact on an image. These include simple filters such as the Blur, Facet, and Clouds filters. Just select each filter to apply it; it has no options to choose.

- Dialog box-based filters let you choose options galore. These filters come complete with preview windows, buttons, slider controls, and menus. You can distort, pixelate, sharpen, stylize, apply textures, and perform other functions with these filters.

If you install additional filters from third parties, Photoshop lists them at the very bottom of the Filter menu. You can find third-party filters at Web sites such as www.alienskin.com, www.andromeda.com, and www.autofx.com.

Simplifying your edits with the Options bar

The Options bar, shown in Figure 1-10, is a great feature because it eliminates the need to access a separate options palette for each tool. The bar remains available at all times, docked beneath the menu bar (unless you decide to hide it for some bizarre reason), and the options change as you switch tools. If under the menu isn't a good place for it, feel free to move it anywhere you please.

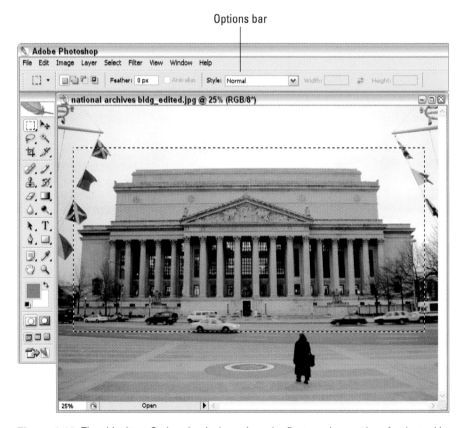

Figure 1-10: The ubiquitous Options bar is dynamic and reflects various options for the tool in use and operation being performed.

Because the Options bar changes its appearance with each active tool, I can't explain all the components you might find there, but every Options bar does have some characteristics in common:

✔ **Gripper bar:** Grab this little bar, on the far left, and drag to undock or dock the Options bar at the top or bottom of the Photoshop window. You can also let the Options bar float anywhere in the working space.

✔ **Tool options:** This box displays the icon of the currently active tool and may include some options for that tool.

✔ **Options pop-up menu:** The Options bar may have a pop-up menu that includes a selection of brush tips (for painting and erasing tools), a flyout-type options menu that lets you select presets (saved settings) for various tools, and additional options, such as the size of the icons used to represent brush tips. You may also reset a particular tool or all tools to their Photoshop default values.

✔ **Bar options:** Additional options, such as mode, opacity, feather, type styles, and fonts are arrayed on the rest of the Options bar.

✔ **Adobe Bridge button:** The Adobe Bridge button (a folder with a magnifying glass and shell icon) allows you to access the cross application Bridge with a mere click. See Book I, Chapter 4 for lots of details.

✔ **Palette Well:** If your monitor has a screen resolution higher than 800 x 600 pixels, the Palette Well appears at the right side of the Options bar. You can drag palettes from their groups into the Palette Well, where only their tabs appear. Click the tab, and the palette appears, ready for use. When you click again in your document, the palette shrinks down to its tab.

The Palette Well is a great tool for keeping your frequently used palettes accessible. I like to keep some palettes, particularly the Layers and Channels palettes, open in the workspace at all times, but some others (such as the Swatches or Styles palettes) don't need to be visible on-screen at all times.

Viewing and navigating the image

A hodgepodge of functions is sprinkled throughout the View menu. Some of them, such as Proof Setup, Proof Colors, and Gamut Warning, won't trouble you until you've become a fairly advanced Photoshop user. For new Photoshop users, the various commands to zoom into and out of the image are likely the most familiar. You can also choose your screen mode, which lets you view your image full screen with the menu bar and palettes, or full screen with just palettes.

You're better off accessing some functions, especially the zoom features, through keyboard shortcuts. See Book I, Chapter 5 for details.

From the View menu, you can select which extras Photoshop displays. You can choose to see (or hide) the following, as shown in Figure 1-11:

Figure 1-11: Viewing and navigating your image are the main tasks on the View menu.

- **Layer Edges:** Displays a blue stroked box that surrounds the boundaries of the content of the selected layer.

- **Selection Edges:** Moving lines that define the boundary of a selection and are very useful for obvious reasons.

- **Target Path:** Lines and curves that define a shape or are used to select part of an image. You definitely want to see them if they need editing.

- **Grids and Guides:** Lines that display on-screen and are great when you're aligning selections, objects, or other components, and potentially distracting when you're not.

- **Smart Guides:** Smart Guides enable you to precisely position and align layer content and only appear when needed.

- **Slices:** Rectangular pieces of an image to which you can optimize or apply Web features. If you slice the image, you probably want to view the results.

- **Annotations:** On-screen notes and audio annotations that you can create and view (or play). Annotations can sometimes be confusing, unless you're already confused; then annotations can help you sort out what's what.

The View menu holds the controls for turning on and off the *snap* feature in Photoshop. (The snap feature makes objects magnetically attracted to grids and guides.) You can also create new guides, lock and clear *slices* (see Bonus Chapter 2 for slice-and-dice information), and turn rulers on or off.

Chapter 2: Getting to Know the Tools Palette

In This Chapter

✏ **Using the Tools palette**

✏ **Taking a look at what each tool does**

✏ **Creating tool presets**

*A*fter you have a good grasp of the overall Photoshop environment (described in Book I, Chapter 1), you're ready to dive into the cache of gadgets that, along with the menus and palettes and dialog boxes, make it all happen. Just as you can use a saw, hammer, and nails to transform a pile of 2 x 4s into a garden gazebo, you can use the Lasso tool, Healing Brush, and Smudge tool to convert a mediocre photo into a masterpiece that's fit to be framed. But remember, behind every garden gazebo is a carpenter who knew how to use the tools required to build it.

Turning On the Tools Palette

You can access the Tools palette by choosing Window➪Tools. Here are a few tips for using the Tools palette:

✏ To quickly hide and show the Tools palette (along with the other palettes), press Tab.

✏ To collapse the Tools palette, double-click the title bar above the feather icon at the top.

✏ To move the Tools palette anywhere within the Photoshop window, drag the title bar above the feather icon.

Selecting tools

To select a tool, simply click it in the Tools palette. A small black triangle in the bottom-right corner of a tool slot indicates that more tools are hidden behind that tool on a *flyout menu,* shown in Figure 2-1. You can also access tools by using keyboard shortcuts (which are listed in the Cheat Sheet at the front of the book).

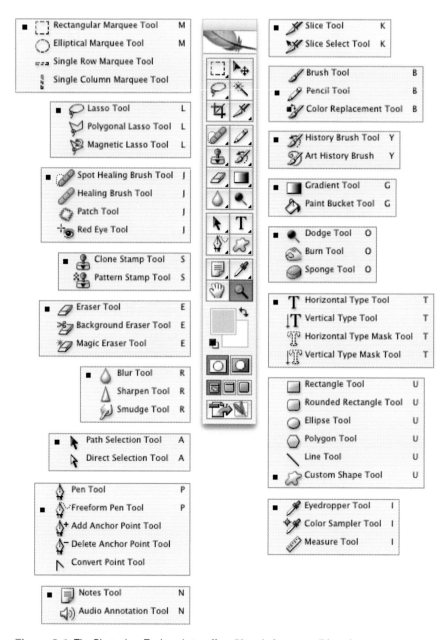

Figure 2-1: The Photoshop Tools palette offers 58 tools for your editing pleasure.

For the most part, you can access a hidden tool by pressing the Shift key along with the keyboard letter of the visible tool. For example, to select the Pencil tool, which shares the flyout menu with the Brush tool, press Shift+B.

If you don't like having to press the Shift key to access a hidden tool, choose Edit⇨Preferences⇨General (Photoshop⇨Preferences⇨General on the Mac) and deselect the Use Shift Key for Tool Switch option. You can then rotate through the tools by pressing the same letter repeatedly.

When you hover your mouse over a tool, color control, or icon, you see a *tool tip*. The tool tip tells you the name of the tool or icon and its keyboard shortcut, if any. Although helpful at first, it can get annoying after a while. Turn it off by deselecting the Show Tool Tips option in the General Preferences dialog box.

Getting to know your tools

The Tools palette is divided into three basic sections: tools, color swatches, and icons for masking modes and viewing options. The next several sections introduce you to the tools. The following list details the other residents of the Tools palette, shown in Figure 2-2:

✔ **Foreground Color and Background Color:** *Color swatches* represent the current foreground and background colors. When using some of the tools, such as the Brush or Pencil, you may apply either of these colors. The small black-and-white swatches represent the default colors. Click the Default Colors icon to reset the colors to the default. Click the curved arrow icon to switch the foreground and background colors. For everything you need to know on color, see Book II, Chapter 3.

✔ **Edit in Standard Mode and Edit in Quick Mask Mode:** The first set of icons allows you to work in either Standard mode (the icon on the left) or Quick Mask mode. I cover Quick Masks, which offer a way to view, make, and edit a selection, in detail in Book VI, Chapter 2.

✔ **Screen Modes:** Standard screen mode, the icon on the far left, is the default setting. This mode enables you to see your entire Photoshop desktop. You can also select Full Screen Mode with Menu Bar, which hides your desktop background and other open images. Or click Full Screen Mode, to the far right, to hide your desktop background, any open images, and the menu bar.

✔ **ImageReady icon:** ImageReady is Photoshop's sister Web graphics program. The arrow pointing to a feather icon is Edit in ImageReady, which launches ImageReady. The feather icon at the top of Tools palette and Photoshop transport you to the Photoshop and ImageReady area of Adobe's Web site, where you can find tips, tech support, upgrades, and news on products and events.

Figure 2-2: The Tools palette's color, viewing, and masking options.

Introducing the Photoshop Tools

I'm just giving you a very brief description of what each tool does. You become more thoroughly initiated with the use of each of the tools as you go through the book. Don't want to go page by page through the book? Okay. Well, you're in luck; I also give you the exact spot where you can find more on each of the tools. For what it's worth, I have organized the tools into logical groupings, although some can cross over into other groups and some are so unique that they don't fit well in any group.

Using selection tools

The selection tools are the workhorses of Photoshop. They allow you to capture and isolate pixels so that you can edit or manipulate just a portion of an image. Marquee tools capture rectangular, elliptical, or single rows or columns of pixels. Figure 2-3 shows an example of an elliptical selection. Whereas the lasso tools make freeform selections, the Magic Wand tool creates selections by picking up pixels of similar colors. And the Move and Crop tools do just what their names describe — move and crop images. See Book III, Chapter 1 for details on all the selection tools but the Move tool and Crop tool. You can find Move tool details in Book III, Chapter 3 and Book V, Chapters 1 and 5. Crop tool details reside in Book II, Chapter 1.

Figure 2-3: The Elliptical Marquee tool (left) lets you make an elliptical selection, while the Move tool (right) enables you to move a selection within your image.

Creating and modifying paths

The path tools create and modify *paths,* which are elements comprised of straight and curved segments and anchor points. You can then use these paths as a basis for a selection or to define a shape.

Because of their precision, using path tools to ultimately create a difficult selection usually yields better results than you can achieve with the selection tools.

The Path Selection and Direct Selection tools select your paths and path components after you draw the path. Figure 2-4 shows examples of using the Pen tool and Direct Selection tool, respectively. For more on the Pen tools, see Book III, Chapter 2.

Corbis Digital Stock
Figure 2-4: The Pen tool creates a path comprised of anchor points and segments, while the Direct Selection tool allows you to select those points and segments and manipulate them.

Using painting tools

The painting tools, in general, allow you to apply color or erase pixels. In the case of the Gradient tool, you can apply multiple colors simultaneously. And with the Art History Brush tool, you paint on a stylized effect rather than color. The Color Replacement tool lets you replace the color of your image with the foreground color. Figure 2-5 shows an example of a heart drawn with the Custom Shape tool, painted with a special effect brush (left), and later (right) partially erased with the Eraser tool.

Figure 2-5: The painting tools can add texture and color to a basic shape, while the Eraser tool erases pixels to reveal your background color.

All the painting tools rely on the Brushes palette for the size, shape, texture, and angle for the tip of the tool. See Book IV, Chapters 1 and 2 for details on most of the painting tools. You find an explanation of the Eraser's Erase to History option in Book II, Chapter 4.

Using tools for cloning and healing

The cloning and retouching tools are the powerhouse tools to break out when you need to do some image repair work. These tools allow you to duplicate portions of your image, paint with a pattern, or seamlessly fix scratches, wrinkles, and other blemishes. The unique History Brush tool lets you actually paint a previous version of your image back into your current image — perfect for undoing mistakes.

Photoshop stole a couple user-friendly healing tools from Photoshop Elements. The Spot Healing Brush quickly removes small blemishes and hickeys of all kinds. The Red Eye tool removes the nasty red reflections in the eyes of your loved ones, as shown in Figure 2-6. Be sure and check out Book VIII, Chapter 3 for info on cloning and healing. You can find History Brush details in Book II, Chapter 4. And for all you need to know about pattern stamping, see Book VI, Chapter 2.

Figure 2-6: The Red Eye tool is a quick and easy way to correct demon eyes.

Creating effects with typographical tools

The type tools pretty much do what their moniker suggests — create type of varying sorts. The Horizontal Type tool and Vertical Type tool create regular old type, plus type on a path, whereas the Mask Type tools create selections in the shape of letters, which you can then fill with images. Figure 2-7 shows text created using both the Horizontal Type and Horizontal Type Mask tools. For type details, see Book IV, Chapter 3.

life's a beach

Corbis Digital Stock

Figure 2-7: You can easily create both vector type (right) or a type mask (left) in Photoshop.

Using focus and toning tools

The focus and toning tools allow you to enhance your image by altering the pixels in various ways. You can lighten, darken, blur, smudge, sharpen, saturate, or desaturate color in selective portions of your image.

TIP

These tools work best for touching up smaller areas rather than the entire image. For example, in Figure 2-8, I used the Smudge tool to spike the groom's hair. Hopefully he doesn't take it personally. To saturate the orange on the right, I used the Sponge tool. See Book VIII, Chapter 2 for all you want to know about focus and toning tools.

Corbis Digital Stock

Figure 2-8: You can make your images stand out from the crowd with the Smudge (left) or Sponge (right) tool.

Creating shapes

The shape tools allow you to create vector-based elements in your image. You can fill these elements with the foreground color or leave them as an empty path.

Although vector-based elements are the heart and soul of the shape tools, you can also create shapes filled with pixels of the foreground color. For shape details, see Book IV, Chapter 1. For more on resolution, see Book II, Chapter 1. Figure 2-9 shows the Custom Shape (left) and Rectangle and Ellipse tools (right) in action.

Figure 2-9: Create shapes from large preset libraries or from your own imagination with the shape tools.

Viewing, navigating, sampling, and annotating tools

Photoshop has an abundance of tools to help you view and navigate your image window. These tools allow you to zoom in (as shown in Figure 2-10) and out, move your image within the window, and measure distances and angles. The Eyedropper and Color Sampler tools let you pick up and sample color respectively — handy for grabbing or evaluating color in an image. The Notes tool and Audio Annotation tool create written and audio notes that you can leave in an image window — useful for collaboration purposes or simply for reminders to yourself. See Book II, Chapter 3 for more on the Eyedropper and Color Sampler tools. For the lowdown on the Measure, Zoom, and Hand tools, see Book I, Chapter 5.

Figure 2-10: The Zoom tool enables you to zoom in and out of your image.

Bonus Chapter 3 covers the Notes and Annotation tools. See the Introduction for details about this book's companion Web site.

Using tools for the Web

Photoshop doesn't have a whole lot of tools dedicated to the preparation of Web images. That's mainly because its companion program, ImageReady, takes up the slack in that department. In the Tools palette, you find the Slice tool and Slice Select tool, which allow you to create and select slices. *Slices* are rectangular sections from an image that you can optimize and turn into Web features. For example, you might slice an image and apply rollovers and image maps to those slices separately for the best viewing experience on your Web page.

See Bonus Chapter 2 for all you need to know on slicing. The Introduction has all the details about this book's Web site.

Saving Time with Tool Presets

Tool presets enable you to create tool settings that you can save and use again. Creating tool presets is a real timesaver if you use specific tool settings on a frequent basis. For example, I make numerous 2-x-2-inch and 2-x-3-inch rectangular selections on images I use in a newsletter. Because I saved the settings as presets, I don't have to redefine them each time I want to select an image for my project.

Creating custom tool presets

Here are the short and simple steps for creating your own custom tool preset:

1. **Choose the tool you want to create a preset for.**

   If a tool doesn't allow for presets, such as the Measure tool for example, the Tool Preset picker button (described in Step 3) is grayed out.

2. **Select the option you want for the tool on the Options bar.**

   For example, if you chose the Rectangular Marquee in Step 1, you may want to choose Fixed Size from the Style pop-up menu and then enter your desired Width and Height.

3. **Click the Tool Preset picker button on the Options bar, as shown in Figure 2-11 (it's on the far left side of the Options bar). Or you can choose Window➪Tool Presets to work through the Tool Presets palette.**

4. **Click the Create New Tool Preset picker button (the dog-eared page icon), or if you're using the Tool Presets palette, choose New Tool Preset from the palette menu.**

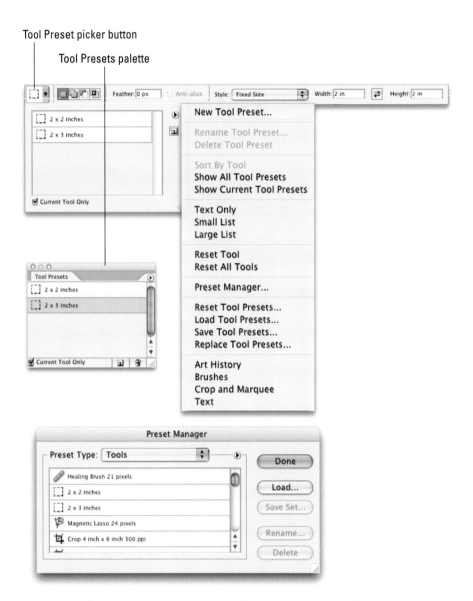

Figure 2-11: Create a custom tool preset for tool settings that you use often.

5. Name the preset and click OK.

Your new preset is now saved and ready for reuse.

6. To select the tool preset, you can do one of three things:

- Click the Tool Preset picker button and select a preset from the picker pop-up menu.

- Select a preset in the Tool Presets palette.

- Select a preset in the Preset Manager. Choose Tools from the pop-up menu and select your preset.

The Tool Presets palette contains a trash can icon that enables you to quickly delete a preset. Select the preset and drag it to the trash.

Managing your presets

You can manage your presets by choosing options from the Tool Preset picker pop-up menu. Table 2-1 describes these options.

Table 2-1	The Tool Preset Picker Pop-Up Menu
Option	*What It Does*
Dock to Palette Well	Places the Tool Presets palette in the Palette Well for easy accessibility.
New Tool Preset	Creates a new preset.
Rename Tool Preset	Renames the preset. (Select the preset in the list and then choose this option.)
Delete Tool Preset	Deletes a preset. (Select the preset in the list and then choose this option.)
Sort by Tool	Groups your presets by tool.
Show All Tool Presets	Shows the presets for all your tools.
Show Current Tool Presets	Shows the presets for the active tool only.
Text Only	Gives you the name of the preset without the icon.
Small List	Shows a small icon, along with the preset name.
Large List	Shows a larger icon with the preset name.
Reset Tool	Closes the active preset and returns to the default tool setting.
Reset All Tools	Returns all tools to their defaults.
Preset Manager	Opens the Preset Manager, which manages all the various libraries of preset brushes, swatches, gradients, styles, patterns, contours, custom shapes, and tools. You can also load other libraries and the custom preset libraries you have created. In addition, you can rename or delete a preset library.
Reset Tool Presets	Deletes all your tool presets at once. If you want to restore the defaults but keep your custom tool presets, choose Append.
Load Tool Presets	Loads tool presets that have been previously saved or acquired elsewhere.

continued

Table 2-1 *(continued)*

Option	What It Does
Save Tool Presets	Saves a custom set of tool presets for later retrieval. The saved file has a .tpl extension.
Replace Tool Presets	Replaces your current tool presets. Allows you to load a .tpl file that replaces your current tool presets.
Art History, Brushes, Crop and Marquee, and Text options	Allows you to either append or replace your current tool presets with the tool presets from each of those individual libraries.

Chapter 3: Starting, Finishing, and Getting It on Paper

In This Chapter

✐ **Opening images**

✐ **Saving images**

✐ **Closing down Photoshop**

✐ **Printing from Windows and Mac**

*A*lthough you can create some interesting images from scratch in Photoshop, most of the time you'll be working with digital pictures that already exist. These may be images captured by your scanner, photos you've grabbed with your digital camera, or snapshots stored on a Kodak Photo CD.

Photoshop offers you lots of different options for opening existing images, creating new images, and saving original files or copies to your hard drive. After you open, edit, and save your files, you may want to transfer those images from screen to paper. This chapter takes you through the steps you need to know to get your photos in and out of Photoshop.

Browsing for Files

If you don't know the exact filename or location of an image, you can use Adobe Bridge to search for and open files. (Check out Book I, Chapter 4 for a complete description of Bridge.) The Adobe Bridge replaces the previous File Browser and is designed to work across all CS2 applications. Finding a file is about as easy as you might expect: Choose File⇨Browse, or press Alt+Ctrl+O (Option+⌘+O on the Mac). Guess what! The Bridge window opens, as shown in Figure 3-1.

You can also just click the new Go to Bridge button, which looks like a folder and magnifying glass, and is on the right side of the Options bar.

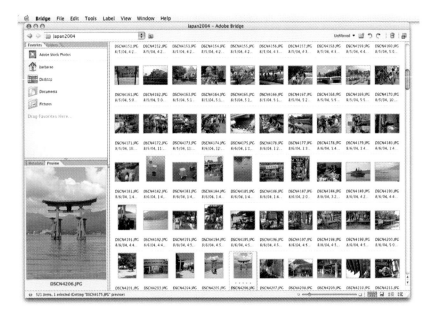

Figure 3-1: The new Adobe Bridge allows you to efficiently search for your images.

To navigate to a folder you want to search, use the folder tree in the upper-left corner of the window or click the Folder tab and locate your desired folder from the list. Click an image in the lightbox area to see it in the Preview window (which shows up on the left side of the Bridge). Photoshop graciously provides information about the file in the Metadata palette that shares a space with the Preview.

When you find a file you're sure you want to open, double-click it, or choose File⇨Open on the Bridge menu.

Opening an Image

If you know where an image file is stored, you can open the file in a similar way to opening a word processing, spreadsheet, or other file. Follow these steps to open a file:

1. **Choose File⇨Open, or press Ctrl+O (⌘+O on the Mac).**

   The standard Open dialog box for Windows or the Mac OS appears. The layout of the dialog box differs slightly between the two. Figure 3-2 shows the Windows version, and Figure 3-3 the Mac version.

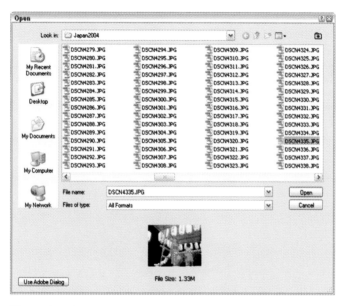

Figure 3-2: Opening a file in Photoshop on a Windows PC.

Figure 3-3: The split window style Mac OS X Open dialog box.

When opening images you now also have the option of choosing between the standard OS (Operating System) or the Adobe dialog box. The Adobe dialog box, shown in Figure 3-4, is like a pared-down mini Bridge, offering various views and the ability to delete items and create folders. Project Tools (the Toolbox icon) enables you to select an item and see its location in Explorer (Windows), the Finder (Mac OS), or in Bridge. You also have access to certain metadata, such as filename, size, and creation dates. Version Cue aficionados also have several tools to use.

Figure 3-4: The Adobe dialog box acts like a mini Bridge.

2. Navigate to the folder that contains your file.

From the Files of Type list (Windows) or Show list (Mac OS), you can choose which types of files you want to display.

To view all image files, choose All Formats (Windows) or All Readable Documents (Mac OS).

3. Click the name of the image file you want to open.

To select multiple files, click the first file and then Ctrl+click (⌘+click in Mac OS X) each additional file.

You may see a preview of the image in the dialog box's Preview window.

4. **After you select the file you want, click the Open button.**

The file opens in Photoshop.

If you choose File➪Open Recent, a submenu lists the last files you worked on. Click a filename to open it or simply type the number next to the filename. You can define the number of files that appear on this menu in the File Handling section of the Preferences dialog box. For the lowdown on how to specify this value, jump ahead to Book I, Chapter 5.

Opening special files

Photoshop needs to know the image format of a file (that is, whether it's a TIFF, PCX, PSD, or JPEG file, for example) before it can open the file. Photoshop uses different methods in Windows and Mac OS to determine the format of an image file:

✔ In Windows, Photoshop looks at the file extension (.tif, .pcx, .psd, and so forth), and if it finds a standard image format extension, it assumes that the file was saved using that format. Note that file extensions are hidden by default in Windows XP. You, like many other users, may have changed the default to display file extensions.

✔ The Mac OS X uses a similar system based on filename extensions. File extensions may or may not be hidden in the Mac OS. Showing or hiding file extensions can be accomplished via any file's Info dialog box. Select the file in the Mac OS X Finder, press ⌘+I, and the Info dialog box pops up. Here you can show or hide the extension for that file, and change what application is associated with that file (and all files with the same extension).

For compatibility reasons, Macintosh applications such as Photoshop usually use the Windows file extension. However, when you move files from one platform to the other, they can easily be misidentified. With Photoshop's Open As feature, you can specify the format you think (or know) that a given file uses. This facility works slightly differently in Windows than in the Mac OS.

Opening special files using the Windows OS

In Windows, follow these steps:

1. **Choose File➪Open As and navigate to the file you want to open.**

2. **From the Open As drop-down list, choose the file format you want to use.**

3. **Double-click the file's icon.**

If you've chosen the right format, the file opens in Photoshop. If the file doesn't open, you may have chosen the wrong format. Choose another and try again.

Opening special files using the Mac OS

The standard Open dialog box includes an Enable option at the top. Choose All Documents from the pop-up menu at the bottom. Then you can choose the file format you'd like to try directly from the Format list.

Opening a Photo CD image

The Eastman Kodak Photo CD format has become a popular image format option because of its flexibility and high quality. Photo CDs store each image in multiple versions as Image Pacs, so you can open the version that has the resolution you need. Your photofinisher can save your images to a CD in Photo CD format for you; Photoshop can't save in this format, however.

Follow these steps to open a Photo CD image:

1. **Choose File⇨Open and navigate to the Photo CD image you want to open.**

2. **Double-click the file's icon.**

   The Kodak PCD Format dialog box appears, as shown in Figure 3-5.

3. **Choose the desired resolution from the Pixel Size drop-down list.**

   In the consumer version, sizes from 64 x 96 to 2048 x 3072 pixels are available.

   Figure 3-5: The PhotoCD format gives you the option of opening various resolution settings.

   The ProCD version of Photo CD has one additional higher resolution: 4096 x 6144 pixels, a whopping 72MB per image! The top resolution in the consumer version is plenty for all but the most demanding applications.

   You can select a color profile tailored to a specific type of image from the Profile drop-down list. (Generally, only advanced users will want to change the default value.)

4. **In the Profile drop-down list, choose the film type for the original image, such as color negative, Ektachrome (E-6), Kodachrome (K-14), and so forth.**

5. **In the Destination Image area, choose a resolution and indicate whether you want the image to open in landscape (wide) or portrait (tall) orientation.**

   Leave the Color Space at the default setting. Only advanced users will want to change the Color Space definition.

6. **Click OK to open the image.**

   In the Image Info area of the dialog box, you can see what type of equipment was used to scan the original as well as the original image type (color negative, transparency, and so forth).

Placing Files

In Photoshop, use File➪Place to put PDF (Portable Document Format), Adobe Illustrator (AI), or EPS (Encapsulated PostScript) files into a layer of their own. These files are often created by programs other than Photoshop, such as Adobe Acrobat, Adobe Illustrator, or CorelDRAW. Although Photoshop can open these files independently, you must use the Place feature if you want to combine them with an existing image.

Follow these steps to place a PDF, Adobe Illustrator, or EPS file:

1. **Open an existing document into which you want to place a file.**

2. **Choose File➪Place.**

   The Place dialog box opens.

3. **Navigate to the file you want to insert and then double-click the file.**

   For some types of files, such as multipage PDF files, you may see a dialog box like the one shown in Figure 3-6, which lets you specify which page you want to place.

   Your image appears in a bounding box in the center of your Photoshop image.

Figure 3-6: Use the Place command when importing a page from a multipaged PDF into an existing file.

4. **You can reposition the artwork by positioning your cursor inside the bounding box and dragging. You can also transform (size, rotate, and so on) your placed artwork if desired by dragging or rotating the handles on the bounding box or by entering values on the Options bar.**

   Be careful, however. If you enlarge your placed image too much, you may degrade the quality of your image. For more information on transforming images, see Book III, Chapter 3. Avoid this by creating a smart object, which I explain in Book V, Chapter 5.

   Note that when you place a file, you cannot edit the text or vector artwork in it. Why? Because Photoshop rasterizes the file, using the resolution of the file into which you placed it. Note too that when art is larger than the Photoshop image, Photoshop downsizes the art so that it fits the image. See Book II, Chapter I for more on resolution.

5. **Choose Anti-Alias on the Options bar if you want to soften the edges of the artwork during the transformation.**

   Not choosing the option produces a hard edge.

6. **Double-click inside the bounding box to commit the placed image to a new layer. You can also press Enter (Return on the Mac) or click the Commit button (the check icon) on the Options bar.**

Creating a New Image

At some point, you'll want to create a new image from scratch. You may want an empty canvas to paint on or need a blank image as scratch space. Or you may want to paste a copied selection into a new document.

Follow these steps to use the New feature to create a new image:

1. **Choose File➪New or press Ctrl+N (⌘+N on the Mac).**

   The New dialog box appears, as shown in Figure 3-7.

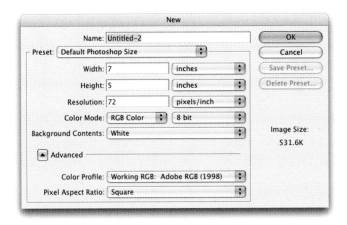

Figure 3-7: Specify all your desired options in the New dialog box.

2. **Type a name for the new file.**

   If you specify no name, Photoshop creates one for you, such as Untitled-1, Untitled-2, and so forth.

3. **Enter the width and height of your image by using one of the following methods:**

   • **Enter the width and height manually.** Type the width and height of your choice in the text boxes. The Preset size automatically reverts to Custom. Note that when you change the units for either the width or height, the other also changes. Press the Shift key to change both width and height independently.

- **Choose a preset size from the Preset pop-up menu.** The document sizes include Default Photoshop Size; common printing sizes such as 4 x 6, 5 x 7, or 8 x 10 inches; display screen sizes such as 640 x 480 pixels or 800 x 600 pixels; digital video and film sizes; plus an array of other popular sizes.

The Clipboard provides the size that corresponds with an image that you have copied. You can also choose to match the size of any open file. Open files are listed at the bottom of the Preset list.

Photoshop also allows you to create a user-defined custom preset based on your defined settings. Click the Save Preset button in the New Document Preset dialog box. Name your preset. Choose any or all the options you want to include in your preset. When you choose not to include an option, Photoshop displays the last used value for that option. Click OK. Your custom preset now appears at the top of the Preset list.

As with other Photoshop dialog boxes, you may change from the default unit of measurement of pixels to another, such as inches.

4. **Enter the resolution for the new document.**

Choosing the right resolution at this point in the creation process is important because if you need to change the resolution later, you degrade image quality. For more information on selecting an appropriate resolution, see Book II, Chapter 1.

Note that Photoshop gives you the size of your image file in the lower-right of the dialog box based on your settings. This information is good to know if you're targeting a specific file size for your image.

5. **From the Color Mode drop-down list, select a color mode.**

Your choices include Bitmap, Grayscale, RGB Color, CMYK Color, and Lab Color.

6. **Choose your desired color depth for your document.**

Only one-bit color depth is available for bitmap images (each pixel is either black or white). The remaining 8-bit and 16-bit color depths are available for the other color modes. For details on modes and color depths, see Book II, Chapter 2.

7. **In the Background Contents drop-down list, select an option for how you want the background layer to be filled.**

Your choices are white, the current background color, or transparent.

8. **Click the Advanced button to display a couple of additional options.**

- **Color Profile** assigns a color profile (a definition of the way color looks in a document) to your new document. The default, Adobe RGB

(1998), is fine when creating a new document unless you have good reason not to otherwise. This setting provides a nice, large gamut (range) of RGB colors.

- **Pixel Aspect Ratio** selects an aspect ratio (the relationship of width to height). The default setting of Square is fine for print or Web images. Images for digital video content may require a non-square aspect ratio such as D1/DV NTSC or others.

9. **Click OK when you finish entering your options.**

Photoshop creates the new image.

Saving a File

Before you exit Photoshop, you'll want to save your file on your hard drive or other media. Don't worry if you forget to do this; Photoshop won't let you exit without first asking you if you'd like to save any files that you've changed or newly created. However, saving files from time to time as you work on them is a good idea so that you always have a recent copy safely stored on your drive.

Follow these steps to save a file:

1. **Choose File⇨Save to store the current file with its present name. Choose File⇨Save As to store a new file never saved or a file already saved with a different name, or even a file with the same name but in a different location.**

   The dialog box appears, as shown in Figure 3-8.

2. **Navigate to the folder where you'd like to store the file.**

3. **Type a name in the File Name (Save As on the Mac) text box.**

4. **Choose a format from the Format drop-down list.**

   Some file formats have special capabilities and requirements. For details on file formats, see Book II, Chapter 2.

5. **In the Save and Color Options areas, select or deselect (if available) the following check boxes as desired:**

   - **As a Copy:** Save the file as a copy.

   - **Annotations:** Include or delete annotations in the saved copy. (See Bonus Chapter 3 for more on annotations. The Introduction has details about this book's bonus material on the Web.)

   - **Alpha Channels:** Include or ignore alpha channels (stored selections). (See Book VI, Chapter 1 for a discussion of channels.)

   - **Spot Colors:** Enable spot colors in the saved file. (For more information on spot colors, see Book IX, Chapter 1.)

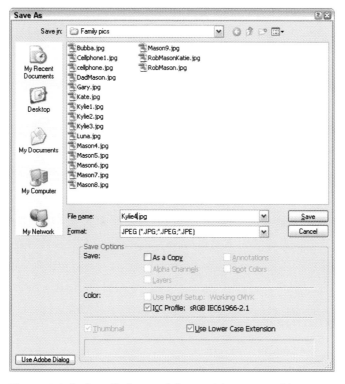

Figure 3-8: Saving a file frequently is one of the smartest things you can do in Photoshop.

- **Layers:** Include layers or simply flatten the image to one layer. (See Book V, Chapter 1 for the lowdown on layers.)

- **Use Proof Setup:** Enable proof setup, which includes an on-screen preview of how the image will look when printed or viewed on a specific device. (See Book II, Chapter 3 for more information.)

- **ICC Profile (Windows)/Embed Color Profile (Mac):** Embed a color profile in the file based on the settings established in your Color Settings dialog box. Leave this value at the default setting, but check out Book II, Chapter 3 for information on the specialized situations when you might want to change it.

- **Thumbnail (Windows only):** Embed a thumbnail image in the file if you've defined thumbnails as optional in Photoshop's Preferences. (You can find more on preferences in Book I, Chapter 5.)

- **Use Lower Case Extension (Windows only):** Use lowercase extensions (that is, `.tif` instead of `.TIF`) regardless of how you type the filename.

6. Depending on which file format you choose, you may get an additional dialog box of options.

For specifics on these file format options, see Book II, Chapter 2.

7. Click Save to store the image.

Closing and Quitting

When your session is finished, you'll want to close up shop and quit Photoshop. PC users, in addition to using the traditional File➪Exit option, can close Photoshop in any of the following ways:

- Choose Close from the Windows Control menu in the upper-left corner of the Photoshop title bar.

- Click the Close (X) button in the upper-right corner of the Photoshop title bar under Windows.

- Press Ctrl+Q.

Mac users can choose Photoshop➪Quit or press ⌘+Q.

With any of these methods, Photoshop asks you, in turn, if you want to save any open file that has not been saved or has not been saved since it was modified in this session. Click the Yes button to close and save the files.

You can also close any open files without exiting Photoshop by pressing Shift+Ctrl+W (Shift+⌘+W on the Mac).

Saving a backup copy

You usually want to have a backup copy of an image safe on your hard drive any time you make changes to a file and, often, periodically throughout a work session. If you change your mind about the modifications you've made to an image, you can always return to the backup copy. Photoshop offers several ways to create such copies:

- **Choose File➪Save As and enter a new name for the file.** Specifying a new location is also a good idea, such as another hard drive or, perhaps a removable storage destination, such as a Zip or CD-R/RW drive.

- **Choose File➪Save As and select the As a Copy check box.** Photoshop simply adds copy to the current filename (for example, myfile.psd becomes myfile copy.psd) and saves the file with that new name.

Photoshop also offers a Layer Comps palette, which enables you to save different configurations of your document by recording the appearance of your layers. For details on this feature, see Book V, Chapter 2.

Getting It on Paper

Hard-copy prints have become a hugely popular output option, thanks largely to the swarm of sub-$200 photo-quality inkjet printers that are vying for your discretionary dollars. Today, anyone can afford a printer capable of producing sparkling prints from digital images. The chief problem is restraining the urge to print everything in sight before your ink tank (and wallet) runs dry.

Actually, making the prints is only a minor puzzle, and one addressed in this section. You can print most images with just a few clicks. Most of the advanced options I discuss in this chapter are needed only for special situations or specialized applications and are not discussed in detail; this section covers only the basics. If you need more detailed information on printing, see Book IX, Chapter 1.

Many photofinishers or service bureaus can make prints from your Photoshop-edited images if you burn them to a CD, save them to a Zip disk, or upload them to an FTP site over the Internet. Adobe has partnered with Shutterfly (www.shutterfly.com) and MyPublisher (www.mypublisher. com) to offer prints of all sizes, calendars, and professionally printed and bound photo books.

Taking a look at printers

You can print Photoshop images on any kind of printer, but, aside from the occasional 200-copy print run of black-and-white "Have You Seen This Kitty?" posters, monochrome laser printers are not high on the list of favored Photoshop output hardware.

More often, you're choosing a full-color printer, probably an inkjet model, but also possibly a dye-sublimation, thermal-wax, or even color laser printer model. Although all these printers produce roughly similar results, they do have some differences, as detailed in the following list:

- **Inkjet printers:** These printers paint the page by spraying a jet of ink one dot at a time, under precision computer control. They produce better results when used with photo paper designed especially for inkjets. Inkjet printers generally provide excellent full-color output, but the cost of consumables (ink and paper) can add up fast.

- **Dye-sublimation printers:** These printers potentially offer better-looking prints, but the printers and materials are more expensive than inkjet printers. They use a continuous *ribbon* of color panels in a roll that is the same width as the print, with each panel used only once. The print head's tiny heating elements can melt dots of dye over a range of 256 values to generate up to 16.8 million colors.

✓ **Thermal-wax printers and solid-ink printers:** These printers use blocks of wax or resin that are melted and sprayed directly onto a page. These devices are generally for advanced-amateur or professional applications.

Printing an image

The process of printing an image in Photoshop is slightly different in the Windows and Mac OS operating systems. The chief differences are in the Page Setup step, in which you select a printer and choose orientation, paper size, and other parameters. The next few sections take a closer look at the Page Setup dialog box in the two operating systems.

Page setup in Microsoft Windows

With Windows applications such as Photoshop, you open the Page Setup dialog box by choosing File⇨Page Setup or by pressing Shift+Ctrl+P. In this dialog box, shown in Figure 3-9, you can select the paper size, orientation (portrait or landscape), and other things, such as which paper tray to use. If you click the Printer button, a second Page Setup dialog box appears. Here, you can choose a specific printer from those attached to your computer or network. Clicking the Properties button takes you to specific options customized for your printer, such as print quality or special effects available with that printer. These vary from printer to printer, so consult your printer's instruction manual.

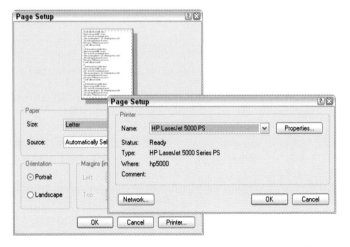

Figure 3-9: Set your desired paper size and orientation in the Windows Page Setup dialog box.

Page setup in the Mac OS

To choose which printer is active in the Mac OS, use the Print Center to access the Page Setup dialog box, shown in Figure 3-10, choose File⇨Page Setup, or press Shift+⌘+P. You can set the page size and orientation, scaling, and additional parameters, depending on your printer.

In Mac OS X, you can also choose a printer directly from the Print dialog box just as you can in Windows. Also in Mac OS X, if you're connected directly to a printer via the USB port, the system automatically detects the printer. If you're on a network, you can use Print Center and select a printer from the Printer list or in the Print dialog box.

Figure 3-10: The Mac Page Setup dialog box offers options for paper size, orientation, and scaling.

Setting printing options

Photoshop has several printing modes to choose from, depending on how much control you need and how much of a hurry you're in. Here are your options:

- ✔ **Print One Copy** is a quick way to print a hard copy using the default settings.

- ✔ **Print** (Ctrl+P, or ⌘+P on the Mac) pops up the standard Windows (or Mac) Print dialog box, with options to choose a new printer, select which pages to print, and so on. The exact options available depend on what printer you are printing to.

- ✔ **Print Online** transports you to Adobe Bridge and automatically launches the Photo Prints command on the Tools⇨Photoshop Services submenu. Note, however, that your images must be in JPEG format.

- ✔ **Print with Preview** (Alt+Ctrl+P, or Option+⌘+P on the Mac) opens an expanded Print dialog box that includes a Preview window and many more options to choose from. You can even access the Page Setup dialog box from this dialog box if you want to change the orientation, paper size, or switch to a different printer. This dialog box is almost identical in Windows, shown in Figure 3-11, and Mac operating systems.

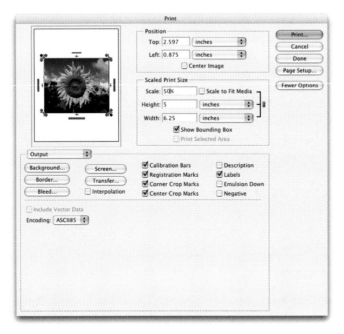

Corbis Digital Stock

Figure 3-11: Print with Preview command gives you more options.

To set your print options, follow these steps:

1. **Choose File⇨Print with Preview.**

   The Print dialog box opens.

2. **Use the Top and Left boxes in the Position area to indicate where you want the image to appear on the page.**

3. **To center the image, select the Center Image check box.**

4. **Click the More Options button and choose Output from the drop-down list located in the Preview area.**

   The other option on the drop-down list, Color Management, controls advanced proofing and color-profile tasks. Check out Book IX, Chapter 1 for information on printing using color management, as well as Book II, Chapter 3 for more detail on general color-management topics.

5. **If you want to scale the image up or down, choose the scale percentage and/or enter height and width values in the Scaled Print Size area.**

   (This doesn't change the physical dimensions of the image, just the print size. But keep in mind that scaling up may give you a less-than-optimum printout.) Additional options include

- **Show Bounding Box:** Places the handles around the image area and allows for visual sizing.

- **Print Selected Area:** Allows you to print only part of a large image.

- **Scale to Fit Media:** Sizes your image to fit on a particular paper size.

6. **Choose the printing options you want to apply:**

   - **Background:** The area surrounding the printed image is called the background, not to be confused with the background color on the Colors palette or the background layer of an image. You can change this color from the default (white) to any other color.

   - **Border:** The dialog box that pops up lets you add a black border around an image in any width from 0 to 10 points, 0 to 3.5 millimeters, or 0 to 1.5 inches.

   - **Bleed:** A bleed is an image that extends right up to the edge of the paper size on one or more edges. In effect, you're cropping *inside* the image area. In practice, most printers don't actually print right to the edge, so to bleed, say, a 5-x-7-inch image, you need to print it on a larger sheet of paper, such as 8 x 10. Clicking the Bleed button opens a dialog box in which you enter a width in inches, millimeters, or points inside the edge of the image.

   - **Screen:** When you click the Screen button, you see the Halftone Screens dialog box that lets you create halftones for color separation. See Book IX, Chapter 1 for more information on color separations.

   - **Transfer:** This is an advanced function used for prepress operations to compensate for the change in dot sizes when halftoned images are printed on a press.

   - **Interpolation:** This option is only available with some printers, particularly PostScript Level 2 (or higher models), to even out the jagged appearance of diagonal lines. Just be aware that interpolation can only help so much and in some cases, it can be damaging. For more on interpolation, see Book II, Chapter 1.

7. **Select options for marking the area outside the print area. These include several items that appear only when the print area is smaller than the paper size:**

   - **Calibration Bars:** This option adds an 11-step grayscale bar outside the image area when printing to a paper size that is larger than the image area. You can use calibration bars to gauge how accurately the gray tones of an image are being reproduced.

   - **Registration Marks:** Registration marks are handy when you're printing with multiple plates for color separations, such as those used in four-color or duotone processes. These marks help keep the plates aligned so the image is printed properly.

- **Corner Crop Marks:** Clicking this box prints crop marks at the corners of the image, which indicate where trimming should take place. You can see these and other marks in Figure 3-12.

- **Center Crop Marks:** These crop marks show where the page will be trimmed at the top, bottom, and each side.

- **Description:** To include a description on a printout, choose File➪File Info and enter the text you want to appeal. Then check the Description box in this dialog box.

- **Labels:** Selecting this check box prints the document name and channel name on the image.

Corner crop marks   Center crop mark

Registration mark   Label

Corbis Digital Stock

Figure 3-12: Crop marks are handy to print.

8. **Set the options that apply when you're printing to film for color separations, if that's the case.**

Be sure to talk to your service bureau or offset printer representative for their recommendations. For more tips on prepress and printing, see Book IX, Chapter 1.

Here are your choices:

- **Emulsion Down:** The side of a film or photographic print paper that is light sensitive is called the *emulsion* side. You must specify whether you want the emulsion side up or side down for film output. Emulsion Down is the most common film output choice, although some publications may request Emulsion Up. The default is Emulsion Up (the check box is not selected). This option is not available with all printers.

- **Negative:** When you print an image on paper, you usually want a positive image, in which case you should not select the Negative check box. If you're printing the image on film (as is the case if you're printing color separations), your printer will probably request a negative.

Chapter 4: Viewing and Navigating Images

In This Chapter

✔ **Exploring the image window**

✔ **Zooming within an image**

✔ **Moving with the Hand tool**

✔ **Traveling around with the Navigator**

✔ **Selecting screen modes**

✔ **Positioning and measuring precisely**

✔ **Finding images with Adobe Bridge**

*P*hotoshop offers a variety of ways to view your image documents as you work with them. You can pull back to look at the big picture or zoom in to work on a tiny portion of the image in minute detail. A useful Navigator palette is also at hand to show you exactly where you are in an image and help you move to a specific spot with a click of the mouse button. Should you want to align objects precisely on the screen, Photoshop offers grids and guides with some "magnetic" properties. And, if you're having trouble finding the image you want, a new uber-browser, called the Bridge, helps you search visually.

This chapter introduces you to all these viewing and navigating aids, each designed to help you spend less time cruising around the images and more time working with them.

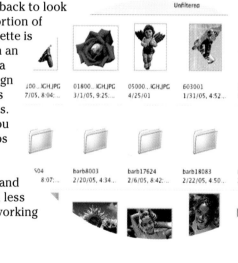

Looking at the Image Window

Each Photoshop image document resides in its own window. A great feature of this window is that you can open multiple image windows for the same image. This feature comes in handy because sometimes you want to look at an image from two perspectives. For example, you may want to get up close and personal with an image to edit pixels, but you still want to view the full image in a fairly large size, as shown in Figure 4-1. In either case, all you need to do is create a new image window for the same image. You can size each window separately, and you can center the window on any portion of the image you like.

Corbis Digital Stock

Figure 4-1: Creating a new image window enables you to view the overall image while editing an area in close-up view.

Here's a quick list of what you can do with multiple windows:

- **Keep different parts of an image straight by creating multiple windows.** Select the document window you want and then choose Window⇨ Arrange⇨New Window for (filename) from the menu bar. You can size and position the new window and zoom in or out without affecting the view of the original window.

- **Keep windows organized by cascading them.** If you find that you've created so many windows that you can't view them all easily, Photoshop can automatically arrange them for you in its working space. Choose Window⇨Arrange⇨Cascade to create an overlapping stack of windows arranged from the upper-left to the lower-right side of your display.

- **Keep from losing important windows by tiling them.** Choose Window⇨ Arrange⇨Tile Horizontally or Vertically to arrange the windows side by side in a horizontal or vertical fashion without overlapping. Photoshop changes the size of the document windows so they all fit on-screen, but doesn't change the zoom amount. The reduced-size windows have scroll bars to let you view the hidden portion of the window.

✔ **Tidy up by closing windows you don't need anymore.** To close a specific window, click its Close button in the upper-right corner of its title bar in Windows (at the top left in the Mac OS).

✔ **Close all windows in one fell swoop.** To close all windows, choose File⇨Close All. You can also close all opened document windows by pressing the Shift key and clicking any open document's Close button. On the Mac, do the same thing by pressing the Option key and clicking the Close button.

✔ **Minimize a document.** In Windows, click the Minimize button (a square with the horizontal line) to minimize a document window. On the Mac, minimize an active document and place the thumbnail in the Dock, choose Window⇨Arrange⇨Minimize. To maximize the image, simply click the image thumbnail in the Dock.

✔ **Bring all Photoshop documents to the front (in Mac OS).** The Mac OS allows you to work in multiple applications and multiple files simultaneously. Sometimes when you switch back into working in Photoshop, your documents may be buried behind non-Photoshop files that are open in the other applications (the files are *interleaved*). Choose Window⇨ Arrange⇨Bring All to Front to bring all your Photoshop documents to the forefront.

✔ **Get your images in a row (in Windows).** Align minimized image windows along the bottom of the screen by choosing Window⇨Arrange⇨ Arrange Icons.

One image, two monitors

For many image-editing enthusiasts and professionals, one monitor simply isn't enough. If you have Windows 2000 or later installed or any recent Mac OS, you can set up your computer so that you can use two monitors to edit an image. The extra space offers advantages for viewing and navigating your images:

In Windows, you can drag the image window anywhere in the Photoshop working space. If you want to drag it to a second display screen (and your video card supports spanning two displays) you have to stretch the Photoshop working space (or application window) across both displays. This works great if both monitors are the same size. But if the monitors are significantly different sizes, it doesn't work so well. Remember that you can, however, move palettes and dialog boxes onto a second monitor.

Although explaining how to set up multiple monitors on various operating systems is beyond the scope of this book, you can likely find details on how to set up an additional monitor in your operating system's Help feature.

Zooming In and Out of Image Windows

Photoshop offers several ways to zoom in or out of an image, but you'll probably find yourself using one method, such as the keyboard shortcuts, almost instinctively. Each method has advantages of its own. The following sections offer a quick discussion of the main zoom features as well as some of the lesser-known zooming tricks.

Zooming with keyboard shortcuts

The keyboard shortcuts are the quickest and easiest way to zoom, after you use them enough to remember what they are. Table 4-1 offers a rundown of the handiest keyboard shortcuts, which work no matter what tool you're using. When you press a keyboard shortcut, Photoshop zooms in or out by one of its preset increments (such as 100 percent, 200 percent, 50 percent, 33 percent, 25 percent, and so forth). The maximum magnification Photoshop allows is 1,600 percent; the minimum magnification is 0.0533 percent.

Table 4-1	Zooming with Keyboard Shortcuts	
To Do This	*Windows Shortcut*	*Mac Shortcut*
Zoom in	Ctrl+ the plus key (Press Ctrl and then the + key.)	⌘+
Zoom out	Ctrl+ the minus key (Press Ctrl and then the - key.)	⌘-
Zoom in to a point centered on where you click the mouse button	Spacebar+Ctrl and click	Spacebar+ ⌘ and click
Zoom out from a point centered on where you click	Spacebar+Alt and click	Spacebar+ Option and click

Using the Zoom tool

Click the Zoom tool in the Tools palette or press Z to activate it. Click anywhere in the image to magnify it by one of the preset magnifications mentioned in the preceding section. Press the Alt key (or the Option key on the Mac) and click with the Zoom tool to zoom out. In either case, the zoom centers on the point you click.

The Zoom tool's big advantage is its zoom selection facility. With the Zoom tool, drag in your image to create a temporary selection. When you release the button, Photoshop zooms in to fill the image window at the highest magnification that includes the selected area.

When the Zoom tool is active, you also have additional zoom tools on the Options bar, as shown in Figure 4-2. Choosing a plus (+) or minus (-) sets the default magnification of the Zoom tool to either enlarge or reduce the image.

Corbis Digital Stock

Figure 4-2: Zoom options include handy buttons for fitting your image on-screen and displaying the image's print size.

As you zoom in and out, Photoshop does not alter the size of the document window, so your image may become too large for its window (in which case scroll bars appear so you can view the rest of the image) or too small (in which case a gray border appears around the image).

Select the Resize Windows to Fit option on the Options bar, and Photoshop automatically changes the size of the document window to show the full document in view, up to the size of the Photoshop working area.

Other ways to zoom

Although you'll likely use the zoom methods mentioned in the preceding section most often, Photoshop offers some other ways to zoom that come in handy from time to time as well:

✓ **Zooming from the View menu:** Choose View➪Zoom In or View➪Zoom Out to enlarge or reduce the image from the menu bar. You can also choose from these options on the View menu:

- Actual Pixels (which shows your image on-screen at a 1:1 pixel ratio)

- Fit on Screen (which enlarges the image to the maximum size that fits on-screen)

- Print Size (which shows the image at the size it will print)

To resize windows to fit on-screen when you're not using the Zoom tool, choose Edit➪Preferences➪General (or Photoshop➪Preferences➪ General in Mac OS X) and select the Zoom Resizes Windows option.

✔ **Typing ratios in the Magnification box:** The Magnification box in the status bar at the bottom of the Photoshop working area (in Windows) or the bottom of each document (in Mac OS) shows the current magnification ratio. Type an exact magnification ratio in this box to produce a custom zoom level. This box is handy if you need a specific amount of enlargement or reduction.

Another Magnification box appears in the Navigator palette, along with some other options for zooming. I describe them later in this chapter.

✔ The following commands live on the Window➪Arrange menu.

- **Match Zoom:** Choose Match Zoom to have all your open documents match the magnification percentage of your active document.

- **Match Location:** Choose this command to match the locations of all your open documents with the location of your active document. For example, if you are viewing the center portion of an image, choosing this command then adjusts the views of all your open documents to the center as well.

- **Match Zoom and Location:** And finally, Match Zoom and Location does both commands simultaneously.

✔ **Magnifing by dragging:** With the Zoom tool, drag over the portion of the image you want to zoom into. A selection marquee appears, and when you release the mouse button, that portion of the image fills your document window. To freeze and then move the selection marquee around the image, begin your drag and then press the spacebar while dragging the marquee to a new location.

Handling the Hand tool

The Hand tool helps you to quickly move around in an image document and works similarly to a scroll bar.

The Hand tool is more of a function than an actual tool because you rarely need to click the Hand tool to use it. Simply press the spacebar while using any other tool, and the cursor changes into the Hand icon, enabling you to move the image around in its window by dragging.

Here are some tips for using this tool:

✔ **Press H to activate the tool:** To activate the Hand tool without clicking its icon in the Tools palette, just press the H key.

✔ **Use the Options bar to change the size of a window:** When the Hand tool is active, the Actual Pixels, Fit on Screen, and Print Size buttons appear on the Options bar. Click these buttons to enlarge or reduce the image window so the whole image fits in the window; make the document as large as it can be in your working space; or make the document appear in the size it will be when printed.

✔ **Use the Hand tool while zooming:** When the Hand tool is active, you can press the Alt key (Option key on the Mac) and click the image to zoom out, or press the Ctrl key (⌘ key on the Mac) and click to zoom in — without needing to press the spacebar as you would with the normal keyboard shortcut.

✔ **Scroll All Windows:** This option enables you to move around all open documents simultaneously.

Double-clicking the Hand tool resizes the document image so its longest dimension expands to fill the screen in that direction. A tall, portrait-oriented image balloons up until the document is as tall as possible in the Photoshop working area. A wide, landscape-oriented image expands its width to fit within the left and right borders of the screen.

✔ **Press the Page Up or Page Down buttons to change the view:** These buttons move the view up or down by a window.

Now that you have become friendly with the Zoom and Hand tools, here is one last tip. If you press the Shift key while scrolling with the Hand tool or zooming with the Zoom tool, all open image windows scroll or zoom together. This trick can come in especially handy, for example, when you create another view of the same document (Window➪Arrange➪New Window).

Cruising with the Navigator Palette

Some Photoshop users don't use the Navigator palette, which is a roadmap to your image document, nearly as often as they could, and there's a simple reason for that: In its default size, the Navigator palette is just too darned small to be of use.

Most new Photoshop users see the tiny Navigator window and decide that working with such a small thumbnail image isn't worth the bother. There's a quick fix, and after you've seen exactly what the Navigator palette can do for you, it may become one of your favorite tools.

Here are the keys to using the Navigator palette:

✔ **Resize the Navigator palette:** Before you begin working with the Navigator palette, grab the size box at the lower-right corner of the Navigator palette and drag it down and to the right to create a jumbo version with a much larger, more viewable thumbnail, as shown in Figure 4-3.

Resizing works really well if you are using a second monitor. Placing the jumbo-sized Navigator palette on the second monitor works great. For more on working with two monitors, see the related sidebar elsewhere in this chapter.

Corbis Digital Stock

Figure 4-3: The Navigator palette is more productive and user-friendly when enlarged.

The Navigator palette is one palette that you probably don't want to relegate to the Palette Well. It's most useful when it is visible at all times. Position the Navigator palette to one side of your image so it's ready for instant use.

✓ **View the thumbnail:** The entire Navigator window shows the full document image, with an outline called a *View box* showing the amount of image visible in the document window at the current zoom level.

✓ **Change the view:** Click anywhere in the thumbnail *outside* the View box to center the box at that position. The comparable view in your main document window changes to match.

✓ **Move the view:** Click anywhere in the thumbnail inside the View box and then drag to move the box to a new position. The main document window changes to match the new view.

✓ **Zoom in or out:** Click the Zoom In button (which has an icon of two large pyramids) or Zoom Out button (which has an icon of two smaller pyramids) to zoom in or out. Or drag the Zoom slider that resides between the two icons. The View box changes sizes as you zoom in or out, and Photoshop magnifies or reduces the view in the original document window to match, as well.

✓ **Specify an exact magnification:** The lower-left corner of the Navigator palette has a Magnification box just like the one in the status bar. It shows the current magnification, and you can type a new value to zoom to the exact magnification level you need.

If the View box color is too similar to a dominant color in your image, you can choose a new color for its outline by selecting Palette Options from the Navigator palette pop-up menu.

Choosing a Screen Mode

Photoshop's working area can become horribly cluttered. And here's a secret: The more adept you become, the more cluttered the desktop becomes. Just when you begin to appreciate a neatly docked Options bar and the convenience of displaying palettes, you realize that you've gobbled up all your free working space.

Photoshop has three different screen modes (or maybe five, depending on what you consider to be a screen mode). Each mode shows or hides some of the elements on the screen at the press of a key or click of the mouse button. Three screen modes are in the Tools palette; two more are hidden but easily accessible. Table 4-2 shows you how to unclutter your screen quickly.

Table 4-2	Cleaning Up Working Space Clutter	
Do This . . .	*. . . To Change to This Screen Mode*	*What's Happening*
Press Shift+Tab	Hide all palettes	All the palettes in your working space — except for the Tools palette and any palettes stowed in the Palette Well — vanish. When you need to access them again, press Shift+Tab again.
Press the Tab key	Hide all palettes and the Options bar	All the palettes (including the Tools palette) and the Options bar vanish, leaving you with a clean workspace showing only the menu bar, application title bar, and any open documents.
Click the Full Screen with Menu Bar icon in the second row from the bottom of the Tools palette	Full Screen mode with menu bar	Only the active document window is visible, along with the palettes, menu bar, and Options bar. The document window is maximized, and the other documents are hidden. (See Figure 4-4.)
Click the Full Screen button to view the image alone, with the menu bar and other components hidden	Full Screen mode	Press Shift+Tab to hide the palettes. Press Tab to hide the palettes and the Options bar.
Click the Normal Screen button	Standard Screen mode	The default Photoshop screen appears, displaying all menus and palettes.

Press the F key to cycle between the three screen modes.

Dynamic Graphics, Inc.

Figure 4-4: Get the effect of viewing your image against a black matboard.

In the Full Screen mode, Standard Screen mode, or Full Screen mode with menu bar, you can still press Shift+Tab to hide the palettes and Tab to hide the Options bar.

If you hide the Tools palette when in either Full Screen mode, you can't click the icons to return. Press Tab or Shift+Tab to reveal the Tools palette, or simply press the F key to cycle among the screen modes.

Getting Precise Layout Results

Photoshop includes numerous useful features that help you lay out your images precisely. There are dozens of reasons to make a selection in a particular place, position an object at an exact location, or align several objects along the same imaginary line. Here are a few examples:

- You want to draw parallel lines exactly 50 pixels apart to create a "window blind" effect.

- You're creating a set of thumbnails that need to be aligned in neat rows and columns.

- You want to create an object that is the exact same size (in one or more dimensions) as another object already in your image.

You have several tools to help you do this, and more.

Creating guides

Guides are nonprintable horizontal and vertical lines that you can position anywhere you like within a document window. Normally, they are displayed as solid blue lines, but you can change guides to another color and/or to a dashed line.

To use guides, choose Edit➪Preferences➪Guides, Grid, & Slices (or Photoshop➪Preferences➪Guides, Grid, & Slices in Mac OS X), as I discuss in Book I, Chapter 5. Guides would be useful even if they were only, well, guides. However, they have another cool feature: Objects and tools dragged to within 8 screen pixels of a guide are magnetically attracted to the guide and snap to it. That makes it ridiculously easy to align objects precisely. Because the objects snap to the guides, you can be confident that you have placed the objects exactly on the guide and not just near it. You can turn off the Snap to Guides feature if you want a little less precision in your arrangements.

To place guides, follow these steps:

1. **Make sure that rulers are visible in your image. Choose View➪Rulers to display them, if necessary.**

   Anytime you create a guide by dragging from the ruler, the Show Guides option automatically switches on. At other times, you can show or hide guides by choosing View➪Show➪Guides, or by pressing Ctrl+semicolon (⌘+semicolon on the Mac).

2. **Click in the horizontal ruler and drag down to create a new horizontal guide. Release the mouse button when the guide is in the location you want.**

3. **Click in the vertical ruler and drag to the right to create a new vertical guide.**

   When you release the mouse button, your new guide stops.

   You can also create a horizontal guide by Alt+clicking in the vertical ruler (Option+clicking on the Mac), or a vertical guide by Alt+clicking in the horizontal ruler (Option+clicking on the Mac). Use whichever method is faster for you.

4. **Use the Move tool (press V to activate it) to reposition your guides.**

   Look for the guides in Figure 4-5.

Using guides

After the guides are in place, here are a few of the things you can do with them:

- **Turn the Snap to Guides feature on or off:** Choose View⇨Snap To⇨ Guides.

- **Lock all guides so you don't accidentally move them:** Choose View⇨ Lock Guides. You can also select Alt+Ctrl+semicolon (Option+⌘+semi-colon on the Mac).

- **Remove all guides and start from scratch:** Choose View⇨Clear Guides.

- **Change a horizontal guide to a vertical guide (or vice versa):** Press the Alt key (Option key on the Mac) as you drag the guide.

- **Align a guide at a precise location on the ruler:** Press the Shift key as you drag a guide to force it to snap to the ruler ticks.

- **Create a new guide in a precise location:** Choose View⇨New Guide, click the Horizontal or Vertical option, and type a distance from the ruler where you want the new guide to reside.

Corbis Digital Stock

Figure 4-5: Nonprinting guides allow you to precisely position your elements.

Using grids

The Photoshop Grid feature offers a convenient canned set of guidelines already nicely arranged for you at preset intervals. You can use a grid for any application where you want to align objects in a pleasing, geometrically precise arrangement.

Grids share some features in common with guides but boast a few differences, too:

- Like guides, grids don't print with your image. They are transparent artifacts used only as reference lines in your image, as shown in Figure 4-6.

- Objects and tools can optionally snap to the lines on a grid, depending on whether you have View⇨Snap To⇨Grid turned on or off.

- You can show or hide grids by choosing View⇨Show (Hide)⇨Grid.

- You can change the color of the grid and choose solid lines, dashed lines, or dots for the grid by choosing Edit⇨Preferences⇨Guides, Grids, & Slices (Photoshop⇨Preferences in Mac OS).

- You can specify the distance between grid lines and the number of subdivisions between grid lines in the Preferences dialog box. For more information on setting grid and guide preferences, see Book I, Chapter 5.

Corbis Digital Stock

Figure 4-6: Grids enable you to arrange elements in geometric order.

Measuring On-Screen

You can measure distances and objects within Photoshop many different ways. The rulers, used in combination with guides, are a good way to mark distances precisely so that you can create objects of a particular size. You can change the increments used for these measurements in Photoshop's Preferences, as I detail in Book I, Chapter 5.

However, Photoshop also has a handy Measure tool you can use to lay measurement outlines in any direction. These lines tell you a great deal more than just the size of the object you're measuring. You can also measure angles and determine the exact coordinates of an object.

When you use the Measure tool, the Options bar offers a read-out of information that includes the following values:

- ✓ **X, Y — the X and Y coordinates of the start of the line:** For example, if you start at the 1-inch position on the horizontal ruler and the 3-inch position on the vertical ruler, the X and Y values on the Options bar are 1.0 and 3.0, respectively. (You select the increments for the X and Y values on the ruler in Photoshop's Preferences.)

- ✓ **W, H — the horizontal (W) and vertical (H) distances traveled from the X and Y points:** A 1-inch long, perfectly horizontal line drawn from the X,1 and Y,3 position shows a W value of 1.0 and an H value of 0.0.

- ✓ **A:** The angle of the first line.

- ✓ **D1:** The total length of the line.

- ✓ **D2:** The total length of the second line.

Measuring an object

To measure an object, follow these steps:

1. **Select the Measure tool.**

   It's tucked away in the Tools palette with the Eyedropper. Press I to cycle among the Eyedropper, Color Eyedropper, and Measure tool until it appears.

2. **Click at a starting location for the measuring line and then drag to the end location.**

   Press the Shift key to constrain the line to multiples of 45 degrees.

3. **Release the mouse button to create the measurement line, as shown in Figure 4-7.**

Figure 4-7: The Measure tool is your on-screen ruler.

Measuring an angle

You can measure an angle by drawing two lines and reading the angle between them from the Options bar. Just follow these steps:

1. **Select the Measure tool.**

2. **Click at a starting location for the first line and drag to the end location.**

   You can press the Shift key to constrain the line to multiples of 45 degrees.

3. **Release the mouse button to create the first line.**

4. **Press the Alt key (or the Option key on the Mac) and click the endpoint of the first line where you want to measure the angle.**

5. **Drag the second line and release the mouse button when it is finished.**

6. **On the Options bar, read the angle between the two lines (A).**

   You can also see the length of each line as D1 and D2, as shown in Figure 4-8.

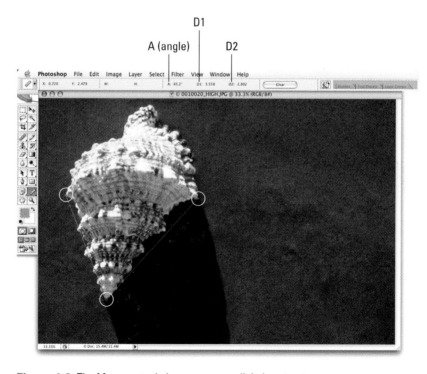

Figure 4-8: The Measure tool also serves as a digital protractor.

Using the Info Palette

The Info palette, shown in Figure 4-9, displays a variety of information, depending on what tool you're using. In CS2, the Info palette got a little beefier with the addition of the display of Status Information and the showing of Tool Hints. To specify which status info options you want displayed, or whether you want Tool Hints shown, choose Palette Options from the Info palette pop-up menu. For example, if you're using the Measure tool, the information in the Info palette dupli-cates the measurements shown on the Options bar. Choosing other tools modifies the Info palette's display to reflect the functions of that tool. Here is some of the information you can find out by keeping the Info palette visible on your desktop:

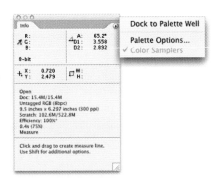

Figure 4-9: The Info palette displays useful file information, such as measurements and color readouts.

- ✔ When using most tools, the Info palette displays the X and Y coordinates of the cursor, as well as the color values of the pixel directly beneath the cursor.

- ✔ When making a selection with the marquee tools, the Info palette shows both the X and Y coordinates of the cursor, as well as the width and height of the selection.

- ✔ When dragging with the Crop or Zoom tools, the Info palette shows the width and height of the marquee used to define the cropping or zoom borders. The Crop tool's current angle of rotation is also displayed.

- ✔ With the Line, Pen, and Gradient tools, the Info palette shows the X and Y coordinates of the starting position for the line, path, or gradient you are defining, as well as the distance (D) of the line you've dragged, the change in X and Y directions (DX and DY), and the angle (A).

- ✔ When you use a transformation command, the Info palette displays the percentage change in the Width, Height, and Angle, Angle of Horizontal Skew (H), and Angle of Vertical Skew (V). For more on transformations, see Book III, Chapter 3.

- ✔ When you use a color adjustment, such as Levels, the Info palette displays before and after color values beneath the mouse cursor. See Book VIII, Chapter 1 for more on color adjustments.

- ✔ After you've made a selection with the Lasso or Magic Wand tools, the Info palette also shows the Width and Height of the selection. Choose Palette Options from the Info palette's pop-up menu (click the triangle in the upper right to open the pop-up menu). Here you can define a second color readout in addition to the default readout, using a different color model if you want, as shown in Figure 4-10. In addition to the regular color modes, the default Actual Color option displays values in the current mode of the document. Proof Color displays values based on the setting chosen in View⇨Proof Setup. The Total Ink option displays the percentage CMYK ink under the cursor based on the settings in the CMYK Setup dialog box in the Color Settings (Advanced). You can also define a measurement increment for the mouse cursor (in inches, pixels, millimeters, and so forth) independently of the increment you've selected in Preferences.

Figure 4-10: Set a different color mode in the Info Palette Options dialog box.

Working with Extras

Extras are the optional items displayed on your screen, such as grids, guides and smart guides, selection and layer edges, annotations, slices, and the *target path* (a line drawn with the Pen tool). Although you can turn on and off the display of each of these options independently, the Extras function helps you to create a set of extras that you want to see or hide. You can then turn them all on or off at once.

The following list explains how to show or hide these extras:

✔ To turn one extra on or off, choose View⇨Show and then choose the extra you want to show.

✔ To show or hide extras in a group, choose View⇨Show⇨Show Extras Options. Select each extra that you want to show in the dialog box that appears, as shown in Figure 4-11.

✔ To show or hide all the extras you've selected in Extras Options, choose View⇨Extras or press Ctrl+H (⌘+H on the Mac).

Figure 4-11: Pick and choose the extras you want to show in your image window.

Managing Images with Adobe Bridge

The new Adobe Bridge, shown in Figure 4-12, is command and control central for, not just Photoshop, but the entire Adobe Creative Suite. While you may initially regret the demise of the Bridge's predecessor — the File Browser — it won't be long before you appreciate the omnipresent power of the Bridge.

Adobe Bridge enables you to visually browse your network, hard drives, and external media to find the exact image you need and has a multitude of viewing, sorting, cataloging, and organizing features to manage all of your assets — photographic, illustrative, video, written, and so on. The Bridge is so multifaceted, that although you can access it from any Adobe application, it is also a stand-alone program.

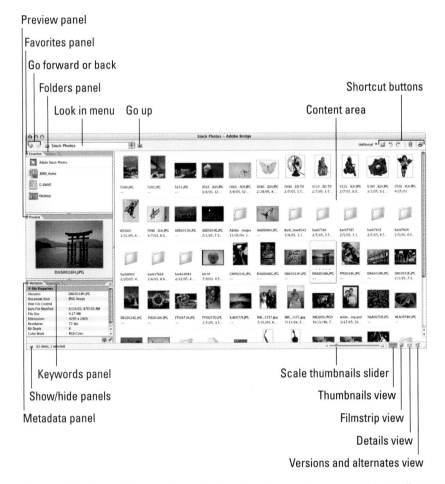

Figure 4-12: Adobe Bridge enables you to visually explore and locate your digital media assets.

Here's a brief description of what the Bridge offers:

- **File Browsing:** View, search, and organize your files. You can open, move, delete, rotate, and even run Photoshop commands such as Contact Sheet and Web Photo Gallery.

- **Version Cue:** If you have the Creative Suite installed, you can use the Bridge to organize and manage your Version Cue projects.

- **Bridge Center:** Again, if you have the Creative Suite, you have access to the Bridge Center, where you can read news in your Web browser, get tips and tricks about Adobe applications, and view your recent folders and files. You can also save file groups (sets of files you want saved as a group even from separate applications).

- **Camera Raw:** You can now open and actually edit Camera Raw files directly from the Bridge and save them in a format that is compatible with Photoshop.

- **Stock Photos:** This new service from Adobe enables you to search and purchase royalty-free stock photography at reasonable prices. Low-resolution images may be tried out for free prior to purchase.

- **Color Management:** Finally, you can use the Bridge to synchronize the color settings across all your Creative Suite applications to ensure color accuracy and consistency.

You can access the Bridge in several ways:

- Choose File⇨Browse from Photoshop.

- Click the Bridge icon at the far left of the Options bar,

- To launch Bridge directly, choose Start⇨Adobe Bridge in Windows (double click the Bridge icon in the Dock or in the Applications/Adobe/ Bridge folder on the Mac).

Brief anatomy of Bridge

Before I dive headlong into the detailed operations of the Bridge, let me give you a brief anatomical breakdown of each of its components, (refer to Figures 4-12 and 4-13):

- **Menu bar:** Commands found on the menu bar allow you to open or delete images, edit an image in ImageReady, add file info, and search for images. You can also label files and append their *metadata* (information about your file). The menu bar also offers options for sorting and viewing files. Finally, on the Tools⇨Photoshop menu you have access to basically the same Automate menu that you find in Photoshop itself.

- **Look In menu:** Across the top left edge of the Bridge is a bar that lists the current location (such as a folder on your hard drive) on display. Click the up and down arrow to view the particular folder's hierarchy as well as Favorites and Recent Folders.

- **Shortcut buttons:** Create a new folder and rotate or delete files with a click of the button. You can also switch to Compact mode (which I explain how to do in the upcoming section "Configuring the Bridge window").

- **Favorites panel:** Located in the upper left, this panel provides easy access to folders as well as Version Cue, Adobe Stock Photos and, if you're a Creative Suite user, the Bridge Center. Drag whatever hard drives or folders you want to include in your Favorites panel.

- **Folders panel:** Also located in the upper left is a panel showing the folder hierarchy on your computer. If an image file is available to your computer, the File Bridge lets you use this palette to find it.

- **Preview panel:** Beneath the Folder and Favorites panels is a preview of the currently selected file. You can reduce or enlarge the preview.

- **Content window:** The largest area is reserved for displaying the content. This window shows thumbnail images of all the files, along with information, in the currently selected folder. In addition, any subfolders are shown with a folder icon.

- **Keywords panel:** This feature lets you tag your images with keywords, such as the names of people or places, to enable easier locating and sorting of images.

- **Metadata panel:** The Metadata panel shows information about your images. The File Properties section shows items such as filename, date of creation, date last modified, image format, size, and so on. Any file information for images added via File⇨File Info displays in the IPTC section of the Metadata palette. Likewise, you can also enter or edit file information directly in the IPTC section in the Bridge. Finally, the Camera Data section displays information associated with your digital photos, such as the make and model of your camera, exposure, and ISO speed. You can also display other types of metadata, such as Camera Raw information, by choosing them in the Preferences dialog box accessed via the Metadata palette pop-up menu.

In Bonus Chapter 3 on this book's companion Web site, you can find out about the Notes and Annotations feature (an alternative to keywords) and advanced features of the Metadata panel. See the Introduction for details about this book's Web site.

- **Viewing controls:** At the bottom of the Bridge window is a slider that reduces or enlarges the content thumbnails. The remaining four buttons change the view from thumbnails, to filmstrip to details to versions and alternates (for Version Cue users).

Configuring the Bridge window

The Bridge, being as enormous and full-featured as it is, is surprisingly flexible when it comes to how you configure its various panels. Here's a rundown of how to customize your Bridge window:

✓ To size the entire Bridge window, diagonally drag any corner or edge of the window. On the Mac, drag the lower-right corner.

✓ To resize panes, drag the bar that divides them. Position your cursor over the bar (it changes to a double-headed arrow) and click and drag the bar to size the pane.

✓ To view just the Content window containing the thumbnails, click the Show/Hide Panels button (double-headed arrow) located in the bottom-left corner of the Bridge window.

✓ You can drag and regroup the tabbed panels in the Bridge just as you can with Photoshop palettes. To collapse a panel, double-click its tab.

✓ After you configure your Bridge, you can save it as a workspace preset that you can then call up at anytime. For example, you may want one workspace for working with photos and yet another when working with layout or word processing files. Simply choose Window➪Workspace➪ Save Workspace. Provide a name, a keyboard shortcut, and click Save. To access the workspace, choose Workspace and then select the name of your saved preset. You may also choose from a few preset workspaces designed for specific tasks. For example, if viewing files is your most important task, then choose the Lightbox preset, shown in Figure 4-13. Not happy with a workspace? Choose delete or simply reset your Workspace back to the default.

Figure 4-13: The Lightbox workspace focuses on the best viewing configuration in the Bridge.

You can also go the conventional route and choose the panel you want to show or hide on the View menu.

Using the menu bar and buttons

The menu bar is a visual testimony to the numerous capabilities of the Bridge. The next several sections provide a rundown of what you find on each menu.

File menu

Here's what you find on the Bridge's File menu:

- **New Window:** If you want one window to remain displayed as is, choose this command to create another Bridge window.

- **New Folder:** This command creates a new folder in the location listed in the Look In menu. You can also click the New Folder button in the top right of the Bridge window.

- **Open:** After you select a thumbnail in the Content window, you can choose the Open command to open the image in Photoshop, or another CS2 application. Of course, you can also simply double-click the selected file(s). To open multiple files, just press Ctrl (⌘ on the Mac) while selecting. To select a group of contiguous files, Shift+click the first and last files to select those and all the files in between.

- **Open With:** Select a file and choose the Open With command. Select your program of choice from the submenu.

- **Open in Camera Raw:** Select a Camera Raw file and choose this command to edit the raw settings.

- **Eject:** Select external media, such as CDs or USB flash drives, and choose Eject.

- **Close Window:** When you have enough of the Bridge, choose this command.

- **Move to Trash:** If you want to eliminate a file, select it and choose this command. Kiss it goodbye by emptying the trash. You can also click the trash can icon in the top right of the Bridge window. Remember that when trashing things via the Bridge, you are actually deleting them from the desktop as well.

- **Return to (program):** Choose this command to leave the Bridge and return to your program of choice.

- **Reveal in Finder:** This command brings up your operating system's window and reveals the location of the selected file.

- **Reveal in Bridge:** This command visually escorts you to where your selected file resides.

✓ **Place:** Select a file, choose Place and then choose one of the CS2 applications, such as InDesign. That program then imports your selected file.

✓ **Add to Favorites:** You can choose to add or remove a folder from your Favorites. If you're not familiar with Favorites, it is a special folder that lists your favorite files, folders, programs, and drives for quick and handy access. You can easily find the Favorites panel in the Folders panel and the Look In menu. And depending on your operating system, you'll come across numerous ways to access your Favorites.

✓ **File Info:** This feature lets you add some of your own metadata, such as title, author, copyrights, dates, credits, and so on. This information can come in handy for photographers and reporters. You can also edit (replace, append, save, and delete) advanced data such as EXIF (Extended File Information) properties and TIFF properties. But feel free to leave this data as it is.

✓ **Versions** and **Alternates:** These two commands display files saved as Versions or Alternates for Version Cue workflows.

✓ **Rotate Counterclockwise or Clockwise buttons:** Click either button to rotate the image in the content window.

Many commands, such as Open, Move to Trash, Rotate, and Label are available via a context menu. Simply select an image or folder and right-click (Control+click on the Mac) to access the menu.

Edit menu

On the Bridge's Edit menu, here are your options:

✓ **Preferences:** Mac users can find the Preferences window on the Bridge menu, rather than Edit. Briefly, **General** preferences control the way the Bridge looks and feels. For example, you can control how light or dark to make the Content window for your files. Metadata preferences control which type of data is displayed in the Metadata panel. Read on to find out more on metadata. You can assign names and keyboard shortcuts to your colored **Labels**. Specify which application to use to open files of certain types. The **File Type Associations** is specific to the Bridge only. **Advanced** settings have to do with miscellaneous items, such as the number of recently visited folders to display and more advanced options such cache settings. I suggest leaving those settings at their default unless you are certain you want to change them.

✓ **Undo/Cut/Copy/Paste/Duplicate:** I lumped these commands together because they are all self-explanatory. Undo undos your last executed command. Select a file and cut, copy, duplicate, or paste it from or into your folder.

✔ **Select All/Deselect All:** These two commands quickly select or deselect all the files in your selected folder.

✔ **Select Labeled/Unlabeled:** Selects all labeled or unlabeled images located in your selected folder. Use the Label menu to attach ratings or labels to selected images.

✔ **Invert Selection:** Selects everything that is currently not selected.

✔ **Find:** This command enables you to find files in selected folders for a subfolder, based on a variety of criteria such as filename, dates, labels, or keywords. Click Find and the files matching your criteria appear in the Bridge Content window.

✔ **Search Adobe Stock Photos:** This command transports you (provided you have an Internet connection up and running) to Adobe's Stock Photo portion of the Bridge where you can search for and purchase royalty-free stock photos.

✔ **Apply Camera Raw Settings:** If you have Camera Raw images, you can open them directly in the Bridge and apply settings such as Exposure and Lighting and then save them in a Photoshop-compatible file format.

✔ **Rotate:** The rotate commands rotate your images in varying degrees and direction. Note that when you rotate your images, the rotation is shown in the Bridge only when you open the image. When you open the image, Photoshop then applies the rotation. You can also click the rotate buttons.

Tools menu

Here are the offerings on the Tools menu:

✔ **Batch Rename:** Choose this command to rename multiple image files within a folder in one execution. You can choose to rename the files and keep them in the same folder or move them to a new folder. Click the Choose button to select that folder. Next, designate how your files are named. Choose an option from the pop-up menu or type your own. Next, choose the starting number for renamed images and check whether you want to enable the naming convention to be compatible with another platform.

✔ **Version Cue:** This menu command is for Creative Suite users working with Version Cue, Adobe's collaborative workflow feature. The menu offers all the Version Cue commands, such as creating a new project or marking that a file is in use and can be found on the submenu.

✔ **Photoshop Services:** You can access Adobe's partners and service providers online to order products, such as prints and photo books.

✓ **Photoshop:** All the features are the same as those on the Photoshop File⊅ Automate menu. The Batch Processor command is on the File⊅Scripts menu. See Book IX, Chapter 2 for more on contact sheets, picture packages, Photomerge, Merge to HDR, Batch Processor, and PDF Presentation. For more on Web Photo Gallery, see Bonus Chapter 2. For more info on batch processing, see Book II, Chapter 5.

✓ **Cache:** *Cache* is memory that stores frequently used data, such as thumbnails and file info, to allow for quicker loading when you display a previously viewed image or folder. Building cache for a subfolder enables you to store the information for a selected folder. If you purge the cache, you delete ranking and thumbnail information, thereby creating more disk space. Exporting cache lets you export to the folder selected in the Look In bar. Cache allows you to burn a CD without generating thumbnails.

✓ **Append Metadata** and **Replace Metadata:** Allow you to add or substitute existing metadata based on a template. To create a template, choose File⊅File Info. In the File Info dialog box, enter all your desired data. Then choose Save Metadata Template from the dialog box pop-up menu. Name the template and click Save.

Label menu

The Label menu offers commands for rating and labeling your files:

✓ **Rating:** Rank your files using the one to five star system. Use the View⊅ Sort menu or the Unfiltered drop-down menu at the top left of the Bridge window to choose your desired ranking. Those ranked files then display in the Content window.

✓ **Labels:** Label your files for quick identification and organization. Again, use the View⊅Sort menu and Unfiltered drop-down menu to choose and view the labeled files.

View

Here's what the View menu has to offer:

✓ **Compact View:** Select this option to get a pared-down Bridge with just a Content window — no panels.

✓ **Slide Show:** This neat option leaves the Bridge interface and displays just the images, full screen, from your selected folder.

✓ **As Thumbnails/Filmstrip/Details/Versions and Alternates:** These options display your content in the format specified. Thumbnail images view is the default setting.

✔ **Favorites/Folders/Preview/Metadata/Keywords Panel:** Display and hide these panels as you see fit.

✔ **Sort:** From this menu, select the criteria by which you want to sort your files. The default is by the name of your file, but a ton of other options, such as label, rating, or date are up for grabs. After you select the criteria, the Bridge displays your files accordingly.

✔ **Show Thumbnail Only:** This option shows just the thumbnail of the image without the accompanying data such as filename, date, and so on.

✔ **Show Hidden Files:** Select this option to see files that Photoshop doesn't recognize.

✔ **Show Folders:** This option enables you to view folder icon thumbnails in addition to image thumbnails.

✔ **Show All Files/Graphic Files/Camera Raw Files/Vector Files:** Leave your viewing option at all files or be more specific and show just Graphic, Camera Raw, or Vector (for example Illustrator) files.

✔ **Refresh:** If you've renamed a file, the order of your files isn't updated in the Bridge's window. Choose Refresh or press F5, to get your files in order. Note that you can also choose Refresh from the Folders panel pop-up menu.

Window

If you've configured the Bridge just to your liking and want to save it as a workspace for future retrieval, choose Workspace⇨Save Workspace. You can also choose from preset workspaces that are configured for specific tasks, such as optimum viewing of thumbnails or pinpointing metadata.

You should be aware that Photoshop has bestowed the Content window with lightbox powers. You can drag images around to reorder, group, or rank them. What the heck? You can just drag them around to give them a little exercise if you want. Sitting in the Bridge window all day can make a file a little stiff.

Using keywords

Keywords are descriptive labels that you attach to files. They help to categorize your images, enabling you to more efficiently and quickly locate your desired files. Here is the lowdown on creating and using keywords.

✔ To create a new keyword set (a categorical folder which contains keywords), click the folder icon at the bottom of the Keywords panel or choose New Keyword Set from the Keywords panel pop-up menu. Name your set and press Enter (Return on the Mac).

✔ To create a new keyword, select your desired keyword set, click the dog-eared page icon at the bottom, or choose New Keyword from the Keywords panel pop-up menu. Type the keyword you want to add, as shown in Figure 4-14, and press Enter (Return on the Mac).

✔ To rename an existing keyword set or keyword, select it and choose Rename from the Keywords panel pop-up menu. Provide a new name and press Enter (Return on the Mac).

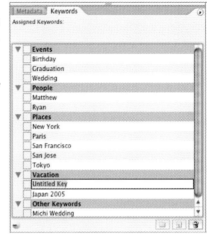

Figure 4-14: Creating a new keyword.

Note that renaming a keyword in the panel doesn't also rename it if you've applied it to a file.

✔ To delete a keyword set or keyword from the panel, select it and click the trash can icon or choose Delete from the Keywords panel pop-up menu. Again, deleting the keyword doesn't delete it from any files that you've previously applied it to.

✔ To apply a keyword, select the file or files and check the box to the left of the keyword in the panel.

✔ To remove a keyword from a file, select the file(s) and deselect the keyword in the panel.

✔ To apply all the keywords in a set, select the files and select the check box to the left of the keyword set.

✔ To search for images labeled with certain keywords, choose Find from the Keywords panel pop-up menu. Choose your desired folder or disk from the Look In menu or click the Browse button to navigate to your desired location. Select your criteria from the pop-up menu, choose either Contains or Does Not Contain, and enter your text,

Figure 4-15: Searching for an image by using a keyword.

as shown in Figure 4-15. To add additional criteria fields, click the plus sign. When finished, click the Search button. All images containing your entered keyword appear in the Content window of the Bridge.

Right-click (Control+click on the Mac) on a keyword in the panel and select Find from the context menu. The keyword is automatically entered in the Find field.

Chapter 5: Customizing Your Workspace and Preferences

In This Chapter

☞ Saving your workspace as a preset

☞ Customizing keyboard shortcuts and menus

☞ Defining preferences in Photoshop

☞ Managing settings with the Preset Manager

*N*ow, more than ever, Photoshop lets you have it your way without having to make a trip down to the local burger shack. You can easily customize the look of your workspace, specifying everything from the location of palettes to the arrangement of dialog boxes when you begin a session. You can even store these physical layouts and recall them anytime you like. And now in addition to customizing your keyboard shortcuts, you can also customize your menus to highlight certain workflow commands.

Photoshop also makes it easy to choose how certain tools and features operate. You can choose how the cursors for tools such as brushes look, tell Photoshop your preferred way of storing files, and specify just how much memory you'd like to set aside for image editing. You can set all these preferences once and then forget them, or you can change them from time to time as your needs change. This chapter shows you how to customize your workspace and preferences so that Photoshop works your way.

Creating Workspace Presets

Photoshop is a complicated program; the more you learn, the more complicated (and routine) your activities become. For one project, you may find yourself using the Styles palette repeatedly to add special effects to layers. For your next project, you may never use the Styles palette but require frequent access to the Paths palette to create curves that you use to make selections. And so it goes.

Use custom workspaces to save time and effort, or to instantly clean up a messy desktop.

Custom workspaces come in handy if you share a computer with students, family members, or coworkers. Those who prepare images for both Web and print have different needs that may call for special workspaces, too.

You can now even start with one of the new preset workspaces. Photoshop CS2 offers preset workspaces for various workflows, such as retouching, Web design, working with type, and many others. These presets modify menu and/or keyboard shortcuts. Palettes, however, remain untouched. You can select a preset, then establish your palette preferences, and then save the modified workspace as your own custom workspace. Read on to find out how.

You can tailor your workspace in these ways:

✐ **Combine palettes to group together the ones you use most often.** Drag a palette's tab into another palette group to add it to that group. If the Layers, Channels, and History palettes are the ones you use most often, you might want to group them together. You can also hide palettes that you rarely use for a particular project, tuck them away in the Palette Well, or minimize them to their title bars.

Move a palette out of the way quickly by Shift+clicking its title bar. The bar snaps to the nearest screen edge.

Before saving your workspace preset, show or hide the palettes as you prefer them and move them to the locations you want on your screen.

✐ **Position dialog boxes.** Photoshop's menu bar dialog boxes pop up in the same location they appeared the last time you used them. You may want to drag them to a specific place on your screen and store that location when you save your workspace preset. When I'm working with a large image, I sometimes position dialog boxes on the screen of my second monitor to maximize the area for the image on my main display.

✐ **Customize the Options bar.** You can grab the gripper bar at the left edge of the Options bar and drag it to another location. For example, you can dock the bar at the lower edge of your screen or have it float in a specific place on your Photoshop desktop. You can also double-click the title bar of the floating Options bar to collapse it so that only the active tool's icon is showing. Photoshop stores these settings with your workspace preset.

✐ **Set Photoshop's font size.** You can now even change the size of the font for text that is displayed on the Options bar, palettes, and tool tips. Choose Edit⇨Preferences⇨General (Photoshop⇨Preferences⇨General on the Mac). Choose Small, Medium, or Large from the UI Font Size pop-up menu. The change takes place the next time you start Photoshop.

Saving and Deleting Workspace Presets

After you set up your custom workspace, you can save it by choosing Window➪Workspace➪Save Workspace. In the Save Workspace dialog box that appears, type a name for your saved workspace.

You now have the additional options of selecting which components — palette locations, keyboard shortcuts, and menus — you want to capture in your custom workspace, as shown in Figure 5-1. After you check your desired settings, click the Save button.

Figure 5-1: Choose which components to save in your custom workspace.

Your saved workspace now appears as a listing on the Workspace submenu.

Want to return to the way Adobe sees the world of Photoshop? Choose Window➪Workspace➪Default Workspace. If you decide to revert any of your workspace components to the default settings, choose Window➪ Workspace➪Reset Palette Locations or Reset Keyboard Shortcuts or Reset Menus.

To delete a saved workspace, choose Window➪Workspace➪Delete Workspace. In the Delete Workspace dialog box that appears, choose the name of the workspace you want to remove from the drop-down list. Click the Delete button, and your preset is gone, gone, gone.

Customizing Keyboard Shortcuts

For those of you who are like me — I avoid using a mouse and prefer the ease and speed of keyboard shortcuts — Photoshop offers customizable keyboard shortcuts. You can assign shortcuts to menu commands, palette commands, and tools. You can edit, delete, or add to the Photoshop default set or create your own custom set. Here are the steps to work with keyboard shortcuts:

1. **Choose Edit➪Keyboard Shortcuts.**

   You can also choose Window➪Workspace➪Keyboard Shortcuts and Menus. Then click the Keyboard tab. The Keyboard Shortcuts dialog box appears, shown in Figure 5-2.

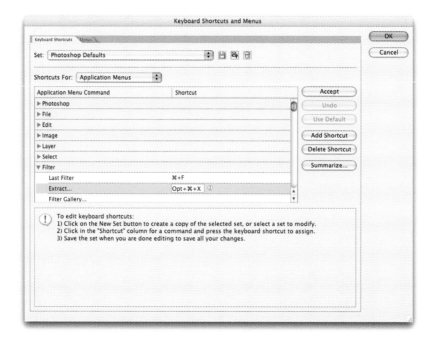

Figure 5-2: Customize keyboard shortcuts for enhanced productivity.

2. **Choose between the Photoshop Defaults set or the new Working with Type set. You can also create a new set by clicking the New Set button (the disk with a down arrow icon).**

   Clicking New Set makes a copy of the selected set for you to then edit and customize. If you choose a new set, name the set (leaving it with a .kys extension), and keep it stored in the Keyboard Shortcuts folder.

3. **Choose Application Menus, Palette Menus, or Tools from the Shortcuts For drop-down list. Click the triangle to expand the menu.**

4. **Select your desired command from the list. Type the shortcut keys you want to assign to that command in the shortcut field. If you type a keyboard shortcut that is already assigned to that command, you can simply type over it.**

   If the keyboard shortcut you type is already being used, Photoshop warns you that if you accept the shortcut, it will be removed from the original command.

5. **Click Accept or the Add Shortcut button.**

   If you later change your mind and want to use the original keyboard shortcut (if there was one), click Use Default. If you decide you don't want the shortcut at all, click Delete Shortcut. And if you make a mistake, just click Undo.

Application and Palette menu commands must include a Ctrl (⌘ on the Mac) and/or an F key in the keyboard shortcut.

6. **When you finish, click the Save Set button (the disk icon).**

   If you want to delete the set, click the Delete Set button (the trash can icon).

7. **Click the Summarize button to save the keyboard shortcut set as an .htm file, which loads in your Internet browser. You can then print the file and keep it as a handy reference of your shortcuts.**

8. **Click OK to exit the dialog box.**

Customizing Menus

In CS2, Adobe's taken the customization club to yet another level by adding the ability to customize menus. You have the choice of colorizing chosen menu items or hiding the menu items altogether, as shown in Figure 5-3.

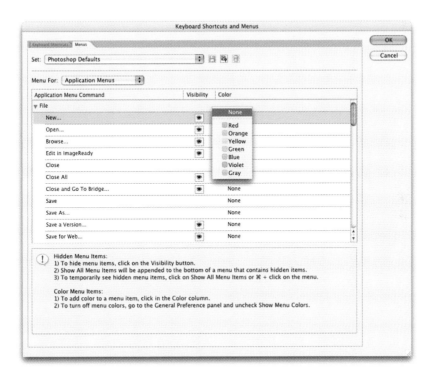

Figure 5-3: Colorize menu items that you frequently access for quicker identification.

The following steps explain how to make the Photoshop menus your own:

1. **Choose Edit➪Menus.**

   You can also choose Window➪Workspace➪Keyboard Shortcuts and Menus. Then click the Menus tab. The Menus dialog box appears (refer to Figure 5-3).

2. **In the Set drop-down list at the top, choose the Photoshop Defaults set or one of the presets. Or to create a new menu, click the New Set button (the disk with a down arrow icon).**

   Clicking New Set makes a copy of the selected set for you to then edit and customize. If you choose a new set, name the set (leaving it with a .mnu extension), and keep it stored in the Menu Customization folder.

3. **Choose Application Menus or Palette Menus from the Menu For drop-down list. Click the triangle to expand the menu.**

4. **Select your desired command from the list and choose one of the following options.**

   • To hide or show a menu item, click the Visibility button. Be careful not to hide the really critical commands, such as Open or Save and especially not Edit➪Menus.

   • To add color to a menu item, click the Color Swatch (or the word None) and choose a color from the drop-down list.

5. **When you finish making changes, click the Save Set button (the disk icon).**

   To delete a menu set, click the Delete Set button (trash can icon).

   Or to create a new set based on the current menu, click the Save Set As button.

6. **In the Save dialog box, enter a name for the set and click Save.**

7. **Click OK to exit the dialog box.**

If you've hidden some menu items and decide you want to temporarily show them while working in Photoshop, choose Show All Menu Items from the menu with the hidden items.

To turn menu colors off (they're on by default) choose Edit➪Preferences➪General (Photoshop➪Preferences➪General on the Mac) and deselect Show Menu Colors.

Setting Your Preferences

Photoshop stores settings for many different options in various Preferences files on your hard drive. The first time you run Photoshop after a new installation, you probably want to customize Preferences to suit your own needs.

You can access the Preferences dialog box by choosing Edit⇨Preferences (Photoshop⇨Preferences on the Mac). The first group of settings that appear in the submenu are the General Preferences (shown in Figure 5-4). You can choose any of the other Preferences dialog boxes from the submenu. You can also move between the dialog boxes by clicking the Prev or Next buttons that appear in each of the Preferences dialog boxes. The next several sections give you a rundown of what you can do with the settings in the different Preferences dialog boxes.

Figure 5-4: The General Preferences dialog box specifies a lot of the "look and feel" of your Photoshop interface.

When the General Preferences dialog box is visible, you can switch to the other Preferences dialog boxes by pressing Ctrl+1, Ctrl+2 (⌘+1, ⌘+2 on the Mac), and so forth. These shortcuts can be useful if you need to frequently access particular dialog boxes.

Setting general preferences

The General Preferences dialog box is where you select some options that are, well, general in nature. You can select some choices from drop-down lists, and others are check boxes you can select or deselect to activate or disable that option. Here's a rundown of options in the upper part of the dialog box:

✔ **Color Picker:** Choose the familiar Adobe Color Picker to select precise colors or work with the Windows or Macintosh system color pickers, as desired. You might want to use the Windows or Apple color picker, for example, if you've previously defined some custom colors outside Photoshop and now want to make them available for a Photoshop project.

✔ **Image Interpolation:** When Photoshop resizes an image, it must either create new pixels (when making the image larger) or combine existing pixels (to make the image smaller). To do this, the program examines neighboring pixels and uses the information to derive the new or replacement pixels. You can select the type of mathematical algorithm Photoshop uses to do this, though you likely want to stick with the default option, Bicubic (Better). You can find out more on interpolation and the other algorithms in Book II, Chapter 1.

✔ **UI Font Size:** Specify the size of the text displayed in dialog boxes, palettes, and so on. Choose from Small, Medium, or Large.

✔ **History States:** Photoshop remembers how your document looks at various stages of editing, storing all the image information on your hard drive and listing the individual *states* in the History palette. (For more information on using the History palette, see Book II, Chapter 4.) Keeping track of every change you make requires lots of memory and hard drive space, so you can specify how many resources to use by typing a value into this box. The default is 20 (the max is 1000). If you have resources to burn and frequently find yourself stepping way back in time to modify or delete a step, you can type a larger number. If your resources are skimpy and you don't anticipate making many changes to earlier steps (or are willing to take frequent snapshots or save interim images), you can enter a smaller number.

In the Options section of the General Preferences dialog box, you find nearly a dozen check boxes that you can select or deselect, as described in the following list:

✔ **Export Clipboard:** When this feature is active, Photoshop transfers its private clipboard (used only within Photoshop) to the general Windows or Macintosh Clipboard so that you can paste information into other applications. If you activate this option, switching from Photoshop to other applications takes a little longer, and Photoshop's clipboard contents replace whatever was in your system Clipboard when you switched.

The clipboard is generally a poor vehicle for moving image data between applications because the transferred information may not be of the best quality. Instead, save your file and open it in the other application. If you do this, you can turn off the Export Clipboard option, saving you some time when switching between applications.

✔ **Show Tool Tips:** Photoshop can display little pop-up reminders about tools and other objects on your screen. If you find these reminders distracting, deselect this check box to turn off tool tips.

 ✓ **Zoom Resizes Windows:** Select this check box if you want your document windows to grow and shrink to fit your document as you zoom in and out. Deselect this check box if you want the document's window to always remain the same size; you might want to deselect the check box if you frequently work with several documents side by side and don't want them to change relative size as you zoom in and out.

 ✓ **Auto-Update Open Documents:** When you're working on an image and move to another application (such as ImageReady) to work on the same image, you'll probably want the changes made in the other application to reflect in the document still open in Photoshop. Select this check box so that Photoshop monitors the document and updates its version whenever the document is changed in the other application.

 ✓ **Show Menu Colors:** Check this option to have the ability to view customized menus in color.

 ✓ **Resize Image During Paste/Place:** By default, when you place or paste files that are larger than the document they are being pasted or placed into, the files are resized to fit. Uncheck this option to have the file import with its exact dimensions, as shown in Figure 5-5.

Not resized

Resized

Figure 5-5: Check the Resize Image During Paste/Place to have your image automatically resized upon import.

✔ **Beep When Done:** I remember the bad old days when computers were slow and Photoshop would take a minute or two to apply the Gaussian Blur filter or perform calculations when merging even moderate-sized image layers. The Beep When Done signal was my cue to stop watching television and resume working with Photoshop. Although most operations are a lot faster today, if you're working with very large images or simply like to be notified when a step is finished, the beep option can be useful (or incredibly annoying to your coworkers).

✔ **Dynamic Color Sliders:** The sliders in the Color palette change colors to match the settings you make. If your computer is on the slow side, you can turn off this feature to improve performance.

✔ **Save Palette Locations:** Select this check box if you want Photoshop to restore your most recent palette locations the next time you start up. Deselect this check box if you always want your palettes in the same location each time you begin working.

✔ **Use Shift Key for Tool Switch:** When this feature is active, you can change from one tool in the Tools palette to another in the same group (say, to change from the Gradient tool to the Paint Bucket tool) by pressing the Shift key and the keyboard shortcut for that tool.

✔ **Automatically Launch Bridge:** Check this option to have Adobe Bridge (technically a stand-alone program) automatically launch when Photoshop is launched. See Book I, Chapter 4 for details about the Bridge, which is new in Photoshop CS2.

✔ **Zoom with Scroll Wheel:** This handy option enables your mouse scroll wheel to become a zooming tool, regardless of which tool you are using.

In the History Log section, you can have Photoshop record all your editing commands. The History Log feature is handy if you want to present a finished, fully edited image to a client or manager, but need to be able to show the steps of how you got there. Or maybe you want a record of the steps, so you can repeat them on other images and don't want to rely on your memory.

You have a few formats in which you can save your history log:

✔ **Metadata:** Saving the log to metadata (information embedded in your image file) allows you to view the log in the Bridge window. For more on the Bridge, see Book I, Chapter 4.

✔ **Text File:** You can save the log to a text file. Click the Choose button to provide a name and location for the file.

✔ **Both:** This option saves the log as both metadata and a text file.

✔ **Edit Log Items:** You choose Sessions Only, Concise, or Detailed. The Sessions Only option records your editing until you close the file or quit Photoshop. The Concise option keeps a comprehensive log (multiple sessions), but in short and sweet steps. The Detailed option provides a comprehensive, detailed log. For example, a concise log entry may be just Crop, whereas a detailed log entry may be Crop. To rectangle and then also provide the original and cropped dimensions, the angle and the resolution values.

The last option in the General Preferences dialog box is the Reset All Warning Dialogs button. If you've turned off the display of certain warnings by selecting the Don't Show Me This Dialog Box Again check box, you can reactivate all the warnings by clicking this button.

Deciding how you want files handled

The options in the File Handling Preferences dialog box, shown in Figure 5-6, control how Photoshop handles files as they are opened and closed. Here's the lowdown on these options:

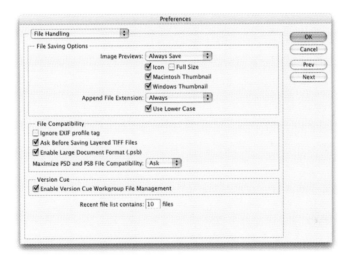

Figure 5-6: The File Handling Preferences dialog box offers settings for opening and saving files.

- ✔ **Image Previews:** Storing a preview thumbnail with an image can speed up browsing for the image you want. You can tell Photoshop to save a preview by default or to ask you first (in case you want to create images that are a little smaller in size, especially for the Web). Or you can also choose not to ever save a preview. Mac users need to select the kinds of image previews they need. Select the Icon option to enable an image icon to appear on the desktop. Select the Macintosh Thumbnail option to see a preview in the Open dialog box. Select the Windows Thumbnail option to see a preview in a Windows OS dialog box. Finally, select the Full Size option to save a low-resolution version of the file to use in applications that can open only low-resolution (72 ppi) Photoshop images.

✔ **Append File Extension:** You can select whether the file extensions appended to filenames (such as `.psd`, `.tif`, and so forth) are consistently uppercase or lowercase, as you prefer. On Macs, you can choose whether to add extensions by selecting from the Always, Never, or Ask When Saving options. If you want cross-platform compatibility with PCs or prep Web graphics, select the Always option. Mac users, select the Use Lower Case option to save extensions as lowercase characters.

✔ **Ignore EXIF Profile Tag:** When this option is selected, Photoshop ignores the sRGB tag that many digital cameras add to their EXIF (camera) data. The sRGB tag is widely used, but not well respected among many high-end digital photography professionals.

✔ **Ask Before Saving Layered TIFF Files:** Photoshop can save an advanced type of TIFF file that includes layers, exactly as with its own native PSD files. However, many applications cannot read these files. If you always open TIFF files in Photoshop and don't mind creating larger TIFF files in the process, you can disable this option. Otherwise, Photoshop asks you for confirmation each time you want to save a TIFF file that contains layers.

✔ **Enable Large Document Format (`.psb`):** Photoshop can now create documents up to 300,000 x 300,000 pixels. You can save these humongous files as TIFFs (up to 4GB) or in the new `.psb` or Photoshop Raw formats, with no limitation in size.

✔ **Maximize PSD File and PSB File Compatibility:** Photoshop lets you choose an option for file compatibility.

Not all applications can handle the more sophisticated features that may be stored in a PSD file (such as fancy layer effects). If you frequently open PSD files in applications other than later versions of Photoshop, you may want to set this option to Always. Keep in mind that you may lose some features when you choose this option. Choose Ask to have Photoshop prompt you when you save a file as to whether you want the option. Or select Never to ignore the option completely.

When you maximize compatibility, Photoshop saves a *composite* (flattened) version along with the layered file to ensure that older applications (such as Version 2) can read the files. However, this option also makes your file size balloon enormously. In addition, when you save in this mode, you get an annoying warning that your file may not be read by future versions of Photoshop. This silly warning appears every time you save a layered PSD file.

The PSB (large file) format is like the PSD format in that it supports most Photoshop features. Currently, only Photoshop CS and CS2 can open PSB files. Again, keeping this option checked ensures maximum compatibility with any future programs that may accept this format.

If you plan to use your PSD files in InDesign or Illustrator, you should have the maximize compatibility feature selected because the performance of these programs is faster when a composite is along with the layers.

✔ **Enable Version Cue:** Select this option if your computer is located on a network and you need to share your files with others in your workgroup by using a server.

✔ **Recent File List Contains:** Type a value from 0 to 30 to specify the number of recently used files you want displayed in the Recent File list on the File menu.

Adjusting your display and cursors

This Display & Cursors Preferences dialog box, shown in Figure 5-7, enables you to set several options that control how cursors display on-screen and three display parameters that may affect how quickly your computer completes an operation. The following list describes these options:

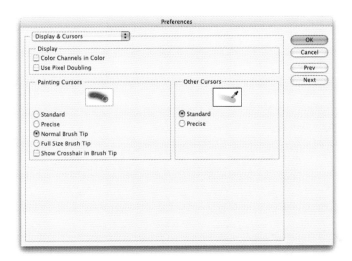

Figure 5-7: Choose the way your cursors are displayed — from crosshairs to brush tips.

✔ **Color Channels in Color:** When selected, this option tells Photoshop to show each of the color channels (for example, Red, Green, and Blue or Cyan, Magenta, Yellow, and Black) in their respective colors in the Channels palette. In most cases, you won't want to use this feature. You need to be able to see the channels in their grayscale form to perform image-editing tasks such as converting from color to grayscale, channel masking, or for selective sharpening on certain channels. Book VI, Chapter 1 introduces channels.

✔ **Use Pixel Doubling:** Many dialog boxes and tools have preview windows that show the effect of the settings you're working with. With this feature active, Photoshop doubles the size of the pixels in the preview only, reducing the resolution of the preview but speeding display.

✔ **Painting and Other Cursors (shown in Figure 5-8):**
Choose the Standard option to show a tool's cursor as an icon representing the tool itself (although I don't know why you'd want to do this).

> Use Precise to switch to a cursor that has crosshairs, which is useful for positioning the center of a tool's operational area in a particular place.

> The new Normal Brush Tip displays a 50% point for the brush tip, which means that the diameter of the brush tip reflects feathering of 50% or more. The wispier feathered areas of 50% or less are outside the diameter area shown.

> Full Size Brush Tip, a new feature in CS2, displays the full size of the diameter of the brush tip.

> Show Cross Hair in Brush Tip, another new setting, is a great hybrid. It shows a cross hair in the center of either of the brush tips — great for precision retouching.

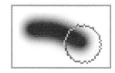

Most users prefer to set the painting cursors to Brush Size and the other cursors to Precise. Some folks do complain that precise cursors are hard to see against some backgrounds, but you can always press the Caps Lock key to toggle precise cursors on or off.

Figure 5-8:
Photoshop CS2 offers five brush tips.

Adjusting transparency and gamut

Photoshop uses colors and patterns to represent information about an image that is normally invisible, such as areas that are transparent, or parts of an image that contain colors that cannot be represented by your current display or printing system. The Transparency & Gamut Preferences dialog box, shown in Figure 5-9, enables you to tailor these displays to your own preferences.

For example, transparency is typically shown on-screen by using a gray-and-white checkerboard pattern. You can change the pattern and colors if you prefer another type of display.

Here is a rundown of the options you find in this dialog box:

✔ **Grid Size:** You can choose small, medium, large, or no grid at all. You may want to switch from the default medium-sized grid to a large grid if you're using a very high-resolution setting (such as the 1920 x 1440 pixel setting I use on my monitor) so the grid is a little easier to see. (I don't bother with this, myself.) Or you can switch to a smaller grid if you're working at a 640 x 480 or an 800 x 600 resolution.

✔ **Grid Colors:** The default light grid is the least obtrusive, but you can switch to a medium or dark grid if you want. Also, you are not limited to gray-and-white checkerboard squares. To choose custom colors, double-click the white and gray squares below the Grid Colors list.

✔ **Use Video Alpha:** If you have a video board that supports chroma keying, select this option to be able to view video in the transparent portions behind a layer.

✔ **Gamut Warning:** You can adjust the color used to represent out-of-gamut colors and to specify the transparency for the warning color. Double-click the Color box to set the hue and choose the transparency with the Opacity slider. The gamut warning is generally used before converting RGB images to CMYK to see which colors will be lost. For more information on color gamuts, see Book II, Chapter 2.

A *gamut* is the range of colors that can be displayed or printed. In Photoshop talk, out-of-gamut colors generally are those that can't be represented by cyan, magenta, yellow, and black and, therefore, can't be printed. To turn gamut warnings on or off, choose View➪Gamut Warning.

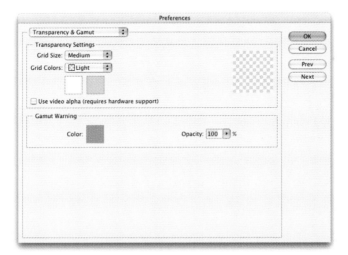

Figure 5-9: Specify how transparency and out-of-gamut (or range) colors are displayed in the Transparency & Gamut Preferences dialog box.

Setting measurement preferences

In the Units & Rulers Preferences dialog box, shown in Figure 5-10, you can set the units used to measure things on-screen (inches, pixels, millimeters, and so forth) and to define a default column size when typing text in multiple columns. In addition, you can define the resolution of the image when you choose File➪New and select Default Photoshop Size from the Preset Sizes list. (See Book I, Chapter 3 for more on preset sizes.)

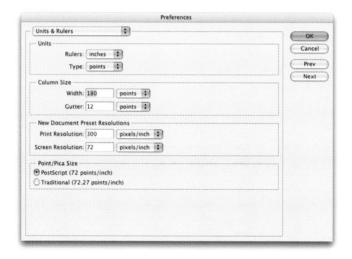

Figure 5-10: Specify your units of measurement and default Photoshop resolution settings from the Units & Rulers Preferences dialog box.

In the Units area of the dialog box, you find these options:

- ✔ **Rulers:** Select the measurement units Photoshop uses for rulers. Your choices are pixels, inches, centimeters, millimeters, points, picas, or percent. The most popular sizes are inches and millimeters, but if you're working with publications and specifying in picas, you might prefer that increment instead. If you're prepping Web graphics, you may prefer to have your rulers incremented in pixels.

- ✔ **Type:** Choose the measurement used to represent the dimensions of type. Point size is almost universally used, but pixels and millimeters are also available. You may want to use pixels if you're trying to fit type into a specific-sized area of an image.

In the Column Size area, you can specify the following:

✔ **Width:** The width of the column in inches, centimeters, millimeters, points, or picas.

✔ **Gutter:** The width of the area separating columns, also in inches, centimeters, millimeters, points, or picas.

In the New Document Preset Resolutions area, you can set the following:

✔ **Print Resolution:** The default is 300 pixels per inch, a good setting to keep. You can change to another value and use pixels per centimeter as a measurement if you want.

✔ **Screen Resolution:** Generally, 72 pixels per inch works with most images that are prepped for screen viewing. You can select another resolution and use pixels per centimeter if you like.

Changing the resolution of an image after you created it can impact the sharpness of your image and degrade quality. Choosing the final resolution you want when you create a document is best, whether you specify the resolution manually or use these presets.

In the Point/Pica Size area, you can choose whether you want to use a measurement of 72 points per inch (which first became relevant in the Macintosh realm and spread as desktop publishing became widespread) or the traditional 72.27 points per inch definition used in the precomputer era. Unless you have a special reason to choose otherwise, use the Postscript (72 points per inch) option.

Setting up guides, grids, and slices

Guides are nonprinting lines you can create on your screen to make it easier to align objects. *Grids* are vertical and horizontal lines in the background that make lining up objects even easier. *Slices* are sections of an image you can create for Web page graphics so that each slice can be loaded and treated separately (usually in a table or similar arrangement). For more information on using grids and guides, see Book I, Chapter 4. Figure 5-11 shows the Guides, Grid & Slices Preferences dialog box.

In the Guides and Smart Guides area, you can set these options:

✔ **Color:** Either select a color from the drop-down list or click the color sample swatch to choose your own color. You may want to change the default color if that color is too similar to a dominant color in your image.

✔ **Style:** Select from lines or dashed lines. If you work with images that contain many horizontal and vertical lines that extend across most of an image, dashed lines may be more visible.

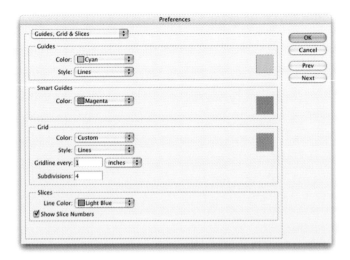

Figure 5-11: Change the colors and styles of your guides and grids for maximum contrast against your image in the Guides, Grid & Slices Preferences dialog box.

In the Grid area, these are your options:

- **Color:** Select a color from the drop-down list or click the color sample patch to define a specific hue.

- **Style:** You can choose lines, dashed lines, or dots.

- **Gridline Every:** Choose the distance between gridlines.

- **Subdivisions:** Select the number of subdivisions for each gridline.

In the Slices area, these are your choices:

- **Line Color:** From the drop-down list, choose a color for the lines that surround each slice.

- **Show Slice Numbers:** If you select this check box, Photoshop adds a slice number to the display of slices, which makes it easier to keep track of individual slices.

For a full explanation of slices, check out Bonus Chapter 2.

Plug-Ins and Scratch Disks

Plug-ins and scratch disks are a couple of unrelated options combined in a single dialog box, shown in Figure 5-12. Briefly, *plug-ins* are mini software programs that add features to Photoshop. *Scratch disks* are free areas on your hard drive(s) that Photoshop uses as virtual memory when it is short on RAM. Read on to find out more.

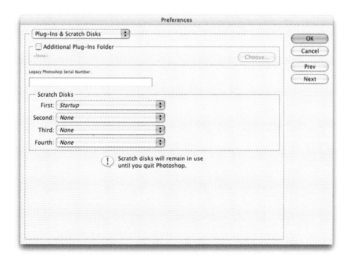

Figure 5-12: Photoshop allows you to specify auxiliary drives as scratch disks after you exhaust your RAM.

Plug-ins

The Plug-Ins folder is where Photoshop stores all your filters and other plug-in add-ons. A default folder is created when you install Photoshop.

Photoshop allows you to specify an additional folder to search other than its own Plug-Ins folder. This additional folder may come in handy if you want to keep your third-party add-ons separate from Photoshop's native plug-ins. An auxiliary plug-ins directory (not nested within Photoshop's own Plug-Ins folder) can simplify managing those extra filters, and you can turn off their use (potentially speeding up Photoshop's load time) by deselecting the Additional Plug-Ins Folder check box in this dialog box. You can also use this option when you have some plug-ins installed for another application and want to share them with Photoshop without having to make extra copies in your Photoshop Plug-Ins directory.

To activate a new plug-ins directory, select the Additional Plug-Ins Folder check box and then click the Choose button. In the dialog box that appears, navigate to the folder you want to use and select it. Click OK. You then need to exit Photoshop and restart the program to activate the new directory.

If you have a plug-in or folder you'd like to deactivate, use a tilde (~) as the first character of the plug-in or folder name. Photoshop ignores the plug-in(s) or folder(s) specified. Just remove the tilde from the name to activate the plug-in or folder. This can come in handy if you're having a program glitch and want to deactivate your plug-ins to troubleshoot whether they are causing the problem.

Scratch disks

Scratch disks are areas on your hard drive that Photoshop uses to substitute for physical RAM when you don't have enough RAM to work with the images you have opened. Scratch disks are no replacement for physical memory, but Photoshop will need scratch disks many times, even if you have huge amounts of memory.

Photoshop uses your startup drive (the drive used to boot your operating system) as its first scratch disk by default. That may not be the best choice because your startup drive is usually pretty busy handling requests of your operating system and, if you're running Windows, requests for Windows's own virtual memory scheme (your so-called *swap file* or *paging file*). Ideally, your scratch disk(s) should be a different hard drive and, preferably, the fastest one you have available.

If you have more than one hard drive, choose one other than your startup drive as your first scratch disk. Select your fastest drive; for example, select a FireWire 800 or USB 2.0 drive over one using the original, slow, USB 1.1 connection. If you have an Ultra-DMA EIDE drive or, better yet, a SCSI drive, use that. Although Ultra-DMA drives have transfer rates that rival even the speediest SCSI models, SCSI can be better because the SCSI bus is designed for multitasking. You often get better performance than with an EIDE drive that shares one of the two EIDE channels with other devices.

If you don't have a second hard drive, you can improve scratch disk performance by creating a partition on an existing drive for use as a scratch disk. Remember to keep the scratch disk defragmented (that is, with the files all organized together on your hard drive) by using your favorite defragmentation utility.

Adobe changed the format for serial numbers with Photoshop 7, and if you have old plug-ins that require a valid Photoshop serial number, you can enter the serial number from an older version into the space provided in this dialog box.

Changing Memory and Cache Settings

The perennial question: How much memory does Photoshop require? The perennial answer: As much as you can cram into your computer! Memory is so inexpensive right now you have no excuse for not having at least 512MB of RAM, and more is even better if you're using an operating system that can handle extra memory efficiently, such as Windows XP and Mac OS X. Version CS2 runs at its best with a gigabyte of RAM.

When you cram your RAM, you want to make sure Photoshop can use as much as you can spare. You can use the Memory & Image Cache Preferences dialog box, shown in Figure 5-13, to allocate your memory.

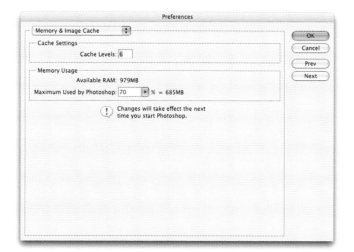

Figure 5-13: Use the Memory & Image Cache Preferences to allocate the maximum amount of RAM Photoshop gobbles up.

Managing memory

Here's how to allocate RAM:

1. **Choose Edit⇨Preferences⇨Memory & Image Cache.**

   The Memory & Image Cache Preferences dialog box opens (refer to Figure 5-13).

2. **In the Memory Usage area, change the Maximum Used by Photoshop parameter.**

   Use a value of 50 to 80 percent, depending on how much memory you have to waste. Allocating more to Photoshop reduces the RAM for other applications, so if you have other programs that need lots of memory, choose a prudent value.

3. **Click OK to apply the option.**

4. **Exit Photoshop and relaunch the program to activate the new setting.**

Setting aside memory for storing screen images

You can also set aside the amount of memory for storing screen images in the Memory & Image Cache dialog box, to speed up redraws of a reduced-view image on your screen as you make changes. You have two options. You can specify the number of copies of your image stored in memory, from the default value of 6 up to 8 levels.

Using the Preset Manager

Many of the palettes and tools Photoshop works with can use settings that you store on your hard drive as presets. For example, you can create custom colors and brush tips, build your own gradients, create a library of shapes, or compile a set of styles to apply to layers.

You'll want to become familiar with the Preset Manager, which provides a central management tool for all the options that are individually available from the palettes and tools themselves. Just as with the tools, you can select, edit, and delete presets. The only thing you can't do with the Preset Manager is actually create a preset. You must do this with the Tool Preset picker or Tool Presets palette. For more details, see Book I, Chapter 2. Here are some tips on using the Preset Manager, shown with its pop-up menu in Figure 5-14:

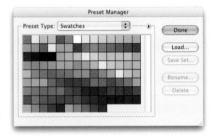

Figure 5-14: The Preset Manager is the central management tool for all Photoshop presets for all palettes.

✔ To show the Preset Manager, choose Edit➪Preset Manager. To hide it, click Done.

✔ To select a specific type of preset to work with, choose it from the Preset Type drop-down list.

✔ To modify a preset, choose the option from the pop-up menu available in each preset's dialog box. Click the right-pointing arrow to the left of the Done button to access the preset pop-up menu.

✔ To load an existing set of presets from your hard drive, click the Load button and navigate to the presets you want to access. You can also choose a preset library listed on the pop-up menu of each preset type.

✔ To store a new or modified group of settings, click the Save Set button and type a name.

✔ To give a particular preset a new name, select the setting in the dialog box, click the Rename button, and type the new name.

You can rename multiple settings consecutively by clicking and Shift+ clicking the items that you want to rename and then clicking the Rename button. Photoshop asks you to supply a new name for each, in turn.

✔ To quickly load the default preset library for any tool or palette, choose Reset *[name]* Preset from the Preset Manager pop-up menu. You can also replace your current preset library with another.

✔ Different preset display options are available on the Preset Manager pop-up menu.

Book II

Image Essentials

To me, when people say that a bit of information is *essential,* they mean, "Hey, you really gotta know this stuff or else!" Well, technically, you could skip this book and Photoshop wouldn't be any wiser, but I don't recommend it. In this book, I cover the nitty-gritty of topics like resolution, image modes, and file formats. Fun? Nope. Dry? Most likely, unless you're the type who gets excited about pixel dimensions. But having a good handle on the information in this book is critical to ensuring good-looking images.

I show you how to safely size your images without causing them to turn to mush. You can also find information on cropping images and increasing canvas sizes, as well as an important chapter on both applying color and color managing your files. If you want to know more about how to undo your mistakes, you'll want to check out the chapter on the History palette. And finally, if all this information makes your head spin and you need a breather, look at the chapter on Actions. Actions can automate a lot of your frequently executed Photoshop techniques, giving you more time to stop and smell those roses you just photographed.

Chapter 1: Specifying Size and Resolution

In This Chapter

- ✔ Comparing pixel and vector images
- ✔ Working with the Image Size command
- ✔ Resizing with the wizard
- ✔ Adjusting the canvas size
- ✔ Cropping an image

Size and resolution are slippery subjects. A digital image's size may refer to its file size, how big you want it to be on a printed page (such as 3 x 5 or 8 x 10 inches), the size you want it be on-screen (full screen or just part of the screen), or how densely packed the pixels are (its resolution). To use Photoshop's tools so that an image looks good in print or on-screen, you need to know not only what type of size you're working with, but also what the image's resolution is and how both of these factors might affect the image's appearance.

Given all the factors in size and resolution, it's not surprising that Photoshop has evolved into a Swiss Army knife. It offers multiple tools for specifying, viewing, or changing an image's size. In this chapter, I give you a bit of background in both size and resolution so that you know what tools to use and how to use them. In Book IX, you can find out how to use the basics I cover here in order to tailor size and resolution specifically for print.

I also explain how to change image size without harming your image. Yes, you can harm your image. Not intentionally, of course. But it can happen quicker than you can close a dialog box. However, with a firm understanding of how pixels live and breathe, you can ensure that your images are safe from any undue damage.

Putting Images under the Microscope

Digital images fall into two camps, *vector* images, which are created based on mathematical formulas, and *raster* images, which are made up of pixels. Photoshop allows you to produce both types of images and even to combine both types within a single file.

Table 1-1 gives you the skinny on vector and raster images. For the details, keep reading.

Table 1-1	Characteristics of Vector and Raster Graphics			
Graphic Type	*How It Works*	*File Size*	*Image Degradation Possible?*	*Resolution Dependent?*
Vector	Mathematical formulas precisely locate and connect geometric objects and segments	Usually smaller	No	No
Raster	Breaks pieces of an image into a grid made up of pixels	Usually larger	Yes	Yes

Even though Photoshop can produce vector graphics, its primary mission is to create awe-inspiring raster images. And because the issue of resolution is so critical to raster images, this chapter primarily discusses methods for sizing and resizing raster images. I cover producing vector art in more detail in Book IV, Chapter I.

Vector images

One cool thing about vector images, also called object-oriented images, is that when you zoom in on them, they don't look blocky. That's because vector images are comprised of *segments* — curved or straight — and *anchor points* — elements that indicate the endpoints of the segments — that are defined by mathematical objects called *vectors*. Vectors use a unique mathematical formula to define the specific location of an object as well as its geometric shape. Vector images, one of which is shown in Figure 1-1, are usually the product of drawing programs, such as Adobe Illustrator, but Photoshop is also capable of producing a vector or two.

Figure 1-1: Graphics that need clean lines, such as logos, typographic illustrations, and line art, work great in vector format, such as my logo.

Here is some additional information about vector graphics:

- ✔ **A curve is still a curve, even at 20,000 feet.** Because they are mathematically defined, vector graphics can be sized and otherwise transformed without an inkling of quality loss. Take that little 2-inch spot illustration and size it up to mural size, and it appears identical.

- ✔ **You can get pretty pictures in small packages.** Vector images can be small in file size because the file size depends on the complexity of the vector objects, not the size of the illustration.

- ✔ **Vector images are independent — resolution independent, that is.** Not only can they be transformed and printed without a degradation in quality, but they also have no built-in resolution — they take on the resolution of the output device. For example, print my logo in Figure 1-1 to an *imagesetter* (a high-end printing device used for color separations) at 2400 dots per inch (dpi), and the image comes out at 2400 dpi. Print it to a 300 dpi laser printer and what do you get? A 300 dpi image.

Because your monitor can display images only on a grid, vector images display on-screen as pixels. This accounts for the jagged appearance you sometimes see when you zoom into a curved vector object. But don't worry; it prints just fine.

Raster images

Raster images are usually the result of the digitizing of *continuous-tone* images, such as photographs or original painted or drawn artwork. Raster images are comprised of a grid of squares, which are called pixels. Pixel is short for PICture Element and is the smallest component of a digital image. If you've ever looked at a bathroom wall made up of those small square tiles reminiscent of the '40s, you're familiar with what a grid of pixels looks like: Each pixel lives in a specific location on that grid and contains a single color. When you edit a raster image, you are editing one or more pixels rather than an object-oriented shape.

But how do you fit a round peg in a square hole? By faking it. Unlike the true mathematical curve possible when drawing vector shapes, raster images must try to approximate a curve by mimicking the overall shape with square pixels. That means the elliptical shapes of my beanie, shown in Figure 1-2, have to fit within this system of squares. Fortunately, the pixels' mimicry is indecipherable with high-resolution images viewed at a reasonable distance. But when you zoom in, you can see that a curve in an image (like the curve of my beanie) is indeed comprised of square pixels.

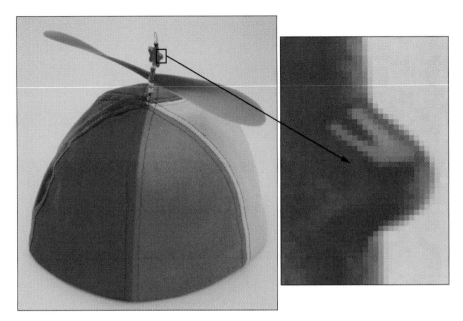

Figure 1-2: Raster images are composed of a grid of square pixels.

Raster graphics work great for photorealistic or painterly images where subtle gradations of color are necessary. On the downside, because they contain a fixed number of pixels, raster graphics can suffer a degradation of quality when they're enlarged or otherwise transformed. They are also large in file size.

Bitmap images are resolution dependent. Because they contain a fixed number of pixels, the resolution of the device they are being printed to is only one of two factors that influence the quality of the image. The quality of the output also depends heavily on the resolution of the image. For example, an image with 72 dots per inch (dpi) doesn't look any better printed on a 600 dpi printer than it does on a 1200 dpi printer. Likewise, a 300 dpi image doesn't look as good printed on an old 72 dpi dot matrix printer as it does on a 1200 dpi printer.

Viewing Raster Images On-Screen

When you view images on-screen, pixel dimensions come into play — especially if you're putting images on the Web — because the display of images is based on 1 image pixel per 1 screen pixel. The most important issue, then, is making sure that your image fits inside your (or your audience's) monitor when viewed at 100%.

When you view an image on-screen, the display size is determined by the pixel dimension, plus the size and setting of the monitor. You therefore need to determine what monitor resolution your audience is likely using and size your graphics accordingly. Table 1-2 illustrates how an 800-x-600-pixel image might display differently, depending on monitor resolution.

Table 1-2	Displaying an Image on Different Monitors	
Size of Monitor	*Resolution*	*How Does an 800 x 600 Pixel Image Display?*
17-inch monitor	1024 by 768 pixels	The image fills part of the screen.
	800 x 600	The image fills the screen, with each pixel appearing larger.
15-inch monitor	800 x 600	The image fills the screen.
		Larger images can't be viewed in their entirety.

You may also hear monitor resolution being referred to in graphic display standards, such as VGA (640 x 480 pixels), XGA (1024 x 768 pixels), UXGA (1600 x 1200), and so on.

Resolution is measured in pixels per inch, or *ppi*. You may also run across the term samples per inch (*spi*), often used when talking about scanners. Another term you see often is dots per inch (*dpi*). Dots per inch is always used in reference to printers, imagesetters, and other paper-outputting devices. You may hear people refer to dpi as *printer resolution*.

When displaying images on-screen, the recommended resolution setting is somewhere between 72 ppi and 96 ppi, even though resolution isn't really a factor in preparing screen images. That's just because monitors display somewhere in the 72 to 96 ppi range.

So if you change the physical dimensions of an image, then it is always at a one to one ratio with the monitor. If you view an image whose resolution is higher than that of the monitor, the image appears larger on-screen than in print. For example, try opening (or dragging and dropping) a 300 pixel-per-inch (ppi) JPEG file into a browser window. It explodes on your screen. Because the monitor can display only 72 to 96 ppi, it needs a ton of space to show all the pixels.

Using the Image Size Command

A time will come when you need to mess with the resolution or dimensions of an image. You may want to

✔ Change the file size.

✔ Make sure the resolution is appropriate for print.

✔ Adjust the dimensions so that they're just right for viewing on-screen.

✔ Change the width, height, and/or resolution of your image for printing or some other kind of output.

Photoshop, being the powerhouse that it is, certainly allows you to size an image in all these ways with the Image Size command on the Image menu. Follow these steps to resize your image:

1. **Open the image and then choose Image➪Image Size.**

   The Image Size dialog box opens, as shown in Figure 1-3. This is where the magic happens.

2. **Note the current state of your image, and decide whether any of the following values need to change in order to get a nice-looking image for the desired output (print or the Web):**

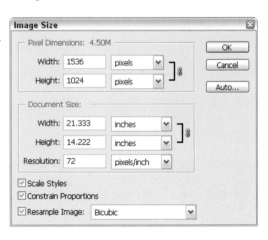

Figure 1-3: The Image Size dialog box is the one of the most important in Photoshop.

   • **The current pixel dimensions and the resulting file size:** Mine shows 1536 pixels in width and 1024 pixels in height for a file size of 4.5M (or megabytes).

   • **The current document size:** This is the size of your image when it prints on media, such as paper.

   • **The resolution:** Mine is 72 ppi, which is good for displaying on-screen or on the Web but inadequate for printing. I will see some *pixelation* (visible little squares) on my printout. Therefore, to print, I need to reduce the size of the image so that my total pixels are packed into a smaller area, so that the image has clean lines.

3. **Make sure the Constrain Proportions check box is selected.**

   The chain and bracket icon in the Document Size area indicate that the Constrain Proportions check box is selected. Nine times out of ten, you want your image to stay proportional. With the option selected, changing one value in the Document Size area makes the other values change automatically so that the proportions stay intact.

   You can also select the Scale Styles check box, which allows you to scale or not scale any effects or styles that you have applied to your layer(s).

Note that this option is available only if you have checked Constrain Proportions. For more on styles, see Book V, Chapter 4.

4. **Make sure that the Resample Image check box is deselected.**

When you *resample,* you add or delete pixels in the image. Although sometimes you need to resample, doing so isn't good for your image (I explain why in the next section).

5. **Enter any new values in the dialog box.**

For example, because I want to print my image, I enter a new value of 300 pixels per inch for my resolution in the Document Size area. Note how the other values automatically changed, as shown in Figure 1-4.

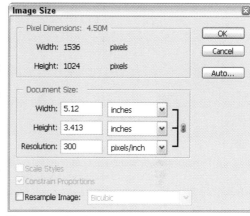

6. **Click OK.**

You won't notice any difference in the way your image appears on-screen because you haven't added or deleted any pixels; you've merely compacted them into a smaller space.

Figure 1-4: The Constrain Proportions option prevents your image from becoming distorted when sized.

Book II Chapter 1

Specifying Size and Resolution

Congratulations! You have just safely resized your image. You can proudly say, "No pixels were harmed in the making of this image."

Resampling Images

Resampling means you are changing the pixel dimensions of an image. When you *downsample* (or resample down), you are eliminating pixels and therefore deleting information and detail from your image. When you resample up (or upsampling), you are adding pixels. Photoshop adds these pixels by using *interpolation.* Interpolation means Photoshop analyzes the colors of the original pixels and "manufactures" new ones, which are then added to the existing ones.

You can specify the interpolation method in the Image Size dialog box. The default that appears in the dialog box is based on the interpolation method you specified in your General Preferences dialog box. Here are your five choices:

- **Nearest Neighbor:** This method is fast and provides for the smallest file size, but it is less precise and therefore of the lowest quality. This method works by copying the color of the nearest pixel. It can result in jagged edges, so use it only for images with non-anti-aliased edges (hard edges).

- **Bilinear:** Considered a medium-quality method, it works by averaging the color of the pixel above, below, and to the right and left of each pixel.

- **Bicubic:** This method is the slowest but most precise. It averages the color of the pixel above and below and the two on the right and left of each pixel. It provides a smoother transition between pixels but also increases the contrast between pixels to reduce blurriness.

- **Bicubic Smoother:** Like Bicubic, but provides an even smoother transition between pixels and therefore increases the amount of blurriness. A good method to use when upsampling images. Can slightly affect the sharpness of the image.

- **Bicubic Sharper:** Also similar to Bicubic, but applies less anti-aliasing and therefore less blurriness as well. This method applies just a little softening to pixel edges. This is a good method when downsampling an image.

A potpourri of image size do's and don'ts

Here are some tips and tricks to keep in mind when you're messing around with image size and resolution settings:

- **Use the Unsharp Mask filter when you resample.** Choose Filter⇨Sharpen⇨ Unsharp Mask. This filter heightens the contrast between pixels to give the illusion of sharpening or forcing the image more in focus.

- **Don't change your settings — just use Print with Preview.** If you want to leave the size and resolution settings untouched, but need to print your image at a different size, use the Print with Preview command. For details, see Book I, Chapter 3.

- **Start out with the proper dimensions.** It goes without saying, but I'll say it anyway.

You want to try to enter the proper dimensions and resolution when creating a new document. You don't want to find yourself in the unfortunate situation of creating your file at 72 ppi, spending hours getting it just perfect and then remembering that you were supposed to prep it for print and really needed it to be 300 ppi. Make sure that you scan images at a high enough resolution too.

- **Don't use a higher resolution than you need.** All you do is create an unnecessarily huge file with a slower print time. In some cases, it may actually make your printout look darker and muddier.

- **Look no further than this book.** Use the handy, dandy table of recommended resolution settings for a variety of output devices in Book IX, Chapter 1.

If you really must resample, I recommend leaving the method set to Bicubic Smoother. Notice I said if you really must. Here are some reasons why you might choose to add or delete pixels:

✔ You no longer have access to the original artwork, which you could rescan at the proper resolution and size.

✔ You no longer have access to the original high-resolution version of the file.

✔ You absolutely cannot substitute the low-resolution image with another of higher resolution.

Resampling isn't a recommended activity, especially when it pertains to upsampling. I mean as smart as Photoshop is, having to manufacture pixels is not an exact science. Your image tends to lose detail and sharpness and get blurry and mushy. Notice the overall blurriness and goopy edges that are an unfortunate side effect of interpolation, as shown in Figure 1-5. The bottom line is your resampled image never looks as good as the original. Downsampling isn't as scary. You are deleting pixels, and therefore detail, but the degradation is virtually undetectable to the eye.

Book II
Chapter 1

Specifying Size and Resolution

Original   Resampled

Figure 1-5: Fuzzy, blurry images are a result of resampling images.

Adding pixels to an image

To add pixels to an image, follow these steps:

1. **With your desired image open, first choose Image⇨Duplicate to make a copy of your original. With the duplicate active, choose Image⇨Image Size.**

   The Image Size dialog box appears; see Figure 1-6.

   This is where the havoc happens. Be careful!

2. **Make sure that the Resample Image option is selected.**

   The Width and Height in the Pixel Dimensions area are now text boxes into which you can enter values as well. They are no longer fixed values, as they are when Resample Image is deselected.

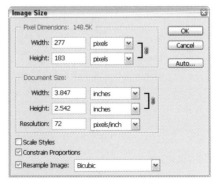

Figure 1-6: Checking Resample Image enables Photoshop to add pixels to your image.

3. **Enter a higher value for the resolution, and if desired, enter a higher value for the width or height.**

   I entered a resolution of 300 ppi.

   Note how the pixel dimensions increased dramatically as did the file size (from a mere 148.5K to 2.52M), as shown in Figure 1-7.

   If you get all discombobu-lated when working in the dialog box, press Alt (Option on the Mac). The Cancel button changes to a Reset button. Click it, and you're back to where you started. This is a good shortcut to remember, as it holds true for many of Photoshop's dialog boxes.

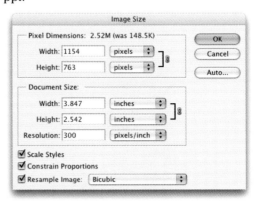

Figure 1-7: Increasing the pixel dimensions in an image causes your image to degrade in quality.

4. **Leave your Interpolation method set to Bicubic Smoother, which is a good option when upsampling.**

5. **Click OK.**

Photoshop now goes through its interpolation ritual and churns out a newly resampled image. Do a side-by-side comparison to the original, looking at both at 100% view. Your original should look a whole lot better than the resampled image. And for a real shocker, try printing out the two images and seeing what kind of degradation takes place.

Taking pixels out of an image

When you *downsample* you eliminate pixels and therefore delete information and detail from your image. Although I have emphasized the pitfalls of resampling up, you can sometimes damage your image by downsampling, as well.

Granted, downsampling is sometimes necessary when converting high-resolution print graphics into Web graphics. For example, you may be forced to take images used for a corporate brochure and repurpose them into content for the company's Web site. You probably won't notice much degradation in image quality because the images are just being viewed on-screen. In addition, downsampling can occasionally camouflage the moiré patterns caused by scanning halftones (for more on halftones, check out Book VII, Chapter 1). However, you can downsample to the extreme where the images look horrid even on-screen, as shown in Figure 1-8. But just remember, you should never need to make an image smaller than 72 ppi.

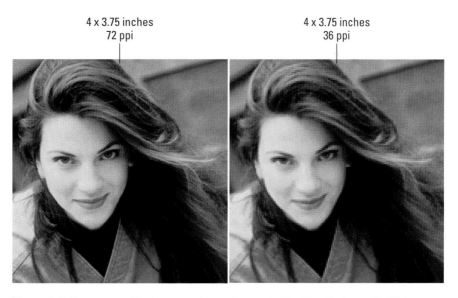

4 x 3.75 inches
72 ppi

4 x 3.75 inches
36 ppi

Figure 1-8: You may need to downsample your images to 72 ppi for display on the Web.

To remove pixels from an image, follow the steps in the preceding section and change the image settings accordingly.

If you have to downsample your image significantly, for example to 25% of its original size, you get better results if you do several successive 50% downsamples, applying an Unsharp Mask filter on the image in between each image sizing. For more on the Unsharp Mask filter, see Book VII, Chapter 1.

Resizing Images with the Resize Image Wizard

You find the Resize Image Wizard (Resize Image Assistant on the Mac) on the Help menu on the Photoshop menu bar. When selected, the wizard/assistant dialog box appears and asks you questions about your intended use for the image. The wizard/assistant then guides you through the image-sizing process. If you happen to choose options that the wizard doesn't like, you get a warning that your changes are likely to lower your image quality. You can then go back and try another setting.

Beginners might find the Resize Image Wizard a good tool to start with, but the wizard doesn't offer quite the control that the Image Size dialog box does. In addition, you can't see all your options on one screen and must continually go back and forth between screens when entering different values. If you're comfortable working with the Image Size dialog box, I recommend using it instead of the wizard.

When you finish changing settings and choosing options, the wizard/assistant creates a new file called `Resize Wizard_1` (`Resize Assistant 1` on the Mac), leaving your original unharmed. Like any kind of wizard, this one is pretty savvy, but I recommend having a firm understanding of proper output resolution (see the beginning of this chapter for info on that topic) before you use the wizard/assistant. And actually with that firm understanding, you can do manually everything the wizard/assistant can do and more. Remember the old adage, knowledge is power.

Although using the Resize Image Wizard is fine, try to avoid using File⇨Automate⇨Fit Image. This command resizes your image dimensions while leaving the resolution the same. And if you've read earlier sections of this chapter, you know this is also called resampling — not a nice thing in image-editing circles.

Changing the Canvas Size

I've probably harped on you to the point that you're slightly paranoid, or at least ultraconscious, of using the Image Size command. Well, you can relax now because the Canvas Size command is as safe as can be. Unlike the Image Size command, which enlarges or reduces the dimensions or resolution of your image, the Canvas Size command merely changes the size of the *canvas,* or page, on which the image sits.

When you increase the size of the canvas, Photoshop fills the expanded area outside the image with your chosen color. Increasing your canvas size can come in handy if you are trying to add a frame or border around your image. If you make the canvas smaller, Photoshop *crops* (cuts away) the image.

Here are the quick and easy steps to changing your canvas size:

1. **Choose Image⇨Canvas Size.**

   The Canvas Size dialog box, shown in Figure 1-9, appears. The current size of your canvas appears at the top of the dialog box.

Figure 1-9: Increasing your canvas size adds to the area around your image.

2. **Enter new values in the Width and Height text boxes.**

   You can also change the unit of measurement by using the pop-up menus. Select the Relative check box to specify an amount of space for Photoshop to add around your image. This feature is handy when adding equal amounts of canvas around images with fractional measurements.

3. **Specify your desired anchor placement.**

The anchor shows how the image sits inside the canvas. By default, Photoshop centers the image and adds the canvas around it. Click any of the other eight squares to have Photoshop add the canvas asymmetrically around the image, as shown in Figure 1-10.

If you reduce either the Width or Height value and click OK, an alert box appears asking if you really want to proceed

Figure 1-10: You can increase the size of your canvas symmetrically or asymmetrically around your image.

because you will be clipping the image. This is actually another way of cropping an image, albeit not one you will use everyday.

4. **Choose your canvas color from the Canvas Extension Color pop-up menu and click OK.**

   Choose from Foreground, Background, White, Black, Gray, or Other. If you select Other, Photoshop transports you to the Color Picker where you can choose any color you desire. Note that the small swatch to the right of the pop-up menu displays the current background color. You can also click this swatch to access the Color Picker, which I explain how to use in Book II, Chapter 4.

Cropping an Image

Even a novice photographer knows that cropping an image can make a composition stronger. *Cropping* entails cutting away background clutter or endless expanses of empty space in order to focus in on your desired subject.

This simple process can transform a ho-hum photograph into a visually exciting one. Take a look at my example in Figure 1-11. I mean, it doesn't take an Ansel Adams to figure out which image is stronger. (It would be even better if the fence weren't in the background,

Figure 1-11: Cropping is one of the easiest ways to improve the composition of your image.

but hey, that's nothing that a little Photoshop retouching can't take care of. Check out Book VIII; it's all about retouching and restoration techniques.)

Using the Crop tool

The most popular way to crop an image is by using the Crop tool. This simple tool is as easy and effective to use as a T square and X-ACTO knife, and without the possibility of bodily injury. Select the Crop tool in the Tools palette or press C on the keyboard. Then follow these steps:

1. **With the Crop tool, drag around the part of the image you want to keep and then release your mouse button.**

   As you drag, a *marquee* (a dotted outline) appears displaying the cropping boundaries. Don't worry if your cropping marquee isn't exactly correct. You can adjust it in the next step.

   Notice how the area outside the cropping marquee appears darker than the inside in order to better frame your image. Adobe calls this a *shield*. You control the color and opacity (the amount of transparency) of the shield by adjusting the settings on the Options bar. If, for some strange reason, you don't want the shield, deselect the check box. Figure 1-12 shows a great example of way too much background clutter. I dragged around the only thing I want to retain — the birthday girl.

Cropping marquee

Handle   Shield

Figure 1-12: The area around your cropping marquee appears darker so you can better frame your image.

2. **Adjust the cropping marquee by dragging the handles.**

The small squares on the sides and corners of the cropping marquee are called *handles*. When you hover your mouse over any handle or the marquee itself, your cursor changes to a double-headed arrow, indicating that you can drag.

To move the entire marquee, position your mouse inside the marquee until you see a black arrowhead cursor and then drag. Adjust the marquee until you're satisfied.

You can also drag the origin point (the circle icon in the center) to change the axis of rotation.

If you move your mouse outside the marquee, the cursor changes to a curved, double-headed arrow. Dragging with this cursor rotates the marquee. This feature can be extremely useful when you need to rotate and crop a crooked image. By using the Crop tool, you can perform both commands in one step and often more quickly and accurately. Just be aware that rotation, unless it's in 90-degree increments, resamples your image, which, if done repeatedly, can damage your image (see the earlier section, "Resampling Images," for more on resampling). Getting the rotation right the first time around is for the best.

3. **Double-click inside the cropping marquee.**

You can also just press Enter (Return on the Mac) or click the Commit (check mark icon) button on the Options bar. Photoshop discards the area outside the marquee, as shown in Figure 1-13. If you want to cancel the crop, just press Esc or click Cancel (the slashed circle icon) on the Options bar.

Figure 1-13: Eliminating background clutter allows you to hone in on your subject.

Cropping with the Marquee tool

If you get bored using the Crop tool, you can also crop a selected area by choosing Image⇨Crop. Simply make a selection with any of the tools and then choose this command. Although using the Rectangular Marquee tool for your selection makes the most sense, you don't have to.

You can use Image⇨Crop with any selection — circular, polygonal, kidney bean, even feathered. Photoshop can't crop to those odd shapes, but it gets as close to the outline as it can. For all you need to know on selections, see Book III, Chapter 1.

Using the Trim command

The fabulous Trim trims away transparent or solid-colored areas around your image. Choose Image⇨Trim, and a dialog box appears. Select Transparent Pixels (for layered images), Top Left Pixel Color, or Bottom Right Pixel Color as a basis for the trim. Next, instruct Photoshop to trim away the Top, Bottom, Left, or Right side(s) from the image.

Sure-fire cropping tips

Even though cropping is about as simple an image-editing maneuver as you can get, you need to know about a few other options:

- If you need a nonrectangular cropping marquee, select the **Perspective** check box on the Options bar. This feature allows the corner handles to move independently.

- The **Front Image** option enables you to crop one image so that it's the exact same size as another image. Open two images and crop the first one. Click Front Image. Photoshop enters the width, height, and resolution values from the first image on the Options bar. Drag the Crop tool on your second image and adjust the marquee as desired. Double-click inside the marquee. Photoshop automatically crops your second image to match your first.

- If your image doesn't contain any layers — that is, it consists only of a background — any cropped areas are permanently deleted from your file. However, if your image consists of one or more layers (see Book V for the lowdown on layers), you have the choice of deleting or hiding your cropped area. **Delete** eliminates the cropped areas, whereas **Hide** just hides the cropped area. You can see the cropped area if you move the layer with the Move tool. Another way to see the hidden area is to choose Image⇨Reveal All. Photoshop expands the canvas to show all areas in all layers. These options are available only while the crop marquee is active.

- If you want to crop an image to an exact measurement, enter a value in the **Width**, **Height**, and **Resolution** text boxes on the Options bar. Note that these options are available only when the Crop tool is active and you haven't yet dragged a cropping marquee. But again, be careful about the value you use for the Resolution setting. Remember, resampling is not a good thing. To remove the entered settings, click the **Clear** button on the Options bar.

This command works great for quickly eliminating black-and-white borders around images, as shown in Figure 1-14.

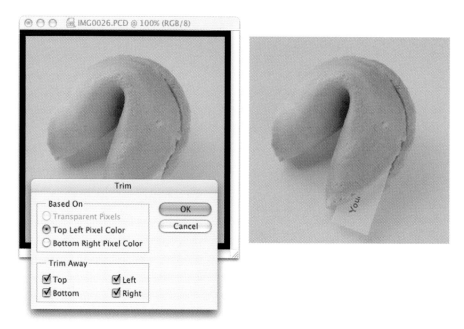

Figure 1-14: Use the Trim command to slice off borders.

Using the Crop and Straighten Photo Command

Choose File⇨Automate⇨Crop and Straighten Photos. Photoshop then looks for rectangular areas in your document, extracts each one into its own document, and then straightens those individual images, as shown in Figure 1-15.

The Crop and Straighten Photos command is fabulous if you want to save time by scanning multiple images initially into one document (and the command works on single images as well). This command is a real manual labor time saver, and I wholeheartedly endorse it.

Figure 1-15: The Crop and Straighten command extracts and straightens your images into separate files.

Chapter 2: Choosing Color Modes and File Formats

In addition to choosing a size and resolution (discussed in the previous chapter), you need to decide on a color mode and file format for your image. This decision is usually based on the final use for the image. Are you importing it into a page layout program for offset printing? Posting it on a Web page? Using it for a newspaper article?

When you know an image's final destination, you can make intelligent choices of which color mode and file format are best. This chapter gives you some background information to help you make those choices so that you don't end up having to do extra work, spend extra time, or waste extra money.

Selecting a Color Mode

Every file has a color mode, also called an *image mode* or just plain *mode*. To determine the color mode of an image, look in the title bar of the image window or choose Image⇨Mode. Color modes define the color values used to display the image. Photoshop offers eight different modes and allows you to convert images from one mode to another. The color mode you choose for a particular image depends on a couple of factors:

✔ **The file format you plan to save it in.** Some modes call for specific file formats. You may find that a certain format is unavailable because your file isn't in the appropriate color mode.

✔ **The end use for the image.** Do you plan to post the image on the Web? Or are you putting it in a brochure that will be offset printed? For more on prepping images for print, see Book IX, Chapter 1.

Basic RGB and CMYK color theory

When you view an RGB image, you are looking at an image comprised of three colors — red, green, and blue. These colors are

✔ The primary colors of light

✔ The colors that correspond to the three types of cones inside your eyes

✔ The colors that comprise white light from the sun

✔ The colors your monitor uses when displaying images

The CMYK color scheme is based on the light-absorbing quality of ink on paper. In theory, a white light hits these inks. Some visible wavelengths are absorbed, or subtracted, while others are reflected back to your eyes. CMYK images comprise various percentages of only four colors of ink — cyan, magenta, yellow, and black. These colors correspond to the inks used in the offset printing process.

The next few sections provide a brief description and example of each mode and any file format or usage connections.

Color modes affect the number of colors that are displayed, as well as the size of the file and the number of channels. One or more channels, which is where the color data is stored, represent each mode. Grayscale images have one color channel — Black. CMYK images have four color channels — Cyan, Magenta, Yellow, and Black. For the lowdown on channels, see Book VI, Chapter 1.

RGB Color

Uses: RGB is the gold standard for most scanners, all monitors, digital cameras, and some desktop inkjet printers. And it's the primary color mode (with Indexed Color being secondary) to use with any images to be viewed on-screen (whether on the Web or in any kind of multimedia presentation).

File formats: Just about every file format, except GIF, can handle an image in RGB mode.

RGB is a very good overall work mode. Images in RGB mode have full access to all Photoshop commands, including filters and image adjustments. RGB images contain values of 0–255 for each of three colors — red, green, and blue. With 8 bits of color information for each of the three colors, these 24-bit images can reproduce up to 16.7 million colors on-screen. And 48-bit images (16 bits per color) can display even more. Most scanners also scan images in RGB, all monitors display in RGB, and some desktop inkjet printers prefer to print

RGB (rather than CMYK) images. **Remember:** The RGB mode in Photoshop varies according to the RGB Working Space setting you have selected in the Color Settings dialog box. For details on color settings, see Book II, Chapter 3.

CMYK Color

Uses: CMYK is the standard for images that are color separated for offset printing.

File formats: CMYK can handle just about every format except GIF.

CMYK images, shown in Figure 2-1, contain a percentage of one or more four-process color inks — cyan, magenta, yellow, and black. Darker colors have higher percentages, whereas lighter colors have lower percentages. Pure white is created when all four colors have a value of 0%. Many other composite printing devices also require images to be in CMYK mode. Again, like RGB mode, remember that the CMYK mode in Photoshop can vary according to the CMYK Working Space setting you have selected in the Color Settings dialog box.

Corbis Digital Stock

Figure 2-1: CMYK is the mode needed for offset printed images.

Make sure that you do all your image editing in RGB mode, where you have access to the full range of filters. When you complete your editing, convert the image from RGB to CMYK. (For details, see "Converting from RGB to CMYK," later in this chapter.)

Grayscale

Uses: Grayscale mode, shown in Figure 2-2, is for black-and-white (and all shades of gray in between) images.

File formats: All the most commonly used file formats accept Grayscale mode.

Grayscale images contain up to 256 levels of gray. Each pixel has a brightness value

Corbis Digital Stock

Figure 2-2: Images in grayscale mode contain 256 levels of gray.

ranging from 0 (black) to 255 (white). You can scan an image in Grayscale mode, or you can convert color images to grayscale. If you convert a color image to grayscale, Photoshop discards all the color information, and the remaining gray levels represent the luminosity of the pixels. (Check out the "Converting to grayscale" section, later in this chapter.) You can also convert a grayscale image to a color image, which, while it doesn't convert your grayscale image to color, it allows you to apply color on top of the grayscale image.

Monotone, Duotone, Tritone, and Quadtone

Uses: Because printing presses can print only about 50 gray levels per ink color, duotones, which use two to four inks, are used to increase the range of tones of grayscale images. Duotones are often created by using black and spot colors (premixed inks), although you can also use process colors. For more on spot colors, see Book IX, Chapter 1.

File formats: The only file formats that can save duotones, tritones, and quadtones are native Photoshop, Photoshop 2.0, EPS, PDF, Large Document Format, or Photoshop Raw.

These modes create one-color, (monotone), two-color (duotone), three-color (tritone), shown in Figure 2-3, and four-color (quadtone) images. Note that Photoshop lumps all the various "tone" modes under duotone. You can find a pop-up menu in the Duotone options dialog box where you can select the various options. Unlike RGB and CMYK images where the components of the image display with different colors, the monotones, duotones, tritones, and quadtones have the colors mixed throughout the image. The colored inks are used to reproduce tinted grays, not the different colors you find in RGB and CMYK images.

Corbis Digital Stock

Figure 2-3: Tritone images use three inks that are mixed throughout the image.

To access the Duotone mode, you must first convert the color image to grayscale by choosing Image⇨Mode⇨Grayscale. Then choose Image⇨Mode⇨Duotone. In the dialog box that appears, choose Monotone, Duotone, Tritone, or Quadtone from the pop-up menu. Next, select ink colors — either spot or process — by clicking the swatches. Finally, you can adjust the curves settings and tell Photoshop how to distribute the ink(s) among the various tones. Note that you do not have access to the individual color channels in Duotone mode. The only manipulation that you do is with the curves settings.

If you are new to these modes, you need to know that Photoshop offers numerous preset duotones, tritones, and quadtones. To access these presets, click the Load button and go to the Duotones folder (which is located in the Presets folder in the Photoshop folder). Sometimes printing these types of images can be challenging so starting with these presets is a good idea if you're inexperienced.

Indexed Color

Uses: Indexed Color mode is primarily for Web graphics and multimedia displays.

File formats: Indexed Color mode supports a variety of formats, with GIF being the most popular. Other formats supported include Photoshop, Photoshop 2.0, Photoshop Raw, BMP, EPS, ElectricImage, Large Document Format, PCX, PDF, PICT, PICT Resource, PNG, Targa, and TIFF.

Indexed Color mode, shown in Figure 2-4, uses 256 colors or less; what graphics aficionados call 8-bit color. When you convert an image to indexed color, Photoshop builds a Color Lookup Table (CLUT), which stores and indexes the color. (Note the Color Table option in the Mode menu.) If a color in the original image isn't in the table, Photoshop chooses the closest match or makes a new one from the available colors. The small amount of colors reduces the file size, which is why the GIF file format, a very popular Web graphics format, uses this mode. (See the "GIF" section, later in this chapter.)

The Indexed Color mode does not support layers, and editing capabilities are limited. For more on indexed color, see Bonus Chapter 1. The book's Introduction has details about the companion Web site.

Corbis Digital Stock
Figure 2-4: Indexed Color mode uses 256 colors or less.

Lab Color

Uses: Lab Color mode provides a consistent color display, which is ideal for high-end retouching of images.

File formats: You can save an image in Lab Color mode in native Photoshop, Photoshop Raw, EPS, TIFF, PDF, JPEG 2000, Large Document Format, or Photoshop DCS 1.0 and 2.0 formats. You can save images containing 48 bits (16 bits per channel) in Photoshop, Photoshop Raw, Large Document Format, and TIFF formats.

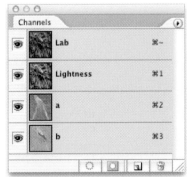

Lab Color mode is usually thought of as the internal color mode Photoshop uses when converting from one color mode to another — for example, when going from RGB to CMYK. It is also the mode preferred by color-retouching experts because it is considered to be *device independent* (it appears consistent on various devices).

Lab Color mode consists of a lightness channel and two additional channels, *a* and *b*, shown in Figure 2-5, which contain the range of color from green to red (a) and blue to yellow (b).

Figure 2-5: Lab color mode is the preferred editing mode for color experts due to its device independency.

Bitmap

Uses: This mode is best for scanned line art (that is, art composed entirely of lines, such as a line drawing of a camera you might see in a manual) and signatures (your John Hancock). A quick tip: When scanning line art be sure and crank up your scanning resolution to 1200 dpi or so to ensure a good quality bitmap image.

File formats: Photoshop, Photoshop 2.0, EPS, TIFF, PDF, BMP, PNG, GIF, PNG, PCX, PICT, PICT Resource, Portable Bitmap, and Wireless Bitmap.

Bitmap images contain pixels that are either black or white, exclusively. You must convert color images to grayscale before you can access Bitmap mode. Upon choosing Image⇨Mode⇨Bitmap, a dialog box appears, offering options for resolution and method. The various methods give different appearances, one of which is shown in Figure 2-6, so try each one to see which you prefer. When

Corbis Digital Stock

Figure 2-6: Bitmap mode allows you to choose a method such as Pattern Dither.

you choose Custom Pattern, you can then choose a pattern from the drop-down menu.

If you save a file in Bitmap mode as an EPS (see "EPS," later in this chapter), you can convert the white areas in the image to transparent areas. Transparency allows you to overlay the file over a background containing color or an image, and only the dark pixels show.

Multichannel

Uses: Multichannel mode is for special printing needs or as an intermediate mode when converting between different color modes.

File formats: The only file formats available for multichannel images are native Photoshop, Photoshop 2.0, Photoshop DCS 2.0, Large Document Format, or Photoshop Raw formats.

The Multichannel mode, shown in Figure 2-7, comprises multiple grayscale channels, each containing 256 levels of gray. Whenever you delete or mix channels, you end up with a multichannel image. You can also convert any image with more than one channel to this mode. In a multichannel image, each channel becomes a spot channel, with 256 levels of gray.

Corbis Digital Stock

Figure 2-7: Deleting or mixing channels creates a multichannel image.

For more on channels, see Book VI, Chapter 1.

**Book II
Chapter 2**

**Choosing Color
Modes and
File Formats**

Converting to a Different Color Mode

Sometimes, your image starts out in one color mode and then you find you need to convert the image to another mode. Maybe you need to strip the color out of an image you're submitting to the local newspaper. Or maybe you need to convert your RGB image to CMYK to get it ready for an offset print job.

When you convert modes, you are permanently changing the color values in your image, so save a backup image just in case.

The next few sections offer pointers for the most common conversions you'll make. If you want to convert an image into an indexed color for the Web, your best bet is to use the Save for Web option, which I cover in Bonus Chapter 1.

Converting from RGB to CMYK

As I mention several times in this book, CMYK is the image mode necessary for high-end composite printing and offset printing. You first want to perform all your necessary image-editing tasks in RGB mode for the following reasons:

- The image size is smaller because RGB mode has only three channels.

- The RGB color space provides more device independence because it isn't reliant on inks.

- You have full accessibility to filters.

- RGB mode provides a large color gamut, so Photoshop preserves more colors after it makes image adjustments.

When you finish editing the image in RGB mode, you can convert the image from RGB to CMYK (you can perform any fine-tuning in CMYK mode if necessary). If you're new to this procedure, you may be surprised at what can result. Because the color *gamut* (range of colors) of the RGB model (16.7 million) is much larger than that of CMYK (approximately 55,000), you may see a color shift, which may range from slight to major.

The extent of the shift depends on the colors in the RGB image and how many of them are *out of gamut*. Photoshop replaces RGB colors that are out of gamut with the closest match available within the CMYK gamut, often replacing the electric blues, fiery reds, and sunny yellows with duller, muddier CMYK equivalents. Unfortunately, you can't do anything to prevent this. It is just the way of the world of color. However, if you can select colors (rather than acquiring them from a scan), be sure that you don't select any colors that are out of gamut to begin with. You can also *soft proof* colors (preview the effects of your CMYK conversion without actually converting) by choosing View➪Proof Setup➪Working CMYK. Check out Book II, Chapter 3 for details about selecting colors and soft proofing.

Converting to grayscale

You can convert a color image to grayscale a multitude of ways, as shown in Figure 2-8. The next few sections cover a few that you may want to try out.

Image⇨Mode⇨Grayscale   Lab mode   Best channel

Corbis Digital Stock
Figure 2-8: Photoshop gives you many ways to convert a color image to grayscale.

Quick-and-dirty method

Choose Image⇨Mode⇨Grayscale. Photoshop then asks you whether you want to discard color information. Click OK. If your image contains multiple layers, Photoshop asks whether you want to merge your layers. If you want to keep your layers, click the Don't Merge button.

Although this method does the job in stripping color from your image, you may be left with an image that is flat and lacking contrast. You can apply a Levels adjustment (choose Image⇨Adjustments⇨Levels) to boost the contrast, or you can try one of the other conversion methods.

Be aware that you can no longer apply color to your image after you convert it. If you choose a color in the Color palette, the color appears gray in the foreground and background color icons. If you *want* to apply color to your grayscale image, convert it back to RGB or CMYK mode.

Lab Color mode method

This method most likely provides a better grayscale image than the quick-and-dirty method. Make sure that you finish all your edits requiring layers before you follow these steps:

1. **Choose Image⇨Mode⇨Lab Color.**

   As I mention earlier, converting to Lab Color mode converts the channels into a lightness channel and *a* and *b* channels containing ranges of color.

2. **Delete the *a* channel.**

   The *b* channel then changes its name to Alpha 2.

3. **Delete the Alpha 2 channel.**

   That leaves you with the lightness channel, which is now named Alpha 1.

4. **Choose Image⇨Mode⇨Grayscale.**

   Your color image is now a grayscale one. Note that if your image contains multiple layers, Photoshop flattens the layers when you convert to grayscale.

Best channel method

If you look at the individual channels in the image, one often stands out as being a very good grayscale image by itself. (If channels are a mystery to you, check out Book VI, Chapter 1 for details.) You may find that the Red channel provides a good grayscale image when the subject is people, because humans have a lot of red in their skin. Or you may find the Green channel looks good in a scenic shot. The Blue channel rarely yields a nice image, though. Most of the crud picked up in a digital image finds its way into the Blue channel.

In the Channels palette, select each channel and view its contents. Find the channel that looks the best and then choose Image⇨Mode⇨Grayscale. Photoshop asks you if you want to discard all the other channels. Click OK. Like with the Lab Color method, if your image contains multiple layers, Photoshop flattens the layers when you convert to grayscale.

You can also use the Channel Mixer to create custom grayscale images. For more on the Channel Mixer, see Book VI, Chapter 1.

Using the Conditional Mode Change command

Photoshop enables you to specify instances where one mode changes into another so that you can utilize the conversion command in an *action*. Briefly, an action is a collection of recorded and saved commands that you can replay again and again. For details on actions, see Book II, Chapter 5. Sometimes when you incorporate a mode conversion as part of an action, you get an error message because the file you're opening may not have the same mode you specified as the *source* mode in the action. For example, you may have specified CMYK as your source mode in the action. But if the action opens a file in Grayscale mode, you get an error message, because the Grayscale mode of the file doesn't match the CMYK source mode. The Conditional Mode Change command takes care of this problem. Here's what you do to add this command to your action:

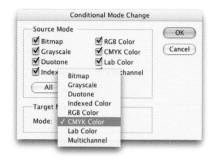

1. **Start creating and recording your action.**

2. **Choose File⇨Automate⇨ Conditional Mode Change.**

   The Conditional Mode Change dialog box, shown in Figure 2-9, appears.

Figure 2-9: Include the Conditional Mode Change command in your action to ensure all images are processed regardless of the image's mode.

3. **Select the mode(s) you want as valid for the source mode. Other options include the All or None buttons to select all modes or no modes.**

4. **Select your desired target mode from the Mode pop-up menu.**

5. **Click OK.**

   If all goes well, Photoshop incorporates the Conditional Mode Change command as a step in your action.

Choosing the Right File Format

A critical component in saving a file is choosing the file format. The file format is the way the file's data is represented and saved. Photoshop generously offers numerous file formats to choose from. Some you'll use frequently, and others you'll never set eyes on. I provide quite a bit of detail on the formats you'll use most frequently

Note that if a file format doesn't appear in the Open, Save, or another dialog box, you may need to install the plug-in for that particular format.

TIFF

TIFF, *Tagged Image File Format*, is by far one of the best and most useful formats. One of the great qualities of TIFFs is that they are and have always been totally cross-platform. In addition, almost every program on the planet can import TIFFs. Okay, so that's a slight exaggeration. Almost every word processing, presentation, page layout, drawing, painting, and image-editing program can import TIFFs. This file format works especially well for printed or color-separated images.

Photoshop allows you to save layers and transparency (explained in detail in Book V) and also use various methods of compression. You have the option of having Photoshop warn you that including layers increases your file size. To enable this option, select the Ask Before Saving Layered TIFF Files check box in the File Handling section of the Preferences dialog box. Photoshop saves the layers along with a flattened version of the image. Be aware that some applications may display only the flattened version (in which case transparency isn't preserved).

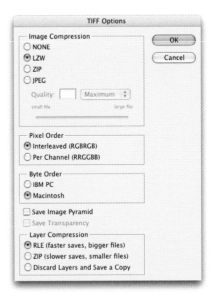

It should come as no surprise that the most commonly used format offers a variety of options — all of which are available in the TIFF Options dialog box (shown in Figure 2-10). The following sections give you everything you need to know about your various options so that you can make an informed decision based on your intended uses for the image.

Figure 2-10: The TIFF dialog box offers a multitude of options for saving TIFFs.

Image Compression

Compression makes your file sizes smaller, but at a cost. If your files are unusually large, compressing them makes your files save and open more slowly. Note that TIFFs can be up to 4GB in file size. Be careful, however, because older versions of Photoshop and other applications don't support file sizes larger than 2GB.

Photoshop offers three methods of compression, besides the option of None, which of course leaves your image uncompressed:

- **LZW:** This method has been around for eons and is a *lossless* compression scheme, which means that data is not deleted to make your file smaller. LZW is especially good for compressing images with large areas of a single color. Most programs that support TIFF also support LZW compression, so you can use this method without much hesitation.

- **Zip:** Zip compression is also a lossless method and is popular in the Windows arena. Like LZW, it works well with images that have large areas of a single color.

✔ **JPEG:** This method, while popular and very effective, is a *lossy* compression process. When compressing, JPEG deletes data to reduce the file size. (That's where the *loss* in lossy comes from.) JPEG compression is a cumulative compression scheme which means that it recompresses every time it saves. Over time this can degrade image quality.

I recommend that you stick with LZW compression if possible. If you need to create a JPEG however, minimize the degradation of lossy compression by leaving your image in either TIFF or native Photoshop file formats while editing. Then when you're completely done editing and you need to compress the image, save the file as a JPEG at a high to maximum quality setting.

Pixel Order

Specify how Photoshop arranges the data in the color channels of the TIFF file. Interleaved stores the samples from individual channels interleaved with each other (for example RGBRGBRGB). Planar stores them consecutively (for example RRRGGGBBB). Previously Photoshop wrote all TIFFs as interleaved. But planar offers better compression and speed, and Adobe swears that all applications support the format.

Byte Order

Byte order is the way bits of data are arranged and stored. Specify whether you want to save the TIFF for a Mac or a PC. If you want to be able to use the image on both platforms, select IBM PC. Macs are much more forgiving when exchanging files.

Save Image Pyramid

This option allows you to save multiple resolutions of an image. The top of the pyramid is the lowest resolution, and the bottom of the pyramid is the highest resolution. If the program supports them, you can choose to open any of the resolutions. Photoshop can open only the image at the highest resolution within the file. I recommend leaving this option deselected.

Save Transparency

Select this option to preserve transparent areas when the TIFF is opened in other applications. Of course, those applications must also support transparency. If you open a TIFF with transparency in Photoshop, the transparent areas are *always* preserved whether or not you select the option. Note that this option is disabled if your image has no transparent areas.

Layer Compression

If your file has layers and you choose to save them, you have the choice of RLE (Run Length Encoding) or Zip compression. Because RLE compression is also lossless, you have the choice of faster saves (RLE) or smaller files (Zip). The last choice is for Photoshop to discard the layers, thereby flattening the image and then saving it as a copy. Your original layered file also remains intact. This option is disabled if your image has no layers.

JPEG

JPEG, the acronym for *Joint Photographic Experts Group*, is a file format that uses lossy compression (explained in the "Image Compression" section). The JPEG file format offers 13 compression settings — the higher the quality, the less the compression, and vice versa.

JPEG compression is very effective. It can squeeze your file size to practically nothing. But because the compression is lossy, I don't recommend this format for high-end printing. JPEG supports RGB, CMYK, and Grayscale image modes.

If you want to post your image on the Web, you have to save it as a JPEG, GIF, or PNG. JPEG works great with photographic images that have a wide range of colors. You're better off using the Save for Web feature when saving as a JPEG. You think 13 levels of compression is a lot? With Save for Web, you get around 100 levels of compression along with some other options. Check out Bonus Chapter 1 for the lowdown on all the JPEG options and settings. The Introduction offers details about the book's companion Web site.

JPEG 2000

JPEG 2000 is a cousin to standard JPEG; it provides a few more bells and whistles, including better compression rates and more quality settings. In addition to the standard lossy compression algorithms, JPEG 2000 also offers lossless compression, shown in Figure 2-11, and can support 16-bit images, alpha and spot channels, and transparency (8 bit-images only). You can save this format using the following image modes: RGB, CMYK, Grayscale, and Lab Color. If you want to utilize this file format, be sure to install this optional plug-in that is on the Photoshop CS2 Install CD.

One of the coolest features of this format is its support of a *Region of Interest (ROI)*. This feature allows you to selectively choose a region of an image that you can then optimize to ensure the best quality. You save an alpha channel (explained in Book VI) to define that vital portion of the image where detail retention is critical. You can then compress the rest of the image more heavily and with lesser quality, resulting in a smaller file size. For more details on JPEG 2000, see Bonus Chapter 1.

Figure 2-11: The JPEG 2000 format is a souped-up version of an old favorite.

Although praising the qualities of JPEG 2000 is all well and good, be warned that you currently need a plug-in to view these files on the Web. In the future, this format is sure to become a standard for the Web and digital cameras.

GIF

GIF is another file format used for Web graphics. While GIFs support transparency, on the down side you must save GIFs in the Indexed Color mode, which comprises 256 colors or less. Although this format is great for making tiny files, it's not so great for continuous-tone images where the number of colors displayed is critical. Therefore, the GIF format is usually reserved for illustrations (spot illustrations, buttons, logos, and so on) and type with large areas of flat colors and sharp details. For the whole story on GIFs, see Bonus Chapter 1.

EPS

EPS is short for *Encapsulated PostScript*. PostScript is a page-description language developed by Adobe and used by many printers. The EPS format can contain both vector and raster graphics. (For details on vector and raster graphics, see Book II, Chapter 1.) EPSs tend to create larger file sizes and do not have a built-in compression scheme like JPEGs or TIFFs. EPS is the recommended file format for creating color separations for high-end, four-color print jobs. This is also the file format to use for images with clipping paths (explained in Book III) and those with a Duotone mode. In addition to duotones, EPS supports Lab Color, CMYK, RGB, Indexed Color, Grayscale, DCS, and Bitmap modes. It does not support alpha channels. Finally, EPS is the format of choice for importing to and from drawing programs such as Illustrator, FreeHand, and CorelDraw.

Here are the options when saving in the EPS format, as shown in Figure 2-12:

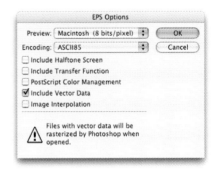

Figure 2-12: When saving an EPS, specify your options.

- ✔ **Preview:** If you import your EPS into another application, this option provides a low-resolution image for you to view. I recommend choosing 8-bit TIFF, which works on both PC and Mac.

- ✔ **Encoding:** This option specifies the way an image is sent to the PostScript printer. Choose Binary if you can; it produces smaller files and keeps all original data. If you're having printing problems, choose ASCII. JPEG compresses the file, but discards data and may cause color-separation problems. Avoid it if possible.

- ✔ **Include Halftone Screen and Include Transfer Function:** Use these options for offset print jobs. Let your friendly service bureau or commercial printing expert specify these options.

- ✔ **Transparent Whites:** If your image is in Bitmap color mode, this option allows white areas to appear transparent.

- ✔ **PostScript Color Management:** This option converts the file's color data to the printer's color space. I do not recommend selecting this option if you are importing your image into a document that is color managed. For more on color management, see Book II, Chapter 3.

- ✔ **Include Vector Data:** When selected, this option preserves any vector graphics, such as type and shapes. However, it is preserved only when you import the file into another program. If you reopen the EPS in Photoshop, however, your vector data is rasterized.

- ✔ **Image Interpolation:** This option anti-aliases (softens the edges) of low-resolution images when printed.

PDF: The universal donor

PDF is the acronym for *Portable Document Format*, which is the native format of Adobe Acrobat. This format, developed by Adobe, can contain editable text, vector, and raster data. PDF files are often used for electronic documentation that will be downloaded from the Web. You've probably noticed that every Adobe Help document is in PDF format, and if you're a Web user, you've probably downloaded more than a few PDFs. Even the government, notoriously slow to catch on to new technology, has embraced PDF. The military uses PDFs for technical documentation. And all your tax forms are available as downloadable PDFs.

You might be thinking, "So what. I'm into images, not documents." Well, hold on a second. PDFs can be extremely useful in the imaging world as well. Anyone with a computer running Windows, Mac OS, or Unix can read a PDF. All you need to view a PDF file is Adobe Acrobat Reader, which is available as a free download from the Adobe Web site. If you save your image as a PDF and e-mail it (or post it on the Web as a downloadable file) to a colleague, manager, client, or friend, that person can see your image — colors, fonts, and all — exactly like you see it. The other nice thing about PDFs is that they have an automatic compression process that makes the files small and manageable for mail transfer or loading on the Web.

When you save a file as a Photoshop PDF, you have all the same save options of the native Photoshop format. PDF supports layers, alpha channels, and annotations, so select these options if you have any. It also supports the same image modes as the native Photoshop format. In addition, you can now also save 16-bit images as PDF. After choosing your initial options, you then get an alert dialog box that informs you that the settings you just chose may be overridden by the settings you choose next.

The Save Adobe PDF dialog box replaces the PDF Options dialog box, and offers even more options than ever before. The options you find in this dialog box are similar to the ones in other Adobe applications, such as Illustrator and InDesign.

At the top of the dialog box are settings for presets, standards, and compatibility as shown in Figure 2-13:

✓ **Adobe PDF Preset:** Choose a preset setting from the pop-up menu. Photoshop then kindly gives you a description of that setting and what versions of Acrobat can open that PDF. The default setting of High Quality Print creates PDF files suitable for good quality printing on desktop printers. Unless you want to specifically create a PDF to view on-screen or e-mail for approval purposes, in which case you choose Smallest File Size, stick with the default as an overall setting.

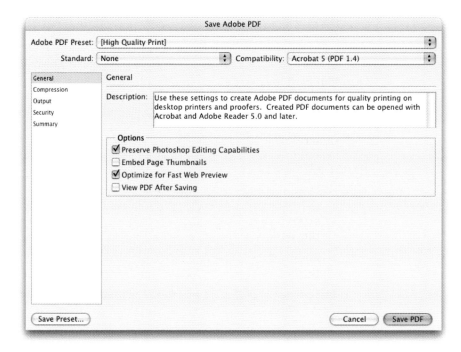

Figure 2-13: The new Save Adobe PDF dialog box offers a smorgasbord of options.

PDF/X is an ISO (*International Organization for Standardization*) standard for graphic content exchange designed for the prepress purpose workflow. This subset of PDF enables what Adobe calls a *blind exchange* of files, meaning that all content and criteria that makes up the PDF is enclosed in one file. The advantage of this format is that it eliminates much of the font and color issues that could potentially lead to printing problems. Ask your service provider or offset print house if it prefers one of the PDF/X formats, instead of the generic PDF, for final file output. For specifics on the criteria of each of the PDF/X formats, check the Acrobat Help file.

✏ **Standard:** Accept the default associated with your chosen preset or choose a flavor of PDF/X from the pop-up menu. Remember you only need to consider this option if you are preparing a PDF for high-resolution printing and handing the file to a service bureau or offset printer. Again, for more details about the criteria of each PDF/X, see Acrobat Help.

✏ **Compatibility:** Specify the version of Acrobat you want your file to be compatible with. If you are not sure if your recipient has the latest version of Acrobat, then play it safe and choose a lower version. Note, however, that Acrobat 4 and 5 do not support layers. And Acrobat 3 doesn't support transparency. When you change either the Standard or Compatibility options, (Modified) is added to your preset name.

In addition to the options along the top described in the preceding list, this massive, multi-tiered dialog box offers the following categories where you can refine your choices if you wish:

✓ **General:** The General category of settings contains the PDF presets, editing options, Acrobat version compatibility choices, and viewing options. Here's the rundown:

- **Preserve Photoshop Editing Capabilities:** This option enables you to reopen and edit the PDF in Photoshop. All Photoshop data is saved within the PDF file. This flexibility comes with a price. Checking this option makes your file size larger.

- **Embed Page Thumbnails:** Creates a thumbnail of the image that is then displayed in the Photoshop Open and Place dialog boxes.

- **Optimize for Fast Web Preview:** Optimizes the file for faster viewing in your browser.

- **View PDF After Saving:** After saving, the PDF opens in Acrobat or Acrobat Reader.

✓ **Compression:** The PDF format, by nature, includes excellent compression, but you can compress and downsample your image even further to reduce (or maybe to simply adjust) the size of the PDF file. You can find details about downsampling in Book II, Chapter 1. Remember that if optimum print quality is a concern, you are better off not downsampling your image at all.

✓ **Output:** The Output area covers how to handle the color data in your file when you export to PDF. I recommend keeping the default settings of your presets, unless you are really sure of what you're doing. An understanding of color management, explained in Book II, Chapter 3, helps you interpret the options in this area.

✓ **Security:** If want to apply some restrictions on who can open your PDF and what they can then do with it, you've come to the right spot. You can assign a password for opening the file in either Acrobat or Photoshop, but if you forget the password, there is no way to extract it from your file. Make sure you write it down somewhere! You can also choose whether you want your user to be able to print or change the document.

✓ **Summary:** This option gives you a total run down of all your specified options and alerts you of any thing it finds not so kosher.

Note that Acrobat 4 users cannot open PDFs with 128-bit RC4 encryption (Acrobat 5, 6, and 7).

You can now also combine multiple images into a single, multipaged PDF document or slide show. This is a great way to e-mail images to coworkers, family, and friends. Choose File⇨Automate⇨PDF Presentation. For more details, see Book IX, Chapter 2.

Photoshop

Of course, I can't forget the native Photoshop format (.psd). This format offers a lot of benefits. First of all, along with TIFF and PDF, Photoshop allows you to save layers in your image. The other formats flatten the layers into a single background. This format works well if you are going to spend a considerable length of time working on your image. The Photoshop format also supports all image modes, is the fastest format for opening and saving, and offers all the various save options.

Like TIFF, the Photoshop format uses a lossless compression process, although it's invisible to you. If you need to open a file in an older version of Photoshop, be sure to save it as a native Photoshop file. Finally, almost all drawing and layout programs now support the importing of Photoshop files.

Photoshop Raw

This format is designed to transfer images among applications and platforms. The Photoshop Raw format can be useful if you want to transfer an image to or from a mainframe computer or other type of device that doesn't support the standard graphic formats. Don't confuse it with the Camera Raw format I describe later in this chapter. The Photoshop Raw format supports CMYK, RGB, and Grayscale images with alpha channels. It also supports multichannel and Lab Color images without alpha channels. The format allows for any pixel or file size, but it doesn't support layers.

You may never have to save a file in the Photoshop Raw format. And you may not want to after you read the options involved in saving in this format. The Photoshop Raw format imports and exports files in an uncompressed, binary format. The format does not specify image size, color mode, or bit depth. It is simply comprised of bytes that represent the color information in the image. Each pixel is represented by a brightness value, with 0 being black and 255 being white. The format then includes the total number of color channels in the image, plus any other channels, such as alpha channels. In order to save a file in the Photoshop Raw format you must specify certain settings in the Photoshop Raw Options dialog box:

✔ **File Type (Mac OS only):** This four-character ID identifies the file type. PRAW is the default ID for the Photoshop Raw format. Leave this default setting.

✔ **File Creator (Mac OS only):** Another four-character ID that tells the operating system which application created the file. Leave the default setting of 8BIM (Photoshop's code), unless you know the special file creator ID for the application you plan on using the file with. Many Mac applications have file creator IDs registered with the Apple Computer Developer Services group.

✔ **Header:** This parameter specifies how many bytes of information appear in the file before the image data starts. The default setting of 0 means there is no header. If, for example, you enter 2, two zeros are entered at the beginning of the file as placeholders. When you open the Photoshop Raw format, you can then replace those placeholders with a header. I recommend leaving the value at 0.

✔ **Save Channels In:** Choose between Interleaved Order and Non-interleaved Order. The default setting of Interleaved Order stores the color data sequentially by pixels. In other words, in an RGB image, the first byte is red for the first pixel, the second byte is green for the second pixel, the third byte is blue for the third pixel. Non-interleaved Order stores the color data by channel. In this case, the first byte is red for the first pixel, the second byte is also red for the second pixel. Once the Red channel is complete, it then goes and saves the Green and then the Blue channel.

Your choice depends on the requirements of the application that opens the file.

Camera Raw

The Camera Raw file format is the format used by many digital cameras to capture and save image data and also the image's metadata. In fact, this format captures everything about an image. Each camera has its own proprietary raw image format. Fortunately, Photoshop can support most camera models, especially higher-end cameras.

Camera Raw files utilize a lossless scheme to capture and save image data, similar to TIFFs. This is advantageous, because no data is lost through compression as it is with the JPEG format. Camera Raw files also have the advantage of being smaller than uncompressed TIFFs. Of all the digital camera file formats, only Camera Raw images contain the actual, unadulterated data captured by the digital camera's sensor without any camera adjustments, filters, and other processing. Many hard-core photographers consider this file format to be the pure digital "negative," so to speak. They prefer to analyze, manipulate, and adjust the image data themselves rather than leaving those decisions to the mercy of the camera. This file format also prevents the loss of any image data that can sometimes occur when a file is converted from its native format to a more commonly used format such as TIFF or PSD. But note that Camera Raw is able to save your files as DNG (Digital Negative), TIFF, PSD, or JPEG formats if you desire.

In the previous version of Photoshop, the Camera Raw plug-in was directly incorporated into Photoshop, enabling you to work efficiently with Camera Raw data. In the new version of Photoshop, Adobe has added further enhancements to Camera Raw through the combination of Camera Raw 3.0 and Adobe Bridge, shown in Figure 2-14. For more on Bridge, see Book I, Chapter 5.

Corbis Digital Stock

Figure 2-14: The Camera Raw format has been given a bevy of new capabilities in this version of Photoshop.

Here is just a brief sampling of some of the new capabilities of Camera Raw:

✔ Select multiple Camera Raw files in the Bridge and edit the settings in one fell swoop.

✔ Make Camera Raw adjustments in white balance, exposure, shadows, contrast, saturation, sharpness, and so on. Your settings are applied to all selected files.

✔ Save your Camera Raw files in the Bridge or import them into Photoshop for further enhancements.

✔ Rate your files inside Camera Raw (similar to how you could rate files in the File Browser).

✔ Crop your Camera Raw images.

✔ Camera Raw files are processed in their own thread, which means you can do double duty — editing some files while saving others simultaneously.

If, by chance, the Camera Raw feature doesn't support your particular camera model, contact Adobe to see if it will be supporting your model in the near future. If your camera doesn't capture images in the Camera Raw format at all, don't worry. You're fine with TIFF or JPEG. However, if your camera is capable of saving images in Camera Raw format, you want to check out its capabilities. Visit www.adobe.com/products/photoshop/cameraraw.html for a downloadable User Guide, a Q&A file, and great tutorials showing all you need to know about working with Camera Raw.

PICT

PICT, for *Macintosh Picture,* is a format developed by Apple as its main format for Mac graphics. It is based on the QuickDraw screen language. And although many Mac programs support PICT, I don't recommend using it for any images that you plan to print. PICTs are notorious for being absurdly slow in the printing department. Today, PICT images are usually used for graphics that are incorporated into slides, screen presentations (such as PowerPoint), multimedia projects, and digital video. PICT supports RGB (with a single alpha channel), Indexed Color, Grayscale, and Bitmap (without alpha channels) image modes.

Make sure that QuickTime is running if you want to save a file as a PICT. In the PICT File Options dialog box, you have options for resolution and compression. Resolution uses the default option; otherwise, you delete colors from your image and can't access the compression settings. The compression settings for PICT are more limited than those for the regular JPEG format and cause even more image degradation than with JPEGs. To minimize the damage, always select the maximum quality setting.

BMP

BMP is a standard Windows file format commonly used for saving images that you want to make part of your computer's resources, such as the wallpaper that you see on your Windows desktop. BMP is also a format used by computer programmers. BMP supports RGB, Indexed Color, Grayscale, and Bitmap image modes.

Here are your options when saving a BMP file:

- **File Format:** Choose between Windows and OS/2.

- **Depth:** Although you can select a bit depth, I recommend leaving the default setting Photoshop has selected for you.

- **Compress (RLE):** The compression scheme used is lossless, which is great, but don't select this option if you are creating wallpaper. Windows won't recognize it.

- **Flip Row Order:** This option enables Windows to recognize the file by reading the first row of pixels first and the last row last. It is for programmers who are coding for Windows applications. Leave it deselected unless you're one of them.

Don't worry about the Advanced Modes option. It is even more eggheady than the other options and strictly programming territory.

Large Document Format (PSB)

Work with humongous files? Then you'll be pleased to know that the Large Document Format supports files of any size. Besides the Photoshop Raw and TIFF file formats, the Large Document Format is the only other format that can save files over 2GB. What's even better is that the coveted features, such as layers, layer effects, and filters, are all supported by this format. If you want to work with large files, just make sure you have the Enable Large Document Format option selected in the File Handling panel of your Preferences.

You knew it was too good to be true, right? Just remember that Large Document Format files can be opened in Photoshop CS or later, only. So make sure any recipients of your files have the latest and greatest version of Photoshop. This limitation isn't confined to older versions of Photoshop either. Be forewarned that many other applications fall to their knees when presented with a file size larger than 2GB.

Chapter 3: Using and Managing Color

Color in Photoshop takes on two personalities. On one hand, choosing colors and applying them is easy, fun, and stress free. On the other hand, managing color — that is, making what you see on-screen match what comes out on paper (or in your browser) — can be difficult and frustrating.

Unfortunately, you have to be well-versed in both picking great colors and managing colors for print. (What's the use of creating the next *Mona Lisa* in Photoshop only to find it looks like a fifth-generation, color, Xerox copy?) In this chapter, I start by showing you how to define and apply color; then I ease you into the world of color management.

If you haven't already read the section on color theory in Book II, Chapter 2, you might want to give it a gander before you dive into this chapter. Knowing a little color theory may make this chapter a little more, er, *palette-able*.

Dealing with Foreground and Background Colors

Photoshop has two categories of color — a *foreground color* and a *background color*. You apply the foreground color when you use the type tools, the painting tools, or the shape tools. The foreground color is also the beginning color of a default gradient applied by the Gradient tool. The background color is the color you apply with the Eraser tool (assuming you don't have layers) and is the ending color of the default gradient. When you increase the size of your canvas, you fill the additional canvas with the background color (also assuming you don't have layers). You find the swatches that represent the two color categories in the lower part of the Tools palette, as shown in Figure 3-1.

The default color for the foreground is black; the background is white. Click the small icon labeled in Figure 3-1 to return the colors to the defaults or simply press the D key. That's easy to remember. To switch the foreground and background colors, click the curved arrow in the Toolbox or press the X key.

Here are a few tips about using tools with foreground and background colors:

- **Blend the foreground and background with the Gradient tool.** When you drag with the Gradient tool across the canvas and the gradient is set to the default, you get a blending of the foreground and background colors.

- **Fill selected areas with the foreground color.** Just click your canvas with the Paint Bucket tool to select areas based on a Tolerance setting and fill those areas with the foreground color.

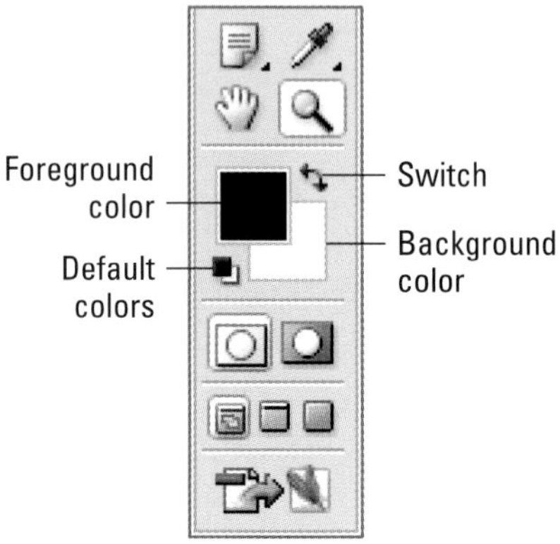

Figure 3-1: Photoshop color swatches are at the bottom of the Tools palette.

- **Apply the background color by erasing.** If you are working on a background rather than a layer, you can use the Eraser tool to apply the background color. Some people prefer to say you are erasing to the background or canvas color.

If you use the Eraser tool on a layer, you erase to transparency. See Book V for the scoop on layers.

- **Add more background to your canvas and fill it with the background color.** When you enlarge your canvas size, Photoshop, by default, automatically fills the added canvas with the background color.

If you enlarge a layer, the extra canvas is transparent. See Book II, Chapter 1 if the word *canvas* seems foreign to you.

Defining Color

Like most everything else in Photoshop, you can choose color in several ways. I explain each of the following color definition options in upcoming sections:

✓ Click a color in the Color Picker.

✓ Move the sliders in the Color palette.

✓ Sample color from your image (or elsewhere) with the Eyedropper tool.

✓ Grab a color from the Swatches palette.

Poking around Color Picker

When you click either the Foreground or Background color swatch in the Tools palette, you're transported magically to the Color Picker. This huge dialog box, shown in Figure 3-2, allows you to select a color from the color spectrum (called a color slider) or to define your color numerically.

Color field   Color slider   Color values

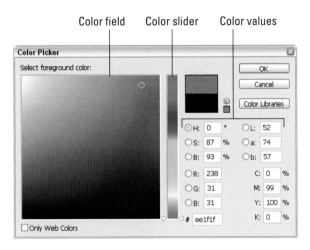

Figure 3-2: Using the Color Picker is one of the many ways to specify color in Photoshop.

Choosing a color visually is fine for Web or multimedia work, but not recommended for print work. Among other reasons, your monitor uses an RGB (red, green, blue) color model, whereas printers use a CMYK (cyan, magenta, yellow, and black) model. For more on this and other color management issues, see "Color Management Essentials," later in this chapter. For the basics of color theory, see Book II, Chapter 2.

To choose a color visually, follow these steps:

1. **Click either the Foreground or Background color swatch in the Toolbox.**

   The Color Picker dialog box appears (refer to Figure 3-2).

2. **Drag the color slider to get in the ballpark for the color you want.**

3. **To fine-tune your choice, click in the large square on the left.**

This square area is called a *color field*. The circular icon targets your selected shade. The dialog box displays your new chosen color as well as the original foreground or background color.

The numeric values also change accordingly to represent the exact shade you've chosen.

Alternatively, if you know the numeric values of the color you want to use, you can plug in the values in the text boxes on the right side of the Color Picker. For example, RGB values are based on brightness levels, from 0 to 255, with 0 being black and 255 being the pure color or white. CMYK values are based on percentages (1–100) of the four process colors — cyan, magenta, yellow, and black. You can enter the hexadecimal formula for Web Safe colors.

4. **When you're satisfied with the color, click OK to exit the Color Picker.**

You can do pretty much the same thing in the Color palette that you can do with the Color Picker. I prefer the Color palette, so I go into more detail about it in the next section.

Mixing with the Color palette

To open the Color palette, shown in Figure 3-3, choose Window➪Color. A couple of swatches in this palette may look vaguely familiar. That's because they represent the foreground and background colors, just like the swatches in the Tools palette. And just like the Tools palette swatches, if you click the swatches in the Color palette, the infamous Color Picker appears. But forget the Color Picker; you don't need to go there. Everything you need is right here in this tiny palette.

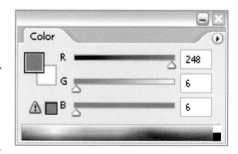

Figure 3-3: The Color palette is a compact, but efficient way to choose colors.

Before you use the Color palette to define your colors, you should know which color model you want to use. Here is a short description of each:

✔ **RGB (Red-Green-Blue)** is the model for anything that's viewed on-screen — from multimedia and slide presentations to content for the Web. Occasionally, you can use it for printing with desktop inkjet printers.

✔ **CMYK (Cyan-Magenta-Yellow-Black)** is the color model used in printing.

✔ **Web Color** is the model used strictly for the Web. If you choose this model, make sure that you also choose Make Ramp Web Safe from the Color palette options menu.

✔ **HSB (Hue-Saturation-Brightness),** which I don't cover in Book II, Chapter 2, is based on percentages of saturation and brightness and an angle (0 to 360 degrees), which corresponds to a location on the color wheel.

✔ **Lab (Lightness, a, b)** color model contains three channels: one for lightness, one (a) that contains colors from green to red, and one (b) that contains colors from blue to red. Lab is more complex to understand and work with than the other models and is the color model of choice for high-end color experts. By the way, Lab is also Photoshop's "native" color mode.

✔ **Grayscale** is the color model for working strictly in black and white and shades of gray. You'll get one slider, K, which represents black. Move the slider to get shades of gray, including complete white and black.

When defining a color according to a color model, I think the Color palette is the way to go. Here are the quick and easy steps to define a color by using the Color palette:

1. **Open the Color palette by choosing Window⇨Color.**

2. **Make sure the color swatch you want to define, Foreground or Background, is selected on the left side of the Color palette. (A double outline appears around the selected swatch.)**

3. **Select your desired color model from the Color palette pop-up menu by clicking the arrow in the upper-right corner.**

   You'll probably be using RGB, CMYK, or Web Color the majority of the time.

   If you want to use the RGB color model but also want to ensure that any color you choose is printable, select CMYK Spectrum from the Color palette options menu. By default, all the colors in the ramp are printable. Just be sure to choose your colors by clicking in the ramp.

4. **In the Color palette, move the sliders for each component of the color model or enter a numeric value.**

   You can also select a color by clicking inside the color ramp at the bottom of the Color palette. Click the small swatches at the far right end of the color ramp to change your color to black or white.

5. **To make sure your desired color works with the color mode you've selected, keep an eye open for an alert icon.**

   If you're working in RGB or CMYK, this alert icon is known as the *gamut alarm* and looks like the triangular warning shown in Figure 3-3. Its appearance is Photoshop's way of saying, "Hey, you! That color you mixed won't print like you think it will because it's out of gamut." Remember *gamut* is the range of colors a device can either display or print.

   Because the RGB color model has a much wider gamut than the CMYK color model, some of the colors can only be viewed on-screen and not reproduced on paper.

If a color is out of gamut, Photoshop offers you a substitution. Inside a little square to the right of the gamut alarm icon, the closest printable color to the one you chose appears.

If you're working in Web Colors, be on the lookout for a small cube icon. Click either the icon or the square to use the closest Web-safe color. The cube indicates that the color you mixed is not a Web-safe color. Clicking the cube tells Photoshop that you want to use its Web-safe alternative instead. A Web-safe color ensures that the color will not dither (mixing available colors to simulate a missing color) when displayed in the browser.

6. **Click either the icon or the square if you want to use the closest printable color rather than your original choice.**

Grabbing color from the Swatches palette

Another way to define a foreground or background color is by clicking a color in the Swatches palette, shown in Figure 3-4. Choose Window➪Swatches to bring up the palette.

You can have any tool active when you use the Swatches palette to define a color because as soon as you move the tool over the Swatches palette, it temporarily changes to an eyedropper icon that samples the color.

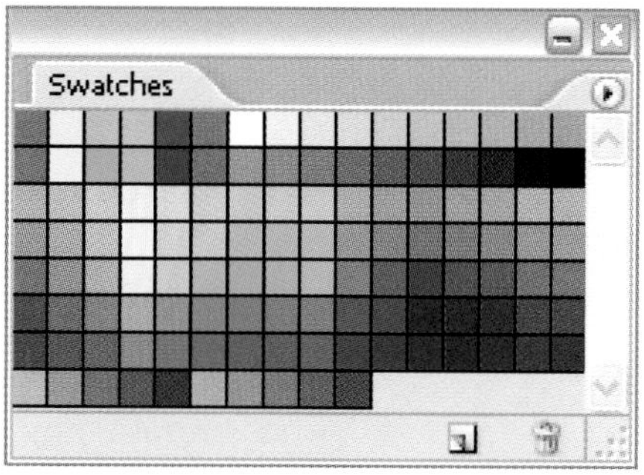

Besides being a way to select your foreground and background colors, the Swatches palette acts like a traditional artist's paint palette in digital form by letting you store as many colors as you want in the palette for later use.

Figure 3-4: The Swatches palette allows you to grab and store colors.

To change the background color, either select the background swatch icon in the Color palette or simply Ctrl+click a swatch (⌘+click on the Mac).

Here are some of the things you can do with the Swatches palette:

- ✓ **Customize the Swatches palette's display.** You can choose how to display the Swatches palette by choosing Small or Large Thumbnail (swatch thumbnails) or Small or Large List (swatch thumbnails along with a name) from the Swatches palette pop-up menu (click the right-pointing triangle in the upper right to open the menu).

- ✓ **Use preset colors.** To load a particular preset swatch library, choose it from the list on the Swatches palette pop-up menu. Click Append to add the library to the existing swatches or OK to replace the existing swatches. You find libraries specific for Web graphics and for implementing spot colors such as those created by Pantone, Toyo, and Focoltone. You can also select Load Swatches from the Swatches palette pop-up menu. In the Load dialog box, navigate to the Color Swatches folder by following this path: Adobe Photoshop⇨Presets⇨Color Swatches; and select your desired library.

You can also work with swatches by using the Preset Manager. For more on the Preset Manager, see Book I, Chapter 5.

✔ **Customize your own Swatches palette.** To add a color to the Swatches palette, do one of the following:

- Click the New Swatch icon at the bottom of the Swatches palette.

- Choose New Swatch from the Swatches palette pop-up menu. Name your swatch and click OK.

- Click an empty spot in the Swatches palette (your cursor changes to a paint bucket icon). Name your swatch and click OK. Or Alt+click (Option+click on the Mac) on an empty spot to add the color and bypass the Name dialog box.

✔ **Delete swatches that you don't want anymore.** To delete a swatch, drag it to the trash can icon at the bottom of the Swatches palette.

✔ **Create your own library of swatches.** To save a set of swatches as a library, choose Save Swatches from the Swatches palette pop-up menu. Navigate to the folder where you want to save the library.

✔ **Save swatches to share with other Adobe Creative Suite applications.** Choose Save Swatches for Exchange from the Swatches palette pop-up menu, and your color palette is saved in a format that you can then load into sister applications such as Illustrator and InDesign.

I recommend saving libraries in a subfolder of the Presets folder. Follow this path: Adobe Photoshop⇨Presets⇨Color Swatches; then create your own folder, name the file, and click Save.

✔ **Restore your default swatch libraries.** To return to the default library of swatches, choose Reset Swatches from the Swatches palette pop-up menu. You can choose to either replace or append to the current library.

Book II
Chapter 3

**Using and
Managing Color**

Lifting and sampling color

Photoshop lets you change foreground or background colors by lifting them from the image with the Eyedropper tool. Using the Eyedropper tool comes in handy when you want to sample an existing color in an image for use in another element. For example, if I want my text to be the same color as the flower in my image, I click a petal with my Eyedropper tool, which then lifts (samples) the color and makes it my new foreground color. I then create my type, which uses that foreground color. Voilà — color coordination at its finest.

Here are some handy tips for using the Eyedropper tool to suck up color from one place and use it elsewhere in your image:

✓ **Choose any color you want from any image that's open.** If you have multiple images open, you can also click inside an image that you're not working on. In fact, if that doesn't knock your socks off, you can lift any color you see on-screen, even from a file in another application, such as Illustrator, or from your desktop. Just drag your Eyedropper from the image window onto the color you want to sample.

✓ **Choose your sampling area.** You have only one option (found on the Options bar) to worry about when using the Eyedropper tool. You have the option of selecting the color of just the single pixel you click (Point Sample). Or Photoshop averages the colors of the pixels in a 3-x-3- or 5-x-5-pixel radius.

✓ **Make colors Web safe with a right-click of your mouse button.** For you Webbies out there, if you right-click (Control+click on the Mac) your image to bring up the context menu, you have one more option — Copy Color as HTML. This option converts the sampled color to a hexadecimal color code that's safe for the Web and copies the code to the Clipboard so that you can paste the code into an HTML file.

✓ **Toggle between the Eyedropper and other tools.** For your productive painting pleasure, when you're using the Brush, Pencil, Color Replacement, Gradient, Paint Bucket, or Shape tool, pressing Alt (Option on the Mac) allows you to temporarily access the Eyedropper tool. Release the key and return to your original tool.

✓ **Toggle between the background and the foreground.** If the foreground color swatch is active, press Alt+click (Option+click on the Mac) with the Eyedropper tool to lift a new background color. If the background color swatch is active, pressing Alt+click (Option+click on the Mac) lifts a new foreground color.

To use the Eyedropper tool, you first need to decide whether you want to change the foreground or background color. Then follow these steps:

1. **Select the foreground (or the background) in the Tools palette or the Color palette.**

2. **Select the Eyedropper tool in the Tools palette (or press the I key).**

   Fortunately, the Eyedropper looks exactly like a real eyedropper.

3. **Click the color in your image that you want to use.**

   That color becomes your new foreground (or background) color.

Using the Color Sampler tool to measure color

 The Eyedropper's cousin, the Color Sampler tool, looks like an eyedropper with a small target next to the icon. It also shares the Eyedropper's flyout menu.

The moniker of "Sampler" is kind of misleading because this tool only *measures* the colors you click. Aside from merely obtaining the numeric value of a color, another use of the Color Sampler tool is to monitor changes to your image after you apply color-correction techniques and filters.

Follow these steps to use the Color Sampler tool:

1. **Select the Color Sampler tool in the Tools palette and then click the color you want to measure.**

   Note the target icon that appears on your image. It is labeled as #1.

   Photoshop automatically opens the Info palette and shows you the numeric values for that color, as shown in Figure 3-5.

2. **Repeat Step 1 up to three more times for a total of four targeted colors.**

   Target icons appear for your second, third, and fourth samples.

3. **With the Color Sampler tool, drag the targets to sample new areas of your image if you want. Delete a target by Alt+clicking (Option+ clicking) it.**

   You can actually measure a fifth color by just moving the Color Sampler cursor around the image. The numeric value displays in the upper portion of the Info palette.

Color target icons

Corbis Digital Stock

Figure 3-5: The Color Sampler tool measures up to five colors in your image.

Color Management Essentials

Grab some Tylenol. You're about to delve into the rather confusing and some-times cantankerous world (or as some users would call it — underworld) of color management. It is, by far, the biggest headache of every graphics pro-fessional's day-to-day experience. And I'm sure quite a few home users also scratch their heads wondering why their digital photo looked so great on-screen and turned into a muddy mess on paper.

Reproducing color is not an exact science. In fact, sometimes you would think it takes an act of voodoo magic to get the output you want. Don't throw up your hands and live with whatever output comes out the other end; if you can't change the color, you can at least change your attitude toward color. Getting a handle on color management requires four things — some knowledge, some patience, a significant amount of time to experiment and test, and, most importantly, acceptance. Acceptance of the unfortunate fact that we don't live in a WYSIWYG world: What you get in one medium is sometimes merely an approximation of what you see in another.

Why? Well, I start with the basic gripe of many users as they look disap-provingly at their printout — "But it didn't look like that on the screen!" As detailed in Book II, Chapter 2, there are two major color models — RGB (Red-Green-Blue) and CMYK (Cyan-Magenta-Yellow-Black). The RGB color model (16.7 million colors), which all monitors use, has a significantly wider range of color (called a *gamut* in computer lingo) than the CMYK color model (approximately 55,000 colors) that is used by printers. The result is that many of the colors you see on-screen fall outside the CMYK gamut and there-fore cannot be reproduced on paper. And in some cases, some CMYK colors fall outside the RGB gamut. Programs such as Photoshop try to do their best by providing colors that are the closest match. But those bright and vibrant colors that are out of gamut are matched with duller, darker versions at best.

And if that difference alone isn't enough to complicate matters, hardware devices that share the same color model can possess different gamuts within the same color model. For example, the RGB color space of a monitor can differ from the RGB color space of a scanner. Not only that, but you can also have different color spaces within the same type of device. A 15-inch generic monitor won't display color equal to a 21-inch Sony Trinitron monitor. Likewise, an Epson printer may not share the same color space as a Hewlett-Packard or Lexmark printer. So when you take into account the differences that can occur between platforms, monitors, printers, browsers, scanners, applica-tions, paper and other substrates, or any of the almost infinite number of possible permutations, it makes you want to return to the days of quill and parchment. Techies often call this mind-numbingly large number of possible inconsistencies *device-dependent* color. In other words, the color is depend-ent upon the hardware device. And device-dependent color varies. That's just the cold, harsh reality, and nothing's changing that.

But Adobe, being the kind and benevolent software megagiant that it is, has developed (first introduced in Version 5.0) a color management system designed to be *device independent.* The five-cent explanation of this system is that you first identify your working color spaces. Photoshop then *tags* your files with that color space by embedding a color profile (also known as an ICC profile) with your files. The program then analyzes any color space in which you either view or output a file and makes adjustments on the fly so that the color is viewed and printed reasonably accurately and consistently, in theory, independent of the device. Photoshop also reads the embedded color profile (or lack thereof) of any file you open and addresses how you wish to deal with that profile if it doesn't match your working color space.

In the upcoming sections, I give you the 25-cent explanation — which I hope is enough to get you started in managing color. If color management is an extremely critical workflow issue to you, I recommend buying a book or two strictly devoted to nothing but managing color. It is well worth the money.

Setting up your work environment

One aspect of color management that people often overlook is setting up a good working environment for digital image editing. You may wave your hand impatiently and say, "Yeah, yeah, I just want to get to the important stuff." This is the important stuff.

Don't worry. Setting up a good work environment won't cost you much. Just do these things:

- ✔ **Keep your computer desktop a neutral gray.** Colors and patterns behind your images influence the way that you perceive those images. Creating a neutral, gray desktop is the closest you can get to mounting your work on gray, black, or white mat board (and not neon green or paisley) the way professional graphic designers and photographers do.

- ✔ **Keep your lighting as consistent as possible.** For example, avoid working on images in full, bright afternoon sun and then again under a single desk lamp late at night. Likewise, view on-screen images and your printed output under the same lighting.

- ✔ **Keep the walls of your work environment as neutral as your monitor desktop.** You don't have to paint your office gray, but try to avoid lots of colorful posters and artwork around and behind your monitor.

- ✔ **Speaking of monitors, if you are using an LCD (flat screen) monitor, be sure you are sitting directly in front of it.** Color shifts quite a bit on LCDs if you are viewing it at even a slight angle. So no slumping in your chair!

- ✔ **Keep a swatch book (or two) handy, such as those from Pantone or Trumatch, to choose your colors.** Don't make a decision based on what you see on-screen. These books give you a true representation of how color looks when printed on paper.

Be prepared for a healthy monetary investment when you buy a swatch book. These little buggers can cost anywhere from $75 to $200. You can purchase swatch books from some larger art supply stores or order them online. You can purchase Pantone books from www.pantone.com. Do a search for others such as Trumatch, Focoltone, and Toyo.

✔ **Take some time to test your *workflow* (production methods) and your computer system.** Scan images using multiple settings, print images using multiple settings, and view your images using different browsers on different monitors and different platforms.

Get to know the strengths and limitations and quirks of every piece of your equipment. Experiment with Photoshop. I know, I know, you have a life. But trust me, it's an investment with great returns.

Calibrating your monitor

Calibrating your monitor and creating an ICC profile of your monitor ensures that your monitor doesn't display any red, green, or blue *colorcasts* (a trace of color) and that it provides as neutral a gray screen as possible. Calibration is incredibly important if you want to standardize your image display — knowing that how you view your image today will be how you view your image tomorrow or next week.

If you really want to do a great calibration job, consider investing in a combination hardware/software calibration package. These products used to be really pricey, but you can get a decent package for around $250. You can choose from several manufacturers, including ColorVision (www.colorvision.com).

If more software isn't within your budget, you can use the simple calibration tool that comes with Photoshop (Windows) or your system software (Mac). Turn on your monitor and let it warm up at least an hour. Then, open the utility to begin calibrating your monitor.

If you're a Windows user, you can use Photoshop's Adobe Gamma utility. Look for it in the Control Panel on the Windows Start menu. If for some reason you don't locate it in the Control Panels, you can find it by going to Program Files\Common Files\Adobe\Calibration and then double-clicking the Gamma file. You can either use the Gamma utility's wizard, shown in Figure 3-6, which walks you through the calibration process by asking you a series of questions, or manually calibrate your monitor by using sliders in the Adobe Gamma control panel.

If you're a Mac OS X user, you can use the Display Calibrator Assistant. Choose Apple⇨System Preferences⇨Displays⇨Color. Click the Color tab and then click the Calibrate button. Answer the questions in the Display Calibrator Assistant. (See Figure 3-7.)

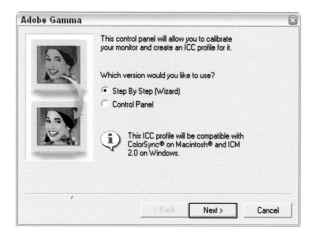

Figure 3-6: The Adobe Gamma utility helps Windows users quickly calibrate their monitors.

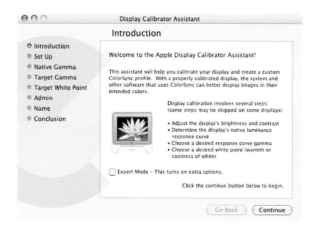

Figure 3-7: Mac users can use the Display Calibrator Assistant to calibrate their monitors.

Both utilities, Adobe Gamma and the Display Calibrator Assistant, help you remove any colorcasts and get as neutral a gray background as you can. They also create a profile of your monitor for Photoshop, Illustrator, and other programs so that those applications know how your monitor displays color.

TIP

When you calibrate your monitor, display an image for which you already know the color values. For example, use an image that you've worked with and for which you have a good print and then use that image each and every time you calibrate. Your goal is to match the digital image on your screen to the printed image. You should calibrate every so often because monitors can drift and degrade. Some experts say weekly; others are more liberal and say monthly is fine.

Not only is letting your monitor warm up a prerequisite before you calibrate, it is also a good idea before you sit down to tackle any image adjustment work.

Establishing Your Settings

After you have calibrated your monitor (see the preceding section) and adequately arranged your work environment, you need to nail down the color settings and make sure that they're the right match for your intended output.

You establish these settings in the Color Settings dialog box, the rather intimidating dialog box shown in Figure 3-8. To open it, choose Edit➪Color Settings. In the Color Settings dialog box, you can choose from predefined settings established for specific types of output, or you can customize your own settings to fit your individual needs. The following sections offer more details about the settings you can choose in the Color Settings dialog box.

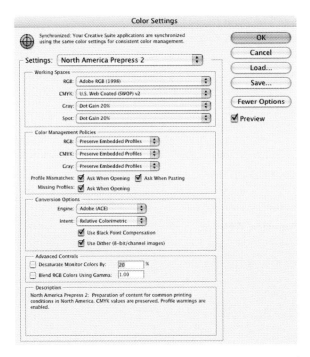

Figure 3-8: The Color Settings dialog box is command central for establishing your color management system.

As you're perusing the dialog box, hover your cursor over any item, and a great description of that item appears at the bottom of the dialog box.

Handling Photoshop's predefined settings

In the Color Settings dialog box, Photoshop allows you to take the easy route and choose from a long list of predefined color settings based on your desired output. After you set up the predefined settings, Photoshop provides all the appropriate working color spaces and color management policies you need to get good color results.

Being the smart program that it is, Photoshop won't steer you down the wrong path with its predefined settings. The only way you can mess up the predefined settings is if your output doesn't match the setting. For example, the Web Graphics Defaults setting isn't appropriate for your high-end, four-color print job, because these two mediums use color in completely different ways (see Book II, Chapter 2 for details if you're curious why this is so).

Be sure and click the More Options button in the Color Settings dialog box to access the full set of predefined color settings. Here is a brief description of each setting in the Settings drop-down list at the top:

- **Custom:** Allows you to manually assign your own settings. When you define a custom configuration, save your settings so that you can reload them later if necessary.

- **Monitor Color:** Emulates the color of most video applications. Reserve it for screen images only. Avoid it for producing print images.

- **North America General Purpose 2:** Provides all-purpose general color settings for screen and print images in North America. Uses the same CMYK, Grayscale, and Spot working spaces as the North America Prepress 2, but uses the Web standard of the sRGB for the RGB working space.

- **North America Prepress 2:** Provides color settings for print images in North America. Preserves the CMYK working space and brings any profile warnings to your attention.

- **North America Web/Internet:** Gives color settings for Web images in North America. Uses sRGB for the RGB working space.

- **Color Management Off:** Deactivates Photoshop's color management system. I recommend this setting for video output only, but not for anything else, unless you're a color guru and know what you're doing.

- **ColorSync Workflow (Mac only):** Uses ColorSync 3.0 Color Management System and ColorSync profiles. It's not recognized by the Windows platform.

- **Emulate Acrobat 4:** Emulates Acrobat 4 and earlier versions.

Book II
Chapter 3

Using and Managing Color

- **Emulate Photoshop 4:** Turns off color management and emulates the Photoshop 4 display. Photoshop 4 didn't employ color management.

- **Europe General Purpose 2:** Provides general color settings for screen and print images in Europe.

- **Europe General Purpose Defaults:** Provides general color settings for using Adobe software in Europe.

- **Europe Prepress 2:** Provides color settings for print images in Europe. Preserves the CMYK working space and brings any profile warnings to your attention.

- **Europe Prepress Defaults:** Provides settings to be used for printing in Europe.

- **Europe Web/Internet:** Gives color settings for Web images in Europe. Uses sRGB for the RGB working space.

- **Japan Color for Newspaper:** Provides settings to be used for newspaper presses in Japan. Preserves the CMYK working space and alerts you to any profile warnings.

- **Japan Color Prepress:** Provides settings to be used for printing in Japan. Uses the Japan Color 2001 Coated CMYK profile, which provides for 350% total ink coverage.

- **Japan General Purpose 2:** Provides general color settings for screen and print images in Japan.

- **Japan General Purpose Defaults:** Provides general color settings for using Adobe software in Japan.

- **Japan Magazine Advertisement Color:** Gives color settings for preparing images using the color standards of the Japanese Magazine Publisher Association.

- **Japan Prepress 2:** Provides color settings for print images in Japan. Preserves the CMYK working space and brings any profile warnings to your attention.

- **Japan Prepress Defaults:** Provides settings to be used for printing in Japan. Uses the Japan Standard v2 CMYK profile, which provides for 300% total ink coverage.

- **Japan Web/Internet:** Gives color settings for Web images in Japan. Uses sRGB for the RGB working space.

- **North America General Purpose Defaults:** Provides general color settings for using Adobe software in North America. Uses the same CMYK, Grayscale, and Spot working spaces as the North American Prepress Default, but uses the same RGB working space as the Web Defaults.

- **Photoshop 5 Default Spaces:** Uses the default color settings found in Photoshop 5, the first version to use color management.

✔ **U.S. Prepress Defaults:** Provides the settings for printing in the United States. This is a good overall selection if you use Photoshop mainly for print work.

✔ **Web Graphics Defaults:** Provides the settings for Web graphics. If you use Photoshop primarily for Web content, this setting is a good option because it reflects the average PC monitor.

Note that the Web and Prepress defaults have big differences and the Prepress and Prepress 2 defaults have subtle differences. But, you can always use a predefined setting as a starting point and adjust whatever individual settings you need to. Note that if you do, your predefined setting name automatically changes to Custom.

Indicating your working spaces

If you choose one of the predefined color settings from the Settings drop-down list, Photoshop plugs in all the necessary remaining options in the dialog box. (If you select the Custom option, Photoshop leaves whatever settings were there previously because it knows you are going to choose your own settings anyway.)

When you chose one of the predefined color settings, the first group of settings Photoshop plugged in were your working spaces. *Working spaces* are the color profiles associated with the RGB, CMYK, Grayscale, and Spot color modes. If you choose the Custom color setting, you need to choose your own working spaces.

Each of the four working spaces is equally important, so I advise you to read all the following sections — and read them in order — if you're serious about color management.

RGB working spaces

Table 3-1 gives you a quick view of your RGB working space options.

Table 3-1	RGB Working Space Options	
Working Space	*What It Does*	*Recommendation*
Monitor RGB	The default setting for the predefined setting of Color Management Off and Emulate Acrobat 4. Sets the working space to your current monitor space (which it gets from the monitor profile you established during calibration). Forces Photoshop to turn off color management.	I don't recommend this setting unless you have a specific need to use it.

continued

Table 3-1 *(continued)*

Working Space	What It Does	Recommendation
ColorSync RGB	Sets the working space to the profile specified in the Apple Color Sync control panel. The default setting for the ColorSync Workflow predefined setting.	For Macintosh only.
Adobe RGB (1998)	The default setting for all the Prepress predefined settings. It is the best color profile to use for viewing 24-bit images and for converting RGB files to CMYK. Provides a large gamut of RGB colors.	I recommend this setting for all print work and as an overall setting if you're unsure what to choose.
Apple RGB	The default setting for the Emulate Photoshop 4 predefined setting. Can also be used for older Mac OS scanners and monitors.	Unless you're the proud owner of a 13-inch Apple monitor, I'd avoid it.
ColorMatch RGB	Use this working space only with Radius Pressview monitors.	I don't think I need to give you a recommendation on this one! You Radius Pressview users know who you are.
sRGB	The default setting for Web Graphics Defaults. This color profile represents a standard, Trinitron PC monitor — the monitor of choice for many of the world's Web surfers. Can also be used with Windows scanners. Avoid it for print work due to its limited RGB color gamut.	If your goal is to ensure your Web graphics look relatively the same in Los Angeles as they do in Bangladesh, sRGB is a good profile to use.

After you set RGB working spaces, don't forget that you also have to configure the other three working spaces, as described in the following sections.

CMYK working spaces

CMYK working spaces are a little more involved than RGB options, listed in the preceding section. They serve a threefold purpose:

- CMYK is the color space to which Photoshop converts your RGB file when you choose Image⇨Mode⇨CMYK.

- CMYK is the color space you view your RGB image in when you choose View⇨Proof Setup⇨Working CMYK (see the upcoming section on soft proofing colors).

- The CMYK color space determines how a CMYK file is displayed on an RGB monitor.

Europe, Japan, and the United States have specific color profiles for printing. Those four CMYK options are divided between those for coated and uncoated paper, and sheet-fed or Web printing presses. The latter two have different percentages of ink coverage and paper stock. There is also a ColorSync Generic CMYK profile for Macs only. I would leave the setting at U.S. Web Coated (SWOP)v2 unless your commercial printer tells you otherwise.

Grayscale working spaces

Grayscale working spaces have to do with two parameters — *viewing* and *dot gain* of grayscale images (Image➪Mode➪Grayscale). You can choose Gray Gamma 1.8 for a Macintosh monitor or Gray Gamma 2.2 for a PC monitor. You can also view an image according to how it will print, based on typical dot gain.

Dot gain is how much ink the paper absorbs, thereby increasing the size of every halftone dot. When continuous-tone images are digitized, they are converted into a series of dots known as a *halftone*.

If you're preparing graphics for the Web, you may want to set your working space to Gray Gamma 2.2 — whether or not you're using a Mac — because most of the Web surfers worldwide are PC users.

For print work, leave the setting at Dot Gain 20% unless your commercial printer tells you otherwise.

Don't forget — you still have to adjust another working space.

Spot working spaces

Spot working spaces have to do with spot colors. Spot colors are premixed inks that are printed in addition to, or in lieu of, the four process colors — cyan, magenta, yellow, and black. Unless your commercial printer tells you otherwise, stick with a setting of Dot Gain 20%.

Working with your newly defined settings

After you define your color profiles in the Color Settings dialog box, understanding how these newly established settings affect how Photoshop works is helpful. Although the settings typically affect how Photoshop works in the background, you nevertheless might want to be aware of the following key changes:

- ✔ **By default, any new images you create use the color profile you selected in the Color Settings dialog box.** Every file you create on your computer now uses the colors within the gamut of your color profiles (either RGB or CMYK, depending on your document color mode). Overall, this default setting should make managing color in Photoshop easier. For example, if you mostly work with multimedia or Web images and have specified your color settings accordingly, you don't need to think about each color displaying accurately, because you've set the defaults to reflect that color mode. But if you want to prep an image for print, those defaults won't work, and you need to change your individual working spaces to those that are print oriented or to a preset, such as North American Prepress.

✔ **The color settings you choose are applied to any untagged images (images that don't have an embedded color).** An example of an untagged image is a Photoshop file created before Version 5 — that is, before Photoshop supported embedded color profiles.

✔ **Your settings also define how Photoshop converts your images from one working space to another.** For example, say you chose North America Prepress 2 from the Settings drop-down list in the Color Settings dialog box. In this case, the default for CMYK is U.S. Web Coated (SWOP) v2, which is a specific CMYK setting for a Web printing press and coated paper, among other things. (You see this setting in the Working Spaces area of the Color Settings dialog box.) When you convert an RGB image to CMYK (Image➪Mode➪CMYK) prior to sending it off to the printer, Photoshop automatically tags the image with the U.S. Web Coated (SWOP) v2 color profile.

✔ **When you save a file, make sure that you select the ICC Profile (Embed Color Profile on the Mac) option in the Save dialog box, if it's available (see Figure 3-9).** (Some file formats don't support color profiles.) This ensures that Photoshop tags the file with the specified color profile and that its origins are always known.

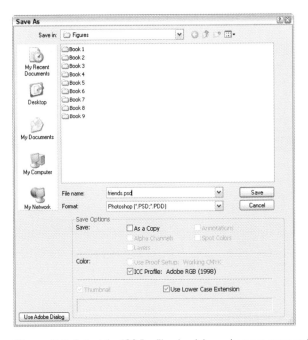

Figure 3-9: Select the ICC Profile check box when you save an image.

Setting Color Management Policies

After you establish working color spaces, the next step is to establish the default color management policy for each color mode. In other words, you need to tell Photoshop how to interpret and manage the color profiles of files it opens.

Photoshop looks at the color profile of that file, compares it to your working spaces, and then employs the default policies you have established. If the file has the same color profile as yours, there isn't an issue. You're good to go.

But sometimes this isn't the case:

- **The file you open has no profile.** These can be older files, files that were created with color management turned off, or files created in other applications that do not employ color management.

- **The file you open has a color profile that doesn't match your working space.** Say that you have a Web designer friend, and his settings are based on the Web Graphics Defaults. He gives you a file, and you open it in Photoshop on your computer. You do mostly print work, so your settings are the U.S. Prepress Defaults. Photoshop then displays an alert that says the file has an embedded color profile that doesn't match your current RGB working space — his working space is sRGB and yours is Adobe RGB (1998). The alert then goes on to describe the default policy that is invoked on the file, as shown in Figure 3-10.

Figure 3-10: Photoshop alerts you when you open a file whose color profile doesn't match yours.

Again, if you have selected a predefined setting, the policies have already been established for you, and those should work fine. I do recommend, however, that you change the policies of one of the predefined settings. If you choose Web Graphics Defaults, the Color Management Policies options are all set to Off. Unless you have a good reason not to, change these to Convert to Working RGB. Remember color management is a good thing.

To set your color management policies, follow these steps:

1. **Open the Color Settings dialog box by choosing Edit⇨Color Settings.**

2. **In the Color Management Polices area, choose from the following three options for each color mode:**

   - **Off:** This option turns color management off for any new files you create, import, or open. However, if the opened or imported file's color profile matches your current working space, the profile is preserved.

- **Preserve Embedded Profiles:** This option displays the files in their original embedded color space. No color conversion occurs. Untagged files remain untagged but use the current working space for display.

- **Convert to Working RGB (or CMYK or Grayscale, depending on your image mode):** This option converts any files with missing or mismatched embedded profiles to your working RGB space. Untagged files remain untagged but use the current working space for display.

3. **Decide whether you want to check the Ask When Opening check box for Profile Mismatches.**

If you do not select the Ask When Opening option for Profile Mismatches, Photoshop displays the Embedded Profile Mismatch alert message (see Figure 3-11), describing what default policy will occur. You can then select the Don't Show Again check box, and from that point forward, Photoshop executes the policy without displaying an alert. For files with missing profiles, Photoshop simply invokes the default policy without an alert.

Figure 3-11: Checking the Ask When Opening option allows you to override your default color management policy setting.

If you select the Ask When Opening option for Profile Mismatches, Photoshop not only displays an Embedded Profile Mismatch alert, but also provides you with options for handling the color of that file, thereby overriding the default policy, as shown in Figure 3-11.

The options in the alert are similar to the default policies of the Color Settings dialog box. Here's a brief explanation of each option in the alert:

- **Use the Embedded Profile (Instead of the Working Space):** Photoshop displays the file in its original embedded color space and does not perform any color conversions.

- **Convert Document's Colors to the Working Space:** Photoshop converts the file from its embedded color space to your working color space.

- **Discard the Embedded Profile (Don't Color Manage):** Photoshop doesn't utilize any color management when opening files but displays the file in your working space.

Be cautious about making any CMYK conversions. If you encounter a Profile Mismatch with a CMYK image, you probably want to preserve the image's embedded profile unless you're absolutely sure it should be converted to another CMYK working space. But, if the image doesn't have a profile, then by all means convert it to your CMYK working space.

4. Decide whether you want to check the Ask When Pasting box for Profile Mismatches.

If you select the Ask When Pasting option for Profile Mismatches, Photoshop prompts you when you drag and drop layers or selections that have the same color mode (see Book II, Chapter 2 for more on modes), but different color profiles. In the Paste Profile Mismatch alert dialog box, you have two options:

- **Convert (Preserve Color Appearance):** Photoshop converts and matches the appearance of the color rather than the RGB numerical values. For example, the RGB color of R 152, G 122, B 250 may be a different shade of purple in one RGB working space versus another. If you preserve the numerical values, the shades won't match. If you preserve the appearance, Photoshop attempts to maintain the two shades.

- **Don't Convert (Preserve Color Number):** Photoshop does not convert the appearance of the color but instead matches the RGB numerical values.

If you don't select the Ask When Pasting check box, Photoshop pastes the color appearance between RGB images and pastes the numerical values between CMYK images.

5. Decide whether you want to select the Ask When Opening check box for Missing Profiles.

If you do select the check box, Photoshop displays a Missing Profile alert and also provides you with the following options, as shown in Figure 3-12:

- **Leave As Is (Don't Color Manage):** This leaves the image untagged and without a color profile, but displays the image in your working space.

Figure 3-12: Photoshop alerts you when opening an image without a color profile and asks you how you want to proceed.

- **Assign Working RGB (or CMYK or Grayscale, depending on your image mode):** *your working space:* Photoshop tags the image with your working space and displays it in that working space. If you change your working space, the image retains the old working space.

- **Assign Profile:** This option allows you to assign any color profile contained within the pop-up menu. You can use this option if you know where the untagged image originated. For example, if you scanned your image and your scanner doesn't embed profiles, you can assign the scanner profile.

Unless you have a specific reason not to, I recommend that you assign your working RGB space to those orphan files.

6. If you're done working in the Color Settings dialog box, click OK to exit.

I recommend selecting the Ask When Opening and Ask When Pasting check boxes. That way you know when a profile mismatch occurs and you have the choice of picking your course of action, which includes overriding the defaults you set in the policy settings. This allows you to evaluate whether you want to preserve or convert on a file-by-file basis. For example, if you're a print designer, and a Web designer gives you a file, you get a profile mismatch alerting you that the file has the sRGB color space and that it doesn't match your working space of Adobe RGB (1998). If you're going to use the image as-is for Web content, you tell Photoshop to preserve the embedded profile and not to make any conversion. But if you want to repurpose the image (for, say, a logo), you have to instruct Photoshop to convert the file to your working RGB space. (Of course, ultimately, you have to also convert the image mode to CMYK for printing purposes.)

To find out the color profile of an image, choose Document Profile from the pop-up menu at the bottom of the image window (which I describe in detail in Book I, Chapter 1). Also if an image has a color profile that differs from your working space, an asterisk appears in the title bar. An untagged image displays a pound sign.

By the way, when you select the More Options, you have a few additional options regarding color conversion engines and rendering intents, which are methods of color translation. I recommend putting your trust in Photoshop and leaving these options at their defaults, unless you're a bona fide color expert.

Getting Consistent Color among Adobe Applications

If you have a complete Adobe workflow like I do, you'll want to use the same Color Settings for all your Adobe applications. Illustrator, InDesign, GoLive, and Acrobat share a similar Color Settings dialog box. They have a few minor differences, but nothing major. If an element doesn't exist in one application's Color Settings dialog box, Adobe merely plugs in the default setting. You can choose the same predefined color setting from the Settings pop-up menu in each application or you can now use a shortcut. Read on.

With the advent of the new Adobe Bridge, getting consistent color across all your Creative Suite 2 applications is merely a button click away. Simply launch Bridge and choose Edit➪Creative Suite Color Settings. In the Suite Color Settings dialog box, shown in Figure 3-13, you can immediately tell whether the color settings across all your CS2 applications are "synchronized." (*Synchronized* is Adobe's cool name for *the same*.) If they aren't and you want the settings to be the same, first click the Show Expanded List of Color Settings Files to ensure you have the full list of possibilities. Then just choose your desired predefined color setting from the list and click the Apply button. Bridge then ensures that each CS2 application uses that color setting. You can also choose a previously saved custom setting. Just make sure you save it to the right place. If you want to see where your saved color settings files reside, just click the Show Saved Color Settings Files button. Note that it isn't mandatory that you synchronize your color settings. You may want to have different settings in InDesign, a page layout program, than you have in GoLive, a Web page creation application. Note that in the Color Settings dialog box in each CS2 application, a message is displayed at the top to let you know whether your suite color settings are synchronized.

Figure 3-13: Getting consistent color among your Adobe Creative Suite 2 applications is now a matter of a few clicks in Adobe Bridge.

You can save your custom Color Settings in Photoshop by clicking the Save button in the Color Settings dialog box. To ensure that all your Adobe applications can access the settings file, save it to a default location:

- For Microsoft Windows, the default location is the `Program Files/ Common Files/Adobe/Color/Settings` folder.

- For Mac OS X users, the default folder is `User/CurrentUser/Library/ ApplicationSupport/Adobe/Color/Settings`.

Note that you can also place saved custom Color Settings files that you have received from other people (for example, reps from your offset print house) in this location as well.

Proofing Colors in the Final Output (Soft Proofing)

Photoshop allows you to preview on-screen how your image will look on a variety of output devices. First, choose View⇨Proof Setup and select your desired setup. The Working options are based on the working spaces you specified in the Color Settings dialog box.

- **Macintosh RGB** and **Windows RGB** display your image as it will appear on a standard Macintosh or Windows monitor. This setting can come in handy when you want to see how your Web graphic will generally look on another platform.

- **Monitor RGB** allows you to view the image by using your current monitor's color space. This setting essentially turns off your RGB working space and lets you see the image without any color management.

- **Custom** allows you to choose a specific device. For example, choosing U.S. Web Coated (SWOP)v2 lets you to see how your RGB images will look when they're converted to CMYK for printing.

After you have chosen your setup, choose View⇨Proof Colors to view the image in your chosen working space. For the most reliable results, use a good quality monitor and set up a good viewing environment as well. Also keep in mind that although soft proofing is a good thing, it is not a substitute for a good quality hard copy proof. Some things, such as the type and quality of paper, certain inks, and so on cannot be accurately simulated on-screen.

Chapter 4: Time Travel — Undoing in Photoshop

In This Chapter

⊮ **Undoing and redoing**

⊮ **Exploring the History palette**

⊮ **Erasing with the Erase to History option**

⊮ **Brushing back in time with the History Brush tool**

*W*hen Tom Wolfe said, "You can't go home again," he wasn't talking about Photoshop. If you change your mind about something you've done and want to return to your starting place (or any point in between), Photoshop is very forgiving. My favorite image editor offers many different ways to reverse actions, undo what you did, reapply effects you've cancelled, and generally change your mind as often as a new apartment owner deciding where to put the couch.

This chapter helps you master Photoshop's powerful time-traveling features, including the Undo command, the History palette, and tools such as the Art History Brush and Eraser.

Undoing What's Done with the Undo Command

Your first stop in your journey through time is the Undo/ Redo command. This command simply reverses the last action you took or reapplies it if you just undid something. For example, if you apply a brush stroke you don't like, use Undo to remove that stroke. Then if you immediately change your mind, you can redo it.

To undo your last action, choose Edit➪Undo or simply press Ctrl+Z (⌘+Z on the Mac).

Use Undo/Redo to toggle an effect on and off to compare the before and after effects quickly, such as the adjusted and unadjusted version shown in Figure 4-1, by pressing the Undo/Redo shortcut keys rapidly. When you decide which way to go, stop. This procedure works best if you choose to press Ctrl+Z (⌘+Z on the Mac) to apply both Undo and Redo.

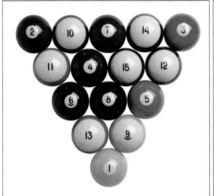

Corbis Digital Stock

Figure 4-1: Flip back and forth between edited and unedited versions of your image by using the Undo/Redo command.

Remember that Undo/Redo works only for a single command. If you do anything else after applying a command and then change your mind, you have to resort to one of the other time-travel techniques described later in this chapter.

If an action can't be undone or redone, Undo/Redo is grayed out and unavailable. However, you can often use the History palette to remove the action. See "Working with the Almighty History Palette," later in this chapter.

If you want to free the memory used by the Undo command, choose Edit⇨Purge⇨Undo. If the item is grayed out, the buffer is already empty. Note that this action cannot be undone, so only do it if Photoshop is acting sluggish.

Reverting to What's Saved

Revert replaces your current file with the last saved file, effectively wiping out everything you've done since the file was last saved. You can revert to the last version of the file by choosing File⇨Revert (or by pressing F12). Although you lose all the changes in your current file when the last saved version replaces it on-screen, the Revert command is stored on the History palette. You find out how to remove a command from the History palette in the next section.

Working with the Almighty History Palette

Undoing and redoing commands are kid's stuff next to the power of the almighty History palette. Think of this tool as a recipe listing all the steps (depending how many you specified in your preferences) you took to cook up your image in its present state. Using the History palette, you can browse through the recipe and return to any step in the list to begin work anew from that point.

Understanding states and snapshots

You can't go too far in your use of the History palette without understanding two important concepts, as well as how the concepts are different:

- **States:** States are just another way of saying steps. At any given point in your image-editing activities, Photoshop saves your individual edits into states.

  By default, Photoshop remembers 20 states for an image. You can increase the number to as many as 1,000 in the General Preferences dialog box. Choose Edit⇨Preferences⇨General (or Photoshop⇨Preferences⇨General in Mac OS X) and enter a new value in the History States box. Keep in mind that boosting this number can eat up your available memory quite quickly. A better choice may be to leave the states set to 20 and instead save snapshots of your image, as I describe in the following sections. Remember that when you reach the limit of 20 steps, the oldest step (at the top of the list) drops off to make room for the latest one at the bottom.

- **Snapshots:** You can save temporary copies of an image, each containing all its various states. For example, say you make six edits to an image before you take a snapshot. The snapshot shows the image, but it also contains a complete history of the six states. Make a few more changes, and take another snapshot: The new snapshot contains the six states you made previously, as well as any new ones. See "Taking Snapshots," later in this chapter, to find out how to use snapshots.

When you have these concepts down, you can get to the business of understanding how the individual tools in the History palette use states and snapshots to help you go back in time (and back to the future again) to undo, redo, and modify each miniscule edit you make to your images.

Introducing History palette options and tools

The History palette has several components you should know about, as shown in Figure 4-2:

- **Snapshot thumbnail:** This is a miniature image of the most recently saved *snapshot* image, which is a copy of your document with all the current states included. (For more on snapshots, see "Taking Snapshots," later in this chapter.)

- **Source state column:** Click in this column next to a particular snapshot or state, and when you begin painting with the History Brush tool or when erasing with the Erase to History option, Photoshop uses the snapshot or state you select as the source.

- **History state:** This is a particular step or edit in your document's list of steps. An icon appears in this column showing what kind of action occurred in that state.

- **Active state marker:** This slider points to the currently active state. You can drag it up or down to change the current state.

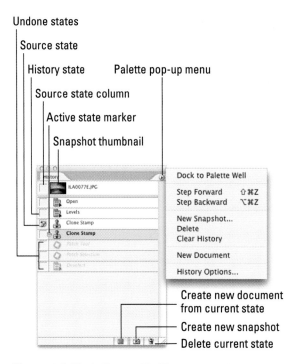

Undone states

Source state

History state   Palette pop-up menu

Source state column

Active state marker

Snapshot thumbnail

Dock to Palette Well

Step Forward ⇧⌘Z
Step Backward ⌥⌘Z

New Snapshot...
Delete
Clear History

New Document

History Options...

Create new document
from current state

Create new snapshot

Delete current state

Figure 4-2: The indispensable History palette lets you undo up to 1,000 steps.

✏ **Create new document from current state:** Click this icon to create a duplicate copy of your image at the currently selected state. Your new document starts out with a clean slate and an empty history list.

✏ **Create new snapshot:** Click this icon to store an image of your document, preserving all the states listed.

✏ **Delete current state:** Click this icon to remove a selected state.

✏ **Undone states:** These are the grayed-out states that are undone when you select an earlier state in the list.

✏ **Open state:** This is the original document when first opened.

✏ **Current history state:** This is the active state you've selected in the history list.

Viewing an Image's Various States

You can move back to any state listed in the History palette, remove a state to cancel a step, or perform other time-travel stunts with the History palette. The following sections outline some basic time-shifting techniques you should know.

Going back to a particular state

To go back in time and resume editing at a particular point, just click the state you want to return to. All subsequent states appear grayed out, or what Adobe calls *undone*. Then begin editing your image as usual. As soon as you perform a new step, all the states that follow your re-entry point vanish. It's like applying the Undo command to a group of steps with one click.

If you intentionally (or accidentally) begin editing while a previous state is high-lighted, and you change your mind, immediately undo your first action — press Ctrl+Z (⌘+Z on the Mac). The subsequent steps that were removed reappear.

Reviewing your image at different states

To review how your image looked at various previous states, just click the state you want to take a look at. (You can also drag the active state marker up and down the list.) The document image immediately changes to reflect that earlier state. You can move back and forth between any point in the history list if you like. As long as you don't make any editing changes during your time-traveling jaunt, your current history list is preserved.

Removing a state

To remove a state and all the steps that follow it, select the state and then press the Delete key or click the trash can icon.

Clearing all states

You can clear all the states from the palette by choosing Clear History from the palette pop-up menu. To delete all the states except the last one in the history list, as well as keep the snapshots you've saved, choose Edit⇨Purge⇨ Histories. You can clear or purge your history list when you don't need the states that are included anymore, to save memory or to return to the original state of your document. Just be sure you're really, seriously, not interested in going back again later to make changes because this command cannot be undone, with one exception. You can undo your clearing or purging only if you choose Edit⇨Undo immediately after you execute the command.

Navigating the history list

You can move up and down the history list even if the list isn't visible on your screen. The Edit⇨Step Forward and Edit⇨Step Backward commands move forward and back in the history list. The best way to access these commands is to use the keyboard shortcuts:

- Press Alt+Ctrl+Z (Option+⌘+Z on the Mac) to move backward in time (upward in the history list).
- Press Shift+Ctrl+Z (Shift+⌘+Z on the Mac) to move forward in time (down the history list).

Looking at the History Options Dialog Box

The History palette has five options that change its behavior. To access these options, choose History Options from the History palette pop-up menu to open the History Options dialog box, shown in Figure 4-3. For a rundown of the various settings, see Table 4-1.

Figure 4-3: Check the Automatically Create First Snapshot setting.

Table 4-1	Setting History Palette Options	
Option	*What It Does*	*Recommended Setting*
Automatically Create First Snapshot	This option, selected by default, tells Photoshop to create a snapshot of the image when you first open it, before you make any changes. You can return to this snapshot at any time by clicking its name in the History palette.	Checked. Consider it free insurance — you can always return to your original image if necessary.
Automatically Create New Snapshot When Saving	This option tells Photoshop to create a new snapshot each time you save the image.	Depends. If you're like me and save every couple of minutes, you probably won't want to select this option; otherwise, you end up with a palette full of unwanted snapshots.
Allow Non-Linear History	This option makes editing or deleting a state without removing all the states that follow it possible. When the Non-Linear History capability is active, you can edit an intermediate state in the history list, leaving the other steps below it unchanged.	Unchecked. Use this option with caution because steps are inter-dependent. A change you've removed may form the basis for another edit later on, so deleting it can cause weird results.
Show New Snapshot Dialog by Defaul	This option ensures that Photoshop asks you for a name for any new snapshot you create.	Checked. Applying names to snap-shots makes reminding yourself of the state of the image when you saved the snapshot easy. Even if this option is unchecked, however, you can still access the dialog box by pressing the Alt (Option on the Mac) key when you click the camera icon.
Make Layer Visibility Changes Undoable	This new option records the toggling on and off of the visibility of your layers.	Unchecked. Showing and hiding layers doesn't affect image pixels.

Taking Snapshots

Snapshots are duplicates of your image at a particular point in time, similar to saving a document under an alternate name. (Photoshop automatically names the snapshots generically Snapshot 1, Snapshot 2, and so on.) However, snapshots are temporary copies, available only during your current work session.

Snapshots are a handy way to alternate between versions of an image when you're making major changes. For example, if you plan to apply several filters and adjustments that will drastically modify your image, you may want to save a snapshot before you use the filters and apply the adjustments and save another one after you've applied them. You can then click either snapshot to switch from one version to the other quickly, as shown in Figure 4-4.

The second you close a file, the snapshots you've taken disappear forever. If you want a more permanent way of saving versions of your file, see the section on using the Layer Comps palette in Book V, Chapter 2.

PhotoDisc

Figure 4-4: Use snapshots to compare before and after images when you apply a filter or adjustment.

To take a snapshot, follow these steps:

1. **Select the state at which you want to take a snapshot.**

   The state can be the most recent one with all your latest editing changes, or an earlier state.

2. **Choose New Snapshot from the palette pop-up menu.**

   The New Snapshot dialog box opens, as shown in Figure 4-5. Photoshop names your first snapshot Snapshot 1.

3. **In the Name box, enter a name for the snapshot, preferably one that helps you remember the contents of that particular snapshot.**

   You can add or change the name of the snapshot later by double-clicking the snapshot name in the history list.

4. **If you like, choose a snapshot sub-type in the From menu (refer to Figure 4-5).**

   Full Document, which is the default, creates a snapshot of all the layers in the image at the currently selected state. It'll probably suit your needs and takes up the least memory. You can also take a snapshot of merged layers or just the current layer. Book V explains working with layers.

Figure 4-5: Save your image's appearance at a certain point with a snapshot.

5. **Click OK to create the snapshot.**

If you no longer need a snapshot, select the snapshot and click the trash can icon, drag the snapshot to the trash can icon, or choose Delete from the palette options menu.

Restoring Part of an Image

Although the concept may seem like quantum physics, you can erase and brush on an image by using previously saved states or snapshots.

What? Okay, let me try this again. You can erase portions of an image to a history state, as well as paint on an image from a history state. This means that traveling through time doesn't have to be an all-or-nothing thing; you can erase or paint portions of a different state onto your currently active state.

For example, suppose you applied a blur filter to a face and decide later you want to make the eyes sharp again. You can use the Eraser tool with the Erase to History option, or the History Brush tool, to paint over the eyes with information from an earlier state before you blurred them, as shown in Figure 4-6.

Using the Eraser with the Erase to History option

You'd want to use the Eraser with the Erase to History option when a portion of an earlier state or snapshot contains information that you want to include in an image that has otherwise been extensively edited. To erase and restore to a portion of an earlier state or snapshot, just follow these steps:

Book II
Chapter 4

Time Travel —
Undoing in
Photoshop

Corbis Digital Stock

Figure 4-6: You can easily restore portions of your edited image back to its original pristine state.

1. **In the History palette, click in the far-left column of the state or snapshot you want to use as the source for the Eraser tool with the Erase to History option.**

   A brush icon appears in the History palette, indicating that Photoshop will use this state as the source for the Eraser tool with the Erase to History option.

2. **Select the Eraser tool.**

3. **Choose the Erase to History option on the Options bar.**

4. **Choose any other Eraser tool options you want to use, such as Brush size and type, Mode, Opacity and Flow percentages, or Airbrush.**

   Under Mode, you have the choice of using Brush, Pencil, or Block tip for your brush.

5. **Select the layer in the Layers palette and the state you want to erase in the History palette.**

6. **Begin to erase.**

   Photoshop removes the image in the layer and replaces it with the image in the state you specified as the source in Step 1.

You can convert the Eraser tool temporarily to use the Erase to History option by pressing the Alt key (Option key on the Mac) when you erase or paint.

Using the History Brush tool

You can also use the History Brush tool to apply an image area from a different state or snapshot to your current state. You'd want to use this tool to restore a portion of an image to an earlier state, while leaving the rest of the heavily modified image alone. The History Brush has an advantage over the Eraser tool, in that you have access to the many different blend modes. Just follow these steps:

1. **In the History palette, click in the far-left column of the state or snapshot you want to use as the source for the History Brush tool (refer to Figure 4-2).**

   A brush icon appears, indicating that Photoshop will use this state as the source for the History Brush tool.

   In my example, I chose my original image just after cropping it.

2. **Select the History Brush tool in the Tools palette.**

   You can also press Y or Shift+Y to select the tool.

3. **On the Options bar, choose any other brush options you want to use, such as Brush size and type, Mode, Opacity and Flow percentages, and Airbrush.**

   For details on the brush options, see Book IV, Chapter 1.

4. **Select the layer in the Layers palette and select the state that you want to paint on in the History palette.**

5. **Begin to paint.**

   Photoshop paints over the image in the layer with the image from the state you specified as the source in Step 1. In Figure 4-7, I painted my original faces using a 10-15% opacity setting over my Water Paper filtered image.

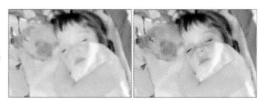

Figure 4-7: Painting with the History brush.

When Photoshop won't let you go back

Sometimes you may see a No symbol when trying to use the Eraser with the Erase to History option, the History Brush tool, or the Fill with History command. You must be sure that your current image is the same file size (same number of pixels) as the state you are trying to go back to. Actions such as cropping, trimming, using the Image Size or Canvas Size commands, or rotating any amount other than 180 degrees can prevent you from going back to a previous state. However, if you happen to have a square image, you can rotate in 90-degree increments and still use the Eraser with the Erase to History option.

Using the Fill to History feature

If you can easily select the area you want to replace with a specific state, you can use the Fill to History feature. Suppose you didn't like the sky in a particular image. You selected the sky area and then added clouds by using the Clouds filter. Now you want to put the original sky back, but don't want to reverse any of the other edits you performed in the meantime. Just follow these steps to replace an area by using the Fill to History feature:

1. **Select a state as the source for the Fill to History function in the History palette.**

    For example, select the state that has the original sky.

2. **Choose the current state and use your favorite selection tools to select the area you want to replace.**

    For example, if you remembered to save your original sky selection when you originally added clouds, you can choose Select⇨Load Selection and retrieve that selection. Book III covers selection tools in detail.

3. **Choose Edit⇨Fill and then select History from the Use pop-up menu.**

4. **Click OK to fill your selection with the image area from the selected state.**

Book II
Chapter 4

Time Travel — Undoing in Photoshop

Using the Art History Brush tool

The Art History Brush tool is an interesting variation on the plain old History Brush tool. Both paint over an image by using information from a previous state. The Art History Brush tool, however, includes several choices on the Options bar that let you apply brush stroke effects to your image as you paint:

- ✔ **Style:** The Style menu contains various-shaped brush stroke styles, such as Tight Short, Loose Medium, Dab, or Loose Curl.

- ✔ **Area:** This option controls the area covered by the paint stroke independently of the brush size you select. The larger the size, the more area covered.

- ✔ **Tolerance:** This option adjusts the amount of the change applied to your image. A low tolerance value lets you apply strokes anywhere in the image, regardless of color values. A high tolerance limits Art History strokes to areas that are very different from the source state or snapshot, making your image not quite as dramatically different from the original.

The result of using these options is an interesting hand-painted effect that you can control quite easily after you have some practice.

The Art History Brush tool often works best when you use a state that is quite different from the state you're painting over. For example, you can apply a heavy filter that makes the image almost unrecognizable and then use that filtered image to paint with the Art History Brush tool. You can even completely fill an image with color or texture and work with that.

To paint with the Art History Brush tool, follow these steps:

1. **Apply any effects you want to use to a chosen state.**

   I started by applying a Cutout filter to my sunflower.

2. **Click in the far-left column in the History palette to select the state you want to use as the source for the Art History Brush tool, as shown in Figure 4-8.**

3. **Select the Art History Brush tool from the Tools palette.**

   You can also press Y or Shift+Y to select it.

4. **Select from the choices on the Options bar.**

   Several of the options, such as Brush, Mode, or Opacity, are similar to the options available with the ordinary Brush tool. The new options are Style, Area, and Tolerance.

5. **Paint with the brush to get the effect you want.**

Don't forget that you can use the History palette to reverse Art History strokes that you change your mind about!

Figure 4-8: The Art History Brush lets you paint back to history with artistic flair.

Chapter 5: Creating Actions for Productivity and Fun

In This Chapter

✓ Working with actions

✓ Playing presets

✓ Recording a new action

✓ Editing and organizing actions

✓ Processing batches of files

✓ Creating droplet applets

*P*ractice makes perfect, but when repeating the same steps in Photoshop over and over, the result is often tedium and impatience. You wouldn't want to have to reinvent the wheel each time you wanted to go for a spin around the block, so why repeat the labor needed to carry out specific tasks if you don't have to?

Photoshop lets you record steps by using a fast and fun feature called *Actions*. Photoshop actions are similar to the macro recording features found in your word processing or spreadsheet program, but they're usually easier to create and have capabilities custom-tailored for image editing and customization. In addition, Photoshop has presets for popular actions such as creating a wood frame, simulating water reflections, or providing a molten lead look. This chapter shows you how to take advantage of Photoshop's presets and its macro recording and editing capabilities.

Using the Actions Palette

Not surprisingly, a palette is dedicated to the automation of various chores. To view the Actions palette, choose Window➪Actions (or press F9), or click the Actions tab in its palette group or in the Palette Well. You can view the Actions palette in two different modes, Button and List, each of which is useful in its own way. You can access the mode you're not currently using via the Actions palette pop-up menu.

Button mode, shown in Figure 5-1, is a convenient, compact mode that hides all the inner workings of the actions, presenting only a button face that you can click to trigger a particular macro. Button mode is fast and easy; just click and go.

Figure 5-1: Button mode allows for a compact view of the Actions palette.

List mode, shown in Figure 5-2, is the default display in which each action is shown as a folder-like heading. You can open the heading to reveal all the steps within the action or collapse the heading to hide them. You need to be in List mode when you record an action and when you edit individual steps. List mode also lets you perform only some of the steps in an action.

When you're working in List mode, the Actions palette has these three columns:

- ✓ **The leftmost column contains check boxes that you can select or deselect to include or exclude actions, or steps within an action.**

- ✓ **The second column toggles on or off the display of dialog boxes in actions.** Some actions include options you can select while running the macro. For example, the Vignette (Selection) action, which creates a faded frame around a selection, includes a dialog box that lets you specify the width of the fading. This dialog box is shown

Figure 5-2: The Actions palette lets you create and store actions — a set of recorded steps that automate repetitive tasks.

only when you select the dialog box column; if you deselect the column, the action uses a default value. Adobe refers to this as Modal control.

- ✓ **The third and widest column shows the name of the set of actions (folder icon) or the individual action.** Click the right-pointing arrow to the left of the action's name to reveal the individual steps of the action. If you have assigned any keyboard shortcuts to your action, they also appear in this column.

At the bottom of the Actions palette in List mode, you find six icons, not all of which are available at all times. The following list describes the icons from left to right:

- ↙ **Stop Playing/Recording:** This icon is active when you're recording an action. Click it to stop recording (or to stop playing back an action).

- ↙ **Begin Recording:** Click this icon to begin recording an action (as described in more detail later in this chapter).

- ↙ **Play Selection:** Click this icon to begin playing a selected action. Playback begins at the step selected; you can choose the action's name to start the action at the beginning, or expand the action and select any step to begin playback at that point.

- ↙ **Create New Set:** Click this icon to create a new action set (as I describe later in this chapter).

- ↙ **Create New Action:** Click this icon to begin a new action.

- ↙ **Delete:** Click this icon to remove a selection action or step.

You can also find all these commands on the Actions palette pop-up menu.

Introducing Preset Actions

Preset actions are actions that have been created by the kind folks at Adobe and come with Photoshop. You can also get other preset actions from Adobe's Web site as well as third party vendors. You may need to load an action into the palette so that it's ready to use. After an action is loaded, you can apply all the steps in one fell swoop by playing the action. The following sections explain how to work with preset actions in more detail.

Loading preset actions

Photoshop's preset actions are located in a series of files in the Actions folder. The default actions are loaded by, um, default, when you first open Photoshop. However, other preset actions are available for you to open and use. They include actions, such as Frames (for putting frames around your images), Text Effects (for enhancing your text), and Image Effects, where you can give your image the appearance of being aged or neon, for example.

Follow these steps to load preset actions:

1. **In the Actions palette, click the palette pop-up menu arrow and choose Load Actions.**

   Photoshop opens the Photoshop Actions folder in the Load dialog box. This folder contains several sets of actions presets.

2. **Select one of the actions sets.**

3. Click the Load button.

Photoshop's additional actions presets also appear at the bottom of the Actions palette pop-up menu. You can add any of them to your current list of actions by choosing the set's name.

The new actions presets appear in the Actions palette, appended after the default actions that are already there. You can show or hide the actions in the Default Actions or Image Effects sets by clicking the expand/collapse arrow in the third column.

You can also make actions available or unavailable for an entire set by clicking the first column in the Actions palette next to the action set's folder icon.

Here are some other tidbits about loading and working with preset actions:

✔ Any action sets that you create yourself (as I describe later in this chapter) appear in the pop-up menu if you save them in the Photoshop Actions folder. If you saved them somewhere other than the Photoshop Actions folder, you can navigate to that folder by using the usual file navigation commands.

✔ To remove the existing actions and replace them with the set you are loading, choose Replace Actions from the palette pop-up menu.

✔ To reset the Actions palette to the Default Actions set (removing all other sets you may have loaded), choose Reset Actions from the palette pop-up menu.

✔ To clear all actions from the Actions palette, choose Clear Actions from the palette pop-up menu. (You might want to do this when creating your own set of actions from scratch.)

✔ To rename an action set, select it and choose Set Options from the palette pop-up menu.

Try a Google search for Photoshop Actions and you're presented with a barrage of user created actions, ranging from functional to funky. You can then save these actions to your computer so that you can then load them into Photoshop. Remember to check any file you download from the Internet for viruses and other malware, using an antivirus or similar utility.

Playing a preset action

You perform an action on an image by playing it. To play a preset action, just open the file you want to apply the action to and then do one of the following:

✔ In Button mode, click the action you want to play. There are no other options.

✔ In List mode, select the action you want to play and then click the Play Selection button at the bottom of the Actions palette. You can also choose Play from the palette pop-up menu.

If you want to play back just one step of an action, say, for testing purposes, select the step you want to play in List mode and then Ctrl+click (⌘+click on the Mac) the Play button in the Actions palette. You can also simply double-click the step in the list while holding down the Ctrl key (the ⌘ key on the Mac).

If all goes well, you see your original image transformed with a mere click of the mouse, as shown in Figure 5-3.

Original	Oil pastel action applied

Corbis Digital Stock

Figure 5-3: Photoshop comes with a wide array of interesting preset actions that can quickly transform your image.

Creating a New Action

When you create an action, you automate a series of steps. The hardest part about creating a new action is figuring out what functions you want to automate. Think about steps that you carry out over and over, and whether you could be more productive if you had an action that could do them for you. For example, you might want to create your own action to reduce images to a constant 500 pixels wide for display in an eBay auction. However, performing color correction tasks for your eBay images is more difficult to automate, because your images may vary in their original color and contrast.

After you decide what you want to automate, examine the actual steps so that you can record them. After that, creating a new action involves little more than starting Photoshop's macro recorder and carrying out the steps you want to include in the action.

 I highly recommend while you're working out the kinks in your action to do so on a copy of your original file. That way if things go awry, your original file is safe from harm.

Here are the steps to follow to create a new action:

1. **Open an image.**

2. **Display the Actions palette in List mode by unchecking Button Mode from the palette pop-up menu.**

3. **Click the Create New Action button at the bottom of the Actions palette.**

   You can also choose New Action from the palette pop-up menu.

   The New Action dialog box opens, as shown in Figure 5-4.

   Figure 5-4: Name your new action and specify your other options.

4. **In the Name text box, enter a name for the action.**

5. **From the Set pop-up menu, choose the actions set. If you have more than one actions set open, choose the actions set in which you want to place the new action.**

   An *action set* is merely a folder that contains individual actions for organizational purposes. Feel free to use an existing set or create your own.

6. **(Optional) To associate the action with a function key shortcut, choose the name of the function key from the Function Key drop-down list.**

   This step associates the action with a button on the keyboard. Function keys like F2, F3, and so on are very useful for actions you perform all the time.

   Select the Shift or Ctrl (⌘ on the Mac) check box to use either of these keys along with the function key.

   Any keyboard shortcut you assign to an action overrides the default function already assigned to the keyboard shortcut. You can revert to the original shortcut by choosing Edit⇨Keyboard Shortcuts. See Book I, Chapter 5 for details.

7. **From the Color drop-down list, select a color to mark your action in Button mode.**

   This option enables you to group related actions by color.

8. **Click the Record button in the New Action dialog box to begin recording.**

9. **Carry out all the steps you want to record.**

10. **Click the Stop Playing/Recording button at the bottom of the Actions palette to finish the action.**

    Your new action appears in the Actions palette in both List and Button modes.

Editing and Managing Actions

The first thing you need to do after you create a new action is to try it out by opening an image and clicking the Play button in the Actions palette. If the action doesn't perform as you expect, you may need to edit your action to fine-tune it. You also may need to edit an action to add features or change the action's behavior in some way. For example, you might decide that you want your resizing action to change the size to 45 percent rather than 50 percent. Photoshop enables you to edit your actions fairly easily. Also keep in mind that certain actions won't run on certain files. For example, if your action involves adjusting the opacity of a layer and you run it on an image without layers, it won't work. You would have to include a step to include the creation of a layer first.

You have a lot of editing options; you can change the action's name, keyboard shortcut, or color-coding of an action. That's easy enough: Just double-click the action name in the Actions palette to enter a new name, or select the action, choose Action Options from the palette pop-up menu, and change the information as desired. You can also hold down the Alt key (Option key on the Mac) and click the action's name in the Actions palette to open the Actions Options dialog box.

Re-recording an action

As easy as editing an action is, often your best option is to simply re-record the action from scratch. If the action is not long or complex, you can often re-record it in less time then editing the existing action takes. You can re-record an action two ways:

- **Create a new action from scratch:** Perform all the steps again to replace the old action with a new one, saving the action with the same (or a different) filename.

- **Use the clever Record Again feature:** Photoshop runs through the steps you already recorded, opening the appropriate dialog boxes used the first time around so you can enter new values.

This Record Again method is very handy if you just want to change some of the parameters but keep the steps the same and in the same order. You don't even have to remember what steps you used. Photoshop runs through them for you as you record the steps, or macro, again.

To re-record a macro with the Record Again option, select the name of the macro you want to re-record and choose Record Again from the palette pop-up menu. As the different dialog boxes appear, enter the values you want and click OK until the macro is finished.

Editing an action

You can also edit individual steps of an action. Here are some of the editing changes you can make:

✔ **Move a step:** To move a step from one place in the action to another, click the action you want to relocate and drag it to its new place in the action list.

✔ **Add a step in the middle:** To add a new step in the middle of an existing action, select the step that you want to precede the new step. Click the Record button and perform the steps you want to add. Click the Stop Recording button when you finish.

✔ **Add a step to the end:** To add a new step at the end of an existing action, select the name of the action, click the Record button, and perform the steps you want to add. Click the Stop Recording button when you finish.

✔ **Remove a step:** Click the step you want to delete and either drag the step to the trash can icon, or click the trash can icon and click OK in the dialog box that pops up. (Press the Alt key [Option key on the Mac] to bypass the dialog box and delete the step without confirmation.) You can also select a step and choose Delete from the palette pop-up menu.

✔ **Duplicate a step:** Press the Alt key (Option key on the Mac) and drag the step you want to duplicate to another location in the Actions palette. Photoshop then creates a copy of the step, leaving the original step where it was, as shown in Figure 5-5.

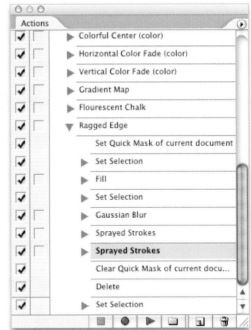

Figure 5-5: Duplicate a step in an action.

You can remove or duplicate an entire action by using the procedures described in the preceding list for removing a step and duplicating a step.

Slowing down action playback

When you play back an action to test it, the action may run too quickly for you to see exactly what is going on. To slow things down, choose Playback Options from the palette pop-up menu and choose a playback speed in the Playback Options dialog box.

Select Accelerated to zip through an action at normal speed; Step by Step to command Photoshop to stop between actions so you can examine what has happened, or Pause For to create a short pause before moving on. Make sure and specify how many seconds you want to pause for. If you want to get really fancy, you can select the Pause for Audio Annotation check box and use your microphone to describe what each step does.

Creating sets and saving actions

If you create your own sets of actions, you may want to include them in custom sets that you can load or remove as needed. Just follow these steps:

1. **Display the Actions palette in List mode.**

2. **Click the Create New Set button in the Actions palette or choose New Set from the palette pop-up menu.**

   The New Set dialog box appears.

3. **Enter a name for your actions set.**

4. **Drag any existing actions you want to include from their locations in the Actions palette to a new location within your new set folder.**

5. **Create any new actions you want to include within the new set.**

6. **Select the name of the set and choose Save Actions from the palette pop-up menu.**

7. **Save the set in the Photoshop Actions folder or another folder of your choice.**

Batch Processing Actions

Photoshop's Batch feature lets you apply an action to a group of files. Suppose you want to make changes to a series of files. You could open each file in Photoshop, play the desired macro, and then save the file. But that might take a few minutes, or much longer if you have a lot of files to process. If you want to keep your original file, too, you have to remember to save each file in a new folder. Batch processing can automate tedious chores like this for you.

To check out this useful tool, copy some files (at least five or six) to a new folder and follow these steps:

1. **Make sure that all the files are in a single folder of their own.**

   Photoshop by default works on all the files in a folder. You have to use the Bridge if you want to choose only some of them using the Batch feature. You can find out more about the Bridge in Book I, Chapter 5.

2. **Choose File⇨Automate⇨ Batch.**

   The Batch dialog box opens, as shown in Figure 5-6.

3. **From the Set pop-up menu, choose the set that contains the action you want to apply.**

   If you have only one set of actions loaded, it appears by default.

4. **Choose the action you want to apply from the Action pop-up menu.**

5. **From the Source pop-up menu, choose Folder.**

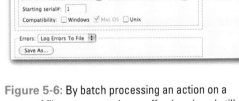
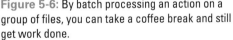

   You can also select Opened Files to process files you already opened in

Figure 5-6: By batch processing an action on a group of files, you can take a coffee break and still get work done.

Photoshop; Import to process a series of files captured with your scanner or transferred from your digital camera; or Bridge to process files you selected in the Bridge. File Browser is a good method for processing files that do not appear in the same folder.

6. **Click the Choose button, navigate to the folder you want to use, and click OK (in Windows) or Choose (in Mac OS).**

7. **Select other options in the Source area, as desired. Here's a description of your choices:**

   • **Override Action "Open" Commands:** Normally, Photoshop automatically opens each of the files in the selected folder and processes them, so your action doesn't need to contain an Open command. However, if the macro *does* contain an Open command, you want to select this option. Photoshop then overrides Open commands in the actions that use specific files, rather than the batched files.

TIP

- **Include All Subfolders:** Select this option to process files in subfolders within the folder specified.

- **Suppress File Open Options Dialogs:** Select this option to have Photoshop disregard any options that could be possibly selected upon opening a file.

- **Suppress Color Profile Warnings:** When Photoshop opens a file that contains its own color profile, it asks whether you want to use that profile or Photoshop's default profile. Selecting this check box suppresses that choice; Photoshop always uses its own default color profile. I explain color profiles in Book II, Chapter 2.

8. **In the Destination area, tell Photoshop what to do with each file after it is processed with the macro. Choose one of the following options from the drop-down list:**

   - **None:** Leaves the file open on your Photoshop desktop without saving it (unless the action itself contains a Save command).

   - **Save and Close:** Closes the files in the same folder where Photoshop found them. Your original file is overwritten, so use this option only when you don't want to save the original or have another copy.

   - **Folder:** Saves the document in a folder.

9. **If you chose Folder in Step 8, click the Choose button and navigate to a destination folder for your files.**

10. **Select the Override Action "Save As" Commands check box to ignore any Save As parameters in the action and use the filenames of the files as specified in the File Naming section described in Step 11.**

11. **In the File Naming section, specify how you want Photoshop to create the filenames for the new, processed files by choosing from the pop-up menus.**

    You can choose options from six pop-up menus, depending on how long and complicated you want the filenames to be. Here are a few suggestions:

    - You usually want to choose Document Name from the first pop-up menu. If you do that, Photoshop retains the document name of the original file. If your documents are named `Sunset.tif`, `Sunrise.tif`, and `Winter.tif`, for example, the processed versions are given exactly the same names.

      You can apply other choices in the pop-up menus, such as consecutive serial numbers or mm/dd/yy choices, if you want. The serial numbers choices create consecutive numbers, either 1-, 2-, 3-, or 4-digit numbers, as well as serial letters, such as a, b, c or A, B, C for each file created.

    - You'll usually stick with the file's extension in the second pop-up menu. Choose extension to apply a lowercase version of the file's original extension, or EXTENSION to apply an uppercase version.

- Use the four additional pop-up menus if you want to create longer and more complicated filenames.

  For example, if you choose Document Name in the first pop-up menu, 4 Digit Serial Number in the second pop-up menu, ddmmyy in the third pop-up menu, and extension in the fourth pop-up menu (refer to Figure 5-6), the `Sunset.tif`, `Sunrise.tif`, and `Winter.tif` files are renamed `Sunset0001030305.tif`, `Sunrise0002030305.tif`, and `Winter0003030305.tif` if they're saved on March 3, 2005.

When processing large numbers of files, these naming tools can help you keep track of when and how the files were created.

12. **Select the Windows, Mac OS, or Unix check box to specify what operating system you want the saved filenames to be most compatible with.**

13. **From the Errors pop-up menu, choose whether you want Photoshop to stop processing a batch when it encounters an error or whether you want it to simply continue and list the errors in a file. If you choose the latter option, click the Save As button to specify a log file and location for the log.**

If you want to apply several different actions to a single set of files, or to apply the same action to multiple folders of files, just create an action that includes multiple batch-processing directives. To process multiple folders, you can also deposit shortcuts (in Windows) or aliases (in Mac OS) to each of the additional folders in the main source folder, and then select the Include All Subfolders check box in the Source area.

14. **When you're done selecting options in the dialog box, click OK to start the batch processing.**

Creating Droplets

Droplets are drag-and-drop mini applications, or applets, in macro form that can exist outside of Photoshop on your desktop, on your taskbar, or within a folder. They're always available so that you can apply them to any image files you want. Think of them as batches waiting to happen.

All you need to do is drag the file or files you want to process onto the droplet. Photoshop doesn't even have to be open at the time. When you drop the file or files, the droplet opens Photoshop and carries out the steps in the action embedded in the droplet's instructions. You must use an existing action as the core of the droplet.

To create a droplet, follow these steps:

1. **Choose File⇨Automate⇨ Create Droplet.**

   The Create Droplet dialog box opens, as shown in Figure 5-7.

2. **In the Save Droplet In area, click the Choose button and enter a name and location on your hard drive for the droplet application.**

   The location isn't of over-riding importance because after you create the droplet, you can drag it to your desktop, a toolbar, or wherever you like.

   The rest of the Create Droplet dialog box is the same as the Batch

Figure 5-7: Drag and drop files onto droplets, mini applications that reside outside Photoshop.

Processing dialog box (described in the steps in the preceding section), except that you don't have to specify a source. Droplets use the files dropped on them as their source files.

3. **In the Play area, choose the actions set, action, and options.**

4. **Select a destination from the Destination pop-up menu.**

5. **Specify any filenaming options you want.**

6. **Specify how Photoshop should process errors.**

7. **When you finish, click OK to create the droplet.**

   To use the droplet, just select the file, files, or folders you want to process and drag them to the droplet applet.

Book III
Selections

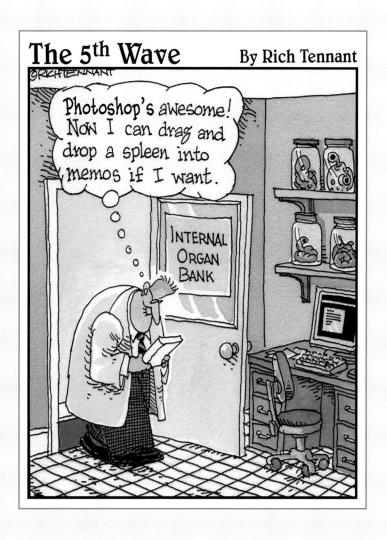

*I*f there's one technique that separates the really good Photoshop users from the wannabes, it's the ability to make a top-notch selection. Pick up any tabloid and you'll agree with me that a lot of those wannabes seem to be gainfully employed! This book, along with Book VI, gives you a complete arsenal of selection commands, methods, and techniques. In this book, I give you information on how to create and modify selections and paths by using various Photoshop tools, such as the Marquee, Lasso, Magic Wand, and Pen tools. After you go through this book, you can put those wannabes to shame.

Chapter 1: Making Selections

*N*o matter how much you learn about Photoshop, if you can't make a good selection, your work will look like it belongs with the creatively, but poorly, composed images in those weekly tabloid rags. You know what I'm talking about — those pictures that go alongside headlines like "Bat Boy Wins Bake-Off" and "Woman with 16 Fingers Wins Typing Contest."

Making accurate selections is the key to creating and editing images effectively so that the end result looks flawless. Fortunately, Photoshop offers a bevy of tools and techniques for creating selections, from the simple to the complex. Photoshop offers three basic methods of creating a selection: using a selection tool or method, using the Pen tool, or creating a mask.

In this chapter, I give you the foundation you need to use the selection and pen tools. In fact, the rest of Book III covers these tools in detail. I cover the more complex method of masking in Book VI.

Defining Selections

The tools I discuss in this chapter require you to take a little piece of a larger image so that you can dig in and make some serious edits. Defining a selection means that you specify which part of the image you want to work with. Everything within a selection is fair game for manipulation and is considered *selected*. Everything outside the selection is protected, or *unselected*. Simple enough, right? Well, you can also have partially selected pixels. Confused yet? A *partially selected* pixel has usually been anti-aliased, feathered, or masked. (I cover anti-aliasing and feathering later in this chapter. You can find out about masking in Book VI.)

When you use a selection tool to define a selection, a moving dotted outline called a *selection marquee* appears.

Marqueeing When You Can

Photoshop geeks call the selection marquee by a variety of names. Sometimes it's referred to as a marquee, other times as a selection, and you might even hear people call it a selection outline, an outline, selection edges, or just plain old edges. A favorite name for these dotted lines is marching ants. Throughout the book, I usually call them *selection marquees*. Boring? Maybe. Accurate? Yup. Whatever you want to call the selection marquee, how you create one depends on the particular marquee tool or command you use.

The marquee tools are the easiest selection tools to use — so I suggest that you use them when you can.

In the Photoshop repertoire of tools, you find four types of marquee tools: Rectangular Marquee, Elliptical Marquee, Single Row Marquee, and Single Column Marquee.

Using the Rectangular Marquee tool

The Rectangular Marquee tool creates rectangular or square selections. It's a good tool to use when you want to zero in on an image, plucking it out of a larger background to provide a better focal point.

Here's how to make a selection with the Rectangular Marquee tool:

1. **Select the Rectangular Marquee tool from the Tools palette (also known as the Toolbox).**

   You can also use the keyboard shortcut — press the M key.

2. **Drag from one corner of the area you want to select to the opposite corner.**

   As you drag, the selection marquee appears. The marquee follows the movement of your mouse cursor (a crosshair, or plus sign, icon). For example, in Figure 1-1, I dragged from the lower-left corner to the upper-right corner.

3. **Release your mouse button.**

   You now have a full-fledged rectangular selection.

If you want to create a perfect square, press the Shift key after you begin dragging. When you have your desired selection, release the mouse button and then the Shift key.

Marquee cursor

Figure 1-1: The Rectangular Marquee selects part of your image.

If you want to drag your selection from the center outward instead of corner to corner, press the Alt key (Option on the Mac) after you begin dragging. When you have your desired selection, release your mouse button and then release the Alt (Option on the Mac) key.

Using the Elliptical Marquee tool

The Elliptical Marquee tool is designed for elliptical or circular selections. You can easily select objects such as clocks, balls, and full moons with this tool.

When you select with the Elliptical Marquee tool, you don't drag from corner to corner; you drag from a given point on the ellipse, which makes the process a little tougher. Here are the steps:

1. **Select the Elliptical Marquee tool from the Marquee flyout menu in the Toolbox.**

   You can also use the keyboard shortcut. If the Elliptical Marquee tool is visible, press the M key. If the Rectangular Marquee is visible, you must press Shift+M.

2. **Position the crosshair near the area you want to select and then drag around your desired element.**

   As you drag, the selection marquee appears.

   You may find it easier to create an elliptical selection by pressing the Alt (Option on the Mac) key and dragging from the center outward. First click the mouse button, and then before you move the mouse, press Alt (Option on the Mac) and drag. Release your mouse and then the key when you have your desired selection. If you want to draw from the center out and you want a perfect circle, press the Shift key as well. When you have your desired selection, release your mouse button and then the Shift+Alt (Shift+Option on the Mac) keys. This technique works for creating squares also.

3. **When you're satisfied with your selection, release your mouse button.**

   Your elliptical selection is alive and well, as shown in Figure 1-2. If you need to move the selection marquee to better center your selection, click and drag inside the marquee.

   You can also move a selection with any of the marquee tools by pressing the spacebar while you're drawing.

   If the selection isn't quite the right shape and size, jump to Book III, Chapter 2 to find out how to make perfect selections.

   Corbis Digital Stock

   Figure 1-2: The Elliptical marquee is the tool of choice for selecting round objects.

Using the Single Column and Single Row Marquee tools

The Single Row and Single Column Marquee tools select a single row or single column of pixels. If you don't go blind using them, these tools can occasionally come in handy for selecting and repairing a thin scratch or fold line on an image or for getting rid of an artifact such as a colored line that has somehow appeared on a scanned image. (You can find out more about making repairs in Book VIII.)

To use either of these tools, simply choose a row or column of pixels on your image and click it. You don't have to do any dragging, but it does help to zoom into your image so that you can better position the tool on the offending row or column.

For more on zooming, see Book I, Chapter 4. Check out Figure 1-3 to get familiar with a single row selection.

Corbis Digital Stock

Figure 1-3: The Single Row Marquee tool selects just one row of pixels.

The Single Row and Single Column Marquee tools don't have keyboard shortcuts, so you're stuck with having to click the tools to select them.

**Book III
Chapter 1**

Making Selections

Using the marquee options

If drawing from the center outward or creating a perfect circle or square doesn't give you enough control, you may want to take a look at the marquee settings provided by the Options bar. These options allow you to make even more precise selections by specifying exact measurements.

You must select the options on the Options bar *before* you make your selection with the marquee tools.

For now, you can ignore the first five icons on the left side of the Options bar, as shown in Figure 1-4. The first icon has to do with tool presets, which I cover in Book I, Chapter 2. The next four icons are the selection state icons, which I discuss in Book III, Chapter 3.

Figure 1-4: Specify all your marquee settings on the Options bar.

Here's the lowdown on each of the remaining options:

✔ **Feather:** Feathering softens or feathers the edges of a selection. The amount of softening depends on the radius — the higher the radius, the softer the edge as shown in Figure 1-5. The *radius* measures how far in all directions the feather effect extends.

Feather radius 4 pixels   Feather radius 20 pixels

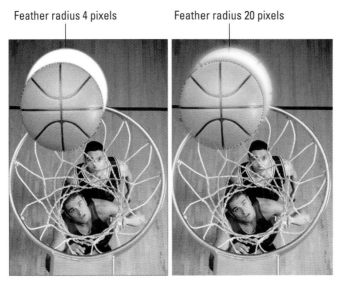

Corbis Digital Stock

Figure 1-5: Applying a feather to your selection blurs the edges.

You can use feathers to create a subtle and natural transition between selections or to create a special effect where an image slowly fades out to the background or to transparency. To feather as you are selecting, select the Feather option on the Options bar before using the marquee tools. You can feather a selection after the fact by using the Select menu. Check out Book III, Chapter 2 for more feathering details.

✔ **Anti-alias:** Whereas feathering completely blurs edges, anti-aliasing just slightly softens the edge of an elliptical selection so that very hard, jagged edges aren't quite so prominent, as shown in Figure 1-6. You don't have an option for entering a pixel value for anti-aliasing. An anti-aliased edge is always 1 pixel wide.

I recommend keeping the Anti-alias option selected, especially if you plan to create composite images. Anti-aliasing helps in creating natural-looking blends between multiple selections.

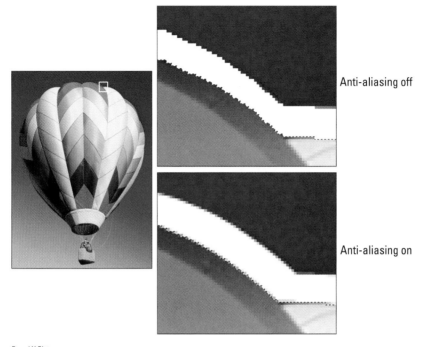

Anti-aliasing off

Anti-aliasing on

Brand X Pictures

Figure 1-6: Anti-aliasing slightly softens your selection edges.

✓ **Style:** The Style drop-down list contains three settings:

- The *Normal* setting enables you to freely drag a selection to any desired dimension.

- The *Fixed Aspect Ratio* option allows you to specify a ratio of width to height in a selection. For example, if you enter 2 for width and 1 for height, you *always* get a marquee selection that's twice as wide as it is high, no matter what the size.

- And finally, select *Fixed Size* to specify exact values for the Width and Height. This option comes in handy when several images need to be the same exact size, as in a row of headshots in a corporate brochure.

✓ **Width and Height:** When you select a Fixed Size from the Style drop-down list, the Width and Height text boxes are available for you to enter values. To swap between the Width and Height values, click the double-headed arrow button.

Even though the default unit of measurement in the Width and Height text boxes is pixels (px for short), you can enter any unit of measurement that Photoshop recognizes — pixels, inches, centimeters, millimeters, points, picas, or percents. After the number, simply type the word or abbreviation of your desired unit of measurement. Photoshop even lets you enter mixed units of measurements, so if you want a selection 100 pixels by 1.25 inches, you can do so.

Lassoing When You Can't

Unfortunately, not much in life is rectangular or elliptical in shape. Most of the time, you have to deal with irregular shapes with *extrusions* and *protrusions* (otherwise known as bumps or bulges) of some sort or another. That's where the lasso tools come in handy. This group of tools allows you to make freeform selections.

Photoshop offers three lasso tools: the Lasso tool (which I call the regular Lasso to distinguish it from the others), the Polygonal Lasso tool, and the Magnetic Lasso tool. Each of the lasso tools has its own special purpose in the realm of freeform selections. But in the category of simplicity, they're all almost as easy to use as the marquee tools. All you have to do is drag around the part of the image you want to select. Just don't indulge in too much caffeine. A steady lasso hand is a good lasso hand.

The selection you make is only as good as how accurately you can trace around your desired element. If you don't make an exact selection the first time around, you can always go back and make corrections (which I cover in Book III, Chapter 3).

If, when making a selection, you find yourself fighting with your mouse (and losing), you may want to invest in a digital drawing tablet, such as a Wacom tablet. Using the stylus and the tablet can make mastering tools such as the Lasso a whole lot easier.

The Lasso and the Polygonal Lasso tools both have only two choices on the Options bar to worry about — Feather and Anti-aliased. These options work exactly like they do with the marquee tools. To find out more, check out the earlier section, "Using the marquee options."

To make a selection by using the Lasso tool, here's what you do:

1. **Select the Lasso tool from the Tools palette.**

   It's the tool that looks like a rope. You can also use the keyboard short-cut; press the L key.

2. **Position the cursor somewhere on the edge of the element that you want to select.**

   The hot spot (the lead point) of the lasso cursor is the end of the rope.

Zoom in on the image a bit if the element and the background don't have a lot of contrast.

In my example, I started at the top of the butte, as shown in Figure 1-7.

3. **Trace around the element, trying to capture only what you want to retain in your selection.**

As you trace, a line forms that follows the movement of your mouse.

Don't release your mouse button until you complete the selection by closing the loop or returning to the starting point. When you release your mouse button, Photoshop thinks you're done and closes the selection, as shown in Figure 1-8.

4. **Continue tracing until you return to your starting point; release the mouse button.**

Recognizing that you're now done, Photoshop presents you with a selection marquee that matches your lasso line (see Figure 1-9).

Selecting straight sides with the Polygonal Lasso tool

Whereas the regular Lasso tool is great for selecting undulating, curvy elements, the Polygonal Lasso tool shines when it comes to the more regimented, straight-sided subjects, such as city skylines, buildings, and stairways.

Lasso cursor

ImageState

Figure 1-7: The Lasso tool is for freeform selections.

Closed selection marquee

Figure 1-8: Don't release your mouse button too soon.

Unlike the regular Lasso tool, the Polygonal Lasso tool has rubber-band-like qualities, and instead of dragging, you click and release the mouse button at the corners of the object you're selecting. It's like a digital connect the dots. Bonus: less manual dexterity required.

Figure 1-9: After tracing around your object, release your mouse and Photoshop presents you with a selection marquee.

The following steps show you how to select with the Polygon Lasso tool:

1. Select the Polygonal Lasso tool from the Tools palette.

You can also use the keyboard shortcut. Press the L key and then press Shift+L until you get the Polygonal Lasso tool. It looks like the regular Lasso tool, but it has straight sides.

2. With the Polygonal Lasso tool selected, click to establish the beginning of the first line of your selection.

A corner is always a good place to start.

3. Move the mouse and click at the next corner of the object. Then continue clicking at the various corners of your object.

The line stretches out from each corner you click like a rubber band.

4. To close your selection, return to the first point you clicked and click one last time.

When you place your cursor over the starting point, a small circle appears next to your cursor, a sure sign that you're at the right place for closing the selection. A selection marquee that matches your Polygonal Lasso line appears, as shown in Figure 1-10.

Figure 1-10: The Polygon Lasso tool is perfect for selecting straight-sided objects.

Which tool do you use if you have an object with both curves and straight sides? You can have two, two, two tools in one! Press the Alt (Option on the Mac) key to have the Polygonal Lasso tool temporarily transform into the regular Lasso tool. Then drag to select the curves. Release the Alt (Option) key to return to the Polygonal Lasso tool. This trick works with the other Lasso tools as well.

Attracting with the Magnetic Lasso tool

The last member of the lasso tool trio is the Magnetic Lasso, which I admit can be kind of tricky to use and sometimes even downright obstinate. The Magnetic Lasso tool works by analyzing the colors of the pixels between the elements in the foreground and the elements in the background. Then it snaps to the edge between the elements, as if the edge had a magnetic pull.

The Magnetic Lasso tool performs best when your image has a lot of contrast between the foreground and background elements — for example, a dark mountain range against a light sky or a shadow against a stucco wall.

The Magnetic Lasso tool also has some unique settings, which you can adjust on the Options bar, to tame its behavior. I cover those settings in the next section, "Adjusting the Magnetic Lasso options." For now, follow these steps to use the tool:

1. **Select the Magnetic Lasso tool from the Tools palette.**

   You can also use the keyboard shortcut: Press the L key and then press Shift+L until you get the Magnetic Lasso tool. The tool looks like a straight-sided lasso with a little magnet on it.

2. **Click the edge of the object you want to select.**

You can start anywhere; just be sure to click the edge between the element you want and the background you don't want.

3. **Move your cursor around the object, without clicking.**

The Magnetic Lasso tool creates a selection line similar to the other lasso tools. It also adds little squares called *points* along that selection line, as shown in Figure 1-11. These points pin down the selection line the way you might section off an area of your yard with ropes and stakes.

- If the Magnetic Lasso tool starts veering off the edge of your object, back up your mouse and click to force a point down on the line.

- If the Magnetic Lasso tool adds a point where you don't want one, simply press your Backspace (Delete on a Mac) key to delete it.

4. **Continue moving your mouse around the object; return to your starting point and release the mouse button to close the selection.**

As with the Polygon Lasso tool, you see a small circle next to your cursor indicating that you're at the correct place to close the selection. The selection marquee appears when the selection is closed.

Magnetic Lasso point

Figure 1-11: The Magnetic Lasso tool detects the edge of your object.

Adjusting the Magnetic Lasso options

The Magnetic Lasso tool comes equipped with a few settings on the Options bar that control the sensitivity of the tool.

I recommend starting out by messing around with the Magnetic Lasso tool using its default settings. If the tool isn't cooperating, then play with the options.

The first icon has to do with tool presets, and the next four icons are the selection state icons (check out Book III, Chapter 2). The Feather and Anti-alias options work like they do with the marquee tools (see the earlier section, "Using the marquee options"). The following list explains the remaining options:

- ✔ **Width:** This option, measured in pixels from 1 to 256, determines how close to the edge you have to move your mouse before the Magnetic Lasso tool recognizes the object you're selecting. Decrease the value if the object's edge has a lot of indentations and protrusions or if the image is of lower contrast. Increase the value if the image is of higher contrast or has smoother edges.

  When using the Magnetic Lasso tool, you can change the Width value from the keyboard by pressing the left bracket ([ ) key to lower the value and the right bracket ( ]) key to increase the value.

- ✔ **Edge Contrast:** Measured in percentages from 1 to 100, this option specifies the required contrast between the object you're selecting and its background before the Magnetic Lasso tool hugs the edge between them. If your image has good contrast between the foreground and background, use a higher percentage.

- ✔ **Frequency:** This setting, measured in percentages from 1 to 100, specifies how many points to place on the selection line. The higher the percentage, the greater number of points. If the object you want to select has a fairly smooth edge, keep the percentage low. If the edge is jagged or has a lot of detail, a higher percentage may be more effective in getting an accurate selection line.

- ✔ **Tablet Pressure (pen icon):** If you own a pressure-sensitive drawing tablet, select this option to make an increase in stylus pressure cause the edge width to decrease.

Performing Wand Wizardry

The Magic Wand. The name is intriguing, isn't it? Any tool that has the audacity to call itself the Magic Wand must be so powerful that it can grant your every selection wish with a mere swoosh. Unfortunately, it's not quite so awe-inspiring. A better name for this tool would be the Click-'n-Select tool. You click your image, and the Magic Wand tool makes a selection, which contains areas of similar color, based on the color of the pixel you clicked.

Simple enough. What's not quite so simple is how to determine how *similar* the color has to be to get the Magic Wand tool to select it. That's where the important Tolerance setting comes in. Before you tackle tolerance (and find out how it affects the Magic Wand tool's performance), you first need to get the hang of using the Magic Wand tool.

Selecting with the Magic Wand tool

As with the Magnetic Lasso tool, the Magic Wand tool works best when you have high-contrast images or images with a limited number of colors. As shown in Figure 1-12, a black-and-white checkered flag is a perfect example of something that the Magic Wand tool effectively selects. I click once on the top of a black square, and the Magic Wand tool picks up all the other surrounding black pixels. I can now easily change the color of my black squares to red or yellow in one fell swoop.

Figure 1-12: The Magic Wand tool works best on images with limited colors.

As you can see, Figure 1-13 is a poor candidate. This image contains a ton of colors and no real definitive contrast between the scale and the background. Although it takes only one click to select the black squares on the flag, other high-contrast candidates may take a few clicks. And some images may need a tweak or two of the Tolerance setting, described in the next section.

Figure 1-13: Trying to select an image with a lot of color variation can be an exercise in futility.

Setting your tolerance

Sometimes an image may contain a few shades of a similar color. Consider a cloudless sky for example. A few shades of blue make up the bright blue yonder. With the Magic Wand tool, if you click a darker shade of blue in the sky, Photoshop selects all similar shades of blue, but the lighter shades remain unselected. This is usually a sure sign that you need to increase your Tolerance level. The *Tolerance* setting determines the range of color that the Magic Wand tool selects.

Tolerance is based on brightness levels that range from 0 to 255:

- ✔ Setting the Tolerance to 0 selects one color only.
- ✔ Setting the Tolerance to 255 selects all colors — the entire image.

To use the Magic Wand tool and adjust Tolerance settings, follow these steps:

1. **Select the Magic Wand tool from the Tools palette.**

   The Magic Wand tool looks like the weapon of choice for many Disney characters. You can also use the keyboard shortcut; press the W key.

2. **Click the portion of the image that you want to select; use the default Tolerance setting of 16.**

   The pixel that you click determines the base color. The default value of 16 means that the Magic Wand tool selects all colors that are 32 levels lighter and 16 levels darker than the base color.

   If you selected everything you wanted the first time you used the Magic Wand tool, stretch your arm and give yourself a pat on the back. If you didn't (which is probably the case), go to Step 3.

3. **Enter a new Tolerance setting on the Options bar.**

   If the Magic Wand tool selected more than you wanted it to, lower the Tolerance setting. If it didn't select enough, raise the setting.

4. **Click again the portion of the image that you want to select.**

   Changing the tolerance doesn't adjust your current selection.

   The Magic Wand tool deselects the current selection and makes a new selection based on your new Tolerance setting, as shown in Figure 1-14. If it still isn't right, you can adjust the Tolerance setting again. I regret that I can't give you a magic formula that you can use to determine the right value. It's all about trial and error.

Using the Magic Wand Options bar

If you get a selection close to what you want, stop there and then use the selection-refining techniques I discuss in Book III, Chapter 2. But before you do that, you need to know about the other Magic Wand settings on the Options bar. Besides Anti-alias, which I discuss in the earlier section, "Using the marquee options," the three remaining options are as follows:

- ✔ **Contiguous:** When you turn on this option, the Magic Wand tool selects *only* pixels that are adjacent to each other. If you turn off the option, the Magic Wand tool selects all pixels within the range of tolerance, whether or not they're adjacent to each other.

Book III
Chapter 1

Making Selections

Figure 1-14: Finding the right Tolerance is the key to selecting with the Magic Wand.

✓ **Sample All Layers:** This option is valid only when you have multiple layers in your image. (For more on layers, see Book V.) If you have multiple layers and this option is on, the Magic Wand tool selects color from all visible layers. If you turn off this option, the Magic Wand selects colors from the active layer only.

✓ **Sample Size:** Although this option affects the Magic Wand tool, it appears on the Options bar *only* when you select the Eyedropper tool. (For more on the Eyedropper, see Book II, Chapter 3.) Select the Eyedropper tool and, in the Sample Size pop-up menu that appears, choose from the following:

- **Point Sample:** Samples just the color of the pixel you clicked

- **3 by 3 Average:** Averages the color of the pixel you clicked and the surrounding 8 pixels

- **5 by 5 Average:** Averages the color of the pixel you clicked and the surrounding 24 pixels

Chapter 2: Creating and Working with Paths

*A*lthough the Marquee, Lasso, and Magic Wand tools are fun, friendly, and pretty easy to wield, sometimes they don't quite have the horsepower to make that really precise selection. So either you spend a lot of time cleaning up what you've selected (see Book III, Chapter 3 for more on that topic), or you live with a ho-hum selection. That's where the Pen tool and its related cronies come to the rescue. The Pen tool creates paths, which you can then convert into selections.

Because the Pen tool (and related path-editing tools) offers control and precision, it is very capable at nailing that accurate selection. The only problem is that the Pen tool is a far cry from fun, friendly, and easy. Many new users try the Pen a few times, but end up muttering in disgust and returning gratefully to the Lasso tool. However, I guarantee that if you dedicate a good chunk of time to mastering the Pen tool, you'll soon turn your elite little nose up at the simple Lasso tool.

Introducing Paths

Unlike the other selection tools, the Pen tool doesn't initially produce a selection marquee. When you select the Pen tool and start clicking and dragging around your image, you create a path. Paths have three types of components — anchor points, straight segments, and curved segments.

Curved paths are called *Bézier paths* (after Pierre Bézier who, in the 1970s, invented the equation used for CAD/CAM programs). They are based on a mathematical cubic equation where the path is controlled by direction lines that end in direction points (often referred to as *handles*), as shown in Figure 2-1. The length and angle of direction lines control the pitch and angle of the Bézier curve.

Figure 2-1 and the following list introduce the different kinds of anchor points that Photoshop puts at your disposal and show you exactly what they do. You can use some or all of these anchor points in a single path:

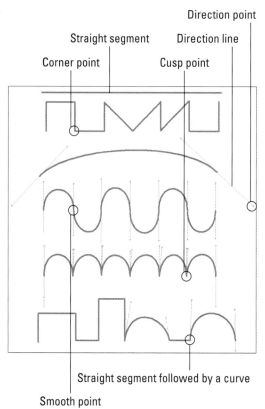

Figure 2-1: The Pen tool creates Bézier curves, which are comprised of many different components.

- ✔ A true corner point has no direction lines. Use corner points when selecting objects with straight sides, such as stairs or barns.

- ✔ A smooth point has two direction lines pointing in opposite directions but dependent on one another. Use smooth points when selecting objects that have alternating curves, such as a sea of rolling waves.

- ✔ A cusp point has two direction lines that are independent of one another. Use cusp points when selecting an object with curves going the same direction, such as the petals on a daisy.

- ✔ A point between a straight segment and a curve is a corner point with only one direction line.

After you create a Bézier path, you can then edit the path by moving, adding, deleting, or converting anchor points and by manipulating the direction lines. You can also transform paths by choosing Edit➪Transform Paths. With transforming, you are able to scale, rotate, skew, distort, or change the perspective of the path (see Book III, Chapter 3 for details).

The path hovers over the image in its own space. You control it via the Paths palette, where you can save it, duplicate it, stroke it with color (apply color to the edge only), fill it with color or a pattern, and most importantly, load it as a selection. I say "most importantly" because nine times out of ten, you painstakingly create a path as a means to an accurate selection marquee. You may use the path as a clipping path one other time: to hide a part of a layer or part of an entire image. I cover clipping paths in the last section of this chapter.

Creating a Path with the Pen Tool

The best way to get the hang of the Pen tool is to dive right in and work with it. You'll want to start with straight lines, which are very easy, and then move on to the more difficult curves. The more you practice with the Pen, the more comfortable and proficient you'll become. It definitely is an example of the old adage "you get out what you put into it."

Knowing your Pen tool options

Although every path consists of three basic components — segments, points, and direction lines — the Pen tool enables you to use these components to create a few different types of paths. See Book IV, Chapter 2 for more information on the following options, accessible from the Pen tool's Options bar. You must choose one of the following:

Book III
Chapter 2

Creating and
Working with Paths

- ✔ **Shape Layers:** This option creates a shape on a new layer that's called, not surprisingly, a shape layer. After you create the path that defines the shape, Photoshop fills the shape with the foreground color and stores the path as a vector mask in the Paths palette. A shape layer is a unique entity.

- ✔ **Fill Pixels:** This option is available only when you're using the shape tools. It allows you to create a shape and fill it with the foreground color, but it does not create a shape layer nor does it retain the path.

- ✔ **Paths:** This option enables you to create a traditional path that hovers over the image. The path you create is a *work path*, which is temporary, appears in the Paths palette, and is unsaved. If you're creating a path that you'll eventually load as a selection, this is your option.

Creating your first work path

Making a work path is the easiest of the three options, and you'll use it frequently after you get the hang of using the Pen tool. The following steps show you how to create a simple, straight path:

Rarely (if ever) will you create a work path that's a single, straight line. Please keep reading the other sections in this chapter.

1. **Open an image you want to practice on.**

   I suggest choosing an image that has an element with both straight edges and curves, if you want to also practice creating curved paths later.

2. **Select the Pen tool from the Tools palette.**

   Or you can just press the P key.

3. **On the Options bar, click the Paths button.**

   You can see this button in Figure 2-2.

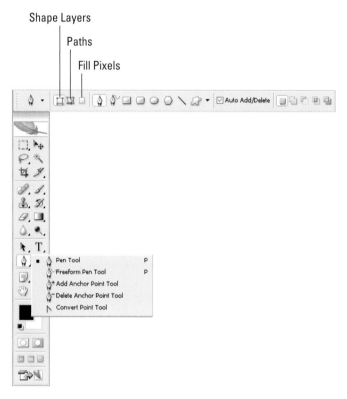

Figure 2-2: When using the Pen tool, be sure and choose your desired path type from the Options bar.

4. **To create a straight line, click and release your mouse button at the points where you want the line to begin and to end, leaving anchor points at those positions.**

You don't need to do any dragging to create straight segments. As you click and add your anchor points, Photoshop creates straight segments that connect the anchor points, as shown in Figure 2-3.

Anchor points

Straight segment

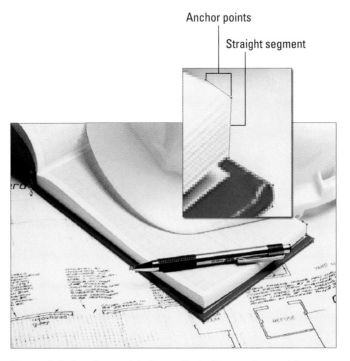

Figure 2-3: Drawing straight lines with the Pen requires nothing more than clicks with the tool.

5. **To draw a constrained line — horizontal, vertical, or 45° angle — press the Shift key as you click.**

6. **To end the path, click the Pen tool in the Tools palette to deselect it.**

 Or use this very handy shortcut: Press the Ctrl key (⌘ on the Mac), which gives you the Direct Selection tool (the white arrow), and then click away from the line. Release the Ctrl key (⌘ on the Mac), and the Pen tool reappears.

 When you deselect the path, you're free to start another, unconnected path if you need to.

 Continue on to the following sections if you want to add other kinds of segments to the path. Otherwise, skip to "Closing a path," later in this chapter.

Drawing curves

You're probably never going to create a simple work path that doesn't have curves as well as straight lines. I mean, not much in life is perfectly linear. Most things have undulations here and there. Picking up from the preceding section, here's how to create curved paths:

1. **If you are adding onto a previously created open path, make sure that you position your cursor on the last anchor point you created on that open path to continue.**

   You see a slash mark or small square appear next to your cursor. If you are starting a new path, position the cursor where you want the curve to begin.

2. **In both cases, drag toward the direction that you want the bump of the curve to go. Release the mouse button when you're done.**

   If you are creating a new path, an anchor point and two direction lines, which have direction points at their ends, appear. If you are adding a curve to your straight segment, an anchor point and one direction line with one direction point appear. The direction lines and direction points control the angle and pitch of the curve.

   How do you know how far you should drag? You can do what I do and use the rule of thirds. Imagine that your curve is a piece of string that you have stretched and laid out in a straight line. Divide that line into thirds. The distance you drag your mouse cursor is approximately one-third the length of that line.

   How do you establish the angle? Drag straight from the anchor point for a steeper curve and at an angle from the anchor point for a flatter curve. The element in my example is a flatter curve; therefore I dragged up and to the right at an angle of about 4.5 degrees, as shown in Figure 2-4.

3. **Move the cursor to the end of the curve and drag in the opposite direction, away from the bump.**

   You now see another anchor point and a set of two direction lines and points. Photoshop creates the curve segment between the anchor points, as shown in Figure 2-5.

   If you drag both direction lines in the same direction, you create a curve shaped like an S.

   On the Options bar, click the down-pointing arrow at the end of the row of tools and choose the Rubber Band option. With this option selected, Photoshop draws a segment between the last anchor point you create and wherever your cursor is located, giving you a kind of animated preview of how the path will appear. I personally find the option distracting, but some users love it.

4. **To draw more alternating curves, just repeat these steps, dragging in an opposite direction each time.**

Anchor point

Direction line

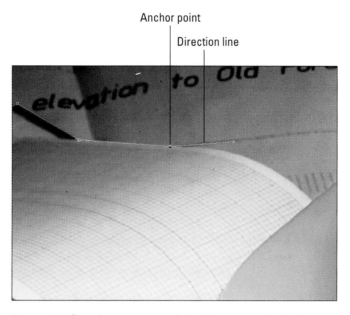

Figure 2-4: Dragging at an angle of about 4.5 degrees begins the path of the flat curve.

Second anchor point

Curve segment

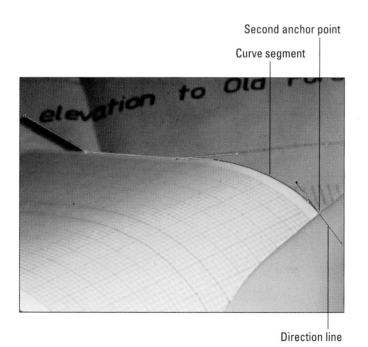

Direction line

Figure 2-5: Finish the curve by dragging in the opposite direction.

Connecting a straight segment to a curve segment

If you need to create a straight segment after creating a curve (or vice versa), you need to convert the point where the path changes from curved to straight. To convert a point, follow these steps:

1. **Position your cursor over the second anchor point in the existing curve and press the Alt key (Option on the Mac).**

   You see a caret (which looks like an upside down *V*) next to the Pen cursor.

2. **Click and release your mouse button over the anchor point.**

   The bottom direction line disappears. You have converted a smooth point into a corner point with one direction line. This action now allows you to create a straight segment.

   It's no coincidence that the tool icon for the Convert Point tool is also a caret. Whenever you see a caret symbol in Photoshop, it's an indication that you are converting an anchor point, from smooth to corner or vice versa.

3. **Move your mouse to the end of the straight edge you want to select and click and release.**

   You can press the Shift key if you want the line to be constrained horizontally, vertically, or at an angle with a multiple of 45 degrees.

   Photoshop connects the two anchor points with a straight segment, as shown in Figure 2-6.

Corner point with one direction line

Straight segment

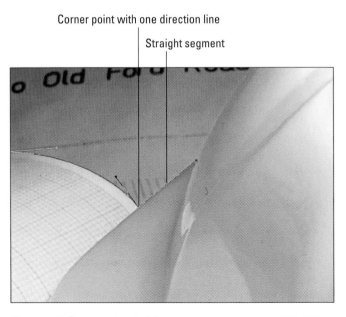

Figure 2-6: To connect a straight segment to a curve segment, you must first convert the point.

Connecting curve segments with cusp points

If you need to create a curve that goes in the same direction as a curve that is adjacent to it, you need to take a couple additional steps:

1. **Convert the point — this time from smooth to cusp — by positioning your cursor over the second anchor point in the existing curve and pressing the Alt key (Option on the Mac).**

2. **Drag toward the bump of the curve. Release the mouse button and then release the Alt (Option on the Mac) key.**

   Essentially, your actions are pulling the direction line out from the anchor point. Both direction lines move to the same side of the anchor point, yet are independent of each other, creating the cusp point, as shown in Figure 2-7.

3. **Move your cursor to where you want the curve to end and drag away from the bump to create your second curve.**

Try to keep anchor points on either side of the curve, not along the top. It is also good to try to use the fewest number of anchor points possible to create your path. That way, the path results in a much smoother curve. It also creates a smaller file size and reduces the possibility of printing problems.

To draw a curve after a straight segment, first position your cursor directly on the last anchor point of the straight segment. Drag toward the bump of the curve you need to draw. A direction line appears. Position your cursor where you want the curve to end and drag away from the bump.

Book III
Chapter 2

Creating and
Working with Paths

Cusp point

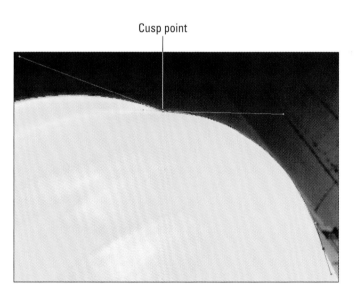

Figure 2-7: You can connect two curves that go in the same direction with a cusp point.

Closing a path

To close the path, return to your first anchor point and click. You see a small circle next to your Pen cursor, indicating that you're closing the path when you click.

Congratulations! You are now the proud owner of a work path (see Figure 2-8). Don't worry if the path isn't perfect; you find out how to edit paths in an upcoming section. If your path is perfect and you want to save it now, skip ahead to the section, "Working with the Paths Palette."

If your path is incomplete and you need to continue drawing it, either click or drag on the endpoint with the Pen tool. You see the appearance of a slash mark or small square next to the Pen cursor.

Creating subpaths

You can also create a series of lines or curves. For example, you may want to create a border consisting of some decorative curve shapes, which you could later stroke with color. You can then save these *subpaths* under a single path name. To create a series of subpaths, simply end one path before starting another. Make sure that the paths are not hidden when you do so; otherwise, Photoshop eliminates the previous path when you start another.

Figure 2-8: To close your work path, return to your first anchor point and click.

Working with the Paths Palette

Working hand in hand with the Pen tool is the Paths palette. You can think of it as a kind of Command and Control Center for your paths. Although it isn't mandatory, opening up your Paths palette, shown in Figure 2-9, is a good idea before you create a path so that you can stay apprised as to what is happening with your image. To open the palette, choose Window➪Paths.

The icons at the bottom of the Paths palette from left to right, as shown in Figure 2-9, are

Saved path

- ✓ Fill Path
- ✓ Stroke Path
- ✓ Load Path as Selection
- ✓ Make Work Path from Selection
- ✓ Create New Path
- ✓ Delete Current Path

The following sections highlight some of the stuff you can do with the Paths palette.

Figure 2-9: The Paths palette allows you to save, delete, stroke, fill, and make selections from your paths.

**Book III
Chapter 2**

Creating and
Working with Paths

Creating a path

When you create a path, it automatically appears in the Paths palette as a work path.

Remember that a work path is temporary and unsaved, and you can have only one work path in the Paths palette at a time.

If the work path is selected when you begin another path, your actions are added to the current work path. But if the existing work path is hidden and you begin drawing another path, that new work path replaces the existing one.

Creating a new path

You can save yourself a lot of grief if you make sure that your path is saved before you start. If you select New Path from the Paths palette pop-up menu *before* you create the path, Photoshop automatically saves the work path, and it becomes a saved path or named path. You can also just click the Create New Path icon at the bottom of the Paths palette.

Saving a work path

To save a work path, double-click the path in the Paths palette. Or choose Save Path from the Paths palette pop-up menu (click the triangle in the upper right to open the menu). Then provide a name in the Save Path dialog box and click OK.

After you save your path, you can reload it at any time. Unlike layers, paths take up very little storage space, so don't hesitate to save them. Plus, you don't want to go through all that work again if you don't have to. Unlike work paths, you can have as many saved paths as your heart desires.

Deleting, duplicating, and renaming a path

To delete a path, drag the path to the trash can icon at the bottom of the palette. Or choose Delete Path from the Paths palette pop-up menu.

You can duplicate a saved path by choosing the path in the Paths palette and selecting Duplicate Path from the Paths palette pop-up menu. You can also drag the saved path on top of the Create New Path icon at the bottom of the palette.

To rename a path, double-click the path name in the Paths palette. Then enter the new name directly within the palette.

Stroking a path

You can use the Stroke Path command to paint a stroke along the path. You can choose which painting or editing tool to use to stroke the path. Follow these steps:

1. **Select the path in the Paths palette. Then choose Stroke Path from the Paths palette pop-up menu.**

   Or press the Alt key (Option on the Mac) and click the Stroke path with the brush icon (an outlined circle) at the bottom of the palette.

   You can also click the Stroke Path icon without the Alt (Option on the Mac) key. Note that this option bypasses the dialog box in Step 2 and just strokes your path with whatever setting you used previously.

2. **In the dialog box that opens, choose one of the 16 painting or editing tools you want to use to apply color to the stroke. Click OK.**

   Make sure that you verify your chosen tool's settings on the Options bar because Photoshop uses those settings to stroke your path. Photoshop also applies your current foreground color to the stroke.

   If you're using a pressure-sensitive drawing tablet, you can select the Simulate Pressure check box to create strokes with varying widths. If everything has gone well, you end up with a stroked path like the one shown in Figure 2-10.

If you select one or more paths with the Direct Selection tool, the Stroke Path command changes to Stroke Subpath(s), enabling you to stroke only the selected paths.

Filling a path

You can fill the interior of a path with color by choosing the Fill Path command. Follow these steps:

Figure 2-10: Photoshop allows you to easily apply a stroke of color to your paths.

1. **Select the path in the Paths palette and choose Fill Path from the Paths palette pop-up menu.**

   A dialog box gives options for Contents, Opacity, Blending, and Rendering. Briefly, for your Contents, choose between colors, pattern, or history. (For more on the Contents and Opacity options, see Book IV, Chapter 2.)

   Or you can press the Alt key (Option on the Mac) and click the Fill Path with Foreground Color icon (a solid circle) at the bottom of the palette. You can also click the Fill icon without the Alt (Option on the Mac) key. This option bypasses the dialog box and just fills your path with whatever setting you used previously.

2. **In the dialog box, leave the Blending Mode option set to Normal.**

   Using the Layers palette to apply your blend modes is better because you have more flexibility (see Book V for more on layers). Here is the scoop on the remaining options:

   - The feathering option gradually blurs the edges of the fill into the background. Enter the Feather Radius in pixels. The more pixels, the greater the blur or feather.

   - The anti-alias option just slightly softens the very edge of the fill so it doesn't appear as ragged.

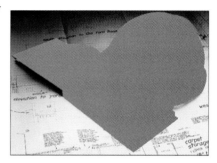

If you select one or more paths with the Direct Selection tool, the Fill Path command changes to Fill Subpath(s), enabling you to fill only the selected paths.

3. **After you set your options, click OK.**

   Your path now is filled, similar to mine, which is shown in Figure 2-11.

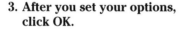

Figure 2-11: If stroking your path with color isn't enough, you can fill it instead.

Loading Paths as Selections

Creating a path is usually the means to an end — an accurate selection. Therefore, you'll frequently use the Paths palette to load your path as a selection.

Follow these steps to get the lowdown on how to do just that. Open an image, make a selection by using the Pen tool, and get started.

1. **Choose Make Selection from the Paths palette pop-up menu.**

   Alternatively, you can also press Alt (Option on the Mac) and click the Load Path as Selection icon in the Paths palette.

   To bypass the Make Selection dialog box, simply click the Load path as Selection icon at the bottom of the Paths palette.

2. **In the Make Selection dialog box, you can**

   - Feather your selection by entering a pixel value in the Feather Radius box. (For more on feathering, see Book III, Chapter 3.)

   - Leave the feather radius at 0 for a hard-edged selection.

   - Select the Anti-aliased option. This option slightly softens the edge of the selection so that it doesn't appear so jagged. (It's my personal recommendation.)

   If you happen to have another selection active when you load your current path as a selection, you can choose to add, subtract, or intersect with that other selection.

After the path is made into a selection, as shown in Figure 2-12, it acts like any other selection.

If you need a selection refresher, see Book III, Chapter 1. If you want to save your selection (saving a selection creates an alpha channel), jump ahead to Book VI, Chapter 1 where I explain details on working with channels.

Figure 2-12: The main reason to create a path is to achieve an accurate selection.

Here's one of my favorite shortcuts. To quickly load the path as a selection, select the path and then press Ctrl+Enter (⌘+Return on the Mac). You can also Ctrl+click (⌘+click on the Mac) on your path name in the Paths palette to do the same. Just be aware that you bypass the dialog box and its options when you use the shortcuts.

Turning a Selection into a Path

Although you probably won't use this option nearly as often as you use the option to turn a path into a selection, the option is, indeed, available: You can create paths from existing selections.

Creating a path from a selection can come in handy if you need to save a path as a clipping path (areas of the image outside the path are hidden).

1. **If you've been reading from the beginning of this chapter, you probably have a selection on-screen ready and raring to go. If you are just jumping in, go ahead and select the desired element in your image.**

2. **With the selection marquee active, select Make Work Path from the Paths palette pop-up menu.**

3. **In the dialog box that appears, enter a Tolerance value.**

   You can also create a path from a selection by pressing Alt (Option on the Mac) and clicking the Make Work Path from Selection icon in the Paths palette. If you just click the icon, you also make a path, but you bypass the dialog box.

   The Tolerance value controls how sensitive Photoshop is to the nooks and crannies in the selection when it creates the path:

   • The lower the value, the more sensitive it is, and the more closely the selection follows your path.

   • Too low a value, such as 0.5, may create too many anchor points.

   • Too high a value, such as 10 (the max), rounds out your path too much. Start with the default setting of 2.0.

   You can always tweak the path later (check out "Editing Paths" later in this chapter).

4. **If the path is still showing, simply click in the gray area below the path names in the Paths palette.**

   This action deselects the path.

5. **Select the work path in the Paths palette and choose Save Path from the Paths palette pop-up menu. Name the path and click OK.**

**Book III
Chapter 2**

**Creating and
Working with Paths**

Using the Kinder Freeform Pen

Confession: There is a more amicable incarnation of the Pen tool — the Freeform Pen tool. This tool is kind of a hybrid Lasso/Pen tool. Just drag around the element you want to select, and the tool creates an outline that follows your cursor, exactly like the Lasso.

After you release your mouse button, Photoshop provides the anchor points, lines, and curves for that path, exactly like the Pen.

In my humble opinion, the Freeform Pen rates just an okay. The downside is that you are back to needing a really steady hand in order to get an accurate selection. The tool is probably one notch better than the Lasso tool because you do get a path that you can refine before you load it as a selection. But I'd rather pay my dues and get skilled with the regular Pen.

Here are some Freeform Pen tips:

✔ To create straight segments with the Freeform Pen, press Alt (Option on the Mac) while pressing the mouse button and then click to create the anchor point.

✔ Pressing Alt (Option on the Mac) temporarily turns the Freeform Pen into the regular Pen. When you want to return to drawing curves, release Alt (Option on the Mac), keeping the mouse button pressed.

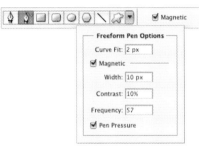

Be careful: If you release Alt (Option on the Mac) after releasing the mouse button, Photoshop ends your path, and you can do nothing about it.

The following sections give you the scoop on the options, which you can find by clicking the down-pointing arrow on the Options bar, that go hand in hand with the Freeform Pen tool (see Figure 2-13).

Figure 2-13: The Freeform Pen is a cross between the Lasso and the Pen tools and requires a steady hand to create paths.

Curve Fit

The Curve Fit option lets you adjust the amount of error Photoshop allows when trying to fit your cursor movement to a path. You can enter a value from 0.5 to 10 pixels; the default setting is 2 pixels.

At the default setting, Photoshop doesn't register any movement of your cursor that is 2 pixels or less. Setting the value to 0.5 pixels makes the Freeform Pen very sensitive to your movement and forces the tool to very closely follow the edge.

The disadvantage of this option is that using it also causes a lot of unnecessary anchor points. Although a value of 10 pixels corrects this problem by making the option less sensitive, your path may not be as accurate.

I recommend trying the Freeform Pen at each of these settings and then getting a feel for the kind of path it makes.

Magnetic

When selected, the Magnetic option makes the Freeform Pen act much like the Magnetic Lasso tool. Click anywhere on the edge of the element you want to select. Release your mouse button and then move the cursor around the edge. The tool snaps to the edge of your element, creating anchor points and segments. You can

- **Manually control the magnetism:** If the Freeform Pen tool starts to veer off course, you can manually force down an anchor point by clicking.

- **Create straight segments:** To create straight segments, again press Alt+click (Option+click on the Mac) to temporarily get the regular Pen. Alt+drag (Option+drag on the Mac) to temporarily access the regular Freeform Pen. To return to the magnetic Freeform Pen tool, release Alt (Option on the Mac), click again, and continue moving the cursor.

To close a path with the magnetic Freeform Pen, double-click or return to your starting anchor point.

Width, Contrast, Frequency, and Pen Pressure

The Width, Contrast, and Frequency settings are specifically for the Magnetic option and work just like the Magnetic Lasso options. Width specifies how close to the edge (1–256) the tool must be before it detects an edge. Contrast (1–100) specifies how much contrast must be between pixels for the tool to see the edge. And Frequency (5–40) specifies the rate at which the tool lays down anchor points. For more details, see Book III, Chapter 1.

The Pen Pressure option is available only if you're using a pressure-sensitive drawing tablet and allows you to adjust how sensitive the tool is based on how hard you press down with the stylus.

Book III
Chapter 2

Creating and Working with Paths

Creating Paths without the Pen

I want to let you in on a fun way to create paths. Yes, I said fun. You have to assume by fun I mean no Pen tool is involved in the method.

You can grab any of the shape tools and create a work path. Before you do, however, be sure to click the Paths icon on the Options bar. It's the icon that looks like a Pen cursor with a square path around it. Drag the shape tool of choice on your canvas and presto, an instant path. These shapes can come in handy for creating small spot illustrations, logos, and Web buttons.

Follow these steps:

1. **Open an existing image and select a shape tool.**

   In the example shown in Figure 2-14, I used the Custom Shape tool.

2. **Choose a shape from the shape preset library on the Options bar and open an image.**

   I chose a fish shape.

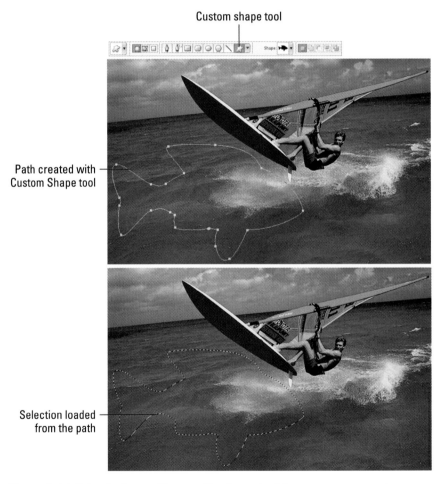

Figure 2-14: Using the Custom Shape tool is a fun and painless way to create paths.

3. **Using the Shape tool, drag a path in your image window.**

   You can then use the Paths palette to load the path as a selection. See "Loading Paths as Selections," earlier in this chapter.

4. **Choose Layer➪New➪Layer via Copy.**

   You've just put the selection on its own layer. You can hide your original background image by clicking the eyeball icon in the Layers palette. For more on layers, see Book V.

5. **If you want, add some type with the Type tool.**

   If you want to give your type some motion, click the Create Warped Text button on the Options bar. You can also apply drop shadows, bevels, and other effects by choosing Layer➪Layer Style.

   I chose the Flag style warp in the Warp Text dialog box.

   I also applied a Bevel and Emboss and Drop Shadow Layer Style to both the selection and the type. (For more on type, see Book IV, Chapter 3.)

6. **Delete the original image.**

   When I was done, the image in Figure 2-15 was what I ended up with — fun and very easy.

**Book III
Chapter 2**

**Creating and
Working with Paths**

Figure 2-15: After adding some type and a few effects, you have a fun composite image.

Editing Paths

Often, it is easier and less time consuming to try to get a reasonably
decent, but not perfect path with the
Pen tool. Then after you have that, go
back and edit your path for more accuracy. And while following the Eyeball-It-
Then-Fix-It strategy is valuable anytime
in your Photoshop career, it is especially true when you're first learning
to use the Pen tool.

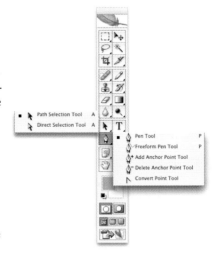

Figure 2-16: The compadres of the Pen
tool help to refine your paths to perfection.

Photoshop offers you a bevy of editing
tools that can make your path repair
a snap. These tools even share the
same flyout menu as the Pen tool. In
addition, the arrow tools, which Adobe
calls the Path Selection and Direct
Selection tools, are also extremely
helpful when it comes to fine-tuning
your path. In fact, you may find, like
I do, that the Direct Selection tool is
one of your favorite tools — so simple
to use, yet so functional. Figure 2-16
shows both sets of tools.

To edit a path, follow these steps:

1. **If you can't see the path you
   want to edit, select the path in
   the Paths palette.**

   This activates the path.

2. **To see the individual anchor
   points so that you can edit
   them, select the Direct
   Selection tool (remember, it's
   the white arrow). Click anywhere along the path.**

   You now see the individual
   anchor points and segments
   that comprise the path. Most of
   the anchor points, if not all, are
   hollow because they are unselected, as shown in Figure 2-17.

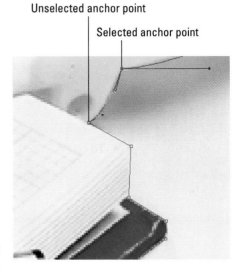

Figure 2-17: Hollow anchor points are
unselected, while solid points are selected.

3. **If you need to move an anchor point, click it with the Direct Selection tool. When selected, the point becomes solid, also shown in Figure 2-17. Drag to move the anchor point. If you need to, you can move a curved or straight segment in the same fashion.**

4. **If you're in need of some major repair and need to move an entire path, use the Path Selection tool (the black arrow).**

   You can also select multiple paths by pressing the Shift key while clicking the paths.

   REMEMBER

   If you move any part of the path beyond the boundary of the image canvas, it is still available — just not visible. Use the Zoom tool to zoom out until you see the hidden portion of the path.

5. **Manipulate the direction lines to change the shape of the curve. First, click the anchor point of the curve to select it. Then click and drag the direction point going the same direction as the bump.**

   By lengthening or shortening the direction line, you can control how steep or flat the curve is. By rotating the direction line, you change the slope of the curve, as shown in Figure 2-18.

   • To add an anchor point in your path, use the Add Anchor Point tool. Click in the path where you need an anchor point. This tool always adds a smooth point, no matter where you click.

   • To delete an anchor point, select the Delete Anchor Point tool, position the cursor over the anchor point and click it. The anchor point disappears while keeping your path intact.

   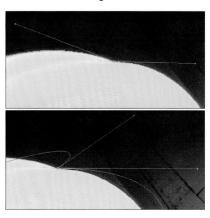

   Figure 2-18: By manipulating the direction lines, you can change the shape of a curve.

   • To convert an anchor point from smooth to corner or vice versa, select the Convert Point tool. Position your cursor on your desired anchor point. If the anchor point is a corner point, drag away from the anchor point to create the direction lines that create a smooth point. If the point is a smooth point, simply click and release on the anchor point to convert it into a corner point. To convert a smooth point to a cusp point, make sure the direction lines are showing and then drag a direction line to break it into independent direction lines. And finally, to convert a cusp point back to a smooth point, just drag out from the anchor point.

Book III
Chapter 2

Creating and
Working with Paths

- To copy a path, first select it with the Path Selection tool. Then press Alt (Option on the Mac) and drag away from the path. As you drag, you carry a copied path with you.

- To delete a path, select the path with the Path Selection tool and press the Backspace key (Delete key on the Mac). You can also select a point on the path with the Direct Selection tool and press Backspace (Delete on the Mac) twice.

Using the Options Bar

Quite a few options appear on the Options bar when the Pen tool or Path Selection/Direct Selection tools are active. Here is the scoop on those options:

➤ The **Auto Add/Delete option** enables you to add or delete an anchor point with the regular Pen tool.

➤ **Show Bounding Box** places a box around the path, allowing you to transform the path. The bounding box isn't a path or part of your image. It is merely a visual guide to assist you in transformations. You can scale it by dragging the handles or rotate it by dragging just outside the box. Press Ctrl (⌘ on the Mac) and drag a handle or side to distort or skew the path. For more on transformations, see Book III, Chapter 3.

➤ The **path state buttons** (Add, Subtract, Intersect, and Exclude) combine all visible paths by adding, subtracting, intersecting, or excluding paths. Click your desired button to direct Photoshop on how to control the overlapping portions of the path(s) when you convert it to a selection. For example, clicking the Add button selects all areas whether or not they overlap. Clicking Intersect selects only the overlapping areas.

➤ The **Combine button** allows you to group paths together as a single unit. Select your desired paths and click the Combine button. When you select any one of the paths, all the paths within the group are selected as well.

➤ The **Align and Distribute buttons** align two or more paths and distribute three or more paths. The icons give you a good visual cue as to how the alignment or distribution will appear.

Chapter 3: Modifying and Transforming Selections and Paths

In This Chapter

- ✏ **Adding and subtracting from a selection**
- ✏ **Using the Select commands**
- ✏ **Feathering selections**
- ✏ **Moving and cloning a selection**
- ✏ **Transforming selections and paths**

*I*f you're like me, you may find it tough to get the perfect selection the first time around. I mean, all you need is one too many cups of coffee, and that Lasso tool seems to take on a mind of its own. That's okay. Photoshop is way too benevolent to leave you hanging with a mediocre selection. A multitude of techniques are available to modify and transform your selections. You can add or remove pixels from your selection, scale your selection outline, smooth out jagged edges, or switch what is selected for what isn't. Knowing how to clean up and modify your selections helps you to nail your desired element with precision.

If you haven't already thumbed through the first two chapters of Book III and gotten a good grasp of how to create selections by using the mighty Photoshop Tools palette, go ahead and browse those chapters now.

Achieving Selection Perfection

Although the selection tools, such as the Lasso and Magic Wand, usually do a pretty fair job at capturing the bulk of your selection, making a really accurate selection often requires another sort of tool — concentration. Give your selections a little extra attention, and you'll be amazed by the results. By adding and subtracting from the outline here and there, you can refine a selection and ensure that you capture only what you really want — and nothing that you don't.

The following few sections show you how to use keyboard shortcuts, along with your mouse, to make perfect selections. If you're not one for keyboard shortcuts, you can use the four selection option buttons on the Options bar to create a new selection, add to a selection, subtract from a selection, or intersect one selection with another. All you need to do is grab the selection tool of your choice, click the selection option button you want, and drag (or click if you're using the Magic Wand or Polygon Lasso tool).

When adding to a selection, a small plus sign appears next to your cursor. When subtracting from a selection, a small minus sign appears. When intersecting two selections, a small multiplication sign appears.

Adding to a selection

If your selection doesn't quite contain all the elements you want to capture, you need to add those portions to your current selection.

For you keyboarders, to add to a current selection, simply press the Shift key and drag around the pixels you want to include with the regular Lasso or the Rectangular or Elliptical Marquee tool. You can also press the Shift key and click the area you want with the Magic Wand tool.

To include an area with straight sides in your selection, you can press the Shift key and click around the area with the Polygon Lasso tool. And although you may not have much need to do it, you can also press the Shift key and click with the Single Column or Single Row Marquee tool. I wouldn't use the Magnetic Lasso tool to add to a selection; it's way too cumbersome.

You don't have to use the same tool to add to your selection that you used to create the original selection. Feel free to use whatever selection tool you think can get the job done. See Book III, Chapters 1 and 2 for details on selection tools and methods.

Here are the steps to use for adding to a circular selection:

1. **Make your initial elliptical selection. Select the larger circle with the Elliptical Marquee tool. Make sure and press the Alt key (Option on the Mac) to draw from the center out.**

   See the left image in Figure 3-1.

2. **To add the smaller circular area, first press the Shift key to add to the selection, and then press the Alt key (Option on the Mac) to draw from the center out.**

3. **Drag around the smaller selection with the Elliptical Marquee tool.**

   The resulting selection is shown in the example on the right in Figure 3-1.

Figure 3-1: The original selection appears on the left, and the selection after adding is on the right.

Subtracting from a selection

Just as you can add to a selection marquee, you can also subtract, or take a chunk out of a selection. To subtract from a current selection, press the Alt key (Option on the Mac) and drag around the pixels you want to subtract with the regular Lasso or the Rectangular or Elliptical Marquee tool.

Press the Alt key (Option on the Mac) and click the area you want to remove with the Magic Wand tool.

To subtract a straight-sided area, press the Alt key (Option on the Mac) and click around the area with the Polygon Lasso tool.

You can press the Alt key (Option on the Mac) and click with the Single Column or Single Row Marquee tool. The Single Column and Row Marquee tools come in handy when you want to get rid of just the very edge of a selection.

In the left example of Figure 3-2, I first selected the frame with the Polygon Lasso tool. I didn't use the obvious tool of choice — the Rectangular Marquee tool — because the frame was not completely straight. To deselect the inside of the frame from the selection, I pressed the Alt key (Option on the Mac) and clicked at each corner of the inside of the frame with the Polygon Lasso tool, resulting in the selection shown in the right example of Figure 3-2.

 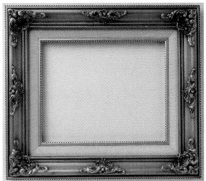

Figure 3-2: Press the Alt (Option on the Mac) to delete from your existing selection.

Intersecting two selections

What happens when you press the Shift and Alt (Option on the Mac) keys together? Not a collision, but an intersection. Pressing both keys while dragging with the Lasso or Marquee tool or clicking with the Magic Wand tool creates the intersection of the original selection with the second selection.

To retain only the part of an image where two selections overlap, press Shift and Alt (or Shift and Option on the Mac) and then drag.

You can select a portion of an image with a tool such as the Polygon Lasso tool. Then press the Shift and Alt (Option on the Mac) keys at the same time and drag with the Rectangular Marquee tool. The resulting intersection of the two selections appears.

Getting the Keys to Behave

Photoshop has a little glitch in its way of doing things. Well, not so much of a glitch as a conflict. With so many ways of doing things with Photoshop, somewhere along the line you may have to jigger with Photoshop to get it to do what you want. For example, how does Photoshop know whether you want to create a perfect square or add to a selection when you press the Shift key?

Let me lay this out for you:

- ✔ When you make an initial selection with the Rectangular or Elliptical Marquee tool, pressing the Shift key constrains the proportions of the selection, thereby allowing you to create a perfect square or a perfect circle.

- ✔ If you press Alt (Option on the Mac) with either of these tools, you can draw from the center out.

- ✔ If you press Alt (Option on the Mac) with the Lasso tool, the Lasso temporarily becomes the Polygon Lasso tool.

Unfortunately, despite numerous requests, the ability to read users' minds wasn't a Version CS2 upgrade feature. The following sections show you what you have to do to get Photoshop to recognize your wishes.

Adding a perfectly square or circular selection

To add a perfectly square or round selection to an existing selection, follow these steps:

1. **Press Shift and drag with the Rectangular or Elliptical Marquee tool.**

   Your selection is unconstrained.

2. **As you drag, keeping your mouse button pressed, release the Shift key for just a moment, and then press it again.**

   Your unconstrained selection suddenly snaps into a constrained square or circle.

3. **Release the mouse button before you release the Shift key.**

   If you don't release the mouse button before you release the Shift key, the selection shape reverts back to its unconstrained form.

Deleting from an existing selection while drawing from the center out

To delete part of a selection while drawing from the center out, follow these steps:

1. **Press Alt (Option on the Mac) and drag with the Rectangular or Elliptical Marquee tool.**

2. **As you drag, keeping your mouse button pressed, release the Alt (Option on the Mac) key for just a moment, and then press it again.**

**Book III
Chapter 3**

**Modifying and
Transforming
Selections and Paths**

You are now drawing from the center outward.

3. **Release the mouse button before you release the Alt (Option on the Mac) key.**

   See Figure 3-3.

TIP

Use this technique when you're selecting a doughnut, tire, inflatable swim ring, and other circular items with holes in the middle.

Using the Select Menu

Although you can add, subtract, and intersect selections with the Shift and Alt (Option on the Mac) keys and the selection option buttons on the Options bar, you can do much more with the commands on the Select menu, shown in Figure 3-4. Here you find ways to expand, contract, smooth, fuzz, and turn your selection inside out. You can also use this menu to automatically select similar colors and create selection borders. And I show you how to do this in the next few sections. With this kind of knowledge, imperfect selections will soon be a thing of the past.

Selecting all or nothing

The Select All and Deselect commands are pretty self-explanatory. To select everything in your image, choose Select⇨All. To deselect everything, choose Select⇨Deselect. The key commands Ctrl+A (⌘+A on the Mac) and Ctrl+D (⌘+D on the Mac), respectively, come in very handy and are easy to remember.

Figure 3-3: Deleting from an existing selection and drawing from the center out simultaneously is possible.

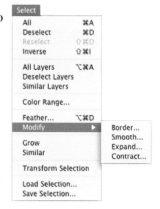

Figure 3-4: The commands on the Select menu.

REMEMBER

In most cases, you don't have to select everything in your image. If you don't have an active selection marquee, Photoshop naturally assumes to apply whatever command you execute to the entire image.

Deleting a straight-sided selection

If you have an existing selection, pressing Alt (Option on the Mac) with the Lasso tool subtracts from the selection. If you want to subtract a straight-sided selection from an existing selection, you can press Alt (Option on the Mac) and begin to drag. Then quickly release Alt (Option on the Mac) and then select the Polygon Lasso tool. But this can be tricky and is really unnecessary. I recommend just grabbing the Polygon Lasso tool itself to delete your straight-sided selection. Ditto for adding and getting intersections with straight-sided selections.

Reselecting a selection

If you have taken 20 minutes to carefully lasso a spiny sea anemone from its ocean home, the last thing you want is to lose your coveted selection marquee. But that is exactly what happens if you accidentally click the canvas when you have an active selection tool in hand. The selection marquee disappears.

Sure, you can choose Edit⇨Undo if you catch your mistake right away. And technically, you can access the History palette to recover your selection (see Book II, Chapter 4 for more on history). A much easier solution is to choose Select⇨Reselect. This command retrieves your last selection.

Besides immediately bringing back a selection you accidentally deselected, the Reselect command can come in handy if you decide to select an element again for a second time. For example, if you do such a great job retouching your spiny anemone that you decide to add, by cloning, another anemone to your image, go ahead. It's all up to you. By using the Reselect command, you can easily load the selection again rather than start the selection from scratch.

The Reselect command only works for the last selection you made, so don't plan to reselect a selection you made last week — or even ten minutes ago — if you've selected something else in the meantime.

Swapping a selection

**Book III
Chapter 3**

Modifying and Transforming Selections and Paths

Sometimes selecting what you don't want is easier than selecting what you do want. For example, if you're trying to select your pet dog, photographed against a neutral background, why spend valuable time meticulously selecting him with the Pen or Lasso tool, when you can just click the background with the Magic Wand tool? (Don't forget to use the Shift key to select bits of background you might have missed the first time.)

After you select the background, just choose Select⇨Inverse. Presto, you now have Fido the Retriever selected and obediently awaiting your next command, as shown in Figure 3-5.

Figure 3-5: Sometimes you want to select what you don't want and then inverse your selection.

Feathering a selection

In Book III, Chapter 1, I described how to *feather* (blur the edges) a selection when using the Lasso and Marquee tools by entering a value in the Feather box on the Options bar. This method of feathering requires that you set your Feather radius *before* you create your selection.

Unfortunately, using this method, a problem arises if you want to modify the initial selection. When you make a selection with a feather, the marquee outline of the selection adjusts to take into account the amount of the feather. That means that the resulting marquee outline doesn't resemble your precise mouse movement. As a result, modifying, adding, or subtracting from your original selection is pretty tough.

A much better way to feather a selection is to make your initial selection without a feather, as shown in the top image of Figure 3-6. Clean up your selection as you need to, and then apply your feather by choosing Select⇨ Feather. Enter a Feather Radius value and click OK. The resulting selection appears in the bottom image of Figure 3-6.

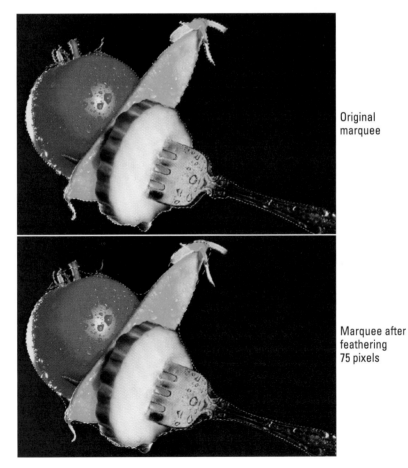

Original marquee

Marquee after feathering 75 pixels

Book III
Chapter 3

Modifying and
Transforming
Selections and Paths

Figure 3-6: Cleaning up your selection is easier prior to applying a feather.

The radius is how far out in all directions the feather extends. A radius of 8 means the feather extends 8 pixels to the right, left, up, and down from the selection outline. A large feather radius makes the image appear to fade out.

Using the Modify commands

The Select Modify menu contains a group of modification commands that are lumped categorically. With the exception of the Contract command, you probably won't use these options every day. But when you do use them, you'll find that they prove useful. Here is the lowdown on each command:

✔ **Border:** This command selects the area around the edge of the selection marquee. You specify the width of the area, from 1 to 200 pixels, and you get a border marquee, like the top image in Figure 3-7. Choose a foreground color, choose Edit➪Fill, pick Foreground Color from the Use drop-down list, and then click OK to fill your border with color, as shown in the bottom image in Figure 3-7. By the way, you can also achieve a similar look by choosing Edit➪Stroke.

As you can see in Figure 3-7, the Border command creates an anti-aliased (or soft-edged) selection.

Figure 3-7: The Border command creates a marquee from 1 to 200 pixels wide, which you can then fill with color.

✔ **Smooth:** If your selection marquee seems a bit ragged around the edges, try selecting the Smooth command to round off the nooks and crannies. Enter a sample radius value from 1 to 100 pixels. Photoshop examines each selected pixel and then includes or de-selects pixels in your selection based on the range specified by the radius amount. If most of the pixels are selected, Photoshop includes the strays; if most of the pixels are unselected, Photoshop removes the pixels. Start with 2 pixels and, if that doesn't seem like enough, increase it by a few more pixels or so.

Use this command with great caution. The results can be mushy, ill-defined selections.

✔ **Expand:** This command allows you to increase the size of your selection by a specified number of pixels, from 1 to 100. This command can come in handy if you just missed the edge of a circular selection and want to enlarge it, as shown in Figure 3-8.

✔ **Contract:** To shrink your selection by 1 to 100 pixels, choose Contract. I use this command a lot, in conjunction with the Feather command, when compositing multiple images.

After you make a selection, contract it and then feather it before you drag it onto the canvas. This technique helps to create a nice, natural-looking transition between the various images in your composite. The amount you decide to contract and feather varies according to the resolution of your images. For example, if you're using low-resolution (72 dpi) images, you may want to use 1 pixel for the Contract amount and 0.5 pixels for the Feather amount; higher resolution images may warrant 2 to 3 pixels for the Contract amount and 1 to 2 pixels for the Feather amount. (For more on compositing images, see Book V on layers.)

**Book III
Chapter 3**

**Modifying and
Transforming
Selections and Paths**

Figure 3-8: The Expand command increases your selection, enabling you to pick up missed pixels around the edges.

Applying the Grow and Similar commands

The Grow and Similar commands are close cousins to the Magic Wand tool. (For more on the Wand and Tolerance, check out Book III, Chapter 1.) If you're familiar with the modus operandi of the Magic Wand tool, you know that you rarely get the perfect selection on the first click. That's because you are making an intelligent guess as to what Tolerance setting picks up the pixels you want.

The Grow command compensates a little for the Magic Wand tool's inaccuracy. For example, if you need to include more in your selection, you can increase the Tolerance setting and try again — press Shift and click the area you need to include. Or you can choose Select➪Grow. The Grow command increases the size of the selection by including adjacent pixels that fall within the range of Tolerance.

The Similar command is like Grow, only the pixels don't have to be adjacent to be selected. The command searches throughout the image and picks up pixels within the Tolerance range, wherever they may fall.

Both commands use the Tolerance value that is displayed on the Options bar when you have the Magic Wand tool selected. Adjust the Tolerance setting to include more or fewer colors by increasing or decreasing the setting, respectively.

Moving and Cloning Selections

When you have your selection refined to the ultimate in perfection, you may then want to move it or clone it. To move a selection, simply grab the Move tool (the four-headed arrow) at the top right of the Tools palette, and then drag the selection.

Sounds easy enough, right? When you move the selection, however, be warned that the area where the selection used to reside is now filled with the background color, as shown in Figure 3-9. This is provided, of course, that you are moving both the selection outline and the image pixels. You can move just the selection outline (without the pixels), as I explain in an upcoming section. Also note that if you are moving a selection on a layer, you are left with transparent pixels. When you use the Move tool, your cursor icon changes to a pair of scissors, letting you know that you are cutting out the selection.

Figure 3-9: When moving a selection with the Move tool, you leave a hole that reveals the background color.

Cloning

If the idea of leaving a big hole in your image doesn't appeal to you, you can copy and move the selection, leaving the original image intact, as shown in Figure 3-10. Just press Alt (Option on the Mac) and drag with the Move tool. This action is often referred to as *cloning* because you're essentially making a duplicate of a selected area and then moving that duplicate elsewhere.

Figure 3-10: Press the Alt (Option on the Mac) to clone your selection and not leave a nasty hole.

When cloning, your cursor icon changes to a double-headed arrow, notifying you that you are duplicating the selection. If you want to move your selection in small increments (1 pixel), press your arrow keys while you have the Move tool selected. Press Shift along with an arrow key to move 10 pixels. And of course, adding the Alt (Option on the Mac) key to the key commands allows you to clone a selection while you move it.

You can temporarily access the Move tool by pressing the Ctrl (⌘ on the Mac) key when you have any tool selected, except for the Hand tool, pen tools, slice tools, Path Selection tool, Direct Selection tool, and shape tools. Likewise, press Alt (Option) along with Ctrl (⌘) with any of these tools to clone and move a selection.

Moving the selection outline, but not the pixels

If all you want to do is move the selection marquee without moving the pixels underneath, you want to avoid using the Move tool. Instead, grab any selection tool — the marquee tools, the lasso tools, or the Magic Wand tool — and then click inside the marquee and just drag. That way you move only the outline of the element, not the element itself. You can also use the arrow keys to nudge a selection marquee.

You can move and clone selections within a single image or among multiple images. To move a selection from one image to another, choose Edit➪Cut, activate the second image, and choose Edit➪Paste. To clone a selection, simply drag the selection with the Move tool from one image window and drop it onto another image window.

Transforming Pixels

After you perfectly select your element, you may find you need to resize or reorient that element. *Transforming* involves the scaling, rotating, skewing, distorting, warping, flipping, or adjusting of the perspective of your pixels. Although you may consider the distortions on the Transform menu somewhat mundane when compared to the fun and flashy Liquify command (which I describe in Book VII, Chapter 3), I'm sure you'll find them a lot more practical and useful in your daily digital-imaging chores.

Here's how to transform a selection:

1. **Create your selection.**

   I'll leave this task up to you; just use your now well-honed selection expertise.

   You can also apply transformations to a layer or to multiple layers (for more on this topic, see Book V).

2. **Choose Edit➪Transform.**

   If all you want is a single transformation, this command is adequate. However, if you want multiple transformations, you're wise to stick with the Free Transform command, which I cover later in this section.

3. **Choose a transformation type from the submenu, as shown in Figure 3-11:**

Figure 3-11: The Transform submenu offers a variety of transformation options.

- **Scale:** Increases or decreases the size of your selection

- **Rotate:** Freely rotates your selection in either direction

- **Skew:** Distorts your selection on a given axis

- **Distort:** Distorts your selection with no restrictions on an axis

- **Perspective:** Applies a one-point perspective to your selection

- **Warp:** This new option is like a mini-Liquify command where you can distort your selection by manipulating a mesh grid that overlays on your image

- **Rotate 180°, 90° CW (Clockwise), or 90° CCW (Counterclockwise):** Rotates the selection by specified amounts

- **Flip Horizontal or Vertical:** Flips your selection along the vertical and horizontal axes, respectively

As soon as you select your desired distortion and release the mouse button, a box called the *bounding box,* or *transform box,* surrounds your selection, complete with handles on the sides and corners. Note that you don't get a bounding box with the Flip transformation (which just gets applied to your image).

4. **Depending on which transformation type you chose in Step 3, drag a handle.**

- **Scale:** Corner handles work best for this transformation. Press Shift to scale proportionately. Press Alt (Option on the Mac) to scale from the center.

- **Rotate:** Move your cursor outside the bounding box. When the cursor becomes a curved arrow, drag CW or CCW. Press Shift to rotate in 15-degree increments.

- **Skew:** Drag a side handle.

- **Distort:** Drag a corner handle.

- **Perspective:** Drag a corner handle.

- **Warp:** Drag any control point or line on the default custom mesh grid to distort your selection. In fact, you can pretty much drag anywhere on the image, even in between mesh lines, to apply the warp. You cannot, however, add or delete control points.

With the new Warp transformation you have some additional options. On the Options bar, you find a drop-down menu with various warping styles such as arch, wave, and twist. In fact, these are the same styles you find on the Warp Text menu (see Book IV, Chapter 3). When you choose one of the styles, Photoshop then applies the mesh grid for that style. Here is the lowdown on the remaining options:

- **Change the warp orientation:** Change the direction of some styles, such as wave, flag, and fish.

- **Bend:** Increase the value to increase the distortion.

- **H% and V%:** Increase the percentages to increase the Horizontal (H) and Vertical (V) distortions.

- **High Quality:** Keep this option checked to enable Photoshop to use a more detailed and complex algorithm when interpolating image data.

- **Switch between free transform and warp mode:** Click this button to switch between the Free Transform box and the Warp mesh grid.

Choosing Rotate 180°, 90° CW, or 90° CCW or Flip Horizontal or Vertical just executes the command. Handle-dragging isn't necessary.

Photoshop executes all the transformations, except warp, around a point called the *reference point*. The reference point appears in the center of the transform box by default.

You can move the center point anywhere you want, even outside the bounding box. In addition, you can set your own reference point for the transformation by clicking a square on the reference point locator on the Options bar. Each square corresponds with a point on the bounding box.

5. **You can choose a second transformation type from the Edit⇨Transform submenu, if desired.**

If you're an ultraprecise type of person, you can also numerically transform the selection by entering values on the Options bar.

In Figure 3-12, I executed all the transformations at the same time.

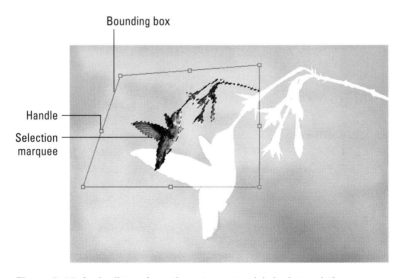

Bounding box

Handle

Selection marquee

Figure 3-12: Apply all transformations at once to minimize interpolation.

Be sure to execute all your transformations in one fell swoop if possible. In other words, don't scale a selection now and then five minutes later rotate it and then five minutes later distort it, because every time you apply a transformation to an image, you are putting it through an interpolation process. You want to limit how many times you interpolate an image because it has a degrading effect — your image starts to appear soft and mushy. Only flipping or rotating in 90-degree increments is interpolation free. For more on interpolation, see Book II, Chapter 1.

6. **After you transform your selection to your liking, do one of the following: Double-click inside the bounding box; click the Commit button on the Options bar; or press Enter (Return on the Mac).**

   To cancel the transformation, press Esc or click the Cancel button on the Options bar.

   Your image is now magically transformed. Note that if your image isn't on a layer, you can leave a hole filled with the background color after your image is transformed. Check out Book V to avoid this calamity.

To repeat a transformation, choose Edit⇨Transform⇨Again.

Transforming Selection Marquees

To transform just the selection marquee without affecting the underlying pixels, make your desired selection and then choose Select⇨Transform Selection. Photoshop doesn't have a submenu with individual transformations to choose from. Instead, you must apply the transformations like you do with the Free Transform command: by using the keyboard shortcuts. You can also enter values on the Options bar to transform numerically, or you can access the context menu. To move the selection marquee and the bounding box, simply drag inside the marquee or nudge it by using the keyboard arrow keys. Transforming selections is particularly handy when you're trying to select elliptical objects. Getting a precise selection the first time around is often hard, so applying a transformation is often necessary. For example, in Figure 3-13, I scaled, rotated, and distorted the marquee around my clock to get a more accurate selection.

Figure 3-13: You can easily transform a selection marquee without affecting underlying pixels.

Book III Chapter 3

Modifying and Transforming Selections and Paths

Distorting selected pixels with Free Transform

The Transform menu isn't the only way to distort selected pixels. A much more efficient way is to use the Free Transform command, also on the Edit menu. Like the Transform command, the Free Transform command surrounds your selection with a bounding box. Within the bounding box, you can scale, rotate, skew, distort, or apply perspective without having to choose the individual distortions. You just have to use the right keyboard shortcuts. To scale and rotate, use the same method as the Transform commands. Here's the scoop on the rest:

- **Skew:** Ctrl+Shift+drag (⌘+Shift+drag on the Mac) on a side handle.

- **Distort:** Ctrl+drag (⌘+drag on the Mac) on any handle.

- **Perspective:** Ctrl+Shift+Alt+drag (⌘+Shift+ Option+drag on the Mac) on a corner handle.

Unfortunately, if you want to rotate by degree while free transforming, you need to enter the numeric values of your desired rotation on the Options bar.

Transforming Paths

After the bounding box is around the path, the transformation technique for paths is the same as it is for selections and selection marquees, except that you can apply the distort, perspective, and warp commands only to whole paths. The major difference between transforming paths and selections is in how you first select the path.

All paths

To select all paths:

1. **Choose Window⇨Paths.**

2. **Click the pathname in the Paths palette.**

3. **Choose Edit⇨Transform Path and choose your desired transformation from the submenu.**

   You can also choose Edit⇨Free Transform Path.

Single path

To select a single path:

1. **Choose Window⇨Paths.**

2. **Click the pathname in the Paths palette.**

3. **Choose the Path Selection tool.**

4. **Click the path with the Path Selection tool.**

5. **Choose Edit⇨Transform Path and choose your desired transformation from the submenu.**

   You can also choose Edit⇨Free Transform Path. In Figure 3-14, I transformed the path by rotating it.

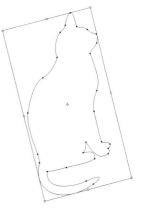

Figure 3-14: Apply transformations to paths.

Part of a path

To select part of a path:

1. **Choose Window⇨Paths.**

2. **Click the pathname in the Paths palette.**

3. **Choose the Direct Selection tool.**

4. **Select the points you want with the Direct Selection tool.**

5. **Choose Edit⇨Transform Points and choose your desired transformation from the submenu.**

Book III
Chapter 3

Modifying and
Transforming
Selections and Paths

Putting It Together

Removing a Person (Without Getting in Trouble with the Law)

Sometimes you may want to take an element out of a picture so that you can maintain the viewer's focus on something else. Or maybe you just don't want the element in the image. But remember, if you simply delete an unwanted element without cloning, you leave a huge space (colored with the background color) where the element was. Not smooth.

In the following steps, I show you how to seamlessly remove an unwanted element (in this case, a person) from an image.

continued

continued

When you first attempt this technique, start with an image that has an element that isn't physically attached to something that you want to keep in the image.

1. **Open an image that contains something that you want to remove.**

2. **Use the selection tool of your choice to select the element that you want to remove.**

   In this step, you're creating a selection marquee that you use to clone another area of the image.

   You don't have to be super-precise, so feel free to grab the Lasso tool. If you need a Lasso refresher, see Book III, Chapter 1. When you make your selection, be careful not to cut off any portion of your element. Otherwise, you leave some stray pixels — a dead giveaway that something was once there. Using the Lasso tool, I made a rough outline around the little boy, as shown in the following figure.

Selection marquee

3. **Position your cursor inside the selection marquee, press the mouse button and then the Shift key, and drag your selection to move it horizontally (or vertically if the image warrants it) to an area of the photo that you want to clone.**

   Notice how the selection marquee, shown in the following figure, is the only thing that I moved.

Area to be cloned

4. **With the Move tool selected, position your cursor inside the selection marquee, press Alt+Shift (Option+Shift on the Mac), and then drag to move the cloned area on top of the element that you're removing. Carefully match up the edges, release your mouse button, and then release the Alt and Shift keys (Option and Shift on the Mac).**

5. **Choose Select⇨Deselect.**

   The cloned area now covers the element that you want to remove, as shown in the following figure. In the example, the beach/ocean selection now covers the little boy.

Cloned area covers boy

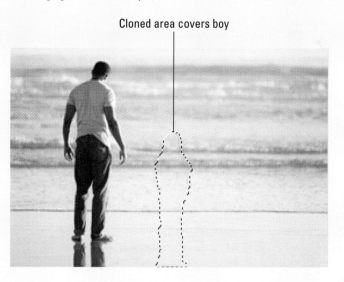

continued

Book III
Chapter 3

Modifying and
Transforming
Selections and Paths

continued

Depending on your image, you may want to choose Select➪Feather and enter 1 or 2 pixels before you move the cloned area. Doing this softens the edges and smoothes out the transition between the cloned area and the background. (See the section, "Feathering a selection," in this chapter for more on feathering.) I didn't feather my selection because it didn't really need it. Try it both ways to see which looks better. Use the History palette to undo your steps, if necessary (see Book II, Chapter 4 for more on the History palette).

The final step is to clean up any telltale signs that the element was there.

6. **Choose the Clone Stamp tool and select a medium-size feathered brush from the Brushes palette, press Alt (Option on the Mac), and click a good area next to a flaw; release Alt (Option) and then click the flaw.**

If the Clone Stamp is a mystery to you, be sure to check out Book VIII, Chapter 3.

Repeat this step until you fix all the flaws and the clone blends in seamlessly with the background. Don't get carried away with the Clone Stamp tool, or you end up with a smudgy mess. Being light-handed is a good thing, as I was in the now retouched image. Nobody can tell that only one man stands where two people once stood.

Book IV

Painting, Drawing, and Typing

The 5th Wave — By Rich Tennant

©RICHTENNANT

Jeez-that's impressive! Let's see that airbrush effect again.

*L*ike a Swiss Army knife, Photoshop does it all. This book describes all you need to know about Photoshop's drawing and painting tools. I first give you the lowdown on the ubiquitous brush. The brush — which is found not only in the Brush tool itself, but within several other painting and editing tools — has more variations than you can shake a stick at. I also cover how to create vector shapes with the Shape tools and how to fill and stroke your selections with color. If one color is not enough, keep reading until you get to the section on gradients and patterns. I give you the steps for using the many Photoshop presets and also for creating your own gradients and patterns. And because man doesn't communicate by images alone, you can find lots of useful information about creating type. Not just regular old run-of-the-mill type, mind you (which is covered of course), but type on a path, type with shadows and bevels, type filled with images, type warped into shapes — you get the . . . um . . . picture.

Chapter 1: Painting and Drawing with Photoshop

In This Chapter

✓ **Making pencil sketches and brush strokes**

✓ **Using Brush presets**

✓ **Managing brushes with the Brushes palette**

✓ **Understanding vectors**

✓ **Creating basic and custom shapes**

✓ **Setting geometry options**

*Y*ou're definitely going to want to brush up on your painting and drawing techniques now that you don't have to worry about messing up your clothes. Painting is one of the basic skills you need to work in Photoshop. After you master the art of painting strokes and working with brushes, you're well on your way to mastering more advanced techniques, such as masking, which benefit from strong painting skills. (I introduce the full range of brush tools in Book I, Chapter 2.)

Going hand in hand with painting, of course, is drawing. Photoshop's shape tools add an important dimension to your drawing capabilities. This chapter introduces you to a plethora of tools and techniques. I start with painting and then move on to drawing. Embrace both and they can serve you well.

Introducing the Pencil and Brush Tools

The Pencil and Brush tools are like peanut butter and chocolate. Not only do they work well together, but they also share many important traits. Just as important, however, are their differences. You can access these tools in the Tools palette. Press B, and the Brush tool appears by default. To access the Pencil, press Shift+B. You can toggle between the tools by pressing Shift+B again. Find out more about using these tools in the following sections.

Finding out what the Pencil tool does

The Pencil and Brush tools are very much alike, except that the Pencil tool has hard edges by default (as shown in Figure 1-1) and the Brush tool can have soft, feathered edges. The Pencil tool also has the ability to erase itself!

Figure 1-1: The Pencil tool draws hard-edged strokes and is perfect for digital sketches.

You can do all the following with the Pencil tool:

- Drag the mouse to draw freehand lines.

- Click at one point, release the mouse button, and then Shift+click at a second point to draw a straight line between the points. As long as you keep the Shift key depressed, you can keep clicking to draw straight lines between each of the points.

- Press the Alt key (the Option key on the Mac) and click in any area of your drawing to switch the foreground color to that hue.

The Pencil tool also offers the Auto Erase option, which you activate from the Options bar at the top. Auto Erase is a handy feature that lets you remove portions of your pencil strokes without switching to the Eraser tool. When you have Auto Erase turned on, the operation of the Pencil tool is slightly different from the default. The effect of either of the following actions is that Photoshop erases lines you've drawn:

✔ When you click in any area of the drawing other than an area that is foreground colored (for example, the pencil lines you've already drawn), the Pencil tool begins drawing a line in the foreground color (this is the default mode).

✔ When you click in any area of the drawing that is foreground colored (such as the pencil lines you've drawn), the Pencil tool draws by using the background color.

Because the Pencil tool doesn't use soft-edged lines to draw, anything other than straight vertical or horizontal lines has rough, jagged edges, as shown in the close-up image in Figure 1-2. *Jaggies* aren't objectionable in some cases, especially in higher resolution images, but if you zoom in on an area containing pencil lines, the jaggies are readily apparent. I show you how to modify the characteristics of the lines drawn with the Pencil tool later in this chapter in "Working with the Brushes palette."

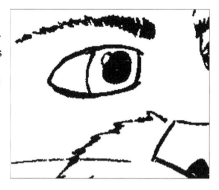

Figure 1-2: Zooming in on hard-edged strokes displays jagged edges.

Using the Pencil tool

If you're ready to start using the Pencil tool, keep in mind that lines that aren't vertical or horizontal look jagged up close. But this doesn't necessarily pose a problem in all cases, especially when working with Web graphics. Those same hard edges can lend themselves to producing crisp edged images for display in a browser window. To try out the Pencil tool, work your way through these steps:

1. **Activate the Pencil tool by choosing it from the Tools palette. (It shares a flyout menu with the Brush tool.)**

   You can press Shift+B to make it appear if it's hidden underneath the Brush tool.

   The Pencil tool's current brush tip (usually the 1-pixel brush unless you select something else) is shown in the Brush Preset picker on the Options bar.

   Click the arrow in the Brush box to summon the Brush Preset picker palette if you want to choose a different-sized pencil tip.

2. **If you want to draw using anything other than Normal mode, choose a mode from the Mode options menu.**

   Modes other than Normal cause colors to interact and blend in different ways. You can find more about modes in Book V, Chapter 3.

3. Choose an opacity for your pencil strokes.

If you want whatever is in the background to show partially through your strokes, choose an opacity of less than 100 percent by using the slider or by typing an opacity percentage directly into the text box.

4. Click and drag with the mouse to create your pencil lines.

Painting with the Brush tool

The Brush tool is a basic tool used throughout Photoshop in various incarnations, so you'll want to master its use as quickly as possible.

The most important difference between the Brush and the Pencil tools is that, by default, the Brush tool produces soft-edged lines that Photoshop renders smoother by a process known as *anti-aliasing*. This technique substitutes partially filled pixels along the edges of lines to produce the illusion of gradual fading. Our eyes merge the transparent pixels together, so the line looks smooth rather than hard-edged.

Although jaggy edges are most apparent in diagonal lines, Photoshop applies anti-aliasing to brush stroke edges even in horizontal and vertical lines. The fuzzier the brush, the more semi-filled pixels used to produce the effect, as you can see in Figure 1-3.

The Brush tool shares most of the basic features found in the Pencil tool, except the Auto Erase feature is not available:

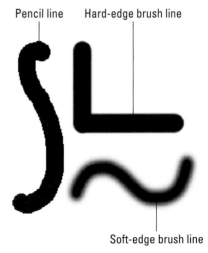

Figure 1-3: Strokes from the Pencil and Brush vary in the softness of their edges.

- ✔ Activate the Brush tool from the Tools palette or by pressing B (or Shift+B if you used the Pencil tool last).

- ✔ Choose a brush tip from the Brush Preset picker on the Options bar.

- ✔ Select a mode and opacity from the options on the Options bar.

- ✔ Drag to paint, click and Shift+click to paint straight lines, and press the Shift key while dragging to constrain the Brush tool to horizontal or vertical lines.

- ✔ Press the Alt key (the Option key on the Mac) and click in any area of color to switch the foreground color to that color.

The Brush tool has several other options to select from:

- **Flow:** *Flow* determines how quickly the Brush tool applies the paint. You can set a flow rate from 1 to 100 percent by using the Flow slider or by typing a percentage directly into the text box. You might think of it as controlling how wet or liquid the paint is. At low flow rates, Photoshop applies the paint slowly so the color is not as dark; at higher flow rates, the paint quickly reaches its full strength as you drag.

- **Airbrush:** Click the Airbrush button on the Options bar to switch the Brush tool (as well as many of the other tools that use brush tips) to Airbrush mode. This mode produces the spray effect you get with a traditional airbrush. The longer you hold down the mouse button, the more paint that pumps out of the tool, and the wider the airbrush effect spreads, as shown in Figure 1-4.

- **Toggle the Brushes Palette:** At the far right of the Options bar is a button (a palette icon) that shows or hides the Brushes palette. It's a quick way to access this valuable palette, and is also available with the Pencil tool and other tools that use brush tips. I show you how to use the Brushes palette later in this chapter.

Figure 1-4: Using the Airbrush option with the Brush tool enables you to create smoky strokes.

Working with the Brushes palette

You'll find the Brushes palette extremely useful for changing the characteristics of preset brush tips and for creating your own. You can also access and select brush presets, as I discuss later in this chapter.

You can view the Brushes palette in several ways:

- Choose Window⇨Brushes from the menu bar.
- Click the Brushes palette tab in the Palette Well.
- Click the Brushes palette button on the right side of the Options bar.
- Press F5 to toggle the Brushes palette open or closed.
- Grab the Brushes palette's tab and drag it out of the Palette Well and onto your Photoshop desktop. This mode keeps the Brushes palette visible until you put it away by dragging it back to the Palette Well, clicking its close box, or rendering it hidden with Window⇨Brushes.

The Brushes palette displays a list of brush properties on the left and includes a brush stroke preview at the bottom of the palette.

The largest pane in the dialog box is the upper-right area that shows various types of information, such as the size and type of brush tip, or the different controls offered for any of the twelve different properties you can set.

Click the Brush Presets label in the upper-left. The various preset previews appear in the right panel.

Choosing a brush tip shape

When you have Brush Tip Shape selected in the left column of the Brushes palette, a scrolling box shows the available brush tips, as shown in Figure 1-5. You can use the palette pop-up menu to choose various views, including text only, small and large thumbnails, small and large lists, and stroke thumbnail. (To access the pop-up menu, click the triangle in the upper-right of the palette.)

The twelve brush parameters that you can choose to apply and edit are arrayed in the left column. You can select any of these options to apply them to the currently selected brush. Select an option to edit its characteristics. Note that you must select the parameter name to access the options. Toggling the parameter on by checking the check box doesn't work. Here are the characteristics for Brush Tip Shape:

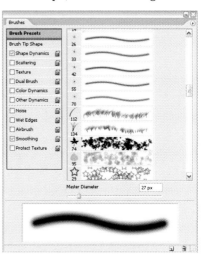

Figure 1-5: The Brushes palette offers a multitude of different brush tips.

- ✏ **Shape Dynamics:** These controls include the amount of jitter (randomness or variation) produced when you draw a stroke, amount of fade, the size, the jitter angle, the roundness, and other options. The higher the value, the greater the amount of variance for each option. Some of these apply only when you are using a pressure-sensitive digital tablet. Check your digital tablet's instruction manual for more information on how to customize brushes for your tablet. The Flip X and Flip Y jitter option flips the brush shape across the horizontal axis (X) or the vertical axis (Y). For example, if your brush shape is an L shape and you select Flip X, your brush shape is a backwards L. Check Flip Y and your brush shape is an upside down L shape. Check both and it's an upside-down, backwards L shape.

- ✏ **Scattering:** This parameter controls the amount and position of brush marks in a stroke. The higher the value, the higher the number of brush marks and the farther apart they are. When you have Both Axes selected,

Photoshop distributes the brush marks radially, as if on a curve. The Count controls the number of brush marks at each spacing point. The higher the value, the greater the number of marks.

✔ **Texture:** This control allows you to impart a texture pattern (using the foreground color) to a brush stroke, either one of Photoshop's preset textures or one of your design. Select Invert to reverse the light and dark pixels in the pattern. Scale sizes the pattern in each stroke. Texture Each Tip renders each tip as it is stroked, giving a more saturated effect. Depth controls how prominent the pattern appears against the brush stroke. Minimum Depth specifies the minimum depth that the paint of each stroke shows through the pattern. Mode lets you choose one of Photoshop's blending modes, as I describe in Book V, Chapter 3. You can find more about creating and working with patterns in Book III, Chapter 3.

✔ **Dual Brush:** You can use two tips to draw with a single brush. This option lets you select the characteristics of the second tip by using the same type of attributes — such as diameter, spacing, and scatter — applied to the first tip. You can also specify a blending mode between the two tips.

✔ **Color Dynamics:** This control uses your foreground and background colors to adjust how the color varies during a stroke, allowing you to create a multicolored brush. Slight variations give the stroke a more natural, organic look. You can introduce slight (or major) jitter to the hue, saturation, brightness, and purity of the colors, as well as some randomness between the foreground and background colors as you draw a stroke. Without color dynamics, the stroke color remains constant.

✔ **Other Dynamics:** These introduce randomness into the opacity and flow factors of a brush, again making the brush stroke look more natural and less machine-generated. You'll want to experiment with all the dynamics to see exactly how they can affect your image. Note that the Flow and Opacity settings in the Brushes palette do not override those settings on the Options bar.

Here's a list of brush tip characteristics, which you also find on the left side of the Brushes palette:

✔ **Noise:** Adds random pixels to brush tips, giving them texture and an organic quality. This option is more apparent in feathered brushes.

✔ **Wet Edges:** The brush tip leaves a stroke that looks more like watercolor, with paint building up along the edges.

✔ **Airbrush:** Gives the brush tip a soft, airbrushed look.

✔ **Smoothing:** Smoothes out the curves when drawing arcs with the brush. Again, this option is more noticeable when you use a pressure-sensitive drawing tablet.

✔ **Protect Texture:** Ensures that all brush tips that use a texture use the same texture. This allows you to switch back and forth between brush tips while painting and still achieve a consistent texture.

Book IV Chapter 1

Painting and Drawing with Photoshop

Figure 1-6 shows the range of possibilities these options offer.

You can lock any of the brush characteristics by clicking the small lock icon to the right of the characteristic. This ensures that the settings don't change after you have your brush just so. This works especially well if you want the size of your brush to be correlated with the amount of pressure you apply to a stylus when using a drawing tablet. By locking settings, you override any specifications set by preset brushes. You can choose the Reset All Locked Settings option from the Brushes palette pop-up menu to bring back the default settings of the brush. And finally, to clear all brush options, select Clear Brush Controls from the Brushes palette pop-up menu.

If you really like a brush that you have created, feel free to save it as a preset that you can access again and again. Simply choose New Brush Preset from the pop-up menu on the Brushes palette or from the Brushes drop-down palette on the Options bar.

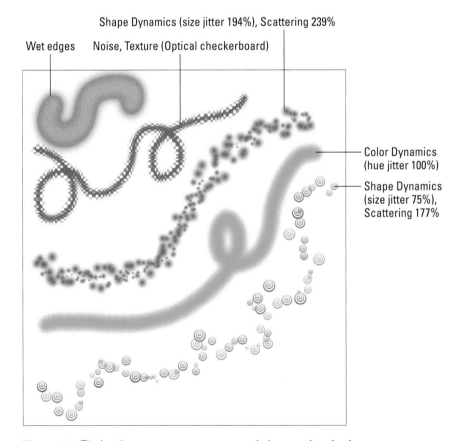

Figure 1-6: The brushes you can create are as varied as your imagination.

Using the preset brushes

Photoshop has two brush palettes, in a sense. In addition to the Brushes palette, there is the Brush Preset picker, shown in Figure 1-7. It is tucked away on the Options bar and appears when you click the down-pointing triangle next to the box that displays the currently active brush tip.

Photoshop has a large number of predesigned brush presets that you can use. The default set includes six round, hard-edged brushes (which still have softer edges than the Pencil tool) and a group of twelve round soft-edged brushes. There are also airbrush, spatter, and natural media brush tip presets, as well as a group of brush tip shapes such as stars, leaves, and other shapes. And Photoshop CS2 has even more brush libraries, so go crazy.

Figure 1-7: The Brush Preset picker offers a mini Brushes palette for quick and simplified access to brush tips.

A preset brush's pixel diameters are shown as text below a thumbnail image of the brush shape when the palette's display is in default mode. To use one of these brush tips, just click the Brush Preset picker arrow on the Options bar and choose the tip you want from the scrolling preset list. You can augment your choices with any of the following options:

✒ Move the Master Diameter slider to change the diameter of the selected brush. This is a quick way of getting a slightly larger or smaller brush when none of the presets meet your needs exactly. For example, the largest hard-edged brush preset is 19 pixels in diameter. You can click this brush tip and move the slider to the right to get a hard-edged brush in any size up to 2500 pixels.

To change the brush size from the keyboard when a tool is active, press the] key (the right bracket) to increase the size and the] key (the left bracket) to decrease the size. The amount of change varies according to the initial size of the brush. To adjust the size more dramatically, continue to press the bracket key.

✔ Choose the Use Sample Size option to get brush strokes of equal size. Depending on the size settings in your Shape Dynamics characteristics, when you use a scatter brush, such as a fish or flower, you get random variations in sizes. Select the Use Sample Size option before you use the brush to get a consistently sized stroke every time based on a preset sample size. Note that you must select the option each time you use the brush and you must also click, not drag, the brush for each individual stroke to be equally sized.

✔ Choose any of the libraries of additional brush tip presets provided with Photoshop. Click the Brush Preset picker's pop-up menu and choose one of the other brush libraries shown at the bottom. They have names like Special Effect Brushes and Faux Finish Brushes. Select one to append the brushes to your current set or to replace the current set with the library you select (a dialog box appears that offers a choice of either action).

You can also manage brush tip libraries by using the Preset Manager. See Book I, Chapter 5 for information on using the Preset Manager.

✔ Select your own custom library of brush tips that you've created. Click Load Brushes to append new brushes to your current collection or to replace them with the new library.

✔ If the Hardness option is available, adjust the slider to make the brush more (higher) or less (lower) fuzzy.

In addition to the presets Photoshop offers, you can create your own presets to use when you need them. Book I, Chapter 2 explains how to create your own presets.

Viewing preset brushes

You can change the way brushes are shown in the Brushes Preset picker and Brushes palette by choosing a viewing mode from the picker's or palette's pop-up menus:

✔ **Text Only:** This displays the names of the brush tips in several columns (depending on how wide you've made the pop-up palette).

✔ **Small Thumbnail:** This is the default view, with a thumbnail image of the brush tip and its diameter in pixels.

✓ **Large Thumbnail:** This view provides a closer look at the brush tip.

✓ **Small list:** This view shows a single-column list of the brush tips with their text names.

✓ **Large list:** The larger list adds thumbnails so you can see the brush shape.

✓ **Stroke thumbnail:** This view shows a typical ess stroke by using the selected brush so you can see how it looks when applied.

Putting It Together

Colorizing Black-and-White Images

Just as there are valid artistic reasons for shooting a photo in black and white, there are equally reasonable rationales for changing a grayscale image into a color one. Perhaps the picture is an old one, taken before color film was widely used, and you'd like to colorize it. Or you may come across a monochrome image that would look even better in color. Photoshop lets you restore black-and-white pictures to their original colors or create whole new color schemes. If you can imagine an image in color, use Photoshop to add the hues you want to see.

IT Stock Free

Book IV
Chapter 1

Painting and
Drawing with
Photoshop

continued

continued

In my example, which you can find on this book's Web site (see the Introduction for details), I chose a black-and-white photo of an adorable boy. Instead of a full-color treatment that attempts to duplicate a color photograph, I want to apply a technique that mimics the hand-colored look of the venerable Marshall's Photo Coloring System of pigments, photo oils, spot colors, retouch pencils, and other products so popular in the '50s and '60s and enjoying a rebirth today. Although I've worked with a Marshall's kit myself, Photoshop is a lot faster, easier, and way less messier.

1. **Open a grayscale image in Photoshop.**

2. **Choose Image⇨Mode⇨RGB Color to convert the grayscale image to a full color image (even though it presently still lacks any color).**

3. **Choose Layer⇨New Layer.**

   This creates a new transparent layer to paint on. Although you can paint directly on an image layer or a copy of an image layer, using an empty layer is safer and gives you more flexibility in backtracking when you make a mistake. For more information on working with layers, consult Book V.

4. **In the New Layer dialog box that appears, name the layer.**

   You can paint all your colors on a single layer, but you may find that using a separate layer for each part of the face lets you fade that color in and out as required to blend smoothly with your other hues.

5. **Select the Color mode from the Blend Mode drop-down list in the Layers palette, shown in the figure.**

   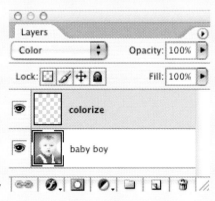

   Photoshop uses this mode to combine the painting layer with the image layer, enabling you to apply color while retaining the details of the underlying image.

6. **Select a color you want to apply from the Swatches palette. Use the Color palette to mix your own.**

   You find information on color in Book II, Chapter 3.

7. **Select the Brush tool in the Tools palette.**

8. **Click the down arrow next to the Brush Preset picker on the Options bar and choose a brush from the list.**

   Hard-edged brushes appear first and the soft-edged brushes follow. I would start with a soft-edged brush.

   The Airbrush option on the Options bar creates a very subtle and soft effect. Just be sure you pick the kind of brush that works best for the area of the picture you're colorizing. (Use a small, fuzzy brush for smaller areas, and use a bigger, sharper brush for more defined lines and wider areas.)

9. **Paint all the parts of the image where you want to apply color.**

   If you make a mistake, you can erase the bad strokes without affecting the underlying grayscale image because you're painting on a separate layer.

   In my example, I chose a nice, light blue color to change the color of the boy's eyes, shown in the figure. A small fuzzy brush is perfect for a small area such as the eyes.

   Change brushes as necessary by clicking the Brush Preset picker on the Options bar and choosing a larger or smaller brush.

   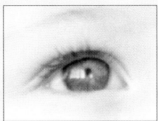

10. **When you finish with that area of the image, create a new layer for each of the main components of the photograph and repeat Steps 4 through 9 with an additional color.**

    I painted the eyes, lips, cheeks, hair, and hair highlights separately because creating natural, subtle effects with people's skin, hair, and eyes takes a special touch:

    - **Eyes:** When painting the eyes, paint only the irises and leave the pupils their original black color. Don't paint over the catchlights in the eyes, either. (*Catchlights* are reflections of light sources, such as windows or the flash.)

    - **Lips:** Color the inner surface of the lips a darker, rosier pink than the outer surface. Lips look best when portrayed in at least two shades. Don't forget to color the gums with an even lighter pink.

    - **Hair:** Hair looks best when the highlights and darker portions are slightly different colors.

    - **Cheeks:** To put a little blush in the cheeks, choose the Airbrush option on the Options bar and work with a relatively large brush size. Apply a good dash of color to each cheek, and a lighter bit of color to the forehead and chin. (I used a 300-pixel brush for this high resolution image.)

    I left the clothes and background uncolored to emphasize the focal point is the boy's face.

11. **For the overall skin tone, I chose a different technique using the Hue/Saturation command. This technique works especially well with those who have naturally dark complexions. You can choose to paint the skin with a brush or use this technique:**

    - Duplicate the grayscale image layer and then choose Image➪Adjustments➪Hue/Saturation.

    - Choose the Colorize option and move the Hue slider to the left to produce a sepia tone. I set my Hue to 36. Set Saturation to 25 percent and click OK to colorize this layer.

continued

Book IV
Chapter 1

Painting and
Drawing with
Photoshop

continued

TIP

- Use the Eraser tool to remove everything in the colorized layer that isn't skin. In my example, I removed the hair, background, eyes, lips, teeth, and dress. This result is a nice sepia tone to the face.

  Be sure to pick a color that's as close to real life as possible. If the subject has darker skin, you may need to move away from rosier blush tones.

12. **When you finish coloring your layers, you can experiment with different opacity levels for each colorized layer to see if more transparent hues might look better.**

Drawing with Vector Shapes

While I am a big fan of photos and all the pixels that comprise those photos, some times you need to call on a vector or two. Maybe you need to create a simple line art graphic for a Web page. Or perhaps you want to add a logo onto a poster. In these instances, drawing a vector shape with the pen or shape tools is the way to go.

Before you begin creating vector shapes in Photoshop, having a firm grasp on the basics of pixels versus vectors is a big help. Vectors describe a shape mathematically; pixel images, on the other hand, describe the same shape in terms of a map of pixels. The key difference is that, as you increase the size of a pixel-based image, it begins to look blocky. Because vector images are based on mathematical formulas, they look good at any size. Figure 1-8 shows both types of images. I explain the difference between vector and pixel-based images in more detail in Book II, Chapter 1.

Vector image   Pixel image

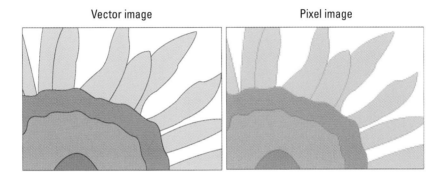

Figure 1-8: Photoshop images fall into one of two camps — vector or pixel.

When you create vector objects in a program like Photoshop, they are comprised of paths, which are in turn made up of anchor points and straight and curved segments, or *lines*. You can create these points and lines by working with the preset shapes or by creating your own shape. The presets are easier to work with, but the custom shapes enable you to be more creative. In the following sections, I walk you through the steps for creating vector shapes as well as the various options.

Drawing a preset shape

Follow these steps to draw a preset shape in your document:

1. **Choose the shape tool of your choice from the Tools palette.**

   You can also press U and choose the shape tool from the Options bar. You can choose from the following shape tools (shown in Figure 1-9):

   • **Rectangle/Ellipse:** The rectangle and ellipse have no special parameters on the Options bar; however, they both behave much like their counterparts among the selection tools. For example, you can press the Shift key while dragging a shape to produce a perfect square or circle; press the Shift key plus the Alt key (Option key on the Mac) to draw the shape outward from the center. You have other geometry options that let you determine how you draw the shapes (unconstrained, fixed size, from center, and so forth).

Shape tools

Shape mode Custom Shape palette

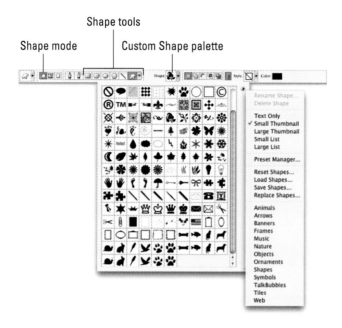

Figure 1-9: The shape tools and Options bar give you everything you need to make shapes from simple squares to ornate *fleur de lys*.

- **Rounded Rectangle:** This shape has the same options as the rectangle shape, with the addition of a box in which you can type the radius of the circle used to round off the corners of the rectangle.

- **Polygon:** This shape includes a box in which you can enter the number of sides you'd like for the polygon, in the range of 3 to 100, as well as geometry options.

- **Line:** You can give the line shape a width from 1 to 1000 pixels and assign a layer style and/or fill color. You can also enter parameters for an arrowhead at either or both ends.

- **Custom:** You find numerous preset custom shapes to choose from. As with any shape, you press Shift to constrain proportions or Alt (Option on the Mac) to draw from the center out.

2. **Choose the mode of shape you want to draw from the three icons on the Options bar.**

   Here's a list of ways in which you can create a shape (all options are on the Options bar):

- **Shape Layers:** Click this icon to create the shape in a new layer of its own. When you choose this mode, icons appear on the Options bar that let you choose a layer style and/or fill color.

Shape Layers is a good choice if you want to keep your shapes in separate layers so you can manipulate them further. (Some options include making the shapes appear to have been added together, subtracted from, and so on.) Photoshop links shapes in a shape layer to a *vector mask,* which can show or hide portions of an image. You find out more about shape layers and vector masks later in this chapter. The shapes remain scalable until you change them into pixels by choosing Layer⇨Rasterize⇨Shape.

- **Paths:** Click this icon to create the shape on an existing layer. The shape appears as a path that you can edit by using the pen tools and the Paths palette. For everything you need to know about paths, check out Book III, Chapter 2.

- **Fill Pixels:** Click this icon to create a shaped area filled with the foreground color. This option *doesn't* produce a vector shape, but instead fills the shape with pixels. The process is similar to filling a selection created with the Rectangular or Elliptical Marquee tools or painting on your canvas with a painting tool. When you choose this mode, the Options bar includes choices that let you specify a blending mode, the transparency of the filled area, and whether you want the area anti-aliased. You cannot edit a shape created with this option, except to modify the pixels.

3. **Select your options — both on the Options bar (if any) and in the geometry options drop-down palette, which also resides on the Options bar.**

   The Options bar changes to reflect each type of shape; each type has its own options, which are listed in Step 1. For detailed explanations on the various geometry options, see "Setting geometry options."

   If you chose the Custom Shape tool in Step 1, click the down-pointing arrow to access the drop-down shapes palette. Choose the shape of your choice. You can access more preset shape libraries via the pop-up menu at the top of the palette (refer to Figure 1-9).

4. **Drag in the document to draw the shape you've defined.**

   The shape appears in the image window. If you chose the Shape Layer mode in Step 2, the shape also appears in the Layers palette in its own layer. A rectangle filled with the foreground color appears in the image column, and the shape itself is shown in the mask column as a vector mask, as you can see in Figure 1-10. The green layer of color peeks through my vector mask, which is in the shape of a leaf.

Figure 1-10: When you create a shape layer you are creating a layer of color that shows through a vector mask (path) in the form of your shape.

Drawing multiple shapes in a shapes layer

After you create a shape layer, you can draw additional shapes in the layer, adding to the vector mask associated with that layer. You can add, subtract, overlap, and intersect shapes in exactly the same way you do with selections, as described in Book III, Chapter 3. Here's how it works:

1. **After you create the first shape, as I explain in the preceding section, select your desired state button on the Options bar:**

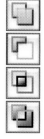

   - **Add to Shape Area:** Combines and joins two or more shapes

   - **Subtract from Shape Area:** Subtracts one shape from another shape

   - **Intersect Shape Areas:** Creates a shape only from the areas that overlap

   - **Exclude Overlapping Shape Areas:** Creates a shape only from the areas that do not overlap

2. Grab your desired shape tool and draw the next shape.

Press the Shift key to temporarily switch to Add to Shape Area while drawing a new shape. Press the Alt key (Option on the Mac) to temporarily switch to Subtract from Shape Area. This works just like adding or subtracting selections.

Setting geometry options

Geometry options for your shapes (rectangle/rounded rectangle, ellipse, polygon, line, and custom) help define how the shapes look. Click the down-pointing arrow on the Options bar to access the geometry options. The following sections show you what you can do with these options.

Rectangular shape geometry options

Here are the Geometry options for the rectangle and rounded rectangle shapes, as shown in Figure 1-11:

Figure 1-11: Geometry options define how your particular shape appears.

- ✔ **Unconstrained:** When you have this option (the default) selected, Photoshop defines the size and proportions of the rectangle as you drag.

- ✔ **Square:** Select this button to constrain the shape to a perfect square. (You can also press the Shift key to do the same thing on the fly.)

- ✔ **Fixed Size:** This option lets you draw rectangles only in fixed sizes. Specify the exact size by entering a width and height.

- ✔ **Proportional:** This option lets you define an aspect ratio, or proportion, for the rectangle. Type 3 into the W box, and 4 into the H box, and you're constrained to drawing any size rectangle with fixed proportions in a 3:4 ratio.

- ✔ **From Center:** Select this option to expand the shape from the center point you click.

- ✔ **Snap to Pixels:** This option aligns the shape to the pixels on your screen.

Elliptical shape geometry options

The ellipse shape has the same options that are available for rectangles (also shown in Figure 1-12). Of course, instead of being able to create a perfect square, you can restrain the shape to be a perfect circle. Also, the Snap to Pixels option (available for rectangles) doesn't exist for ellipses.

Polygon shape geometry options

These are the geometry options for the polygon shape, as shown in Figure 1-12:

- **Radius:** You can enter the radius of a circle used to round off the corners of a polygon when you have the Smooth Corners option selected.

- **Smooth Corners:** Choose this option to round off the corners.

- **Star:** Select this option to create a star shape — that is, a polygon where the sides indent inward rather than extend outward from the corner points.

- **Indent Sides By:** The value entered here determines the amount the sides indent inward.

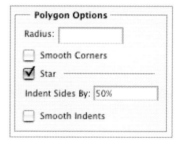

Figure 1-12: Choose between a polygon or a star.

- **Smooth Indents:** This option rounds off the inner corners created by indenting the sides.

- **Sides:** Indicate the number of sides for your polygon or the number of points for your star.

Line geometry options

The line's geometry settings include whether to put arrowheads at the start or end of the line, or both, as shown in Figure 1-13. Figure 1-13 also shows how changing the width, length, and concavity settings affect the arrowhead shapes.

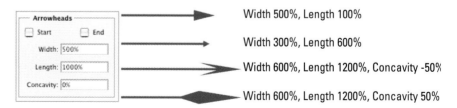

Figure 1-13: By specifying the width, length and concavity, you can change the appearance of your arrowheads.

Custom shape geometry options

The custom shape options are similar to those you find for the other geometry shapes with a couple of additions, shown in Figure 1-14:

✔ **Defined Proportions:** When you use this option, Photoshop limits any shapes created using this new custom shape to the *proportions* you use when you create it now. That is, you can change the size of a new shape but only in proportion with the original custom shape you create.

Figure 1-14: You can size your shape without losing its original proportions by checking the Defined Proportions option.

✔ **Defined Size:** When you use this option, Photoshop limits any shapes generated based on this new custom shape to the size you set now.

Creating your own custom shape

You can create your own custom shape by defining the shape using a vector mask, work path, or saved path. You can find out more about creating work paths and saved paths in Book III, Chapter 2. To create a shape and add it to your shape library, follow these steps:

1. **Choose the Pen tool from the Tools palette, or press Shift+P until the Pen tool is selected.**

2. **Select the Shape Layers icon on the Options bar and use the Pen to draw the shape you want to create.**

   Book III, Chapter 2 describes the techniques for adding, removing, and adjusting the shapes of curves with the Pen tool.

   Photoshop automatically places the shape you create in its own shape layer as a vector mask. Find out more about what you can do with a vector mask in the following section, "Using vector masks."

3. **In the Paths palette, select the path or vector mask you want to convert into a custom shape.**

4. **Choose Edit⇨Define Custom Shape from the menu bar.**

   The Shape Name dialog box appears, as shown in Figure 1-15.

5. **Enter a descriptive name for your new shape in the dialog box and then click OK.**

   The new shape appears in the custom shapes pop-up palette on the Options bar.

6. **Choose Save Shapes from the palette's pop-up menu to store your new library on your hard drive.**

Although you can't create a shape with the Preset Manager, you can use it to manage the shapes in your shape library.

Figure 1-15: Create your own shapes when you tire of the presets.

Using vector masks

When you create a shape in Shape layer mode, Photoshop automatically saves the shape as a *vector mask*. Essentially, a shape layer has two components. First, Photoshop entirely fills the layer with color. Then, Photoshop places the shape, which (again) is comprised of a path, on top. The thumbnails in the Layers palette visually display this concept. The color peeks through the outline of the shape, and Photoshop hides (or masks) the rest of the layer. So in other words, vector masks clip away the color of a shape layer. If you delete a vector mask, you are left with just a layer of solid color.

Like all vector objects, vector paths print at the full resolution of the printer and are resolution independent.

You can edit a shape that Photoshop has saved as a vector mask at any time. Simply click the vector mask thumbnail to select it. Then use the shape and pen tools to edit the shape.

Here are some additional things you can do with a vector mask:

- ✔ To remove a vector mask, drag its thumbnail in the Layers palette to the trash can icon at the bottom of the palette. You can also select the layer and choose Layer⇨Delete Vector.

- ✔ To enable or disable a vector mask, Shift+click its thumbnail in the Layers palette, or select the layer and choose Layer⇨Disable (or Enable) Vector Mask. Photoshop marks the thumbnails of disabled vector masks with an X.

- ✔ You can convert a vector mask to a layer mask by selecting the layer and choosing Layer⇨Rasterize⇨Vector Mask.

Manipulating shapes

You can manipulate shapes you create by using a variety of tools. Here's a quick list of the things you can do:

✔ **Move:** Choose the Move tool (press V) to move shapes in their layer.

✔ **Delete:** Select a shape and press Delete to remove it.

✔ **Adjust anchor points:** Use the Direct Selection tool to manipulate anchor points, directional handles, lines, and curves.

✔ **Transform shapes:** Use Edit⇨Transform Path or select the Show Bounding Box option on the Options bar to transform shapes. For more information, see Book III, Chapter 3.

✔ **Align and distribute shapes:** Use active buttons on the Options bar when you have the Move tool selected to change alignment and distribution along an imaginary line (shown on the button).

✔ **Clone a shape:** Press Alt (Option on the Mac) and move the shape with the Path Selection tool.

You find more information on manipulating shapes in Book III, Chapter 2.

Remember that if you select the Fill Pixels option on the Options bar, you're stuck without editing capabilities.

Chapter 2: Filling and Stroking

In This Chapter

↙ **Filling and stroking selections**

↙ **Filling or stroking paths**

↙ **Building and applying gradients**

↙ **Creating and applying patterns**

*P*hotoshop offers several ways to create elements, such as geometric shapes, out of pixels and filling and stroking them are two of the most venerable commands at your disposal. You can also paint geometric elements on your canvas by hand, or convert vector shapes to pixels (see Book IV, Chapter 1 for more on that topic). But if you need pixels arranged into regular circles, ellipses, and polygons, the Fill and Stroke facilities of Photoshop are worthy of your consideration.

Here's how they work:

↙ The Fill command adds color or a pattern to a selection of any shape or form you have created.

↙ The Stroke command applies color around the selection outline only.

This chapter shows you how to create these objects by filling and stroking selections and paths, how to add smooth gradient blends, and the best ways to apply patterns. After reading this chapter, you will have your fill of different strokes.

Another way of filling is through the use of a fill layer, which you can use to fill a shape. Because fill layers work a little differently from the types of fills discussed in this chapter, I cover them in Book V, Chapter 1.

Filling a Selection with a Solid Color

When you just want to add a solid color, you use either the foreground or background color. (These colors appear at the bottom of the Tools palette, as I explain in Book I, Chapter 2.) The following steps show you the basics of filling a selection with either the foreground or background color (you have plenty of other filling options, which I discuss later in the chapter):

1. Create your selection on a layer.

See Book III for all you need to know about selections and Book V for the scoop on layers.

2. Choose a fill color as the foreground or background color.

Choose Window➪Color. Use the color sliders to mix your desired color. For more on choosing color, see Book II, Chapter 3.

3. Choose Edit➪Fill.

The Fill dialog box, shown in Figure 2-1, appears. Here, you can select whether to fill with the foreground or background color. You also can choose color, black, 50 percent gray, white, history, or pattern.

4. Click OK.

The foreground (or background) color fills the selection.

Figure 2-1: You can fill your selection with color, history, or a pattern.

 You can also choose a blend mode, the opacity of the fill, and whether to fill the entire selection or only portions of the selection that contain pixels (the nontransparent areas). I recommend not adjusting your blend mode and opacity in the Fill dialog box, but instead creating a new layer for your fill and adjusting those settings in the Layers palette, where you have more flexibility.

Filling Options and Tips

After you make a selection, you're ready to use one of the filling options. You can use the Fill dialog box (as described in the preceding section) to fill the selection with the foreground or background color; you can also choose to fill the selection with color, black, white, or gray. Photoshop is full of shortcuts and options. Here are just a few:

✔ With the selection active, press Alt+Delete (Option+Delete on the Mac) to fill it with the foreground color. All areas within the selection, including transparent areas, fill with the color.

✔ Fill only the pixels in a selection with the foreground color, leaving any transparent pixels transparent, by pressing Alt+Shift+Backspace (or Option+Shift+Delete on the Mac). For more on transparency, see Book V, Chapter 1.

Lock the transparent pixels in a layer (and its selections) by clicking the Transparency icon in the Lock area of the Layers palette.

✔ If you're working on the Background layer, you can also fill the selection with the background color by pressing the Delete key. (Pressing Delete on other layers creates a transparent area that shows the image in the layer underneath the selection.)

✔ By choosing the Color option in the Fill dialog box, you access the Color Picker where you can select any color of the rainbow to fill your selection with. For more on using the Color Picker, see Book II, Chapter 3.

✔ Choose the Pattern option in the Fill dialog box to fill the selection with a pattern. Click the arrow next to the pattern swatch and select a pattern from the pop-up palette. Click the pattern palette pop-up menu to choose more pattern libraries.

✔ Select the History option in the Fill dialog box to restore the selection to a state or snapshot of the image. For more on working with the History palette, see Book II, Chapter 4.

✔ Paint part or all the interior of the selection by using any of the brush tools, as shown in Figure 2-2. This option lets you partially fill a selection by using a bit of flexibility and creativity. When you paint a selection with brush tools, Photoshop confines the paint inside the boundaries of your selection. For more on painting, see Book IV, Chapter 1.

✔ Pour color from the Paint Bucket tool into the selection.

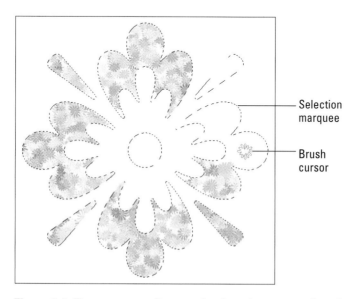

Selection marquee

Brush cursor

**Book IV
Chapter 2**

Filling and Stroking

Figure 2-2: The marquee confines your brush strokes to your selected area.

Pouring with the Paint Bucket Tool

The Paint Bucket tool, available from the Tools palette where it shares a flyout menu with the Gradient tool, operates much like a combination of the Brush tool and the Magic Wand tool, as you'll see from looking over its options. To use it, select the tool (press Shift+G until it's active) and click inside the selection you want to fill. Here are your options, all of which are on the Options bar:

- **Fill:** You can choose whether to fill with the foreground color or a pattern.

- **Pattern:** When you've chosen Pattern from the Options bar, you can select a preset pattern, load patterns from your pattern libraries, or create a pattern of your own. You find more information on patterns later in this chapter.

- **Mode:** You can select a fill mode, too. You find more information on these modes in Book V, Chapter 3.

- **Opacity:** Adjust this value to make your fill semitransparent.

- **Tolerance:** Like the Magic Wand tool, you can choose a tolerance level that specifies how similar in brightness a pixel must be before it is selected for painting. You can find more information on tolerance levels in Book III, Chapter 1.

- **Anti-alias:** Choose this option to blend the paint in smoothly with the areas not filled.

- **Contiguous:** When selected, the paint fills only pixels that are touching within your selection. When deselected, paint fills all pixels within the brightness tolerance you specify within your selection.

- **All Layers:** This option applies paint to pixels in all layers that are within the selection and brightness/tolerance levels you specify.

As with other tools that fill, you can prevent the Paint Bucket tool from filling the transparent pixels. Just select the Transparency icon in the Lock area of the Layers palette.

Stroking a Selection

Stroking enables you to create outlines of selections, layers, or paths. Stroking a selection creates a border around the selection. It's up to you to decide whether to put the border inside, outside, or centered on the selection. (Photoshop doesn't care either way.)

To stroke a selection, follow these steps:

1. **Choose a foreground color and make a selection.**

   (Stroke can't automatically use the background color, although you can select that color in the dialog box.)

2. **Choose Edit➪Stroke.**

3. **In the Stroke dialog box, adjust the settings and the options, as shown in Figure 2-3.**

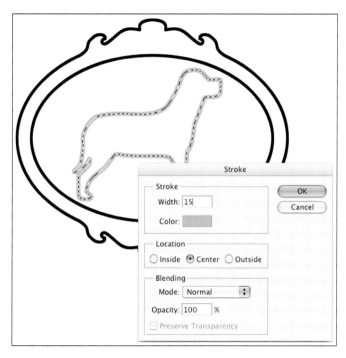

Figure 2-3: Apply strokes to your selection up to 250 pixels wide.

✐ **Width:** You can select 1 to 250 pixels. You can also type a value by using another measurement, such as inches, but Photoshop converts it to pixel values before applying.

✐ **Color:** Click in the Color box to select the hue you want from the Color Picker.

✐ **Location:** Select where Photoshop should apply the stroke.

✐ **Mode:** This determines how the stroke merges with other colors.

    ✔ **Opacity:** The default value is 100 percent. If you want the stroke to be semitransparent, type another value.

    ✔ **Preserve Transparency:** Choose this option to apply the stroke only to nontransparent pixels.

  4. Click OK to apply the stroke.

I recommend leaving the blend mode and opacity setting options in the Stroke dialog box alone. Instead of adjusting these settings, create a new layer for your stroke and then choose a different blend mode and opacity setting in the Layers palette. This maximizes your ability to make edits.

Working with Gradients

A *gradient* is a wonderful blend of colors that you can apply to a layer or selection, gradually fading from one hue to another. Gradients can involve more than two colors, producing a veritable rainbow of variations. You can apply gradients by using preset selections of colors, or you can create your own gradient.

You can create the following gradient effects:

✔ **Foreground to background:** The gradient is a transition from the current foreground color to the background color.

✔ **Foreground to transparent:** The gradient is a transition from the current foreground color to transparent, allowing whatever is under the transparent portion to show through.

✔ **Black to white:** The gradient is a transition from black to white.

✔ **An array of colorful selections:** This includes rainbows, coppery sheens, and other effects.

You can load other libraries of gradients from the Gradient palette menu's libraries. They have names such as Color Harmonies, Metals, and Special Effects. For more information on managing preset libraries, see Book I, Chapter 5.

In addition to being able to control the appearance and application of a gradient, you also have the opportunity to adjust the Gradient tool's options, all of which are on the Options bar:

✔ **Mode:** Select any of Photoshop's blending modes.

✔ **Opacity:** Choose how transparent the gradient is.

✔ **Reverse:** Reverse the order in which the colors are applied.

✔ **Dither:** Add *noise,* or random information, to produce a smoother gradient that prints with less *banding* (color stripes caused by the limitations of the printing process to reproduce a full range of colors).

✔ **Transparency:** This option determines whether Photoshop ignores the gradient's transparency settings when you apply a gradient. If you deselect this option, all portions of the gradient are fully opaque. I show you how to add transparency to a gradient later in this chapter.

Applying a preset gradient to a selection

Here's how to apply a preset gradient:

1. **Choose the layer from the Layers palette and/or make the selection you want to apply the gradient to.**

2. **Select the Gradient tool from the Tools palette, or press G or Shift+G until the Gradient tool becomes active.**

3. **Choose one of the preset gradients from the Gradient Picker dropdown menu on the Options bar.**

4. **Choose the gradient type by clicking one of the icons on the Options bar. Figure 2-4 illustrates each gradient type.**

   Linear: Blends the colors of the gradient from start color to end color in a straight line.

   Radial: Blends the colors from start to end in a circular arrangement.

   Angle: Creates a counterclockwise sweep around the starting point, resembling a radar screen.

   Reflected: Blends the colors by using symmetrical linear gradients on either side of the starting point.

   Diamond: Blends the colors outward in a diamond pattern.

Figure 2-4: You can choose from five gradients.

5. **Choose any other options you want from the Options bar.**

   I explain these options in "Working with Gradients," earlier in this chapter.

6. **Place the cursor at the position in the layer or selection where you want to place the starting color of the gradient.**

7. **Drag in any direction to the point you want to place the end color.**

   Longer drags result in a subtle transition between colors, whereas shorter drags result in a more abrupt transition. Press the Shift key to restrain the direction of the gradient to an even 45-degree angle.

Book IV
Chapter 2

Filling and Stroking

8. **Release the mouse button to apply the gradient.**

The gradient I created is shown in Figure 2-5.

Figure 2-5: Indulge your love of color with Photoshop gradients.

Customizing and editing gradients

Although Photoshop includes dozens of different gradient presets, you may want to create your own. Perhaps you'd like to create a gradient with your company colors or build one to match the predominant colors in an image. Or you might want to create a gradient that includes more than two colors. The Gradient Editor lets you create your own gradient preset, using two or as many colors as you want, which you can save and reuse at any time.

The Gradient Editor has lots of options, but it's easy to use when you know what all the controls and options do. Follow these steps to create a simple smooth gradient:

1. **Select the Gradient tool from the Tools palette.**

2. **Click in the gradient sample window itself (not the arrow) on the Options bar.**

The Gradient Editor dialog box opens, as shown in Figure 2-6.

3. **Pick an existing gradient preset from the Presets windows to use as your basis for your new gradient.**

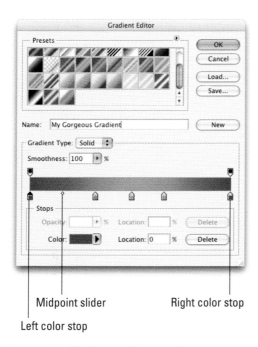

Midpoint slider   Right color stop

Left color stop

Figure 2-6: The Gradient Editor enables you to create custom gradients.

4. Choose Solid or Noise from the Gradient Type pop-up menu.

As soon as you start to edit the existing gradient, the name of the gradient changes to Custom. A Noise gradient is one containing random colors. Because the colors are random, each time you create a noise gradient the result is different. You can choose which color mode to use and how rough the gradient is and select a range of acceptable colors.

5. Adjust the Smoothness slider. Drag the slider (click the right-pointing arrow) or enter a value to determine how smoothly to blend your colors into one another.

If you chose Noise in the previous step, the slider changes to Roughness. This option affects how smooth or abruptly one color transitions into another.

6. You can set the following options only if you chose Noise in Step 4.

- **Color Model:** Select your desired color model or limit the range of colors by adjusting the sliders. See Book II, Chapter 2 for more on color models.

- **Restrict Colors:** Limits the colors to printable CMYK colors only. Again, see Book II, Chapter 2 for details.

- **Add Transparency:** Lets you include transparency in your gradient, if desired.

- **Randomize:** Changes the colors in your gradient. Each time you click Randomize, you get a new set of colors.

7. **To begin defining the color of the starting point for your gradient, first click the left color stop button under the gradient bar.**

   The triangle on top of the stop turns black to indicate you are working with the starting point of the gradient. Remember because Noise gradients are random, you cannot define the colors.

8. **Choose the starting color by using one of these methods:**

   - Double-click the left color stop and select a color from the Color dialog box that appears.

   - Double-click the Color box in the Stops area of the dialog box and choose a color from the dialog box.

   - Choose Foreground, Background, or User Color from the Color pop-up menu in the Stops area of the dialog box.

   Keep in mind that if you select color with the Foreground or Background option when you change the foreground or background color, the color in the gradient changes automatically. The change doesn't affect any gradients you've already created, but it does affect any future gradients. However, when you open the Gradient Editor again, you can revert to your original foreground or background color by selecting the User Color option.

   - Position the cursor (it appears as an eyedropper icon) anywhere in the gradient bar to select a start color from the bar, or position the cursor anywhere within an image on your screen, and then click to select the color under the cursor.

9. **Click the end point color stop at the right side of the gradient bar and use any of the methods described in Step 8 to choose the end color of the gradient.**

10. **Change the percentage of one color to the other by moving the starting or ending point's color stops to the left or right. Drag the midpoint slider (a diamond icon) to adjust where the colors mix equally, 50-50.**

    You can also change the position of the midpoint by typing a value into the Location box.

    Because the center point of the gradient is halfway between the start and end points, the gradient proceeds smoothly from one color to the other, meeting to blend evenly in the middle. Moving the color stops and the midpoint changes the proportions.

11. **Want to add another color? Just click below the gradient bar at the position you want to add the next color. Define a color for the new color.**

12. **Repeat Step 11 for additional colors.**

    Heck, you can keep going like this for hours.

13. **Move all your color stops to the left or right to assign percentages for the additional colors. Then adjust the midpoint sliders between the colors.**

14. **If you change your mind, you can redefine the color or click the Delete button.**

    You can also remove a color stop by dragging it down or up from its position on the gradient bar.

15. **Once your edits are complete, give your gradient a name if you prefer and click the New button.**

    Your gradient is added to the Presets menu. Figure 2-7 shows an example of a unique gradient I created in the Gradient Editor.

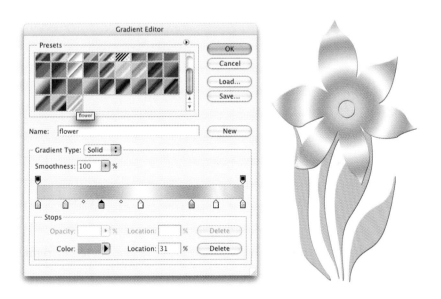

Figure 2-7: The Gradient Editor gives you more creative license than the presets.

Adding transparency to a gradient

By default, a gradient has 100-percent opacity in the start color and progresses to 100-percent opacity in the end color. If you like, you can have the gradient fade out to transparency so that the portion of the image under the gradient shows through. To add transparency to a gradient, follow these steps.

1. **Create a gradient, as described in the two previous sections.**

2. **Select the left opacity stop.**

   This stop is located just above the gradient bar, as shown in Figure 2-8.

Opacity stop

Figure 2-8: Lighten your gradients by adjusting the opacity of your colors.

3. **Use the Opacity slider to specify the amount of transparency for the gradient at its start point.**

   You can also type a value into the Opacity box.

4. **Select the right opacity stop and slide the Opacity slider or enter a percentage in the text box to specify transparency for the gradient at its end point.**

   The lower the percentage, the less opaque the color.

5. **Move the opacity stops to the right or left to adjust the position where Photoshop applies each stop's opacity setting.**

6. Click above the gradient bar to add more opacity stops if you want to vary the transparency of the gradient at different points.

For example, you could fade transparency from 100 percent to 50 percent back to 100 percent to produce a particular effect. Figure 2-9 shows a gradient with varying levels of transparency.

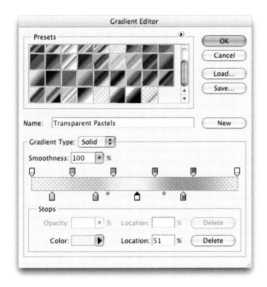

Figure 2-9: Transparency gives a gradient a different look.

Gradients ordinarily proceed smoothly from one color to another. If you'd like a less homogeneous appearance, adjust the Smoothness slider to a value of less than 100 percent (click the right-pointing arrow to access the slider).

Managing and Saving Gradients

If you're smart, you'll want to store the gradients you create so that you can use or edit them again later. Here are some tips for managing your gradients:

✔ To save a gradient, click the Save button in the Gradient Editor dialog box. You save the current presets, including your new gradient, under the current library's name or another one that you choose.

    ✔ To load gradient presets into the Gradient Editor, click the Load button and select the name of the gradient library you want to add to the Presets list.

    ✔ To add an additional set of presets to the current presets, choose the name of the presets from the Gradient Editor's pop-up menu.

For more information about managing gradient presets with the Preset Manager, see Book I, Chapter 5.

Working with Patterns

Patterns are textures or repeating configurations of pixels that you can use to fill selections or layers, apply with painting tools, smear around your image with the Pattern Stamp, or use as a basis for the Healing Brush and Patch tools. Photoshop offers a large selection of patterns, and you can create your own in two different ways.

You select patterns from palettes that appear on the Options bar for many of the tools just mentioned, much like brush tips and gradients, and you manage them in much the same way, using the Preset Manager (see Book I, Chapter 5). The following sections show you how to apply a preset pattern and create your own.

Applying a preset pattern

Although you can apply patterns by using many different tools, this chapter sticks with applying patterns as fills. To fill a layer or selection with a preset pattern, follow these steps.

1. **Choose the layer or selection you want to fill with a pattern.**

2. **Choose Edit➪Fill and select Pattern from the Use pop-up menu.**

3. **In the Custom Pattern palette, select the pattern you want to fill with.**

   • Choose a pattern from the drop-down palette, as shown in Figure 2-10.

   • Replace the current patterns with new patterns by choosing Replace Patterns from the palette pop-up menu (click the right-pointing arrow at the right side of the dialog box). Then choose the new pattern library from the dialog box that appears.

   • Append new patterns to the current set by choosing Load Patterns from the palette pop-up menu.

   • Append one of the preset libraries furnished with Photoshop by choosing the pattern from the list at the bottom of the palette menu.

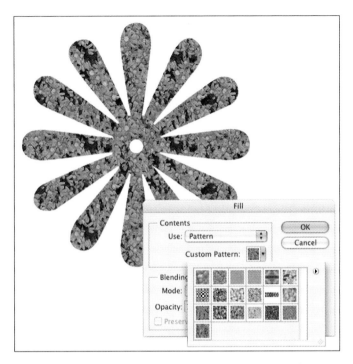

Figure 2-10: Fill your selection with purple daisies or one of the many other Photoshop preset patterns.

4. **Choose any other fill options you want to apply, such as Mode, Opacity, or Preserve Transparency.**

   The Preserve Transparency option prevents Photoshop from filling the transparent areas on your layer with a pattern.

   I recommend adjusting the Mode and Opacity settings in the Layers palette rather than the Fill dialog box. This allows you the maximum flexibility if you want to make edits later.

5. **Click OK to fill the layer or selection with the chosen pattern.**

Creating a new pattern

You can create your own pattern, basing it on an existing image or on one you create yourself. Select a small portion of an image to build an abstract pattern, or use a recognizable object to define that object as a pattern stamp. You can use anything from a logo to your signature as a pattern.

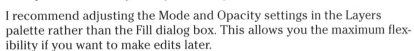

**Book IV
Chapter 2**

Filling and Stroking

To create your own pattern, follow these steps:

1. **Open the image that contains the area you want to use as a pattern, or create an image from scratch.**

2. **Make any modifications to the image to produce the exact pattern that you want.**

3. **Use the Rectangular Marquee tool to select the area you want to convert into a pattern.**

   If you don't make a selection, Photoshop uses your entire image as a basis for the pattern.

   Note that if you are using a selection to define your pattern you must use a rectangular selection. Note that you cannot use a feathered selection of any kind.

4. **Choose Edit➪Define Pattern.**

5. **Enter a name for your pattern in the Define Pattern dialog box.**

   Your new pattern appears in the Pattern palette for use.

Using the Pattern Maker filter

The Pattern Maker filter is an advanced tool that provides even more ways to customize your patterns. This easy-to-use dialog box, shown in Figure 2-11, helps you build a pattern that fills an entire layer of your choice. The cool part is that you can create a whole series of different patterns and review them to find the one you like best.

Figure 2-11: The Pattern Maker enables you to create patterns that tile seamlessly.

As with creating a pattern from a selection, you must use a rectangular shape to build your new pattern. If your selection is irregular or feathered when you enter the Pattern Maker dialog box, Photoshop forces a rectangular selection around your irregular or feathered selection.

The most valuable feature of the Pattern Maker is that it creates patterns that tile smoothly. That is, you can repeat the pattern as many times as you need to fill an area, and the boundaries between sections blend together smoothly. The Pattern Maker command is on the Filter menu.

To create a pattern using this filter, just follow these steps:

1. **To apply a pattern to an existing image, first make a copy of the layer that contains the image area you want to convert to a pattern.**

   To apply the pattern to a new image, select the area you want to use with the Rectangular Marquee tool and choose Edit⇨Copy. Then choose File⇨ New, choose Custom from the New File dialog box, click OK to create the new file, and paste (Edit⇨Paste) the selection into the new image.

2. **Choose Filter⇨Pattern Maker.**

3. **Select the area to be used as the basis for the pattern.**

4. **If you're creating the pattern in the current layer, choose the Rectangular Marquee tool from the dialog box's Tools palette, and select the portion of the image you want to convert to a pattern.**

   You can drag the selection marquee around the image, use the zoom features to change the magnification, or drag the image around by using the Hand tool.

5. **If you want to completely fill the layer with tiled versions of the pattern, specify the size of the tile by typing values in the Width and Height boxes in the Tile Generation area. You can also enter the offset (None, Horizontal, or Vertical) to use and the amount of that offset. If you'd rather have only a single, non-tiled image, click the Use Image Size button.**

6. **Set other options:**

   - **Smoothness:** Set a value to determine how smooth the edges of the patterns are blended with the surrounding tiles.

   - **Sample Detail:** This parameter controls the maximum size of details in the pattern.

   - **Preview:** Choose whether to display the original image or the generated patterns in the Preview window.

- **Tile Boundaries:** If you want, you can insert a line between tiled images to show their boundaries. Select the Tile Boundaries option and, if you like, choose a color for the boundary that will show up well against your sampled image.

7. **Click the Generate button to create a pattern from your selection. You can click the button multiple times to create multiple pattern variations.**

   Photoshop displays all the different patterns you generate in the Tile History panel in the lower-right corner of the dialog box.

   You can review patterns in a slide-show manner by clicking the Previous, Next, First, and Last arrows.

8. **If you see a pattern you want to save, click the floppy disk icon at the bottom-left edge of the Tile History panel.**

9. **You can get rid of patterns that you don't like by selecting them and then clicking the trash can icon at the lower-right edge.**

   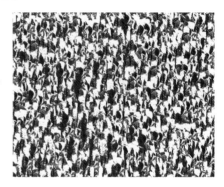

   Tile History can save up to 20 generated patterns.

10. **Click OK if you want to apply the pattern to your document. You can also click the disk icon at the bottom of the Tile Generation area to save the currently selected tile.**

    A typical pattern is shown in Figure 2-12.

Figure 2-12: If you tire of Photoshop's preset pattern, easily create your own with the Pattern Maker.

Chapter 3: Creating and Editing Type

In This Chapter

✏ **Discovering different kinds of type**

✏ **Exploring the type tools**

✏ **Entering and editing text**

*P*hotoshop has morphed into a surprisingly good tool for creating type used in images. The last few releases have added features that let you create paragraphs of text or simple lines of text used as headlines or labels. You can change the spacing between characters, warp your type, check your spelling, or create selections in the shape of text. Drop shadows, beveled type, and other special effects are yours quickly and easily. And you can even place text on or inside a path.

You may still want to use Adobe Illustrator or InDesign to create professional layouts where you can keep text and image files separate, or where you have to place buckets full of text at small point sizes. But if what you're looking for is a great-looking image that includes great-looking snippets of text, Photoshop can do the job. This chapter introduces you to Photoshop's basic type tools as well as its more advanced type capabilities.

Selecting a Type Mode

The text you create in Photoshop can be categorized in several different ways, but ultimately, you're either adding just a little text (such as a word or single line of text) or a lot (maybe a paragraph or so). Accordingly, Photoshop separates type into two modes:

✏ **Point type:** Use this mode to create a headline or label. You can create point type by clicking in your image and typing; the line appears as you type and grows to whatever length you need (even if that length is wider or taller than your image). Point type never wraps around to a new line. To wrap to the next line, you must insert a hard return.

✔ **Paragraph type:** Use this mode to enter longer blocks of text on an image. It's (unsurprisingly) similar to the kind of type you're accustomed to working with in word processing programs. In Paragraph mode, all the text goes into a resizable bounding box, and if a line is too long, Photoshop automatically wraps it around to the next line.

The Point type and Paragraph type modes each operate a bit differently, although they share many features and options. I explain each of them separately later in this chapter.

Understanding Different Kinds of Type

Whether you're using Point type mode or Paragraph type mode, you can choose several type options, each designed to help you work with, display, print, and edit text. These options determine how Photoshop expresses text in a file:

✔ **Vector type:** All text in Photoshop is initially created as *vector* type. Vector type provides scalable outlines that you can resize without producing jaggy edges in the diagonal strokes. You can also edit type in this mode, adding or subtracting characters or adjusting attributes, such as kerning and tracking. Vector type is always of optimum quality and appears crisp and clean. (See Book II, Chapter 2 for more details on vector and rasterized images.)

✔ **Rasterized type:** When Photoshop converts vector type into pixels, it's *rasterized.* When text is rasterized, it is no longer editable, but is, rather, a frozen graphic of what the text looks like. When you've finished editing vector type and want to merge the text with the other pixels in an image (or to perform some manipulations that can be done only with rasterized text), you can transform the vector type into pixels by rasterizing it. You can't resize rasterized type without losing some quality or risking a bad case of the jaggies.

✔ **Pixel fonts:** Pixel fonts are tiny fonts designed for display at small sizes on computer screens, especially Web sites. Pixel fonts are designed so every pixel corresponds to a pixel on your screen. These fonts, with names like MINI 7, MiniSerif, and Tenacity, are created in fixed sizes (say, 7 pixels high for MINI 7 or 10 pixels high for Tenacity and PixelDust). Diagonal lines are avoided as much as possible, with the font designs favoring horizontal and vertical strokes. As a result, pixel fonts look crisp and clear at small sizes without *anti-aliasing* (smoothing around the edges). Indeed, you shouldn't use anti-aliasing with pixel fonts, nor should you attempt to resize or rescale them. You can buy or download pixel fonts, install them on your computer, and use them just as you use other fonts. You can see some examples of pixel fonts in Figure 3-1.

FFF NADADOR BOLD

FFF MANAGER BOLD

FFF HARMONY

FFF FORWARD

Exploring the Type Tools

Strictly speaking, Photoshop has four type tools (found in the Tools palette), but two of them are simply vertically oriented versions of the main two text implements. You can use either Paragraph or Point type mode with any of the type tools:

Figure 3-1: Unlike traditional fonts, pixel fonts are designed to fit into the pixel grid of your screen.

✔ **Horizontal Type:** Use this tool to enter point or paragraph type oriented horizontally on your screen. If you want text that is oriented at an angle other than vertical, you can rotate it by choosing Edit⇨Transform⇨Rotate after you enter the text. This tool creates the type on its own type layer, except when used in Bitmap, Multichannel, or Indexed Color modes, which don't support layers. (Book II, Chapter 2 covers these modes.)

✔ **Vertical Type:** The Vertical Type and Vertical Type Mask tools (described next) are handy for entering Asian characters. However, you can also use this tool to enter Roman character point type oriented in a vertical column. You can also use the Vertical Type tool to create columns of paragraph text, but the results look a little strange. After you enter your text columns, you can rotate the text to an orientation other than vertical by choosing Edit⇨Rotate. Like the Horizontal Type tool, this tool creates type in its own type layer, except with file modes that don't support layers.

✔ **Horizontal Type Mask /Vertical Type Mask:** These tools operate identically to their siblings described in the two preceding bullets, with two exceptions. Instead of adding filled type, both the Horizontal and Vertical Type Mask tools create a selection border in the shape of the type you enter. Both tools add a selection marquee to the current active layer. You can do anything with a type selection that you can do with any other selection, including saving it (Select⇨Save Selection) for reuse later. You find a longer discussion of the type mask tools later in this chapter.

The Horizontal and Vertical Type tools have some interesting options, which I explain in the next section. You can also set controls in the Paragraph and Character palettes, which I discuss later in this chapter.

**Book IV
Chapter 3**

**Creating and
Editing Type**

Entering Text in Point Type Mode

If you're image oriented (and why wouldn't you be if you're using Photoshop?), you're probably not planning to include a novella with your graphics.

Point type is great for headlines, labels, and similar small amounts of text. You can also use it to create logos and headings for Web pages. The Web is one place that text that isn't tack-sharp can still do the job.

Although a Photoshop image is generally not the place you want to insert a whole lot of text, you can add larger blocks of text that are professional and effective — read "Entering Text in Paragraph Type Mode," later in this chapter. You can modify how point type and paragraph type are displayed by using the Paragraph and Character palettes.

To enter point type, just follow these steps:

1. **Open a saved image or create a new Photoshop document.**

2. **Select either the Horizontal or Vertical Type tool from the Tools palette, or press T to select the type tool if the one you want is active.**

   Press the Shift key and then T to cycle through the four available type tools until the one that you want is active.

   Your cursor looks like an I-beam, similar to one you see in a word processing program.

3. **Click the area of the image where you want to insert the text.**

   This is called the insertion point.

   A small horizontal line about one-third of the way up the I-beam shows where the baseline (on which the line of text rests) is for horizontal type. If you select the Vertical Type tool, the cursor is rotated 90 degrees. The baseline is centered in the I-beam and represents the center axis of the vertical column of text you type.

4. **Choose any of the type options from the Options bar, Character palette, or Paragraph palette. To access the palettes, click the Character and Paragraph toggle button on the Options bar or choose either palette on the Window menu.**

   I describe these options later in the chapter.

5. **Type your text. Press Enter (or Return on the Mac) to begin a new line.**

   Lines of point type don't wrap around. When you press Enter or Return, you're inserting a hard carriage return that doesn't move. You have to remove hard returns if you want to change the length of the lines you type.

6. **When you finish entering the text, click the Commit (the check icon) button on the Options bar.**

   A new type layer with your text is created. Note the layer that appears in your Layers palette, as indicated by the T icon.

Entering Text in Paragraph Type Mode

Paragraphs are best allocated to captions or text descriptions that accompany an image. Large amounts of text in an image don't look their best because when you rasterize the type, even the most carefully entered text may have a fuzzy look.

Paragraph type is similar to the text you're accustomed to entering within a word processing program, except that it's contained inside a border, called a text box or a *bounding box*. As you type into a text box, the lines of text wrap around to fit the dimensions of the box. If you resize the box, Photoshop adjusts the wrapped ends to account for the new size.

You can type multiple paragraphs, use typographical controls, and rotate or scale the type. You can easily resize paragraph type (and point type, too) by entering a new point size value in the Character dialog box without having to reselect all the text. Just make sure the text layer is selected in the Layers palette and the Text tool is active. This works for all the other text characteristics as well.

To enter paragraph type, follow these steps:

1. **Open a saved image or create a new Photoshop document.**

2. **Select either the Horizontal or Vertical Type tool from the Tools palette, or press T to select the type tool if the one you want is active.**

   Press the Shift key and then T to cycle through the four available type tools until the one you want is active.

   Your cursor looks like an I-beam, similar to one you see in a word processing program.

3. **Insert and size the text box by using one of the following methods:**

   • Drag to create a text box of an arbitrary size. After you release the mouse button, you can drag any of the handles at the corners and sides of the box to customize the size.

   • Press the Alt key (Option key on the Mac) and drag a box of any size. The Paragraph Text Size dialog box appears. You can enter the exact dimensions of the box you want to create. When you click OK, a bounding box of the size you specified appears, complete with handles for resizing the box later, if you choose.

4. **Choose the type options you want from the Options bar, or Character or Paragraph palettes.**

5. **Enter your text. To start a new paragraph, press Enter (or Return on the Mac).**

   Each line wraps around to fit inside the bounding box, as you can see in Figure 3-2.

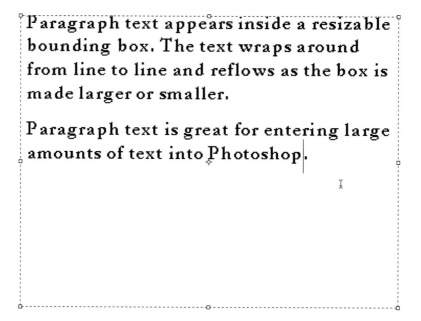

Paragraph text appears inside a resizable bounding box. The text wraps around from line to line and reflows as the box is made larger or smaller.

Paragraph text is great for entering large amounts of text into Photoshop.

Figure 3-2: Paragraph text automatically wraps to conform to your bounding box.

   If you type more text than fits in the text box, an overflow icon appears. You can resize the text box by gripping any of the eight handles and dragging.

6. **Click the Commit button on the Options bar (the button looks like a check mark).**

   Photoshop creates a new type layer.

Creating Type on or in a Path

The last version of Photoshop brought us the long awaited ability to place type in and on a path. The way you create path type in Photoshop is very similar to the way you create path type in InDesign and Illustrator. Here's how.

1. **Grab the Pen or Shape tool. Choose the Paths option from the Options bar and create your path.**

   Note that you can also copy and paste an existing path or import a path from Illustrator or other compatible drawing program.

2. **With the regular Type tool (either Horizontal or Vertical), click on or inside the path.**

   Your type cursor changes to indicate the path type. Note that if you are filling a path with type, you see a bounding box appear.

3. **Type your desired text and marvel at how the type glides along or inside the path, as shown in Figure 3-3.**

   Commit the type by clicking the Commit button on the Options bar. After you commit the type, the path itself doesn't display unless you stroke or fill it with color, as I did with my smaller heart.

Figure 3-3: Make a visual statement with your type by putting it on or in the path of your choice.

**Book IV
Chapter 3**

**Creating and
Editing Type**

4. **To adjust the starting point for the text, click the starting point with the Path Selection tool and drag the type to a new position.**

   The path appears along with an I-beam/black arrow cursor.

5. **Edit the text (changing characters, colors, alignment, and so on) just as you would with regular type.**

6. **Adjust the path by using any of the path tools — the Direct Selection tool, the Convert Point tool, and so on.**

   The type magically reflows along the newly adjusted path.

To create regular point or paragraph type when clicking near a path, press the Shift key when clicking, telling Photoshop you don't want path type.

Using the Options Bar

The Options bar contains a group of options, shown in Figure 3-4. Some (but not all) of these options are duplicated in the Character palette. Those options that appear in both places are the most frequently used options. Talk about convenience.

Figure 3-4: The text options on the Options bar.

Your options, from left to right, include

- **Change the Text Orientation:** Use this handy button to toggle between vertical and horizontal text orientations. Just select the type layer you want to transform and click. This option works with point type and paragraph type, although the results you get from switching the paragraph type to vertical orientation may look odd.

- **Font Family:** Select the font/typeface you want from the drop-down list.

  Photoshop CS2 has graciously provided us with a WYSIWYG font menu. You'll notice that after the font name, the word "sample" is rendered in the actual font. You also find one of these abbreviations before the font name: a, Adobe Type 1 (PostScript) fonts; TT (TrueType); O (OpenType). Those with no abbreviations are Bit Mapped fonts.

- **Font Style:** Some fonts can have additional styles, such as light or demi-bold, other styles are assigned as separate typefaces. Only the styles available for a particular font appear in the list. You'll notice that the font style also now supports a WYSIWYG menu (that is, what you see is what you get).

If a font you want to use doesn't offer bold or italic styles, you can simulate either or both by choosing a faux style in the Character palette.

✔ **Font Size:** Choose the size of the text from this list, or type a size in the text box. Generally, text sizes are shown in points, with 72 points equaling approximately 1 inch. (A 36-point font is ½-inch in size at 72 ppi.)

If you don't like points, you can switch to millimeters or pixels in the Units and Rulers Preferences dialog box. (You can find instructions for doing this in Book I, Chapter 5.)

✔ **Anti-aliasing:** This list includes four different types of smoothing to use on your text, plus *none* (which leaves your text unsmoothed). For small type, try Sharp to avoid your type from being too fuzzy around the edges. But the exact results depend on the typeface, so be sure and take a gander at your type. Bonus Chapter 1 explains anti-aliasing in detail. See the Introduction for details about the Web site.

✔ **Text Alignment:** Three buttons specify whether Photoshop aligns your Horizontal Type tool text left, center, or right. When you use the Vertical Type tool, the buttons transform into Top, Center (vertically), and Bottom choices.

✔ **Text Color:** Click in this box to select a color from the Color Picker.

✔ **Create Warped Text:** This option lets you warp and bend text by using 15 different types of distortion.

✔ **Toggle Character and Paragraph Palettes:** Click this button any time a type tool is active to show or hide the Character and Paragraph palettes.

✔ **Cancel:** Click this button (or press the Esc key) to cancel the text entry you're making.

✔ **Commit:** Click this button to apply the text to a type layer.

Working with the Character Palette

The Character palette, shown in Figure 3-5, is a tabbed palette, usually paired with the Paragraph palette, which lets you format the appearance of individual type characters. Five of the options in the Character palette are exactly the same as those on the Options bar. The duplicated features include font family, font style, font size, anti-aliasing, text color. The other

Figure 3-5: The Character palette offers type specification options galore.

menus, buttons, and text boxes provide additional functions. I discuss these options in the following sections.

Leading

Leading is the amount of space between the baselines of consecutive lines of type, usually measured in points. (The *baseline* is the imaginary line on which a line of type rests.) You can choose a specific amount of leading or allow Photoshop to determine the amount automatically by choosing Auto from the Leading menu.

Wider line spacing can make text easier to read (as long as you don't go overboard!) or be used for artistic effect. Tighter line spacing makes for more compact text but can decrease readability if your tightening goes too far.

When you select Auto Leading, Photoshop multiplies the type size by a value of 120 percent to calculate the leading size. So Photoshop spaces the baselines of 10-point type 12 points apart. You can change this automatic value by clicking the Paragraph palette and choosing Justify from the palette's menu. A dialog box appears with several values. Type the amount you want in the Auto Leading box. If all this seems confusing, I recommend experimenting with leading to get a true idea of how various values affect the space between lines of text.

Tracking

Tracking is the amount of space between letters in a string or line. You can specify negative tracking to squeeze all the letters together more closely, or positive tracking to let them spread out a bit.

Don't confuse tracking with *kerning,* which deals with the space between two individual letters. Tracking sets a value to evenly space all the letters you select, and kerning helps you close or widen the gap between two individual letters.

One use for tracking is to help lines of text fit a specified horizontal space, and you can make this technique work if you use it judiciously. Beginners typically overdo tracking, squeezing letters together so tightly they touch, or spreading them apart so that wide gaps appear. You can see examples of tracking in Figure 3-6.

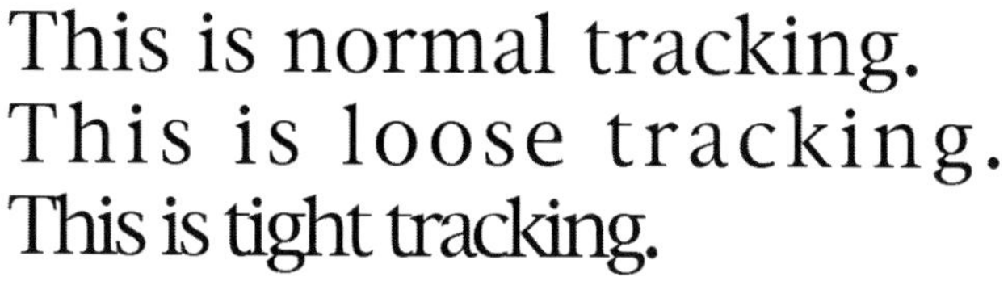

This is normal tracking.
This is loose tracking.
This is tight tracking.

Figure 3-6: Tracking adjusts the spaces between your selected letters.

To track a set of characters or a line, select the text you want to squeeze or expand, and either choose a value from 0 to –100, or 0 to 200, from the Track menu, or type a specific value in the Track text box. Each unit is equal to $\frac{1}{1,000}$ of an em (the width of an em dash in a particular typeface), so a setting of –100 reduces the space between characters by $\frac{1}{10}$ the width of an em dash (quite a lot!).

Kerning

Kerning is a technique for adding or removing space between pairs of letters to make them fit together more closely and aesthetically. For example, the letters A and V are a natural fit and often look better when kerned slightly. If you choose Kern⟹ Metrics, Photoshop automatically tries to kern the characters to provide an attractive look, like that shown in Figure 3-7. Note that the kerning tables are built into the individual font. Be warned that cheap fonts sometimes have poorly created kerning tables or no tables at all — another good reason to stick with quality fonts.

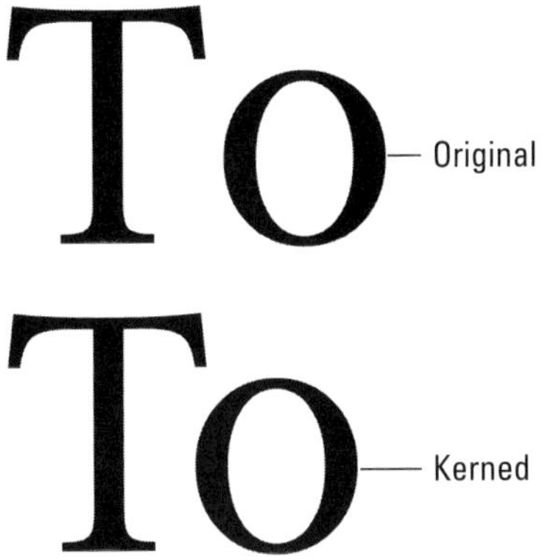

To — Original

To — Kerned

Figure 3-7: Kerning a pair of letters can enhance their appearance.

To manually kern letters, click a point between the two characters and either choose a percentage from 0 to –100, or 0 to 200, from the Kern menu, or type a specific value in the Kern text box. As with the Track menu, the values represent $\frac{1}{1,000}$ of an em.

Vertical and Horizontal Scale

The Vertical and Horizontal Scale options represent the relationship between the height and width of the text. By default, this relationship is 100 percent. To make the width of the type proportionately 50 percent more than the height, you enter 150 percent into the Horizontal Scale box. You can see examples of scaling in Figure 3-8.

Be careful about using the scale options. Type designers create fonts with very specific proportions. When you deviate from those proportions, you can destroy what was once a beautifully designed typeface.

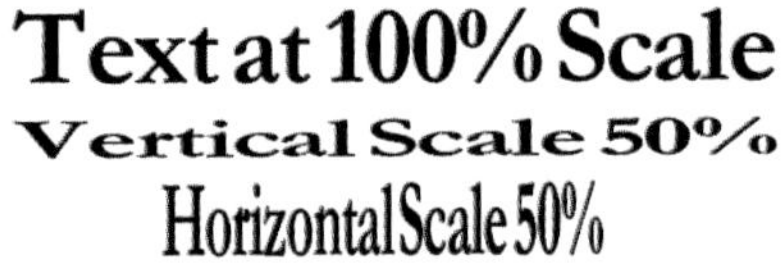

Text at 100% Scale
Vertical Scale 50%
Horizontal Scale 50%

Figure 3-8: Be wary of using Vertical or Horizontal Scale.

Baseline shift and text attributes

The Baseline option adjusts the height above or below a typeface's normal baseline. You usually employ this option to create superscripts and subscripts. A bar with several buttons in the Character palette lets you turn on or off several type attributes with a single click. Table 3-1 covers the many text attributes.

Table 3-1		Character Palette Text Attributes
Icon	*Name*	*What It Does*
T	Faux Bold	Creates a fake bold. ***Warning:*** Applying faux styles can distort the proportions of a font. It is really best to use fonts as they were originally designed and if there is no bold option, *c'est la vie*.
T	Faux Italic	Creates a fake italic. As with faux bold, take caution when using to prevent distortion.
TT	All Caps	Changes the case of the characters in selected text to all capitals, or back to their normal case when you turn it off.
T$_T$	Small Caps	Creates uppercase letters about the size of lowercase letters in a font. Less obtrusive than full-size caps in text passages. Photoshop either uses the small caps characters built into many fonts or creates faux small caps for you.
T^1	Superscript	Raises a character automatically to create a superscript, as in E=MC^2. You'll probably also want to reduce the size of the character.
T$_1$	Subscript	Lowers the character below the baseline, creating a subscript. Usually, subscripts are reduced in size, as in H$_2$O.
T	Underline	Underlines the selected characters.
T	Strikethrough	Provides a ~~strikethrough~~ effect to the selected characters. In legal applications, strikethrough is widely used to show sections that have been removed, but in their original context.
English: USA	Character Set	Selects the language you want to use for Photoshop's spell checker and for hyphenation. The option includes variations, such as English: USA or English: UK, and French or Canadian French.

You can also find the preceding attributes on the Character palette pop-up menu. And the menu lists a few other attributes that are not displayed directly in the palette:

- ✔ **Change Text Orientation:** Rotates your text horizontally or vertically.

- ✔ **Standard Vertical Roman Alignment:** Displays the text in the standard alignment we are used to seeing — across the page.

- ✔ **Fractional Widths:** This setting is the default display. When type gets small, the spacing between characters may vary by fractions of a pixel. Photoshop has to favor one pixel or the other and sometimes the appearance is strange. Overall, however, it provides the best spacing for the legibility and appearance of the type. But, for small type to be displayed on the Web, the readability may be impaired due to some characters running together and words having gaps.

- ✔ **System Layout:** Displays the text using the operating system's default text handling, similar to what you see in WordPad or SimpleText. This option doesn't allow fractions of pixels and removes any anti-aliasing. This is a good option for text to be displayed on the Web.

- ✔ **No Break:** Prevents words from breaking at the end of lines. You may want to select this option to prevent words such as proper names, dates, initials, and so forth from breaking. Select your text and then choose the option.

- ✔ **Old Style to Fractions:** When you work with OpenType fonts, you may find that they include tables of various font attributes. These tables allow you to apply various styles, such as true, diagonal fractions, alternate Old Style numerals, fancy cursive type uppercase letters (Swash and Titling), ligatures (designed to fix the kerning of certain awkward letter combinations such as fi and tt), and ornamental fonts (think dingbats or wingdings) such as leaves and flowers.

- ✔ **Reset Character:** Choose this option to reset your character attributes (font family, size, style, and so on) back to Photoshop's default.

Working with the Paragraph Palette

You can use the Paragraph palette, shown in Figure 3-9, to format any or all paragraphs in a type layer. Simply select the paragraph or paragraphs that you want to format by clicking in an individual paragraph. You can drag a selection to select multiple paragraphs; or click a type layer containing the paragraphs to format all of them at once.

The Paragraph palette's pop-up menu gives you access to Justification and Hyphenation dialog boxes. You can use these to customize the default settings Photoshop uses for these functions. As a side note, if you're not familiar with the word *glyph* used in the Justification dialog box, it is another word for a font character.

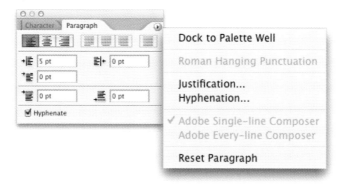

Figure 3-9: Use the Paragraph palette to align and indent your text.

Changing paragraph alignment

At the top of the Paragraph palette, you see a set of seven alignment buttons. Three align nonjustified text. They include the following:

- ✔ **Left Align Text:** All text is even with the left margin and allowed to be ragged on the right side of the column.

- ✔ **Center Text:** Text is evenly centered in its column and ragged on both right and left edges.

- ✔ **Right Align Text:** All text is even with the right margin and allowed to be ragged on the left side.

With vertical type, these choices align the text to the top, a center axis, and the bottom of a column.

Changing paragraph justification

The other four options in the Paragraph palette produce justified text, in which Photoshop inserts spaces between characters as necessary so each line is flush on both left and right sides. The options apply only to the last line of text in each paragraph. You can choose to make this last line flush left, flush right, centered, or force justified on both sides with spaces inserted by Photoshop. This last option sometimes calls for some manual tweaking to avoid a final line that is squeezed or expanded too much. Note that you can apply justification options to paragraph type only, not point type.

With vertical type, the justification choices are top aligns, center aligns, bottom aligns, or force justifies the last line of text.

Changing paragraph indentation

The next three options in the Paragraph palette let you enter an amount of indentation between the sides of the text bounding box and the actual text. You can specify the amount of indentation from the left, right, and for the first line of the paragraph (creating a first line that is indented more than the others in the paragraph). For vertical type, the indentations are rotated 90 degrees.

Changing spacing between paragraphs

The next two options in the Paragraph palette let you specify the amount of space between paragraphs. You can specify the amount of space before every paragraph, the amount after every paragraph, or both.

Breaking long words across two lines

The final option in the Paragraph palette is the Hyphenate check box, which specifies whether Photoshop hyphenates words that are too long to fit on a line or leaves them intact. Turning on hyphenation can prevent awkward spacing, particularly with justified text that would otherwise contain a lot more spaces between characters to make a line fit.

The Paragraph palette's pop-up menu has a few additional options:

- **Roman Hanging Punctuation:** Controls whether punctuation marks (quotations, dashes, colons, and so on) appear inside or outside the margins. Select this option to have the punctuation marks appear outside.

- **Adobe Single-line Composer:** Composition includes using a host of parameters, such as word and letter spacing and hyphenation to determine where a line should break. This option composes type one line at a time and offers more manual control over where lines break. The option favors compressing or expanding word spacing over hyphenation, but prefers hyphenation over compressing or expanding letter spacing. This is the default setting.

- **Adobe Every-line Composer:** Looks at multiple, possible breaking points for a range of lines. The option can optimize earlier lines in the paragraph to avoid weird breaks later on in the paragraph. Emphasis is given to even spacing of letters and words over hyphenation. This option can provide more even spacing and fewer hyphens.

- **Reset Paragraph:** Resets all the paragraph attributes back to the Photoshop default.

**Book IV
Chapter 3**

**Creating and
Editing Type**

Editing Text

You can apply all the options described in this chapter as you enter text, or later, when you're rearranging words or fixing typos and other errors. To make changes to the text itself, just follow these steps:

1. **Open a saved image or create a new Photoshop document.**

2. **Select the Type tool.**

3. **Select the type layer you want to modify, or click in the type in the document.**

4. **You can begin typing at the place you clicked, backspace to eliminate characters, or drag the mouse from the insertion point to select characters to copy, delete, or format.**

5. **When you're done entering your changes, click the Commit button.**

Finding and replacing text

You can make global changes in a text layer, switching all occurrences of a set of characters to another string. For example, you might have typed Ghandi a few dozen times before remembering that the Mahatma's name is spelled Gandhi. To replace text, follow these steps:

1. **Open a saved image or create a new Photoshop document.**

2. **Select the type layer you want to modify.**

3. **Choose Edit⇨Find and Replace⇨ Text.**

   The Find and Replace Text dialog box appears, as shown in Figure 3-10.

4. **Type or paste the text you want to replace in the Find What box.**

Figure 3-10: Make global changes to your text with the Find and Replace command.

5. **Enter the replacement text in the Change To box.**

6. **If you want the search to locate only text that exactly matches the case of the Find string (that is *FREEdom* but not *Freedom*), choose the Case Sensitive option.**

7. **To ignore the search word embedded in another word (say, to find *the* but not *there* or *they*), choose Whole Word Only.**

8. **Click Find Next.**

9. **As each string is found, select whether you want to**

- **Change:** This changes only the string of text just located. Click this button if you are looking for one particular occurrence.

- **Change All:** This changes all occurrences of the search text with the replacement string in your text.

- **Change/Find:** This changes the found text and then looks for the next occurrence.

Checking your spelling

Photoshop can check your spelling by using an internal dictionary that you can update with words of your own. Even though you're not likely to enter huge amounts of text in Photoshop, that's no excuse for misspelling the words that you do include. Indeed, because it's so difficult to change text after you've rasterized a text layer, the spell checker can save you a great deal of work. Here's how to use it:

1. **Open a saved image or create a new Photoshop document.**

2. **Make sure that you've specified the correct language in the Character palette's language menu.**

3. **Select the text that you want to check, or select a type layer to check all the text on that layer.**

4. **Choose Edit⇨Check Spelling.**

5. **When Photoshop identifies a possible error in the Not in Dictionary box, click Change to substitute the recommended correction for the word that is spelled incorrectly.**

   Or you can choose from one of these options:

   - **Ignore:** Leaves the word alone and continues to check the next text.

   - **Ignore All:** Ignores all instances of the word for the rest of the spell-check session.

   - **Suggestions:** Choose a different word from the Suggestions text box, or type in the correct spelling yourself.

   - **Change All:** Corrects all occurrences of the misspelled word.

   - **Add:** Adds the unfamiliar word to Photoshop's dictionary.

   Deselect the Check All Layers option to check only the currently selected layer.

6. **Click Done when you finish.**

   The Check Spelling dialog box closes.

Masking, Shaping, and Warping Type

You can do a lot more with type than create labels, captions, or paragraphs of text. Type can become an integral part of the decorative design, especially when you stylize, warp, or otherwise transform it in interesting ways.

Your Photoshop text can have character, too, communicating messages with more than just words. The text of a beach scene can appear to be wavy or watery and translucent. Halloween type can take on a ghostly or spooky appearance. Type can be romantic, otherworldly, cheerful, or comical. It all depends on how you create and apply it.

This chapter shows you some of the tricks you can perform by masking, warping, and shaping your type so your words come to life and add something special to your images.

Playing with type layer opacity

Layers are the stacks of digital overlays on which each of the elements of your image reside. (Check out Book V, Chapter 1 for the lowdown on layers.) You can change the transparency of a type layer the same as you can with any other layer in Photoshop, reducing the opacity (transparency) of the type so it allows the underlying layer to show through. Take a look at Figure 3-11, which shows type at varying levels of opacity over an image.

100% opacity

80% opacity

60% opacity

40% opacity

20% opacity

Corbis Digital Stock

Figure 3-11: Varying the opacity of your type is as easy as dragging a slider.

Changing the opacity of a type layer can convey an idea of gradual visibility of words onto an image. When working with opacity in multiple layers of type, you can create a sort of non-animated fade-in, each with a greater opacity. Figure 3-12 shows an example of this effect.

Corbis Digital Stock

Figure 3-12: Gradually fade your type to get the message across.

Another way to alter the transparency of type is to use a layer mask. (Check out Book VI, Chapter 3 for more information on layer masks.) By using a layer mask, you can customize your transparency with maximum flexibility and still edit the text to change the wording, font size, font, or anything else. Simply apply a gradient or grab a brush and paint on the layer mask. I used the fun Drippy Water Color Brush and painted on my layer mask, as shown in Figure 3-13.

PhotoSpin

Figure 3-13: Creating a layer mask on your type layer gives you more flexibility with your transparency effects.

The first Putting-It-Together project in this chapter shows you another way to use type opacity to create a ghostly effect.

Creating fade effects

To create a "fade out" image, just follow these steps:

1. **Enter the words** Fading out slowly **(or other text of your choice) into a new type layer.**

   You find out how to enter text earlier in this chapter.

2. **Choose Layer➪Layer Mask➪Reveal All.**

   This creates a mask that can show or hide some of the layer. With Reveal All selected, the layer defaults to showing everything on the layer without hiding any of it.

3. **Press D to make sure that Photoshop's colors are the default black and white.**

4. **Choose the Gradient tool from the Tools palette.**

   Or press Shift+G until it is active.

5. **Select the Linear Gradient from the Options bar.**

6. **Click the Gradient Picker (down-pointing arrow) and choose the Foreground to Background gradient.**

   This is, by default the first one in the palette, unless you have changed the defaults.

7. **Click the layer mask's icon in the Layers palette to make sure it is active.**

8. **Click the right side of the type layer and drag to the left side.**

   Photoshop creates a gradient in the layer mask that is black on the right and fades to white on the left, as shown in Figure 3-14. That means the mask is most transparent on the left side (where the mask is white) and least transparent on the right side (where the mask is black). It reveals more of the original type on the left and fades it out on the right, as you can see in the figure.

Figure 3-14: Fade your text gradually by applying a gradient on a layer mask.

Putting It Together

Ghosting Your Type

Need some ghostly, semitransparent type? You can twist, transmogrify, and transform your text by using Photoshop's arsenal of features. Create your type from scratch in an empty document or add the type to an existing picture or background. (You can find my example image on this book's Web site.) For the heck of it, these steps show you how to add ghostly writing to an existing image. Just follow these steps:

PhotoSpin

1. **Open the background image you want to overlay with the ghost type.**

   Any image, ectoplasmic or not, will do.

2. **Choose the color you want to use for your text from the Swatches palette.**

   Black or orange are good Halloween colors, but you can use any contrasting color.

   You can also sample a color from your image with the Eyedropper tool. Simply click your desired color and it then becomes your new foreground color.

3. **Choose the Horizontal Type tool from the Tools palette and then click the area where you want to add the text.**

   The vertical cursor that appears is the same size that the text will be.

4. **Choose a font, style, and size from the drop-down list on the Options bar.**

5. **Select an anti-aliasing method to help smooth the edges of your type.**

   Anti-aliasing, which I cover earlier in this chapter, softens a hard edge by adding partially transparent pixels.

6. **Type your text.**

   The text appears on top of the background.

7. **Click the Commit button (the check icon) on the Options bar to insert the text you've typed into a layer of its own.**

continued

Book IV
Chapter 3

Creating and Editing Type

continued

8. **To change the opacity of the type, adjust the Opacity setting in the Layers palette.**

To make additional changes to the text, use a filter. For example, if you want to make the text wavy, use the Wave filter on the Filter⇨Distort menu. Or you can use other filters from the array discussed in Book VII. Just remember, when you do a warning pops up, informing you that the type layer must be rasterized (converted from editable text to pixels) first. Click OK and you're on your way.

9. **When you're satisfied with the look, save your image for additional editing later, or choose Layer⇨Flatten Image to combine the text and background.**

Creating type outlines

In addition to its Vertical and Horizontal Type tools (discussed earlier in this chapter), Photoshop includes Vertical and Horizontal Type Mask tools. These function almost identically to their conventional counterparts, with one important exception: Type mask tools don't create a new layer. Instead, they create a selection within the currently active layer, like the one shown in Figure 3-15.

Figure 3-15: Type mask tools create selection marquees from your letter shapes.

You can treat the selections created with the type mask tools just as you can any other selection. Try the following:

- Move type mask selections around your document when any of the selection tools are active.

- Store type selections as alpha channels by choosing Select⇨Save Selection. I introduce selections in Book III, Chapter 3. You can find out how to save selections in Book VI, Chapter 1.

- Skew type selections (or change them in some other way) by using Select⇨Transform. You can find more information on transforming selections in Book III, Chapter 3.

- Convert a selection into an editable path, as described in "Transforming type into vector shapes and paths," later in this chapter.

- Use the selection to cut or copy portions of an image in text-shaped chunks, as shown in Figure 3-16. You can find out how this last suggestion works by following the steps in the Putting-It-Together project at the end of this chapter, in which you find out how to literally carve your words in stone.

PhotoSpin
Figure 3-16: Use a type mask to create type from an image.

Rasterizing type the other way

In addition to rasterizing a type layer in the usual way, you can also rasterize it by merging it with a non-type layer. For example, if your type layer appears immediately above a text layer that has already been rasterized, you can merge the layers by pressing Ctrl+E (⌘+E on the Mac).

You may also come across the opportunity to rasterize a type layer because Photoshop reminds you to. Some commands, particularly filters, operate only on pixels. When you try to use them, you may see a warning dialog box. Often, the dialog box includes an option for immediately converting the type layer to raster form.

Rasterizing your type layer

The Type tool creates editable type layers. You can change the wording, spacing, font, font size, and other factors as much as you want, as long as the type remains in a type layer.

However, after you make all the changes you want, you may need to convert your type layer to pixels in the form of rasterized type. After they're rasterized, you can apply filters, paint on the type, and apply gradients and patterns. Rasterizing type layers allows you to merge the type with other pixels in your image and, eventually, flatten the image to create a finished document suitable for use with other programs.

After you convert your type to pixels, you can no longer edit the type. Nor can you resize the text without risking jaggies. You want to rasterize your type only when you're certain you won't need to edit or resize it. Make a copy of the type layer before you rasterize it and toggle off the visibility of the copy, and make sure you save an unflattened copy of the document with all layers intact. That way if you need to edit the type, you have the layered file with the unrasterized text. For more on layers, see Book V.

To rasterize your type, select the type layer that you want to convert to pixels. Then choose Layer⇨Rasterize⇨Type. The type is shown in the Layers palette on a transparent background.

Transforming type into vector shapes and paths

By default, regular type created with the Type tool is vector-based type, not bitmapped, rasterized type. But you can also convert regular type (each character) to individual vector shapes. The individual characters then become shapes defined by vector masks. You can edit the shapes like any shapes created with the shape tools, by manipulating anchor points and straight and curved segments. See Book IV, Chapter 1 for the lowdown on shapes. And you can also convert regular type to work paths where each character becomes a path, editable like any other path with the selection arrows and pen tools. Type is usually converted into a path in order to create a clipping path based on the type (see Book III, Chapter 2). For more on paths, see Book III, Chapter 2.

So again, you can convert regular nonrasterized vector type to Photoshop line/curve-oriented shapes in the form of a vector mask or work path. You convert type to vector shapes and paths in order to edit it with the pen tools. Here are the ways to do that:

- To convert type to an editable work path, choose Layer⇨Type⇨Create Work Path.

- To convert type to shapes, choose Layer⇨Type⇨Convert to Shape.

Here are the chief things to know about type converted into a shape or path:

- Like type layers, you can resize it without producing jagged diagonal lines.

- You can edit the shape of the charac-ters, but you cannot edit the text itself, as shown in Figure 3-17.

- You must rasterize the converted type before you can merge it with pixel-based layers or apply special effects with filters. You can apply layer styles to any kind of type, how-ever. Be sure to check out Book V, Chapter 4 for all you need to know about layer styles.

- If you have converted your type into a shape, it becomes a vector mask exactly like other vector masks in Photoshop, and you can edit the shape of the characters by using the pen tools. You can find detailed infor-mation on editing vector masks in Book VI, Chapter 1.

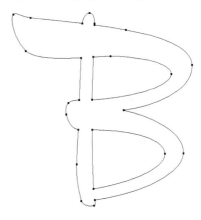

Figure 3-17: Converting your type to a path allows you to alter the shape of the letters.

Book IV
Chapter 3

Creating and
Editing Type

Wreaking havoc on your type

Photoshop's great automated Warp feature can twist your type in predictable ways that are not only repeatable but, thanks to the controls in their dialog boxes, customizable as well. The cool part is that even though type has been warped, it remains fully editable until you rasterize it. All you need to do to warp your text is click the Warp icon on the Options bar. This opens the multifaceted Warp Text dialog box, shown in Figure 3-18.

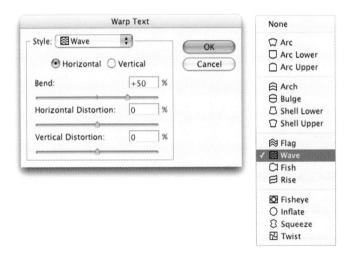

Figure 3-18: Choose from a number of warp styles.

Web developers take note: You cannot warp text that has faux styles applied (found in the Character palette).

You find a whole list of special effects, such as Arc, Arch, Bulge, Flag, Wave, Fish, Fisheye, and Twist. Each of these effects provides a special look to your type, as shown in Figure 3-19.

Each effect has a dialog box of its own that allows you to set

Figure 3-19: Even after warping your text it remains fully editable.

the parameters for the amount, direction, degree of distortion, amount of bend, and so forth. You can watch your type warp right on-screen and tailor the distortion as you like. You can apply most asymmetrical warp effects to type in either horizontal or vertical directions. Fisheye, Inflate, and Twist are among those that can't be rotated, because their effects are already oriented in horizontal and vertical directions that you can control with sliders.

Putting It Together

Carving Your Type in Stone

You can use the Type tool to create selections shaped like text and then use images themselves as textures for the type. For example, if you were creating a floral-themed Web page, you could use pictures of flowers as the fill for your text. A type selection can cut out any part of a picture for use any way you want.

Corbis Digital Stock

Follow these steps to carve letters into a stone texture image:

1. **Open the stone texture image you want to use.**

I'm using a sandstone wall, but you can use other kinds of stone, wood, or any texture that interests you. Best of all, the embossed look that results is only one of many different looks you can achieve simply by making small changes in the Layer style that you apply to the text.

2. **Choose the Horizontal Type Mask tool from the Tools palette and then click in the area where you want to enter your text.**

3. **Choose the font, font style, font size, and other text parameters from the drop-down lists on the Options bar.**

4. **Enter the text you want to use onto the texture you've chosen. Then click the Commit button (check mark icon) on the Options bar to set your text.**

The selection in the shape of the text appears where you typed the text.

continued

Book IV
Chapter 3

Creating and
Editing Type

continued

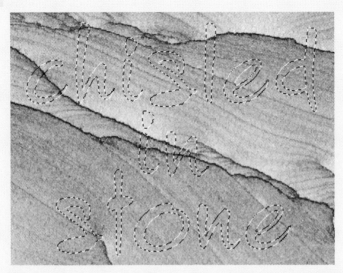

Corbis Digital Stock

5. **Press Ctrl+C (⌘+C on the Mac) to copy the selected area of your chosen texture (the brick in the shape of the text in my example), and then press Ctrl+V (⌘+V on the Mac) to paste a text-shaped section of that texture in a layer of its own.**

The text blends in with what's in the background layer (in my example, the stone) and is invisible (for now).

6. **Choose Layer➪Layer Style➪Bevel and Emboss to open the Layer Style dialog box.**

In the Layer Style dialog box, you find dozens of different effects that you can create.

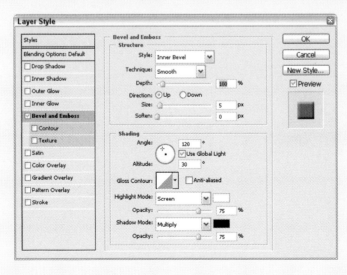

7. **Experiment with the settings in the Layer Style dialog box to try out different looks and to achieve various effects.**

   🖝 **Choose the kind of beveling or embossing you want from the Style and Technique drop-down lists in the Structure area.**

   I choose Inner Bevel and Chisel Hard to produce a dramatic, hard-edged embossing effect.

   🖝 **Move the Depth slider to the right to increase the depth of the bevel.**

   I set the value at 500% for a raised effect. A lower value produces a less 3-D effect, while a higher value produces a more drastic 3-D effect.

   🖝 **Select the Contour check box on the left side for an even more pronounced 3-D look.**

   🖝 **In the Shading area, you can adjust controls that allow you to change the apparent angle of the illumination that produces the bevel's shadow.**

   I moved the angle to 95 degrees (roughly straight overhead), but I left the other controls alone.

   You can find details about how to use the other options in the Layer Style dialog box in Book V, Chapter 4.

8. **Click OK to apply the effects that you've chosen.**

9. **As a last touch, choose Image⇨Adjustments⇨Levels to darken the text layer to make it stand out even more distinctly from the background.**

   For more info on how to use the Levels adjustment see Book VIII, Chapter 1.

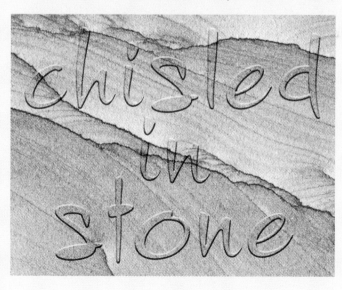

**Book IV
Chapter 3**

**Creating and
Editing Type**

Book V
Working with Layers

The 5th Wave — By Rich Tennant

RICHTENNANT

"Please Dad – do we have to hear the story of Snow White and her 7-layer composite again?"

*L*ayers are like modern appliances. Sure, you could live without a microwave, a dishwasher, and a vacuum cleaner, but cooking and cleaning would take a lot longer, and it wouldn't be nearly as convenient. Layers give Photoshop users the ultimate in editing flexibility. This in turn saves production time, giving you more time to let your creative juices flow.

In this book, I give you information about how to create and edit layers. You see how to take multiple images and create single composite images. I also cover how to manage your layers by using layer sets and layer comps. And you find out how to enhance your layers by using adjustment layers, layer styles, blend modes, and various opacity settings. Finally, you'll want to check out the chapter on the new Smart Objects. These new objects allow you to transform objects indefinitely without loss of quality.

Chapter 1: Creating Layers

In This Chapter

- Backgrounds versus layers
- Taking at look at the types of layers
- Working with the Layers palette
- Creating layers
- Compositing with multiple layers
- Transforming layers

*P*eople are often surprised and even downright shocked when I tell them that pretty much everything they can do with layers they can also do without them. Not using layers would be more technically challenging and a heck of a lot more tedious, but you could still get the job done. The benefit to using layers is that you have tremendous flexibility. The changes you make to the pixels on the individual layers are permanent, but the interaction between the pixels on different layers is dynamic. You can make endless edits as long as those layers exist. Layers make working in Photoshop a lot more forgiving, allowing you to make changes quickly and productively.

But hey, it's not just the technical and practical aspects that make layers so wonderful. Layers also allow you to express your creative side, compositing several images into one, with just a drag of the mouse. The only downside to layers is that each one makes your file size grow and therefore can start to slow your system performance. And you can save layers in only a few file formats. But the downsides are a small price to pay for something that makes your image-editing life so much easier.

Getting to Know the Layers Palette

In terms of a real-world analogy, think of layers as sheets of acetate, similar to those clear plastic sheets used with overhead projectors. You draw different elements on the various sheets. What you draw on one sheet doesn't affect the other sheets. You can show just one sheet, or you can stack several on top of one another to create a combination image. You can reshuffle the order of the sheets, add new sheets, or delete old sheets. Any space on the sheet that doesn't have a mark on it is clear, or transparent.

That's how layers work in Photoshop. You can place elements on separate layers, yet show them together to create a combination image, or *composite*. You can also add, delete, or rearrange layers. And unlike sheets of acetate, you can adjust how opaque or transparent the element on the layer is, as well as change the way the colors between layers interact (blend modes).

Just as with every other important aspect of Photoshop, the program houses layers in a single location, called a palette. It's time to formally meet the powerful palette that controls the operations of layers. To display the Layers palette, shown in Figure 1-1, choose Window⇨Layers or, easier yet, press F7.

Active layer

Type layer

Figure 1-1: Layers give you tremendous editing flexibility.

The order of the layers in the Layers palette represents the order in the image. The top layer in the palette is the top layer in your image, and so on.

For some tasks you can work on only one layer at a time. For other tasks, you can work on multiple layers simultaneously.

Here's the lowdown on how to work with the Layers palette:

✓ **Select a layer:** Simply click its name or thumbnail. Photoshop then highlights the *active layer*.

✓ **Select multiple contiguous layers:** Click your first layer and then Shift+click your last layer.

✓ **Select multiple non-contiguous layers:** Ctrl+click (⌘+click on the Mac) your desired layers.

✓ **Select all layers:** Choose Select⇨All Layers.

✓ **Select layers of similar type:** Select a layer and then choose Select⇨Similar Layers.

✓ **Deselect all layers:** Choose Select⇨Deselect Layers or click in the area below the bottom layer or background.

✓ **Select the actual element (the non-transparent pixels) on the layer:** Ctrl+click (⌘+click on the Mac) the layer's thumbnail in the palette. If you forget this handy shortcut, you can also choose Select⇨Load Selection. Make sure that the layer name that appears in the Channel pop-up menu is [layer name] Transparency and click OK.

✓ **Create a new blank layer:** Click the Create a New Layer icon at the bottom of the palette. See the next section for more on creating layers.

✓ **Create an adjustment or fill layer:** Click the Create a New Fill or Adjustment Layer icon at the bottom of the palette. See "Introducing Different Types of Layers," later in this chapter, for more on these layers.

✓ **Duplicate an existing layer:** Drag the layer to the Create a New Layer icon at the bottom of the palette. See the next section for more on creating layers.

✓ **Rename a layer:** When you create a new layer, Photoshop provides default layer names (Layer 1, Layer 2, and so on). If you want to rename a layer, simply double-click the layer name (the name not the thumbnail) in the Layers palette and enter the name directly in the Layers palette. This renaming shortcut works throughout Photoshop (the Channels palette, the Paths palette, and so on). You can also select the layer and choose Layer Properties from the Layers palette options menu or choose Layer⇨Layer Properties.

✓ **Determine what layer holds the element you want to edit:** Select the Move tool and Ctrl+click (⌘+click on the Mac) the element. Photoshop automatically activates the appropriate layer. Or you can right-click (Control+click on the Mac) the element. A context menu appears, telling you what layer the element resides on, and then enables you to select that layer.

You can use the keyboard shortcut Alt+] (right bracket) (Option+] on the Mac) to move up one layer; Alt+[(left bracket) (Option+[on the Mac) to activate the next layer down. Press Shift+Alt+] (Shift+Option+] on the Mac) to move to the top layer; press Shift+Alt+[(Shift+Option+[on the Mac) to move to the background or bottom layer.

✔ **Adjust the interaction between colors on layers and adjust the transparency of layers:** You can use the blend modes and the opacity and fill options at the top of the palette to mix the colors between layers and adjust the transparency of the layers. For details, see Book V, Chapter 3.

✔ **Delete a layer:** Drag it to the trash can icon at the bottom of the Layers palette. You can also choose Layer⇨Delete⇨Layer or choose Delete Layer from the palette options menu.

✔ **Change the size of the layer thumbnails:** Choose Palette Options from the palette options menu and select a thumbnail size.

The remaining icons at the bottom of the Layers palette allow you to link layers, create layer styles, layer masks, and layers groups, all of which warrant sections of their own. See Book V, Chapter 4 for more on layer styles and Chapter 2 for more on layer sets. Check out Book VI, Chapter 3 for more on layer masks.

The preceding list represents just the tip of the iceberg. You can also view and hide layers, link, lock, color-code, rearrange, merge, flatten, and animate layers. Book V, Chapter 2 covers most topics in detail.

Looking at the Background and Layers

When you create a new image with white or background colored contents, scan an image into Photoshop, or open a file from a stock photography CD, Kodak Photo CD, or your own digital camera, you basically have a file with just a *background*.

An image contains only one background, and you can't do much to it besides paint on it and make basic adjustments. You can't rearrange the background in the stack of layers — it's always on the very bottom of the Layers palette. You can't change the opacity, or blend mode of a background either. What you can do is convert a background to a layer, and then the world's at your feet.

To convert a background into a layer, follow these steps:

1. **Double-click Background in the Layers palette.**

   In addition, you can choose Layer⇨New⇨Layer from Background. Note that the name Background is italicized in the Layers palette, as shown in Figure 1-2.

PhotoSpin

Figure 1-2: A newly opened image in Photoshop contains only a background.

2. Name the layer or leave it at the default name of Layer 0.

You can also color-code your layer by choosing Layer Properties from the palette pop-up menu. All this does is make your layer stand out more noticeably in the Layers palette.

3. Click OK.

Photoshop converts your background into a layer, as indicated in the Layers palette. Note that the layer name is no longer italicized, as shown in Figure 1-3.

When you create a new image with transparent contents, the image doesn't contain a background but instead is created with a single layer. You can also convert a layer into a background by selecting it and then choosing Layer⊅New⊅Background from Layer. Note that this option is available only when no background exists.

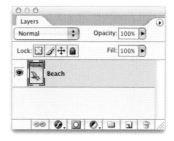

Figure 1-3: Double-click the background to convert it into a layer.

Introducing Different Types of Layers

Although turning the background into a layer (discussed in the previous section) is a popular activity, Photoshop refers to *layers* in the plural for a reason. Image editing would be no fun if you didn't have a variety of different layers to mess around with.

Photoshop offers five types of layers. Four of the five have very specific purposes in the life of your image. Some you may never use, and some you'll use only occasionally. But the vanilla-flavored type, which you'll use the most, is simply called a layer. Read on to find out more.

Using plain vanilla layers

The regular layer is the one that most closely matches the acetate analogy. You put various elements on separate layers to create a composite image. You can create blank layers and add images to them, or you can create layers from images themselves. You can create as many layers as your computer's RAM lets you. And sometimes layers are created automatically by a specific action.

Because each layer in an image is a separate entity, you can edit, paint, transform, mask, or apply a filter on a layer without affecting the other layers. And once an element is on a layer, you no longer have to make a selection (get the selection outline) to select it — you simply drag the element with the Move tool. The element freely floats in a sea of transparency. Because showing "clear" areas or transparency is impossible on a computer monitor, Photoshop uses a gray-and-white checkerboard, by default, to represent the transparent areas of a layer.

Because you'll work with regular layers on a daily basis, I spend the majority of Book V discussing them.

Playing around with layer masks

A *layer mask* is like a second sheet of acetate that hovers over a layer. You can use layer masks with regular layers, adjustment layers, and fill layers. For example, you may paint on a layer mask (typically with black, white, and various shades of gray) to selectively hide or display an adjustment (or an image on a regular layer). Any black areas on the mask hide the adjustment, any white areas show the adjustment, and anything in between (gray) partially shows the adjustment. I cover layer masks in detail in Book VI, Chapter 3.

Using adjustment layers

An adjustment layer is a special kind of layer used expressly for color correction. What's great about adjustment layers is that you can apply that color correction without permanently affecting any of your layers. Adjustment layers apply the correction to all the layers below them, without affecting any of the layers above them.

Because the color correction actually resides on a layer, you can edit, delete, duplicate, merge, or rearrange the adjustment layer at any time. You have more flexibility in your image-editing chores and more freedom for experimentation. In addition, none of this experimentation harms your image because it takes place above the image on an adjustment layer.

Photoshop has 12 kinds of adjustment layers, and you can use as many as your heart desires. The adjustments offered are the same adjustments you find on the Image⇨Adjustments menu. For specifics on each adjustment and what it corrects, see Book VIII, Chapter 1. Here's how to create an adjustment layer:

1. **Open an image of your choice.**

   Because you're applying an adjustment layer, you may want to use an image that is in need of some color correction. In the case of adjustment layers, you don't need to convert your background into a layer. I chose an image that was oversaturated.

2. **Choose Layer⇨New Adjustment Layer. From the submenu, choose your desired adjustment. Name the layer if you want, leave the other options at their defaults, and click OK.**

   For my example, I chose Hue/Saturation.

   You can also just click the Create a New Fill or Adjustment Layer icon (the black and white circle icon) at the bottom of the Layers palette and choose an adjustment from the pop-up menu.

   The dialog box pertaining to your adjustment appears.

3. **Make the necessary corrections and click OK.**

   After you close the dialog box, the adjustment layer appears in the Layers palette, shown in Figure 1-4. The adjustment layer icon and a thumbnail appear on the adjustment layer. The thumbnail represents a layer mask. For more on layer masks, check out the "Playing around with layer masks" sidebar in this chapter.

Adjustment layer

Layer mask thumbnail

Adjustment icon

Corbis Digital Stock

Figure 1-4: Applying your corrections to an adjustment layer, rather than directly on the image, allows for more editing flexibility.

In my example, the layer mask is all white, so my adjustment shows up full strength over my entire image. Note that you can also apply an adjustment layer to a selected portion of your image. Like regular layers, you can adjust the opacity, fill, and blend modes of an adjustment layer. For more on these options, see Book V, Chapter 3.

If you want to view your image without the adjustment, click the eye icon in the left column of the Layers palette to hide the adjustment layer. You can find more on viewing layers in Book V, Chapter 2. If you want to delete the adjustment layer, simply drag it to the trash can icon in the Layers palette or choose Delete from the Layer menu or Layers palette options menu.

Editing adjustment layers

After you create an adjustment layer, you can easily edit it. Simply double-click the adjustment layer circle icon in the Layers palette or choose Layer⊅Layer Content Options. In the dialog box that appears, make any edits and then click OK. The only adjustment layer that you cannot edit is the Invert adjustment. It is either totally on or totally off.

To change the content of an adjustment layer, choose Layer⊅Change Layer Content and select a different adjustment layer from the submenu. Editing and changing the content works the exact same way for fill layers (which I discuss in the next section).

Isolating your adjustments

If you don't use an adjustment layer when you make color corrections, the correction you apply affects only the *active* layer (the layer highlighted in the Layers palette). This may be the way to go if you want to just tweak the color on a single layer.

Here are some tips for using and isolating adjustment layers:

✔ **Correct part (but not all) of a layer:** To enable the adjustment layer to correct only a portion of a layer, make a selection before you create the adjustment layer. The adjustment affects only the pixels within the selection outline.

This is referring to the pixels within the selection outline *on each layer that resides below the adjustment layer.* In addition to making a selection, you can also create and select a closed path (see Book III, Chapter 2 for more on paths).

✔ **Create a clipping group:** When you create a *clipping group* of the layers you want to adjust, you can place the adjustment layer in or at the bottom of the clipping group, and it affects only those clipped layers. In a clipping group, the bottommost layer acts as a mask for the layers in the group. For more on clipping groups, see Book V, Chapter 4.

✔ **Create a layer group:** You can create a *layer group* (described in Book V, Chapter 2) and place the layers you want adjusted in that group. Then make sure that the blend mode is set to any mode except Pass Through. For more on modes, see Book V, Chapter 3.

Taking advantage of fill layers

A *fill layer* lets you add a layer of solid color, a gradient, or a pattern. Like adjustment layers, fill layers also have layer masks, as indicated by the mask icon thumbnail in the Layers palette.

You can create as many fill layers as you like, just as you can with regular layers and adjustment layers. You can also edit, rearrange, duplicate, delete, and merge fill layers. And you can blend fill layers with other layers by using the opacity, fill, and blend mode options in the Layers palette.

Like an adjustment layer, to confine the effects of a fill layer to a portion of the image, make a selection or create and select a closed path before you create the fill layer (see Book III, Chapter 2 for more on paths). And editing or changing the contents of a fill layer is similar to editing or changing the contents of an adjustment layer (see the preceding section for details).

Here's how to create a fill layer:

1. **Open an image of your choice.**

   In this case, open an image that would look good with a border or text. For my example, I created the word *fujiyama* by using the Horizontal Type Mask tool (for details, see Book IV, Chapter 3). If you don't have an active selection, the fill layer encompasses your entire canvas.

2. **Choose Layer➪New Fill Layer. From the submenu, choose your desired adjustment. Name the layer, leave the other options at their defaults, and click OK.**

   For my example, I chose Pattern from the submenu.

   You can also just click the Create a New Fill or Adjustment Layer icon at the bottom of the Layers palette and choose a fill from the pop-up menu.

3. **Follow the steps that correspond with the option you chose in Step 2:**

   • **Solid Color:** Choose your desired color from the Photoshop Color Picker. (For more on color, see Book II, Chapter 3.)

   • **Gradient:** Choose a preset gradient from the pop-up palette or click the gradient preview to display the Gradient Editor to create your own gradient. Set additional gradient options as desired. (For gradient details, see Book IV, Chapter 2.)

   • **Pattern:** Select a pattern from the pop-up palette. Click Scale and enter a value or drag the scale slider. I scaled my Crayon on Vellum pattern 120%, as shown in Figure 1-5. Click Snap to Origin to position the origin of the pattern with the document window. Finally, select the Link with Layer option to specify that the pattern moves with the fill layer if you move it. I chose Pattern in my example in Figure 1-5.

   Figure 1-5: Choose from a variety of preset patterns for your fill layer.

4. **Click OK.**

   After you close the dialog box, the fill layer appears in the Layers palette, as shown in Figure 1-6. Similar to adjustment layers, you'll notice the layer mask that was created on the fill layer. In my example, the word *fujiyama* appears white on the layer mask, thereby allowing my pattern to show through. The remaining areas are black, hiding my pattern. I added a couple of layer styles (Drop Shadow and Inner Bevel) to my type to jazz it up a bit. If you want to do the same, jump ahead to Book V, Chapter 4.

Figure 1-6: Your chosen fill shows through your selected areas.

If you want to delete the fill layer, do one of three things: Drag it to the trash can icon in the Layers palette; choose Delete from the Layer menu; or choose Delete Layer from the Layers palette options menu.

One final note. You can also rasterize a fill layer to convert it to a regular raster image. Choose Layer⇨Rasterize⇨Fill Content. A raster image enables you to use painting tools or filters on the layer.

Making use of shape layers

Believe or not, Photoshop isn't just about photos and painting. It also has a whole slew of shape drawing tools — six to be exact. You can fill those shapes with solid color, gradients, or patterns. When you create a shape, it resides on its own unique shape layer. A shape layer contains a *vector mask,* similar in concept to the adjustment layer mask described earlier.

If you look at the Layers palette, you can see that the Shape layer has two thumbnails: One is entirely filled with color, and the other contains the path of the shape, as shown in Figure 1-7. To state it simply, the color is peeking through the path of the shape, and the rest of the layer is hidden or masked. The paths that comprise a shape are *vector paths;* when printed, they retain their smooth curves without the jagged edges you often see from bitmap editing programs. Although you can edit, move, and transform shapes, your ability to edit shape layers is limited. To apply filters and other special effects, you must first *rasterize* the shape layers — that is, convert the vector paths to pixels. For more details on shapes, see Book IV, Chapter 2.

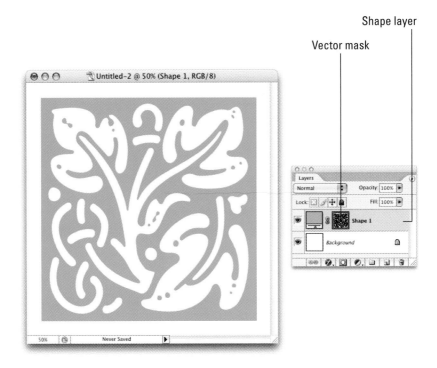

Figure 1-7: On a shape layer, color peeks through a path and is hidden everywhere else.

Using type layers

To create type, such as the type shown in Figure 1-8, click your canvas with the Type tool (horizontal or vertical) and type your desired text. After you commit your text by pressing Enter on the numeric keypad or clicking the Commit button on the Options bar (it looks like a check mark), you've created a type layer. In the Layers palette, you see a layer with a T icon, indicating that it's a type layer. Initially, the name of the type layer corresponds to the text you typed (you can change the layer name if you like). Like shapes, the text in Photoshop is true vector type and, if left in that format, always prints smooth and without the jaggies.

Figure 1-8: Type layers automatically appear when you create and commit type.

Another great thing about type in Photoshop is that it is live; you can edit the text at any time. You can also change the orientation, apply anti-aliasing (softening of the edges), create paths from the type, and even warp it into various distortions. You can also convert the type to a shape. And like regular layers, you can move, rearrange, copy, and change the layer options (opacity, fill, and mode) of a type layer. If, however, you want to apply certain special effects, such as filters, you must first *rasterize* (convert into pixels) the text. For everything you need to know about type, see Book IV, Chapter 3.

Making Layers

As I mention earlier in the chapter, good, old-fashioned, regular layers are the backbone of the world of layers. The next few sections take a look at the various ways to create these layers.

Creating a new layer

If you want to create a new blank layer, click the Create a New Layer icon at the bottom of the Layers palette. You can also create a new layer by choosing New Layer from the palette options menu or by choosing Layer⇨New⇨Layer. The latter method prompts you with a dialog box to name your layer and includes other options for grouping, color-coding, blending, and opacity (all of which I explain in other chapters in Book V). Provide a name for your layer and click OK. If you chose one of the first two methods, a layer with the default name of Layer 1 appears in the Layers palette.

You can also create an entirely new document with a layer by choosing File⇨New. In the New dialog box, select the Transparent for the Background Contents option. Your new file then appears with Layer 1 instead of a background.

When you click the Create a New Layer icon, the layer is added above your active layer. By pressing the Ctrl key (⌘ on the Mac) when you click, Photoshop adds the new layer below the active layer.

Your new transparent layer is now ready for content. You can put content on the new layer several ways:

- ✓ Use one of the painting tools and paint directly on the layer.

- ✓ Make a selection on another layer or the background (for the difference between the two, see the previous sections in this chapter) within the same document or from another image entirely and then choose Edit⇨Copy. Select your new blank layer in the Layers palette and then choose Edit⇨Paste.

✓ Make a selection on another layer (or the background) within the same document or from another image and then choose Edit➪Cut. Select your new blank layer and then choose Edit➪Paste. Just remember that Photoshop deletes the selection from the source and adds it to your new layer, as shown in Figure 1-9.

✓ Transfer an entire image to your new layer by choosing Select➪All and then either Edit➪Copy or Edit➪Cut. Select your new blank layer and then choose Edit➪Paste.

Figure 1-9: Cutting and pasting a selection from one layer to another leaves a transparent hole on the original layer.

Using Layer via Copy and Layer via Cut

Another way to create a layer is to use the Layer via Copy command on the Layer menu. Make a selection on a layer or background and choose Layer⇨ New⇨Layer via Copy. The copied selection is placed on a new layer with the default name of Layer 1. You can do the same with the Layer via Cut command, but in this case, Photoshop deletes the selected area from the source layer or background and places it on the new layer. The source layer is left with a gaping transparent hole (refer to Figure 1-9). If you used the background for the source, your background color fills the space. Remember that you can use these two commands only within the same image. You cannot use them between multiple images.

Duplicating layers

If you want to duplicate an existing layer, first select it in the Layers palette. Then drag the layer to the Create a New Layer icon at the bottom of the palette. You can also duplicate a layer by choosing Duplicate Layer from the palette options menu or by choosing Layer⇨Duplicate Layer. Like with creating a new layer, the latter method prompts you with a dialog box to name your layer and includes other options. Provide a name for your layer and click OK. If you chose either of the first two methods, Photoshop provides the default name of the original layer with Copy appended to the name. Duplicating layers can be especially handy when you want to experiment with a special effect but don't want to harm your original image.

Compositing with Multiple Images

Often when working with layers, you are not confined to using a single image. I mean, you can do only so much to that family portrait taken down at the local photo studio. But take your family and put them in front of the ruins at Machu Picchu or the summit at Mount Everest (you can even add faux snow with a technique shown in Book VII), and you have endless hours of fun. When you get the hang of working with several images, you'll find that it opens a whole new door of creative possibilities. And you're not limited to just plain old snapshots. You can incorporate type, vector illustrations, and scans of just about anything you can place on a scanning bed. Apply some layer styles, maybe a filter or two (see Book VII), and you have an image worthy of some major wall space.

Copying and pasting images

Earlier in the "Making Layers" section, I explain how to use the Copy, Cut, and Paste commands within the same image or between two different images when you want to fill a new blank layer with content. You can also use the Copy and Paste commands without having a blank layer first. When you copy and paste a selection without a blank layer, Photoshop automatically creates a new layer from the pasted selection. You can go about your merry way and perform all your layer creations by using only those commands. However, I rarely use them when working with multiple images. I prefer the drag-and-drop method, which I describe next.

The Copy Merged command on the Edit menu creates a merged copy of *all* the visible layers within the selection.

Dragging and dropping layers

To copy an entire layer from one document to another, simply select the layer in the Layers palette, grab the Move tool, and drag and drop that layer onto your destination document. Photoshop automatically introduces the dropped layer as a *new* layer above the active layer in the image. You don't need to have a selection outline to copy the entire layer. However, if you want to copy just a portion of the layer, make your desired selection, as shown in Figure 1-10, before you drag and drop with the Move tool. If you want the selected element to be centered on the destination image, press the Shift key as you drag and drop. See the sidebar, "Bypassing the clipboard" for more on dragging and dropping.

Bypassing the clipboard

Yes, you can always cut and paste or copy and paste a layer from one image to another, but I prefer to drag and drop rather than copy and paste between two images. By dragging and dropping, you bypass the temporary storage area for copied and stored data, the *clipboard*. (Whenever you copy or cut a selection, Photoshop stores the selection on the clipboard until you are ready to paste it to its new home.) So what's wrong with that? Well, nothing, unless you're working with high-resolution images. Storing images on the clipboard, even on a temporary basis, can slow down your system. Keeping your clipboard clear of data ensures that Photoshop is running lean and mean so that you can drag and drop more images, selections, and layers, quicker and more efficiently. If you want to hold a little spring cleaning on your clipboard, you can always choose Edit⇨Purge⇨ Clipboard, which empties your clipboard of any stored data. Take my advice and try the drag-and-drop method. I guarantee that, like me, you'll be flexing your trigger finger — all the better to drag and drop even faster.

What if you have multiple elements on one layer and want to select only one of the elements to drag and drop? Simply grab the Lasso tool and draw around the object. You don't have to be super precise, but don't include any portion of the other elements on the layer. Then press the Ctrl key (⌘ key on the Mac) and press the up-arrow key once. The element will then become neatly selected. Not only can you drag and drop the element, but you can also move or edit it without affecting the other pixels on the layer.

Figure 1-10: Dragging and dropping a selection keeps your clipboard lean and mean.

Using the Paste Into command

You may occasionally want to place an image on a separate layer, yet have it fill a selection. That's where Edit➪Paste Into comes into play. This command enables you to insert a copied or cut selected image into a selection outline.

For example, if you want to make it appear as if a snake is poking its head out of the opening of a cave, or a bottle poking out of a can, as shown in Figure 1-11, Paste Into is your command. Be sure to check out the Putting-It-Together project in this chapter to get more practice at this practical technique.

Layer mask

PhotoSpin

Figure 1-11: Use the Paste Into command to make one layer appear as though it is emerging from another.

Follow these steps to insert a copied or cut selected image into a selection outline:

1. Make the selection on the layer that you want the image to fill.

I'll call this the destination layer.

2. Select the image that will fill that selection.

I'll call this the source image.

Note: The source image can be within the same image or from another image.

3. Choose Edit⇨Copy.

4. Return to the destination layer and choose Edit⇨Paste Into.

Photoshop converts the selection outline on the destination layer into a layer mask. The pasted selection is visible only inside the selection outline. In my example, my bottle is showing only inside my selection. The bottom of the bottle is hidden, making it look like my bottle is sitting inside the can.

Transforming Layers

When compositing multiple images, you will no doubt have to scale some of your image to fit it into your layout. Fortunately, Photoshop makes scaling an easy chore by providing you with the Transform and Free Transform commands on the Edit menu. Transforming layers is almost identical to transforming selections except that you don't need to make a selection first. After an element is on a layer, you can just choose the appropriate transformation command and off you go. In addition, you can apply a transformation to multiple layers simultaneously if you link the layers first. Because I explain each transformation in excruciating detail in Book III, Chapter 3, check that out if you need more detail.

Try to perform all your transformations in one execution. Don't go back numerous times and apply various transformations. Each time you transform pixels, you are putting your image through the interpolation process (manufacturing pixels). Done repeatedly, your image may start to turn into mush. And if not mush, it will not be as pristine and crisp as it was before.

If your image looks jagged after you transform it, you may have your preferences set incorrectly for your interpolation method. Choose Edit⇨ Preferences⇨General (Photoshop⇨Preferences⇨General on Mac OS X) and select the Bicubic option from the Interpolation pop-up menu. Bicubic enables a smoother appearance to your interpolated pixels.

When the Move tool is active, you can transform a layer without choosing a command. Simply select the Show Transform Controls option on the Options bar. This option surrounds the contents (or an active selection) of the layer with a bounding box with handles. Drag these handles to transform the contents.

Putting It Together

Creating Layers and Using the Paste Into Command to Make a Collage

If you remember your elementary-school days, you probably remember cutting out a bunch of pictures from magazines and pasting them on a piece of construction paper. Well, with Photoshop, the idea of a collage isn't much different, but the activity is a little more refined.

Maybe you want to let loose your artistic side. Or maybe you need to combine several images into one as part of a job. Whatever your reason, you can use the steps here to get started on your first collage. And by the way, if *collage* is too froufrou a word for you, you can substitute it with *composite* — as in the definition of "derived from many components." I usually do.

Creating a collage takes many steps. Throughout Book V, you find several ongoing Putting-It-Together projects, all of which lead you to a finished collage. Be sure to save your collage file so that you can work on it as you make your way through this book.

If you're short on photos, you can go to www.gettyimages.com. Be sure to register so that you can have access to a huge gallery of free *comping images*. Comping images are small, low-resolution images used for internal corporate or personal noncommercial use only.

To create the first layer of your collage, follow these steps:

1. **Decide on two images you want to use in your collage and open them by choosing File⇨Open.**

I recommend picking an image to use as your main canvas and then opening up a supporting image that you can select and then drag onto that main image. However, if you want, you can also start with just a blank document. For my example, I decided on a travel theme and opened an image of the Grand Canyon and another image of a passport, as shown in the figure.

2. **Choose Window⇨Layers to open the Layers palette.**

Always be sure that the Layers palette is visible whenever you're creating a composite from multiple images. You need to see what is happening as you drag and drop, and you need to be aware of what layer you are working on at all times.

3. **Select the desired element in the supporting image.**

Feel free to use whatever selection method suits your fancy, but remember, the finished collage will look only as good as its individual selections. For more on making selections, see Book III.

Because the contrast between my passport and the background behind it was very good, I grabbed the Magic Wand tool, set the Tolerance to 50, and clicked the passport. I then pressed the Shift key and, with the Lasso tool, circled the remaining pixels in the gold type that the Magic Wand tool didn't pick up, as you can see in my figure.

4. **Choose Select⇨Modify⇨Contract and enter a value. Then choose Select⇨ Feather and enter a value.**

   Contract the selections lightly (I chose a value of 1 pixel) before you apply a feather (I chose a 0.5 pixel value) to avoid picking up some of the background during the feathering process.

TIP

Using a small feather helps to avoid the harsh, looks-like-I-cut-it-out-with-a-pair-of-pinking-shears look.

continued

continued

5. **With the Move tool, drag and drop the selection onto the background.**

   The Layers palette shows that you've produced a layer. You'll notice that your main image remains as the background below the layer, as shown in the figure.

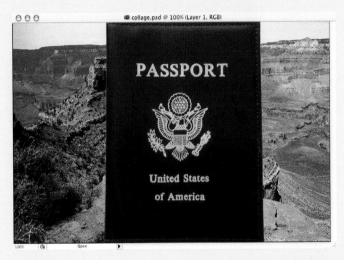

Don't worry if your element isn't the right size. You can find a Putting-It-Together project in Book V, Chapter 2 that shows you how to scale the layer.

6. **Choose File⇨Save. Name the file *collage* and make sure the format is Photoshop.**

   Keep the file in a handy spot on your hard drive so that you can find it when you're ready to do more with your collage.

I've already shown you how to create a layer by dragging and dropping a passport onto a background image of the Grand Canyon. The process I'm demonstrating here is a little different. It entails pasting one selection into another.

Sticking with my travel theme, I opted to take the image of a compass and paste it into the background so that the compass looks like it's peaking out from the side of the canyon.

To paste one selection into another on your collage, follow these steps:

1. **Choose File⇨Open. Select the file you saved from the last exercise. Also open a new supporting image.**

2. **Choose Window⇨Layers to open the Layers palette.**

   Always keep the Layers palette visible whenever you are creating a composite from multiple images.

3. **Select the part of the supporting image that you want to use.**

Feel free to use whatever selection method you desire, but try to get as accurate a selection as you can.

For my compass image, I used the Elliptical Marquee tool, while pressing the Alt key (Option on the Mac), to draw from the center out to select the bottom portion of the compass. With the same tool, I pressed the Shift key and then the mouse button and then the Alt key (Option) to add the top portion of the compass, as shown in the figure.

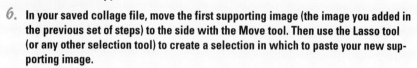

4. **Contract and feather the selection (as described in Step 4 in the previous set of steps).**

Unless you're going for some special effect, be consistent with the treatment of the edges of each of your elements in your composite.

5. **Choose Edit⇨Copy.**

6. **In your saved collage file, move the first supporting image (the image you added in the previous set of steps) to the side with the Move tool. Then use the Lasso tool (or any other selection tool) to create a selection in which to paste your new supporting image.**

I want the compass image to look as if it is peeking up from behind the side of the canyon, so I made a selection in the cliffs of the Grand Canyon, as shown in the figure.

continued

continued

7. **Choose Edit⇨Paste Into.**

   If you use the Move tool to move the pasted image around the canvas, you see that the pasted image is invisible outside the boundaries of the selection outline, as you can see in my collage.

   Don't be concerned if your element isn't the right size. I show you how to scale your layer in Book V, Chapter 2.

   The Layers palette shows a second thumbnail next to the compass thumbnail. This thumbnail represents the layer mask created automatically when you pasted into a selection. A layer mask allows portions of the layer to show and be hidden. In my example, the white areas on the layer mask are where my compass shows through. Those white areas happen to correspond to the selection I made in Step 6. The black areas represent where my compass would be hidden if I were to move it into those areas. For more on layer masks, see Book VI, Chapter 3.

8. **Choose File⇨Save.**

Chapter 2: Managing Layers

In This Chapter

✔ Viewing, moving, and shuffling layers

✔ Aligning and distributing layers

✔ Linking and locking layers

✔ Creating layer sets

✔ Flattening and merging layers

✔ Using the Layer Comps palette

Hopefully, you had the time and inclination to check out the first chapter of Book V. That's where you get all the basic information on creating layers. In this chapter, you get the scoop on how to manage the layers you've created. And unlike some coworkers, clients, or family members, layers are downright agreeable to being managed, even micromanaged for that matter. The beauty of layers is that they're so darn easy to get along with. You can hide them, shuffle them around, link and lock them, herd them into groups, and even smush them together into one loving, collective layer. Yes, Photoshop has a whole slew of ways to get your layers in the orderly and organized fashion you deserve.

Often, hiding all the layers in your image except for the one you want to edit is useful. You can focus on the element at hand without the distraction of all the other components of the image. You can hide a layer with a single quick click of the mouse button, as I describe in the following list:

✔ **Hide all the layers but one:** Select the layer you want to display. Alt+click (Option+click on the Mac) the eye icon for that layer, in the left column of the Layers palette. To redisplay all the layers, Alt+click (Option+click on the Mac) the eye icon again.

✔ **Hide an individual layer:** Click the eye icon for that layer, as shown in Figure 2-1. To redisplay the layer, click the blank space in the eye column.

Figure 2-1: You can hide and show individual layers to better focus your tasks.

You can also hide layer styles or entire layer groups by using the same method as with layers. You can find out more about layer groups later in this chapter. For the lowdown on layer styles, see Book V, Chapter 4.

Only layers that are visible will print. This can be useful if you want to have several versions (each on a separate layer) of an image for a project within the same document. You can view selective layers, print them, get approval from the powers that be, and then delete the layers with the scrapped versions. Only one file to manage — even I can handle that.

If clicking is just too strenuous for you, try this neat trick. *Drag* through the eye column to hide or display multiple layers in one fell swoop. Now that's technology.

Rearranging Layers

You can shuffle the order of layers like clear sheets of acetate used with overhead projectors. The *stacking order* of the layers in the Layers palette corresponds to the order of the layers in the document. If you want to move a layer to another position in the stacking order, drag the layer (or layer set) up or down in the Layers palette. As you drag, you see a fist icon. Release your mouse button when a highlighted line appears where you want to insert the layer.

Alternatively, you can change the order by selecting the layer (or layer set) and then choosing Layer➪Arrange. Then select one of the following commands from the submenu:

- **Bring to Front** and **Send to Back** send the layer to the very top or very bottom of the stacking order.

- **Bring Forward** and **Send Backward** move the layer one level up or down.

- **Reverse** switches the order of your layer stack if you have two or more layers elected.

If your image has a background, it always remains the bottommost layer. If you need to move the background, first convert it to a layer by double-clicking the name in the Layers palette. Enter a name for the layer and click OK.

Moving Layer Elements

Rearranging layers is different from moving the content on the layer. Because the elements on a layer are free floating on a bed of transparency, it's a piece of cake to move the element whenever necessary. Moving the element has no effect on any of the other layers, and it doesn't harm the image one iota.

To move an image on a layer, just drag it with the Move tool (arrow pointer with a tiny four-headed arrow), located in the Tools palette; it doesn't get any simpler than that. Here are a few more handy tips when moving an image and using the Move tool:

- **Move the layer in 1-pixel increments:** Press an arrow key (located between the keyboard and keypad) with the Move tool selected. To move the layer in 10-pixel increments, press Shift as you press the arrow key.

- **Find out what layer holds the element you want to move (or edit in some other way):** If you have the Auto Select Layer option checked in the Options bar, select the Move tool and click the element. Photoshop automatically activates the layer the element resides on. If you do not have this option checked, then Ctrl+click (⌘+click on the Mac) the element. Or you can right-click (Control+click on the Mac) the element. A context menu appears, telling you what layer the element resides on, and then enables you to select that layer from the context menu. Note that it will also list the background layer.

This technique works only on pixels that have an opacity of 50% or more. If you click pixels with opacities of 50% or less, Photoshop burrows down into successive layers and selects the first layer below on which it encounters a pixel with an opacity of 50% or more.

✔ **Switch to a layer when you click with the Move tool on any part of a layer:** Select the Auto Select Layer option on the Options bar. But be careful if you use this option, especially if you have a lot of overlapping elements; you may inadvertently select a layer when you don't want to.

✔ **Display a bounding box with handles around the elements on your layer:** Select the Show Transform Controls check box on the Options bar. This box can be useful if all your elements are melting into one another in an indistinguishable conglomeration.

I recommend keeping this option checked so that you essentially have the same controls (scale, rotate, and so on) you have if you chose Edit⇨Free Transform. For more on transformations, see Book III, Chapter 3.

Putting It Together

Transforming and Moving Layers in a Collage

When you have a couple of images in your collage (see the Putting-It-Together projects in Book V, Chapter 1), you can start transforming them to your liking. Moving and scaling are the manipulations you'll probably do the most. Photoshop enables you to transform layers without affecting any other layer within the image. (For more on transformations, see Book V, Chapter 1 and Book III, Chapter 3.) Here's how to tweak images:

1. **Choose File⇨Open. Select your saved collage file.**

2. **Choose Window⇨Layers to open the Layers palette.**

3. **In the Layers palette, select the layer you want to transform.**

In my example, I chose the layer that has the passport on it.

4. **Choose Edit➪Free Transform.**

By choosing Free Transform rather than Transform, you interpolate the image only once, rather than twice. For more on interpolation, see Book II, Chapter 1.

5. **Shift+drag a corner transformation handle to scale the image down to the desired size but maintain the proportions, which reduces the amount of distortion.**

I reduced the passport in my example to about half its original size.

6. **Position the cursor just outside the handle until a curved arrow appears. Rotate the image the desired amount.**

The figure shows my example; I rotated the passport about 45 degrees.

7. **When you transform the selection to your liking, double-click inside the transform box or press Enter (Return on the Mac).**

8. **Transform the element that has a layer mask. In the Layers palette, choose the layer and follow Steps 4 through 7.**

In my example, that's the compass layer.

Be sure to click the layer's thumbnail and not the layer mask thumbnail. Otherwise, you transform the layer mask thumbnail instead of the element.

9. **When you transform the selection to your liking, double-click in the transform box.**

I scaled the compass slightly so that the top of the compass became visible. Then I rotated the compass to show more of the compass face rather than the cover.

10. **Choose File➪Save.**

continued

continued

You probably already have a pretty good sense of the possibilities (which are infinite) available to you when you create and change collages. Of course, you can always add more stuff to a collage and rearrange the layers as needed. Just follow these steps:

1. **Choose File⇨Open and select your collage file. Also open another image.**

   I chose a boarding pass image.

2. **Choose Window⇨Layers to open the Layers palette if it isn't already visible.**

3. **Select the desired element in the supporting image.**

   It goes without saying that making the selection accurate can only enhance your composite. I selected the boarding pass with the Polygon Lasso tool.

4. **Contract and feather the image's edges and use the Move tool to drag the selection into the collage file.**

   For the most professional appearance possible, use consistent values for modifing and feathering all the selections in this composite.

5. **Position and transform the selection as needed.**

   Follow the directions provided in the preceding steps list. In my example, I scaled the boarding pass to the same size as the passport, rotated it clockwise, and positioned it a little lower than the passport.

6. **In the Layers palette, rearrange your layers if needed by selecting a layer and dragging it above another layer.**

   In my image, I dragged my passport layer above my boarding pass layer, as shown in the following figure.

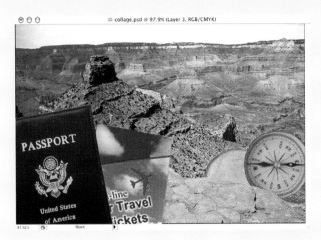

Because the layers are independent entities, you can shuffle them indefinitely like a deck of cards.

7. **Choose File⇨Save.**

Aligning and Distributing Layers

If you are a precision junkie like me, you'll appreciate Photoshop's ability to align and distribute your layers. These commands can be especially useful when you need to align items such as navigation buttons on a Web page or a row of headshots for a corporate publication.

Here are the steps to align and distribute your layers:

1. **In the Layers palette, select the layers you want to align, as shown in Figure 2-2.**

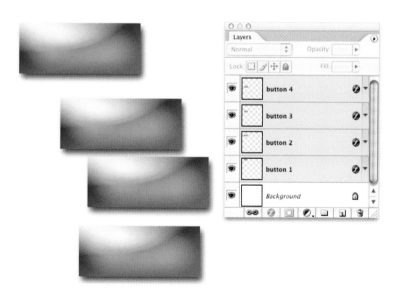

Figure 2-2: Select the layers you want to align in the Layers palette.

Note that it is no longer necessary to link your layers before aligning and distributing them.

2. Choose Layer➪Align and select one of the alignment commands.

Photoshop provides you with handy little icons that illustrate the various alignment types. You also find these icons as buttons on the Options bar when you have the Move tool selected, as shown in Figure 2-3. Feel free to use either method.

Figure 2-3: The Options bar offers different alignment buttons.

Note that, depending on which alignment type you choose, Photoshop aligns to the layer element that is the farthest to the top, bottom, left, or right. If you align to the center, Photoshop splits the difference among the various layer elements.

3. In the Layers palette, select three or more layers that you want to distribute.

This command evenly spaces the layers between the first and last elements in either the row or column.

4. Choose Layer➪Distribute and select one of the distribute commands.

Again for the word-challenged, there is an icon illustrating the distribution types. And like alignment, you also find the distribute icons as buttons on the Options bar when you have the Move tool selected. You can see the buttons from Figure 2-2 precisely aligned and evenly distributed in Figure 2-4.

Figure 2-4: The aligned and evenly distributed buttons.

You can also align a layer to a selection outline. First, make your desired selection in the image. Then select a layer or layers in the Layers palette. Choose Layer➪Align Layers to Selection and choose an alignment type from the submenu. Note that the Align to Selection command doesn't appear in the Layer menu until you have both layers and an active selection outline.

Linking Layers

With Photoshop CS2, you'll find that the need to link layers in most cases is now unnecessary. Simply select multiple layers and apply your command — moving, scaling, rotating, and so on. Occasionally, however, you may want to link layers so that they stay grouped as a unit until you decide otherwise.

To link layers, follow these short steps:

1. **Select the layer or layer groups in the Layers palette.**

2. **Click the Link Layers icon at the bottom of the Layers palette, as shown in Figure 2-5.**

   A link icon appears to the right of the layer name in the Layers palette.

   To remove a link, click the Link Layers icon again.

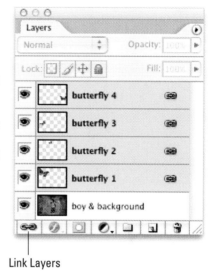

Link Layers

Figure 2-5: Use the Link command if you need a longer-term grouping of your layers.

If you find the need to quickly select all the linked layers in your Layers palette, select just one of the layers and then choose Select Linked Layers from the Layer menu or Layers palette pop-up menu. This can come in handy, for example, when working on Web pages with lots of linked layers containing buttons or labels in a navigation bar.

Putting It Together

Selecting Layers in a Collage and Adjusting Their Size

When you're working on composites, you may find the need to adjust the size or angle of more than one layer. You can select the layers you want to scale or rotate and transform all the layers at the same time. This strategy enables you to adjust all the layers the same amount at the same time — thus ensuring that they stay proportional in size. If you want to be certain that all the layers stay selected during the transformation process, you can link them for extra insurance.

continued

continued

1. **Open your saved collage file.**

   Make sure that the Layers palette is visible.

2. **Select the layers you want to transform. If you want to link them, simply click the Link Layers icon at the bottom of the Layers palette.**

   In my example, I selected Layers 1 and 3 — my passport and boarding pass.

3. **Choose Edit⇨Free Transform and Shift+drag the corner transformation handle to scale the layers. When you're satisfied, double-click inside the transform box or press Enter (Return on the Mac).**

   Because both layers are selected, any transformation you apply, including moving and scaling, affects both layers, as shown in the figure.

4. **Save the file when you're done.**

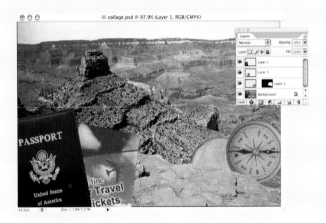

Locking Layers

After you get your layers the way you want them, you may want to lock them to prevent them from being changed, as shown in Figure 2-6. To lock a layer, select it in the Layers palette and select one or more of the lock options at the top of the Layers palette. See Table 2-1 for details about each option.

You can also choose Layer➪Lock Layers or choose Lock Layers from the Layers palette pop-up menu.

When you select the Lock All option, a solid, dark gray lock icon appears on the layer, indicating the layer is fully locked. When you select any of the other lock options, the lock appears light gray and hollow, indicating the layer is partially locked.

By default, the background is locked and cannot be unlocked until you convert the background into a layer by choosing Layer➪New➪Layer from Background. In addition, by default, type layers have the Lock Transparent Pixels and Lock Image Pixels options selected. These options are grayed out and cannot be deselected. However, if you need to paint on the type layer, you can always rasterize it, thereby removing all locking options. For more on type, see Book IV, Chapter 3.

Fully locked

Partially locked

Lock Options

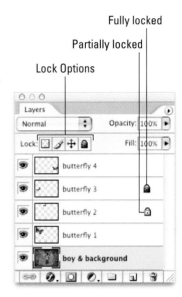

Figure 2-6: Locking prevents unwanted edits.

Table 2-1		Lock Options in the Layers Palette
Button	*Name*	*What It Does*
	**Lock Transparent Pixels**	Prevents you from painting or editing any transparent areas on your layer. To quickly select or deselect the Lock Transparent Pixels check box, press the forward slash key (/).
	Lock Image Pixels	Prevents you from painting or editing your layer. You can still select, move, or transform items on the layer.
	Lock Position	Prevents you from moving and transforming the layer but gives you free rein on everything else.
	Lock All	Prevents you from painting, editing, moving, or transforming your layer. (But you can still make selections.)

Color-Coding Layers

To visually distinguish your layers in the Layers palette, Photoshop lets you color-code your layers or layer sets, as shown in Figure 2-7. Choose Layer⇨Layer Properties or choose Layer Properties from the Layers palette pop-up menu. Choose a color from the drop-down list and click OK.

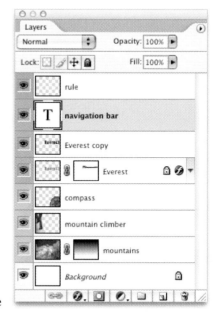

Figure 2-7: Color-coding layers helps to visually identify and organize your layers.

For a great time saver, right-click (Ctrl+click on the Mac) the layer's eyeball icon and you get a context menu listing the colors.

I find that color-coding works especially well with layer groups. First, organize your layers into groups, such as navigation buttons, type, images, border, background, and so on. Then assign a color to each group. By using the same color-coding system from one project to the next, you can get a little productivity boost by instinctively knowing where to find your elements.

Creating Layer Groups

I don't know about you, but having a file cabinet full of neatly labeled manila folders containing all my vital paperwork is very satisfying. It's compact. It's organized. It's "at the ready," as they say in the military. Fellow geeks can revel in Photoshop's digital answer to the manila folder, which enables you to organize layers into *layer groups*. You can expand or collapse layer groups to see or hide their contents. In their collapsed state, layer groups are a great antidote for the annoying scrolling that one must do in an abundantly layered file. And groups enable you to apply opacity settings, blend modes, and layer styles to multiple layers at a time.

To create a layer group, click the Create a New Group icon (the folder icon) at the bottom of the Layers palette, shown in Figure 2-8. You can also choose New Group from the Layers palette pop-up menu or choose Layer⇨New⇨ Group. The latter two methods prompt you for a group name in addition to a few other options (similar to regular layers). You can color-code your group and specify a blend mode and opacity setting. Note that the default mode is Pass Through, which lets the blend modes applied to the individual layers remain intact. If you choose any other mode, it overrides all the layers in the group.

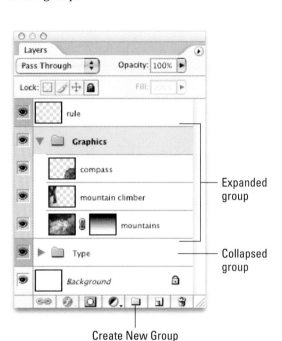

Expanded group

Collapsed group

Create New Group

Figure 2-8: Grouping layers provides better layer manageability.

After you create your group, drag your layers into the group folder in the Layers palette. If the group is collapsed when you drag or if you drag a layer on top of the group icon itself, Photoshop places the layer at the bottom of the layer group. If the group is expanded, you can drag the layer to a specific location within the group. To collapse or expand the group, click the triangle icon to the left of the folder icon.

Although layer groups are pretty straightforward, keep these few points in mind:

- As with regular layers, you can select, duplicate, show, hide, lock, and rearrange layer groups. See other sections in this chapter for more on these commands.
- You can nest layer groups. Create (or drag) one layer group into another layer group.

✔ You can create a layer group from selected layers. Select the layers you want in a group and choose New Group from Layers from the Layers palette pop-up menu or choose Layer⇨New⇨Group from Layers. Name the group and click OK.

✔ If you select a layer within a group and then choose Layer⇨Arrange, the command applies to the stacking order only within the layer group.

✔ You can merge layer groups. Select the group and choose Merge Group from the Layers palette pop-up menu or choose Layer⇨Merge Group. For more on merging, see the next section.

✔ You can rename your group by double-clicking the group name in the Layers palette. Or choose Layer⇨ Group Properties or choose Group Properties from the Layers palette pop-up menu.

✔ In addition, you can lock layers within a group. Choose Lock All Layers in Group from the Layers palette pop-up menu or choose Layer⇨Lock All Layers in Group.

Flattening and Merging Layers

Being the true layers evangelist that I am, I have spent the last two chapters touting the glories of layers. And they are wonderful. But they do have a dark side. They can make your file go from slim and trim to bulky and bloated. You not only get a larger file size that slows your computer system performance, but you're also limited to the file formats that allow you to save layers: Photoshop's native format (.psd), TIFF (.tif), Large Document Format (.psb), and PDF (.pdf). If you save your file in any other format, Photoshop smashes your layers down into a background. This file limitation often forces users to save two versions of every layered file — one as a native Photoshop file and one as something else, such as EPS or JPEG, to import into another program. For more on file formats, see Book II, Chapter 2. To curb large file sizes or use layered images in a wider range of formats, you have a couple of options:

✔ **Merging layers** combines visible, linked, or adjacent layers into a single layer (not a background). The intersection of all transparent areas is retained. You can merge layers or layer groups. You can also merge adjustment or fill layers (see Book V, Chapter 1 for details), but they cannot act as the target layer for the merge. Merging layers can help decrease your file size and make your document more manageable. You're still restricted to the layer-friendly file formats, however.

✔ **Flattening an image** combines all visible layers into a background. Photoshop deletes hidden layers and fills any transparent areas with white. Flattening is usually reserved for when you're completely finished editing your image.

When you convert an image from one color mode to another, it may cause the file to flatten. Look out for the warning dialog box that prompts you of this result and go back and save a copy of your file as a native Photoshop file, thereby preserving your layers.

Merging layers

You can merge your layers several ways. Here's the first option:

1. **Ensure that all the layers (and layer sets) you want to merge are visible, as shown in Figure 2-9.**

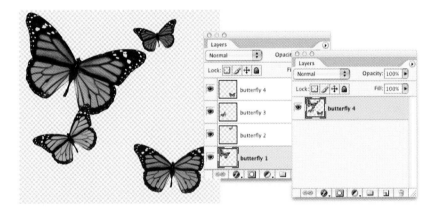

Figure 2-9: Merging layers can make your file size a lot smaller.

2. **Choose Merge Visible from the Layers palette pop-up menu or the Layer menu.**

   All visible layers are smushed into a single layer, as shown in Figure 2-9. The newly merged layer takes on the name of the topmost layer.

   Press Alt (Option on the Mac) when choosing Layer⇨Merge Visible. Photoshop merges those layers onto a new layer.

You can also merge layers using this method:

1. **Position the layer or layer groups you want to merge adjacent to each other in the Layers palette.**

2. **Select the top layer of those you want merged.**

3. **Choose Merge Down from the Layers palette pop-up menu or the Layer menu. If the top layer is a layer group, the command is called Merge Group.**

   Note that Merge Down merges your active layer with *all* layers below it, so make sure that every layer underneath your active layer should be merged.

Stamping layers

Stamping layers is the ability to merge elements of one or more layers into a target layer while leaving other layers untouched. Normally, the selected layers are stamped down into the layer directly below them. To stamp layers, follow these steps:

1. **Move the layer or layers you want to stamp above the layer you want to stamp into. Both layers must be visible.**

2. **Select the top layer and press Ctrl+Alt+E (⌘+Option+E on the Mac).**

   If you want to stamp all visible layers, select the layer that will contain the merged elements and press Shift+Ctrl+Alt+E (Shift+⌘+Option+E on the Mac). You may need to borrow a friend's fingers for that keyboard combo.

Flattening layers

To flatten an image, follow these steps:

1. **Ensure that all the layers you want to retain are visible.**

   Photoshop discards all hidden layers.

2. **Choose Layer⇨Flatten Image, or choose Flatten Image from the Layers palette pop-up menu.**

   Your flattened image is filled with the background color and appears as a background layer in the Layers palette, as shown in Figure 2-10.

   Note that Photoshop doesn't prompt you with a warning like, "Are you sure you really want to do this?" But if you mistakenly flatten your image, you can undo the command immediately by choosing Edit⇨Undo. If you've gone ahead and performed another action, then undo your mistake by using the History palette (see Book II, Chapter 4).

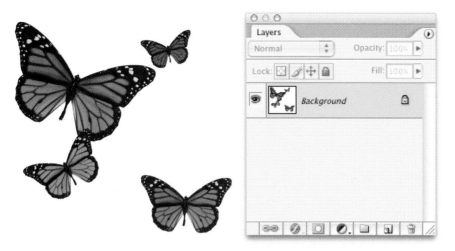

Figure 2-10: Flatten your layers only if you're reasonably sure you won't need individual layers any longer.

 Putting It Together

Checking Your Collage for Flaws and Consolidating Layers

When you begin a project, you may think you know what you want the final result to look like. But as your creative juices start flowing, you may decide that something doesn't look right. For example, as I was working on my collage, I discovered that the sky behind and above the canyon was a little on the ordinary side.

1. **Open the saved collage file and open a new image that you want to incorporate into the collage.**

In my example, I thought the sky needed some kick, so I opened an image that contained a sky I liked.

2. **Select the part of the image that you want to add to your collage as shown in the figure.**

continued

continued

Most of the time, consistency is key. In my example, however, I didn't need to feather the image. Because I'm going to paste it into the old sky, the edges of the element won't be seen.

3. **Using the Move tool, drag the selection into the collage.**

Because I'm pasting the image into the background image, I first needed to make the selection I wanted to paste into. I used the Magic Wand tool. After a couple of additional Shift+clicks, I selected the entire sky behind the canyon. Then I copied and pasted the image (using the Edit⇨Paste Into command) into its new location, as shown in the figure.

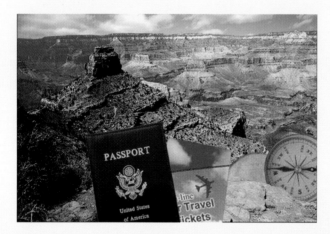

When you're close to finalizing your collage, you might want to consolidate layers. Minimizing the number of layers makes projects easier to manage and your file size smaller, which is great when you get ready to add the finishing touches to your collage.

Be sure that before you merge your layers, you will never have to manipulate them separately, especially if the elements on the layer overlap each other, as mine do.

To consolidate two layers, follow these steps:

1. **Select the layers in the Layers palette.**

2. **Choose Merge Layers from the Layers palette pop-up menu.**

   The two layers merge and become one.

3. **Choose File⇨Save.**

Working with the Layer Comps Palette

The Layer Comps feature doesn't really add more layer functionality, but because it shares a similar moniker, I explain it in this minibook.

What Layer Comps does do is enable you to create and save multiple versions of your project within a single master file. Through the Layer Comps palette, Photoshop records all the vital statistics of your layers, including their visibility, position, and blending options. These statistics come in handy when you want to show a client or art director various design versions within a single document. That's right. No longer do you have to save the various renditions of a design or project in multiple files. Just be aware that layer comps do add to your file size.

The following steps walk you through the day-to-day operation of the Layer Comps palette:

1. **Choose Window⟹Layer Comps to display the palette, shown in Figure 2-11.**

2. **Create all your desired layer content. Note that if you perform all your editing on just a Background layer, you cannot save the document as a layer comp.**

Corbis Digital Stock

Figure 2-11: The Layer Comps palette enables you to create and save multiple versions of a project within a single document.

3. **When you have a version of the document that you want to save as a comp, click the New Layer Comp button at the bottom of the palette or choose New Layer Comp from the palette pop-up menu.**

The New Layer Comp dialog box appears.

To create a comp and bypass the options dialog box, hold down the Alt (Option on the Mac) key when you click the New Layer Comp button.

Note if you execute certain commands, such as changing the size of the document (cropping, using Image Size or Canvas Size, and so on) or rotating by any amount other than 180 degrees, you get a warning alarm icon, which informs you that you won't be able to fully restore the layer comp.

4. **Name your layer comp, and choose the attributes you want recorded — Visibility, Position, and Appearance (Layer Style) of the layers. You can also add an optional comment about the configuration you are capturing, as shown in Figure 2-12. Click OK.**

Note that if you add a comment, you see a triangle just to the left of the layer comp name (refer to the sunflower solo comp shown in Figure 2-11). Click the triangle to see your comment in the palette.

Figure 2-12: Add project details in the Comment field of the New Layer Comp dialog box.

5. **Continue creating your various configurations of the document, capturing a layer comp after each.**

6. **To display a particular layer comp, click in the left column in the Layer Comps palette.**

In the column on the left side of the palette, you see a document icon, which indicates that particular layer comp is selected.

7. **To efficiently cycle through all your layer comps, Ctrl+click, (⌘+click for Mac) all your comps in the palette to select them all.**

You can also click the first layer comp and then Shift+click the last layer comp, which automatically selects all files in between. Then click the Apply Next Selected Layer Comp or Apply Previous Selected Layer Comp icon at the bottom of the Layer Comps palette.

You can also, less efficiently, apply layer comps by selecting the particular layer comp and choosing Apply Layer Comp from the palette pop-up menu. The document icon moves to that layer, and Photoshop displays that layer comp.

Here are a few more Layer Comp tidbits:

✔ To **rename** a layer comp, simply double-click its name in the palette.

✔ To **delete** a layer comp, select it and click the trash can icon in the Layer Comps palette. You can also drag the layer comp to the trash can icon or choose Delete Layer Comp from the palette pop-up menu.

✔ To **duplicate** a layer comp, select it and drag it onto the New Layer Comp icon in the palette or choose Duplicate Layer Comp from the palette pop-up menu.

✔ To **update** a particular layer comp with the currently active configuration of the document, select the layer comp and then choose Update Layer Comp from the palette pop-up menu or click the Update Layer Comp button at the bottom of the palette.

✔ To **display** your document at its latest configuration (but not necessarily the latest saved layer comp), choose Restore Last Document State from the palette pop-up or simply click the Last Document State icon in the Layer Comps palette.

✔ To rearrange the order of the layer comps, simply drag it to a new location in the palette.

Photoshop offers you a variety of great ways to output your layer comps. Here is the lowdown on each:

✔ **Choose File➪Scripts➪Layer Comps to Files:** Select this command and Photoshop exports your layer comps to individual files. In the dialog box, shown in Figure 2-13, provide a destination and prefix name for your file. Indicate whether you want to include Selected Layer Comps Only (you must select them before you choose the command). Leave that option deselected to have Photoshop export all layer comps. Then choose your desired file type and specify whether you want to include ICC Profiles (see Book II, Chapter 2) and Maximize Compatibility (see Book I, Chapter 5). Click Run and then sit back and watch the magic happen.

Figure 2-13: Run a script to have Photoshop automatically export your layer comps into individual files.

✓ **Choose File⇨Scripts⇨Layer Comps to PDF:** Choose this command to export your layer comps as a multipage PDF file. Photoshop saves each layer to a separate PDF page. In the dialog box, click the Browse button to provide a filename and destination. Indicate whether you want to include only selected layer comps. Then choose your options for your PDF Slide Show presentation. Specify the amount of time you want in between pages and whether you want the show to loop (keep playing continuously). Click Run. Photoshop runs the script and saves the PDF to your destination.

✓ **Choose File⇨Scripts⇨Layer Comps to WPG:** This option exports your layer comps to a Web Photo Gallery. In the dialog box, click Browse and choose a destination for your file. Next, specify a gallery style and whether you want to export only the selected layer comps. Click Run. Photoshop does its scripting thing and automatically launches a Web Photo Gallery in your default browser, displaying each layer comp both as a thumbnail and as a larger image.

Chapter 3: Playing with Opacity and Blend Modes

In This Chapter

- ✔ Adjusting opacity and fills
- ✔ Applying blend modes for effects
- ✔ Setting the blend options

*I*n this chapter, I show you how to let down your hair and get those creative juices flowing. Yes, I'm about to say the "F" word: Fun.

This chapter, along with Book V, Chapter 4, focuses on how to tweak the layers you've made. Maybe you want to make one of your layers semitransparent so that you can see the layer beneath it; or say you want to try blending the colors between a couple layers in a way that is slightly offbeat. Look no further.

Although some techniques in this chapter may reek of complexity, keep in mind that you don't need to totally understand them. Take these techniques as far as you want. And remember there's no substitute for good old experimentation. Before you jump into these techniques, it helps to have a handle on the methods of layer creation and management that I explain in Book V, Chapters 1 and 2.

If you want to play around with blend modes and opacity but you're not ready to commit just yet, make a backup copy of an image. (It helps to use an image that contains layers, of course.) You can play around without permanently hurting the image. If the results of your activities offend you, you can always choose File⇨Revert. And try, try again.

Adjusting Layer Opacity

By far one of the easiest ways to make your image look oh so sophisticated is to have one image ghosted over another, as shown in Figure 3-1. Creating this effect is a snap with the Opacity option in the Layers palette. You adjust the opacity in two ways:

Figure 3-1: Adjusting the opacity enables one image to ghost over another.

✏ Select your desired layer in the Layers palette. Then either access the slider by clicking the right-pointing arrow or enter a percentage value in the Opacity text box.

✏ You can also double-click a layer thumbnail, choose Layer⇨Layer Style⇨ Blending Options, or choose Blending Options from the Layers palette pop-up menu. (Click the triangle in the upper-right corner to open the menu.)

Either of these methods brings up the Layer Style dialog box, where you can enter a value or drag the slider for opacity.

The Opacity setting allows you to mix the active layer with the layers below it in varying percentages from 100% (completely opaque) to 0% (completely transparent). Remember that you can adjust the opacity only on a layer, not a background.

You can also change the Opacity percentage by using keyboard shortcuts. With any tool active, except a painting or editing tool, press a number key. Press 5 for 50 percent, 25 for 25 percent. If you are entering a two-digit value, just be sure you type the numbers quickly or else Photoshop interprets the numbers as two different values. You get the picture. Note that for the default of 100 percent, you must press 0.

Adjusting the Fill Opacity

In addition to adjusting the regular opacity for a layer, you can also adjust the fill opacity. Fill opacity works a little differently from regular opacity. The regular Opacity setting affects layer styles (see Book V, Chapter 4) and blend modes (see the following section, "Creating Effects with Blend Modes"), which have been applied to the layer. Fill opacity, however, affects only the pixels or shapes that reside on the layer. It doesn't affect the styles or blends. As you can see in Figure 3-2, the drop shadow and emboss styles in the bottom example show through full strength.

Figure 3-2: Fill opacity (bottom) affects only layer pixels, not styles or blend modes that have been applied to the layer.

To adjust the Fill Opacity setting, select your desired layer in the Layers palette and enter a value in the Fill Opacity text box or drag the pop-up slider. The other methods for adjusting fill opacity are similar to the regular opacity option.

Creating Effects with Blend Modes

Photoshop's 23 blend modes (25 when working with the painting and editing tools) determine how the colors in different layers interact with each other. Blend modes can produce a multitude of interesting, sometimes even bizarre, effects. And what's more, you can easily apply, change, or discard blend modes with no permanent damage to your layers.

Most options in the Blend Mode pop-up menu (located on the Layers tab) in the Layers palette are the same as those on the Mode pop-up menu on the Options bar. The exceptions are the Behind and Clear modes, which you can find only on the Options bar because they are available only for use with painting and editing tools.

I urge you to pick an image with a few layers and apply each blend mode to get a good handle on what the various blend modes do. In fact, try a few different images, because the effects may be subtle or intense depending on the colors in the image. Throw in some different opacity percentages, and you're on your way to endless hours of creative fun.

You'll find these modes called *blend modes, painting modes, brush modes, layer modes, calculations,* or just plain *modes.* They are usually referred to as *blend modes* or *layer modes* when used with layers and painting modes, and *brush modes* when used in conjunction with a painting or editing tool.

General blend modes

In the General category, you find the following modes, which are shown in Figure 3-3 and explained in Table 3-1.

Table 3-1	General Blend Modes
Blend Mode	**Description**
Normal	You're probably very familiar with the Normal blend mode by now. It is the default that lets each pixel appear in its very own unadulterated state. The other three modes are used only in certain circumstances.
Dissolve	The effects of Dissolve can be seen only with a layer that has an opacity setting of less than 100% — the lower the opacity, the more intense the effect. The effect is created by allowing some pixels from lower layers, which are randomized, to show through the target layer.

Blend Mode	Description
Behind	Available only with a painting or editing tool active. Type must be rasterized, and Lock Transparency must be deselected. Allows you to edit or paint only on the transparent areas of the layer, giving the illusion that the strokes are behind the layer.
Clear	Available only with a painting or editing tool active. Type must be rasterized, and Lock Transparency must be deselected. Allows you to edit or paint with transparency, giving the appearance that holes are being punched into your image.

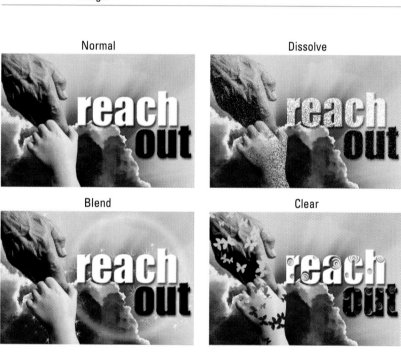

Normal   Dissolve   Blend   Clear

Figure 3-3: The Behind and Clear blend modes are available only with a painting or editing tool.

Blend modes that darken

Overall, the blend modes in this category all produce effects that darken your image, as shown in Figure 3-4. However, one of my favorite uses for the Darken blend mode is a little different. Scan a handwritten letter or sheet of music and layer it over an image. Apply the Darken blend mode to the letter or sheet music layer. The white areas of the paper become transparent, and only the letters or musical notes display, creating a nice composite image. Table 3-2 describes these modes.

Figure 3-4: These blend modes darken, or burn, your layers.

Table 3-2	Blend Modes That Darken
Blend Mode	*Description*
Darken	If the pixels on the layer are lighter than those below, the lighter pixels turn transparent. If the pixels on the layer are darker, they display unchanged. A great mode for superimposing scanned text or line art because it allows the white color of the paper to essentially drop out, leaving only the dark letters or lines.
Multiply	Burns the layer into the layers underneath. The Multiply mode darkens all colors where they mix. With layers, it is comparable to sticking two slides in the same slot in a slide projector. If painting, each successive stroke creates a darker color, as if drawing with markers.
Color Burn	Darkens the layers underneath and burns them with color. Increases contrast. Blending with white pixels has no effect. Like applying a dark dye to your image.
Linear Burn	Darkens the layers underneath by decreasing the brightness. Similar to Multiply but tends to make portions of your image pure black. Blending with white pixels has no effect.

Blend modes that lighten

If you have blend modes that darken, well, having those that lighten just makes good sense. So if you have the need to throw some digital bleach on your brightly colored pixels, try out a couple of these blend modes, which I describe in Table 3-3. Figure 3-5 shows examples of these effects.

Figure 3-5: These blend modes lighten, or dodge, your layers.

Table 3-3	Blend Modes That Lighten
Blend Mode	*Description*
Lighten	If the pixels on the layer are darker than those below, the darker pixels turn transparent. If the pixels on the layer are lighter, they display unchanged. The opposite of Darken.
Screen	Lightens the layer where it mixes with the layer underneath. Blending with black pixels has no effect. Like putting two slides in two different projectors and pointing them at the same screen. The opposite of Multiply.
Color Dodge	Lightens the pixels in the layers underneath and infuses them with colors from the top layer. Like bleaching your layer. Blending with black pixels has no effect.

continued

Table 3-3 *(continued)*

Blend Mode	Description
Linear Dodge	Lightens the layers underneath by increasing the brightness. Similar to Screen but tends to make parts of your image pure white. Blending with black pixels has no effect.

Lighting blend modes

This group of blend modes plays with the lighting in your layers. Some of these blend modes, like Overlay and Pin Light, are reserved for the occasional wacky special effect. The following list shows and explains each mode:

- ✓ **Overlay:** Multiplies the dark pixels in the top layer and screens the light pixels in the underlying layers. Enhances the contrast and saturation of colors.

Overlay

- ✓ **Soft Light:** Darkens the dark pixels and lightens the light pixels. If the pixels on the top layer are lighter than 50% gray, the lighter pixels are lightened further. If the pixels on the top layer are darker than 50% gray, the mode darkens pixels. Blending with black or white results in darker or lighter pixels but doesn't make parts of your image pure black or pure white. Similar to Overlay, but softer and subtler. Like shining a soft spotlight on the image.

Soft Light

- ✓ **Hard Light:** Multiplies the dark pixels and screens the light pixels. Like shining a bright, hard spotlight on the image. If the pixels on the top layer are lighter than 50% gray, they are screened. If the pixels on the top layer are darker than 50% gray, the mode multiplies the pixels. Can be used to add highlights and shadows to an image. Blending with black or white gives you black and white.

Hard Light

- ✓ **Vivid Light:** If the pixels on the top layer are darker than 50% gray, this mode burns, or darkens, the colors by increasing the contrast. If the pixels on the top layer are lighter than 50% gray, the mode dodges, or lightens, the colors by decreasing the contrast. A combination of Color Burn and Color Dodge.

Vivid Light

✓ **Linear Light:** If the pixels on the top layer are darker than 50% gray, the mode burns, or darkens, the colors by decreasing the brightness. If the pixels on the top layer are lighter than 50% gray, the mode dodges, or lightens, the colors by increasing the brightness. A combination of Linear Burn and Linear Dodge.

Linear Light

✓ **Pin Light:** Replaces the colors of pixels, depending on the colors in the top layer. If the pixels on the top layer are darker than 50% gray, the mode replaces pixels darker than those on the top layer and doesn't change lighter pixels. If the pixels on the top layer are lighter than 50% gray, the mode replaces the pixels that are lighter than those pixels on the top layer, and doesn't change pixels that are darker. A combination of Darken and Lighten and useful for special effects.

Pin Light

✓ **Hard Mix:** Similar to Vivid Light, but reduces the colors to a total of eight — Cyan, Magenta, Yellow, Black, Red, Green, Blue, and White. Although the results depend on the mix of existing colors on the top and bottom layers, this mode creates a highly posterized effect.

Hard Mix

Blend modes that invert

If the preceding blend modes are a tad too tame for you, you may want to check out the "Inverters" — Difference and Exclusion (described in Table 3-4). These blend modes invert your colors and can produce some interesting special effects, as shown in Figure 3-6.

Difference Exclusion

Figure 3-6: The Difference and Exclusion blend modes invert colors.

Table 3-4	Blend Modes That Invert
Blend Mode	*Description*
Difference	Produces a negative or inverted effect according to the brightness values on the top layers. If the pixels on the top layer are black, the mode doesn't change the colors of the underlying layers. If the pixels on the top layer are white, the mode inverts the colors of the underlying layers. Can produce bizarre results.
Exclusion	Similar to Difference, but with less contrast and saturation. If the pixels on the top layer are black, the mode doesn't change the colors of the underlying layers. If the pixels on the top layer are white, the mode inverts the colors of the underlying layers. Medium colors blend to create gray.

HSL color model blend modes

These blend modes use the HSL (Hue Saturation Lightness) color model to mix colors. My favorite blend mode in this group is Color, which allows you to apply color to images without obscuring the tonality. Table 3-5 lists these modes, and Figure 3-7 shows their effects.

Figure 3-7: These blend modes use the Hue Saturation Lightness color model to mix colors.

Table 3-5	HSL Color Model Blend Modes
Blend Mode	**Description**
Hue	Blends the luminance (brightness) and saturation (intensity of the color) of the underlying layers with the hue (color) of the top layer.
Saturation	Blends the luminance and hue of the underlying layers with the saturation of the top layer.
Color	Blends the luminance of the underlying layers with the saturation and hue of the top layer. This mode is great for colorizing grayscale (with a color mode set to RGB) images because it preserves the shadows, highlights, and details of the underlying layers.
Luminosity	Blends the hue and saturation of the underlying layers with the luminance of the top layer. Preserves the shadows, highlights, and details from the top layer and mixes them with the colors of the underlying layers. The opposite of Color.

Working with the Advanced Blending Options

If you want to get serious about layers, then you need to know about the Advanced Blending Options, which you can find in the Layer Style dialog box. These options allow you to tailor the way your layer styles and blend modes interact with your layers. Getting to the advanced options is just like accessing opacity and blend modes: You can double-click a layer thumbnail, choose Layer⇨Layer Style⇨Blending Options, or choose Blending Options from the Layers palette pop-up menu. The massive Layer Style dialog box rears its multipaneled head, as shown in Figure 3-8.

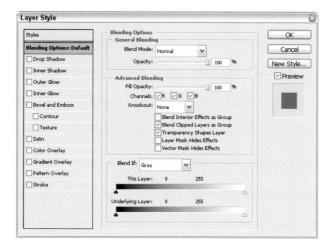

Figure 3-8: The Layer Styles dialog box is home to Advanced Blending Options.

(By the way, if you're ready to know about more blending features, skip to Book V, Chapter 4, where I cover layer styles.)

Advanced options to blend with

The advanced options are not for the faint of heart. To be frank, the options are, well, advanced, so you might find them a tad too eggheady for your taste, but if not, here you go:

- **Fill Opacity:** I cover this in "Adjusting the Fill Opacity," earlier in this chapter.

- **Channels:** This option allows you to restrict your blending options to specific channels only. For all you need to know about working with channels, check out Book VI.

- **Knockout:** This option allows you to specify which layers have holes in them so that you can view the layers underneath. You first have to use the Fill Opacity option to set the opacity of the knockout. The lower the opacity, the more the hole shows; therefore, set it to 0% (as in my example in Figure 3-9) to see all the way through. Set the Knockout to Shallow to create a hole through one layer set (see Book V, Chapter 2) or a clipping group (see Book V, Chapter 4). Set the Knockout to Deep to create a hole all the way through to the background. If you're just working with layers, and not sets or clipping groups, the knockout cuts through to the background. If there is no background, it cuts through to transparency.

Figure 3-9: A knockout cuts holes in your layers to enable you to view the layers underneath.

- **Blend Interior Effects as Group:** This option applies the blend mode of the layer to interior layer effects, such as inner glows, satin and color overlay, and so on. Deselect this option, and the blend mode does not affect the layer effects. You can see the difference in Figure 3-10.

- **Blend Clipped Layers as Group:** The blend mode of the bottom layer in the clipping group affects all the other layers in the group. Deselect this option, and each layer retains its own blend mode and appearance.

- **Transparency Shapes Layer:** Confines layer effects and knockouts to opaque areas of a layer. Deselect this option, and the mode applies layer effects and knockouts to the entire layer. (See Figure 3-11.)

Blend Interior Effects as Group selected

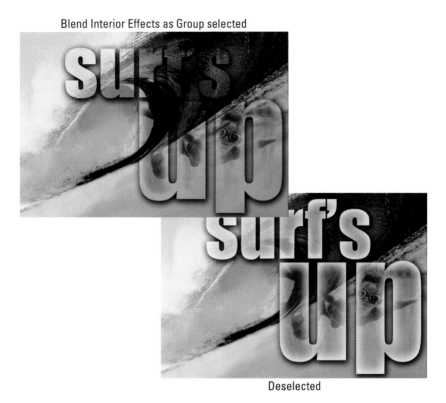

Deselected

Figure 3-10: The Blend Interior Effects as Group option applies the blend mode of the type layers to the layer's inner glow, bevel and emboss, and color overlay.

Transparency Shape Layer selected   Deselected

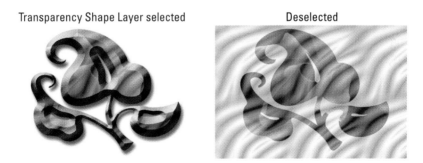

Figure 3-11: The Transparency Shapes Layer restricts layer styles to the opaque areas of a layer.

✔ **Layer Mask Hides Effects:** Confines layer effects to the area designated by the layer mask. (For more on layer masks, see Book VI, Chapter 3.)

✔ **Vector Mask Hides Effects:** Confines layer effects to the visible area designated by a vector mask. (For more on vector masks, see Book VI, Chapter 3.)

Blend If options

By using the slider bars, you can specify which colors are visible in the active layer and which colors show through from the underlying layers. You can choose a specific channel from the Blend If pop-up menu to apply the option to a single channel. The default channel of Gray affects all channels in the image. The two sliders at the bottom of the Layer Style dialog box do the following:

✔ **This Layer:** Allows you to set a blending range. In other words, you can hide certain colors according to the brightness values in the active layer. By dragging the black triangle to the right, you exclude darker colors. By dragging the white triangle to the left, you exclude lighter colors.

✔ **Underlying Layers:** Forces the colors from the underlying layers to show through the active layer. Again, dragging the black and white triangles excludes ranges of colors.

Excluding and forcing colors can result in some harsh color transitions. You can provide for a smoother transition between blended and unblended areas by splitting the slider into two parts. This allows the pixels to gradually fade to transparency. Alt+drag (Option+drag on the Mac) on either the black or white triangle in either slider bar to split the triangle into two halves. The left and right triangles mark the beginning and end of the blending range, where pixels fade into or out of view.

Putting It Together

Fine-Tuning and Adjusting Opacity Settings in Your Collage

If you've followed along with the Putting-It-Together projects I discuss in Book V, Chapters 1 and 2, you may have a collage that you're pretty satisfied with. You just need to make the final tweaks and finally go to sleep (or get home to your spouse and children).

One of the most important tweaks you can make is to opacity. Here's how to adjust the opacity settings on some of the layers:

1. **Open your saved collage file.**

If the Layers palette isn't already visible, open it.

2. **Select a layer in your collage and move the opacity slider to the left or to the right.**

If you want the layer to be more opaque, move the slider to the right. If you're interested in making the layer more transparent, move the slider to the left.

I chose Layer 4 and adjusted the opacity to 75%. I like the blue sky in my collage, but it's a tad too vibrant in comparison to the rest of the image. Adjusting the opacity tones down and allows the blue to blend in more naturally.

3. **Save the file and move on to the next layer you want to adjust.**

If you have more complicated opacity settings to adjust, keep reading.

4. **Select the background layer and then choose Duplicate Layer from the Layers palette pop-up menu. Click OK to close the Duplicate Layer dialog box.**

Making a copy of the background is great because it allows you to add a blend mode, as you'll do in the next step, and then adjust it to get just the right amount of the effect.

For example, if you want to define an element in your collage, but applying it directly on the layer produces too intense of an effect, make a copy of the layer. I wanted to pump up the definition of the canyon in my collage, but when I used the blend mode directly on the background, the result looked too harsh.

By the way, I couldn't resist the urge to include a pair of hiking boots in my collage.

continued

continued

5. **Select the background copy layer and choose a mode (such as Vivid Light) from the Mode pop-up menu in the Layers palette.**

   The definition likely looks great but the contrast is over the top.

6. **Adjust the opacity to tone it down.**

   I changed the opacity in mine to 35%.

7. **When you're satisfied with the opacity and contrast, save the collage file.**

Chapter 4: Getting Jazzy with Layer Styles and Clipping Groups

*A*fter you have all the basic elements in your layered composite image, you may want to give it a little pizzazz and finesse. Maybe a headline would pop out a little more if you beveled the edge, or maybe that silhouetted image would take on a little more dimension if you placed a drop shadow behind it. This chapter is where you find out how to do that and more. (If you're wondering how to create a composite image with layers, see Book V, Chapters 1, 2, and 3, which introduce the basics of creating composites with layers.)

Layer Styles Basics

In the old days, creating a drop shadow in Photoshop took a concerted effort. And beveled or embossed type? Well, let's just say you really had to have the inside scoop on some Photoshop tricks. Now, however, Photoshop makes creating these kinds of effects as easy as selecting an option.

In this chapter, you may see the terms *effect* and *style* used interchangeably. Technically, however, Adobe says that after layer effects are applied to a layer, they become part of a layer's *style*. You can save and load styles, but not effects. So if you apply a bunch of effects and want to be able to easily recreate the look, then save it as a style.

You can apply layer effects to regular layers, shape layers, fill layers, and type layers, but not to backgrounds, locked layers, or layer groups. For more on backgrounds, see Book V, Chapter 1. For details on locking layers and creating layer sets, see Book V, Chapter 2.

Layer effects are *dynamically linked* to the contents of a layer. If you move or edit the contents of the layers, the effects are updated. When you apply effects, they become part of the layer's style. A styled layer has a florin symbol (which looks like a fancy letter *f*) next to the layer's name in the Layers palette. You can expand (to view the individual effects) or collapse the layer style by clicking the triangle icon next to the florin. If you create a style so fantastic that you want to save it for later use, you can do that by saving a custom style as a preset and storing it in the Styles palette (see "Creating your own style," later in this chapter). Feel free to cut loose and have some fun. Layer styles are completely non-destructive. By that I mean they don't muck around with your actual pixel data. If you don't like them, edit them. If you really don't like them, delete them, and you're back to your original unstylized image.

Introducing the Many Layer Styles

Layer effects fall into a few categories. You can add shadows, glow effects, beveled and embossed edges, overlay colors and patterns, and, of course, tweak to your heart's content. This section introduces the various effects that you can apply. Later in this chapter, I explain how you apply each layer style and tweak its settings.

Shadows add a soft drop or inner shadow to a selection or the contents of a layer. You can adjust the blend mode, color, opacity, angle, size, and contour to suit your needs. Figure 4-1 shows examples of both types of shadows.

Drop Shadow   Inner Shadow

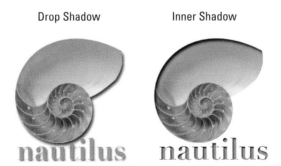

Figure 4-1: Add dimension by applying an inner or drop shadow to your object or type.

Glows add a soft highlight that appears on the outside or inside edges of a selection or the contents of a layer, as shown in Figure 4-2. Like shadows, you can fine-tune the appearance by adjusting numerous options.

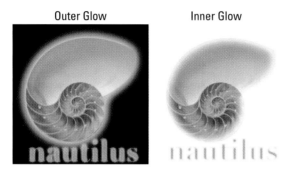

Outer Glow   Inner Glow

Figure 4-2: Inner and outer glows add a soft highlight to edges.

Bevels create a 3-D edge on either the outside or inside edges of a selection or the contents of a layer, giving the element some dimension. Similarly, **emboss** effects make elements appear raised off or punched into the page. **Satin** creates a satiny or draped fabric effect over your element. All these effects (shown in Figure 4-3) offer numerous options to adjust their appearances.

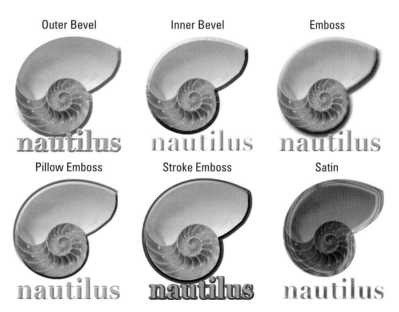

Outer Bevel   Inner Bevel   Emboss

Pillow Emboss   Stroke Emboss   Satin

Figure 4-3: Bevel and Emboss make your element look raised or punched.

Overlays apply a fill of color, a gradient, or a pattern over your selection or the contents of your layer, as shown in Figure 4-4. You can adjust the opacity of the overlay, among other options, so that your original element shows through more clearly. You can also surround your element with a **stroke** consisting of a color, gradient, or pattern.

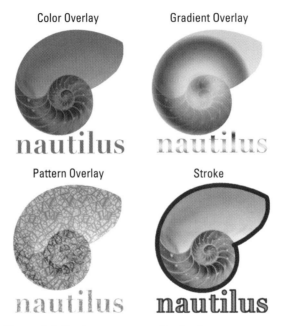

Color Overlay   Gradient Overlay

Pattern Overlay   Stroke

Figure 4-4: Overlays cover your object or type.

Applying a Layer Effect

Follow these steps to apply a layer effect:

1. **Select your desired layer in the Layers palette.**

2. **Choose Layer⊅Layer Style and choose an effect from the submenu.**

   You can click the Layer Style icon in the Layers palette and choose an effect from the pop-up menu.

   An intimidating Layer Style dialog box with a ton of options rears its head, as shown in Figure 4-5.

3. **Select the Preview check box on the right so you can see your effects as you apply them.**

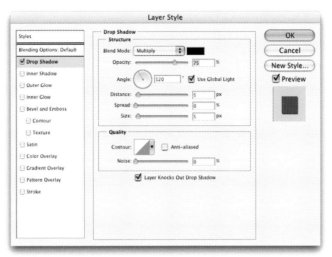

Figure 4-5: The Layer Style dialog box allows you to easily turn
effects off and on with a mere check of a box.

4. **To accept the default settings, just click OK. Or you can experiment
   with the settings.**

   You can use sliders, or you can enter values in the text boxes. The upcoming sections in this chapter describe the options and settings in detail.

5. **After you refine your effect settings, click OK.**

   Photoshop applies your effect to your layer, as indicated by the florin.

Managing and Editing Layer Styles

You can always just apply the layer effect with Photoshop's default settings,
but what fun is that? To edit a style, double-click the Effect name, double-click
the layer thumbnail or double-click the Layer Style icon in the Layers palette
and make your desired adjustments in the Layer Style dialog box. If you double-
clicked the layer thumbnail or the icon, be sure and select your desired effect
from the left side of the dialog box to get access to your effect's settings.

The following sections give you the details on each of the options. But a picture
is worth a thousand words. Experiment to really see these effects come alive.

Managing layer styles

Here are a few pointers to keep in mind when working with and editing layer
styles:

- **Choose several effects at one time:** Simply select the check box for the effect on the left side of the Layer Style dialog box. To access the options for each effect, you must click the effect name so that it is highlighted.

- **Remove an effect:** Deselect the check box associated with it.

- **Move a style onto a separate layer:** By default, layer styles are attached to a layer. To put a style on a separate layer, select the styled layer and choose Layer⇨Layer Style⇨Create Layer. You see a new layer in the Layers palette with a name, such as `Layer 0's Drop Shadow`.

Although separating a style onto its own layer may give you more manual editing capability and allow you to apply filters, you lose all editing ability with the Layer Style dialog box. Also, the style won't dynamically update when you change the layer itself. Your style basically becomes just a generic mass of colored pixels.

- **Copy and paste effects onto other layers:** Select the layer containing the effect and choose Layer⇨Layer Style⇨Copy Layer Style. Select the layer, or layers, on which you want to apply the effect and choose Layer⇨ Layer Style⇨Paste Layer Style. Even easier, you can also just drag and drop an effect from one layer to another.

- **Hide effects:** Choose Layer⇨Layer Style⇨Hide All Effects.

- **Display hidden effects:** Choose Layer⇨Layer Style⇨Show All Effects. You can also click the eye icon next to the style in the Layers palette.

- **Remove all the effects on a layer:** Choose Layer⇨Layer Style⇨ Clear Layer Style. You can also drag the *Effects bar* (what Adobe calls the name Effects), or florin, to the trash can icon in the Layers palette.

- **Remove a single effect:** Double-click the effect in the Layers palette and deselect it in the Layer Style dialog box. You can also just drag and drop the single effect to the trash can icon in the Layers palette.

- **Resize a layer effect:** Choose Layer⇨Layer Style⇨Scale Effects. Select Preview and enter a value between 1 and 1,000 percent. This command allows you to scale the effect without scaling the element.

Editing drop shadow or inner shadow effects

If you used the default settings to apply your drop shadow or inner shadow and want to do some tweaking, edit at will by following these steps:

1. **In the Layers palette, double-click the Effect name. Or you can also double-click the layer thumbnail or the Layer Style icon (florin).**

   The Layer Style dialog box opens. If you double-clicked the layer thumbnail or the Layer Style icon, you need to select Drop Shadow or Inner Shadow on the left side of the dialog box.

2. **Change the Blend Mode setting to adjust how the colors of the shadow mix with the colors of your elements.**

   Usually the default mode of Multiply works best.

3. **Adjust the Opacity setting to change how transparent the shadow appears.**

4. **To choose a shadow color, open the Color Picker by clicking the swatch to the right of the Blend Mode setting.**

5. **Establish the angle of your light source.**

6. **Select the Use Global Light option to ensure that all the shadows and highlights of all your elements are consistent.**

   You don't want one layer to look like it's 6 a.m. and another to look like it's 2 p.m. The neat thing is that if you change the angle on one layer style, all the styles you've applied to your layers adjust to that new angle dynamically.

7. **Specify how far the shadow is offset from your element with the Distance setting.**

8. **Adjust the Spread or Choke and Size settings to specify the boundary, intensity, and size of the shadow.**

9. **Select the Layer Knocks Out Drop Shadow option if you have a transparent object on top of the shadow.**

   This option prevents the shadow from showing through the object.

10. **After you refine your effect settings, click OK.**

    Your effect is edited and ready to go, as shown in Figure 4-6.

    You can also choose to apply various contours and noise to your shadow. See "Playing with Contours," later in this chapter, for details.

Figure 4-6: Effects such as shadows are live, enabling you to edit them at any time.

Changing default inner and outer glow effects

The inner and outer glow effects possess many of the same settings as the shadows. But unlike shadows, glows offer the option of using a gradient. This can produce an interesting halo effect, as shown in Figure 4-7.

PhotoSpin

Figure 4-7: Colorize a glow with a gradient.

Follow these steps to edit your own glow:

1. **Double-click the layer thumbnail or the Layer Style icon (florin).**

   The Layer Style dialog box opens.

2. **Specify Blend Mode, Opacity, Color, Spread, and Size settings.**

   If you are editing an inner glow effect, you see the options of Source (Center or Edge) and Choke rather than Spread. The Center option applies the glow over the entire image except the edge, whereas the Edge option applies only to the element's edge. The Choke option behaves similarly to the way the Spread option behaves.

3. **Choose a preset gradient from the Gradient drop-down palette or click the Gradient Editor button to edit or create your own gradient.**

   Book IV, Chapter 2 explains the Gradient Editor in detail.

4. **In the Technique option, choose either the Softer or Precise setting.**

   Choose Softer to apply a blurred glow. This option doesn't preserve detailed edges of the element.

   Choose Precise to create a glow that is good for hard-edge elements, such as type. This option does preserve the details.

5. **Use the Range and Jitter options for the Contour setting.**

   For more on contours, see the "Playing with Contours" section, later in this chapter.

6. **After you refine your effect settings, click OK.**

   Your effect is edited and ready to rock.

Editing Bevel and Emboss Effects

Because Photoshop offers five bevel and emboss styles, you have, of course, a ton of options. Some are similar to those found with the shadow and glow effects, whereas others are unique. The Layer Style dialog box is divided into four panels.

Structure

This panel contains the most relevant options:

✓ The **Technique** settings of Smooth, Chisel Hard, or Chisel Soft determine how soft or hard the edge of the bevel is. Chisel Hard works well with type and harder-edged elements. You can see an example of each in Figure 4-8. I used a depth of 700% and a size of 8.

Smooth   Chisel Hard   Chisel Soft

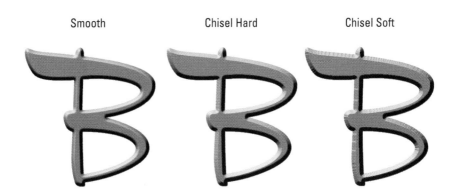

Figure 4-8: Choose from three types of bevels.

✓ **Depth** affects how raised or sunken the edge of the bevel or pattern appears.

✓ For the **Direction** settings, Up positions the highlight along the edge closest to the light source and the shadow on the opposite edge. Down does the opposite, positioning the shadow near the light source.

✔ **Size** controls the size of the bevel or emboss effect.

✔ **Soften** blurs the shading of the effect.

✔ **Angle** is the same as with Drop Shadow.

Shading

Because of the 3-D nature of bevel and emboss effects, Photoshop has settings for Highlight and Shadow (each with separate Blend Modes and Opacity options) and Depth. Because bevels and embosses are more dimensional, an additional setting of Altitude affects the light source.

Texture

In the Texture panel (click Texture on the left side of the dialog box), you can apply a pattern onto your layer that creates a texture, as shown in Figure 4-9. Adjust the scale and depth of the pattern, and link the pattern to the layer if desired. If you link the pattern and layer, the pattern moves when you move the layer. The Snap to Origin command aligns the pattern origin with the document if you have selected the Link with Layer option. If you don't select the option, the Snap to Origin command aligns the pattern to the upper-left corner of the layer.

Figure 4-9: Textures add patterns onto your elements.

Contour

Contours change the distribution of the colors in the effect, as shown in Figure 4-10. You can use the various presets offered to create interesting, and sometimes bizarre, shadows, glows, bevels, and other effects. For details on contour and its various iterations, see the upcoming section, "Playing with Contours."

Figure 4-10: A Rolling Slope Descending contour.

Editing Satin Effects

You can adjust the blend modes, opacity, angle, distance, and size — all of which I explain in the preceding sections. You can also adjust the contour, which is discussed later in "Playing with Contours."

Changing Overlay Effects

Shadows, being based in reality, are the kinds of effects you will find yourself using frequently. On the other hand, you'll probably use overlay effects only occasionally, if at all. In most cases, overlays are reserved for the realm of the special effect. But in case you need to apply an overlay, here are the options:

- **Color Overlay:** Adjust the Blend Mode, Opacity, and Color settings of the overlay. This effect, along with the Gradient Overlay and Pattern Overlay, is best used with an opacity setting of less than 100% or a Blend Mode other than Normal. That way, the elements underneath aren't totally obliterated.

- **Gradient Overlay:** Choose a preset gradient from the drop-down Gradient picker, or click the Gradient swatch to access the Gradient Editor to create your own. The Align with Layer option uses the bounding box of the layer to calculate the gradient. Specify the angle, style (Linear or Radial), and scale of the gradient. Reverse flips the gradient. Adjust the Blend Modes and Opacity settings.

- **Pattern Overlay:** Choose a preset pattern from the Pattern picker drop-down palette. Snap to Origin and Link with Layer work the same as with Bevel and Emboss. Choose Blend Modes and Opacity settings. Figure 4-11 shows a fabric pattern overlay on a rose.

Figure 4-11: I created this fabric rose with the Denim pattern and an Overlay blend mode.

Changing Stroke Effects

Specify the size of your stroke in pixels and whether you want it to ride the outside, center, or inside of the edge of the element. Determine the Blend Mode and Opacity settings. And finally, specify whether to fill your stroke with a color, gradient, or pattern. Choose your desired color, gradient, or pattern from the corresponding options

Playing with Contours

Several of the layer effects have various options for contours. *Contours* change the distribution of the colors in the effect. The default setting for all the effects, except satin, is *linear contour*. In an effect with a linear contour, the opacity drops off in a straight line.

But you're not limited to the linear contour option. Click the arrow of the Contour option, and you find a variety of preset contours, as shown in Figure 4-12. Click the palette arrow, and you can load the complete contour preset library by selecting Contours at the bottom of the submenu. You can also click the Load Contours command to load other libraries you may have saved previously or acquired from friends, colleagues, or third-party vendors.

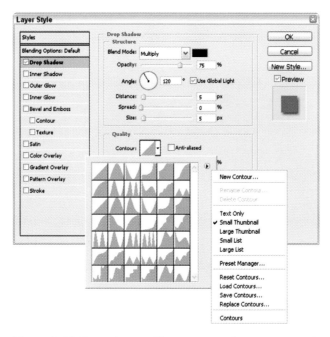

Figure 4-12: Choose from a wide assortment of preset contours for your layer styles.

The presets offer contours like ring, rolling, sawtooth, and steps, all of which create rings of transparency within the shadows and glows. If you use contours with bevel and emboss effects, you can create nooks, crannies, bumps, and lumps that are highlighted and shaded.

You can also find options for naming and deleting contours as well as saving, loading, resetting, and replacing contour libraries. Choosing different contours can create fun and funky shadows and glow, as shown in Figure 4-13.

Adjusting contour settings

Of course, you're using Photoshop, the Swiss Army Knife of the graphics-editing world, so you can do a whole lot more than choose a preset contour and apply it to a layer. Depending on the effect you're working with, you can change the appearance of the contour in a variety of ways:

Figure 4-13: A Ring-Triple contour on the drop shadow of my beveled text and oval adds a metallic touch.

- ✐ **Noise:** Randomizes the colors of selected pixels in the drop shadow to give a gritty effect.
- ✐ **Anti-aliasing:** Slightly softens the edge pixels of a contour.
- ✐ **Range:** Controls how much of the glow is targeted for the contour. Reduce the Range setting to get a less feathered, tighter, and larger glow.
- ✐ **Jitter:** Doesn't affect the appearance of the default glow, but with other gradients, the Jitter setting varies the color and opacity of selected pixels to give a roughened effect.
- ✐ **Invert:** Turns the colors of the satin effect inside out.

✏ **Gloss Contour:** Changes the distribution of color in the effect over the layer. It creates a metallic effect when used with the Bevel and Emboss styles. The indented Contour option, which appears below the Bevel and Emboss style in the Styles list, does the same for the edges of the layer. It creates shaded and highlighted nooks and crannies when used with the Bevel and Emboss styles.

Modifying contours with the Contour Editor

If the preset contours just don't do it for you, feel free to create your own by following these steps:

1. **Open the Contour Editor dialog box, shown in Figure 4-14, by clicking the Contour thumbnail in the Layer Style dialog box.**

2. **Click the line on the mapping line to add points and drag the line to adjust the slope.**

   You can also select a point on the mapping line and enter values in the Input and Output boxes.

3. **To create a sharp corner instead of a curve, select a point and click the Corner option.**

4. **When you have the contour to your liking, click the New button, give it a name, as shown in Figure 4-15, and click OK.**

   Photoshop saves your custom contour as a preset and makes it available in the Contour palette.

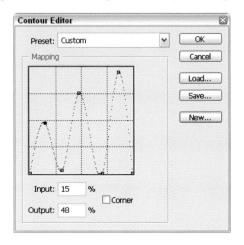

Figure 4-14: Create a custom contour if the presets don't meet your needs.

Figure 4-15: Name your custom contour.

You can save custom contours for reloading later or for trading with friends and neighbors. (Try giving them away on Halloween.) Photoshop saves contours as a .shc file in the Contours folder in the Presets folder in the Photoshop application folder.

Applying and Modifying Preset Styles

In addition to layer effects, Photoshop also offers you a multitude of preset layer styles that you can access via the Styles palette, shown in Figure 4-16.

You can also access these styles by using the Style picker drop-down palette on the Options bar, when the Pen or shape tools are active and you have the Shape Layer option selected. And you find the Styles palette nestled in the Layer Style dialog box as well.

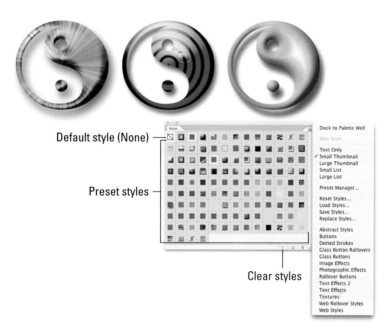

Default style (None)

Preset styles

Clear styles

Figure 4-16: Use the Styles palette to apply effects such as Angled Spectrum (left), Striped Cone (center), and Star Glow (right).

Here are the many splendid ways to apply a preset style:

🖝 Select the layer and click a style in the Styles palette.

🖝 Drag and drop a style from the Styles palette onto a layer in the Layers palette.

🖝 Drag and drop a style directly onto the image window. When your cursor is over the element to which you want to apply the style, release your mouse button.

✏ Double-click the layer thumbnail in the Layers palette. Select Styles in the upper-left side of the Layer Style dialog box. Choose a style from the palette. Click OK to close the Layer Style dialog box.

✏ If you're using the Pen or one of the shape tools, select the Shape Layer option. Then select a style from the Style picker drop-down palette on the Options bar before drawing the shape.

By default, applying a style over another style replaces it. To add a style along with another, press the Shift key while clicking or dragging the style.

Managing preset styles

Here are some additional points to remember when using the Styles palette. You can do any of the following:

✏ **Load another Style preset library:** In the Styles palette, the Style picker drop-down palette, or the palette in the Layer Style dialog box, you can choose Load Styles from the palette pop-up menu to add a library to your current preset list (refer to Figure 4-16). Select the library and click Load. You can also choose Replace Styles. Even easier, just choose a preset library from the bottom of the menu and click OK to replace or append your current list.

✏ **Use the Preset Manager to load preset style libraries:** You can also rename, delete, and save whole libraries of presets. See Book I, Chapter 5.

✏ **Return to the default library of presets:** Choose Reset Styles.

✏ **Choose a viewing option for your palette:** You can choose Small or Large Thumbnail or Small or Large List. And, of course, there's also Text Only, but what fun is it if you can't see the presets?

✏ **Rename a preset style:** Double-click the style in the Styles palette. If you're in Thumbnail view, type a new name in the dialog box and click OK. If the view is set to list, simply type a new name directly and press Enter (Return on the Mac). You can also choose Rename Style from the Picker in the Layer Style dialog box, or the Style picker drop-down palette on the Options bar. Or if you like, click the Rename button in the Preset Manager.

✏ **Save a set of preset styles as a library:** Choose Save Styles from the Styles palette pop-up menu, from the Layer Style dialog box pop-up menu, or from the Style picker drop-down palette pop-up menu on the Options bar. Name the library, navigate to the Styles folder in the Presets folder in the Photoshop folder, and click Save.

✏ **Delete a preset style:** Drag the style to the trash can icon in the Styles palette or Alt+click (Option+click on the Mac) the style. You can also choose Delete Style from the Layer Style dialog box, or the Style picker drop-down palette on the Options bar.

↙ **To clear a style (that is, remove it from the layer):** Click the Clear Style button in the Styles palette. You can also click the Default Style (None) swatch in the stand-alone Styles palette or the ones located in the Layer Style dialog box or on the Options bar.

↙ **Change the style or color of the currently active shape layer:** Click the link icon on the Options bar and select a different style or color. This option allows you to experiment with different styles for that shape. Also, the color swatch on the Options bar changes as the foreground color changes.

Conversely, deselect the link icon, and Photoshop won't change the style of the active shape layer when you select a different style. This option allows you to choose a different style or color for a new shape layer without affecting the previous shape layer. If you have the link icon deselected, the active shape layer determines the color swatch on the Options bar.

Saving your own style

If you get bored using the preset style libraries or if you really went to town and created a custom style that you think is so fabulous that you'll want to use it again and again, you can easily save it to the Styles palette. Here's all you need to know about saving custom styles:

1. **Create your own custom style by applying layer effects and/or styles to your layer.**

   Starting with an existing preset style and modifying the settings to suit your needs is also easy.

2. **After you complete your style, click the Create New Style button in the Styles palette or choose New Style from the palette pop-up menu.**

   You can also drag your selected layer from the Layers palette onto the Styles palette or simply click in an empty space in the Styles palette. Or you can double-click the layer thumbnail to open the Layer Style dialog box where you can click the New Style button.

3. **In the New Style dialog box, shown in Figure 4-17, name your style and select your desired options.**

   The Include Layer Effects check box includes any effects you applied via the Effects section of the Layer Style dialog box — drop shadows, bevels, and so on.

   The Include Layer Blending Options check box includes any blending you did using the Blending Options section of the Layer Styles palette. Photoshop adds your new style to the end of the Styles palette. If you wish to edit your custom style, you must select each individual effect in the Layers palette and adjust the settings in the Layer Styles dialog box.

Alt+click (Option+click on the Mac) to create a new style and bypass the dialog box. Your style gets the default name of Style 1.

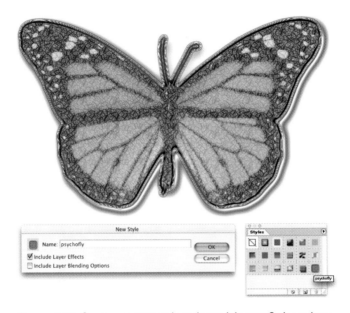

Figure 4-17: Create a custom style and save it in your Styles palette.

Clipping Layers into Masks

In a *clipping mask,* the bottommost layer, also known as the base layer, acts as a mask for the layers above it. The layers in the group clip to the opaque areas of the base layer and do not show over the transparent areas of the base layer.

At this point, you might be saying, "Huh?" Rather than trying to decipher the definition, a better way to understand a clipping mask is to just create one. Follow the steps in this section, and I know that instead of "Huh," you'll be saying "Yeah, baby," just like Austin Powers.

Creating a clipping mask works well if you want to fill type with different images on multiple layers.

Using the steps that follow, I created a new document with a white background. I took the Custom Shape tool and, choosing the Fill Region option (see Book IV, Chapter 1 for more on shapes), drew a heart on my second layer. I then added a drop shadow and inner bevel to my heart for added dimension, but this step isn't mandatory.

I then opened an image of an island and dragged and dropped that image onto my composite. I opened an image of some dolphins, selected a couple dolphins, and dragged and dropped them onto my composite.

And, finally, I created some type and applied a drop shadow and inner bevel to the type, as shown in Figure 4-18.

Figure 4-18: In a clipping mask, layers clip to the opaque areas of a base layer.

Follow these steps to create your own clipping group:

1. **Open or create an image that has several layers.**

2. **Press Alt (Option on the Mac) and position your mouse cursor over the line dividing two layers in the Layers palette.**

   Your cursor changes to two overlapping circles with a small arrow icon. You can also choose Layer➪Create Clipping Mask.

3. **Click your mouse button.**

   I did this three times: in between my type and the dolphin layer, in between the dolphin and the island layer, and in between the island layer

TIP

Managing clipping masks

Here is some clipping mask trivia:

- To remove a single layer from the clipping mask, you can simply Alt+click (Option+click) the line between the two layers in the Layers palette. Or you can select the layer and choose Layer➪Release Clipping Mask. Both commands remove the selected layer and any layers above it from the clipping group.

- To ungroup all the layers in the clipping mask, select the base layer and choose Layer➪Release Clipping Mask.

- You can also apply clipping masks to adjustment and fill layers. If you clip between a regular layer and an adjustment layer, or a regular layer and a fill layer, the adjustment or fill layer affects only the pixels of the adjacent underlying layer, instead of all the underlying layers. For more on adjustment and fill layers, see Book V, Chapter 1.

and my heart shape. Notice how all my images and my type clip to the base layer (the heart shape) in the Layers palette (refer to Figure 4-18).

Nothing outside the boundaries of the heart shape is visible on any of the layers in the clipping mask, as shown in Figure 4-18. The down-pointing arrow icon indicates that the layers are clipped. The clipping group takes on the opacity and blend mode of the base layer.

 Putting It Together

Adding Text and Layer Styles to a Collage

If you've been reading Book V faithfully, then you may have a nearly complete collage on your hands. If you're at all interested in using words with your images, then now (at the end of the project, not the beginning) is the time to add them. Adding type can turn a good composite into a dynamite and cohesive image that conveys exactly what you want. I'm no Shakespeare and can't help you create the perfect tag line, but I can show you how to add text to your collage. Adding layer styles gives you versatility in the kinds of effects you can apply to styles, so I show you how to apply those to a collage. To add and adjust type, follow these steps:

1. **Open the saved collage file.**

   Make sure that the Layers palette is open.

2. **Select the Eyedropper tool from the Tools palette. Click a color in the collage that you like.**

The color you sampled is now the foreground color.

3. **Select the Type tool. On the Options bar, select a font, style, point size, and other formatting options.**

I recommend choosing an easy-to-read serif font and applying a bold style to it. I'm using Times Bold, and I set the point size to 100.

I set the anti-aliasing to Crisp and the Alignment to Left, but you can explore your options until you're dizzy (or your deadline passes).

4. **Click inside your image and type some text.**

I typed Go outside for my travel collage.

5. **Select the Move tool from the Tools palette and position the type in the collage.**

I put my text in the upper-left corner.

6. **Adjust your settings as you desire.**

If you want to add a second, smaller line of text, grab the Type tool again and reduce the point size from the Options bar. You can change other settings, as well.

7. **When you're satisfied with your changes, click under the first line of text and type your next line.**

Under Go outside, I typed and play, as shown in the figure.

With the Move tool, fine-tune the position of the type.

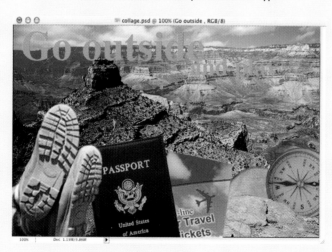

continued

continued

When you're satisfied with the size, style, color, and appearance of the type in your collage, you can make some more large-scale changes by creating layer styles. Follow these steps:

1. **Add a drop shadow and make sure that you have selected Global Light so that all the layers use the same angle.**

   In the Layers palette, first select the layer that includes the first line of text. Then choose Layer⇨Layer Style⇨Drop Shadow. Make sure the Drop Shadow box is selected in the left column.

   You can change the angle so that the light source is coming from one direction or another (mine's set at 120% so that the light's coming from the left).

2. **Add bevels and embossing.**

   Click the Bevel and Emboss style in the left column.

   Make sure that you actually select the style and not just the box; otherwise, the right panel with all the options won't appear.

   In my example, I selected Inner Bevel from the Style pop-up menu in the right panel. Then I selected Chisel Soft from the Technique pop-up menu. My idea was to give the type a carved-in-stone look.

3. **Click OK when you're satisfied with the styles you've created in the layer so far.**

4. **Apply the same styles to the layer where the second line of text is, as shown in the figure.**

TIP

To get the exact same settings without having to make every adjustment again, right-click (Control+click on the Mac) the florin (the f symbol) on the first layer you worked on and choose Copy Layer Style from the context menu. Select the second type layer and right-click (Control+click on the Mac) on the layer name and choose Paste Layer Style from the context menu.

5. **Make any last adjustments and choose File➪Save.**

You're all done. If you feel like it, keep adding to or refining the collage as you learn new tricks.

Chapter 5: Working with Smart Objects

*P*hotoshop has decided to borrow a great feature from its Webby cousin Adobe GoLive. With the advent of Smart Objects, Photoshop has significantly cut your editing time while letting you transform your objects without fear of quality loss. With Smart Objects, you create the art once and then if you want to show the art again, you use what are called *instances*. These instances can be linked to your original art. This makes editing a breeze. If this feature sounds familiar, it's probably because, besides GoLive, Adobe Illustrator uses *symbols,* a similar type of object. Read on to find out more about this feature — the ultimate in digital recycling.

Introducing Smart Objects

A Smart Object is actually what Adobe refers to as a *container,* in which a bitmap (raster) or vector image's source data is embedded. So in essence, a Smart Object is composed of two files, one inside the other. Adobe uses the analogy of a new file, the *child*, which is embedded into the original file, the *parent*. This source data of the child is contained in the Smart Object parent but keeps all its native characteristics and is fully editable.

Here are a few advantages of Smart Objects:

✓ **Transform without degradation.** In Book III, Chapter 3, I warn you about the negative side of transformations. When transforming traditional layers, your image goes through the process of resampling, which then causes degradation of quality. With Smart Objects, you can transform your artwork without losing any image quality. Photoshop does this by actually using your *original* source data to render the transformations.

- **Preserve non-native file data.** Photoshop transforms any non-native image information, such as Illustrator vector artwork for example, into a format it can recognize without altering the native data.

- **Edit the Smart Object and all instances are dynamically updated.** If you make changes to the original Smart Object, all instances (duplicates of the original) are automatically changed as well. No need to change them individually. This can be a real timesaver, especially if you've gone crazy with the number of instances you've used, such as on a map or Web home page.

Creating Smart Objects

You can create a Smart Object in a few ways. You can import the artwork via the Place command. You can also copy and paste the artwork from Illustrator into Photoshop. Or you can convert a Photoshop layer into a Smart Object. Finally, you can create one Smart Object from another. I discuss the specific steps for each way in the following sections.

Placing artwork

You may not have much experience in using the Place command in Photoshop because most activities involve opening images and creating new ones. But with the advent of Smart Objects, you may call on this command more frequently. Here's the scoop on placing artwork:

1. **Choose File⇨New and create a new blank Photoshop document using your desired size and settings.**

   If you're unsure about creating a new file, see Book I, Chapter 3. You can also use an existing Photoshop file.

2. **Choose File⇨Place. Locate and select your desired artwork. Click the Place button.**

   If your file is in any format besides Illustrator or PDF, it pops right onto your canvas, as shown in Figure 5-1. Note the bounding box

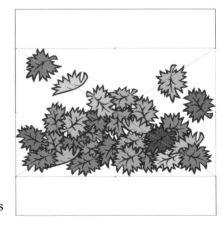

Figure 5-1: Create a Smart Object by placing your artwork into a Photoshop file.

and X around and across the image, which is an indication that the image has been *placed*.

If your file is a native Illustrator or PDF file you get the Place PDF dialog box asking you for additional information, as shown in Figure 5-2. If it is a multipaged PDF you can select the pages or images you want placed. Select your cropping options. Not sure what they mean? Just choose one and view the thumbnail to see how the image appears in relationship to the page. By the way, you can also choose between a Small, Large, and Fit Page thumbnail view.

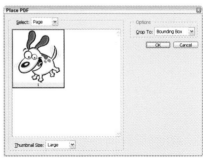

Figure 5-2: When placing an Illustrator or PDF file, specify your options in the Place PDF dialog box.

If you happen to deselect the Create PDF Compatible File option when saving your native Illustrator file, you see a nasty warning in the Place PDF dialog box telling you to go back and resave your file with the option checked and then place the file again. Don't take it personally. Illustrator was programmed based on PDF core code and sometimes doesn't like it when you strip it of the connection.

You can also select the image in the Bridge and choose File⇨ Place⇨In Photoshop. See Book I, Chapter 5 for details on working with the Bridge.

3. **Using the bounding box, transform (scale, rotate, and so on) your image to your desired dimensions and position it on your canvas, as shown in Figure 5-3. Remember you can rest assured that your transformations are applied without degrading the quality of your image.**

Note that if your image is larger than the Photoshop canvas, it's automatically sized to fit within the canvas dimensions. If you need a refresher on transforming and moving, see Book III, Chapter 3.

If you are placing a PDF, EPS, or native Illustrator file, specify the Anti-alias option on the Options bar. Check it to create a softer, blended edge. Uncheck it to produce a hard edge.

Figure 5-3: Transform and position your image before committing it into your file.

4. **After you have your image the way you want it, either click inside the bounding box, press Enter (Return on the Mac), or click the Commit (check mark icon) button on the Options bar.**

When the artwork is committed, the native file data is embedded into the Photoshop file and the artwork is rasterized on its own layer. You'll notice the Smart Object icon appears on those layers, as shown in Figure 5-4.

If you change your mind and don't want to commit the image, press Esc or click the Cancel button on the Options bar.

Smart Object icon

Figure 5-4: The Smart Object icon.

Copying and pasting

Before you copy and paste artwork from Illustrator into Photoshop as a Smart Object, be sure and check the PDF and AICB (no transparency support) options in the File Handling and Clipboard preferences in Illustrator. Leave the default of Preserve Appearances and Overprints checked. By doing so, you can control how your artwork is rasterized in Photoshop. If left unchecked, Photoshop rasterizes the art without your vital input.

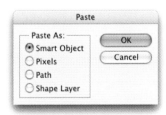

1. **Open your desired Adobe Illustrator file in Illustrator.**

2. **Select your artwork and choose Edit⇨Copy.**

3. **Switch to Photoshop. Open your desired Photoshop document or create a new document.**

4. **Choose Edit⇨Paste.**

5. **In the Paste dialog box, shown in Figure 5-5, select the Smart Object option and click OK.**

Your image is imported and appears in a bounding box, and the Layers palette shows that you pasted the image as a Smart Object, as shown in Figure 5-5.

Figure 5-5: When copying and pasting artwork from Illustrator to Photoshop, specify how you want the artwork pasted.

6. **Using the bounding box, transform (scale, rotate, and so on) your image to your desired dimensions and position it on your canvas.**

   Perspective and Distort transformations are unavailable to Smart Objects.

REMEMBER

If you chose Smart Object in the Paste dialog box in Step 4, remember that you can transform your artwork, without degradation before placing it into Photoshop. Like with the Place command, the native file data is embedded into the Photoshop file, and the art is rasterized on its own layer after the artwork is committed.

Converting a layer into a Smart Object and vice versa

If you want to convert a layer into a Smart Object, follow these steps:

1. **Select your desired layer in the Layers palette.**

2. **Choose Layer⇨Smart Object⇨Group into New Smart Object.**

   You can also choose the command from the Layers palette pop-up menu. After you convert a layer into a Smart Object, you see the Smart Object icon in the lower-right corner of the layer thumbnail.

You can also convert a Smart Object into a layer. You may want to do this if you need to paint on or apply filters to your artwork. Here's how to make the conversion:

1. **Select your desired layer in the Layers palette.**

2. **Choose Layer⇨Smart Objects⇨Convert to Layer, or you can choose Layer⇨Rasterize⇨Smart Object.**

   Note that your Smart Object is rasterized at its current size, so be sure it is the size you want before you execute the command. Your Smart Object icon disappears, and you're left with a normal, run-of-the mill layer.

Creating one Smart Object from another

Sometimes you may want to use one Smart Object as the basis for another. Depending on your needs, you can keep the new Smart Object linked or unlinked to the original. If it remains linked, modifying the original automatically modifies the duplicate. If unlinked, you can modify the original without changing the duplicate. In addition, you're free to change the duplicate without worrying about affecting the original. Here's how to create a Smart Object from another:

1. **Select the Smart Object layer in the Layers palette.**

2. **Create a duplicate Smart Object that is linked or unlinked to the original:**

   An unlinked object: Choose Layer⇨Smart Objects⇨New Smart Object Via Copy.

A linked object: Choose Layer⇨New⇨Layer Via Copy.

A new Smart Object layer appears in the Layers palette, as shown in Figure 5-6.

You can also drag the Smart Object layer over the Create a New Layer icon at the bottom of the Layers palette.

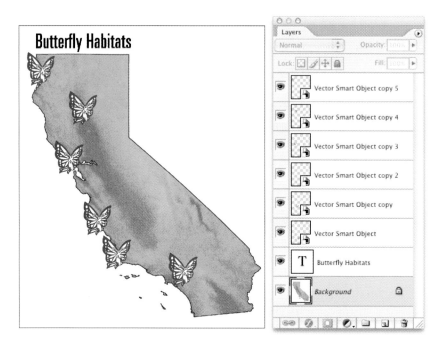

Figure 5-6: You can duplicate a Smart Object and either keep it linked or unlinked to its original.

Editing Smart Objects

One of the great things about Smart Objects is that you can edit the contents, or source data. If the source content is a vector-based PDF, AI, or EPS file and was prepared in Illustrator, it opens in that program. If the source content is raster-based and created in Photoshop, the file opens in Photoshop. (For details on vector versus raster images, see Book II, Chapter 1.)

Here's the 411 on how to edit the contents of a Smart Object:

1. In your document, select the Smart Object layer in the Layers Palette.

2. **Choose Layer➪Smart Objects➪Edit Contents. Or you can simply double-click the Smart Objects layer thumbnail in the Layers palette.**

   A dialog box appears telling you to save your changes and to save the file in the same location.

3. **Click OK to close the dialog box.**

   The Smart Object opens in the program in which it was created, either Illustrator or Photoshop.

4. **Edit your file ad nauseum.**

5. **Choose File➪Save to incorporate the edits.**

6. **Close your source file.**

7. **Return to your Photoshop document, which contains your Smart Object.**

   If all goes as expected, all instances of the Smart Object are updated. For example, my butterflies went from purple in Figure 5-6 to blue in Figure 5-7.

Figure 5-7: The Photoshop document automatically reflects any editing you do to your Smart Object.

Replacing contents

When editing the contents of a Smart Object, you automatically update all instances of that Smart Object in your document. This can be a real productivity enhancer. Just follow these short steps:

1. **Select the Smart Object in the Layers palette.**

2. **Choose Layer➪Smart Objects➪ Replace Contents.**

3. **Locate your file and click the Place button.**

4. **Click OK and the new contents pop into place in the Smart Object container, as shown in Figure 5-8.**

   You find that all instances of that Smart Object are also updated in your document.

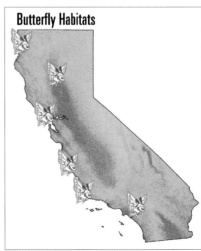

Figure 5-8: I replaced the contents of my blue butterflies to that of a rarer species.

To replace the contents of a single instance of a Smart Object, you have to make sure that the Smart Object is not linked to other Smart Objects. To create an unlinked Smart Object, select the Smart Object instance you wish to change, choose Layer⇨Smart Objects⇨New Smart Object Via Copy. Make your desired replacement and then delete the original Smart Object.

Exporting contents

You can export your Smart Object and save it to a hard drive or external media. Raster, or *bitmap*, data exports in the .psb (large document) format, while vector data exports as a PDF file. Here are the steps:

1. **Select the Smart Object in the Layers palette.**

2. **Choose Layer⇨Smart Objects⇨Export Contents.**

3. **In the Save dialog box, navigate to your destination and click Save.**

   Note that you can open the .psb file only in Photoshop. It won't open in another program.

Book VI

Channels and Masks

The 5th Wave   By Rich Tennant

"I'm going to assume that most of you — but not all of you — understand that this session on 'masking' has to do with Photoshop."

*I*f you got the basics down and are ready for something a little more challenging, this is your book. Here I help you start working with channels and creating masks. Creating masks is one of the most accurate ways to make a selection and is especially useful in tackling more difficult selections.

In this book, I show you different ways of creating a mask, from quick masks to layer masks to channel masks. If you've ever flung your mouse or stylus pen in frustration because you couldn't select the hair on your loved one's photo, you'll be well-served by reading this book and getting up to speed on masking techniques.

Chapter 1: Using Channels

In This Chapter

✔ **Understanding channels**

✔ **Viewing channels**

✔ **Working with the Channels palette**

✔ **Editing channels**

✔ **Creating alpha channels**

✔ **Using the Channel Mixer**

*1*f you're reading this, it probably means that you didn't quickly thumb through this chapter, say "Yuck, boorrrrringgg!" and move on to sexier topics such as blending, filtering, and retouching. You knew that would be a huge mistake.

The wonderful thing about channels is that they offer you greater control and selectivity when doing those very things — blending, filtering, and retouching. Channels bring one more level of control when editing your images. You can use individual channels for layer blending options, filters, and as starting points for masks.

Channels also come into play when saving selections for later use or for adding spot (custom) colors to your image. You can also use channels to turn color images into nicely contrasted grayscale images. And finally, you can play around with the colors in an image by mixing up the channels. So bear with me. The topic of channels may be a bit dry and technical, but in the end, they'll enable you to hold the envious title of Master Editor.

To understand how channels work, you'll find it helpful to know a few things about colors — specifically the various color modes, which I cover in Book II, Chapter 2.

Understanding Channels

When you look at a color image, you see one big, 24-bit, composite collection of colored pixels. Technically speaking, however, Photoshop doesn't see that at all. Photoshop perceives a color image as individual bands of 8-bit, grayscale images. RGB images have three bands; CMYK images have four bands.

I know it's strange to think of a color image as being composed of several grayscale images, but it's true. Each one of these bands, or grayscale images, is a *channel*. Specifically, they're color channels. If you just can't get past the fact that a color image is the sum of several grayscale channels, as shown in Figure 1-1, then just think of channels as holding tanks of color data.

Figure 1-1: A color image is composed of 8-bit grayscale images referred to as channels.

Another way of relating channels to the real world is in terms of hardware. Here's how the most common hardware handles color:

- ✔ When you offset print a CMYK image, the process separates the colors (see Book IX, Chapter 1) into four colors — cyan, magenta, yellow, and black. Paper passes through four individual rollers on the printing press, each roller containing one of those four colored inks.

- ✔ Scanners scan in RGB via a pass of red, green, and blue sensors over your image.

- ✔ CRT Screens display images via red, green, and blue tubes.

In addition to color channels, there are channels called *alpha channels* (covered later in this chapter); others are called *spot channels* (discussed in Book IX, Chapter 1). Photoshop now supports up to 56 channels per file. So knock yourself out! Just remember that each channel you add increases your file size.

Briefly, you can use alpha channels to create, store, and edit selections, defining them not by a selection outline, but by black, white, and varying shades of gray pixels — in other words, a grayscale image. Black pixels represent unselected areas of the image, while white pixels represent selected areas, and gray pixels represent partially selected pixels.

You can create spot channels when you want to add a spot, or custom, color to your image. Spot colors are premixed inks often used in addition to or in lieu of CMYK colors.

TIP

A little bit about bit depth

When you're standing around the water cooler or the color printer, and you hear people talking about a 1-bit or an 8-bit image, they're referring to something called *bit depth*. Bit depth measures how much color information is available to display and print each pixel. A higher bit depth means the image can display more information — specifically, more colors. For example, a 1-bit image can display two color values — black and white. That's why a purely black-and-white image is called a bitmap image. Likewise

✔ An 8-bit image has 256 grayscale levels (2^8). Grayscale images are 8 bit (1 channel, 8 bits).

✔ A 24-bit image has about 16 million colors (2^{24}). RGB images are 24 bit (3 channels × 8 bits).

✔ CMYK images are 32 bit (4 channels × 8 bits). CMYK images, however, are limited to the number of colors that are physically reproducible on paper, which is around 55,000.

Bit depths typically range from 1 to 64 bits.

All images, no matter what their color mode, have at least one channel. Grayscale, Duotone, and Indexed Color (for GIF Web images) modes have only one channel. RGB and CMYK images have three and four channels, respectively. They also contain a composite channel, which reflects the combination of the individual color channels and gives you the full color display.

Working with Channels

As with layers, channels have their own palette that acts as command central for viewing, creating, and managing tasks. The first step is accessing channels by choosing Window⇨Channels. The Channels palette appears, as shown in Figure 1-2.

Viewing channels without a remote

Selecting a channel in the Channels palette automatically makes it show. To select a channel, click the channel thumbnail or name in the palette. To select more than one channel, Shift+click. To show or hide a channel, click in the eye column in the far left of the palette. You can also drag through the column to hide or show the channels quickly.

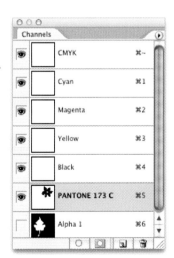

Figure 1-2: The Channels palette stores all of the image's channels, from spot to alpha channels.

CMYK, RGB, and Lab images have a *composite* channel in addition to their individual channels. This composite channel is the combination of all the channels in the image and is named after the color mode. For example, the composite channel in Figure 1-2 is the first one, called CMYK.

Changing the default channel view

The default setting is to view your channels in grayscale. You can, however, view them in color. To do so, choose Edit➪Preferences➪Display & Cursors (Photoshop➪Preferences➪Display & Cursors on Mac OS X) and select Color Channels in Color.

Although this option *graphically* exemplifies the way an image comprises separate color channels, it really does you no good if you want to work with your channels for editing. That's because the color view obscures details and makes measuring the impact of adjustments and filters more difficult. You need to see the channels in their true grayscale form for that.

If you select or show more than one channel, even in the default grayscale view, the channels always appear in color.

To change the size of the thumbnail that appears, choose Palette Options from the Channels palette pop-up menu. Select your desired thumbnail size. If you're working with several channels and you have a dinosaur of a computer, you can also choose None to turn off the thumbnails — to improve its performance.

Duplicating and deleting channels

Duplicating channels is something you may do quite often. I know I do. And of course, deleting channels isn't something you do only if you're a neat freak. Channels take up a lot of memory, so getting rid of the ones you no longer need is always good.

Here are some instances when duplicating channels is a good idea:

- **When you want to create a *channel mask*:** First, you find a suitable channel and then make a duplicate. (For more on this technique, see Book VI, Chapter 3.) You can use channel masks to select difficult elements involving fine details, such as hair, fur, smoke, and so on.

- **When you want to make a backup copy of the channel before doing some editing:** Having a backup just to be on the safe side is always a good idea. For example, you may want to apply an Unsharp Mask filter to one or two channels to improve the focus of the image. For more on the Unsharp Mask filter, see Book VII, Chapter 1.

✔ **To insert a copy of an alpha channel into another image:** For example, maybe you spent an hour creating elaborate alpha channels for shadows and highlights on a product photographed in flat lighting.

You may have 12 products, all the same shape, but different colors that you need to apply those highlights and shadows to. Rather than re-creating the wheel each time, you could simply duplicate the alpha channels into each file.

Duplicating channels

To duplicate a channel, follow these short steps:

1. **Select your desired channel in the Channels palette.**

2. **Choose Duplicate Channel from the palette pop-up menu.**

   The Duplicate Channel dialog box appears, as shown in Figure 1-3.

Figure 1-3: Name and provide a destination for your duplicate channel.

3. **In the Duplicate section, name the channel.**

   You can also drag the channel to the New Channel icon at the bottom of the palette. If you do this, Photoshop provides a default name and bypasses Steps 4, 5, and 6.

   You can also duplicate a channel to another image by dragging the channel. Open your destination image and drag the desired channel from your current image into the destination image window. The duplicated channel appears in the Channels palette.

4. **In the Destination section, select a file from the Document drop-down list. Or choose New to create a new image.**

   You can choose your current image or any open image with the same pixel dimensions (size and resolution) as your current image. (For more on pixel dimensions, see Book II, Chapter 1.)

   If you choose New, Photoshop creates a new image that has a single channel. Provide a name for the file.

5. **Select Invert if you want to reverse the selected and unselected areas of the duplicate channel.**

   You use the Invert option primarily when you duplicate an existing alpha channel. For more on alpha channels, see the upcoming section.

6. Click OK.

The dialog box closes. Your duplicate channel appears in the Channels palette, as shown in Figure 1-4.

Replacing one channel over another

To replace one channel over another, you can use the copy-and-paste method. In your current image, select your desired channel. Choose Select⇨All and then Edit⇨Copy. Select the channel in the destination image that you want to replace and choose Edit⇨Paste. The pasted channel replaces the original one.

Deleting unwanted channels

To delete an unwanted channel — something you definitely want to do because channels can eat up a lot of space — select the channel in the Channels palette and do one of the following:

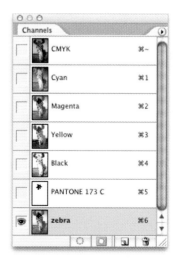

Figure 1-4: You can duplicate channels for masking as well as for backup purposes.

↳ Drag the channel to the trash can icon at the bottom of the palette.

↳ Choose Delete Channel from the palette pop-up menu.

↳ Click the trash can icon and then click Yes.

↳ Alt+click (Option+click on the Mac) on the trash can icon.

Rearranging and renaming channels

Although you can't shuffle or rename color channels, you can do so with spot and alpha channels. To move a spot or alpha channel, simply drag it up or down in the Channels palette. When you see a dark line appear where you want the channel to go, release your mouse button. You can move a spot or alpha channel above a color channel only in a multichannel image. In short, in a multichannel image, each channel becomes an independent spot channel, and the channels no longer have a relationship with each other. Multichannel images also do not support layers. For more details, see Book II, Chapter 2.

To rename a spot or alpha channel, double-click the name in the Channel palette and type a new name. You can also choose Channel Options from the palette pop-up menu.

Splitting channels

You can split the channels of your image into separate images in separate files. For example in Figure 1-5, you see the Red, Green, Blue, Alpha, and Spot channels split into individual channels. Choose Split Channels from the palette pop-up menu. When you do so, your original image closes. The channel files have the name of your original image plus the channel name. You can split channels only on a flattened image — in other words, an image with no individual layers.

**Book VI
Chapter 1**

Using Channels

Figure 1-5: Be sure and save all changes in your original image before you split it because Photoshop closes your file.

You might want to split channels if you need to save your original file in a format that doesn't preserve channels — such as EPS, which doesn't support alpha channels — or you may want to split channels to merge them later on.

Merging channels

You can merge channels into a single image. The channels must be open, in grayscale mode, and have the same pixel dimensions. You can merge channels only when they are flattened images and have no layers.

Merging color channels can create some unique special effects. For example, by mismatching your channels when you merge them, you can create bizarre, and sometimes beautiful, color shifts.

To merge channels, follow these steps:

1. **Open your channel files and activate any one of them.**

2. **Choose Merge Channels from the palette pop-up menu.**

3. **In the Merge Channels dialog box, choose your desired color mode, as shown in Figure 1-6.**

   Any modes that are unavailable are grayed out. That's because you may not have enough channels for that mode.

   Figure 1-6: Choose the color mode and number of channels in this dialog box.

4. **Enter the number of channels you want.**

   When you choose your mode in Step 3, Photoshop automatically fills in the number of channels for the mode. If you deviate and enter something different, the file becomes a multichannel file.

5. **Click OK.**

6. **Select your channels in the dialog box that appears.**

   In my example, the Merge CMYK Channels dialog box appears. If you want to merge the channels normally, make sure that each channel matches (Red for Red and so on). If you want to rearrange the channels, you can mix them as I did in Figure 1-7, so that the Cyan channel is mixed with the Magenta channel, and so on.

   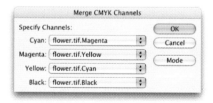

   Figure 1-7: You can mismatch your channels when merging them to create a unique effect.

7. **If you are merging into a multi-channel image, click Next. Repeat for each channel.**

8. Click OK.

You have now merged your files into a single image, which appears in your Photoshop window.

Photoshop closes individual channel files and merges any spot channels as alpha channels.

Check out Figure 1-8 to see how my sunflower went from yellow to magenta just by merging the layers a little differently.

Original   Split and merged

Figure 1-8: When you split and merge channels, you can create botanical specimens from another world.

If you have an image with alpha or spot channels, choose Multichannel from the Mode drop-down list in Step 3 or Photoshop doesn't include those channels in the merged image. After you merge the image, Photoshop gives all the channels the names Alpha 1, Alpha 2, Alpha 3, and so on. To get back to a color composite, choose Image⇨Mode⇨RGB Color or CMYK Color.

Using Painting and Editing Tools with Channels

Sometimes it's better to edit individual channels rather than the composite image. Mediocre flatbed scanners often reproduce an image that is slightly soft or out of focus. You may want to counteract that effect by applying an Unsharp Mask filter. Before you do, you should examine each channel separately. You may find that the Blue channel contains a lot of garbage — artifacts, dithering, and other nasty crud.

Blue channels are notorious for acquiring this junk, so try to avoid applying an Unsharp Mask filter on this channel unless you *really* want to accentuate what's already ugly.

Instead of applying the Unsharp Mask filter on Blue channels, select the Red and Green channels and then choose Filter⇨Sharpen⇨Unsharp Mask. Similarly, you can apply a Gaussian Blur filter to a channel to soften the unsightly pattern (called a *moiré* pattern) caused by scanning a halftone. (See Book VII, Chapter 1 for more on moiré patterns, and filters are covered throughout Book VII.)

While Unsharp Mask and Gaussian Blur are a couple of corrective filters that you'll use frequently, I also find it useful to apply a special-effect filter to individual channels. Sometimes applying a filter to the composite image produces an effect that's, well, overdone. Applying the filter to one or two channels can produce an effect that is subtler and less in-your-face. For example, in Figure 1-9, I applied a filter to just the Blue channel for the flower on the left. Using individual channels can also be useful for applying filters that produce monochromatic images, such as the Graphic Pen or Photocopy filters. If you apply the filter to the entire image, you get a black-and-white image. If you apply it to an individual channel, you retain some color.

Figure 1-9: By editing individual color channels, you can selectively and subtly apply filters (left) or adjust color (right).

You can select a color channel and then edit that channel by using a painting or editing tool to paint in the image. Keep these facts in mind:

- Painting with white adds the color channel's color at full intensity in the composite image.
- Painting with black removes the color in the composite image.
- Painting with a value of gray adds color at varying levels of intensity in the composite image.

For example, if you paint with white on the Blue channel in an existing image, Photoshop adds more blue to the color composite image. But if you paint with black, Photoshop adds yellow to the image because when you remove blue, what's left is the opposite, or complementary, color — yellow. To perform this channel magic, select the Brush tool and then choose your desired brush size from the Options bar. Choose your desired color in the Color palette. Select the channel you want to edit in the Channels palette. You can see the results by selecting the composite channel in the Channels palette. Refer to Figure 1-9 to see how I gave a flower a channel color makeover.

The results are a little different if you try this technique on a blank CMYK canvas. When you paint with black on the Cyan channel, your composite color image displays cyan. When you paint with white, you get no change.

Introducing Alpha Channels

You use alpha channels for selections that are incredibly detailed or that you want to save and reuse. To make that selection, an alpha channel uses black, white, and shades of gray to create a mask. The selected pixels are white, and unselected pixels are black. For example, in the alpha channel of the image shown in Figure 1-10, the selection includes the lanterns and trees; they appear white in the alpha channel. If an alpha channel includes gray areas, those areas are partially selected or partially unselected, depending on whether you think the glass is half full or half empty. The gray areas are selected but appear translucent.

You can create a mask by first duplicating a color channel and then editing that channel with painting and editing tools and filters. (See Book VI, Chapter 3 for more on channel masks.) You can also create an alpha channel by saving a selection you've created. After you create a channel mask or save a selection as an alpha channel, you can load that channel to use it as a selection in any image. The following sections explain how to save a selection as an alpha channel and load a selection. See Book VI, Chapter 3 for more on creating channel masks by duplicating an existing color channel.

Saving a selection as an alpha channel

One of the great things about alpha channels is that you can save them and then retrieve them time and time again. This can be especially handy if you've taken a lot of time and effort to create the selection. Why reinvent the wheel if you want to select the element again in the future? Sure, you can create a mask using Quick Mask mode and Color Range (see Book VI, Chapter 2), but those masks are only temporary.

Original image

Alpha channel mask

Figure 1-10: The alpha channel makes selecting this shape much easier than using the Lasso or Magic Wand tool.

After you make the initial selection, saving it is a piece of cake. Follow these steps:

1. **Make a selection in your image.**

2. **Choose Select⇨Save Selection.**

   You can also click the Save Selection as Channel button (a circle on a square icon) at the bottom of the Channels palette. A new channel appears with the default name of Alpha 1 and bypasses Steps 3 and 4.

3. **Choose a destination image in the Document pop-up menu.**

   You can choose your current image or any other open image with the same pixel dimensions.

4. Choose a destination channel from the Channel pop-up menu.

You can choose a new channel or any existing channel or layer mask. (See Book VI, Chapter 3 for more on layer masks.)

- If you choose New, name the channel.

- If you choose an existing alpha channel or layer mask, select your desired operation: Replace, Add to, Subtract from, or Intersect. These commands add to, subtract from, or intersect your current selection with the existing alpha channel.

5. Click OK.

Your alpha channel is complete and appears in the Channels palette, as shown in Figure 1-11.

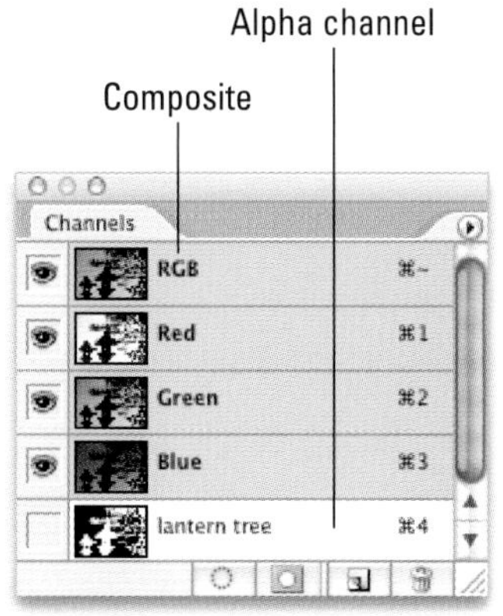

Figure 1-11: Saving your selection as an alpha channel allows you to efficiently reuse the selection.

Loading an alpha channel

No doubt if you've gone through the trouble of creating an alpha channel, it's because you want to easily load, or access, the selection again and again. To load an alpha channel, use any one of these many methods:

- Choose Select⟳Load Selection. Select your document and channel. Click Invert to swap selected and unselected areas. If your image has an active selection, choose how you want to combine the selections.

- Select the alpha channel in the Channels palette, click the Load Channel as Selection icon at the bottom of the palette, and then click the composite channel.

- Drag the channel to the Load Channel as Selection icon.

- Ctrl+Click (⌘+Click on the Mac) the alpha channel in the Channels palette.

- Ctrl+Shift+Click (⌘+Shift+Click on the Mac) to add the alpha channel to an active selection.

- Ctrl+Alt+Click (⌘+Option+Click on the Mac) to subtract the alpha channel from an active selection.

- Ctrl+Alt+Shift+Click (⌘+Option+Shift+Click on the Mac) to intersect the alpha channel with an active selection.

Adding channels can start to bloat your file size, so use them, but use them judiciously. The Photoshop native format and TIFF format compress channel information and therefore are good file formats to use when working with a lot of channels. The only formats that preserve alpha channels are Photoshop, TIFF, PDF, PICT, Pixar, or Photoshop Raw.

Using the Channel Mixer

The Channel Mixer actually does what its name implies — it mixes color channels. This feature lets you repair bad channels and produce grayscale images from color images. It also allows you to create tinted images and more intense special effects. Finally, it allows you to do the more mundane tasks of swapping or duplicating channels.

Although some Photoshop elitists worldwide tout this as an advanced feature not to be mucked with by amateurs, I say, "Give it a whirl." Intimidation is a nasty roadblock to creative fun. Just make a backup copy of an image before diving into the mix:

1. **Select the composite channel in the Channels palette.**

   If you have an RGB image, the composite channel is the RGB channel; for CMYK images, the CMYK channel.

2. **Choose Image⇨Adjustments⇨ Channel Mixer.**

   The Channel Mixer dialog box appears, as shown in Figure 1-12.

3. **For Output Channel, choose the channel in which to blend one or more source (existing) channels.**

   For example, if your Blue channel is lousy, select it from the Output Channel drop-down list.

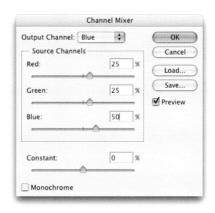

Figure 1-12: Among its many capabilities, the Channel Mixer enables you to repair bad channels.

4. **Drag any source channel's slider to the left to decrease the channel's effect on the Output channel. Or drag to the right to increase the effect.**

   Because my Blue channel contains artifacts and dithering picked up by the scanner, I am raising the Red and Green values from 0% to 25% and lowering the Blue value from 100% to 50%. To retain good contrast, try to use a combo of Red, Green, and Blue values that add up to close to 100%.

You can also enter a value from –200% to +200%. Using a negative value inverts the color data of the source channel.

5. **Tinker with the Constant option to add a black or white channel of varying opacity.**

   Drag the slider to a negative value to get a Black channel. Positive values give a White channel.

   This option brightens or darkens the overall image. I recommend leaving it at 0 most of the time. But try it. It may help.

6. **Select Monochrome to apply the same settings to all output channels producing a color image that has only values of gray.**

   Adjust the individual sliders to mix the values until you are satisfied with the contrast.

   This option is one of the best ways to produce grayscale images from color images because it preserves detail and provides better contrast control.

7. **Click OK to exit the Channel Mixer.**

   After you exit the Channel Mixer, choose Image⇨Mode⇨Grayscale to complete the conversion.

   If you select and then deselect the Monochrome option, you can modify the blend of each channel separately. By doing so, you can create color images that appear to be hand-tinted with color inks. Go for the subtle treatment or a more intensely colored look.

   Swapping color channels can produce some bizarre color effects. For example, try selecting the Red channel from the Output Channel drop-down list. Set the Red source channel to 0 and then set the Green source channel to 100. Try other combinations, Green for Blue, Blue for Red, and so on. Sometimes they can be downright freakish, but occasionally you may stumble on one that's worthy.

Book VI
Chapter 1

Using Channels

Putting It Together

Giving Flat Art Highlights and Shadows

Sometimes you need to give your art — whether it's a photo or another type of image — a little shine and shadow to bring it to life. You can do this by creating and saving your selections as alpha channels and filling them with translucent color. The great thing about alpha channels is that because you save them with your document, you can use them time and time again. Just follow these steps:

continued

continued

1. **Create a simple piece of artwork to use as a basis for your shadows and highlights.**

   I created a pool ball by creating two layers. On each layer, I used the Elliptical Marquee tool to create different-sized circles. I filled each circle with a separate color, as shown in the figure. To follow along with these steps, you can download this image from this book's Web site (see the Introduction for details).

2. **Choose Window➪Channels.**

   The Channels palette appears.

   Be sure to keep this palette visible because you will be creating new channels for the highlights.

3. **Choose the Pen tool from the Tools palette and create a path for the highlight.**

   I created a path for the highlight on the top-left portion of the ball in my example, assuming that the light source is coming from the upper-left corner. If the Pen tool seems like a foreign object to you, check out Book III, Chapter 2.

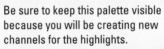

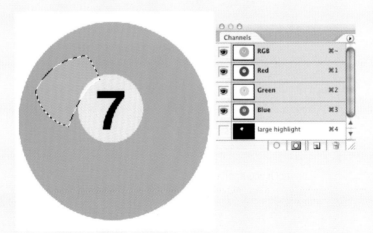

4. **Choose Window➪Paths.**

   The Paths palette appears.

5. **Click the Load Path as Selection icon (a dotted circle) at the bottom of the Paths palette.**

You see your work path disappear and a selection marquee appear.

6. **Choose Select⇨Save Selection.**

The Save Selection dialog box appears.

7. **Name the channel. Make sure the channel is new and click OK.**

An additional channel appears in the Channels palette, as shown in the preceding figure. This new channel is the alpha channel — your saved selection.

8. **Click the Create a New Layer icon (dog eared page) in the Layers palette. Double-click the layer name and rename it.**

I named mine *large highlight*.

Putting your highlights and shadows on separate layers is important so that you can apply different opacity settings and also retain the ability to tweak them later if needed.

9. **Choose Edit⇨Fill, choose the White option for Contents, and leave all the other options at their default settings. Click OK.**

The dialog box closes.

Your highlight is now filled with white. Don't worry; it won't stay this opaque.

10. **In the Layers palette, adjust the Opacity setting to 50%.**

The highlight now appears translucent (refer to the preceding figure).

11. **Choose the Pen tool and create a path for the highlight on the bottom of the object, as seen in the figure.**

Make sure the path matches up to the edge of the object. Use the Direct Selection tool if you need to adjust the anchor points or curve segments of the path.

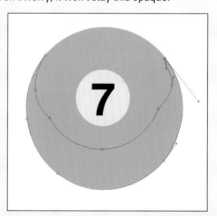

REMEMBER

Book VI
Chapter 1

Using Channels

continued

continued

12. **In the Paths palette, click the third icon from the left at the bottom of the palette.**

The work path disappears, and a selection marquee appears.

13. **Choose Select⇨Save Selection. In the Save Selection dialog box, name the channel. Make sure the channel is new and click OK.**

Mine is called "bottom highlight." Another alpha channel appears in the Channels palette.

14. **Repeat Steps 8, 9, and 10, but only adjust the opacity to 30%.**

15. **Use the Pen tool to create a path for the smaller shadow.**

For example, I created a path on the bottom right of the ball.

16. **Load the path as a selection in the Paths palette and choose Select⇨ Feather. Enter 3 pixels and click OK.**

The idea is to give the shadow a softer edge.

17. **Repeat Steps 6 through 10, but fill the selection with black instead of white and adjust the opacity to 20%.**

The shadow is shown in the figure.

18. **Use a selection tool to add a cast shadow.**

In my example, I used the Ellipse tool, pressed Alt (Option on the Mac), and created an ellipse at the base of the ball, shown in the figure.

Then I feathered the selection 25 pixels before I saved the selection.

The cast shadow needs to have really fuzzy edges, thus the large number of pixels for the feather.

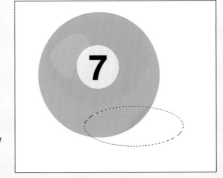

19. **Repeat Steps 8 and 9, filling the selection with black.**

My highlighted and shadowed pool ball is ready to roll, shown in the figure.

If your cast shadow layer is above your object, you have to change the stacking order and move your shadow layer so that it's below your object.

Now that you've spent all this time on the front end creating your alpha channels, you can then save time on the back end by using those alpha channels to apply highlights and shadows to similar artwork.

20. **To load alpha channels, choose Select⇨Load Selection and select your alpha channels from the Channel pop-up menu. Then repeat these steps.**

In my example, I took the highlights and shadows I created with lucky pool ball number 7 and loaded them as alpha channels in pool ball number 5.

Chapter 2: Quick and Dirty Masking

In This Chapter

✏ **Using Quick Masks**

✏ **Working with Color Range**

✏ **Selecting by erasing**

✏ **Extracting an image**

*M*asking is essentially just another way of making a selection. Instead of defining your selection with a selection outline, masks define your selection with 256 levels of gray, which allows you to have varying levels of selection. Photoshop masks or protects unselected pixels from any commands you execute. Photoshop doesn't mask selected pixels, making them fair game to any executed commands.

Different types of masks have different purposes — channel masks, layer masks, and vector masks. You can use them to temporarily make a selection, save and load selections, define vector shapes, selectively apply an adjustment layer or filter, blend one layer into another, and so on. Although selecting with the Marquee, Lasso, Magic Wand, and Pen tools can be fine, you'll soon find that these tools have a limited repertoire: You can't use them with much accuracy on more complex images. That's when you turn to masking.

Most things that pack a powerful punch are either expensive or hard to master, or both. Well, you already forked out a pretty penny for Photoshop. And yes, masking isn't for those who get their selections via a drive-thru window. To help you with the learning curve, in this chapter, I ease you into masking by using Photoshop's automated masking tools. Although they aren't quite as accurate as the hardcore masking I cover in Book VI, Chapter 3, they are easier on you, and with certain images (or a serious time crunch), the quick-and-dirty masking tools get the job done.

Working with Quick Masks

As you can probably guess from the name, Quick Masks allow you to create and edit selections quickly without having to bother with the Channels palette. Although you don't really create an end-product mask per se, the way you go about getting your selection is "mask-like." They are also user friendly in that they allow you to see your image while you're working. You can begin your Quick Mask by using a selection tool or a painting tool. After you have your Quick Mask, you can edit the mask using any painting or editing tool.

Quick Masks are temporary, so if you create one you really like, be sure and choose Select➪Save Selection at the end of the following steps. (Note that you have to be out of Quick Mask mode to do this.) That way you can save the selection as an alpha channel. For more on saving selections as alpha channels, see Book VI, Chapter 1.

Follow these steps to create your very own Quick Mask:

1. **Open a new document and, using any selection tool, select the element you want in your image.**

   Don't worry about getting the selection perfect. You can fine-tune your selection after you have the Quick Mask in place. Note that you can also just paint your mask from scratch. But I think that starting with a selection is easier.

2. **Click the Quick Mask Mode button in the Tools palette.**

   A color overlay covers and protects the area outside the selection, as shown in Figure 2-1. The selected pixels are unprotected.

3. **Refine the mask by selecting a painting or editing tool.**

   Corbis Digital Stock

   Figure 2-1: When using a Quick Mask, a color overlay represents the unselected, or protected, areas.

   Paint with black to add to the mask, thereby making the selection smaller. Even though you are painting with black, your strokes will show up as a red overlay. This red overlay is a visual carryover from back in the day when artists used rubylith (red transparent material) to mask portions of their art during airbrushing. Paint with white to delete from the mask, making the selection larger. Paint with a shade of gray to partially select the pixels. Partially selected pixels take on a semitransparent look, perfect for feathered edges, as you can see in Figure 2-2.

4. **After you finish editing your mask, shown in Figure 2-3, click the Standard Mode button in the Tools palette to exit the Quick Mask.**

Corbis Digital Stock

Figure 2-2: Clean up your Quick Mask.

The overlay disappears and a selection outline appears. Your selection is ready and waiting for your next command. The selection outline correlates with the unmasked or selected areas of the Quick Mask. Don't be surprised if the wispy or soft edges you so diligently selected aren't readily apparent when you switch back to normal editing mode. When you composite your selected image with another, your hard quick masking work will be evident.

Corbis Digital Stock

Figure 2-3: After you refine your mask (left), click the Standard Mode button to convert your mask into a selection outline (right).

Changing Quick Mask options

You can change Quick Mask options by double-clicking the Quick Mask Mode button in the Tools palette.

When you add a Quick Mask to a selection, by default a red overlay covers the selected area. The overlay has an opacity setting of 50%.

In addition to changing the color (to provide better contrast with your image, perhaps) and opacity of the overlay, you can also choose whether you want the overlay to represent the masked (unselected, protected) areas or the selected (unprotected) areas.

Using the Color Range Command

The Color Range command allows you to select similarly colored pixels in a selection or within an entire image. You can think of it as a smarter Magic Wand tool. Unlike the Magic Wand tool, however, Color Range lets you adjust your selection before you ultimately get the selection outline. It does this by using Fuzziness (a cousin of Tolerance), which allows you to select colors relative to how closely they resemble the sampled colors. Photoshop selects all the identical colors, partially selects similar colors, and does not select dissimilar colors. You adjust the fuzziness, and Photoshop adjusts the selection.

Color Range basics

Here are some Color Range command tips before you get started:

✔ You can save and load Color Range settings by clicking the appropriate buttons in the dialog box. But heck, after you have a selection, you can also choose Select⇨Save Selection to save it as an alpha channel.

✔ You can select a color range based on preset colors or tones that you choose from the Select drop-down list. For example, choosing red automatically selects all the red in the image. Choosing midtones selects all the medium-range tones in the image. And Out-of-Gamut (only available for RGB and Lab modes) selects all colors that cannot be printed using CMYK colors. For more on modes, see Book II, Chapter 2.

If you choose the Color Range command when you have an active selection, Photoshop selects only colors within the selection outline and ignores the rest of your image.

Executing the Color Range command

Here's all you need to know about working with the Color Range command:

1. **Choose Select⟶Color Range.**

   The Color Range dialog box appears in full glory.

2. **Choose Sampled Colors from the Select drop-down list and then choose the Eyedropper tool in the dialog box.**

3. **Select a display option — Selection or Image.**

   I recommend leaving the setting at the default of Selection so that you can see the mask as you build it. You can toggle between the two views by pressing Ctrl (⌘ on the Mac).

4. **Either in the image itself or in the image preview in the Color Range dialog box, click to sample your desired colors.**

   The image preview changes to a mask. Black areas show unselected pixels, white areas show selected pixels, and gray areas show partially selected pixels.

   Your goal is to try to make what you want all white and what you don't want all black, as shown in Figure 2-4. And if you want some things partially selected, they can remain gray.

5. **Adjust the selection by adding or deleting colors.**

   You can select or delete as many colors in your image as you want.

   Use the Add to Sample tool (plus eyedropper icon) to add, and use the Subtract from Sample tool (minus eyedropper icon) to delete.

   You can be lazy like me and just stick with the regular eyedropper icon. Simply use Shift and Alt (Option on the Mac) to add and delete.

   Figure 2-4: When using the Color Range command, your desired selection area appears white in the preview box.

6. **Fine-tune the range of colors by dragging the Fuzziness slider.**

   The Fuzziness ranges extend from 0 to 200. A higher value selects more colors, and a lower value selects fewer colors. As you adjust the fuzziness, the mask dynamically updates.

   The Invert option selects what is currently unselected and deselects what is currently selected. And if you totally muck things up, you can reset the dialog box by pressing Alt (Option on the Mac) and clicking Reset.

7. **Choose a Selection Preview from the drop-down list to preview the selection in the image window.**

   - **None** displays the image normally (refer to Figure 2-4).

   - **Grayscale** displays just the grayscale mask.

   - **Black Matte** and **White Matte** display the selection against a black or white background.

   - **Quick Mask** shows the mask over your image, using your Quick Mask settings.

8. **Click OK.**

   Your image appears with a selection outline based on the Color Range mask.

   Now do what you will with your nice, clean selection.

   I decided my Thai dancer needed to be in a more exotic locale, so I transported her (by dragging and dropping with the Move tool onto another image) to a mystical Shangri La, shown in Figure 2-5.

Figure 2-5: With a clean selection made with the Color Range command, you can send people to locales never before visited.

Selective Erasing with the Eraser Tools

The eraser tools let you erase portions of an image to the background color, to transparency, or even to the way your image looked earlier in your editing session. There are three eraser tools — the regular Eraser, the Magic Eraser, and the Background Eraser. All three share a tool flyout menu.

The eraser tools look like real erasers so you can't miss them. But just in case you do, press E and then Shift+E to toggle through the three tools.

When you erase pixels, those pixels are gone. Gone. For good. Before using the eraser tools or the Extract command (coming up in the next section), it might be wise to make a backup of your image. You can save the image either as a separate file or as another layer. That way, if things run amuck, you have some insurance.

The Eraser tool

The Eraser tool allows you to erase areas on your image to either the background color or to transparency. Select it, drag through the desired area on your image, and you're done.

If the image isn't layered and has just a background, you erase to the background color, as shown in Figure 2-6. If the image is on a layer, you erase to transparency.

Figure 2-6: The Eraser tool erases either to the background color (left) or, if on a layer, to transparency (right).

I rate this tool in the same category as the Lasso tool. It's quick, it's easy, but it has limited applications. Use it only for minor touchups. The Eraser tool definitely isn't a tool to use on its own for making accurate selections.

The most useful function I find for the Eraser tool is to clean up my channel masks. Set the mode to Block, zoom into your mask, and clean up those black and white pixels. See Book VI, Chapter 3 for more on channel masks.

These options on the Options bar control the Eraser tool:

- **Mode:** Select from Brush, Pencil, and Block. When you select Brush or Pencil you have access to the Brush Preset picker palette on the far left of the Options bar.

  Use the Brush Preset picker drop-down palette to select from a variety of brush sizes and styles. Block has only one size, a square of 16 x 16 pixels. But because the block size remains constant, if you zoom way in, you can perform some detailed erasing.

- **Opacity:** Specify a percentage of transparency for the erasure. Opacity settings less than 100 percent only partially erase the pixels. The lower the Opacity setting, the less it erases. This option isn't available for the Block mode.

- **Flow:** Set a flow rate percentage when using Brush mode. Flow specifies how fast Photoshop applies the erasure and is especially handy when using the Airbrush option.

- **Airbrush:** Click the button when using Brush mode to turn your brush into an airbrush. With this option, the longer you hold your mouse button down, the more it erases.

- **Erase to History:** This option allows you to erase back to a selected source state or snapshot in the History palette. You can also press Alt (Option on the Mac) to temporarily access the Erase to History option. See Book II, Chapter 4 for more information.

- **Brush Palette:** Click the toggle button to bring up the full Brushes palette.

The Magic Eraser tool

The Magic Eraser tool works like a combination Eraser and Magic Wand tool. It both selects and erases similarly colored pixels:

- **When you click a layer:** The Magic Eraser tool erases pixels of a similar color based on a specified range and leaves the area transparent, as shown in Figure 2-7.

- **When you click an image that has just a background:** The Magic Eraser tool automatically converts the background to a layer and then does the same thing.

- **When you click a layer with locked transparency:** The Magic Eraser tool erases the pixels and replaces the area with the background color.

The Tolerance value defines the range of colors that Photoshop erases, just like it does with the Magic Wand tool. The value determines how similar a neighboring color has to be to the color that you click. A higher value picks up more colors, whereas a lower value picks up fewer colors. In my example in Figure 2-7, I set my Tolerance value to 8 and clicked in the upper left of my image. Photoshop selected and erased only a limited shade of black due to my lower Tolerance setting.

Here are the other options:

Figure 2-7: Clicking with the Magic Eraser simultaneously selects and erases similarly colored pixels.

- **Anti-alias:** Creates a slightly soft edge around the transparent area.

- **Contiguous:** Selects only similar colors that are adjacent to each other. Deselect this option to delete similar-colored pixels wherever they appear in your image.

- **Sample All Layers:** Samples colors using data from all visible layers, but erases pixels on the *active* layer only.

- **Opacity:** Works like it does for the regular Eraser tool.

The Background Eraser tool

The Background Eraser tool is probably the most sophisticated of the eraser-tool lot. It erases away the background from an image and leaves the foreground untouched, in theory anyway.

If you're not careful, the Background Eraser tool erases the foreground and anything else in its path.

Like the Magic Eraser tool, the Background Eraser tool erases to transparency on a layer. If you drag an image with only a background, Photoshop converts the background into a layer.

To use the Background Eraser tool, you need to carefully keep the crosshair in the center of the cursor, also known as the *hot spot,* on the background pixels as you drag. Then Photoshop deletes all background pixels under the brush circumference. But, if you touch a foreground pixel with the hot spot, it's gobbled up as well. As you can see from my example in Figure 2-8, I got a little too close to the man's face in some spots, and it left him a little chewed up.

Here's the rundown on the options, found on the Options bar, for the Background Eraser:

Background Eraser chews up man's face.

Figure 2-8: Be careful when using the Background Eraser or else you can inadvertently eat up pixels.

- ✓ **Brush Preset picker:** Provides various settings to customize the size and appearance of your eraser tip. The size and tolerance settings at the bottom are for those using pressure-sensitive drawing tablets. You can base the size and tolerance on the pen pressure or position of the thumbwheel.

- ✓ **Sampling:** The three settings determine what areas should and shouldn't be erased. The default Sampling: Continuous setting allows you to sample colors continuously as you drag through the image. The Sampling: Once setting erases only areas that contain the color that you first clicked. If the background is pretty much one color, you can try this option. The Sampling: Background Swatch setting erases only the areas containing the background color.

- ✓ **Limits:** The Only setting erases similar colors that are adjacent to one another. The Discontiguous setting erases all similarly colored pixels wherever they appear in the image. The Find Edges setting erases contiguous pixels while retaining the sharpness of the edges.

- ✓ **Tolerance:** Works just like the Magic Eraser Tolerance setting.

- ✓ **Protect Foreground Color:** Prevents the erasing of areas that match the foreground color.

Extracting an Image

The last of the automated masking tools in Photoshop is the Extract command. The name sounds great. You expect that it plucks your desired element right out of the image, cleanly, neatly, and without pain. But to be honest with you, I find the Extract command to be overly complex for the results it provides. You can get lucky and select an image that works well with the command. But frequently, it does a marginal job. When you learn the art of true, manual masking, you may never visit the Extract command again.

Here's how the Extract command works:

1. **Choose Filter⇨Extract.**

   Photoshop brings up the Extract dialog box, shown in Figure 2-9.

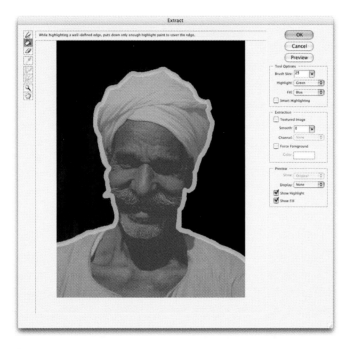

Figure 2-9: When using the Extract command's Edge Highlighter, be sure and overlap the edge of your desired element and the edge of the background.

2. **Select the Edge Highlighter tool, located at the top of the dialog box's Tools palette.**

   You can also press the B key to access the tool.

   Photoshop offers a Smart Highlighting option, in the Tool Options area on the right side of the dialog box.

If your image has a well-defined edge, but the foreground and background colors are similar or the image is highly textured, the Smart Highlighting option helps the Edge Highlighter tool to cling to the edge as you use the tool. You can toggle the option on and off by pressing Ctrl (⌘ on the Mac) when using the Edge Highlighter tool.

3. **Trace around the edges of the element you want to select. As you trace, feel free to change the brush size, again in the Tool Options area.**

Use a small brush for well-defined, sharp edges. Use a larger brush for wispier detailed edges such as hair, fur, leaves, and the like. To change the brush size using keyboard shortcuts, click the left (for smaller) and right (for larger) bracket keys ([and]). Hold down the bracket key, and the brush size changes more dramatically.

Be sure that the highlighted edge overlaps both the element and the background.

You can change the colors of the highlight and fill in the Tool Options settings as well.

I traced around the man in Figure 2-9. Make a complete path around the element. If one or more sides of your element is cropped off the edge, you don't have to highlight that side:

- Use the Hand tool to move your image if needed. You can temporarily access the Hand tool by pressing the spacebar.

- Use the Zoom tool to zoom in. Press Alt (Option on the Mac) to zoom out. You can also Zoom by pressing Ctrl++ and Ctrl+- (⌘++ and ⌘+- on the Mac).

- The Channel option allows you to load an alpha channel as a starting point for the extraction. You can then modify the highlighted area using the Edge Highlighter and Eraser tools.

Beware. For some reason when loading the alpha channel into the Extract dialog box, Photoshop converts the black areas in the mask into the highlighted area but doesn't highlight the white areas. This is the opposite of what you would expect, but it works out just the same. After you complete the highlighted area, fill the unlighted area with the Fill tool (see Step 7).

4. **If you make a mistake as you create your highlighted outline, press Ctrl+Z (⌘+Z on the Mac) to undo your error.**

5. **When you have made your outline, use the Eraser tool to clean up any hiccups in the outline.**

Press the E key to select the Eraser tool from the keyboard. You can have the best of both tools and toggle between the Edge Highlighter and the Eraser tools by pressing Alt (Option on the Mac).

6. **To erase an entire highlight, press Alt+Backspace (Option+Delete on the Mac).**

7. **Select the Fill tool, the second tool in the Tools palette (or press the G key) and click inside the highlighted outline.**

    The outline fills with color (refer to Figure 2-9).

    If by chance the color leaks outside the highlighted edge, you may have a small hole somewhere along the outline. Locate the offending hole and patch it with the Edge Highlighter tool. Click inside the highlighted outline again with the Fill tool. To unfill an area, click inside the same area with the Fill tool.

    As an alternative to using the Fill tool, you can select the Force Foreground option. This option can be useful if the element you want to select is mostly tones of one color. Use the Eyedropper tool to sample the color in the area you want to select. Then use the Edge Highlighter tool to highlight those areas containing your desired color.

8. **Click the Preview button and take a gander at your extracted element (or click OK to skip the preview and get your extraction).**

    If your background is solid and uncluttered, your foreground element has a simple, uncomplicated edge, you can see quite a bit of contrast between the foreground and background elements, *and* if the planets are aligned just so, your results are likely to be pretty good. My example has only a minor bit of background fringe around the moustache and the top of the turban, as shown in Figure 2-10.

9. **If you need to clean up a bit of fringe, give the Smooth option a shot.**

    This option removes stray pixels or artifacts from the selection. A high value smoothes out the edges around the selection, but can cause some undesirable blurring as well. Start with 0 or a small value first, before increasing the Smooth amount.

Figure 2-10: If your image has a simple shape and your horoscope shows a favorable day, you may be pleased with your extracted element.

10. **If you're happy with the results, click OK.**

    Photoshop deletes the masked areas. If your image was a background, Photoshop converts it to a layer, so the selected element will be against transparency.

11. **If you would rather preview your image against something other than the transparent checkerboard, choose another option from the Display drop-down list.**

    You can view the image against a white, gray, black, or other colored background. Or you can view it as a mask. (If you view it as a mask, the white areas represent the selected areas and the black areas represent the transparent areas.)

12. **If you're not happy, choose a view option before you start editing your mask.**

    You can choose between the Original and Extracted view from the Show drop-down list.

    You can also select the Show Highlight and Show Fill check boxes.

13. **To do fine-tuned editing of your image, you have the following tools at your disposal:**

    - Drag with the **Cleanup tool** (press C on the keyboard) to erase background pixels around your extraction by subtracting opacity. Alt+ drag (Option+drag on the Mac) to bring the opacity back. This tool is useful for creating feathered edges.

    - The **Edge Touchup tool** (T is the keyboard shortcut) sharpens the edges of the selection by adding opacity to your selection or subtracting opacity from the background.

    You can adjust the brush size of these editing tools to get the best results.

14. **When you finish editing, click OK to exit the dialog box. If you still have some areas that need some cleanup, use some regular editing tools, such as the Background Eraser and the History Brush tools.**

Putting It Together

Framing a Photo with Quick Mask

Sometimes you may want to add a decorative border or edge to your image. Maybe you're creating a postcard or greeting card and the standard rectangular shape image just doesn't provide enough pizzazz. Although adding a border or edge might look difficult, it is a snap with the Quick Mask command.

1. **Using any selection tool, create a selection on your image.**

I started with a rectangle in my image and then chose Select⇨Inverse to turn the selection inside out.

2. **Click the Quick Mask Mode button in the Tools palette.**

A color overlay covers and protects the area outside the selection, as shown in the figure.

Your selected area is open for you to edit as you so desire.

3. **Grab the Brush tool, choose the Heavy Stipple brush, and set the brush diameter to 168 pixels.**

You can find the Heavy Stipple brush in the Wet Media Brushes library of the Brushes palette.

4. **Paint around the edges of the mask with black to add to the masked area.**

5. **Adjust the Flow setting to 35% to get a semitransparent area, and then click a few more times.**

You could also paint with gray to get the same effect.

6. **Again, adjust your brush diameter, this time to 80 pixels, and add a few random clicks here and there.**

7. **Switch your color to white and repeat the steps, clicking around the image and also in the interior of the mask.**

Because white adds to the selected area, your image starts to show through.

I ended up with a mottled mess, shown in the figure.

You can also apply a filter or adjustment (Image⇨Adjustment) to the Quick Mask. See this technique in action in Book VII, Chapter 2.

8. **Click the Standard Mode button to exit the Quick Mask mode.**

continued

Book VI
Chapter 2

Quick and Dirty Masking

continued

The overlay disappears, leaving you with a selection outline, shown in the figure.

The selection outline correlates with the unmasked or selected areas of the Quick Mask. If you had a feathered mask, such as mine, the selection outline runs halfway between the selected and unselected areas of the mask, creating a soft transition.

9. **Your selection is ready and waiting for your next command.**

In my example, I deleted my selection, thereby filling the hole with my background color of white and leaving me with a stippled image. Note that because my brush was feathered and also varied in the Flow settings, some of my image is also feathered and semitransparent.

Chapter 3: Getting Exact with Advanced Masking Techniques

*I*f you haven't already checked out Book VI, Chapter 2, which covers Photoshop's quick and easy masking tools, you might want to breeze through that chapter first, especially if the word *mask* brings to mind an image from Halloween instead of a selection technique. In this chapter, I dive into some manual masking techniques.

Layer masks are tremendously useful, and if you're like me, you'll find yourself addicted to them. They can be fantastic for blending layers and making multiple images dissolve into one another. Vector masks create shapes defined by vector paths and produce clean, smooth-edged graphic elements.

Channel masks are probably the most time-consuming of the masking lot, but they're powerful and accurate. Like anything in life, the more you practice using them, the faster and better you get.

After you get through this final chapter of Book VI, you'll be familiar with every masking technique Photoshop has to offer. By then, you'll be prepared to use masks to select a very hairy orangutan, dyed green, perched in a tree in a lush rainforest. And how many people can say that?

Working with Layer Masks

Like any other mask, a *layer mask* is a grayscale image that you can edit to your heart's content. Layer masks are excellent for blending layers of images together and creating soft transitions between elements.

For versatility, layer masks are unparalleled. They allow you to gradually brush in transparency and opacity on a selective pixel basis. Paint with black to hide portions of the layer; paint with white to display portions; and paint in varying shades of gray to partially show elements. You can even apply gradients, image adjustments, and filters to your layer masks to create interesting special effects.

After you get the concept of layer masks, you'll never use the eraser tools (covered in Book VI, Chapter 2) again. You won't have to because one of the great things about layer masks is that you can forever edit, or even delete them, with no permanent harm whatsoever to the image.

Creating layer masks

To create a layer mask, select your desired layer and choose Layer⇨ Layer Mask⇨Reveal All or Hide All.

- **Reveal All** creates a mask filled with white, which shows the layer.

- **Hide All** creates a mask filled with black, which hides, or *masks,* the layer and shows nothing but transparency.

You can also click the Add Layer Mask icon at the bottom of Layers palette (which by default selects Reveal All).

You can't add a layer mask to a background layer. You must convert the background layer to a regular layer if you want to use a layer mask on the background of an image.

You can also apply a layer mask. Choose your desired layer and make a selection using one of the selection tools. Choose Layer⇨Layer Mask⇨ Reveal Selection or Hide Selection. You can also click the New Layer Mask button in the Layers palette to create a mask that reveals the selection.

After you create the layer mask, you can grab the painting tool of your choice and apply your grayscale color. *Remember:* Add white to the mask to display the image. Add black to hide the image. Add gray to make the image semitransparent.

Using the Gradient and Brush tools on a layer mask

I must confess: I use two of the layer masking tools more than the others:

- The Gradient tool, set to a linear gradient of black to white or white to black is truly awesome. Simply drag the layer mask to create the gradient. The darker areas of the gradient gradually hide the image, whereas the lighter areas gradually show the image.

✓ The Brush tool, with a large, feathered tip, using the Airbrush option and the Flow set to around 10% is amazing. With these settings in place, you can create feathered edges that blend one layer into another without any harsh lines.

In Figure 3-1, which is an image with two layers (the flag on the bottom and the girl on top), I used a combination of both these tools. I started with the black-to-white linear gradient, which I dragged from the left edge of my image through to the right edge. I then took the Brush tool with a large feathered tip (265 pixels), selected the Airbrush option, set the Flow to 10%, and worked my way around the profile of the girl's face to get rid of some more of the background behind her.

No layer mask

With layer mask

Figure 3-1: Layer masks enable you to seamlessly blend two layers.

To edit a layer mask, click the Layer Mask thumbnail in the Layers palette. Select your desired painting or editing tool, and paint or edit the mask to perfection. Just be sure that you're working on the layer mask, instead of editing the image itself. Otherwise, you apply paint directly to your image. You can tell because you see a layer mask icon next to the eye icon in the Layers palette.

Managing layer masks

Here are some tips to help you work with your layer masks. You can do the following:

- **Load a layer mask:** *Loading* a layer mask means getting a selection outline based on the layer mask. Simply Ctrl+click (⌘+click on the Mac) the Layer Mask thumbnail.

- **View the mask without viewing the image:** Sometimes when you're editing a layer mask, you may find it helpful to see the mask itself without having to view the image, too. For example, in Figure 3-2, I hid the image of the little girl and the flag to see the layer masks. Simply Alt+click (Option+click on the Mac) the Layer Mask thumbnail to view the mask and hide the image on the layer.

Figure 3-2: Check out just your layer mask without the image.

    To redisplay the image, Alt+click (Option+click on the Mac) again or click the eye icon in the far left column.

- **View the layer mask as a red overlay:** If you prefer to see your layer mask as a red overlay (called a *rubylith*), Alt+Shift+click (Option+Shift+click on the Mac) the Layer Mask thumbnail. You can also click the eyeball icon on the layer mask in the Channels palette.

- **Click again with the same keys to remove the overlay:** You can change the opacity and color of the overlay in the Layer Mask Display Options dialog box, which you access by double-clicking the layer mask channel in the Channels palette.

    A rubylith is similar to the red overlay used with Quick Masks, covered in Book VI, Chapter 2.

- **Paste a copied selection into a layer mask:** Simply Alt+click (Option+click on the Mac) the Layer Mask thumbnail. Choose Edit⇨Paste and then Select⇨Deselect. Click the image thumbnail in the Layers palette to return to the image.

The copied selection can consist of anything, but this technique comes in particularly handy when you're copying one layer mask into another.

🗸 **Disable (temporarily hide) or enable a layer mask:** Just Shift+click the Layer Mask thumbnail or choose Layer⇨Layer Mask⇨Disable or Enable.

🗸 **Unlink a layer from its layer mask:** By default, Photoshop links a layer mask to the contents of the layer. This allows them to move together. To unlink a layer from its layer mask, click the link icon in the Layers palette. Click again to re-establish the link. You can also choose Layer⇨ Layer Mask⇨Unlink or Link.

🗸 **Discard a layer mask:** Just drag the Layer Mask thumbnail to the trash can icon in the Layers palette. Click Discard in the dialog box. Or you can choose Layer⇨Layer Mask⇨Delete.

🗸 **Apply a layer mask:** When you apply a layer mask, you fuse the mask to the image. Photoshop replaces all black areas in the mask with transparent pixels and all gray areas with partially transparent pixels; all white areas are image pixels. Drag the thumbnail to the trash can icon in the Layers palette. Click Apply in the dialog box. Or you can choose Layer⇨ Layer Mask⇨Apply.

**Book VI
Chapter 3**

*Getting Exact with
Advanced Masking
Techniques*

 Putting It Together

Making a Photo Gradually Fade from Color to Grayscale

Layer masks are extremely powerful when it comes to blending multiple images so that one seems to dissolve into the others. This time I'm not going to show you how to use a layer mask to blend different images, but rather the same image — one in color and one in grayscale.

1. **Open a copy of your favorite color image, shown in the figure.**

The subject matter isn't critical here, so feel free to whip out that old prom picture.

2. **Choose Image⇨Duplicate.**

Accept the default name and click OK in the dialog box.

continued

continued

3. **With the duplicate image active, choose Window➪Channels.**

4. **View each of the channels to find the one that gives you the best grayscale image.**

   If you need a refresher on channels, see Book VI, Chapter 1. The Red channel gives the best contrast for the portrait in my example. Because skin tones tend to have a lot of red in them, the Red channel usually provides the best grayscale image of a person.

5. **Choose Image➪Mode➪Grayscale and click OK in the Discard Other Channels dialog box.**

   Photoshop has now stripped the color from the image, shown in the figure.

   This is only one way to convert a color image to grayscale. There are lots of others. Check them out in Book II, Chapter 2.

6. **Choose Window➪Layers. With the Move tool and holding down the Shift key, drag and drop your grayscale image onto your color image.**

   This action automatically creates a new layer from the grayscale image. (See Book V for more information about layers.)

   By holding down the Shift key, you keep the two images perfectly aligned.

7. **Close your duplicate image.**

8. **Press D for default colors.**

   This gives you a black foreground swatch and a white background swatch in your Tools palette.

   Now, I show you how to use one of my favorite techniques, a black-to-white gradient, on the layer mask.

9. **Make sure that the grayscale layer you dragged in is the active layer in the Layers palette. Click the Add Layer Mask icon at the bottom of the palette.**

   It's the icon that looks like a dark square with a white circle on top. Photoshop adds a second thumbnail on your layer, indicating that a layer mask has been applied.

   A layer mask acts like a piece of clear acetate over your layer.

10. **Select the Gradient tool. Then select the default gradient of Foreground to Background.**

To get the default gradient, click the Gradient picker on the Options bar and select the first gradient.

It should be a gradient of white to black because it's based on the current foreground and background colors, which reverse when you select the Layer Mask thumbnail. For a gradient refresher, see Book IV, Chapter 3.

11. **Drag the gradient from the top of your image to the bottom.**

Or from left to right. Or at a diagonal. It's your call.

12. **Experiment with long drags and short drags. The angle and length of your mouse movement determine how the layer mask reveals the underlying image.**

In my example, I dragged from the bottom of the image to the top and stopped about two-thirds of the way up.

Where black appears on the layer mask, the grayscale image is hidden. Where white appears on the mask, the grayscale image shows through and everything in between allows the grayscale image to partially show.

continued

continued

Although I used a linear gradient in my example, you can experiment with the other types as well. Radial gradients can provide some interesting effects.

13. **When you complete your mask, save and close the file.**

Creating and Editing Vector Masks

Whereas layer masks let you create soft-edged masks, vector masks create hard-edged masks defined by shapes created by a vector path on a layer. Vector-based shapes produce clean, smooth, and well-defined edges that are never jagged. And you can size and transform vector shapes without ever degrading the appearance of the element. (For an introduction to vector images, see Book IV, Chapter 1.)

You create a vector mask when you create a shape with any one of the shape tools. You can also create a vector mask when you convert type to a shape (Layer⇨Type⇨Convert to Shape). See Book IV, Chapter 4.

Adding a vector mask to a layer

To add a vector mask to layer, follow these steps:

1. **Select the layer in the Layers palette and choose Layer⇨Vector Mask⇨ Reveal All or Hide All.**

   I describe Reveal All and Hide All in the "Creating layer masks" section. Remember that you cannot add a vector mask to a background layer.

2. **On the vector mask, create a path with the Pen tool or grab any shape tool and create a shape.**

   See Book III, Chapter 2 for more on paths and Book IV, Chapter 1 for more on shapes.

   I selected the Custom Shape tool and dragged a sunburst shape on my vector mask. Notice how everything outside the path is hidden, or masked, as shown in Figure 3-3.

   Like layer masks, you can add vector masks only to layers, not backgrounds. If necessary, simply convert your background to a layer by double-clicking background in the Layers palette.

3. **If your vector mask is satisfactory, save your file and then close it.**

Without vector mask

With vector mask

Figure 3-3: Everything outside of a vector mask is hidden, or masked, from display.

Another way to add a vector mask is to select your desired layer, draw a work path with the Pen tool or one of the shape tools, and then select Layer➪Add Vector Mask➪Current Path.

Managing vector masks

Here are a few more vector mask tips. You can perform the following tasks:

- **Edit a vector mask path:** Use the pen tools and the Direct Selection tool, as described in Book III, Chapter 2.

- **Add multiple shapes or paths to the existing vector mask:** All you need to do is just drag another shape with any of the shape tools. Or add another path with the Pen tool.

- **Remove a vector mask from a layer:** Drag the thumbnail to the trash can icon in the Layers palette or choose Layer➪Vector Mask.

- **Disable (temporarily hide) or enable a vector mask:** Shift+click the vector mask thumbnail or choose Layer➪Vector Mask➪Disable (or Enable).

- **Rasterize a vector mask:** Rasterizing (or turning the mask into a pixel-based image) converts the vector mask into a layer mask. Choose Layer➪Rasterize➪Vector Mask.

- **Apply layer styles to vector shapes:** This is a quick and easy way to create buttons for a Web page or a custom logo, as shown in Figure 3-4. Just select the layer, not the vector mask, and choose Layer➪Layer Style. Select your style of choice. For details on layer styles, see Book V, Chapter 4.

Figure 3-4: Adding layer styles to your shapes can make them really shine.

Creating Channel Masks

Photoshop's channel masks are probably the most time-consuming masks to use because they require a lot of manual labor. Not heavy lifting, mind you, but work with the tools and commands in Photoshop.

But, don't get me wrong, it's time well spent. Channel masks can usually accurately select what the other Photoshop tools can only dream about — wisps of hair, tufts of fur, a ficus benjamina tree with 9,574 leaves.

You can create a channel mask in lots of ways, but I'm here to offer you one that works most of the time. To create a channel mask, follow these steps:

1. Analyze your existing channels to find a suitable candidate to use to create a duplicate channel.

This is usually the channel with the most contrast between what you want and don't want. For instance, in my example, the Red channel provided the most contrast between the tree and lanterns, which I wanted to mask, and the background, which I didn't.

After you duplicate the channel, it then becomes an alpha channel.

2. **Choose Image⇨Adjustments⇨Levels.**

   Using the histogram and the sliders in the Levels dialog box, increase the contrast between the element(s) you want and don't want selected.

3. **Choose a tool, such as the Brush or Eraser tool, and paint and edit the alpha channel to refine the mask.**

   See Figure 3-5. I used the a combo of the brush and Eraser set to Block mode to clean up my mask.

4. **When you complete the mask, click the Load Channel as Selection icon (the dotted circle icon on the far left) at the bottom of the Channels palette. Then click your composite channel at the top of the list of channels.**

   This loads your mask as a selection, giving you that familiar selection outline. You can also use one of my favorite keyboard shortcuts: Ctrl+ click (⌘+click on the Mac) directly on the alpha channel to load the mask as a selection.

Channel mask

Original

Corbis Digital Stock

Figure 3-5: Use the Levels and Photoshop painting and editing tools to refine your channel mask.

Your selection is now ready to go.

5. **You can leave it within the original image or drag and drop it onto another image, as I did in Figure 3-6.**

Because my new sky was darker than my original, I also darkened my windmills so the lighting would be more consistent. If you've done a good job, nobody will be the wiser that the two images never met in real life.

Corbis Digital Stock

Figure 3-6: When combining multiple images, masking is usually the most accurate method.

Putting It Together

Masking Hair, Fur, and Other Wispy Things

Hair, fur, fuzz, and other objects with complex or loosely defined edges can prove difficult to select with the run-of-the-mill selection techniques. But that's where masking can save the day. Because a mask allows for a 256-level selection, it does a great job in picking up those illusive strands of hair and such that would otherwise probably be cut off in the selecting process.

Perhaps you've seen those photos where everyone in a composite image appears to have helmet hair? Here are the steps to avoid the Aqua Net look and select even the smallest wisp of hair:

1. **Choose File⇨Open.**

   Select an image that contains something hairy, furry, or fuzzy. A portrait is an ideal choice (unless the subject is hair challenged).

   For your first attempt at this technique, starting with an image that has a pretty simple and uncluttered background is best.

   In my example, I used an image of a pensive, young urban professional shown in the figure.

2. **Choose View⇨Channels. View each channel by clicking the channel name.**

   Each channel is an independent grayscale image and a potential starting point for a mask.

continued

continued

It is best to start with the channel that contains the most contrast between what you want to select and what you don't. If it's a toss-up, go with the channel that makes selecting the difficult part of the image easiest (in my example, that's the hair).

In my example, I'm using the Blue channel.

3. **Choose Duplicate Channel from the Channels palette pop-up menu. Name the channel *mask* and click OK.**

   You've created an alpha channel for the mask, shown in the figure. Now you can edit the mask without harming the original channel.

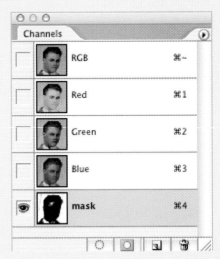

4. **Choose Image⇨Adjustments⇨ Levels and boost the contrast in the image by adjusting the Input sliders for shadows, midtones, and highlights.**

   If you need help using the Levels adjustment, see Book VIII, Chapter 1.

5. **Select the person and his or her hair.**

   You can do that one of two ways:

   ✔ By selecting the person.

   ✔ By selecting the background first and then inverting the selection.

   In a mask, traditionally white represents a selected area, black represents an unselected area, and gray represents a partially selected area.

6. **Adjust the Levels settings by dragging your shadows, midtones, and highlights sliders so that the element you want to select is either all white or all black with a little gray in the wispy areas. In other words, you want to change most of the pixels in the image to either black or white.**

   In my example, because my guy is darker than the background, I adjusted the contrast to make the subject as black as I could while making the background lighter. You can see the result in the figure.

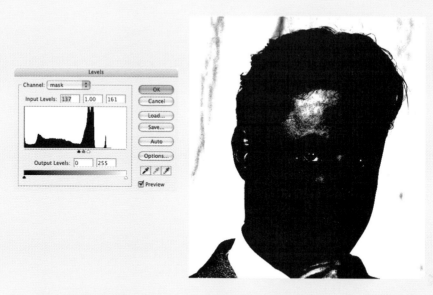

7. **If you think the edges of your image need to be accentuated, you can apply a High Pass filter (Filter⇨Other⇨High Pass) before you apply the Level adjustment.**

   High Pass turns your overall image gray while leaving the edges white.

   Don't use too low a radius value (start with a setting between 8 and 10) or completing the mask can be too time-consuming.

8. **Refine the mask by selecting the Eraser tool and choosing Block Mode from the Options bar.**

   The Block Eraser is a great tool for cleaning up masks. It allows you to paint inside the mask without creating any feathered edges.

9. **Press D for default colors.**

   Remember the Eraser tool paints with the background color, so be sure you have the color you want before you drag. Press X to switch the foreground and background colors.

10. **Clean up your mask by painting with black and white, as shown in the figure.**

continued

continued

Make sure to use short strokes so you can undo any mistakes you make.

11. **Use the Zoom tool if you need to touch up the details.**

The Block Eraser tool has only one size, so you have to zoom in to paint thinner strokes and zoom out to erase a larger area.

Remember to leave some gray around the wispy areas, as seen in the figure; otherwise, they may look chopped off.

Take your time and be as accurate as you can. Patience makes a big difference.

TIP

If you're not sure what you need to paint on the mask and you want to refer to the color image, simply click the composite channel (either RGB or CMYK depending on your image) at the top of the Channels palette. Then click the mask channel again to return to your mask. Or, you can view both the mask and the composite simultaneously. Your mask appears as a red overlay.

Your mask is refined and ready to go.

12. **Click the first icon on the left at the bottom of the Channels palette to load the mask as a selection (or Ctrl+click [⌘+click on the Mac] the channel mask).**

A selection marquee appears around your mask.

TIP

If you want to soften the edge a little, you can choose Select➪Feather and enter a value somewhere between 0.5 pixel (for a low-resolution image) to 2 pixels (for a high-resolution image). Feathering allows for a softer, natural-looking transition between your masked element and the background. I used a 1-pixel feather for my image.

13. **Return to the composite image by clicking the RGB channel (or CMYK if warranted).**

The selection outline appears in your composite image, shown in the figure.

14. **If you need to invert your selection, choose Select⇨Inverse.**

In my example, I just filled my background with a solid color, so I left the background selected.

15. **Choose Window⇨Color and mix a color of your choice. Choose Edit⇨Fill, choose Foreground Color for your Contents, and click OK.**

Photoshop now replaces the background with a solid color. Check the edges to see how clean your mask is.

16. **Make any final edits you need to make.**

My guy looked like he spent too much time at the local tanning booth, so I toned down the redness in his skin by using the Variation commands (see Book VIII, Chapter 1), as seen in the figure.

17. **When you're happy with your channel mask, save and close the file.**

It takes practice to get masking down to a science, but believe me, it's worth your time. Nine times out of ten, a channel mask lends a much better selection than any of the easier, quicker selection tools and techniques.

Instead of filling the background with a color, you can also open a second image and, with the Move tool, drag and drop your masked element into the second image. A couple of things to keep in mind when compositing with two images: First try to use two images whose lighting isn't so dissimilar that it looks artificial. Take into account the time of day, the angle of the light, and so on. Secondly, try to select two images whose levels of focus make sense. If you need to soften one of the images, apply the Gaussian Blur filter. If your mask is good, your person should look right at home in his or her new digs.

**Book VI
Chapter 3**

**Getting Exact with
Advanced Masking
Techniques**

Book VII
Filters and Distortions

The 5th Wave   By Rich Tennant

"Hey- let's put scanned photos of ourselves through a ripple filter and see if we can make ourselves look weird."

Got an image that needs to be sharper or maybe less dusty? How about an image that needs to look like it was wrapped in plastic and then xeroxed on a circa-1970 photocopier? Either way, this is the book that describes the fine-tuning and the folly of filters.

Filters can do wonders in correcting your images, making them look better than the original. And if it's special effects you're interested in, look no further. Filters can make your image look ripped, sprayed, wet, hot — and just about any other adjective you're interested in. If distortions are more your thing, you won't be disappointed with the Liquify command, for which image warping, pushing, bloating, and puckering are daily activities. But whatever you do, don't leave this book without checking out the new Vanishing Point command. This single command alone may be well worth the money you plunked down for Photoshop.

Chapter 1: Making Corrections with Daily Filters

In This Chapter

- Understanding how filters work
- Sharpening soft areas
- Improving an image with blurring
- Smoothing defects with Median and Facet filters

*F*ilters have a long and glorious history, ranging from performing essential tasks (such as removing abrasive particles from the oil in your car's crankcase) to even more important chores involving the pixels in your Photoshop images. In both cases, filters (also called *plug-ins* because they can be installed or removed from Photoshop independently) seize tiny, almost invisible bits of stuff and rearrange them in useful ways. The results are something you'd never want to do without.

This chapter introduces you to the basics of Photoshop's filter facilities and starts you on the road to plug-in proficiency.

You Say You Want a Convolution?

All filters do one simple thing in a seemingly complicated way: They make Photoshop do your bidding. Deep within a filter's innards is a set of instructions that tells Photoshop what to do with a particular pixel in an image or selection. Photoshop applies these instructions to each and every pixel in the relevant area by using a process the techies call *convolution* (creating a form or shape that's folded or curved in tortuous windings), but which we normal folk simply refer to as *applying a filter*.

Corrective and destructive filters

Filters fall into two basic categories, *corrective* and *destructive*:

- **Corrective filters** fix problems in an image. They fine-tune color, add blur, improve sharpness, or remove such nastiness as dust and scratches. Although corrective plug-ins can be fairly destructive to certain pixels, in general, they don't change the basic look of an image. You might not even notice that a corrective filter has been applied unless you compare the new version of the image with the original.

- **Destructive filters** tend to obliterate at least some of an image's original detail (some to a greater extent than others) as they add special effects. They may overlay an image with an interesting texture, move pixels around to create brush strokes, simulate light and shadow to create 3-D illusions, or distort an image with twists, waves, or zigzags. You can often tell at a glance that a destructive filter has been applied to an image: The special effect often looks like nothing that exists in real life.

An unaltered image (such as the image on the left in Figure 1-1) can be improved by using a corrective filter such as Unsharp Mask (center) or changed dramatically with a destructive filter such as Find Edges (right).

Corbis Digital Stock
Figure 1-1: Filters range in variety from the corrective (center) to the destructive (right).

Filter basics

Whether a filter is corrective or destructive, it falls into one of two camps. Here's the scoop:

- **Single-step filters:** The easiest filters to use, single-step filters have no options and use no dialog boxes. Just choose the filter from the menu and watch it do its stuff on your image or selection. The basic Blur and Sharpen filters are single-step filters.

✔ **Mini-application filters:** Most filters come complete with at least one dialog box, along with (perhaps) a few lists, buttons, and check boxes. And almost every mini-app filter has sliders you can use to adjust the intensity of an effect or parameter (see Figure 1-2). These filters are marked in the menus with an ellipsis (series of dots) following their names; as with other menu commands that show those dots, it's an indication that more options are lurking.

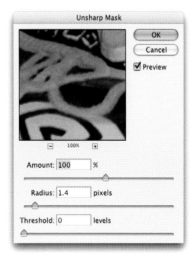

Figure 1-2: Mini-application filters require you to specify various settings before applying your filter.

The controls themselves are easy to master. The tricky part is learning what the various parameters you're using actually do. How does changing brush size affect your image when you're using a brush-stroke filter? What happens when you select a particular pattern with a texturizing filter? You can read descriptions of how various filter controls affect your image, but your best bet is to simply experiment until you discover the effects and parameters that work best for you. Just be sure that you save a copy of the original image; filters do permanent damage to files — modifying, adding, and deleting pixels.

Sharpening What's Soft

Sometimes your images aren't as sharp as you'd like. Sometimes your images have a tiny bit of softening caused by scanning an image or perhaps, by capturing a photo on your digital camera. Or, perhaps, you want only a particular part to be sharper so that it stands out from its surroundings.

All sharpening tools operate by increasing the contrast between adjacent pixels. If you look at a sharpened image side by side with the original version (as shown in Figure 1-3), you see that no new information has been provided. Instead, the contrast is boosted so edges are more distinct. The dark parts of the edges are darker; the light parts at their boundaries are lighter.

Photoshop has five main sharpening tools, only four of which are actually filters, on the Filter⇨Sharpen menu. The fifth, the Sharpen tool, isn't a filter, strictly speaking. It's more like a paintbrush that lets you sharpen areas selectively by using strokes.

Figure 1-3: Sharpening an image boosts the contrast of neighboring pixels and gives the illusion of improved focus.

Sharpen

The Sharpen filter is best used for minimal touchups in small areas. This single-step filter increases the contrast between all the pixels in the image or selection. Although this makes the image look sharper, it can add a grainy look to solid areas that aren't part of the edges.

Sharpen More

The Sharpen More filter, a single-step filter that increases the contrast between pixels even more than the regular Sharpen filter. Like the Sharpen filter, Sharpen More is best relegated to noncritical sharpening because it doesn't do a very good job of sharpening large areas. Also, it doesn't provide the control you need for more intense projects.

Sharpen Edges

The Sharpen Edges filter is a single-step filter that's superior to the Sharpen and Sharpen More filters because it concentrates its efforts on the edges of images, adding sharpness without making the image grainy or noisy. It's best used for quickie fixes.

Smart Sharpen

The newest member of the Sharpen team is definitely a keeper: Smart Sharpen does a great job of detecting edges and sharpening them less destructively. Like the veteran Unsharp Mask filter, this filter gives you a lot of control over the sharpening settings, as shown in Figure 1-4. Here's the scoop on those settings:

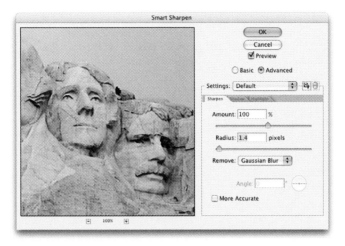

Corbis Digital Stock

Figure 1-4: The new Smart Sharpen filter gives the most control over your sharpening specifications.

⊭ **Preview:** Obviously, keep this option checked so that you can take a gander at what's happening as you sharpen. You'll appreciate the new large Preview window as well.

⊭ **Basic and Advanced:** The only difference between the two views is that with the Advanced view, you are capable of controlling the amount of sharpening in the Shadow and Highlight areas of your image. Use the following controls to fine-tune the amount of sharpening in your light and dark areas:

• **Fade Amount:** Determine the amount of sharpening.

• **Tonal Width:** Specify the range of tones you wish to sharpen. Move your slider to the right to sharpen only the darker of the shadow areas and the lighter of the highlight areas.

• **Radius:** Specify the amount of space around a pixel that is used to determine whether a pixel is in the shadow or the highlight area. Move your slider to the right to specify a greater area.

⊭ **Settings:** You can save your sharpening settings so you can load them for later use without having to re-create them.

⊭ **Amount:** Use this control to vary the amount of edge sharpening. A higher value increases the contrast between pixels around the edges. Your choices range from 1 percent to 500 percent. For subtle amounts of sharpening, anything around 100 percent or less provides the effect you're looking for without making the image appear overly contrasty (yes, that is a technical term) or unrealistic.

✏ **Radius:** This slider controls the width (in pixels) of the edges that the filter will modify. The higher the value, the wider the edge that is affected. Your range varies from 0.1 pixel (for fine control) to 64 pixels (for broader sharpening effects). Your use of this control will vary chiefly on the resolution of your original image. Low-resolution images (100 pixels per inch and lower) look best when you use only a small radius value, from a fraction of a pixel up to three or four pixels.

A small amount of sharpening may produce no visible effect on high-resolution images, especially those with 300 ppi resolution or more. You may need to move the slider to the 5-pixel range before you see any effects. Regardless of the resolution of your image, setting the radius too high may emphasize the edges of your image unrealistically — and it boosts the contrast too much.

A good rule to consider when you select a radius is to divide your image's ppi resolution by 150 and then adjust from there. For example, if you have a 150 ppi image, set the radius at 1 and then tweak from there.

✏ **Remove:** Specify the algorithm to be used to remove the blurriness in the image. Gaussian Blur is the method used by Unsharp Mask and is good for removing that hazy type of blurriness. Lens Blur detects and sharpens the edges and detail in the image and does a good job of reducing those nasty halos that can occur from sharpening. Motion Blur reduces the blurriness that can occur when you move your camera (or your subject moves).

✏ **Angle:** Specify the direction of motion if you choose Motion Blur as your algorithm.

✏ **More Accurate:** Check this option, and Photoshop provides a more accurate removal of blurriness. Takes longer, but worth the wait, as shown in Figure 1-5.

Figure 1-5: Smart Sharpen can take your soft, mushy photo and make it come to life.

Unsharp Mask

Don't feel bad: Everyone is confused by the name *Unsharp Mask* the first time they encounter it. This filter provides a sophisticated attempt to duplicate a sophisticated photographic effect called (you guessed it) *unsharp masking,* in which two sheets of film are sandwiched together to create a final image. One sheet is the original film negative (or a duplicate), and the second is a positive image (the "normal" photograph) that's blurred slightly. When the two are mated together, the light and dark areas cancel each other out, except at the edges — because of the blurring of the positive mask, which causes the edges to spread at those points.

Unsharp masking is a tricky procedure in the darkroom. It's much more precise in the digital realm because Photoshop can easily control the width of the areas to be masked, as well as a relative brightness level to use before beginning to apply the masking effect.

In the Unsharp Mask dialog box, you find two of the same controls that you have with Smart Sharpen — Amount and Radius. You also have another option called Threshold. Threshold controls the difference in brightness that must be present between adjacent pixels before the edge is sharpened. That is, you need to have a distinct contrast between adjacent pixels along an edge in order to sharpen the edge. Your choices range from brightness values of 0 to 255. Selecting a low value emphasizes edges with very little contrast difference (which is usually what you want). You're generally better off leaving this control at 0 unless your image has a lot of noise. Higher values force Photoshop to provide edge sharpening only when adjacent pixels are dramatically different in brightness. Increasing the threshold too much can cause some harsh transitions between sharpened and unsharpened pixels.

In most cases, the Amount and Radius sliders are the only controls you need to use. Threshold is most useful when the first two controls create excessive noise in the image. You can sometimes reduce this noise by increasing the Threshold level a little.

Sharpening always increases contrast, so you should use any of the Sharpening tools before trying other contrast-adjusting tools. When you've sharpened your image to your satisfaction, you can then use the other contrast controls to fine-tune the image with additional contrast (if it's still required).

Book VII Chapter 1

Making Corrections with Daily Filters

Blurring What's Sharp

What, me blurry? The answer is yes, if you have an image that contains unwanted *grain* (the roughness or noise added by the photographic film) or, perhaps, an ugly pattern of halftone dots used in a printed image.

You might need to blur a background to make the foreground seem sharper, or blur a portion of an image to create an angelic glow. Here are your blurring options (all on the Filter➪Blur menu):

✔ **Average:** This single-step filter calculates the average value (or color) of the image or selection and fills the area with that average value. This can be useful for smoothing the values of areas containing a lot of noise.

✔ **Blur:** Also a single-step filter, Blur provides overall blurring of an image.

✔ **Blur More:** This filter provides a significantly increased amount of blurring than the regular, old-fashioned Blur filter.

✔ **Box Blur:** This new Blur filter blurs your image in the shape of, well, a box or square.

✔ **Gaussian Blur:** This filter offers a radius control to let you adjust the amount of blurring more precisely. It's also got a really cool name.

The Gaussian Blur filter is an excellent tool because it gives you a great deal of control over the amount and type of blurring you get. That's especially true when compared to the single-step Blur and Blur More filters, which apply a fixed amount of blur. Use these latter two filters when you simply want to de-sharpen an image a tad, and turn to Gaussian Blur when you're looking for a specific effect.

✔ **Lens Blur:** This filter simulates the blurring that can occur when you capture an image with a camera. For details, see the sidebar "Applying the Lens Blur filter."

✔ **Motion Blur:** This filter simulates the blur you see in objects that are moving.

✔ **Radial Blur:** This filter produces the kind of blur you might get when photographing a revolving automobile tire.

✔ **Shape Blur:** The new Shape blur basically blurs your image according to the shape you choose from the palette. The shape choices you find are the same as those with the Custom Shape tool. Move the Radius slider to the right for a larger blur. You can see an example of different shape blurs in Figure 1-6.

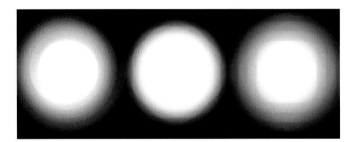

Figure 1-6: The Shape Blur blurs your image in a variety of shapes.

✔ **Surface Blur:** This new filter blurs the surface, or interior, of the image rather than the edges. If you want to preserve your edge details yet blur everything else, this is your filter.

✔ **Smart Blur:** This filter lets you control how Photoshop applies the blur to edges and other details of the image.

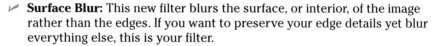

Applying the Lens Blur filter

If you've ever played with the aperture settings on a camera, you're probably well aware that you can determine how shallow or deep your *depth of field* is. Depth of field relates to the *plane of focus* (the areas in a photo that are in front of or behind the focal point that remain in focus) or how in-focus the foreground elements are when you compare them to the background elements. If you use a Lens Blur filter on an alpha channel (see Book VI, Chapter 1 for more on alpha channels), the alpha channel acts as a depth map. This is great for taking a fully focused image and creating a shallow depth of field where the foremost object is in focus and the background elements get blurrier the farther they are from the focal point. You can achieve this by creating an alpha channel filled with a white-to-black gradient — white where you want the most focus, black where you want the least focus or most blur.

Here is a brief description on setting the Lens Blur filter options:

✔ **Source:** If you have an alpha channel, select it from this pop-up menu. The Lens Blur option interprets the various grayscale values of the alpha channel and applies the blur according to the value set in the Blur Focus Distance. Choose Transparency to make an image get blurrier as it gets more transparent. Choose Layer Mask to apply the blur according to the grayscale values on the layer mask (see Book VI, Chapter 3

for more on layer masks). If your image contains none of these options, choose None. Photoshop applies the blur on the image.

✔ **Blur Focal Distance:** Specifies how blurry or in focus an area of the image is. Photoshop places the grayscale values less than the value specified in front of the plane of focus, and those greater than the value specified in back. Drag the slider to specify the value or click the crosshair cursor on the part of the image you want to be in full focus.

✔ **Iris:** The Iris settings are meant to simulate a camera lens. Specify the shape of the lens, as well as the radius (size of the iris), curvature, and rotation of that shape.

✔ **Specular Highlights:** The Lens Blur filter averages the highlights of an image, which, left uncorrected, cause some highlights to appear grayish. These controls help to retain specular highlights, or those highlights, which should appear very white. Set the Threshold value to specify which highlights should be specular, or remain white. Set a Brightness value to specify how much to re-lighten any blurred areas.

✔ **Noise:** Blurring of course obliterates any noise, or *film grain*, an image may have. This can cause the image to appear inconsistent or unrealistic in many cases. Drag the slider to add noise back into your image.

**Book VII
Chapter 1**

**Making Corrections
with Daily Filters**

Smoothing with the Facet and Median Filters

One application for blurring an image is to reduce dust and scratches, or to smooth away sharp edges. Here, I show you how to use the versatile Facet and Median filters to soften an image.

Although the Facet and Median filters smooth images by eliminating some detail, you can compensate for the blurring effect by applying the Smart Sharpen or Unsharp Mask with a low radius setting to sharpen things up a little.

The Facet filter

Facet breaks up an image using a posterizing effect. It gathers up blocks of pixels that are similar in brightness and converts them to a single value, using geometric shapes. (When you posterize an image, you reduce it to a very small number of tones.)

The geometric shapes make the image look more randomly produced, while eliminating much of the banding effect you get with conventional posterizing filters.

The effects of the Facet filter are subtle, and best viewed at close range. The original image in Figure 1-7 contains some dust, scratches, and a few other defects. Instead of retouching them one by one, I used Facet.

Facet is a single-step filter, so you don't need to adjust any controls. Just choose Filter⇨Pixelate⇨Facet and evaluate your results. You can apply the filter multiple times. However, even one application smooths out the picture and eliminates the worst of the artifacts.

If you apply the Facet filter multiple times, your image takes on a kind of pointillist, stroked look that becomes obvious. Using the filter over and over on the same image can yield quite interesting special effects.

The Median filter

The Median filter (look for it on the Filter⇨Noise menu) operates similarly to the Facet filter in that it reduces the difference between adjacent pixels by changing the values of some of them. In this case, it assigns the median values of a group of pixels to the center pixel in the group.

Unlike the Facet filter, the Median filter gives you a bit of control. You can choose the radius of the group that Photoshop uses to calculate the median value.

Median tends to make an image look a bit blurrier because it reduces the contrast of adjacent pixels. However, it does a good job of smoothing the image and removing artifacts.

Original   Single Facet filter

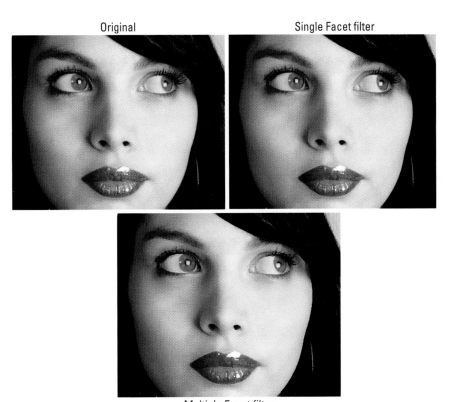

Multiple Facet filter

PhotoSpin

Figure 1-7: The Facet filter can simply eliminate annoying artifacts or convert your image into a "painted" piece.

**Book VII
Chapter 1**

**Making Corrections
with Daily Filters**

Putting It Together

Creating an Angelic Glow

Sometimes, a little blur can add a soft, romantic mood or angelic glow that can improve glamour photos, pictures of kids, or even something as mundane as a flower. The secret is to apply only enough blurring to provide the soft effect you want without completely obliterating your original subject. This assumes, of course, that your subject doesn't *deserve* obliteration, that the kids are your own (or those of a close friend or relative), and are, in fact, of that rare angelic variety.

You won't want to use this effect on other subjects, such as men, who generally like a rugged, masculine appearance. Many senior citizens regard the age lines on their faces as badges of distinction earned over a long, rewarding life. Don't try softening them up with glowing effects, either.

To add an angelic glow to your little angel, just follow these steps:

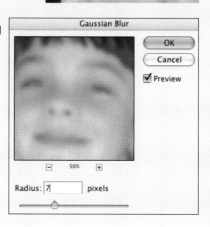

1. **Open the image in Photoshop.**

   I used one of a cute little girl.

2. **Choose Layer⇨Duplicate Layer to create a copy of the image layer.**

3. **Select Image⇨Filter⇨Blur⇨Gaussian Blur.**

   Gaussian blur softens the upper layer, producing an airy glow.

4. **Move the Radius slider to the right to produce a moderate amount of blur, and then click OK to apply the blurring effect, as shown in the figure.**

   I used a value of 7.

5. **In the Layers palette, choose Lighten from the Modes pop-up menu.**

6. **Use the Opacity slider (click the right-pointing arrow to access the slider) to reduce the amount of glow (if it's too much for your tastes).**

   I reduced my Opacity to 65 percent.

7. **Choose Layer⇨Flatten Image to combine all the layers.**

   Experiment with different amounts of Gaussian Blur until you find the perfect glowing effect, as I did in my figure.

When Photoshop applies the Lighten mode as it merges two layers, it looks at each pixel in the top layer — and at each corresponding pixel in the layer below. In the final merged layer, that lower pixel is always the *lighter* of the two. The result is an image in which Photoshop replaces darker pixels with lighter ones, but doesn't change the light pixels at all.

Applying a Filter Again

You can reapply the last filter you worked with — using the same settings — by pressing Ctrl+F (⌘+F on the Mac). (It's also the first command on the Filter menu.) You might want to do this to strengthen the effect of a filter on a particular image, layer, or selection. Or you simply may want to apply the same filter to a succession of images or selections.

To bring up the dialog box for the last filter you applied, press Ctrl+Alt+F (Windows) or ⌘+Option+F (Mac). This shortcut can be very useful when you apply a filter and then decide you want to go back and use different settings. After applying the filter, press Ctrl+Z (⌘+Z on a Mac) to undo, and then press Ctrl+Alt+F (⌘+Option+F on a Mac) to bring up the filter's dialog box. The dialog box opens with the settings you used last time, allowing you to make adjustments and then reapply the filter.

Fading a Filter

Some times you may not want the full effects of a filter applied to your image or selection. Often applying a filter full strength tends to give it that artificial "Photoshopped" look. Photoshop has a handy Fade Filter facility that lets you control the intensity of the filter's effects. You can access this feature by choosing Edit⇨Fade, or by pressing Shift+Ctrl+F (Shift+⌘+F on the Mac). The Fade Filter facility also has a Preview option so you can preview the changes you're making to the original image.

You must fade your filter *immediately after* you use the filter. If you use a painting or editing tool after applying the filter, for example, you won't find Fade Filter on the Edit menu anymore. Photoshop replaces it with Fade Brush or something else.

You can also add a fade effect in the following ways:

- **Adjust opacity settings:** Just about every filter allows you to adjust opacity, so most of the time the Opacity slider is all you need to adjust the strength of the filter applied to your image.

- **Use a blending mode:** Use one of the blend modes in Photoshop to merge the filter effect with the original image. For more on blend modes, see Book V, Chapter 3.

- **Apply a filter to a duplicate layer or a selection on that layer:** Then adjust the opacity of the filtered layer so it merges with the unfiltered layer below it.

  One advantage to this method is that you can selectively erase portions of the filtered image to allow the unaltered portion to show through. For example, you can apply a blur filter to a face and then erase the blurred portion that covers the eyes to make them a focal point of the portrait.

  You could just select the face (minus the eyes) and blur only that with the filter, but using multiple layers gives you more flexibility. You can also fade a filter by using a layer mask to selectively hide or show the filtered area. Find out more about layer masks in Book VI, Chapter 3.

Selectively Applying a Filter

You don't need to apply filters to an entire image or an entire layer. You can achieve some of the best effects when you apply a filter to only a portion of an image, say to an object in the foreground, but not on the background. Your choices include the following:

- **Selections:** Make a selection and apply the filter only to that selection. You can use Quick Mask mode (see Book VI, Chapter 2) to paint a selection. This technique can give you a high degree of control; it even lets you feather the edges of the selection so the filter effect fades out.

- **Channels:** You can store selections as alpha channels, visible in the Channels palette, of course. But you can also choose to apply a filter to only one of the other channels, such as the Red, Green, or Blue channels in an RGB image. This is a good way to create a filter effect that's applied to only one color in an image. (Check out Book VI, Chapter 1 for information about channels.)

Putting It Together

Sprucing Up a Scanned Halftone

Publications use only a limited number of ink colors to reproduce a photograph. Every tone you see in a black-and-white image must be reproduced by using pure black ink and the white (okay, dirty beige) of the paper. Full-color images are represented by combining CMYK (cyan, magenta, yellow, and black). Printers can't use various shades of gray ink to create grayscale photos. They also can't use different strengths of color inks to generate the rainbow of hues you see in an image on-screen. To get at least some of that subtlety, photographs have to be converted to a pattern of dots before they can be printed.

Our eyes blend the dots together to produce the illusion of a grayscale or color image with smooth gradations of tone. However, a problem arises if you want to reuse a photograph and don't have access to the original. Scanners can capture the halftone dots, but the resulting image usually has an unpleasant pattern called *moiré*.

You have several ways of reducing the moiré effect, usually by blurring the image so that the dots merge and the underlying pattern vanishes. Many scanners have a *descreen* setting that partially eliminates the effect, but that setting sometimes actually blurs your image more than you'd like. Fortunately, you can usually do a pretty good job in Photoshop. But remember that, if there is any way possible, scanning from continuous-tone images always yields the best quality.

In the following steps, I demonstrate an easier way (over the years I managed to lose the original negative and print). You can see the dreadful moiré pattern that resulted when I scanned the clip.

To rid your scanned halftone print of bothersome moiré, follow these steps:

1. **Open the image in Photoshop.**

2. **Zoom in so you can see the halftone pattern clearly as you work, as shown in the figure.**

3. **Choose Filter⇨Blur⇨Gaussian Blur.**

   The Gaussian Blur dialog box appears.

4. **Move the Radius slider to the right until the halftone pattern is blurred, and then click OK to apply the blur.**

   I used a value of 1.7 pixels in my figure.

continued

continued

5. **Choose Filter⇨Sharpen⇨Smart Sharpen to restore some of the image's sharpness now that you've eliminated the pattern. Choose Gaussian Blur for the Remove algorithm.**

As long as the Radius value for the Smart Sharpen filter doesn't exceed the radius of the Gaussian Blur that you first applied, the two filters won't cancel each other out. You want the sharpening to make the details of the image crisper without bringing back those blurred halftone dots.

6. **Move the Amount slider to the right to sharpen the image.**

Try to find a setting that does the job without making the image appear unnaturally sharp or show too much contrast. I used 150 percent in my figure.

In most cases, leaving the Threshold at 0 is fine. Calculate a starting Radius value by dividing the ppi (pixels per inch) of the scanned image by 150. If a moiré pattern reappears, reduce the Radius value.

7. **Click OK to apply the sharpness.**

The result of my blur-and-sharpen exercise is shown in the figure.

Chapter 2: Applying Filters for Special Occasions

In This Chapter

✐ **Using the Filter Gallery**

✐ **Applying artsy effects and brush strokes**

✐ **Adding distortion and noise — on purpose**

✐ **Breaking up an image**

✐ **Rendering different effects**

✐ **Sketching and Texturizing images the easy way**

✐ **Putting other filters to work**

*P*hotoshop has dozens of filters that let you enhance your image in unusual ways. You can create Old Masters portraits from common snapshots, shatter your image into a thousand sparkling pieces, create clouds in a cloudless sky, create stained glass, or perform hundreds of other tricks.

The big challenge in using these filters is learning what each filter can do and how to apply it to the best effect. This chapter introduces you to more of those fabulous Photoshop plug-ins — and shows you some typical applications for them. Several Putting-It-Together projects have step-by-step instructions. For the first few examples, I provide you with the settings I used to achieve particular looks. However, filter effects vary greatly when applied to different images, so you'll have to play with the filter controls yourself when you use these techniques with your own images.

You can apply a filter to a layer, selection, or channel. And you can also fade a filter, change opacity settings, and use layer masks to soften the effects of filters. In fact, in some cases, you may *have* to decrease the effect of a filter because full strength can look overdone. On the other hand, when applied selectively, the same filter may look subtle and sophisticated. Although filters can be a blast to play with, you want to exercise some restraint when applying them for a real project. Getting carried away with the effects is easy when often the simplest effect is the most beautiful.

Working in the Filter Gallery

In the last version of Photoshop, we were given an alternative route to access and apply filters, namely the Filter Gallery (a dialog box-like gizmo that Adobe refers to as an *editing window*). To put it on-screen, choose Filter⇨Filter Gallery. Here you can apply multiple filters, as well as edit or delete them later. This feature has made filters more flexible, more user-friendly, and easier to apply.

Here are the steps to get you up and running in the Filter Gallery:

1. **Choose Filter⇨Filter Gallery.**

   The Filter Gallery dialog box appears, as shown in Figure 2-1.

2. **Click your desired filter category folder.**

   The folder expands and displays the filters in that category. A thumbnail illustrating the filter's effect accompanies each filter. To collapse the filter category folder, simply click it again.

3. **Select the filter you want to apply.**

   You can also choose your filter from the filter pop-up menu, shown in Figure 2-1.

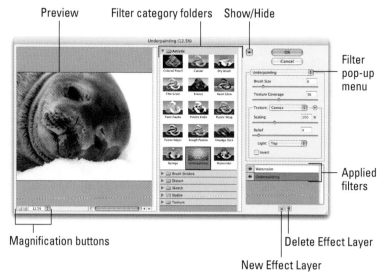

Preview   Filter category folders   Show/Hide

Filter pop-up menu

Applied filters

Magnification buttons

Delete Effect Layer

New Effect Layer

Corbis Digital Stock

Figure 2-1: The Filter Gallery enables you to apply and edit multiple filters within a single dialog box.

4. **Specify any settings associated with the filter.**

   You get a large preview of your image in the left side of the dialog box. Use the magnification controls to zoom in and out of the preview. As you change your settings, the preview dynamically updates itself. To preview a different filter, simply select it.

   Note that if you want your custom settings to be the new default for the filter, simply press the Ctrl key (⌘ key on the Mac). The Cancel button changes to Default. Click it and your settings are now the new default.

5. **When you are happy with the filter, click OK to apply the filter and exit the dialog box.**

6. **If you want to apply another filter, click the New Effects Layer button at the bottom of the dialog box.**

   This duplicates the existing filter.

7. **Choose your new filter, which then replaces the duplicates.**

   Photoshop lists each of the filters you apply to the image in the bottom right of the dialog box.

8. **When you're done, click OK to apply the second filter and exit the dialog box.**

   You can apply as many filters as you want to your image. But often less is more.

Here are some other helpful tips to keep in mind when you're using the Filter Gallery:

✒ To delete an applied filter, select it and click the Delete Effect Layer button (the trash can icon).

✒ To edit an applied filter's settings, select it in the list and make any necessary changes. Click OK to reapply. Note that while you can edit a particular filter's settings, that edit affects any subsequent filters you have made after applying that particular filter.

✒ You can rearrange the order of the applied filters. Simply select and drag the filter up or down within the list.

   Rearranging the order of the applied filters changes the resulting effect of the filters.

✒ To resize the Filter Gallery dialog box, drag the lower-right corner.

✒ To hide the Filter menu and provide the maximum real estate for the preview box, click the arrow to the left of the OK button.

✒ Note that you can also choose any of the filters found in the Filter Gallery from the Filter menu itself. Doing so launches the Filter Gallery automatically — though not all filters are available in the Filter Gallery. You have to access some of them individually from the Filter menu.

Book VII Chapter 2

Applying Filters for Special Occasions

Don't be misled into thinking that the Filter Gallery is like Layer Styles where the styles can be removed and the underlying pixel data is returned to its pristine, original state. Filters change the pixels of an image permanently and after you apply one, you can't remove it. So be sure that you really like what you've done and that you have a backup copy of that precious family photo or critical project image.

Getting Artsy

Quite a few of the Photoshop filters produce artistic effects. You'll find a large collection of them on the Sketch and Stylize submenus. However, the Artistic menu contains 15 versatile filters that you can use to add brush strokes to your images, wrap them in plastic, create poster-like effects, and manufacture other interesting looks.

Many Photoshop users employ these filters to create images that look as if they were painted. What they might not tell you, unless pressed, is that artsy filters can make terrible photos look better — or in some cases, pretty darn good. These filters can disguise a multitude of photographic sins, turning shoebox rejects into pretty decent digital transformations. The photo of a clock in Figure 2-2 is, arguably, not very interesting — and (worse) it's blurry. I moved the camera as I was taking the photo.

Figure 2-2: This photo is not that interesting and slightly out of focus.

To improve this image, I employed filters on the Filter⇨Artistic menu. Try one of the following filters:

✓ **Poster Edges:** A quick application of this filter improves the photo 100 percent. (See Figure 2-3.) The filter not only gives the picture an artsy, poster-like look, but also enhances the edges to make the clock's outline appear sharper.

I set the Poster Edges filter's Edge Thickness to 4, bumped the Edge Intensity up to a value of 6 to create dramatic-looking edges, and set the Posterization level to 6 to allow more tones for a bit more realism.

✓ **Rough Pastels:** This filter, shown in the right photo in Figure 2-3, gives the look of a fine art piece created with oil pastels. I used the settings of 8 for the Stroke Length and Stroke Detail, 100 percent Scale and 20 for Relief. I left my light source at Bottom.

Figure 2-3: The Poster Edges filter (left) and the Rough Pastels filter (right) helps.

- **The Dry Brush:** This filter can add an even more stylistic effect, reducing details down to a series of broad strokes.

- **Colored Pencil:** This filter crosshatches the edges of your image to create a pencil-like effect.

- **Cutout:** This effect assembles an image from what looks like cut-out paper shapes, which resemble a kid's art project.

- **Film Grain:** This photographic effect diffuses an image with thousands of tiny dots that simulate clumps of film grain. (Think of old home movies.)

- **Fresco:** This effect looks (supposedly) like pigments applied to fresh, wet plaster. Okay, I guess . . . if you squint.

- **Paint Daubs:** This effect uses smears of color from your choice of a half-dozen different brush types. Very Jackson Pollock.

- **Plastic Wrap:** This filter can produce a wet look, particularly when you apply it to a selection and then fade the filter so it doesn't overpower the detail in your image.

- **Watercolor:** This is a nice pastel effect that diffuses an image while adding an interesting, watery texture.

Stroking Your Image with Filters

You can find more stroking filters on the Brush Strokes submenu, with some interesting texturizing filters that can spruce up less-than-perfect photos and add a new look to even your best shots.

Choose Filter⇨Brush Strokes to find the stroking filters that can provide hours of fun, including

- **Ink Outlines:** Adobe describes this filter as producing the look of a corroded ink drawing.

- **Spatter:** This filter generates the look you might get from a sputtering airbrush.

- **Accented Edges:** Use this filter to make a subject jump out from its background by emphasizing the edges of all the objects in the picture, as shown in Figure 2-4. I set my Spray Radius to 25 and my Smoothness to 10.

Corbis Digital Stock

Figure 2-4: The Spatter filter gives this portrait a nice airbrush texture.

Putting It Together

Creating Exotic Edges for Your Images

An attractive border can give your image an edge. If you want an edgy look or want to take your work right to the edge, you can apply this next technique faster than you can say, "Overworked metaphor!" Photoshop lets you apply deckled looks and other effects to the borders of your image by using any of several plug-ins built right onto your trusty Filters menu.

Follow these easy steps to the edge of image immortality:

1. **Choose a photo that you think could use a decorative border and open it in Photoshop.**

2. **With the Rectangular Marquee tool, select the portion of the image you're framing, as shown in the figure.**

3. **Double-click the Quick Mask Mode icon in the Tools palette. In the dialog box, choose Selected Areas in the Color Indicates area.**

   The Quick Mask dialog box appears.

4. **Click OK to enter Quick Mask mode.**

   Photoshop highlights the rectangle you selected in color, as shown in the figure.

5. **Choose Filter⇨Blur⇨Gaussian Blur, set the Radius, and click OK.**

   To give the image a softer edge when the selection is deckled, I've set the Radius to 30.

6. **Choose Filter⇨Brush Strokes⇨Sprayed Strokes.**

7. **Adjust the Stroke Length and Spray Radius sliders to acquire the desired effect.**

   The higher the resolution, the higher the value you may need. In this case, I moved the Stroke Length and Spray Radius sliders to the max of 20 and 25 (respectively).

8. **Choose your desired Stroke Direction from the drop-down list.**

   I chose Right Diagonal for my image.

Corbis Digital Stock

REMEMBER

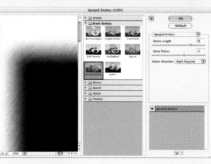

continued

continued

9. **Click OK to apply the effect to the Quick Mask selection.**

After application, the edges of the highlighted area appear frayed, as shown in the figure.

10. **Press Q to exit Quick Mask mode.**

A selection border with stroked edges appears around the selection.

11. **Press Ctrl+C to copy the selected area, and then press Ctrl+V to paste it in a new layer.**

12. **Create a new layer and fill it with the color you would like for the background.**

I filled my background with white.

13. **In the Layers palette, move the layer underneath your deckled image.**

14. **Choose Layer⇨Flatten Image. When prompted, if you want to discard hidden layers, click OK.**

The finished image appears, as shown in the following figure.

Distorting for Fun

With a couple exceptions, Photoshop's Distortion filters twist, turn, and bend your images in surprising ways, turning ordinary objects into wavy images, pinched shapes, and bloated spheres.

The first exception? The Diffuse Glow filter distorts images only to the extent that it imbues them with a soft, romantic, fuzzy look that can make the sharpest image look positively ethereal.

I've never figured out why Adobe dumped this useful filter in the Distort submenu, but there it is. (And here it is applied to a girl in Figure 2-5.)

Corbis Digital Stock

Figure 2-5: Give your photo a heavenly aura with the Diffuse Glow filter (left).

The second exception is the new Lens Correction filter, which fixes distortions caused by the camera lens. In the dialog box, you find settings to correct *barrel* and *pincushion* distortions, where straight lines appear (respectively) bowed out or in. Select the Remove Distortion tool and drag on the image — or you can also drag the Remove Distortion slider. Use the Straighten tool to rotate a tilted image, as shown in Figure 2-6. You can also correct perspective issues by using the Transform sliders of Vertical and Horizontal Perspective. If your images suffer from *vignetting* (where the edges are darker than the center), slide the Vignette slider to correct the problem. Finally, got colored fringe around your subjects? Photographers call this nastiness *chromatic aberration.* Fringe, abberation, whatever it's called — get rid of it by using the Red/Cyan or Blue/Yellow Fringe sliders. The Move Grid, Hand, and Zoom tools help make your adjustments more user-friendly.

Other filters of this ilk can produce wavy images, add pond ripples, pinch images, or transform them into spheres. Check out Figure 2-7 to see distortions of a wall clock.

Corbis Digital Stock

Figure 2-6: Fix the horizon line on those vacation photos with the Straighten tool.

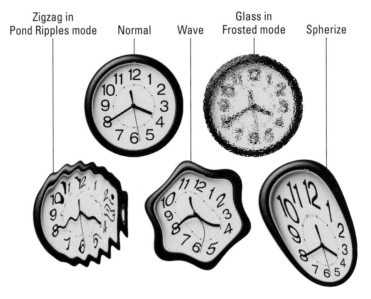

Figure 2-7: A normal clock takes on Dali-esque qualities with various Distort filters.

The Glass filter can do the following to your images:

✔ Add a glass-block texture

✔ Add a canvas texture

✔ Create frosted-glass fuzziness

✔ Break up your image with tiny lenses

 Don't like any of Photoshop's textures? No biggie, you can also load your own texture. Click the Texture pop-up menu (the right-pointing arrow) and choose Load Texture.

Pumping Up the Noise

Noise in images consists of any graininess or texture that occurs, either because of the inherent quality of the image or through the editing process. Noise filters, like the Photoshop Add Noise plug-in, produce random texture and grain in an image. If you're new to image editing, you might wonder why you'd want to add noise to an image in the first place. Wouldn't it be smarter to remove it? Well, sometimes. In practice, you'll find lots of applications that call for a little noise here and there:

✔ **To add texture:** Objects that become too smooth, either because of blurring or other image editing you may have done, often look better when you add some noise to give them a texture. This technique is particularly useful if one object in an image has been edited, smoothed, or blurred more than the other objects in the image.

✔ **To blend foreign objects into a scene:** When you drop a new object into the middle of an existing scene, you'll often find that the amount of grain or noise in the new object is quite different from the objects it's joining.

For example, say you've decided to take a photo of your house and want to insert a certain luxury car in your driveway. Unfortunately, your digital photo of your brother-in-law's luxo-mobile is a lot sharper than the picture of your house. Adding a little noise can help the two objects blend more realistically. You may even forget that the car isn't yours.

✔ **To improve image quality:** Images that contain smooth gradients often don't print well because some printers are unable to reproduce the subtle blend of colors from one hue to another. The result is *objectionable banding* in your printed image: You can see distinct stripes as the colors progress from one to another. Adding a little noise can break up the gradient enough that your printer can reproduce the blend of colors, and the noise/grain itself is virtually invisible on the printed sheet.

Pumping Down the Noise

Although the Add Noise filter adds grain, the other filters in the Noise sub-menu don't add noise at all; instead, they make noise and *artifacts* (flaws such as the dust and scratches on old film) less noticeable. Choose Filter⇨ Noise to find your tools, which include

  ✓ **Despeckle:** This filter makes dust spots in your image less noticeable by decreasing the contrast of your entire image — except at the edges. That translates into a slightly blurry image (which masks the spots) that still retains sharpness along the edges of image components. You end up with a little blur to soften the image, but enough detail in the edges that the picture still looks good.

  ✓ **Dust & Scratches:** This filter concentrates its blurring effect on only those areas of your image that contain scratches and other artifacts. Photoshop performs this magic by looking at each pixel in an image, moving out in a radial direction until it encounters an abrupt transition in tone. (That's a signal that a spot or scratch has been found.) You can specify the radius Photoshop searches for the little culprits, from 1 to 16 pixels. Be careful not to overdo it. Too much of this filter can obliterate the detail in the image. If you journey to the world of mush, try using Edit⇨Fade right after you apply the filter.

While working with any of the Noise filters, being very conservative at first is best. All the Noise filters involve destruction of image data. Remember, that's just the nature of filters in general — changing pixel data. A little bit can help — and be just the effect you're looking for. Just a little bit more, however, may completely wreck things.

  ✓ **Median:** This filter reduces contrast around dust motes, thus hiding them, in a slightly different way. This filter looks at the pixels surround-ing each pixel in the image and replaces the center one with a new pixel that has the median brightness level of that group. The process is a little hard to describe succinctly, but basically, the bright spots darken while the rest of the image isn't affected.

  ✓ **Reduce Noise:** This new filter, shown in Figure 2-8, is designed to remove luminance noise and JPEG artifacts that can appear on digital photos. Luminance noise is grayscale noise that makes images look overly grainy. Here is some info on the options:

    • **Strength:** Specify the amount of noise reduction. Note that you can reduce noise in the Overall image or (if you click the Advanced button) channel by channel.

    Be sure to check out the Blue channel in particular. It's often the channel that captures all the crud.

- **Preserve Details:** A higher number preserves edges and details but reduces the amount of noise removal. Find a happy medium.

- **Reduce Color Noise:** Removes random colored pixel artifacts.

- **Sharpen Details:** Counteracts the fact that removing noise reduces sharpness as well.

- **Remove JPEG Artifact:** Check this option to remove the annoying blocks and halos that can occur from low-quality JPEG compression.

  You can also save and reload your settings.

Figure 2-8: The Reduce Noise filter attempts to remove noise while retaining some sharpness in edges and details.

Book VII
Chapter 2

Applying Filters for
Special Occasions

Breaking Your Image into Pieces

The Pixelate filters in Photoshop break up your images into bits and pieces, providing more of those painterly effects you can get with brush strokes and artistic filters.

The Pixelate submenu includes the Crystallize filter applied to the little girl shown in Figure 2-9, as well as plug-ins that produce color halftone effects, fragmented images, and the Pointillism effect (used in the "Creating Snow and Rain" Putting-It-Together project later in this chapter).

Corbis Digital Stock

Figure 2-9: The Crystallize filter breaks your image into polygonal shapes.

Rendering

In computerese, *rendering* means creating something from nothing, in a way. That's why rendering filters in Photoshop all produce special effects by creating a look, object, or lighting effect that's melded with your original image.

Using the Clouds filter

The Clouds filter can muster a sky full of clouds from scratch with a few clicks of the mouse, as in the now-cloudy picture shown in Figure 2-10. This filter creates clouds using random values from between the foreground and background colors. Indeed, most Photoshop veterans use this filter so much that they have a surprising number of clouds in their images. Find it at Filter⇨Render⇨Clouds. To create a more contrasty cloud effect, press Alt (Option on the Mac) when choosing the command. If you don't like the first set of clouds you get, apply the filter again and again until you do. If you want a more "realistic" sky, try using a dark sky blue for your foreground color and a very light blue, or white, color for your background color.

Need a quick Web background image? Create a 128 x 128 (or some multiple of that size) pixel image and apply the Clouds filter. It tiles seamlessly on your Web page.

Brand X Pictures

Figure 2-10: Got Clouds? Make your own with the Clouds filter.

Creating fibers

This filter can create a textile-like effect out of the thin air. Choose Filter⇨
Render⇨Fibers. In the dialog box, move the Variance slider to increase the
contrast between light and dark areas. Move the Strength slider to increase
the tightness of the weave of the fibers. Click the Randomize button to get
another variation of the effect of the filter.

Using other rendering filters

Other useful filters on the Render submenu (at Filter⇨Render) include

- **3D Transform:** Use this filter to wrap objects around three-dimensional
  shapes such as cubes and spheres — producing (say) a mock-up of your
  favorite championship breakfast cereal with your photo on the front.

- **Difference Clouds:** Use this filter to create puffy objects in the sky (or
  foggy clouds at lower levels). Instead of performing this magical feat the
  way the Clouds filter does, the Difference Clouds filter uses image information to figure the difference in pixel values between the new clouds
  and the image they're joining. The result is a unique cloud effect. Try
  applying the filter repeatedly to create a marbleized effect.

✔ **Lens Flare:** This filter creates the reflection effect that plagues photographers when they point their cameras toward a strong light source, such as the sun. Photoshop mimics several different kinds of photographic lenses, giving you useful flares that can spice up concert photos, add a sunset where none existed, and create other kinds of lighting bursts. In the Lens Flare dialog box, specify a location for the center of the flare by clicking the image thumbnail or dragging the crosshair.

✔ **Lighting Effects:** As a sort of photo-studio lighting setup, this filter uses pixels to do its work. You can set up 16 different lights and manipulate how they illuminate your photo.

✔ **Texture Fill:** This filter fills an area with a grayscale image. Select the filter and open the image you want to use as the texture fill.

Putting It Together

Creating Snow and Rain

Sometimes you may come across a photo that needs a little bit of atmosphere thrown in to give it extra punch. And I mean *atmosphere* literally. By using a couple of filters and a blend mode, you can add some rain or snow to any image. Just follow these steps to create either rain or snow:

1. **Open a color image. It if isn't currently in RGB Mode, then choose Image⇨Mode⇨RGB Color.**

Make sure you're in RGB mode; the blend mode used in these steps doesn't work correctly with CMYK images.

2. **Drag the background layer to the Create a New Layer icon at the bottom of the Layers palette.**

You now see a layer that says *Background copy* in the Layers palette.

3. **Double-click the name *Background copy* and type** Snow.

This isn't a mandatory step. I'm just being ultra-organized.

4. **With the Snow layer active, choose Filter⇨Pixelate⇨Pointillize. In the dialog box, set your cell size to 7 or a value you prefer. Click OK.**

The bigger the cell size, the bigger the snowflakes or raindrops.

For rain, you might try a cell size of 3, which is the minimum, or 4. For snow, try a larger cell size, between 6 and 9. I used a value of 7 in my image.

5. **On the Snow layer, choose Image⇨ Adjustments⇨Threshold. Move the slider all the way to the right, to a max value of 255.**

   This adjustment takes the colored cells and turns them to either black or white.

   By using a value of 255, all brightness values less than 255 turn black and the remaining value turns white.

6. **On the Snow layer, choose Screen from the Mode pop-up menu in the Layers palette.**

   The Screen blend mode lightens the Snow layer, where it mixes with the background. Blending with black pixels has no effect, therefore they drop out, as shown in the figure.

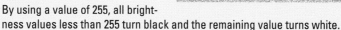

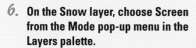

7. **Choose Filter⇨Blur⇨Motion Blur. In the dialog box, specify the Angle and Distance values.**

   If you want the wind to appear to be blowing hard, set the angle more diagonally, around 45 degrees. If you want the weather to appear to be coming straight down, set the angle to 90 degrees. Setting the distance elongates the pointillized cells that you created in Step 4, making them look a little more realistic. For snow, start with a range of about 8 to 12 pixels. For rain, start a little higher, 15 to 25 pixels. I used a value of 12 pixels in my figure.

   If you're creating rain, proceed to Step 8. If you're a snow person, you're done as shown in the following figure.

8. **Choose Filter⇨Sharpen⇨Unsharp Mask.**

   The Unsharp Mask dialog box appears.

9. **Specify the Amount, Radius, and Threshold values.**

   The Unsharp Mask filter gives the illusion of sharpening the focus of the image by increasing the contrast between the pixels.

   I used an amount of 500 percent, a Radius of 1, and kept the Threshold at 0. This gives the raindrops a little more definition.

Book VII Chapter 2

Applying Filters for Special Occasions

continued

continued

10. **Choose Filter⇨Blur⇨Motion Blur. In the dialog box, specify the Angle and Distance values.**

Again, the angle is up to you, but make it consistent with the value that you used in Step 7. Set the distance according to how you want your rain to appear, a moderate spring rain or a torrential, close-to-hurricane type of downpour. In my image that follows, I used 45 degrees and 25 pixels.

Getting Organic with the Sketch Filters

The Sketch filter menu contains a few filters that don't really belong there. That's because many current Photoshop filters were acquired from Aldus Corporation (now defunct), and Adobe had to shoehorn them into the organizational structure of Photoshop. But no matter — they work nonetheless.

If you were to encounter a picture of Michelangelo's *David*, shown in Figure 2-11, you might be tempted to sketch the famous sculpture by using one of the filters you find when you choose Filter➪Sketch.

Normal   Conté Crayon

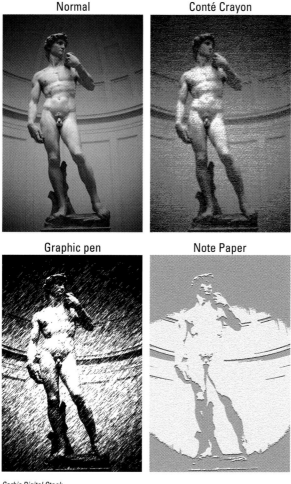

Graphic pen   Note Paper

Corbis Digital Stock

Figure 2-11: Give your digital photos a more organic feel with the Sketch filters.

**Book VII
Chapter 2**

**Applying Filters for
Special Occasions**

Perhaps a Conté Crayon effect or a Graphic Pen and Ink look would be nice. But the Sketch submenu also includes other artistic effects, such as the Note Paper look, a halftone screen, chalk and charcoal, and even a bas-relief effect that turns flat images into a Michelangelo-esque sculpture.

You'll also want to experiment with these other Sketch filters:

- *Chrome* creates a polished chrome effect. Use the Levels adjustment to add more contrast if necessary.

- *Photocopy* gives that infamous, anachronistic look (dating back to the days when photocopiers didn't do a very good job of reproducing halftone images). Creates areas of black and white with little gray value.

- *Plaster* creates a look that resembles molten plastic more than it looks like plaster. The filter uses the foreground and background values to color the image.

- *Stamp* mimics a rubber or wooden-block stamp (not very sketch-like, indeed!).

- *Reticulation* adds texture by reproducing a veritable photographic disaster: The wrinkling of film emulsion that occurs when you move film from one developing chemical to another that has an extreme difference in temperature (think hot developer followed by a bath in cold water). The highlights look grainy; the shadow areas look thick and goopy.

- *Torn Edges* creates the look of ragged paper and colorizes the image, using the foreground and background colors.

- *Water Paper* creates the look of paint-like daubs on fibrous wet paper.

  Even if the Sketch filters don't all produce sketchy effects, they do have one thing in common: They give your images an organic look that's decidedly uncomputer-like.

Putting It Together

Adding Water Droplets and Other Wet Effects

You can find lots of techniques for creating nice, neat round drops of water by using Photoshop. Unless you've just waxed your car and expect a rain shower within moments, however, perfectly beaded water droplets can be fairly rare. In real life, you're likely to encounter some sloppy drops and driblets. This technique simulates that look. You could use it to add sparkling water drops to a flower, create a wet-look texture for artistic effect, or add a three-dimensional *trompe l'oeil* ("fools the eye") optical illusion. Find the flower image I use on this book's companion Web site if you'd like to follow along.

1. **Open a plain, old, bone dry photograph in Photoshop.**

   I'm using a flower photograph, which will look great wet.

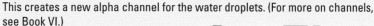

2. **Press D to make sure you have the foreground and background colors in Photoshop set to the default values of black and white.**

3. **Choose Window⇨Channels, choose Create New Channel from the palette menu.**

   This creates a new alpha channel for the water droplets. (For more on channels, see Book VI.)

4. **In the Color Indicates area of the New Channel dialog box, select the Selected Areas radio button, and set Opacity to 100 percent.**

5. **Select Filter⇨Render⇨Clouds to create a motley cloud effect to use as the basis for your random water droplets.**

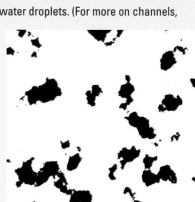

6. **Choose Image⇨Adjustments⇨ Threshold, and then move the slider to create black blotches that will become water droplets, as shown in the figure.**

   I used a value of 83, but, because the Clouds filter produces random results, you may find that a different value works better for you.

7. **Choose Filter⇨Blur⇨Gaussian Blur and move the Radius slider enough to blur the jagged edges of the droplets.**

   I used a value of 3.8 pixels.

8. **Choose Filter⇨Sharpen⇨Unsharp Mask and adjust the Amount and Radius sliders to firm up the edges of the droplets.**

   I found that an Amount of 85 percent and a Radius of about 46 creates soft-edged-but-distinct water droplets, as shown in the figure.

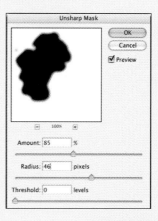

**Book VII
Chapter 2**

**Applying Filters for
Special Occasions**

continued

continued

9. **Ctrl+click (⌘+click on the Mac) on the new channel in the Channels palette to load the selection you've created, as shown in the figure.**

10. **Click the RGB Channel in the Channels palette to return to your full-color picture.**

The droplets appear as selections.

11. **Choose Layer⇨New⇨Layer via Copy to create a new layer for the droplets to reside in.**

12. **Choose Layer⇨Layer Style and select Bevel and Emboss.**

The bevel/embossing effect adds a third dimension to the drops. You can experiment with the depth and size controls to get the exact effect you want. I used the

Inner Bevel style, set to the Smooth Technique in the Structure area of the dialog box. I used the sliders to increase the size of the bevel to 27 pixels, and softened the edges by 11 pixels.

13. **If you like, you can choose Image⇨Adjustments⇨Levels to darken the droplets against their background.**

The final image looks like a print that has been drenched with liquid.

Adding Texture

Photoshop lets you add lots of interesting textures to your images, which are on the Filter⇨Texture menu, such as the cracked canvas effect generated by the Craquelure filter (see Figure 2-12), or the pixel effect produced by the Patchwork filter.

You can find other filters on this menu to help you create mosaic effects, add yet another kind of film grain, and create stained-glass effects in your images. But the most versatile filter in this set is the Texturizer, shown in Figure 2-13. The Texturizer filter enables you to apply various kinds of textures to your images or selections, including Canvas, Sandstone, Burlap, or Brick.

Corbis Digital Stock

Figure 2-12: The Craquelure filter gives an old world painting feel to your image.

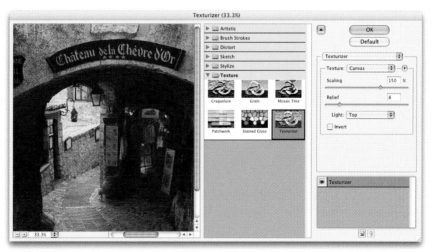

Corbis Digital Stock

Figure 2-13: You can apply either preset or custom made textures to your images with the Texturizer filter.

You can choose the relative size of the texture compared to the rest of your image by using the Scaling slider, and govern the 3-D relief effect. You can even select the direction of the light source that produces the 3-D look, choosing from top, bottom, either side, or any of the four corners of the image. If those variations aren't enough for you, then create your own texture, save it as a Photoshop PSD file, and use that to texturize your image.

You can find a handful of other filters that allow you to load your own textures, including Rough Pastels, Underpainting, and Conté Crayon.

Looking at the Other Filters

The Video and Other categories are the home of the oddest of the odd. For example, the Other submenu is home to the Custom filter, which is no filter at all — but rather a dialog box with a matrix in which you can type numbers that Photoshop uses to process the pixels in your image in unexpected ways. The center box in the matrix represents a pixel in your image; the surrounding boxes represent the pixels that surround that pixel. The numbers you type tell Photoshop whether to darken or lighten pixels. You can experiment to see what will happen, and if you like the effect, tell all your friends that you *meant* to do that.

The High Pass filter, also in the Other category, applies an effect opposite to the Gaussian Blur filter. It finds and keeps the details in the edges where it finds distinct color or tonal differences and turns the rest of the image gray. When converting a continuous-tone image into a bitmap (black and white only) image, applying this filter is useful before applying the Threshold adjustment. See Book VIII, Chapter 1 for more on the Threshold command. It's also handy for creating a channel mask. (See Book VI, Chapter 3 for details.)

Two other filters that help with masking are the Minimum and Maximum filters. The Minimum filter expands the black areas while decreasing white areas (a process known as *choking* in traditional photography). The Maximum filter expands the white portions while decreasing black areas (known as *spreading*). The radius value you enter tells the filter how many pixels to expand or decrease from the edges of your selection.

The Video menu contains its own share of strange filters, including the NTSC Colors filter, which performs the rather obscure function of converting all the colors in your image to match the colors used for television reproduction. (NTSC stands for *National Television Systems Committee*.) You'd use this filter to process digital presentations or slides to be shown on television, if you were really, really particular about how the colors are portrayed.

Chapter 3: Distorting with the Liquify Command

In This Chapter

✒ **Checking out the Liquify window**

✒ **Liquifying an image**

✒ **Protecting/unprotecting with freezing and thawing**

✒ **Canceling your transformations with Reconstruction**

✒ **Extending transformations to other areas**

*L*iquify is the only Photoshop filter that gets a chapter of its own. But then again, Liquify is no ordinary filter; it's the ultimate in image distortion tools, and therefore a good deal more complex than most of its kin on the Filter menu. What other filter has its own hefty tools palette, loads of buttons, several different modes, and more than a dozen option categories with what amount to dozens more variations?

The Liquify command lets you push and pull on parts of your image; twist, turn, and pinch other parts; bloat sections; freeze portions in place so that they remain immune to the transformations going around them; and perform selective reconstructions if you don't like everything you've done. You can perform this magic with a remarkable degree of control, too.

This chapter explores all the features of the Liquify command, and shows you how to use them to create sensational images.

Exploring the Liquify Window

At first glance, the Liquify window is a little daunting. It's a little daunting on second, third, and fourth glances, too. But when you quit glancing and dive into this versatile filter, you'll find that the tools and options make a lot of sense.

The Liquify Tools palette resides at the left side of the Liquify window shown in Figure 3-1. The other options available with Liquify (which I describe later in the section appropriately named "The Options Areas") appear at the right side of the window. The Tools palette includes a dozen tools that you can use to paint and distort your image.

As with Photoshop's main Tools palette, you can activate each tool by pressing a letter associated with its name.

Figure 3-1: The intimidating Liquify window is really quite user-friendly after you get familiar with its tools and settings.

The painting tools

The first group of tools is used to paint distortions on your image. Shown in this list with their keyboard shortcuts in parentheses, the painting tools are (refer to Figure 3-1):

✔ **Forward Warp (W):** This tool is faintly reminiscent of the Smudge tool, but it doesn't blur the pixels quite as much as it pushes them forward as you drag, creating a stretched effect. Use the Warp tool to push pixels where you want them to go, using short strokes or long pushes.

When compared to a tool like the Smudge tool, which tends to destroy detail, the Warp tool can preserve detail within distortions.

 ✔ **Twirl Clockwise (C):** Place the cursor in one spot, press the mouse button, and watch the pixels under your brush rotate like a satellite photo of a tropical storm. Or drag the cursor to create a moving twirl effect. Pixels move faster along the edges of the brush than in the placid center, much like a real hurricane. Adobe gave the Twirl Counterclockwise tool the pink slip. Now to twirl the other way, press the Alt (Option on the Mac) key as you drag or press the mouse button.

Try this technique with the other tools I describe here (with some tools the effect is more obvious than with others). Simply click and press the mouse button. The longer you pressthe mouse button, the more prominent the effect becomes.

 ✔ **Pucker (S):** This tool is the equivalent of the Pinch filter, squishing pixels toward the center of the area covered by the brush as you press the mouse button or drag. To reverse the pucker direction, which essentially applies a bloat, press the Alt (Option on the Mac) key as you press the mouse button or drag.

 ✔ **Bloat (B):** Here we have an analog to the Spherize filter, pushing pixels toward the edge of the brush area as you press the mouse button or drag the mouse. To reverse the bloat direction — doing so applies a pucker — press the Alt (Option on the Mac) key as you press the mouse button or drag.

 ✔ **Push Left (O):** Formerly known as the Shift Pixels tool, this odd tool moves pixels to the left when you drag the tool straight up. Drag down to move pixels to the right. Drag clockwise to increase the size of the object being distorted. Drag counterclockwise to decrease the size. To reverse any of the directions, press the Alt (Option on the Mac) key as you press the mouse button or drag.

 ✔ **Mirror (M):** Formerly known as the Reflect tool, the Mirror tool drags a reversed image of your pixels at a 90-degree angle to the motion of the brush. Press the Alt key (Option key on the Mac) to force the reflection in the direction opposite the motion of the brush (for example, to the left of a brush moving right, or above a brush moving down). This tool is a good choice for producing shimmery reflections.

**Book VII
Chapter 3**

Distorting with the
Liquify Command

⊯ **Turbulence (T):** This tool adds a random jumbling effect to your pixels. You can use the Turbulence tool to re-create maelstroms of air, fire, and water with (well, yeah) clouds, flames, and waves.

The other tools

The remaining tools on the palette perform different functions. Continuing down the Liquify Tools palette (refer to Figure 3-1), these tools are (shown here with their keyboard shortcuts):

 ⊯ **Reconstruct (R):** This tool lets you reverse or alter — completely or partially — the distortions you've made. You can retrace your steps if you went overboard in your warping activities.

 ⊯ **Freeze Mask (F):** Use this tool to protect areas from changes. It paints the frozen area with a red overlay, just like Quick Mask mode.

 ⊯ **Thaw Mask (D):** This tool unprotects areas by erasing the red protective "freeze" tone. This is a lot like erasing areas you've painted in Quick Mask mode.

 ⊯ **Hand (H):** The Hand tool works exactly like the standard Photoshop Hand tool. Click and push the image to move it around within the Preview window. You find more about the Hand tool in Book I, Chapter 4.

 ⊯ **Zoom (Z):** The Zoom tool works exactly like the standard Photoshop Zoom tool. Indeed, you can also zoom in and out by using the spacebar+ Alt+click (spacebar+Option+click on the Mac) and spacebar+Ctrl+click (spacebar+⌘+click on the Mac) shortcuts to zoom in and out. See Book I, Chapter 4, for more on using the regulation Zoom tool.

Separate from the Liquify Tools palette and in the lower-left corner of the Liquify window is a magnification box with a pop-up menu that you can use to select magnifications from 6 percent to 1600 percent. You can also type a specific value to zoom the image to that size. Or if you like buttons, click your way to magnification by using the +/- zoom control buttons.

The Options Areas

At the right side of the Liquify window (refer to Figure 3-1) are some menus and buttons that let you specify options for the tools, for reconstructing and freezing, and for viewing. I point them all out to you here, and cover exactly how to use them later in this chapter.

⊯ **Load Mesh** and **Save Mesh:** Liquify lets you show or hide a criss-cross area called a *mesh,* shown in Figure 3-2. The mesh provides a visual map of the distortions you've applied. The mesh starts out as a square grid and changes as you apply distortions. The mesh lets you clearly see exactly what you've done to the image, and, even better, provides a way to save those distortions on your hard drive so you can load and reapply them to the same (or a different) image later.

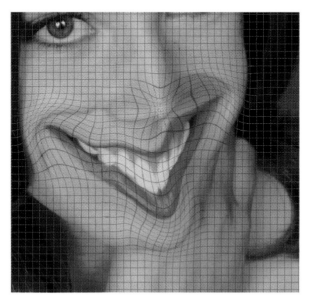

Figure 3-2: The mesh provides a visual map of your applied distortions.

✔ **Tool Options:** You can use the Tool Options area to apply parameters to the painting tools. You can specify the following options:

- **Brush Size:** Specifies the width of the brush.

- **Brush Density:** Specifies how fast the brush effect levels off at its edges. For example, with a feathered brush, the effect is stronger in the center and lighter at the edges.

- **Brush Pressure:** Specifies the speed at which you distort as you drag. Lower is slower.

- **Brush Rate:** Specifies the speed at which you distort as you keep a tool stationary, such as the Twirl tool. Again, lower is slower.

- **Turbulent Jitter:** Determines how tightly the brush jumbles pixels. This option gives the stroke a more natural, organic look.

When you select the Reconstruct tool, you can also choose a Reconstruct Mode from the pop-up menu. (I explain each of these modes later in the chapter.)

If you have a pressure-sensitive stylus tablet, you can also choose to use the amount of pressure you apply to control the width of your brush stroke.

✓ **Reconstruct Options:** Here, you can select one of several reconstruct modes. Reconstruct and Restore All buttons let you reverse all changes made on unfrozen areas (a little at a time) or revert to your last set of distortions. I show you how to use these, too.

✓ **Mask Options:** Consider freezing and masking one and the same when you're immersed in the Liquify dialog box. The mask options let you freeze areas from existing selections, layer masks, transparent areas, or alpha channels in your image. You can also invert the frozen area (thawing frozen portions of the image, and freezing the previously thawed areas), and thaw all the areas that were frozen with one click. Here is the low-down on the options, each of which is indicated by a double-circle icon:

- **Replace Selection:** Allows you to freeze or mask areas of your image based on an existing selection, transparent area, layer mask, or alpha channel. (For more on layer masks and alpha channels, see Book VI, Chapters 1 and 3.)

- **Add to Selection:** Displays the mask in the image and then enables you to add to the frozen areas with the Freeze tool. Adds pixels to the currently frozen areas.

- **Subtract from Selection:** Subtracts pixels from the currently frozen areas.

- **Intersect with Selection:** Masks only those pixels that are selected and currently frozen.

- **Invert Selection:** Inverts selected pixels and currently frozen areas.

  Click None to remove frozen areas. Click Mask All to freeze the entire image. Click Invert All to exchange frozen and thawed areas.

✓ **View Options:** You can show or hide frozen (masked) areas, the mesh, or the image. Also, if you choose the Show Mesh option, you can choose the mesh size and color. If you select the Show Mask option, you can select the color that indicates frozen areas. For example, if your image contains lots of red, you may want to change the freeze color to blue to create more contrast.

Finally, you can also apply a backdrop that shows how the image being lique-fied will appear when merged with other layers. To view your distorted image along with other layers, select the Show Backdrop option, and then select the particular layer you want to view, or choose All Layers from the Use pop-up menu. You can now choose whether you want the backdrop in front, behind, or blended with the distorted image. Specify an opacity percentage for the displayed layers so they won't obliterate the image being distorted. The default (50 percent) allows you to see both well, allowing you to keep track of your distortions.

Transforming an Image

Liquify seems impossibly complex on the surface, but it's as easy to apply as fingerpaint after you play with it a little. Here's a step-by-step scenario of the things you might do to apply some distortion to your own image:

1. **Select and open an image you want to transmogrify with Liquify; select a layer.**

2. **If you don't want to distort the whole layer, you can make your desired selection.**

   You can also use a layer mask, alpha channel, or transparent area to define what portions you want to distort.

3. **Choose Filter⇨Liquify or press Shift+Ctrl+X (Shift+⌘+X on the Mac).**

   The Liquify dialog box appears.

4. **If applicable, load your selection, layer mask, transparent area, or alpha channel in the Mask Options area.**

   Make sure you select the Show Mask option in the View Options area.

5. **You can also select the Freeze Mask tool and paint over the areas that you want to mask or protect.**

   After you freeze an area, you may want to get rid of the freeze highlighting for a while. Deselect the Show Mask option in View Options to turn the display on or off.

6. **In the View Options area, make sure that the Show Mesh and Show Image options are both selected.**

   You can hide any or all of these at any time to get a different view of your image. For example, you might want to hide the frozen areas and mesh to view only your image with the distortions you've applied so far. Or perhaps you might want to look only at the mesh, as shown in Figure 3-3, to get a look at the distortions by themselves. Being able to examine the liquification process in several different ways is one reason that Liquify is so controllable.

7. **If you're having trouble seeing the mesh (or think the mask color will blend in with a dominant color in your image), use the View options to change the size and color of the mesh and the hue of the mask.**

   If you want to see your image distortions against a backdrop, you can select that option as well.

8. **Use the painting tools to apply various effects to your image, as shown in Figure 3-4.**

   Remember to adjust the brush size and pressure to get the exact coverage you want.

**Book VII
Chapter 3**

Distorting with the
Liquify Command

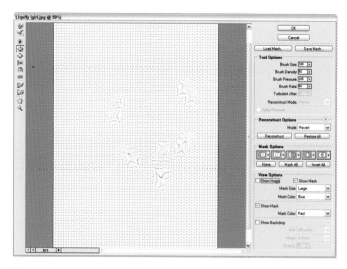

Figure 3-3: You can choose to view just the mesh if you want a good look at how the actual distortions are mapped.

At various points while you work, you may decide you want to freeze parts of the image from further changes (either temporarily or permanently).

Figure 3-4: Use the various Painting tools to apply your desired distortions.

9. **If you decide you want to work on an area again, select the Show Mask option to display the frozen areas again (if necessary). Then select the Thaw Mask tool and erase all or part of the freeze.**

10. **Use the Reconstruct tool or options to partially or fully reverse or modify your distortions.**

    If you want to start over, click Restore All to get back to your original image. All option settings stay as is. Press the Alt key (Option on the Mac) and click Reset to revert back to your original image and reset all options to their default settings.

11. **When you finish, save the mesh you created by clicking Save Mesh. Give the mesh a name and store it on your hard drive.**

    This step is totally optional, but saving your work is a good idea if you really like what you've done.

12. **Apply the distortion to your image by clicking OK and exiting the Liquify dialog box.**

Mastering Freezing and Thawing

Liquify's ability to protect areas by freezing, and unprotect areas by thawing, deserves a closer look. Consider freezing the equivalent to masking. Here's a summary of the things you need to know:

✐ **The easiest way to freeze/unfreeze is to use the Freeze Mask and Thaw Mask tools to paint the areas you want to protect or unprotect, as shown in Figure 3-5.** Use the brush controls to modify how either tool paints or erases. When you set brush pressure to less than 100 percent, the opacity of the mask you're painting determines how frozen that area is. For example, if an area is only 25 percent frozen, using a tool on that area produces only one-quarter the distortion you get in an area that's completely thawed.

✐ **You can use active or saved selections to define a frozen or masked area.** This is a great capability; you can use all the selection tools in Photoshop to define frozen/unfrozen areas before you invoke Liquify. You could, for example, select a portion of your image by using the Magic Wand

Figure 3-5: Protect areas from distortion by freezing them.

tool, another portion using selection marquees or Quick Mask mode, and then save them all (choose Selection⇨Save Selection) as alpha channels. Then, when you use Liquify, choose any of those selections to freeze an area.

✓ **Choose the basis to use for your mask from the pop-up menu of the Replace Selection command.**

You can also choose a layer mask to define your mask. This is a great way to apply your distortions at varying degrees of intensity. Where the mask reveals more, the distortion is more prominent. Where the mask hides more, the distortion is subtler.

✓ **To thaw all frozen areas, click the Thaw All button in the Mask Options area.**

✓ **To freeze all thawed areas, click the Mask All button in the Mask Options area.**

✓ **To reverse your frozen/unfrozen areas, click the Invert All button.** That which was frozen is thawed, and that which was unfrozen is frozen. Amen!

Reconstructing an Image

One of the most powerful capabilities of Liquify is that it can reconstruct your image fully or partially — restoring some or all of the image to its pre-Liquify state. This capability gives you a great deal of control over exactly how Photoshop transforms your image; you can backtrack any part of the transformation exactly the way you want. Here are some of your options:

✓ **To cancel all the changes made on your image (say, you really, really messed up), click the Restore All button in the Reconstruct Options area.** The image returns to its original state (as it was when you first opened the Liquify window) and removes distortions in both frozen and unfrozen areas.

✓ **To change only unfrozen areas of your image to their original states, select the Revert mode in the Reconstruct Options area of the dialog box, and then click the Reconstruct button.** The frozen areas remain distorted, but everything else returns to normal.

Use this option when you're displeased with some sections but like the distortions in others. Freeze the stuff you like, and let Liquify cancel the changes elsewhere.

🛩 **To paint portions of your image back to normalcy, choose Revert mode in the Tool Options area, and then select the Reconstruct tool from the Liquify Tools palette.** You can use the Reconstruct tool to restore the areas that you paint. The image reverts more quickly at the center of the brush, so you have an extremely fine degree of control in how you revert your image. The mesh may help you see exactly what portions are being restored, too.

🛩 **You can also click the Reconstruct button to have Photoshop apply an overall reconstruction.** Click the button and Photoshop reconstructs once. Click again to remove even more distortion.

If you don't necessarily want to reconstruct your image back to its original condition, but rather want to alter, extend, or clone your distortions, you can choose Reconstruct modes other than Revert. See the next section on the other Reconstruct modes.

Extending and Cloning Distortions

Liquify allows you to extend distortions you've made in frozen areas into parts of the image that are unfrozen. If you have an image that has the requisite frozen and unfrozen portions, you should first choose a *mode* — which determines specific ways in which Photoshop extends the image from the frozen areas into the unfrozen area.

Reconstruct modes

The Reconstruct modes include the following four:

🛩 **Rigid:** This mode keeps rigid right angles in the mesh's grid, which can generate some mismatches (Adobe calls those *discontinuities*) at the edges where the frozen and unfrozen portions meet. This mode restores unfrozen areas to close approximations of their original states.

🛩 **Stiff:** Adobe describes this as a *weak magnetic field,* attracting the edges between the frozen and unfrozen areas strongly where they meet, and producing less distortion in unfrozen areas farther away from the edges.

🛩 **Smooth:** This mode smoothly spreads the frozen areas' distortions through the unfrozen areas. It produces a smooth blending effect, as shown in Figure 3-6.

🛩 **Loose:** This mode generates an even smoother blending effect between frozen and unfrozen areas.

Corbis Digital Stock

Figure 3-6: The Smooth mode smoothly blends frozen distortions into unfrozen areas.

Use the Reconstruct tool to expand the frozen-area distortions into the unfrozen area, using the mode you've selected to blend the pixels as you paint. You can drag to paint, or click and Shift+click to paint in straight lines (much as you do with Photoshop's regular Brush tools).

More Reconstruct modes

There are three more Reconstruct modes that work slightly differently from the previous four. These modes more or less clone particular distortions you've already applied elsewhere in the image. Like the Clone Stamp tool, these modes allow you to select part of the distortion and apply (or clone) copies of the selection to other parts of your image:

✓ **Displace:** Displace copies the amount of displacement at the starting point of the distortion to unfrozen parts of your image. You can use this mode to displace parts of your image to a different position in the image.

✓ **Amplitwist:** Amplitwist applies the displacement, *scaling* (sizing up or down), and rotation of the distortion to unfrozen areas to match those that exist at the starting point.

✓ **Affine:** Affine does much the same thing as Amplitwist, using displacement, scaling, rotation, and skew in the distortion to modify unfrozen areas to match those distortions that exist at the starting point.

Each time you click the mouse button, you create a new starting point, so if you are trying to extend a distortion effect from a single starting point, don't release your mouse button until you're done using the Reconstruct tool.

Using Displace, Amplitwist, and Affine

All three of these Reconstruct modes use different combinations of distortion factors — such as displacement, scaling, rotation, or skew. Unlike the other modes, the Reconstruct button isn't available for these three.

You can use these modes only with the Reconstruct tool.

To use Displace, Amplitwist, or Affine, follow these steps:

1. **Open an image to work on, and choose Filter⇨Liquify.**

2. **Choose one of the three modes — Displace, Amplitwist, or Affine — from the Reconstruct Mode pop-up menu in the Tool Options area.**

3. **Choose the Reconstruct tool.**

4. **Click a place in the image where you want to clone the applied distortion.**

5. **Drag with the mouse in the unfrozen areas to apply that distortion.**

6. **To change the origin of the distortions being copied, click again anywhere in a distorted area to choose a new sampling point. Then resume dragging in unfrozen areas.**

   Your image takes on a distorted appearance like the one shown in Figure 3-7.

7. **When you finish, click OK to apply the distortion.**

**Book VII
Chapter 3**

Distorting with the
Liquify Command

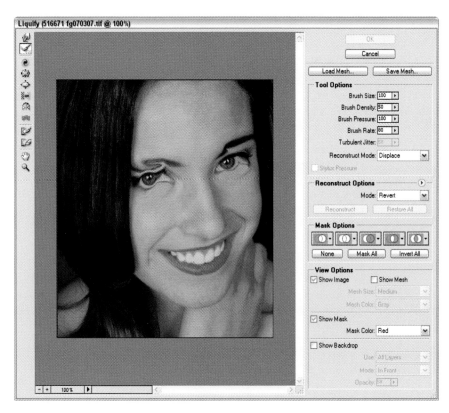

Figure 3-7: Undo your distortions by using one of the various flavors of the Reconstruct tool.

Book VIII
Retouching and Restoration

The 5th Wave   By Rich Tennant

"Why don't you try blurring the brimstone and then putting a nice glow effect around the hellfire."

Although taking the perfect photo is a great goal, it's one that is often just beyond our reach. Not to worry though, if you're a Photoshop owner. In this book, you find out what you need to know about correcting color in all its permutations — contrast, saturation, replacing, remapping, and so on. You find details on using the focus and toning tools to manually adjust the tones, textures, and colors in your images. I also give you details on how you can give your images a digital spa day with the two Healing Brushes and the Patch and Red Eye tools. You learn how to remove blemishes, wrinkles, and every other one of nature's imperfections. After you master these techniques, you'll be on your way to doing your own digital extreme makeovers.

Chapter 1: Enhancing Images with Adjustments

*P*hotoshop can provide magical transformations to images, making them unrecognizable from the original, but sometimes what you really want is simply to make an image look the same as the original — only better. Perhaps the colors are a little too warm, or the shadows a bit inky, but you don't want an image that looks more processed than a freeze-dried floral arrangement. You'd be happy to have everyone admire your image without a clue that you've made major corrections in Photoshop.

Welcome to the world of image enhancements. This chapter concentrates on the things you can do to correct color, contrast, hue, and color saturation. After you master the basic tools, you'll want to explore some even more sophisticated things you can do by using features such as Photoshop's Adjustment Layers (in Book V, Chapter 1), which let you dynamically apply your changes in remarkably flexible ways. But before you dive into image adjustments, you'll want to make sure and remove any flaws, such as dust, scratches, blemishes, and other nasty items, from your image. Check out Book VIII, Chapter 3 to find out about fixing imperfections.

Introducing the Histogram Palette

One of the first things you want to do before you make any color or tonal adjustments to your image is to take a good look at the quality and distribution of the tones throughout your image. I don't mean just eyeballing the composite image on your screen. I'm talking about getting inside your image and looking at its guts with the Histogram palette — and keeping it on-screen so you can see its constant feedback on your image adjustments.

A histogram displays the *tonal* range (also referred to as the key type) of an image, as shown in Figure 1-1. It shows how the pixels are distributed by graphing the number of pixels at each of the 256 brightness levels in an image. On this graph, pixels with the same brightness level are stacked in bars along a vertical axis. The higher the line from this axis, the greater the number of pixels at that brightness level. You can view the distribution for each color channel separately or for the composite image as a whole.

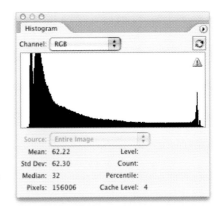

Figure 1-1: The Histogram palette displays how pixels are distributed at each of the 256 brightness levels.

From this graph, you can then determine whether the image contains enough detail in the shadow, midtone, and highlight areas. This information helps you determine what image adjustments you may need to make. The following steps walk you through the basics of using the palette and interpreting the information you find there:

1. **Choose Window⇨Histogram to bring up this graphical wonder.**

   By default, the histogram displays the tonal range of the whole image, in the composite image's color mode, such as RGB, CMYK, Grayscale, and so on. For details on color modes, see Book II, Chapter 1.

2. **Choose Expanded View or All Channels View from the Histogram palette pop-up menu:**

   Compact View, the default, displays only a histogram of the whole image (or your chosen selection or channel) with no controls or statistics.

   Expanded View shows a histogram with statistics and controls for choosing and viewing the histogram of individual channels. This view also has controls for refreshing the histogram to show uncached data, and choosing a selected layer (on the Source pop-up menu). Refer to Figure 1-1 to see this view.

All Channels View, shown in Figure 1-2, displays all the options of the Expanded View, plus shows the individual histograms for each color channel.

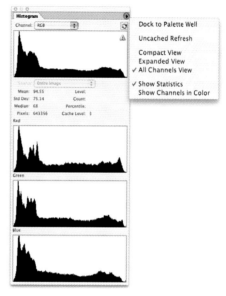

3. **Check the source shown in the Source drop-down list, and choose a different source if needed.**

For example, instead of seeing a histogram for an entire image, you can display the histogram of an individual channel, alpha channel, or spot channel. You can also choose to focus on the selected layer or an adjustment layer. Just select the layer in the Layers palette, and choose Selected Layer or Adjustment Composite from the Source drop-down list.

For more on adjustment layers, see Book V, Chapter 1.

Figure 1-2: The All Channels View displays individual histograms for each color channel, as well as the composite channel.

4. **If the Cached Data Warning icon appears in the upper-right corner of the histogram (refer to Figures 1-1 and 1-2), click the Uncached Refresh button just above the icon to see a histogram the reflects the image's current state.**

The warning lets you know that Photoshop is reading the histogram from cache instead of your image's current state. *Cache* is a reserved, high-speed section of your computer's memory. The image cache allows the histogram to display faster because it is calculating the histogram based on a representative sampling of the pixels in your image.

Unless it is really bogging down your workflow, I recommend viewing your image's histograms using uncached data.

5. **With the Histogram palette displaying the controls and data you want to check, examine the tonal range in the histogram. An image with good tonal range displays pixels in all areas. An image with poor tonal range has gaps in the histogram, as shown in Figure 1-3.**

The rest of this chapter explains ways you can correct color problems that you find.

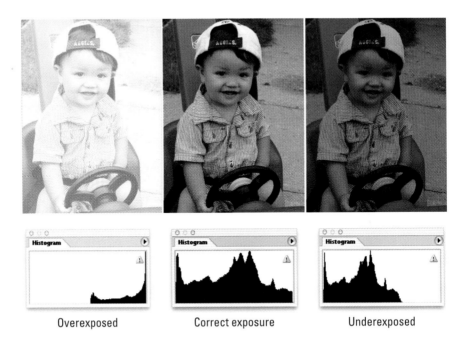

Overexposed   Correct exposure   Underexposed

Figure 1-3: Images with poor tonal range have noticeable gaps in the histogram.

6. If you're into numbers, check the statistics to evaluate your image as well.

See the nearby sidebar for details on interpreting these details.

Position your cursor within the histogram to see statistics about a specific value. Drag your cursor within the histogram to see statistics about a range of values (Photoshop highlights the range).

When you make adjustments based on problems you see in the histogram, be sure to select any Preview options in the dialog boxes of your image adjustments, such as Levels. That way, the Histogram palette displays both the original and adjusted histograms, as shown in Figure 1-4.

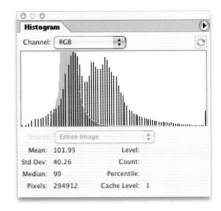

Figure 1-4: Select the Preview option in image adjustment dialog boxes in order to view both the original and adjusted histograms.

Understanding the histogram statistics

The Histogram palette gives you all kinds of statistics about the pixels in your image. Some of these statistics, such as Standard Deviation, may be for those who live in the land of Calculus. But you may be able to glean some useful information from some of the other statistics that can help you in your image-adjusting tasks. Here's a brief explanation of each statistic:

- **Mean:** Average intensity value

- **Standard Deviation:** How much the intensity values vary

- **Median:** Middle value of the intensity value range

- **Pixels:** Total number of pixels used to represent the histogram

- **Cache Level:** The current level of image cache used to calculate the histogram.

The next three statistics display a value only when you position or drag your cursor in the histogram. Each value corresponds only to the portion of the histogram under your cursor.

- **Level:** Intensity level

- **Count:** The total number of pixels corresponding to that intensity level

- **Percentile:** The number of cumulative pixels (in percentages) at or below that level, from 0% (left) to 100% (right)

Choosing Automatic Color Correctors

Photoshop has three automatic correction tools that can, in many cases, improve appearance with a simple click of a menu command: Auto Levels, Auto Color, and Auto Contrast. The upside of these controls is their ease of use: You don't need to know much about levels, color balance, or contrast to use the automatic correctors (that's why they're automatic). But you find out more about each of these characteristics later in this chapter, when I explain how to make adjustments manually.

The automatic controls' ease of use also comes with a downside: None is likely to do as good a job as you can do manually, and sometimes automatic controls even do more harm than good. If you have an average image (one that doesn't require a great deal of correction), you can try them out to see if they help, which I explain how to do in the following sections. If not, you'll want to apply the manual tools explained later in this chapter to produce the exact look you want.

Auto Levels

The Auto Levels command uses a bit of built-in Photoshop intelligence to automatically apply the Levels command (discussed later in the chapter) to your image.

Auto Levels works best with average images that could use a bit of tweaking but have lots of detail in the highlights (brightest portions of an image that contain detail), shadows (the darkest portions of an image that contain detail), and midtones.

Auto Levels defines the very lightest and darkest pixels of each of the three colors as white and black, respectively, and then arranges the midtone pixels in between. Along the way, as it balances the tones in your image, the command may reduce colorcasts or even introduce some. You can fine-tune the color manually after Auto Levels has done its work.

To try out the Auto Levels command, just choose Image⇨Adjustments⇨ Auto Levels, or press Shift+Ctrl+L (Shift+⌘+L on the Mac).

Although Auto Levels can improve your contrast, it may also produce an unwanted colorcast (a slight trace of color). If this happens, cancel the command and try the Auto Contrast command. If that still doesn't improve the contrast, try the Levels command instead. And even better, try your Levels adjustment on an adjustment layer. If it doesn't work, you can always delete it. No harm, no muss. For more on adjustment layers, see Book V, Chapter 1.

Auto Color

The Auto Color command adjusts both the color and contrast of an image, based on the shadows, midtones, and highlights it finds in the image. You usually use this command to remove a colorcast (or bias) or balance the color in your image. Sometimes using Auto Color can be helpful in correcting oversaturated or undersaturated colors as well. You can access the command by choosing Image⇨Adjustments⇨Auto Color, or by pressing Shift+Ctrl+B (Shift+⌘+B on the Mac).

Although Auto Color can do a good job on its own, you can customize the parameters it uses to make its color corrections in the Auto Color Corrections Options dialog box, which I discuss in "Setting Auto Color Correction Options," next in this chapter. See Figure 1-5 to see an image corrected using Auto Levels and Auto Color.

Auto Contrast

Like its manually operated cousin, the Brightness/Contrast command, the Auto Contrast command fiddles with the overall contrast and colors (if you're working with a color image) in an image, rather than making adjustments to each color individually. Auto Contrast converts the lightest and darkest pixels to white and black, respectively, making all highlights in the image lighter and all shadows darker without changing the color values. This command may not do as good a job at improving contrast, but it retains the color balance of an image and doesn't cause any nasty colorcasts.

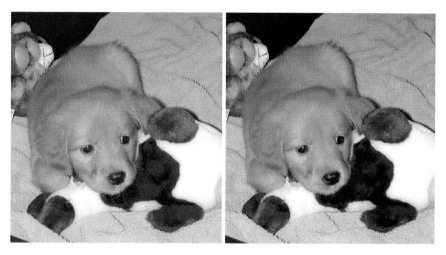

Figure 1-5: Using Auto Levels and Auto Color quickly improved the contrast and colors of this snapshot.

Try using this command on hazy images. If you find it overdoes the adjustment, try choosing Edit⇨Fade and bringing down the Opacity level to blend the adjusted image with your original image. For more on using the Fade command, see Book VII, Chapter 1.

To use Auto Contrast, choose Image⇨Adjustments⇨Auto Contrast, or press Alt+Shift+Ctrl+L (Option+Shift+⌘+L on the Mac).

Setting Auto Color Correction Options

You can use the Auto Color Correction Options dialog box to tweak exactly how Photoshop applies its Auto Levels, Auto Color, and Auto Contrast controls, as well as for the manually operated Levels and Curves commands. You can apply the settings only to a particular image-editing session, or save the settings as defaults for all your Photoshop work.

Click the Options button in either the Levels or Curves dialog boxes on the Edit⇨Adjustments menu. The options available in the Auto Color Correction dialog box are on the advanced side, and this set of tools is best used if you already understand manual color and contrast corrections. You'll want to brush up on your color theory, too, in Book II, Chapter 3.

**Book VIII
Chapter 1**

Enhancing Images
with Adjustments

To customize the automatic options, follow these steps:

1. **Open an image and choose Image➪Adjustments➪Levels or Ctrl+L (or ⌘+L on the Mac).**

   You can also use the Curves command by pressing Ctrl+M (or ⌘+M on the Mac).

2. **Click the Options button in the dialog box to access the Auto Color Correction Options dialog box, shown in Figure 1-6.**

3. **In the algorithm area, click the method you want Photoshop to use to adjust the tones. Your choices include**

   Figure 1-6: Once you know the basics, customize the auto correction options.

   - **Enhance Monochromatic Contrast:** This option applies the same changes to the Red, Green, and Blue channels, making brighter areas appear lighter and shadow areas appear darker, with no changes made to the colors. (This is the method used by the Auto Contrast command.)

   - **Enhance Per Channel Contrast:** This option individually adjusts the red, green, and blue colors so that each has its own best balance of light and dark tones, even if the color balance changes a bit. (This is the algorithm used by the Auto Levels command.)

   - **Find Dark & Light Colors:** This option locates the average lightest and darkest pixels, and uses their values to maximize the contrast of the image. (This is the algorithm used by the Auto Color command.)

4. **Select the Snap Neutral Midtones check box if you want Photoshop to base its gamma, or midtone, correction values around a neutral color located in the image.**

   The Auto Color command uses this option.

5. **In the Target Colors & Clipping area, enter a value in each of the clip text entry boxes.**

   Setting clipping values between 0.5 and 1% eliminates the too-dark and too-light pixels.

   These values adjust the amount of black and white pixels that Photoshop removes from the darkest and lightest areas of the image. This option is useful because every image includes some very dark pixels that contain no real image information, as well as some very light pixels that are completely washed out. Factoring in these two kinds of pixels when you adjust tonal values is a waste. By setting the clipping values at 0.5 to 1%, you leave these no-good pixels out of the picture, so to speak.

6. **Click the Shadows, Midtones, or Highlights swatch.**

   The Color Picker appears, allowing you to set a preferred value for the darkest, medium, and lightest areas.

7. **Select the Eyedropper tool from the Tools palette.**

8. **Move your mouse over the image and locate the dark, middle, or light tone you want to use. Click it when you find it.**

9. **Click OK to exit the Color Picker. Repeat Steps 6 through 8 for each of the three colors you want to change.**

   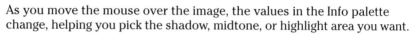

   As you move the mouse over the image, the values in the Info palette change, helping you pick the shadow, midtone, or highlight area you want.

10. **Back in the Auto Color Corrections dialog box, select the Save as Defaults option to store the settings you just made for subsequent use in any Photoshop session.**

    If you don't select the option, Photoshop applies the changes you made only to the current session.

11. **Click OK to exit the Auto Color Correction Options dialog box.**

    Your options are now customized.

Using Simple Color Correctors

Photoshop has several simple manual tools you can use to fix color in ways that are different from the Auto Levels, Auto Contrast, and Auto Color commands. They are the Brightness/Contrast control, Color Balance, Desaturate command, and the ever-popular Variations tool. In the following sections, you find out when to use (and when not to use) each of them.

Avoiding Brightness/Contrast

Beginners gravitate to the Brightness/Contrast control because it seems so intuitive to use. If your image is too dark, move a slider to make it lighter; if it's too light, move the same slider to make it darker. Right? You can fix an image that's overly contrasty or overly flat-looking the same way. Right?

Nope.

In practice, the Brightness/Contrast control is a bad choice for making an image darker or lighter, and for adding or reducing contrast. Its chief failing is that it applies all its changes equally to all areas of your image. For example, you may have a photo that has some shadows that need brightening up but all the middle tones and highlights are just fine. The Brightness slider doesn't take that into account.

Move the slider to the right, and, sure enough, your shadows become brighter. But so do your midtones and highlights, which you probably *don't* want. (See Figure 1-7.) The impulse is to try to fix the bright spots you create with the Brightness slider by fiddling with the Contrast slider. Before you know it, your image is a mess. Be careful.

Although some kinds of pictures you can help a little with the Brightness/Contrast control, you're better off using Levels and Curves, which can tailor your image enhancements to the exact portions of the image you want to work with.

Tweaking with the Color Balance controls

With an understanding of color theory (which I explain in Book II, Chapter 3), you can probably use the Color Balance controls to make some simple changes to the color in your image. The difficult part is in recognizing exactly which color you need to add or subtract from your image in the first place.

Figure 1-7: The Brightness and Contrast command applies its adjustment equally to all areas of your image resulting in undesirable lighter and darker areas.

Colors are subtler than you might think. For example, a slight colorcast toward cyan can look a lot like a slightly green or blue colorcast. Is your image too red, or does it have too much magenta?

Use the Variations command that I describe in the following section to figure out how to tell the various colorcasts apart. The Variations command displays each of the different types of colorcasts in an array so you can compare them.

To use the Color Balance controls, follow these steps:

1. **Choose Image⇨Adjustments⇨Color Balance, or press Ctrl+B (⌘+B on the Mac) to access the Color Balance dialog box.**

2. **Choose the Shadows, Midtones, or Highlights option to select the tones of an image you want to work on.**

   Usually, Midtones is the best choice, unless your image has a colorcast in the shadows or highlights that doesn't affect the overall image.

Resisting the urge to go nuts with sliders

If you're like me, you like clicking options, adjusting values, and sliding sliders back and forth. Thankfully, Photoshop is happy to oblige you with options to make you feel so powerful that you can take on any project.

Was that a sinister laugh I heard? Easy there, partner. I'm about to tell you something that will break your heart at first, but which you'll thank me for later: Always pick a single slider and stick with it when you're trying to compensate for any colorcast. Moving two sliders is a waste because you can accomplish anything you want with just one.

For example, if you move both the Cyan/Red and Magenta/Green sliders an equal amount to the left (adding cyan and magenta), you're actually just adding blue. Moving three sliders is even worse because, depending on the amount and direction of movement, the three are likely to at least partially cancel each other out or multiply the effects. However, if a cast is just in one area, such as the shadows, and a different colorcast in another area, it may be useful to do more than one adjustment.

That can sometimes happen when a subject is close to a colored wall or other object that reflects light onto, say, the shadowed side of a subject.

3. **Make sure you have selected the Preserve Luminosity option.**

   That way, Photoshop modifies the colors of the image, but the brightness and contrast of the tones stay the same.

4. **Move the Cyan/Red, Magenta/Green, or Yellow/Blue sliders to add or subtract color, watching the effects of your adjustments on the original image.**

   The Color Levels boxes show the amount of each color that Photoshop adds and subtracts. Figure 1-8 shows an example of subtracting yellow and green to improve the color in an image.

Figure 1-8: Use the Color Balance adjustment to remove colorcasts from an image.

The colors are arranged by their opposites on the color wheel. Dragging the slider toward Cyan adds cyan to the image and subtracts its complement, red. Dragging toward Green adds green to the image and subtracts magenta.

Fixing Lighting with Shadow/Highlight

The Shadow/Highlight adjustment is a great feature that offers a quick and easy method of correcting over- and underexposed areas in your image. This command works well with subjects photographed with the light source coming from behind (backlit) and consequently have a dark foreground. The adjustment is also helpful for bringing out the detail in harsh shadow areas in subjects shot in bright, overhead light, as shown in Figure 1-9.

Original   Adjusted with Shadow-Highlight

Figure 1-9: The Shadow/Highlight adjustment is a quick way to correct the lighting in your images.

To familiarize yourself with this tool, follow these steps:

1. **Open an image in dire need of repair and choose Image⇨Adjustments⇨ Shadow/Highlight. Note that you can now adjust CMYK images, as well as RGB.**

When the dialog box appears, the correction is automatically applied in your preview. If you don't see any change, make sure you've selected the Preview check box. The default settings in the dialog box are meant to correct backlit images, so they may or may not do the right correction job for you as they are set.

2. **Move the Amount slider to adjust the amount of correction for your Shadows and/or your Highlights.**

The higher the percentage, the lighter the shadows and the darker the highlights. You can also enter a value in the percentage text box.

3. **If you're happy with the results, you can click OK and be done with the adjustment. However, if you crave more control, click the Show More Options check box at the bottom of the dialog box.**

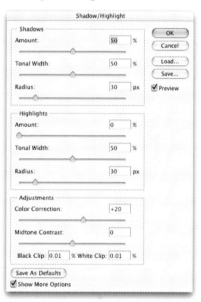

A whole array of sliders magically appears, as shown in Figure 1-10.

4. **Drag the Tonal Width slider to increase or decrease the range of tones adjusted in the shadows or highlights.**

The lower the percentage, the narrower the range of tones that are affected. For example, by using a very low percentage, only the darkest parts of the shadow or the lightest parts of the highlight are corrected. A higher percentage includes a wide range of tones, including midtone areas. The appropriate percentage to use varies among images, so start with the default setting of 50% and work in small increments from there.

Figure 1-10: The Shadow and Highlight dialog box offers controls for adjusting the amount of correction in your shadow, midtone, and highlight areas.

If, when lightening the shadow areas, you find the midtones and highlights getting too light as well, reduce the Tonal Width percentage of the Shadows. But if you start seeing artifacts, you have set the percentage too high.

5. **Drag the Radius slider to increase or decrease the number of pixels used in the local neighborhood.**

To fix lighting, this command lightens or darkens pixels according to the luminance (brightness) of the surrounding pixels, technically called a *local neighborhood*. The best local neighborhood size depends on the particular image, so play with this slider and view the results. If the Radius is too small, your main subject may lack contrast. Conversely, if it's too large, your background may be overly bright or dark. Adobe recommends setting the radius to approximately half the size of the main subject in your image. So if your subject takes up roughly 600 pixels, then set your radius to 300 pixels. Choose View⇨Show Rulers and set your Units to pixels in your Preferences.

6. **Make additional changes in the Adjustments area as needed:**

   - **Color Correction:** Available for color images only, this control enables you to correct the colors in *only* the adjusted portions of your image. Often when you increase or decrease the Amount of Shadows or Highlights, you bring out the "hidden" colors. Generally, higher Color Correction values make colors more saturated, whereas lower values make colors more desaturated.

   - **Brightness:** Available for grayscale images only. Move the slider left to darken and right to lighten.

   - **Midtone Contrast:** Move the slider left to reduce contrast and right to increase contrast. Just be aware that when you increase the Midtone Contrast, you may also undesirably darken shadow areas and lighten highlight areas.

   - **Black Clip/White Clip:** As I explain in "Setting Auto Color Correction Options" earlier in this chapter, setting clipping values between 0.5 and 1% eliminates the too-dark and too-light pixels.

7. **Click the Save As Defaults button to save and make your settings the defaults.**

   If you want to reset the setting back to the original defaults, press Shift and click the Save As Defaults button. You can save as many settings as you want. Click the Load button to reload a particular setting.

8. **Click OK to apply the adjustment and exit the dialog box.**

Adjusting Exposure

This new Exposure adjustment is primarily meant to correct tonal values of High Dynamic Range (HDR) images, which are 32-bit. (In layman's terms, the bits indicate how much information is stored about the color. The more bits, the better the color.) You can apply Exposure adjustments to 16-bit or even 8-bit images as well. This command works by using a linear color space, also know as gamma 1.0, rather than your image's color space, to make tonal adjustments. Figure 1-11 shows an example of an image helped by this new adjustment.

Figure 1-11: Fix tonal values with the new Exposure adjustment.

If you use the Exposure adjustment with 16-bit or 8-bit images, the slider's adjustments may be too drastic. Try pressing the Ctrl (⌘ on the Mac) key over the number field and dragging to access the scrubby sliders, which offers a less dramatic adjustment as you slide the control. Also keep an eye on your images. The Exposure adjustment sometimes clips, or loses, data on lower bit images.

To apply the Exposure adjustment, follow these steps:

1. **Choose Image⇨Adjustments⇨Exposure.**

2. **Adjust any of the following:**

   Exposure: This option adjusts mainly the highlights and pretty much ignores the darkest shadows.

   Offset: This option darkens the shadow and midtone values and leaves the highlights alone.

   Gamma: This option adjusts the image's gamma, or *midtone,* values.

3. **Use the Eyedroppers to adjust the luminance, or *brightness,* values in the image. Note that this is different from Levels where the eyedroppers adjust all the color channels:**

>>   **Set Black Point Eyedropper:** Sets the Offset. The pixel you click becomes the black point.
>>
>>   **Set White Point Eyedropper:** Sets the Exposure. The pixel you click becomes the white point.
>>
>>   **Midtone Eyedropper:** Sets the Exposure. The pixel you click becomes the middle gray value.
>
> 4. **Click the Save button to save the settings to apply later by clicking the Load button.**

Correcting Colorcast with Variations

Photoshop's Variations feature is a variation (so to speak) on the professional photographer's *ring around* (a set of color prints, each made with slightly different color balance) or *test strip* (a single print of an image made so that each section is shown using a different color balance). Both tools let you view several renditions of an image and choose the best one visually by comparing them. You might want to use Variations when you're unsure about exactly how the color is biased, and you want to compare several versions of an image to see exactly what the colorcast is.

Although not as sophisticated as some color correction techniques, the Variations feature has the advantage of being quick and simple, and it doesn't require a lot of training to use.

The Putting-It-Together project that follows walks you through the steps in using the Variations dialog box.

Putting It Together

Correcting Tinted, Faded Photos

In this Putting-It-Together project, I employ the Variations feature to restore the color in a scan of a color print originally made in 1965. Unfortunately, the years have not been kind to this photo; it has a slight, but annoying, greenish tinge that's a result of the magenta dye layer of the print fading. As the magenta fades, the other two color layers, cyan (blue) and yellow, appear proportionately stronger when compared to the magenta that remains and, as you may recall, cyan and yellow make green.

I plan to use the Variations feature of Photoshop to restore the magenta layer in this photo that's green with age.

To correct colorcast in an old photograph by using the Photoshop Variations feature, follow these steps:

1. **In Photoshop, open an old, fading photo that needs color correction.**

   In this case, I'm using an old, faded, greenish-looking picture, shown in the figure, but any colorcast works.

2. **Choose Image⇨Adjustments⇨Variations from the menu bar.**

   The Variations dialog box appears.

3. **Select the Show Clipping option to tell Photoshop to show any areas of the image that will be "overwhelmed" by the correction you're contemplating. That is, no new information is added.**

4. **If you want to use corrections you saved earlier, load those settings by clicking the Load button. Otherwise, skip to the next step.**

5. **Make adjustments with the Fine/Coarse slider.**

   In my example, the greenish picture needs some magenta, so I dragged the Fine/ Coarse slider to the left. I wanted to have a smaller increment of change as I adjust the color.

continued

continued

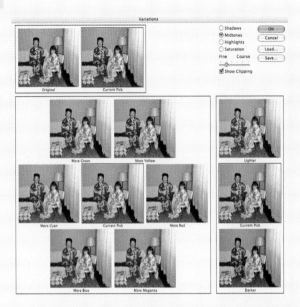

You can also click one of the tick marks to move the slider to that position. Photoshop doesn't allow setting the control to any of the intermediate positions between the marks.

6. **Make sure that you've selected the Midtones radio button, and then click the Preview window containing the amount of color you want to add.**

Watch the Current Pick thumbnail, which reflects the correction.

In my case, I need to click the More Magenta image.

Click several times if your initial application isn't enough or click other Preview windows to add other, additional colors.

Photoshop applies your corrections only to the middle tones of the image. In many cases, that's sufficient. However, sometimes shadows take on a particular hue, or the highlights may gain colorcasts of their own.

7. **Click the Highlights and/or Shadows radio buttons to add colors only to those parts of the photo.**

Variations isn't the best tool to make complex color corrections, so be careful.

You might be able to see a highlight color in the shadows under the pillow, most noticeable in the More Magenta preview. The highlight is the Clipping indicator showing that the change made by that Preview window is too much for that particular area of the picture. That is, Photoshop can't add any more magenta to the highlighted area without losing detail in the image.

8. **Click the Darker preview (in the lower-right corner of the dialog box) to make the photo a little darker.**

The Fine/Coarse slider has no effect on the amount of change Photoshop applies. Instead, you can click the Lighter or Darker preview several times to achieve the look you want.

In my case, only one click is necessary.

9. **Click the Saturation radio button to brighten the colors, and use the Fine/Coarse slider to control how much saturation you add or remove.**

The Variations feature also lets you adjust the purity of color, or *saturation,* of the colors in an image. Now only three previews appear: a less saturated version, the current choice, and a more saturated version. My photo was washed out, or under-saturated, so I clicked the More Saturation button.

10. **To save your settings, click the Save button, apply a name to the settings, and store them in the folder of your choice.**

I recommend saving your settings, especially if you're working on a copy of the original image and want to apply the same corrections later, or if you plan to correct several photos that have the same color defects.

Washing Out Color with Desaturate

Sometimes, you don't want any color at all. Photoshop's Desaturate command can wash all the color out of a layer or selection.

Just because you can do something doesn't mean you should. Use this command with caution because neither the Desaturate command nor Photoshop's Image⇨Mode⇨Grayscale command is the best technique for converting a color image to monochrome. Simply removing the color can produce an image that appears to be too low in contrast, which is another kettle of fish altogether. See Book II, Chapter 2 for a better way to create grayscale images.

However, if you simply want to eliminate the color from a layer or selection image quickly, the Desaturate command does the job. To apply it, select the area you want to operate on and choose Image⇨Adjustments⇨Desaturate, or press Shift+Ctrl+U (Shift+⌘+U on the Mac).

Using the Saturation control in the Hue/Saturation command gives you better control over the degree of desaturation you desire, while leaving the image looking richer. I show you how to play with saturation using the Hue/Saturation controls later in this chapter.

Working with Professional Color Correctors

The simple color correctors I discuss earlier in this chapter usually aren't enough to provide thorough color correction if you have a really problematic image on your hands. Fortunately, Photoshop has the kind of professional tools needed to make sophisticated color corrections required for higher end color printing. You don't have to be a pro to use the Levels or Curves commands, nor to work with the Hue/Saturation controls. But you'll feel like one after you master these powerful tools.

Leveling for better contrast

If you want to adjust tonal values of images (the brightness or darkness of tones) or correct colors (the relationship between the colors), the Levels command is the tool for you. It offers more control than the Auto Levels command, which I discuss earlier in this chapter. The Levels command is also a much more sophisticated tool than the Brightness/Contrast control because you can work with individual tones, brightening or darkening individual tones as you want, and you have a great deal more information to help you make your choices.

Open the Levels dialog box, shown in Figure 1-12, by pressing Ctrl+L (⌘+L on the Mac) or selecting Image⇨ Adjustments⇨Levels. The graph shown in the center of the dialog box is a histogram, which I described in detail in the first section of this chapter. You can use the dialog box, histogram and all, for evaluating and adjusting levels in the following ways:

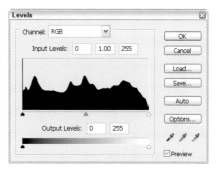

Figure 1-12: The Levels dialog box offers controls for adjusting the contrast in your image.

✓ **Visually check the distribution of dark, midtone, and light values.** I explain how to read histograms in "Introducing the Histogram Palette" at the beginning of this chapter.

✓ **View separate histograms for each channel.** The default histogram displays information for the entire image. To see the histogram of an individual channel, choose it from the Channel pop-up menu. For an RGB image, you can view the Red, Green, and Blue channels. For a CMYK image you can view the Cyan, Magenta, Yellow, and Black channels. You can view the histograms of each channel simultaneously by using the Histogram palette.

✓ **Adjust the black and white points based on the histogram.** The three triangles at the bottom of the histogram, in black, gray, and white, represent the shadow on the left, midtone in the middle, and highlight on the right. Even though they're located where they are, many images have no black tones at the far-left side of the scale, or no white tones at the far-right side.

One of the simplest corrections you can do is to move the black and white sliders so that they actually correspond to the pixels containing dark and light tones. Simply slide the black triangle so that it corresponds to the first true black pixels in the image (the beginning of the histogram), and then move the white triangle to align it with the lightest pixels (the end of the histogram). That ensures that Photoshop doesn't waste tones by allocating them to areas of the image that actually have no image detail. See Figure 1-13 to see an example of an image that was rescued by the use of the Levels adjustment.

✓ **See exactly what happens when you use the Auto Levels command.** When you click the Auto button, which applies the same adjustments as the Auto Levels command discussed earlier in this chapter, Photoshop applies its own suggested changes, resetting the white point and the black point, and redistributing the gray values of the pixels in between. Afterward, the histogram shows that the pixels fill the complete range from white to black.

TIP

**Book VIII
Chapter 1**

**Enhancing Images
with Adjustments**

Figure 1-13: Applying the Levels command to a dark photo dramatically improves the contrast.

Setting black and white points manually

For more control, you can use the Eyedropper tools in the Levels dialog box to set the black and white points. Just follow these steps:

1. **Open an image and choose Image⇨Adjustments⇨Levels.**

   Make sure you have the Info palette open (Window⇨Info), and display the HSB and RGB color modes. (To do this, choose Palette Options from the Info palette pop-up menu and choose HSB and RGB from the Color Readout pop-up menus.) See Book II, Chapters 2 and 3 for more on color modes.

   Remember that you can also apply certain adjustments, such as Levels, via an adjustment layer rather than directly to the image itself. Adjustment layers provide more editing flexibility if you later decide you need to tweak the adjustment. For more on adjustment layers, see Book V, Chapter 1.

2. **Select the White Eyedropper tool and move it around the image while watching the Info palette.**

3. **Look for the lightest white in the image, which may be anywhere from 90 to 100%. Select that point by clicking.**

4. **Using the Black Eyedropper tool, repeat the process outlined in Steps 2 and 3 to select the darkest black in the image.**

   The combination of these two choices redistributes the pixels from pure white to pure black.

   You can also reset the white and black points by moving the position of the white and black triangles on the input sliders (just under the histogram). Or, you can enter numbers in the Input Levels boxes. The three boxes represent the black, gray, and white triangles, respectively. Use the numbers 0 to 255 in the white and black boxes.

5. **Use the Gray Eyedropper tool to remove any colorcasts. Select a neutral gray portion of your image, one in which the Info palette shows equal values of red, green, and blue.**

   Note that the Gray Eyedropper tool is not available when working on grayscale images.

   Although you generally make changes to the entire document by using the RGB channel, you can apply changes to any one of an image's component color channels by selecting the specific channel with the Channel drop-down menu at the top of the Levels dialog box (refer to Figure 1-12). You can also make adjustments to just selected areas. This can be helpful when one area of your image needs adjusting, while others don't. See Book III, Chapter 1 for details on making selections.

6. **Adjust the output sliders at the very bottom of the Levels dialog box.**

   Moving the black triangle to the right reduces the contrast in the shadows and lightens the image. Moving the white triangle to the left reduces the contrast in the highlights and darkens the image.

7. **Adjust the midtones with the gray triangle slider (it appears between the black and white input sliders, just under the histogram).**

   The values you're adjusting are called the *gamma* values.

   Dragging this triangle to the left lightens the midtones. Dragging it to the right darkens the midtones while leaving the highlights and shadows alone. You can also move the gray triangle by entering numbers from 9.99 to 0.1 in the center option box. The default value, 1.0, lies exactly in the middle of the range.

   If you're working with a series of similar images (such as a bunch of video captures), you can save the settings to reuse them later.

8. **Click the Save button to store your settings.**

   This step saves the settings, but doesn't apply them. Just click the Load button to retrieve them.

9. **Click OK to apply your settings and exit the dialog box.**

Adjusting curves for hard-to-correct photos

The Curves command is one of the most advanced Photoshop correction tools available, offering sophisticated control over the brightness, contrast, and midtone *(gamma)* levels in an image; I'm talking about control that is far beyond that offered by the Levels and Brightness/Contrast dialog boxes. This section introduces you to the functions of the Curves command, but you'll want to practice using it a great deal to gain the kind of experience you need to work with it effectively.

Whereas the Brightness/Contrast dialog box lets you change an image globally, and the Levels command allows you to change the shadows, highlights, and midtones separately, Curves goes far beyond either of those settings. It lets you change pixel values at any point along the brightness level, giving you 256 locations at which you can make corrections. You can work with the combined Red, Green, and Blue color channels (or CMYK channels) or apply your changes to the individual colors. Often images that just can't be fixed to your satisfaction with Levels can be helped with the Curves adjustment, as shown in Figure 1-14.

Figure 1-14: The Curves adjustment offers more control and sophistication than many other color correction tools.

Working with the Curves dialog box

You access the Curves dialog box by choosing Image➪Adjustment➪Curves or by pressing Ctrl+M (⌘+M on the Mac). The following tips help you to begin understanding how to interpret the information and use the tools in this dialog box:

✔ The horizontal axis maps the brightness values as they are before image correction.

✔ The vertical axis maps the brightness values after correction.

Each axis represents a continuum of 256 levels, divided into four parts by finely dotted lines. In the default mode, the lower-left-hand corner represents 0,0 (pure black) and the upper-right-hand corner is 255,255 (pure white). By default, the dialog box shows a 4 x 4 grid; Alt+click (Option+click on the Mac) inside the grid to toggle it to a 10 x 10 grid.

✔ Whenever you open the Curves dialog box, the graph begins as a straight line. Unless you make changes, the input is exactly the same as the output, a direct 1:1 correlation.

✔ When you use the Eyedropper tool from the Tools palette to click in the image, a circle appears on the graph to show you the value of the pixel being sampled. At the bottom of the Curves dialog box, you can read the pixel's input and output values.

✔ When you click the Auto button, the darkest pixels in the image (the deep shadows) are reset to black and the lightest areas are set to white. As with the Levels dialog box, this option is the easiest way to make a correction.

✔ The Curves dialog box has black, white, and gray Eyedropper tools you can use to set the black, white, and midtone points, just as you can with Levels.

Adjusting curves

If you click at any point on the curve other than the endpoints, Photoshop adds a control point that shows your position. You can remove a control point by dragging it downward until it is completely off the graph, or by dragging it on top of the next point up or down from it on the graph.

Experiment with the curves to see how they affect the image. For example:

✔ Flattening a curve lowers contrast.

✔ A gently sloped S-shaped curve increases contrast, especially in the highlight and shadow areas. Using a curve like this also helps to define the midtones.

✔ For ultimate control, Photoshop lets you draw a curve with the precise shape you'd like, creating an arbitrary curve or map. Click the Pencil tool in the dialog box, and then draw peaks and valleys in the Curves dialog box. Watch the changes in your original image.

**Book VIII
Chapter 1**

**Enhancing Images
with Adjustments**

Arbitrary maps, such as the one shown in Figure 1-15, create distinctive solarization color effects as Photoshop warps the colors of your image. They are fun to play with, maybe useful now and then, but not nearly as practical as your nice S curves.

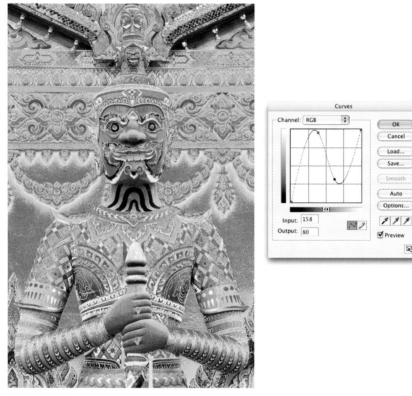

Corbis Digital Stock

Figure 1-15: Going crazy with the Curves maps can result in a solarization-like effect.

Getting colorful with Hue/Saturation

Photoshop's Hue/Saturation controls let you adjust colors based on their hue, saturation, and lightness. The Hue/Saturation dialog box doesn't work with the Red, Green, and Blue (or Cyan, Magenta, Yellow, and Black) channels of an image. Instead, it operates on the different colors, or hues. You can select all the colors (Master) from the Edit pop-up menu, or choose one color to modify.

Three sliders are in the Hue/Saturation dialog box. (See Figure 1-16.)

- **Hue:** Shifts all the colors clockwise or counterclockwise around the color wheel, depending on the direction you move it. I moved my Hue slider to the left to turn my owls green and purple.

- **Saturation:** Increases or decreases the richness of the colors in an image. I moved my Saturation slider to the right to increase the saturation on my owls and make them almost glow.

- **Lightness:** Modifies the brightness values.

ImageState

Figure 1-16: The Hue/Saturation command enables you to adjust colors based on their hue (color), saturation (intensity), or lightness (brightness).

You can adjust any of these values by moving the sliders and watching the results in the image window. The top color bar at the bottom of the dialog box represents the colors in their order on the color wheel before you made any adjustment. The lower color bar shows how the modifications you make affect the colors.

When you select an individual color to adjust, sliders appear between the color bars so that you can define the range of color to be adjusted. You can select, add, or subtract colors from the range by choosing one of the Eyedropper tools and clicking in the image.

The Hue/Saturation dialog box also lets you colorize images, a useful option for creating sepia colored images, as in the Putting-It-Together project that follows.

Using the Colorize option

Use the Colorize option in the Hue/Saturation dialog box to change the color of any selected area to a new, solid color. This is unlike the Hue slider, which changes only individual pixels based on their present color values. Just follow these steps:

1. **Open an image and access the Hue/Saturation dialog box by choosing Image⇨Adjustments⇨Hue/ Saturation, or pressing Ctrl+U (or ⌘+U on the Mac).**

2. **Select the Colorize option.**

3. **Drag the Hue slider in either direction to change a color.**

   Photoshop doesn't colorize pure white pixels and pure black pixels because colorization affects only gray pixels (from a brightness value 1 to 254).

Putting It Together

Making a New Photo Look Old

Black-and-white photography is a newer phenomenon than you might think. Daguerreo-types and other early photographs frequently had a brownish or bluish tone to them. You can create sepia-toned masterpieces of your own. (Or, if you like, you can create a tint in green, blue, or another shade.) Toned pictures can create a mood or otherwise transform a mundane photo into something interesting.

In this Putting-It-Together project, I chose a recent photo of a boy and his donkey in Java, Indonesia. Without any nasty anachronisms, such as automobiles or satellite dishes, aging this image is easy.

Corbis Digital Stock

The Photoshop Hue/Saturation feature is all you need to perform this time-traveling magic. Just follow these easy steps:

1. **Open the image in Photoshop and convert it to black and white by choosing Image⇨Adjustments⇨Desaturate.**

   You choose this command instead of the Image⇨Mode⇨Grayscale command to convert the photo to black and white because you're going to continue to work with it as a color image — the image just won't have colors until you add them.

2. **Choose Image⇨Adjustments⇨Hue/ Saturation.**

   The Hue/Saturation dialog box appears.

3. **Select the Colorize check box so that you can add color to the image.**

4. **Adjust the Hue slider to produce the tone you're looking for.**

   To produce a rich sepia tone, move the Hue slider to the far left. If you prefer green or blue or some other shade, you can experiment with this slider to get the exact color you want.

**Book VIII
Chapter 1**

**Enhancing Images
with Adjustments**

continued

continued

5. **Adjust the Saturation slider to modify the richness of the color.**

I used a setting of 25, as shown in the figure. As you move the slider to the right, the color becomes more pure, until you end up with a striking red at the far-right position.

6. **Adjust the Lightness slider to lighten or darken the photo, depending on your mood.**

Generally, you want to leave the Lightness slider at the default middle position. To create a darker, moodier picture, move it to the left; to produce a more faded look, move it to the right.

7. **When you're satisfied with your changes, click OK.**

Now my photo looks like a vintage postcard.

Corbis Digital Stock

You can create similar effects by using the Photoshop Duotones, Tritones, and Quadtones feature. See Book II, Chapter 2 for more information on these tools.

Matching Color Between Documents

The Match Color command enables you to match colors in a single image or between images — a source image and a target image. But it doesn't stop there. You can also match colors between layers or even selections. You can further refine your correction by adjusting the luminance and color intensity (saturation).

This command is great for getting rid of colorcasts in a single image. It also works wonders for matching the color of the lighting between two images or layers — for example, if you want to realistically composite an image shot under fluorescent lighting and one shot in natural light.

The Match Color command works only with RGB images, but be sure and apply this command before you perform any color conversions.

Here is how to use the Match Color command to match one image with another:

1. **Open the two images you want to match.**

   If you want, you can make selections in one or both of those images — for example, if you are creating a composite image from two separate images and want to match the lighting color or skin tones. Without selections, the overall target image is matched to the source image. In my example in Figure 1-17, I selected an image taken outdoors in natural light and one taken inside under fluorescent lights, which gives it a nasty green colorcast. I want to eventually use the girl in each image in a composite and therefore want to try to match the skin tones.

2. **Make sure your target image (the one that needs to be corrected) is the active file and choose Image⇨Adjustments⇨Match Color.**

   If you are using a specific layer in your target image, select that layer prior to choosing the command. Make sure you have selected the Preview option so you can view your adjustments on the fly.

3. **In the Match Color dialog box, shown in Figure 1-18, choose your source image from the Source pop-up menu in the Image Statistics area. Select None if you're working with only one image (the source image and target image are the same).**

   Remember, the source image contains the colors you want to match in the target image.

4. **If you are using a particular layer in your source image, choose it from the Layer pop-up menu. You can also choose the Merged option to match the colors from all the layers.**

Figure 1-17: The Match Color command lets you match colors within a single image or between two images.

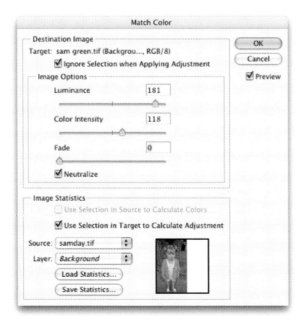

Figure 1-18: Choose your Target and Source images in the Match Color dialog box.

5. **If you have selections in your images, you can select one of the following options:**

   • If you have a selection in your source image but want to match the colors from the whole image, choose the Ignore Selection When Applying Adjustment option. It also applies the correction to the whole target image as well.

   • On the other hand, choose the Use Selection in Source to Calculate Colors option if you want to use the colors in the selection in the source image. Deselect this option to ignore the selection in the source image and match the colors from the entire source image.

   • Select the Use Selection in Target to Calculate Adjustment option if you want to adjust the color only in the selection in your target image.

6. **Select the Neutralize option to remove any colorcasts in the target image.**

   When using the Match Color command, your cursor becomes the Eyedropper tool. This allows you to sample colors on your images and look at the color values in the Info palette while making your adjustments.

7. **Adjust the luminance by moving the slider or entering a value.**

   A higher value increases the brightness in the target image. A lower value decreases brightness.

8. **Adjust the color intensity of your target image.**

   A higher value increases the color saturation, while a lower value decreases the saturation. Moving the slider to 1 desaturates the image to grayscale.

9. **Use the Fade option to control the amount of adjustment that is applied to the target image, moving the slider to the right to reduce the amount.**

10. **If you want to save your settings to use on other images, click the Save Statistics button. Name the file and specify the location.**

    To reload the settings later, click the Load Statistics button and navigate to the file.

11. **Click OK to apply the adjustment and exit the dialog box.**

My image, shown in Figure 1-19, has less of that nasty green cast from the fluorescent lighting.

Figure 1-19: These tones are a better match with the target image.

Switching Colors with Replace Color

The Replace Color command creates interesting creative effects by allowing you to substitute one set of colors for another. It does this by building a mask using colors you select and then replacing the selected colors with others that you specify. You can adjust hue, saturation, and lightness of the masked colors.

Just follow these steps:

1. **Choose Image⊅Adjustments⊅ Replace Color.**

   The Replace Color dialog box appears, as shown in Figure 1-20.

2. **Choose either Selection or Image.**

   • **Selection** shows the mask in the Preview window. The masked area is black, semi-transparent areas are shades of gray, and unmasked areas are white.

   For details on masks, see Book VI, Chapter 2.

   • **Image** shows the full image itself in the Preview window. Use this option if you zoomed in on the original image to select colors more easily, but you still want to be able to see the full image in the preview.

3. **Click the colors you want to select.**

   You can click either the image or the Preview window.

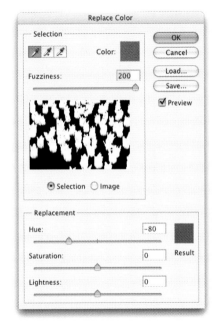

Corbis Digital Stock

Figure 1-20: The Replace Color adjustment enables you to substitute one color for another.

4. **Press the Shift key and click or use the plus (+) Eyedropper tool to add more colors.**

5. **Press the Alt key (Option key on the Mac) or use the minus (–) Eyedropper tool to remove colors.**

6. **To add colors similar to the ones you select, use the Fuzziness slider to refine your selection, adding or subtracting from the selection based on the tolerance value.**

7. **Move the Hue, Saturation, and Lightness sliders to change them to new values.**

8. **When you like the result, click OK to apply the settings.**

Figure 1-21 shows my images before and after replacing color.

Corbis Digital Stock

Figure 1-21: Don't like the color of your flowers? Use the Replace Color command to change it.

Increasing and Decreasing Color

Increasing and decreasing color is a popular Photoshop activity, so having more than one way to do it is no surprise. In addition to the Selective Color command, which I describe in the following section, several other commands are a lot easier to understand — and a lot easier to use.

This is the place to start reading if you want to know all about the Gradient Maps command, and the various color mapper tools, all of which are designed to change the arrangement of the colors in your photos in ways that *don't* produce realistic-looking images. Images that have been color-mapped are certainly interesting to look at.

Using the Selective Color command

The Selective Color command is chiefly of use for manipulating the amount of process colors (that is, cyan, magenta, yellow, and black) used in printing an image. In the Selective Color dialog box, choose the color you want to edit from the Colors pop-up menu. Adjust the CMYK sliders to modify the selected color.

With the Relative method selected, you can add or subtract color. For example, if a pixel is 30 percent cyan and you add 20 percent cyan, Photoshop adds 6 percent cyan to the pixel (20 percent of 30 percent is 6 percent).

With the Absolute method selected, Photoshop bases the amount of change on the exact value you enter. For example, if a pixel is 30 percent cyan and you add 20 percent cyan, the pixel changes to a total of 50 percent cyan.

Using gradient maps

Gradient maps convert your image to grayscale, and then replace the range of black, gray, and white tones with a gradient of your choice, in effect colorizing your image — often in startling ways.

Photoshop maps the lightest tones of your image to one color in the gradient and changes the darkest tones to the other color of the gradient (assuming you're using just two colors for the gradient). Photoshop changes all the formerly gray tones to an intermediate color between the two. When you use multiple colors or fancy gradients, the image really gets interesting. Just follow these steps to try out this feature:

1. **Open an image and access the gradient map, shown in Figure 1-22, by choosing Image⇨ Adjustments⇨Gradient Map.**

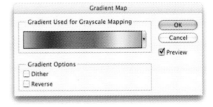

2. **Choose the gradient you want from the gradient list.**

   This list is exactly like the one offered with the Gradient tool. You can edit the gradient used for your map exactly as you do for the

Figure 1-22: A gradient map replaces the tones in your images with a gradient.

   Gradient tool. For more information on choosing gradients, see Book IV, Chapter 2.

3. **Choose either or both of these options:**

   • **Dither** adds random noise to smooth out the gradient and reduces banding.

   • **Reverse** changes the direction of the gradient. Use the Reverse option to create a negative quickly.

4. **Click OK to apply the gradient map.**

   If the effect is a little too intense for your taste, try fading the gradient map (Edit⇨Fade Gradient Mask) and then adjusting the opacity percentage and/or applying a different blend mode.

Adding color with photo filters

Photographers will appreciate the Photo Filter command, which is reminiscent of the analog method of placing a colored filter in front of a camera lens to tweak the color balance and color temperature of the light coming through the lens. This is a great way to make an image appear cooler or warmer. Have a portrait where your subject appears a little too bluish? Apply a Warming filter and bring some rosiness back into his or her cheeks. You can also apply a colored filter to add a tint of color to your image. Figure 1-23 shows how I warmed up an overly cool image.

Corbis Digital Stock

Figure 1-23: Photo Filters adjust the color balance and color temperature of an image.

To apply the Photo Filter adjustment, follow these steps:

1. **Open your image and choose Image⇨Adjustments⇨Photo Filter to apply the filter to the entire image.**

   If you want to apply the filter to one or more layers, choose Layer⇨ New Adjustment Layer⇨Photo Filter.

2. **Make sure you have the Preview option selected so you can view the results.**

3. **In the dialog box, select the Filter radio button to choose a preset filter from the Filter drop-down list, or select the Color radio button to select a custom color for your filter.**

   See Table 1-1 for a brief description of the filters on the Filter drop-down list.

   If you opt for the custom color, click the swatch to choose a color from the Color Picker.

4. **Select the Preserve Luminosity check box if you don't want the filter to darken your image. Note that some photo pros advocate not checking this option.**

5. **Adjust the Density slider to control the amount of color applied to your image.**

   A higher value provides a stronger adjustment. Use the Density control with restraint. Anything above 50% produces a severe effect.

6. **Click OK to apply the adjustment and exit the dialog box.**

Table 1-1	Photo Filters
Name	*Effect of Filters*
Warming filter (85) and Cooling filter (80)	Adjusts the white balance in an image. A photo shot in a higher color temperature of light makes an image blue. Warming Filter (85) makes the colors warmer, more yellow. Similarly, an image shot in light of a lower color temperature benefits from the Cooling Filter (80), which makes the colors more blue.
Warming filter (81) and Cooling filter (82)	Similar to the preceding filters but for minor adjustments.
Colors	These filters adjust the hue of an image. You can choose a color to get rid of a colorcast. For example, if your image is too green, choose magenta. If it is too blue, choose yellow. You can also choose a color to apply a special effect.

Playing with the color mappers

Photoshop also includes some fun-filled color mapping commands, so-called because they change the colors of your image in specific ways. Two of them, Invert and Equalize, don't even have any options. They're akin to single-step filters that you apply and forget. (I cover filters in Book VII.) I show all the color mappers in Figure 1-24.

Invert

Invert simply reverses all the colors and tones in your image, creating a negative image. Photoshop changes black tones to white; white tones to black; dark grays to light grays; and colors to their complements. For example, a light yellow color becomes a dark blue, and so forth.

Some folks mistakenly think they can use this command to create a positive (or color correct) version of a scanned color negative. It isn't so simple because color negatives have an orange mask overlaying the color information. To really do that correctly requires a lot of color correcting and tweaking. If you have sophisticated scanning software you may have a command that does the conversion. A couple third-party Photoshop filters also do the duty. But to do it manually requires a lot of color correcting and tweaking. Something you may not want to try at home!

Invert Equalize Threshold Posterize

Corbis Digital Stock

Figure 1-24: The Color Mappers change the colors in your image in specific ways, such as reversing colors or converting your image to black and white.

Equalize

This command locates the lightest and darkest pixels in an image, defines them as white and black, respectively, and then changes all the other pixels in between to divide the grayscale values evenly. Depending on your image, this process may increase contrast or otherwise alter the color and tones as the values are evenly distributed.

Threshold

Threshold converts your image to black and white, with all pixels that are brighter than a value you specify represented as white, and all pixels that are darker than that value as black. You can change the threshold level to achieve different high-contrast effects.

Posterize

This color mapper creates an interesting graphic effect by reducing the number of colors in your image to a value you specify, from 4 to 255. Low values provide distinct poster-like effects. As you increase the number of color levels, the image begins to look either more normal, or a bit like a bad conversion to Indexed Color.

Putting It Together

Cleaning Up a Line Art Scan

Line art consists of (you guessed it!) lines, rather than the continuous tones of a photograph or painting. Line art can consist of outlines, shapes (like you'd find in a bar chart), patterns (like the fills in the bar chart), or freehand drawings like those produced in pen or pencil.

What you don't want to see when you scan line art is an extra color: the background color of the paper. Often the paper appears as a dull gray, and you may see other artifacts you don't want, such as wrinkles or spots in the paper.

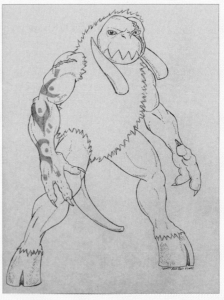

Luckily, Photoshop has a handy Threshold command that you can use to determine which tones appear as black and which are dropped altogether. You end up with a nice black-and-white line art image with all the intermediate tones removed.

Follow these instructions to clean up a piece of line art (to test-drive these steps, download my example image from this book's Web site):

1. **Open a line drawing in Photoshop, as shown in the figure.**

Christopher Blair

2. **Choose Image⇨Adjustments⇨Threshold from the menu bar.**

The Threshold dialog box includes a chart called a *histogram*. The histogram includes a series of vertical lines showing how many of an image's tones are represented by a certain brightness level. You can see that a relatively small number of tones are represented by a brightness value of 93, marked by the gray triangle at the bottom of the histogram. Many more tones are used at the other levels, forming a sloping mountain in the chart.

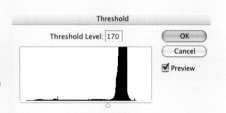

3. **Move the slider to the right until the tones you want to appear in the image are shown.**

   The more you move the slider to the right, the darker the image gets. A threshold of about 170 seems about right for this image.

4. **Click OK to apply the modification.**

   Some small artifacts may remain in your image, as shown in the figure. These are spots and parts of wrinkles that are darker than the page background, approaching the darkness of the line art itself.

5. **To clean up these slight defects, use the Eraser tool.**

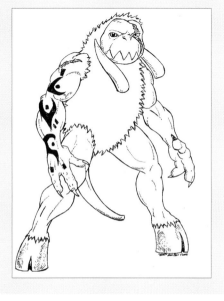

Chapter 2: Repairing with the Focus and Toning Tools

In This Chapter

- ✏ **Dodging and burning**
- ✏ **Manipulating color with the Sponge tool**
- ✏ **Smudging rough spots smooth**
- ✏ **Blurring for effect**
- ✏ **Focusing on sharpness**

*O*ne of the coolest things about Photoshop is the way it offers several tools to accomplish similar end results, but with distinctly individualized looks. The focus and toning tools in Photoshop are examples of this. The focus tools blur, sharpen, and smudge your image in much the same way as the Blur, Sharpen, and Liquify filters (which I cover in Book VII). The toning tools lighten, darken, and change the richness of the color in your image a bit like commands such as Levels, Curves, and Hue/Saturation (covered in Book VIII, Chapter 1).

But where their counterparts operate only on layers or selections, the focus and toning tools let you *paint* the effects you want directly onto your image. Using these tools, you can often create much more subtle, natural looks tailored to meet your exact needs, as I explain in this chapter.

As you work through this chapter, keep in mind all the tips I give you in Book IV, Chapter 1 about using brushes. Most of that information applies to the brush-like focus and toning tools, as well.

Lightening and Darkening with Dodge and Burn Tools

Dodging and burning originated in the darkroom, where photographers salvage negatives containing areas that are too dark or too light by adding or subtracting a bit of exposure as an enlarger makes prints.

An enlarger makes a print by projecting an image of a negative onto a piece of photosensitive paper. During the exposure, the darkroom worker can reduce the amount of light falling onto the paper by placing some object (often a disk shape of cardboard or metal impaled on a piece of wire) in the light-path to *dodge* part of the image. The worker can *burn* other parts of an image by exposing only a small portion through an opening, such as the fingers in a cupped pair of hands. The Dodge and Burn tools in Photoshop adopt their icons from the most popular real-world tools used to achieve these effects in the darkroom.

However, the Photoshop counterparts are a great deal more flexible. For example, the worker in a darkroom varies the size of the dodging or burning tool by moving it up or down in the light path. Unfortunately, the closer the real-world tool gets to the paper, the sharper it appears, forcing the darkroom worker to move the tool more rapidly and frequently to blur the edges of the lighten or darken effects. With the Photoshop Dodge and Burn tools, you can set the size of the tool and its softness independently simply by selecting a brush of the size and hardness or softness you require.

You can also set the Photoshop tools to operate primarily on shadows, midtones, and highlights. You can adjust the degree of lightening and darkening applied by specifying an exposure, too.

The Dodge and Burn tools can be very effective tools, but you can't add detail that isn't there. Keep the following in mind:

- When you lighten very dark shadows that contain little detail, you end up with grayish shadows.
- Darkening very light areas that are completely washed out won't look very good either.

In either case, you want to use the Dodge and Burn tools in moderation, and work only with small areas. To dodge or burn a portion of an image, just follow these steps:

1. **Open an image with under- or overexposed areas and choose the Dodge or Burn tool from the Tools palette.**

   Press the O key to choose the active toning tool, or press Shift+O to cycle through the available toning tools until the one you want is active.

2. **Select a brush from the Brushes palette.**

   Larger, softer brushes spread the dodging and burning effect over a larger area, making blending with the surrounding area easier.

   You can choose the same brushes available with any of the painting tools, including preset brushes from your library.

3. From the Range options, select Shadows, Midtones, or Highlights.

Use Shadows to lighten or darken detail in the darker areas of your image, Midtones to adjust the tones of average darkness, and Highlights to make the brightest areas even lighter or, more frequently, darker.

In Figure 2-1, the original image (left) had mostly dark areas, so I dodged the shadows. I also gave a couple swipes to the lighter areas with the Burn tool.

Figure 2-1: The Dodge and Burn tools are effective when touching up smaller dark and light areas.

4. Choose the amount of the effect to apply with each stroke using the Exposure slider or text box.

5. Paint over the areas you want to lighten or darken with the toning brush, gradually building up the desired effect.

Using a soft-edged brush is often best when dodging and burning. You want to create a realistic, un-retouched appearance.

The Exposure control is similar to the Opacity control offered by other painting tools, but it's especially important with dodging and burning.

 Using a low value is best (I often work with 10% exposure or less) so you can carefully paint in the lightening or darkening you want.

High exposure values work too quickly and produce unnatural-looking, obviously dodged or burned areas in your images.

 For an even softer, more gradual effect, click the Airbrush option on the Options bar.

6. **If you go too far, press Ctrl+Z (⌘+Z on the Mac) to reverse the stroke.**

7. **When you finish, choose File⇨Save to store the image.**

Turning Down the Color with the Sponge Tool

The Sponge tool, which soaks up color like, well, a sponge, reduces the richness or intensity (or saturation) of a color in the areas you paint. It can also perform the reverse, imbuing a specific area with richer, more vibrant colors.

Surprisingly, the Sponge tool also works in grayscale mode, pushing light and dark pixels toward a middle gray, providing a darkening or lightening effect to those pixels. Unlike the Hue/Saturation or Desaturate commands (Image⇨Adjustments), which work only on layers or selections, you can use the Sponge tool on any area you can paint with a brush.

You can use the Sponge tool on an image in subtle ways to reduce the saturation in selected areas for an interesting effect. For example, you may have an object that is the center of attention in your picture simply because the colors are so bright (or even garish). The Sponge tool lets you reduce the color saturation of that area (only) to allow the other sections of your image to come to the forefront. You can also use the Sponge tool to make an artistic statement: You could reduce or increase the saturation of a single person in a group shot to make that person stand out (perhaps as being more colorful than the rest).

To use the Sponge tool, just follow these steps:

1. **Open an image and choose the Sponge tool from the Tools palette.**

   Press the O key to choose the Sponge if it is the active toning tool, or press Shift+O to cycle through the Sponge, Dodge, and Burn tools until the Sponge tool is active.

2. **Select a brush from the Brushes palette.**

   Use large, soft brushes to saturate/desaturate a larger area.

   Smaller brushes are useful mostly when you need to change the saturation of a specific small object in an image.

3. **Select either Desaturate (reduce color richness) or Saturate (increase color richness) from the Mode pop-up menu.**

4. **Choose a flow rate (the speed with which the saturation/desaturation effect builds up as you apply the brush) with the Flow slider or text box.**

5. If you want an even softer effect, choose the Airbrush option.

6. Paint carefully over the areas you want to saturate or desaturate with color.

In Figure 2-2, I saturated one of the Tibetan monks to make him more a focal point and desaturated the others.

Corbis Digital Stock
Figure 2-2: The Sponge tool saturates (increases richness) and desaturates (decreases richness) color.

Smoothing with the Smudge Tool

Although grouped among the focus tools, the Smudge tool performs more of a warping effect, something like the Warp tool in the Liquify dialog box (see Book VII, Chapter 3 for information on this command).

Smudge pushes your pixels around on the screen as if they consisted of wet paint, using the color that's under the cursor when you start to stroke. However, don't view the Smudge tool as a simple distortion tool that produces only comical effects. I use it on tiny areas of an image to soften the edges of objects in a way that often looks more natural than blurring tools. The Smudge tool can come in handy when retouching images to create a soft, almost painted look, as shown in Figure 2-3. Just don't go too gung-ho or you may obliterate detail that you want to preserve.

 Smudged areas may be obvious because of their smooth appearance. Adding some texture using the Noise filter after you smudge is often a good idea, if you want to blend a smudged section in with its surroundings. You find tips on applying Noise in Book VII, Chapter 2.

PhotoDisc

Figure 2-3: The Smudge tool can give your fruit, or other elements, a soft, painted look.

To apply the Smudge tool, just follow these steps:

1. **Open the image and choose the Smudge tool from the Tools palette.**

   Press the R key to select it, or press Shift+R to cycle through the available focus tools (including Blur and Sharpen) until the one you want is active.

2. **Choose the settings you want from the Options bar.**

3. **Select a brush from the Brushes palette.**

   Use a small brush for smudging tiny areas, such as edges. Larger brushes produce drastic effects, so use them with care.

4. **Choose a blending mode from the Mode pop-up menu.**

5. **Choose the strength of the smudging effect with the Strength slider or text box.**

   Low values produce a lighter smudging effect; high values really push your pixels around.

6. **If your image has multiple layers, you can select the Sample All Layers option to tell Photoshop to use the color information from all the visible layers to produce the smudge effect.**

   The smudge still appears only on the active layer, but the look is a bit different, depending on the contents of the underlying layers.

7. **Use the Finger Painting option to begin the smudge using the fore-ground color.**

   You can get some interesting effects with this option.

   You can switch the Smudge tool into Finger Painting mode temporarily by pressing the Alt key (the Option key on the Mac) as you drag.

8. **Paint over the areas you want to smudge.**

9. **Watch the screen carefully as you smudge so that you can redirect your daubs to achieve the look you want.**

   This tool can be a little on the destructive side. If you're looking to preserve reality, use it with restraint. If you want to get wild, go crazy.

10. **When you finish, choose File⇨Save to store your image.**

Softening with the Blur Tool

Adding a little blur here and there can save an image with a few defects. Blurring can also be used for artistic effect — say to add a little motion to a soccer ball frozen in time by too-fast a shutter speed. You can also blur portions of your image to emphasize and focus on a particular element, as shown in Figure 2-4, where I blurred the flowers a bit to draw attention to the butterfly. The Photoshop Blur tool makes painting your blur effects exactly where you want them easy.

The Blur tool doesn't push pixels around like the Smudge tool. Instead, the Blur tool decreases the contrast among adjacent pixels in the area painted.

The mechanics of using the Blur tool and several of its options are similar to those of the Smudge tool. Just follow these steps:

Corbis Digital Stock

Figure 2-4: Use the Blur tool to soften a rough edge or make your element more a focal point by blurring its surroundings.

1. **Open an image and choose the Blur tool from the Tools palette.**

   Press the R key to select it if it happens to be the active focus tool, or press Shift+R to cycle through the Sharpen and Smudge tools until the Blur tool is active.

2. **Select a brush from the Brushes palette.**

   Use a small brush for applying small areas of blur.

   Use larger brushes with caution, say, to blur the entire background to make a foreground object appear sharper in comparison.

3. **Choose a blending mode from the Mode pop-up menu.**

4. **Choose the strength of the blurring effect with the Strength slider or text box.**

5. **If your image has multiple layers, you can select the Use All Layers option to blur based on the pixel information in all visible layers in your image.**

   This can produce a smoother blur when you merge the layers later.

6. **Paint over the areas you want to blur.**

7. **When you finish, choose File⇨Save to store your image.**

Cranking Up the Focus with the Sharpen Tool

In theory, the Sharpen tool is nothing more than the Blur tool in reverse — instead of decreasing contrast among pixels, the Sharpen tool increases the contrast. In practice, however, you need to use this tool with a bit more care. Where blurred areas tend to fade from a viewer's notice (at least in terms of how our eyes perceive them), sharpened areas of an image jump out at people.

If you blur an area a little too much, you may not even notice. But even a small area that has been over-sharpened can change the entire appearance of an image — and not flatteringly.

You can often successfully sharpen small areas with the Sharpen tool. Sometimes the eyes in a portrait can benefit from a little sharpening, as shown in Figure 2-5. Or, you might want to sharpen an area to make it stand out more distinctly against a slightly blurred background.

Here are the simple steps to follow to use the Sharpen tool:

1. **Choose the Sharpen tool from the Tools palette.**

   Press the R key to select it directly if it's the last focus tool used. If not, press Shift+R to cycle through the Blur and Smudge tools to activate the Sharpen tool.

2. **Select the brush of your choice from the Brushes palette.**

3. **Choose a blending mode from the Mode pop-up menu.**

4. **Choose the strength of the sharpening effect with the Strength slider or text box.**

   Using a fairly low value (say, 25% or less) is a good idea because you can build up sharpness slowly, being careful not to overdo it.

   You know you have gone too far with the sharpness when the pixels start to look noisy and grainy.

5. **Use the information on all your layers for Photoshop's contrast-increasing algorithms by selecting the Use All Layers option.**

6. **Paint over the areas you want to sharpen.**

7. **When you finish, choose File⇨Save to store your image.**

Sharpening increases contrast, so be careful when using the Sharpen tool if you plan to also adjust the Levels or Curves controls. Any change that increases contrast in the whole image also boosts the contrast of an area you've sharpened.

Corbis Digital Stock

Figure 2-5: Use the Sharpen tool sparingly and in small areas, such as in the eyes of this portrait.

The Unsharp Mask or Smart Sharpen filters offer more options and better overall control, so unless you really need to paint the sharpening effect, you're usually better off using the filter. If you really want to apply the effect with brushstrokes, you can always apply the Unsharp Mask filter to a whole layer, take a snapshot, undo the filter operation, and then use the snapshot as a source to paint from using the History palette. See Book II, Chapter 4 for information on how to paint from the History palette.

Putting It Together

Fixing an Underexposed Foreground

Sometimes editing tools just don't cut the mustard when it comes to fixing large areas of an underexposed image. Instead, you have to use three tools together to repair the damage: a filter, a fill, and a blend mode.

If you're like me, you've taken at least a couple of photos where your subject was lit from behind, thereby underexposing the foreground and burying the subject in the shadows. You can try the Shadow and Highlight adjustment, on the Image⇨Adjustment menu, which usually does a good job of fixing the problem. But if you're not satisfied with that adjustment, you can follow this old-school method. Or you can even go for a combo plate and use them both. Here's how to bring your subject back into the light:

1. **Open the image in need of repair.**

2. **Choose Image⇨Duplicate.**

3. **Name the file** Repair **and click OK in the dialog box.**

4. **Select Image⇨Mode⇨Grayscale. Click OK to discard the color information.**

Photoshop has now stripped the color from the image. Don't worry; this is just an intermediary step.

5. **On the duplicate image, choose Filter⇨Blur⇨Gaussian Blur. Enter a radius value and click OK.**

For a low resolution image (72 ppi), 5 pixels is enough. For higher resolution images (300 ppi), use 20 pixels. Your goal is to get rid of the detail in the image.

6. **Return to the original image. Choose Select⇨Load Selection.**

Under Document make sure it says Repair.

7. **Choose Gray for the Channel. Select the Invert box. In the Operation area, leave the setting as New Selection. Click OK to load the Load Selection dialog box, as shown in the figure.**

You're loading the only available channel in the duplicate grayscale image as a selection.

A selection outline appears, which corresponds to the blurry gray areas in your duplicate image.

8. **Choose Edit⇨Fill. In the dialog box that appears, shown in the figure, select 50% Gray from the Use pop-up menu. Select Color Dodge from the Mode pop-up menu. Leave the Opacity at 100%. Click OK.**

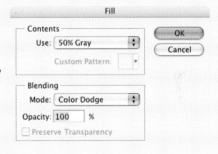

Although Photoshop fills the selection with 50 percent gray, the Color Dodge mode *lightens* the pixels in the image, creating a kind of bleaching effect.

9. **You can now see the subject of your image in a better light, as in my image.**

**Book VIII
Chapter 2**

**Repairing with
the Focus and
Toning Tools**

Chapter 3: Fixing Flaws and Removing What's Not Wanted

In This Chapter

⌐ **Cloning with the Clone Stamp tool**

⌐ **Digital healing with the Healing Brush tool**

⌐ **Applying patches with the Patch tool**

⌐ **Zapping with the Spot Healing Brush tool**

⌐ **Applying color with the Color Replacement tool**

⌐ **Eliminating red eye**

⌐ **Working with Vanishing Point**

*S*ay you want to duplicate an element in your image. That's easy enough, right? Make a selection and copy and paste it into the new location. Presto. That works fine most of the time. But what if the element has a shadow behind it, next to it, over it, or under it? You face the dilemma of having a hard edge on the copied element because the shadow (called a *cast shadow*) is cut off by the selection outline. You could feather the selection, but then you have to make sure that the copied element blends realistically with the background. What a pain. The better method is to clone the element using the Clone Stamp tool. It's quick, easy, and no one will know that only one element was there originally.

Here's another hypothetical situation: What if you already have the right number of elements but some unsightly flaw mars your otherwise perfect image? Or maybe the corporate executive, whose head shot you took last week, has requested a little digital Botox around the eyes and mouth. No problem. You can take care of wrinkles, scars, blemishes, scratches, spots, and any other nasty imperfections in a matter of minutes in Photoshop with the healing tools. And if your flaw is a nasty case of red eye, you can grab the new Red Eye tool and take care of it with a few swipes.

Not into people, but architecture you say? Not a problem. Photoshop's new Vanishing Point feature lets you easily make realistic edits in images with perspective plans, such as buildings.

In this chapter, I reveal secrets of cloning that won't make medical ethicists scream. I show you how to heal scars, scratches, and other imperfections without calling a plastic surgeon. And you can now add or remove windows or doors without forking out a dime to a contractor.

Cloning with the Clone Stamp Tool

Tell Dolly the sheep to move over and make room. The Clone Stamp tool, also known as the Rubber Stamp, one of Photoshop's more popular tools, always arouses a "Wow," "Cool," or similar remark of approval when demonstrated.

Believe it or not, you can also reach for this tool when retouching imperfections such as scratches, scars, bruises, and other minor flaws. In fact, that used to be one of its major functions. In some retouching instances it does a great job, although the advent of the Healing Brush and Patch tools has relegated the Clone Stamp tool more to the pure cloning functions and less to the hard-core retouching jobs.

Using the Clone Stamp tool

The Clone Stamp tool works its magic by taking sampled pixels from one area and *clones* (or copies) them onto another area. Cloning is often better than making a selection, copying, and pasting it because cloning allows you to retain soft edges on details such as shadows, giving you a more realistic duplicate image.

Follow these steps to clone an element without any genetic engineering:

1. **Open an image and select the Clone Stamp tool from the Tools palette.**

   Press the S key on the keyboard.

   You have several options to choose from on the Options bar.

2. **Select a brush and change its size or shape in the Brush Preset picker drop-down palette.**

   For more information on brushes, see Book IV, Chapter 1.

3. **Specify the Clone Stamp tool's brush size to control the area that you're cloning.**

I recommend having your Clone Stamp tool cursor display your Brush Size so you can judge the amount of the area you are cloning. To do so, choose Edit⇨Preferences⇨Display & Cursors (Photoshop⇨ Preferences⇨Display & Cursors on Mac OS X). Select the Brush Size radio button from the Painting Cursors area of the dialog box. I used a 65-pixel, feathered brush.

4. Choose the blend mode of your choice.

Selecting a mode such as Difference, Multiply, or Color can produce some interesting special effects. For more on modes, see Book V, Chapter 3. I left my setting at Normal.

5. To make the clone more or less opaque, use the Opacity slider or text box on the Options bar.

I left the opacity at 100%.

6. Specify how fast the Clone Stamp tool applies the clone by adjusting the Flow rate percentage.

Again I left my option at 100%.

7. Click the Airbrush option for Airbrushing capabilities if so desired.

8. Select or deselect the Aligned option depending on your preference.

With Aligned selected, the clone source moves when you move your cursor to a different location. If you want to clone multiple times from the same location, leave the Aligned option deselected. I left mine selected.

9. Select the Sample All Layers option to clone part of an image with multiple layers.

This tool samples pixels in all the visible layers for the clone. If you leave it deselected, the Clone Stamp tool clones only from the active layer.

10. Alt+click (Option+click on the Mac) the area of your image that you want to clone. By doing this you are defining the *source*.

11. Click or drag along the area where you want the clone to appear, as shown in Figure 3-1.

As you drag, Photoshop displays a crosshair icon along with your Clone Stamp cursor. The crosshair represents the source you are cloning from while the Clone Stamp cursor shows where the clone is being painted. As you move the mouse, the crosshair moves as well. This provides a continuous reference to the area of your image that you're cloning. Keep an eye on the crosshair, or you may clone something you don't want. Try to clone your entire object in one fell swoop so it doesn't get fragmented.

Book VIII
Chapter 3

**Fixing Flaws and
Removing What's
Not Wanted**

Figure 3-1: When using the Clone Stamp tool, drag along the area where you want your clone to appear.

When you successfully complete the cloning process, you have two identical objects. Figure 3-2 shows my identical twin Siberian tigers.

12. Save the image and close it.

Figure 3-2: My twin Siberian tigers are the products of cloning.

Tips for excellent cloning results

Here are a few useful tidbits regarding the Clone Stamp tool:

- **Use the Clone Stamp tool for fixing simple flaws:** To clean up a flaw that is pretty straight, such as a stray hair or scratch, Alt+click (Option+click on the Mac) with the tool to define the source. Then click at one end of the straight flaw and Shift+click at the other end. The cloned source pixels then cover up the flaw.

- **Vary the origin point for sampling often:** If you keep sampling from the same point without ever varying it, the area you're cloning starts to look like ugly shag carpeting. Or at best, starts to appear blotchy and over-retouched.

- **Zoom out once in a while to check how your overall image is looking.** You can avoid those funky telltale clone stamp repetitive patterns and blotches.

- **Clone patterns:** To use the Pattern Stamp tool, which shares the flyout menu with the Clone Stamp tool, select a custom pattern from the Pattern picker drop-down palette on the Options bar. Drag with the Pattern Stamp tool, and you see the pattern appear.

Digital Bandaging with the Healing Brush Tool

The Healing Brush and Patch tools are similar to the Clone Stamp tool. They let you clone pixels from one area and apply them to another area. But that's where the healing tools leave the Clone Stamp tool eating their dust.

The problem with the Clone Stamp tool is that it doesn't take the tonality of the flawed area — the shadows, midtones, and highlights — into consideration. So if the pixels you are sampling from aren't shaded and lit exactly like the ones you're covering, you have a mismatch in color, which makes seamless and indecipherable repairs hard to achieve.

That is, until the Healing Brush tool arrived. This very intelligent tool clones by using the *texture* from the sampled area (the source) and then using the *colors* around the brush stroke as you paint over the flawed area (the destination). The highlights, midtones, and shadows remain intact, and the result of the repair is more realistic and natural — not retouched and phony. Here are the steps to heal your favorite, but imperfect photo:

1. **Open your image and select the Healing Brush tool.**

   My guy, shown in Figure 3-3, looks like he could stand to get some "work done," as they say in Hollywood. Note that you can also heal between two images. Just make sure that they have the same color mode.

2. **On the Options bar, click the Brush Preset picker.**

   In the drop-down palette, select your desired diameter and hardness for your brush tip. You do this several times while retouching your image. Using the appropriate brush size for the flaw you are repairing is important.

3. **Leave the blend mode set to Normal.**

   You can change your blend mode if necessary. The Replace mode preserves textures, such as noise or film grain, around the edges of your strokes. For most simple retouching jobs, such as this one, you can leave it at Normal.

Figure 3-3: The Healing Brush can make these wrinkles practically disappear.

4. **Choose a Source option.**

   You have a choice between Sampled and Pattern.

   - **Sampled,** which you will probably use 99 percent of the time, uses the pixels from the image.

   - Regarding **Pattern,** well, you can probably infer that it uses pixels from a pattern you have selected from the Pattern picker drop-down palette.

   For my example, I am sticking with Sampled because I don't think my guy would look that good with a Tie-Dye or Nebula pattern across his face. He's just way too corporate for that.

5. **Select how you want to align the sampled pixels.**

   When you click or drag with the Healing Brush tool, Photoshop displays a crosshair along with the Healing Brush cursor. The crosshair represents the sampling point, also known as the *source*. As you move the Healing Brush tool, the crosshair also moves, providing a constant reference to the area that you are sampling. However, if you deselect the Aligned option on the Options bar, Photoshop applies the source pixels from your initial sampling point, despite how many times you stop and start dragging. I left Aligned selected in my example.

Select the Sample All Layers option to heal an image using all visible layers. If unselected, you heal only from the active layer.

For maximum flexibility, select the Sample All Layers options and add a new, blank layer above the image you want to heal. When you heal the image, the pixels appear on the new layer and not on the image itself. You can then adjust opacity, blend modes, and make other tweaks to the "healed" pixels.

6. **Establish the sampling point by Alt+clicking (Option+clicking on the Mac). Make sure to click the area of your image you want to clone *from*.**

   In my example, I clicked the smooth area on the chin and portions of the forehead.

7. **Release the Alt (Option on the Mac) key and click or drag over the area of your image that contains the flaw.**

   Pay attention to where the crosshair is located because that's the area you are sampling from.

   In my example, I brushed over the wrinkles under and around the eyes and on the forehead, as shown in Figure 3-4. I also zapped some dark spots here and there. Save the file, close it, and send in your invoice for your digital dermabrasion.

Figure 3-4: In just five or ten minutes, this gentleman lost about ten years.

Patching without Seams

While the Patch tool is similar to the Healing Brush tool in theory, its application method is slightly different. Instead of painting over the flaws with a brush, you select your flawed area and apply a patch to that selection.

The Patch tool does a good job in fixing larger flawed areas or isolated imperfections rather than a few wrinkles or scars here and there. What's more, it's a breeze to use.

Here are steps to patching an area in need of repair:

1. **Open your image and select the Patch tool.**

   It looks like a patch of material. The girl in my image, shown in Figure 3-5, is virtually flawless, although I can't say the same for the wall she is leaning against.

Figure 3-5: The Patch tool can fix the flaws on the wall.

2. Choose Source or Destination on the Options bar.

Choose Source if you want to select the flawed area. Select Destination if you want to select the good area you want to clone from. You can also choose Pattern if you so desire.

3. Drag around the flawed area of your image.

Think of the Patch tool as a kind of super cloning Lasso tool. Drag completely around the flawed area as you would when selecting with the Lasso tool. If you need to, you can apply a slight feather of 0.5 to 2 pixels, depending on the resolution, to soften the edge of the selection. I selected my area without a feather, as shown in Figure 3-6.

Figure 3-6: Drag around the flawed area.

You can actually select your flawed area with any selection tool you like. After you have your selection, then select the Patch tool and proceed to Step 4.

4. Drag your selection to the area on your image that you want to clone (or sample) from, as shown in Figure 3-7.

5. When you release the mouse, Photoshop patches your flawed selection with the cloned pixels.

6. Repeat the process as needed.

After several patches, the wall now looks almost as good as the girl, as shown in Figure 3-8.

Figure 3-7: Drag the selection to the area you want to sample.

**Book VIII
Chapter 3**

**Fixing Flaws and
Removing What's
Not Wanted**

Figure 3-8: The Patch tool repaired the wall.

Zeroing In with the Spot Healing Brush

Whereas the Healing Brush is designed to fix larger flawed areas, the new Spot Healing Brush is designed for smaller blemishes and little imperfections. The tool actually isn't new. It's been borrowed from Photoshop's consumer cousin, Photoshop Elements. The biggest difference between the Healing Brush and the Spot Healing Brush is that the Spot Healing Brush doesn't require you to specify a sampling source. It automatically takes a sample from around the area to be retouched. The good news is it's quick and easy. The downside is that it doesn't give you as much control over the sampling source. Consequently, reserve this tool for small and simple flaws.

Here's how to quickly fix little, nitpicky imperfections with the Spot Healing Brush tool:

1. **Open your image and grab the Spot Healing Brush tool.**

   The small moles in Figure 3-9 are examples of small areas you can fix with the Spot Healing brush.

PhotoSpin

Figure 3-9: Watch these moles disappear.

2. **On the Options bar, click the Brush Preset picker and select your desired diameter and hardness for your brush tip.**

   Try to select a brush that is a little larger than the flawed area you wish to fix.

3. **Choose a blend mode from the Options bar.**

   Like the Healing Brush, you can also choose the Replace mode. Most likely the Normal mode will work the best.

4. **Choose a type from the Options bar.**

   You have a choice between Proximity Match and Create Texture.

   - **Proximity Match:** Samples the pixels around the edge of the selection to use to fix the flawed area.

   - **Create Texture:** Uses all the pixels in the selection to create a texture to fix the flaw.

   Try Proximity Match first and if it doesn't work, undo and try Create Texture.

5. **Choose Sample All Layers to heal an image using all visible layers. If left unselected, you heal only from the active layer.**

6. **Click, or click and drag, on the area you want to fix.**

In Figure 3-10, I used the Spot Healing Brush for the moles and spots on the upper lip and cheeks. But for the mole over the eyebrow, I broke out the Healing Brush. I found I needed more control of the sampling source due to the mole being so close to the hair of the eyebrow.

Figure 3-10: I used the Spot Healing brush and the Healing Brush to remove a few moles.

Colorizing with the Color Replacement Tool

In this new version of Photoshop, the Color Replacement tool was booted out of its home on the healing tools flyout menu and moved to the Brush and Pencil flyout menu. But functionally, it makes more sense to keep it with the flaw fixing brushes, so I talk about it here. The Color Replacement tool allows you to replace the original color of an image with the foreground color. You can use this tool in a variety of ways. Create the look of a hand-painted photo by colorizing a grayscale image. Or maybe you just want to change the color of an object or two, such as a couple of flowers in a bouquet. And although Photoshop now has a bona-fide Red Eye tool, a practical use of the Color Replacement tool is to easily paint away red eye.

The great thing about the Color Replacement tool is that, like the other healing tools, it completely preserves the tonality of the image. The color that you apply doesn't obliterate the midtones, shadows, and highlights as it would if you were using the regular Brush tool. The Color Replacement tool works by first sampling the original colors in the image and then replacing those colors with the foreground color. By specifying different sampling methods, limits, and tolerance settings, you can control the range of colors that Photoshop replaces.

This weapon in the arsenal of retouching tools is a cinch to use. Here are the short steps to replacing color:

1. **Open your image and select the Color Replacement tool. Remember it shares a flyout menu with the regular Brush and Pencil tools.**

   It looks like a brush with a square and two arrows next to it. Use the B (or Shift+B) key to select it from the keyboard.

2. **On the Options bar, click the Brush Preset picker.**

   In the drop-down palette, select your desired diameter and hardness for your brush tip.

3. **Select your desired blend mode.**

   Color is the default mode and works well for most colorizing jobs. Use this mode if you're trying to get rid of red eye.

   Hue is similar to color, but is less intense and provides a lighter effect.

   Set your foreground color to Black in the Tools palette and set the mode to Saturation to convert a color image to a grayscale image.

   Luminosity is the exact opposite of the Color mode and while it can create a beautiful effect between two image layers, it doesn't provide that great of an effect with this tool.

   For a full "scientific" definition of each blend mode, check out Book IV, Chapter 1.

4. **Select your sampling method.**

   The default of Continuous allows you to sample and replace color continuously as you drag your mouse. Choose Once to replace colors only in areas containing the color that you first sample by clicking. And finally, select Background Swatch to replace colors only in areas containing your current Background color.

5. **Select your sampling limits mode.**

   The default of Contiguous lets you replace the color of pixels containing the sampled color that are adjacent to each other only. Discontiguous lets you replace the color of the pixels containing the sampled color wherever it occurs in your image. And Find Edges allows you to replace the color of pixels containing the sampled color while preserving the sharpness of the edges of the objects.

6. **Specify your tolerance percentage.**

   Tolerance refers to a range of color. A higher tolerance lets you replace a broader range of color. A lower tolerance limits the replacement of color only to areas that are similar to the sampled color.

7. **Choose whether you want anti-aliasing.**

   Remember anti-aliasing slightly softens and smooths the edge of the selected or sampled areas.

8. **After you establish your settings, click or drag on your image.**

   Notice how the foreground color, which in my example is black, replaces the original colors of the sampled areas (see Figure 3-11). Of course, the exact effect you get depends on your settings.

Figure 3-11: Use the Color Replacement tool to replace the original color in your image with your current foreground color.

Getting Rid of Dreaded Red Eye

Red eye occurs when the subject of a picture looks directly into the flash, and the unfortunate result is that eerie reddish luminescence in the eyes that says, "I may very well be a demon child."

Many cameras have a red-eye prevention mode that causes the subjects' irises to contract, making their pupils smaller when the second flash (that is, the *real* flash) goes off. Other cameras mount the flash high or to one side of the lens, which also minimizes the chance of red eye. However, these preventive measures are of little solace when you have a great picture that features bright red pupils as its most dominating feature.

If you've been hanging around in Photoshop for a while, you're probably aware that you can get the same result many different ways. This holds true for getting rid of red eye as well. You can use the regular old Brush tool with a Color blend mode and paint away the red. Or you can use the Color Replacement tool with a black foreground to color away the crimson. And now you can use the new Red Eye tool. As with the Spot Healing Brush, the Red Eye tool is another tool that was adopted from Photoshop Elements due to popular demand.

Here's a quick way to get the red out and restore your image to a less zombie-like look:

1. **Open the original photo with red eye showing.**

   I'm using a photo of an unhappy angel, shown in Figure 3-12.

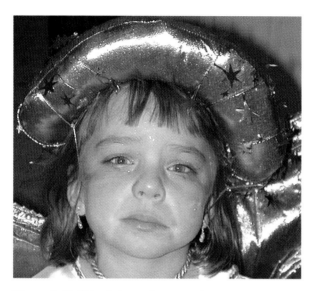

Figure 3-12: This photo needs an exorcist.

2. **Select the Red Eye tool.**

   Using the default settings, click the red portion of the eye in your image, as shown in Figure 3-13. This one click tool darkens the pupil, while retaining the tonality and texture of the eye.

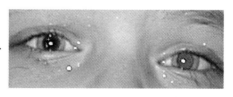

Figure 3-13: Click the red eye with the Red Eye tool to make it vanish.

3. **If you're not happy with the results, tweak one or both of the following options:**

   Pupil Size: Use the slider to increase or decrease the size of the pupil.

   Darken Pupil: Use the slider to darken or lighten the color of the pupil.

4. **If all goes well, your image is now cured of the dreaded red eye, as shown in Figure 3-14.**

The Red Eye tool works only with RGB or LAB color images. For details on these color modes, see Book II.

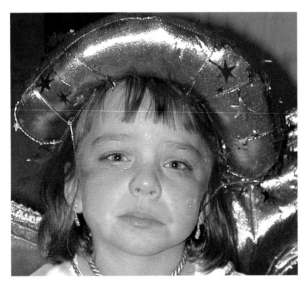

Figure 3-14: The ultimate cure of red eye.

Working with Vanishing Point

Every Photoshop upgrade always has one new feature that everyone "oohs" and "ahhs" over. In CS2 that new feature is Vanishing Point. This awesome command enables you to make realistic edits in images with perspective planes. With Vanishing Point, you specify the planes in your images and then, by using a variety of techniques such as painting or cloning, can add or eliminate objects on those planes.

For example, say you have a building that has only one window on the side. You have a remodeling project in mind where you would like to add more light in the room, so you want to add three more windows on that side. Using Vanishing Point, you can easily add those windows, all of which will be scaled and angled by staying true to the perspective of the side of that building. With Vanishing Point, you can now edit three dimensionally on a two-dimension image. The resulting image is a nice composite to hand over to your general contractor. No more funky cut and paste composites or worse yet, indecipherable hand sketches over photos.

Here are the steps for using this incredible new feature:

1. **Open an image containing perspective planes that needs editing.**

   Creating a new layer is a good idea so that you can isolate your Vanishing Point result from your original image layer. You have further editing advantages if you want to change opacity settings, blend modes, and so on.

If you want only the Vanishing Point results to be applied to a specific part of your image, be sure and make the selection (or add a mask) before choosing the Vanishing Point command.

If you need to paste an element into the Vanishing Point dialog box, be sure and copy the item before choosing the Vanishing Point command. This copied element can be from the same image or a different image. It can also be a text layer.

2. Choose Filter⇨Vanishing Point.

The Vanishing Point dialog box appears, as shown in Figure 3-15.

Create Plane tool

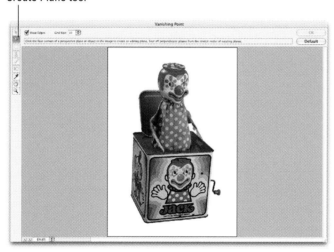

PhotoSpin

Figure 3-15: Boxes are good candidates for working with the Vanishing Point command.

3. Grab the Create Plane tool. Click at each of the four corners of your plane to establish your editing surface. Be as accurate as you can when specifying the plane on your image.

A bounding box with *nodes* at each corner and a grid appears over the plane surface, as shown in Figure 3-16. Feel free to tweak the plane to perfection by moving or resizing the plane using the Create Plane or Edit Plane (black tool) tools. Photoshop informs you if your plane has a problem by displaying a bounding box and grid as red or yellow. Adjust the bounding box until it becomes blue. Move a corner node until the bounding box and grid are blue, which indicates that the plane is valid.

4. Use the Grid Size slider to adjust the size of the grid units to better line up the plane and grid with the elements that may be in your image such as tiles, texture, windows, or doors.

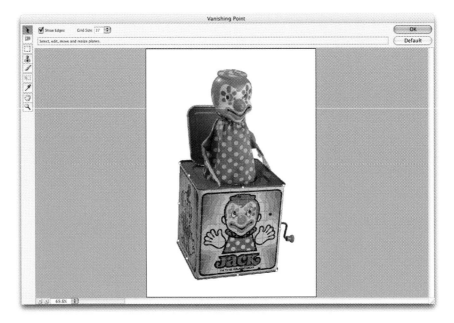

Figure 3-16: Define your editing plane with the Create Plane tool.

5. **If desired, you can use the Create Plane tool and Ctrl+drag (⌘+drag on the Mac) an edge node of the plane to "tear off" a perpendicular plane.**

   This simply means, for example, that you can extend the plane around to another side, as I did in Figure 3-16, and create another plane. This keeps the planes related to each other and ensures that your edit's in the correct scale and angle.

   Note that at this point you can simply create perspective planes and then click OK and bail out. The planes you established appear in the future when you call up the Vanishing Point command again.

6. **After you establish your perspective planes, choose an editing task:**

   • **Make a selection:** Select the Marquee tool and drag a selection in the plane, as I did in Figure 3-17. Specify your selection options, either before or after the selection. You can feather the selection to get soft edges. Or you can adjust the opacity of the selection. You can also choose a Heal option. Move Mode allows you to specify the selection as Destination or Source. Select Destination to select the area you move the marquee to. Source fills an area with the contents of the marquee when you move the marquee and release. If you want to select your entire plan, just double-click the Marquee tool.

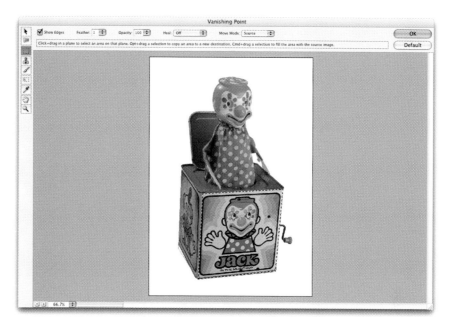

Figure 3-17: Make a selection with the Marquee tool on your plane.

- **Clone:** Select the Marquee or Transform tool and Alt+drag (Option+ drag on the Mac) the selection to create a copy of the selection. Transform (scale, rotate, move) the selection to your liking. Clone as many times as you want. When you move the selection, it adjusts to fit the perspective of the plane, as shown in Figure 3-18.

  Ctrl+Shift+T (⌘+Shift+T on the Mac) duplicates your last clone.

  Note that you have access to multiple undos within the Vanishing Point dialog box. But they are limited to your single editing session. Press Ctrl+Z (⌘+Z on the Mac) to undo.

- **Move a selection:** Grab the Marquee or Transform tool and drag the selection. Press the Shift key to constrain the move.

- **Transform a selection:** To scale the selection, select the Transform tool and move the cursor on top of a node and drag. To rotate, move the cursor next to a node until you see a curved double arrow. Then drag in the direction of your desired rotation. Check the Flip or Flop options to flip the selection horizontally or vertically.

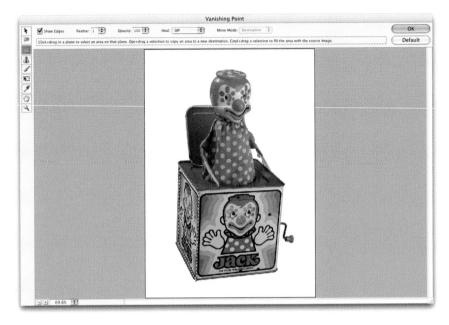

Figure 3-18: Your cloned selection conforms to fit the perspective of the destination plane.

- **Fill a selection with a piece of the image:** With the Marquee tool, Ctrl+drag (⌘+drag on the Mac) and make the selection you want as the source image. You can also choose Source from the Move Mode pop-up menu and drag the selection to the source image. You can then move or clone the selection. If the selection needs to be scaled or rotated, grab the Transform tool.

- **Clone by stamping with part of the image:** This technique works exactly like the regular Photoshop Clone Stamp tool. With the Stamp tool, Alt+click (Option+click on the Mac) the area you want to define as the source for your cloning. Then drag your mouse on the portion of the image where you want the clone to appear. If you drag in a perspective plane, the Stamp tool paints the cloned area in perspective. You can specify options for your brush diameter, hardness, and opacity. Choose a Heal option. The Off option allows you to clone without blending color, lighting, and shading of the surrounding pixels. The Luminance option allows you to clone using the lighting and shading of the surrounding pixels, but keeping the color of the source (or sampled area). And finally, the On option enables you to clone by blending color and lighting and shading of the surrounding pixels. Select Aligned to sample pixels while maintaining the current sampling point even when you release the mouse. Deselect this option to sample pixels from the sampling point of each mouse click.

- **Paint with color:** Select the Brush tool and specify your options, which are similar to the clone options. Click the Brush Color swatch. Choose your desired color from the Color Picker and paint by dragging on your image. As in stamping, the brush size and shape adjusts to stay true to the perspective.

- **Paste a copied element from the clipboard:** Press Ctrl+V (⌘+V on the Mac) to paste your element. With your Marquee tool, position the element on your plane where it adjusts to fit the perspective.

- The **Hand** and **Zoom** tools are for your navigation ease. You can also access the magnification pop-up menu and the plus and minus buttons at the bottom of the window.

7. Click OK.

No one will be the wiser that your composite image, shown in Figure 3-19, doesn't really exist in the real world as we know it. Save your edited image as a native Photoshop (.psd), TIFF, or JPEG to ensure that your perspective planes are saved in the file.

Figure 3-19: Your Vanishing Point edited image looks unedited and untampered with.

Book IX

Photoshop and Print

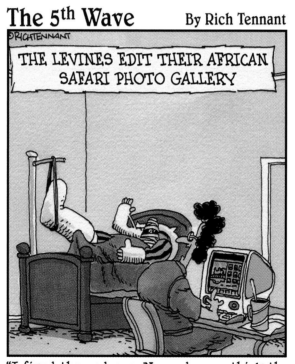

The 5th Wave   By Rich Tennant

THE LEVINES EDIT THEIR AFRICAN
SAFARI PHOTO GALLERY

"I fixed the red eye. Now, do you think the
'Hidden Rhino' photo should come before or
after the 'Waving Hello' photo?"

So you've toiled away and gotten your images picture perfect? Not a flaw, color cast, or stray pixel to be found? Congratulations! It's time to flaunt your editing prowess and share those images with the world. This book gives you the vitals on how to get those images print-ready. You can find information on how to set up images for offset printing. I also explain how to create contact sheets for archiving your images and how to set up picture packages similar to professional portrait studios.

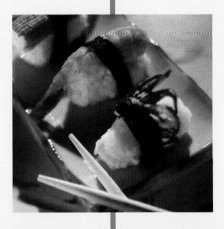

Chapter 1: Prepping Graphics for Print

*P*reparing images for the screen is a snap compared to what you have to go through to get images ripe for the printing process. If all you ever want to do is print your images to a desktop laser or inkjet printer, the task is a little easier, but you still must take some guidelines into account. And prepping your images for offset printing? Well, throw in an additional set of guidelines. It's not rocket science, mind you. If you stick to the basic rules and, more importantly, spend some time developing a good working relationship with your service bureau and offset printer, you're good to go.

Getting the Right Resolution, Mode, and Format

If you're not familiar with the concept of resolution, I suggest taking a look at Book II, Chapter 1. That's where I cover all the basics on resolution, pixel dimension, resampling, and other related topics. For full descriptions on color modes and file formats, see Book II, Chapter 2. That said, the next few sections give you the lowdown on the proper settings for an image that will ultimately go to print.

Resolution and modes

Table 1-1 provides some guidelines on what resolution settings to use for the most common type of output. Remember these are just *guidelines*. They aren't chiseled into stone to withstand the sands of time or anything lofty like that. You need to communicate with your service bureau, offset printer, or client and get specifications and/or recommendations. (See the section, "Working with a Service Bureau," later in this chapter.)

Table 1-1	Recommended Resolutions and Image Modes		
Device	Notes	Recommended Resolution	Mode
Fuji Frontier Photo Printer	Wallets to 10 x 15 inches. Great for printing digital photos.	300 dpi	RGB
Online Photo Printers, such as Shutterfly	Check recommended size and resolution settings on the vendor's Web site.	1024 x 768 for 4 x 6 print; 1600 x 1200 min. for 8 x 10 print	RGB
Digital presses	Brands include Xeikon, Xerox, IBM, Indigo*, Scitex, Heidelberg, and so on.	255 dpi	CMYK
Epson color inkjets	Resolutions depend on the print setting. Epson recommends ⅓ of the horizontal resolution, but do test prints; settings may be higher than you need.	720 dpi x ⅓ = 240 dpi; 1440 dpi x ⅓ = 480 dpi; 2880 dpi x ⅓ = 960 dpi	RGB or CMYK
Color separations	Film separations or direct to plate for offset printing.	2 x lines per inch (lpi); 2 x 133 lpi = 266 dpi; 2 x 150 lpi = 300 dpi; 2 x 175 lpi = 350 dpi**	CMYK and spot colors
Laser printers	Color or B&W printouts.	2 x lpi = 170 dpi	Grayscale or RGB

* Indigo presses can handle a fifth spot color if necessary.

** See the following section, "Screen frequencies."

Screen frequencies

For the appropriate resolution for color separations in Table 1-1, I list the amount of 2 multiplied by the number of lines per inch. The lines per inch, or *lpi,* pertains to the screen frequency of the output device. Screen frequencies are measured in lines per inch in a halftone screen. You can also hear the terms *screen ruling* or *line screen.* When images are printed, they are converted into a series of dots called *halftones.* When you print your halftone, you print it by using a halftone screen of a certain value. The average screen frequency for printing four-color images is 133 to 175 lpi. Therefore, when you multiply that by 2, you need to create your images by using a resolution setting of 266 to 350 dots per inch (dpi).

File formats

As far as file formats go, what you choose depends on a couple of issues:

- What you intend to do with the image. Print it to a laser printer? Order prints from an online photo printer?

- What your service bureau, offset printer, client, director, or other interested parties prefer.

Table 1-2 lists some of the more popular recommended formats for specific jobs, but again, communicate with the parties involved to see what is ultimately the best format to use.

Table 1-2	Recommended File Formats
Job	*Formats*
Color inkjet printouts	EPS, TIFF, PDF, PSD
Color separations	PSD, PDF, EPS, TIFF, DCS 2.0
Spot color separations	PSD, PDF, DCS 2.0 if importing into another application
Magazines/brochures	EPS, TIFF, PDF
Newspapers	TIFF, PDF
Importing to page layout programs	TIFF, EPS, PSD
Importing to illustration programs	EPS, TIFF, DCS, PSD
Slides	TIFF, PowerPoint, PICT, PCX, EPS (some bureaus can't do EPS)
Photo prints	JPEG, TIFF
Word documents	TIFF, EPS
For e-mailing for workflow review	PDF

Working with a Service Bureau

Service bureaus provide a wide variety of services, depending on their size. Some handle photo processing and various photographic output options such as prints (of varying sizes) and slides. Mounting and lamination services may also be provided. Many service bureaus provide scanning services, including high-end drum scanning. A common service is taking scans or digital photos and burning them onto Kodak Photo CDs. Many service bureaus provide output to color separations to film and RC paper. Larger bureaus may even have a digital press to handle a short run (500 or less), on-demand printing need.

Getting the ball rolling

Developing a good working relationship with your service bureau and/or offset printer can save you a lot of time, money, and frustration. These folks are the experts and know their equipment and processes. And believe me, they're only too willing to help. The fewer problems they have with your files, the better they like it. You can do some things to keep the relationship on solid footing:

🖙 **Get a dialogue going about the specs:** If your file is going directly to a newspaper, magazine, or other publication, talk with the art director, graphics production coordinator, or other knowledgeable person about the graphic specifications required. Different service bureaus and offset printers accept files from different applications and files of various formats.

🖙 **Build a lasting relationship:** Consistency is also key. When you find a good bureau or offset printer, stick with it for all your jobs. Jumping from one company to another because a quote came in a little cheaper doesn't always pay off in the long run. If you're a faithful customer, often your service bureau or offset printer will match that lower quote if it can. You don't want to have to relearn what a new company can and can't do and vice versa. And if possible, try to let one company handle your entire job. That way, one company controls the quality from beginning to end, with no finger-pointing if things go bad.

🖙 **Get on the Web:** Many service bureaus have Web sites where you can find a listing of services they offer, price lists, file specs, and even downloadable order forms. Larger offset printers also have Web sites offering general information and online requests for quote applications. Larger offset printers may provide services such as scanning and film-separation output, so be sure to check the Web site for details.

Using a prepress checklist

In addition to communicating with your offset printers and service bureau, you need to do some additional work to prepare your file for print. Here is a handy checklist that you can use whenever you're prepping a file for print. Use it to ensure your file is ready and rarin' for problem-free output. Note that this list isn't all-inclusive when it comes to prepress; I include tips that pertain to Photoshop only.

🖙 **Always transform your images in their native application.** Size, crop, rotate, shear, and reflect art in Photoshop. Transforming images in an illustration or page layout program is complex and can cause the RIP (raster image processing, which converts objects to a series of dots/pixels for printing) to take a long time to process the file.

✓ **Ensure that images can first print from Photoshop.** Do this before importing the images into an illustration or page layout program.

✓ **If you're placing Photoshop EPS images into a page layout or illustration program, set the halftone screen frequency in the destination program instead of embedding it in each image in Photoshop.** Or better yet, don't set any halftone screen frequencies in your images and let your service bureau or offset printer handle setting them in the other program.

✓ **When saving Photoshop images for print purposes, stick to TIFF, EPS, native PSD, or PDF file formats.** If you're unsure of the proper format to use for a specific job, ask your offset printer or service bureau for recommendations.

✓ **Make sure that you have used the proper color mode.** For example, use CMYK for color separations and RGB for slide output. Again, if you're not sure, ask your offset printer or service bureau for recommendations.

✓ **Create vector shapes and paths efficiently.** Printing vector art involves using intense calculations for every anchor point, and overly complex paths can cause problems during the RIP process. Use the fewest number of anchor points possible to create the path and delete any unnecessary or stray points. Leave your flatness setting blank. Photoshop uses the default setting for the output device, which is usually a safe bet.

✓ **Limit the number of typefaces.** Downloading takes time. Limiting the number of typefaces also makes your document look more sophisticated and polished.

✓ **Make sure that all scanning is at the appropriate dpi.** As a general rule, 2 multiplied by the line screen (lines per inch or lpi) equals the dpi to use in scanning the images. If you need to resize your image, be sure to scan it at a higher resolution accordingly. For example, if you need it twice as big, scan it at twice the final resolution needed. When scanning line art, scan at a resolution of 1200 dpi or so to ensure a better black-and-white image.

✓ **If your image is to bleed (extend to the edge of the printed page), take that into account when creating your image.** Note that you need to allow for $\frac{1}{8}$ to $\frac{1}{4}$ of an inch on any side that will bleed to allow for slippages when the paper is cut.

✓ **Always specify colors from a Pantone color swatch chart and then select the color, whether process or spot, in Photoshop.** *Never* trust the way colors look on-screen because of calibration deficiencies and differences between RGB and CMYK color models.

✔ **Make spot color names consistent.** Make sure that the Photoshop spot color names exactly match those of any programs to which you are importing your image, such as an illustration or page layout program. Otherwise, you may get an additional color separation.

✔ **Print and provide laser prints of your file, both separations (if warranted), and a composite print.** Print all with printer marks — crop marks, registration marks, labels, and so on.

✔ **Provide all fonts used in your file.** Provide both screen and PostScript printer fonts, if applicable.

✔ **Choose File⇨Save As for your final save to squccze down to the smallest file size.** Doing a Save As compresses your file as small as possible.

✔ **Organize your files into folders.** For example, put the image files together in one folder, all the fonts in another, and so on. Practice good file management and organization.

✔ **Communicate any trapping needs to your service bureau or offset printer.** For color separations, indicate whether you have created the trapping yourself or if you want the service bureau/offset printer to do it.

Saving and Printing Vector Data in a Raster File

Photoshop allows you to create vector shapes and vector type with the pen tools, shape tools, and type tools (I explain how in Book III). Technically, the vector shapes are clipping paths applied to a bitmap, or *raster,* layer. But the clipping path is *still* a vector path, thereby retaining vector qualities. This vector data is resolution independent, which means that it prints at the resolution of the PostScript output device. Photoshop sends the printer separate images for each type and shape layer, which are printed on top of the raster

Some file format warnings

If you save your file as an EPS or DCS and reopen the file in Photoshop, Photoshop rasterizes the vector data to pixels. Save the original in the native PSD format.

If you save your layered file as an EPS, Photoshop converts your vector type to clipping paths. Extensive and small type creates complex clipping paths, which can be time consuming and sometimes difficult to print. You can either flatten your file or deselect the Include Vector Data option in the Save as EPS Options dialog box. Either choice rasterizes the type into pixels at the resolution of your image. You may want to consider eliminating the type in your image file and applying it either in a drawing or page layout program that can retain vector type.

image and clipped by using their vector paths. The edges of the vector path print at the full resolution of the PostScript printer, but the contents, such as the colored pixels or the image pixels within the vector path, print at the resolution of the Photoshop file (all portions of the type are resolution independent). Therefore, type and shapes always have crisp, hard edges, with curves appearing smooth and never jagged.

Remember that the only file formats that allow you to retain vector data are PSD, PDF, DCS, and EPS. When saving to DCS or EPS, be sure to select the Include Vector Data option in their respective Options dialog boxes. All other file formats rasterize the vector data.

Choosing Color Management Print Options

I highly recommend checking out the color management section in Book II, Chapter 3. There I go into great detail on the concept of color spaces, ICC profiles, and so on. Here, I cover the color management options you find in the Print with Preview dialog box.

Different output devices operate in different color spaces. Monitors, desktop printers, large format printers, film recorders, offset printers, and so on all have their own unique color space. The color management options enable you to convert the color space of your image while printing. So, for example, if the ICC (color) profile of your image is sRGB, you can choose to have your image's color space converted to the color space of your Epson printer when you print.

Unfortunately, I can't tell you what specific settings to choose. This choice is a widely debated topic, and different printers have their strengths, shortcomings, and quirks. Some experts say to let your printer, especially if it is a prosumer or professional-level printer, determine the colors, while others say to let Photoshop handle the duties. My advice is to take an hour and a pack of paper, run test prints to see which settings give you the most accurate result, and stick with those. Try different color spaces for both Source and Print Spaces and compare the printouts. You may even get different results from different types of paper.

When you have some free time, the following steps can help you experiment with the Color Management settings and discover what print settings work best:

1. **Choose File⇨Print with Preview to open the Print dialog box, shown in Figure 1-1.**

2. **Click the More Options button and choose Color Management from the pop-up menu on the far left under the Preview window.**

Figure 1-1: Be sure and specify the settings in the Color Management portion of the Print with Preview dialog box.

3. In the Print area, choose either Document or Proof.

Remember you're experimenting. So choose one, and then try the other.

Document uses the color profile of your image.

Proof by default uses the color profile of your Working CMYK color space, which you defined in your Color Settings dialog box. You can change this profile, however, by choosing Current Custom Setup from the Proof Setup Preset menu in the Options area. You can define this custom option by first going to View➪Proof Setup. For details on proofs, see Book II, Chapter 3.

4. **In the Options area, choose a method of Color Handling.**

The options differ depending on whether you chose Document or Proof in Step 3.

If you chose Document in the Print area, here are your options:

- **Let Printer Determine Colors** sends the document unchanged to the printer, tagged with its color profile. The printer driver then picks an appropriate color profile and converts your document's colors to the final printout. Just make sure you enable color management in your printer dialog box.

- **Let Photoshop Determine Colors** tells Photoshop to handle the color conversion, using the settings you choose from the Printer Profile and Rendering Indent pop-up menus. Photoshop also checks whether or not you selected the Black Point Compensation option with this setting. If so, make sure you disable any color management in your printer dialog box. Choose Separations if you want to print color separations (see the upcoming section). Choose No Color Management and no conversion occurs.

If you chose Proof in the Print area, you see the same options, but they produce different results:

- **Let Printer Determine Colors** works only with a Postscript (PS level 2 or higher) printer, which manages the color conversion of the proof to the print based on your selection of Simulate Paper Color or Simulate Black Ink.

- **Let Photoshop Determine Colors** tells Photoshop to handle the color conversion of the proof to the print, using the printer profile specified in the pop-up menu and your choice of simulation. Unless you have a lot of dark colors, I recommend leaving it on Simulate Paper Color.

5. **If you chose Let Photoshop Determine colors, choose your printer and paper type from the Printer Profile pop-up menu.**

Although you may be able to change the Rendering Indent setting, I recommend leaving this at the default setting of Relative Colorimetric. Also leave the Black Point Compensation check box at the default setting of checked or unchecked (depending on your Color Handling choice) — unless, of course, you're a color guru and have a better reason not to.

6. **Unless you haven't set your CMYK working space yet, you can leave Proof Setup Preset as is. To set the working space, see Book II, Chapter 3.**

Proof Setup Preset reflects the working CMYK space you established in your Color Settings dialog box, along with any custom presets you specified in the View⇨Proof Setup⇨Custom dialog box.

7. When you finish making your selections, click Print.

That's all there is to it. If you want more information on printing, check out Book I, Chapter 3. For more explanation on color management, see Book II, Chapter 3.

If all you want to do is print color prints on your desktop printer, I recommend starting off by choosing Document in the Print area and choosing Let Photoshop Determine Colors for Color Handling. If you have a little time and paper to burn, then print another copy by using Let Printer Determine Colors for Color Space. Do a side-by-side comparison to see which one looks superior. You can also crack the seal on the documentation that came with your printer for any recommendations.

Getting Four-Color Separations

It is necessary to *color separate* your image whenever you plan to print your image to an offset press. Your image must first be in CMYK color mode (choose Image⇨Mode⇨CMYK Color). Then the composite color image gets digitally separated into the four-color channels — cyan, magenta, yellow, and black — and is output. (These colors are also known as *process colors*.) Sometimes, the separation output is onto film, and sometimes, it is output directly to aluminum printing plates. The plates are put on an offset press, paper runs through each of the four inked rollers (cyan first, then magenta, yellow, and finally black), and out comes your composite image.

Getting laser separations

Before you take your image to a service bureau or offset printer to get color separations, it is wise to get what are called *laser separations*. Basically, you are color separating your image, not to film or plates, but to paper.

If your image doesn't separate to paper, most likely it won't to film or plates, either. You can go back and and correct the problem, rather than pay upwards of $80 to $150 an hour to have the service bureau or offset printer correct it for you. Consider laser separations a cheap insurance policy.

Follow these steps to get laser separations from your desktop printer:

1. Be sure your image mode is CMYK. If it isn't, choose Image⇨Mode⇨ CMYK Color.

I'm assuming your image is a four-color image. But it may also be a grayscale, duotone, tritone, or quadtone image, in which case no conversion to CMYK is necessary. (See Book II, Chapter 2, for more on modes.)

If you're new to converting RGB images to CMYK, don't be surprised if your vibrant colors turn muddy and flat. This is because the *gamut,* a fancy word for range of color, for CMYK is much smaller than it is for RGB, and Photoshop converts colors that are out of the CMYK gamut to their closest match. It's a cold, harsh fact that we all have to live with. After the conversion, you have an image with four channels — Cyan, Magenta, Yellow, and Black, like the one shown in Figure 1-2.

Corbis Digital Stock

Figure 1-2: Color images are separated into four process colors — cyan, magenta, yellow and black.

2. **Choose File⇨Print with Preview. In the Print dialog box, click More Options and select Color Management from the pop-up menu on the far left under the Preview window.**

3. **In the Print area, select Document.**

   It should say U.S. Web Coated (SWOP) v2.

4. **Select Separations from the Color Handling pop-up menu.**

   This option prints each channel from the image to a separate plate, or in the case of laser separations, paper.

5. **Select Output from the pop-up menu above the Print area, as shown in Figure 1-3. Then select additional options as you desire.**

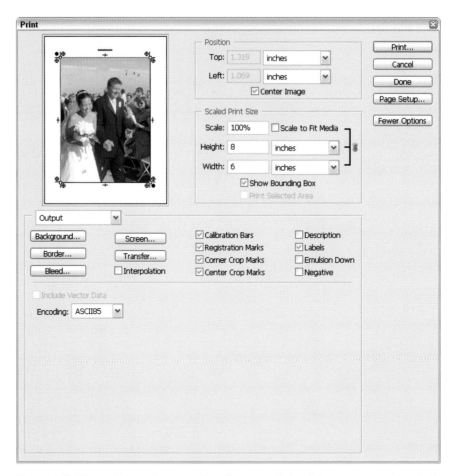

Figure 1-3: When printing color separations, be sure and check the necessary options in the Output section of the Print with Preview dialog box.

For general print options, see Book I, Chapter 3. For additional options, see Table 1-3.

Note that if you're printing to a non-PostScript printer, some of these options may not be available. You see a preview of most of these options as you apply them to your file.

6. Click the Print button.

If all goes well, four pieces of paper, one for each of the four CMYK channels, prints. If you're printing a grayscale, duotone, tritone, or quadtone image, you get one to four pieces of paper, one for each color used. If that doesn't happen, something's amiss, and it's time for troubleshooting. Be sure to take these laser separations with you when you hand over your file to the service bureau or offset printer.

Table 1-3	Output Options	
Option	*What It Does*	*Recommendation*
Screen	Creates a custom halftone screen by changing the size, angle, and shape of the halftone dots.	Leave this set to Use Printer's Default Screen. Let the service bureau or offset printer change it if necessary.
Transfer	Redistributes brightness levels in your image.	I wouldn't mess with this setting unless you're a prepress professional.
Interpolation	Anti-aliases low-resolution images by resampling.	Available only for PostScript Level 2 or laser printers. Leave it deselected.
Calibration Bars	Prints an 11-step grayscale bar outside the image area to gauge how accurately the shades are being printed. When printing separations, this option prints a gradient tint bar and color bar.	Select this option.
Registration Marks	Prints crosshair and target marks outside the image area, allowing you to line up the four plates or pages.	Select this option.
Corner Crop Marks	Adds crops marks at the corners of the image to indicate where to trim the image.	Select this option.
Center Crop Marks	Adds crop marks at the center of each side of the image to indicate where to trim the image.	Select this option.
Labels	Prints the filename and channel name on each plate or page.	Select this option.

continued

Table 1-3 *(continued)*

Option	What It Does	Recommendation
Emulsion Down	*Emulsion* is the side of the film that is light sensitive. Allows the film to be printed with the emulsion side down.	Leave this option deselected for laser separations. When the service bureau or offset printer prints the separations to film or plates, it may select this option.
Negative	Prints black as white and white as black, and every other color inverts accordingly.	Leave this option deselected for laser separations. When the service bureau or offset printer prints the separations to film or plates, it may select this option.
Include Vector Data	See the "Saving and Printing Vector Data in a Raster File" section, earlier in this chapter.	Leave this option selected if you have type or vector paths.
Encoding	This option specifies the method of encoding used to send the image to the printer.	Leave this option at the default of Binary.

Creating Spot Color Separations

Photoshop allows you to add separate channels for spot colors (see Book VI, Chapter 1, for more on channels), which can then be color separated. Spot, or *custom,* colors are premixed inks manufactured by various ink companies, the most popular in the U.S. being Pantone. A spot color is often used for a logo, type, or small illustration. Spot colors are also used when you need to apply metallic inks or varnishes to your print job. Spot colors can be used instead of, or in addition to, the four process CMYK colors.

If you are delving into the world of spot colors, I highly recommend that you choose your color from a printed Pantone swatch book, available from www.pantone.com. Because your screen is an RGB device and you're setting up your file for a CMYK output device, the colors you see on-screen do not match the colors that are ultimately on paper and at best are a ballpark match. For accuracy, you must select the colors from the printed swatch book. For more on working with color, see Book II, Chapter 3.

Creating a spot channel

Follow these steps to create a spot channel:

1. **Create the graphic or type to which you want to apply the spot color on a separate layer.**

2. **Ctrl+click (⌘+click on the Mac) on the thumbnail of the layer to select the graphic and then fill it with any solid color and an opacity of 100 percent.**

3. **With your selection active, choose Window⇨Channels, and choose New Spot Channel from the Channels palette pop-up menu.**

You can apply a spot color only to an active selection. It can't be applied just to a layer.

The New Spot Channel dialog box appears, as shown in Figure 1-4.

Figure 1-4: Adding an additional color separation in Photoshop requires creating a spot color channel first.

4. **In the Name text box, enter a name for your spot color. In the Ink Characteristics area, click the color swatch.**

I recommend naming it according to the spot color you want to use, such as Pantone 7417C.

When you click the color swatch, the Color Picker appears.

5. **Click the Custom button in the Color Picker and select your Pantone color from the Custom Colors dialog box that appears (see Figure1-5). Then click OK.**

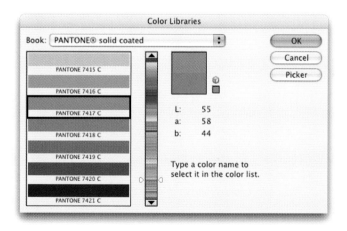

Figure 1-5: Select an appropriate color for the Color Libraries dialog box.

6. **In the New Spot Channel dialog box, select a Solidity value between 0 percent to 100 percent.**

A value of 100 percent represents an ink that is completely opaque, such as a metallic ink, which completely covers the inks beneath it. A value of 0 percent represents a transparent ink, such as a clear varnish. But the solidity value affects only the *screen* view and *composite* prints; it doesn't affect the separations. It can be helpful to see where a "clear" varnish will print.

7. **Click OK to close the dialog box.**

Your spot channel appears in the Channels palette and is filled in the image as well. I created a spot channel for my crest graphic and for the sushiko type (Pantone 7417C), as shown in Figure 1-6.

Figure 1-6: The Channels palette displays the spot channel.

In the printing process, spot colors are overprinted on top of the four-color image, as shown in Figure 1-7. That means that the spot color is applied at the end of the printing process and is printed over the other inks. This can sometimes cause lighter spot colors to darken somewhat.

If you need your spot color graphic to *knock out* the underlying image, create it in an illustration or page layout program. A knock-out is when a hole is left in the four-color image, and the spot ink then fills that hole. It does not print over the other inks.

TIP

Converting an alpha channel to a spot channel

If you want to convert an alpha channel to a spot channel, select the alpha channel in the Channels palette and choose Channel Options from the palette pop-up menu. Rename the channel and select Spot Color. Choose a color from the Custom section of the Color Picker. Click OK. Note that Photoshop converts all areas containing nonwhite pixels (unselected to partially selected areas) to the spot color. Choose Image⇔Adjustments⇔Invert to apply the spot color to the white pixels or selected areas of the alpha channel. For details on alpha channels, see Book VI, Chapters 1 and 3.

Corbis Digital Stock

Figure 1-7: Spot colors are often used for color critical logos
that print on top of your image.

**8. Save the image in the native Photoshop, Photoshop PDF, or Photoshop
DCS 2.0 (Desktop Color Separations) format.**

If the image is being separated directly out of Photoshop, leave it as
a PSD or PDF file. If you want to import it into a different program, such
as PageMaker, InDesign, or QuarkXPress, you must save it as a DCS
file. You also have to go through a few more hoops: If your image is
a duotone, tritone, or quadtone image, you must first convert it to multichannel mode with the Image⇨Mode command.

In the DCS 2.0 Format dialog box, make sure that the Include Halftone Screen and Include Transfer options are not selected.

Import the image into your destination application and set your screen angles.

Editing a spot channel

After you create a spot channel, you can edit it. Select the channel in the Channels palette and use a painting or editing tool to paint with black, white, or any shade of gray, just as you would with an alpha channel. To change any of the options of the spot channel, double-click the spot channel thumbnail, or select it and choose Channel Options from the palette pop-up menu. Choose a different color or solidity.

Chapter 2: Creating Contact Sheets, Picture Packages, and More

In This Chapter

- Creating thumbnail catalogs with contact sheets
- Multiplying images into picture packages
- Using the Photomerge command
- Using the new Merge to HDR command
- Creating PDF presentations

The Contact Sheet II and Picture Package features are two common tasks that are tedious to perform manually. You can use these features to create documents of *thumbnail* images of groups of files and print multiple copies of an image on one sheet, much like the picture packages of 5 x 7s and wallet prints you order from school photographers. Fortunately, the programming wizards at Adobe have made creating contact sheets and picture packages easy, and this chapter leads you through the process.

Cataloging with Contact Sheets

If you're not steeped in photographic darkroom lore (and fewer of us are, in these digital days), the term *contact sheet* might be fuzzy to you. The original purpose of contact sheets was to show the photographer a small image of each picture in a set of negatives so the photographer could compare the images, select which ones to print, and crop them with a grease pencil right on the contact sheet. Contact sheets also made a convenient way of filing away images.

Today, we have more sophisticated ways of previewing and cataloging digital images, including many different image-cataloging programs, such as Adobe's own Photoshop Elements application. Even so, the Contact Sheet II

automated tool in Photoshop works faster than database-type catalog programs (which require you to enter keywords to sort and locate images) and
performs useful tasks, such as the following:

- Prepare Photoshop documents so that you can store them, share them
  with others in digital form, or print them for distribution.

- Create ad hoc catalogs adeptly. Just copy the files you want to include to
  a folder and fire up the Contact Sheet II tool.

- Specify the number of rows and columns in your contact sheet, filling a
  sheet with only a few images (if that's what you want) or packing dozens
  onto a single contact sheet.

- Automatically create multiple sheets if all the selected images don't fit
  on a single sheet.

Using Contact Sheet II

With Contact Sheet II, you can create contact sheets that have many thumbnail images on a single page. You can print the contact sheets or browse
through them electronically. To create a contact sheet catalog of your own
images, follow these steps:

1. **Copy all the files you want to include in your contact sheet into a
   folder on your hard drive.**

2. **Choose File⇨Automate⇨Contact Sheet II.**

   The Contact Sheet II dialog box appears, as shown in Figure 2-1.

   Note that you can find both the Contact Sheet II and Picture Package
   commands on the Tools⇨Photoshop menu in Bridge. The Bridge makes
   for easy and quick visual selection of images to catalog or package.
   Check out Book I, Chapter 5, for more on Bridge.

3. **In the Source Images area, click the Browse button (Choose on the
   Mac) and navigate to the folder containing the images you want to
   include.**

   From the Use pop-up menu, you can also choose Selected Images from
   Bridge or Current Open Documents.

4. **Select the Include All Subfolders check box if you want to include
   images contained in a folder's subfolders.**

5. **Choose your desired unit of measurement from the Units pop-up
   menu. In the Width and Height boxes, enter the dimensions of the
   contact sheet document.**

   Choose the default setting of 8 x 10 inches if you plan to print contact
   sheets on standard-sized paper.

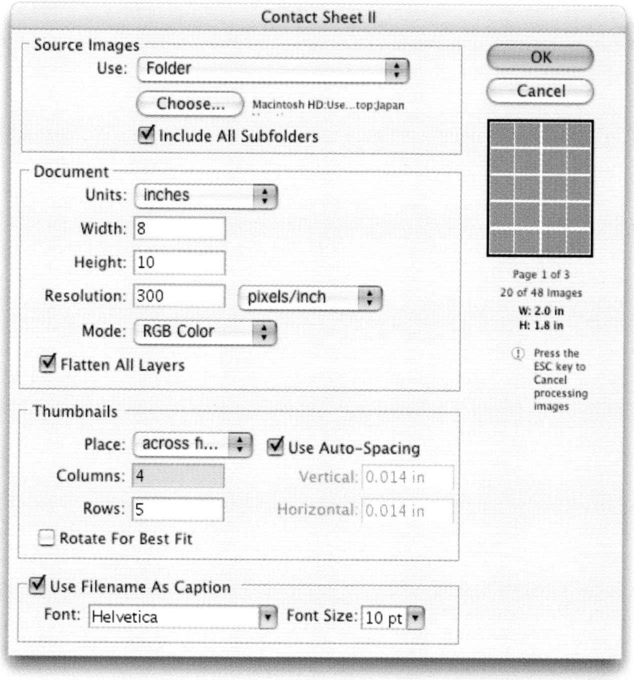

Contact Sheet II

Source Images
Use: Folder ⯆

Choose... Macintosh HD:Use...top:Japan

☑ Include All Subfolders

Document
Units: inches ⯅⯆
Width: 8
Height: 10
Resolution: 300 | pixels/inch ⯅⯆
Mode: RGB Color ⯆
☑ Flatten All Layers

Thumbnails
Place: across fi... ⯅⯆ ☑ Use Auto-Spacing
Columns: 4 Vertical: 0.014 in
Rows: 5 Horizontal: 0.014 in
☐ Rotate For Best Fit

☑ Use Filename As Caption
Font: Helvetica ⯆ Font Size: 10 pt ⯆

OK
Cancel

Page 1 of 3
20 of 48 Images
W: 2.0 in
H: 1.8 in

ⓘ Press the
ESC key to
Cancel
processing
images

Figure 2-1: The Contact Sheet II dialog box allows you to specify
dimensions, resolution, color mode and columns and rows for your
contact sheet.

6. **Adjust the resolutions settings.**

   A setting of 72 pixels/inch works well for contact sheets if all you want is
   just a quick-and-dirty look at them. Use a higher resolution if you want a
   sharper contact sheet. Remember, however that the file size will be larger.

   If you're showing the contact sheets to a client or you want the individual images to look crisp and clear, choose a higher resolution. Also, if
   you want the thumbnails to be larger (with fewer per page), choose a
   higher resolution and adjust the number of columns and rows in Step 10.

   Check out Book II, Chapter 1, for more recommendations on resolution
   settings.

7. **Choose a color mode from the Mode pop-up menu.**

   RGB works best in most cases. However, if your images are black-and-
   white photos, you can create smaller files by selecting the Grayscale
   option.

Check your printer documentation to see the color mode recommended for printing color images. For more on color modes, see Book II, Chapter 2.

8. **Select the Flatten All Layers check box if you want to create a contact sheet with a single layer in which all images and their captions (if any) are merged.**

This option significantly reduces the contact sheet's file size. If you do not select this option, you end up with larger contact sheet files, but you have the additional flexibility of flattening the thumbnails yourself later both with and without captions.

You can now start adjusting the layout. A Preview window at the right side of the dialog box shows roughly how the contact sheet will be laid out.

9. **Select the Across First option from the Place pop-up menu to orient the thumbnails in rows. Down First orients the layout in columns.**

10. **In the Columns and Rows text boxes, enter the number of columns and rows.**

Beneath the small layout preview on the right side of the dialog box are the number of pages in your contact sheet, the total number of images, and the largest possible size of each image.

If you plan to print such a maxi-thumbnail contact sheet, choose a higher resolution (such as 150 to 300 pixels/inch) sharper thumbnails.

11. **Choose the spacing you want between the images.**

Select the Auto-Spacing option to have the default distance of .014 inches vertically and horizontally between each thumbnail option. Deselect the option to enter a custom distance. Select the Rotate For Best Fit option to have Photoshop rotate the thumbnails if necessary to accommodate a better fit based on your specifications.

12. **Choose the Use Filename as Caption option to identify each image easily.**

You can also select the Font and Font Size from the option lists.

13. **Click OK to create your contact sheet. If you change your mind, press the Esc key to quit.**

Figure 2-2 shows a contact sheet with five rows and four columns. Photoshop creates as many pages as necessary to include all the selected images. This can take a few minutes.

Figure 2-2: A digitally created contact sheet.

Pretty as a Picture Package

If you remember having your class pictures taken as a child or have ever gone to a retailer or professional photographer's studio, then you have probably seen the contact sheets that come from these photo sessions. You purchase one of those special deals and wind up with, say, an 8-x-10-inch print, two 5 x 7s, four 4 x 5s, and eight wallet-sized shots.

The number of pictures you get at each of these dimensions isn't pulled out of a hat. That's the number of images at a given size that can fit on a single 8-x-10-inch sheet of photographic paper.

Photofinishers have automated printers that can expose those duplicates onto a standard-sized section of a roll of photographic paper, which is then processed and cut apart by mechanized equipment.

Photoshop can perform much the same magic with your own photos, creating image documents that you can then print as your own picture packages.

This is much easier and faster than you cropping and pasting multiple copies of images onto a single document. Just follow these steps to create your own picture package:

1. **Open the picture you want to use for your picture package in Photoshop.**

   If you want to create multiple picture packages of different images using the same parameters, copy the images to a single folder.

   You have your choice of using files in a folder, an opened file, a specific file, or selected files in Bridge.

2. **Choose File⇨Automate⇨Picture Package.**

   The Picture Package dialog box, shown in Figure 2-3, appears. Again, remember that you can also choose this command from within Bridge.

3. **In the Source Images area, select Frontmost Document to create the picture package from the image that is currently selected in Photoshop, or choose File and select a single file from your hard drive. Click Browse (Choose on the Mac) to navigate to files or folders.**

   If you select Folder to create picture packages from all the files in a folder, all the picture packages must use the same parameters that you enter in the Picture Package dialog box. You can also use images that you have preselected from the Bridge.

4. **If you'd like to include more than one picture in a picture package, such as I have Figure 2-3, click a sample thumbnail in the Layout area of the dialog box.**

   A Select an Image File dialog box appears.

5. **Find the image you want to substitute and click it.**

   The image appears in the thumbnail you chose in Step 4.

6. **Repeat to insert other images in the picture package.**

7. **Choose a setting for Page Size from the list.**

   In most cases, you'll want to use 8 x 10 inches. You can also select 10 x 16 inches or 11 x 17 inches if you have a printer that can handle larger sheets of paper.

8. **Choose a layout.**

   You can fill an entire sheet with only one size photo, if you like, such as two 5-x-7-inch pictures or eight 2.5-x-3.5-inch pictures. Or you can select one of the other combinations, such as two 4 x 5s, two 2.5 x 3.5s, or four 2-x-2.5-inch photos.

9. **Adjust the resolution settings.**

   The default value is 72 pixels/inch. You'll probably want a higher resolution, such as 300 pixels/inch if you plan to print the picture package.

Figure 2-3: The Picture Package feature enables you to create print layouts that rival professional photo studios.

Check your printer documentation to see the recommended resolution. Also check out Book II, Chapter 1, for more on recommended resolution settings.

10. **Choose a color mode from the Mode pop-up menu.**

    RGB is the best choice in most cases. However, if your images happen to be black and white, you can create smaller, more compact picture package files by selecting the Grayscale option. Check your printer documentation.

11. **Select the Flatten All Layers check box to create a picture package with a single layer in which Photoshop merges all images and their labels (if you choose to apply them).**

12. **If you want to apply some text, you can do it in the Label area of the dialog box.**

    Most picture packages don't require text descriptions, but you can choose content such as Filename, Copyright, Credit, and so on.

13. **Select Custom Text from the Content pop-up menu to type your own text.**

14. **Adjust the font settings, position the text, and rotate the text to your heart's content. Use the Opacity drop-down list to adjust the type's opacity.**

15. Click the Edit Layout button to further customize your layout.

In the dialog box, enter a name for your layout. Choose a size from the Page Size menu or enter dimensions in the Width and Height boxes. Choose a unit of measurement. In the Grid area, check the Snap To option to show a grid to help position your image and then specify the size of your grid increments. Click the placeholders, which may or may not contain images, and drag them to your desired location within the page. You can also reposition a placeholder by entering values in the X and Y boxes. Drag a handle to resize the placeholder or enter dimensions in the Width and Height boxes. Note that if you resize a placeholder with an image in it, the image snaps within the placeholder. Click the Add Zone button to add another placeholder. Click Delete Zone or Delete All to delete placeholders. When you are satisfied with your layout, click the Save button.

16. Click OK to create the picture package, ready for printing.

Using the Photomerge Command

The Photomerge command allows you to combine multiple images into one continuous panoramic image. For example, you can take several overlapping photos of a mountain range and put them together into one panoramic shot, as shown in Figure 2-4.

Figure 2-4: The Photomerge command enables you to combine multiple images into one continuous panoramic shot.

If you know you ultimately want to create a Photomerge composition, you can make things easier by making sure that when you shoot your photos, you overlap your individual images by 15 to 40 percent, but no more than 70 percent. Adobe also recommends avoiding using distortion lenses (such as fish-eye) and your camera's zoom setting. Finally, try to stay in the same position and keep your camera at the same level for each shot. Using a tripod and rotating the head can help you achieve this consistency.

Here are the steps to assemble your own Photomerge composition:

1. **Choose File⇨Automate⇨Photomerge.**

   You can also select your desired source images and choose Automate Photomerge from the Bridge menu. Using the Bridge method is a time-saver because you can quickly and visually select your images.

2. **In the first Photomerge dialog box, choose your source files. You can select from Files (uses individual files you choose), Folder (uses all images in a folder), or Open Files (uses all currently open files) from the Use pop-up menu. Click the Browse button to navigate to your desired files or folder.**

   If you want to delete a file from the list, select it and click Remove.

3. **From the list of files, select the ones you want to merge. Select the Attempt to Automatically Arrange Source files option to direct Photoshop to try to compose the panorama automatically. Click OK.**

   Photoshop opens and assembles the source files to create the composite panorama.

4. **Photoshop alerts you if it cannot automatically composite your source files. You then have to assemble your images for yourself, as shown in Figure 2-5.**

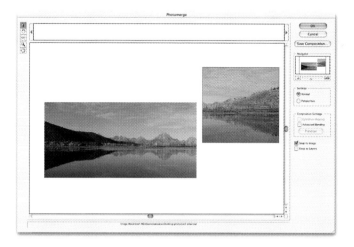

Figure 2-5: Assemble images automatically or manually.

To manually assemble your composition, drag the image thumbnails from the lightbox area onto the work area with the arrow. Or simply double-click on the lightbox thumbnail to add it to the composition. You can also drag an image back into the lightbox to remove it. In addition, you can position the images or rearrange their order also using this same tool. Use the Rotate Image tool, the Zoom and Move View (more commonly known as the Hand tool) tools, and the Navigator view box to zoom in and out of your composition. See Book I, Chapter 5, if you need more details on using these tools.

Select the Snap to Image option to have Photoshop automatically snap overlapping images into place.

5. **To adjust the Vanishing Point, first select the Perspective option in the Settings area. Then, click your desired image with the Set Vanishing Point tool, which you can select from the Photomerge Tools palette on the left.**

   Photoshop then changes the perspective of the composition. By default, Photoshop selects the center image as the Vanishing Point (look for the turquoise border). If needed, you can move the other images.

   Note, however, that when you select the Perspective setting, Photoshop links non-Vanishing Point images to the Vanishing Point image. To break the link, click the Normal setting button or separate the images in the work area. You can also drag the Vanishing Point image back into the lightbox.

6. **Adjust the blending of the composition.**

   Choose Cylindrical Mapping to reduce the bowed distortion you can get when you add perspective to your composition. (Note that you must select Perspective in the Settings area in order to apply cylindrical mapping.)

   Select Advanced Blending to correct the color differences that can occur from blending images with different exposures. Photoshop then blends the colors and tones.

   Click Preview to view your settings. Click Exit Preview to return to the Edit mode. You can also view the results in the final, rendered image.

7. **Select the Keep As Layers option to save each image in the composite as an individual layer.**

8. **Click OK to generate the composite panorama as a new Photoshop file, which opens in Photoshop. Or click Save Composition to save the composite as a .pmg (Photomerge format) file, which you can later open in the Photomerge dialog box.**

   To open a previously saved composite (.pmg file), click the Open Composition button in the Photomerge dialog box.

Using the Merge to HDR command

Have you ever caught an early matinee and emerged mole-like from the pitch black theatre into the bright light of high noon only to have to squint for a while because your eyes burned? Or on the flip side, have you blindly tumbled into your seat, popcorn scattering all over the aisle, into your seat in that same darkened theatre because you just came in from the bright daylight? In both cases, your eyes needed some time to adjust to the abrupt change from extreme dark to extreme light and vice-versa. Cameras suffer from the same problem. But while our eyes can eventually adapt to varying brightness levels, cameras and devices, such as computer monitors and scanners, can only capture a fixed dynamic, or tonal, range. In digital imaging tech talk, dynamic range is the ratio of the darkest and brightest values a device can capture simultaneously.

In the past, digital photography afficionados were hindered when performing higher-end image editing tasks in Photoshop because they were forced to work within a limited dynamic range. Not anymore. Photoshop CS2 now provides support for High Dyanamic Range (HDR) images. HDR images, which contain 32-bits of data per channel, are superior because they can capture a much larger dynamic range — in fact they are able to represent the entire dynamic range of the "real world."

Photographers can now take multiple exposures of an image and then later merge those multiple exposures into a single photo in Photoshop, thereby capturing the entire dynamic range into a single HDR image. Although you can use the Merge to HDR command on 8- or 16-bit images, be aware that only 32-bit images can store all the HDR data.

Adobe offers a few tips to maximize your success with the Merge to HDR command:

- Use a tripod when shooting multiple exposures of the same scene to ensure you're capturing the exact same shot each time.

- Make sure you take enough shots to cover the entire dynamic range of your subject. Shoot for a minimum of three, but try for five to seven, if not more.

- Vary the shutter speed to create different exposures, instead of your aperture or ISO, which can cause noise, vignetting, and altering of depth of field.

- Make sure the exposure difference between the shots is one or two Exposure Value (EV) steps apart. Use one or two f-stops apart as a guide.

- Don't vary the lighting in the shots.

- Don't shoot anything that is moving. The scene needs to be static.

Here are the steps to using this great new feature:

1. **Choose File⇨Automate⇨Merge to HDR.**

   Note that you can also access this command in the Bridge by choosing Tools⇨Photoshop.

   The Merge to HDR dialog box appears, as shown in Figure 2-6.

2. **Choose Open Files, Folder, or Files from the Use pop-up menu.**

3. **If you chose Folder or Files in Step 2, click the Browse button, select the images, and click Open.**

   If you chose an image by accident, simply select it and click Remove.

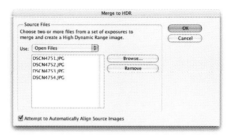

Figure 2-6: Choose two or more files to merge in the Merge to HDR dialog box.

4. **Check Attempt to Automatically Align Source Images if you want Photoshop to try and line up your various exposures.**

   Note that this is a good idea if you shot your photos without the use of a tripod.

5. **Click OK.**

   A second dialog box appears with thumbnails of your chosen images on the left and a large preview of the merged image in the center.

6. **Based on how you like the merged image, you can select or deselect any of the thumbnails in the source area.**

   Photoshop may bark at you that you don't have enough dynamic range to get a "useful" HDR image, in which case you have to bail out.

   You may also get a mini dialog box that asks you to manually set your exposure value. You need to specify your Exposure Time, f-stop (aperture), and ISO (film speed) for all your images.

   If you want to zoom in and out of your images, click the – and + buttons or use the View pop-up menu at the bottom of the Preview window.

7. **In the Bit Depth menu, shown in Figure 2-7, choose your desired bit depth for the merged image. Be sure and leave your 32-bit image set to 32-bit if you want to capture and store the entire dynamic range.**

8. **Use the White Point slider, found on the Bit Depth menu, to set the white point for the merged image if you want to see a better preview.**

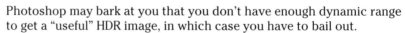

Figure 2-7: Specify your desired bit depth and adjust your white point.

The dynamic range of HDR images surpasses what your monitor can show. So when viewing them, they can look pretty nasty — too dark and undersaturated. If you adjust the preview with the White Point slider, Photoshop provides a better display of the image without altering the image data at all. Remember that if your image is 32-bit, adjusting the white point only affects the preview, not the actual image data. That preview adjustment is then saved in the HDR file and applied whenever the file is opened in Photoshop. But, if your image is 16- or 8-bit, adjusting the white point applies the adjustment to the actual image data itself.

You can also adjust the preview of your HDR images by choosing View➪32-bit Preview Options. Choose either Exposure and Gamma or Highlight and Compression. Exposure and Gamma adjust the brightness and contrast of the image. Highlight and compression compresses the highlight values so they fall within the tonal range of an 8- or 16-bit image. Finally, you can also choose 32-bit Exposure from the status bar pop-up menu at the bottom of the image window, but these adjustments are not stored in the file and are for viewing only.

9. **Click OK.**

Your merged HDR image appears in all its full dynamic glory.

Even if you want to ultimately convert your 32-bit image to 16-bit or even 8-bit, always make your exposure and contrast corrections first and then convert it. You'll get your dynamic range the way you want it. Note that you can choose Image➪Mode➪16-bits or 8-bits/channel. Make your exposure and contrast adjustment in the HDR Conversion dialog box.

Creating PDF Presentations

The PDF Presentation command allows you to use multiple images to create a single, multipaged document or slide show. This feature is great for several reasons. First, your recipient doesn't need to have any specific hardware, software, utilities, or fonts to open and view the presentation. All that is required is Acrobat Reader, a free download from www.adobe.com. In addition, sending a single file containing multiple images is a great way to share your photos with family and friends. You avoid the hassle of having to e-mail your images as separate attachments. Finally, the PDF format offers excellent compression, thereby squeezing your file size down significantly without sacrificing image quality. Just be sure and check your final file size so you don't choke your recipients' e-mail inboxes!

Follow these steps to create a PDF Presentation:

1. **Choose File⇨Automate⇨PDF Presentation.**

   The PDF Presentation dialog box appears, as shown in Figure 2-8.

Figure 2-8: Choose between a multiple paged document or a slide show type presentation for your PDF of images.

Note that you can also access the PDF Presentation in the Bridge by choosing Automate⇨PDF Presentation. Note that if you do not select any images, the command selects all the images displayed in Bridge.

2. **Click the Browse button and navigate to your desired files. If you want to add the files you already have open in Photoshop, select the Add Open Files option.**

   Remove files from the list by selecting them and clicking the Remove button.

3. **Choose either a Multi-Page Document or a Presentation (slide show).**

   A multipage document displays each image on a separate page.

   Note that the PDF Presentation command preserves any notes added with the Notes tool. In addition, Photoshop reimports a multipage document or PDF presentation file with comments that have been added in Acrobat. This is a great tool for presenting projects to clients or management and receiving feedback from those recipients.

4. **If you selected Presentation in Step 3, specify your presentation options.**

   - **Advance Every [5] Seconds:** Establishes how long each image appears on-screen. You can change the default of 5 seconds.

   - **Loop After Last Page:** Enables the presentation to continually run. If not selected, the presentation stops after the last image.

   - **Transition:** From the pop-up menu, choose how you want one image to transition to the next.

5. **Click Save.**

6. **In the Save dialog box, provide a name and location for your presentation. Click Save.**

7. **In the Save Adobe PDF dialog box, shown in Figure 2-9, specify your desired options.**

   This dialog box has been revamped in Photoshop CS2. Book II, Chapter 2, describes all the new options in detail.

8. **Click OK.**

   Photoshop creates your PDF Presentation and prompts you with a message that it was successfully created, if indeed it was. If you didn't choose the View PDF After Saving option in Step 7, launch Acrobat or Acrobat Reader and view your presentation. Figure 2-10 shows an image from mine.

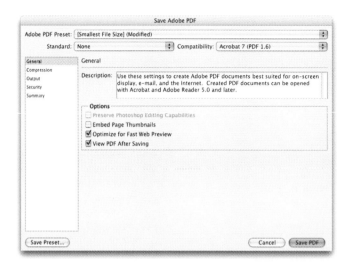

Figure 2-9: The revamped Save Adobe PDF dialog box.

Figure 2-10: PDF presentations offer a quick and easy way to create slide shows.

Index

NOTE: Page numbers beginning with "BC" are on the Web site.

• *M* •

● *T* ●

Don't forget about these bestselling For Dummies® books!

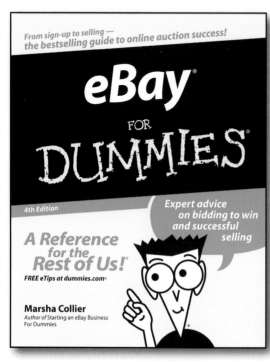

From sign-up to selling —
the bestselling guide to online auction success!

eBay®
FOR DUMMIES®

4th Edition

Expert advice on bidding to win and successful selling

A Reference for the Rest of Us!®

FREE eTips at dummies.com®

Marsha Collier
Author of Starting an eBay Business For Dummies

0-7645-5654-1

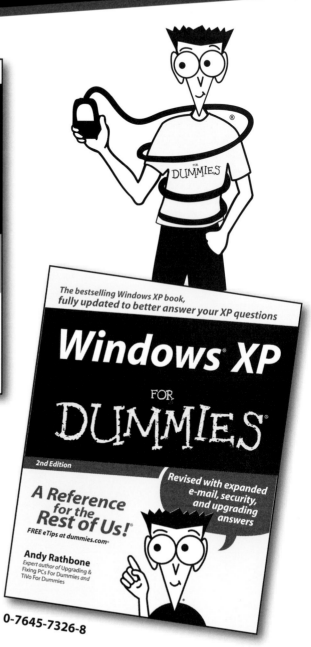

The bestselling Windows XP book, fully updated to better answer your XP questions

Windows® XP
FOR DUMMIES®

2nd Edition

Revised with expanded e-mail, security, and upgrading answers

A Reference for the Rest of Us!®

FREE eTips at dummies.com®

Andy Rathbone
Expert author of Upgrading & Fixing PCs For Dummies and TiVo For Dummies

0-7645-7326-8

Available wherever books are sold. Go to www.dummies.com or call 1-877-762-2974 to order direct.

Don't forget about these bestselling For Dummies® books!

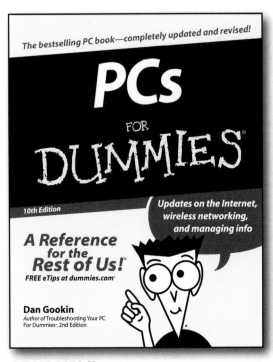

0-7645-8958-X

0-7645-8996-2

Available wherever books are sold. Go to www.dummies.com or call 1-877-762-2974 to order direct.